Middle Childhood Development
A Contextual Approach

MARY JO ZEMBAR
Wittenberg University

LIBBY BALTER BLUME
University of Detroit Mercy

Merrill
is an imprint of

Upper Saddle River, New Jersey
Columbus, Ohio

Library of Congress Cataloging-in-Publication Data

Zembar, Mary Jo.
    Middle childhood development : a contextual approach / Mary Jo Zembar, Libby Balter Blume.
      p. cm.
    Includes bibliographical references and index.
    ISBN-13: 978-0-13-171881-4 (pbk.)
    ISBN-10: 0-13-171881-9 (pbk.)
  1. Child development—Textbooks.   2. Adolescence—Textbooks.   I. Blume, Libby Balter.   II. Title.
    HQ772.Z46 2009
    305.235'5—dc22
                                            2007046607

Vice President and Executive Publisher: Jeffery W. Johnston
Publisher: Kevin M. Davis
Development Editor: Christina Robb
Editorial Assistant: Lauren Reinkober
Project Manager: Mary Harlan
Production Coordination: Thistle Hill Publishing Services, LLC
Design Coordinator: Diane C. Lorenzo
Photo Coordinator: Shea Davis
Cover Designer: Jeff Vanik
Cover Image: Corbis
Operations Specialist: Laura Messerly
Director of Marketing: Quinn Perkson
Marketing Manager: Erica M. DeLuca
Marketing Coordinator: Brian Mounts

This book was set in Utopia by Aptara, Inc. It was printed and bound by Edwards Brothers. The cover was printed by Phoenix Color Corp.

Pearson Education Ltd.
Pearson Education Singapore Pte. Ltd.
Pearson Education Canada, Ltd.
Pearson Education–Japan

Pearson Education Australia Pty. Limited
Pearson Education North Asia Ltd.
Pearson Educación de Mexico, S.A. de C.V.
Pearson Education Malaysia Pte. Ltd.

Merrill
is an imprint of

10 9 8 7 6 5 4 3 2 1
ISBN-13: 978-0-13-171881-4
ISBN-10:   0-13-171881-9

To the Instructor: Why We Wrote This Book

Middle Childhood Development: A Contextual Approach is written for advanced undergraduate courses that focus on the period from ages 6 to 12. By beginning with the period after early childhood and following children's development through early adolescence, we intend this text to be a new and integrative resource for practitioners who work with school-age children from elementary through middle school. A major contribution of the text is to clarify what we mean by middle childhood, early adolescence, and youth. All too often, many textbooks simply ignore the overlaps and ambiguities of this exciting developmental period.

Special features include:

- *A focus on developmental pathways.* We explore the ways in which middle childhood is considered both a stage of development and a transitional period in overview chapters called "Middle Childhood in Context" and "Beyond Middle Childhood: Adolescence."

- *A developmental-contextual orientation.* Each chapter includes key research on the ecologies of home, school, and community highlighted in separate sections called "Contexts of Development" that situate the study of middle childhood in a historical and cultural context.

- *An applied developmental perspective.* Throughout the text, current research is translated into practical applications for educators, parents, and other professionals in the special feature "Guideposts for Working with School-Age Children."

- *Integrated discussion of theories.* Rather than one abstract introductory chapter, psychological theories of development are applied throughout the text to address particular chapter content in integrated sections called "Theoretical Viewpoints."

- *Roadmaps to understanding.* In each chapter, pedagogical boxes called "Roadmap to Understanding Theory and Research" and "Roadmap to Successful Practice" alert students to key illustrations of chapter content.

- *Reflection questions.* Throughout the chapters, students are presented with "Stop and Reflect" questions to encourage continuing integration of the chapter content with their own life experiences.

- *Suggested activities, readings, and electronic resources.* At the end of each chapter, up-to-date suggestions for instructors and students are included that extend the chapter content with opportunities for further learning.

In *Middle Childhood Development: A Contextual Approach*, we examine variations in culture and ethnic background; economic and social opportunity; developmental abilities; and family, neighborhood, and community settings using an applied developmental science approach. Developmental science emphasizes: (a) the integration of complex processes; (b) continuous bidirectional interactions between persons and environments; and (c) interdisciplinary frameworks. We have adopted this applied "lens" to examine middle childhood in order to facilitate several important student objectives:

1. To illustrate the *role of theory* in guiding research and practice
2. To *integrate basic and applied research findings* on middle childhood development
3. To provide practitioners and educators with examples of research-based *prevention and intervention strategies*
4. To position the study of middle childhood as a *reflexive* activity, or one in which readers reflect on their own experiences as valid sources of information
5. To help readers translate their own research questions into meaningful *action and results*
6. To promote *praxis,* or the dynamic interaction between action and critical reflection

Like the study of middle childhood, writing this textbook has created both risks and opportunities. The risks, of course, lie in our hope that instructors and students will find the book useful and stimulating. The opportunities, however, reside in the process itself. Writing this text, we have learned from each other as we applied current literature to the exciting period of middle childhood.

Supplements

The following supplementary materials are available to instructors on the Instructor Resource Center, located at www.pearsonhighered.com:

PowerPoint Slides: These slides include key concept summarizations and other graphic aids to help students understand, organize, and remember core concepts and ideas.

Electronic Test Bank: The Test Bank includes multiple-choice and essay questions for each chapter.

Acknowledgments

We thank our generous and loving families for patiently supporting our seemingly endless writing; we thank the faculty, administrators, and students of our respective institutions, Wittenberg University and the University of Detroit Mercy; we are thankful for the faculty leaves so necessary for completing this project; and we thank our publisher, Kevin Davis, for his continued support.

We would also like to thank the following reviewers for providing helpful suggestions on each chapter: Irene P. Aiken, The University of North Carolina at Pembroke; Alisa Cox, University of Utah; and Ronald L. Mullis, Florida State University.

Mary Jo Zembar
Springfield, Ohio

Libby Balter Blume
Detroit, Michigan

To the Student: How to Use This Book

This text is about middle childhood. It is also about the interplay between basic research and the applied questions that are often asked by parents, teachers, and other practitioners who work with school-age children. Lastly, it is about the real-world contexts of growing up. These three goals are illustrated in Figure P.1, envisioned as pathways to acquiring competence in working with children from ages 6 to 12.

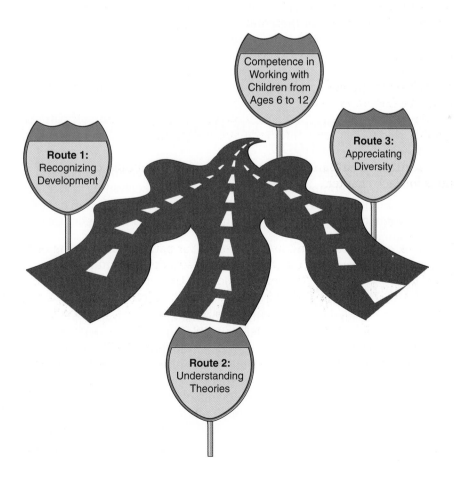

FIGURE P.1
Goals of This Book

The goals of this book can be seen as pathways to acquiring competence in working with school-age children.

GOAL 1: TO RECOGNIZE DEVELOPMENTAL CHANGES IN MIDDLE CHILDHOOD

In chapter 1, we describe the multiple ways in which this age has been defined by the people who work with and care for school-age children. In alternating chapters, the four basic areas of middle childhood development are covered, including physical, cognitive, affective, and social-moral development. The intervening chapters on puberty and health, literacy and achievement, relationships and families, and friendship, play, and peer relations apply developmental research and theory to areas of interest to those who work with school-age children. Chapter 12 concludes the book with a brief view into development beyond middle childhood. Throughout these chapters, current research is translated into practical applications for people working with school-age children.

GOAL 2: TO UNDERSTAND THEORIES OF MIDDLE CHILDHOOD DEVELOPMENT

Specific theories of development are integrated throughout the text in order to better address the particular content presented in each chapter. In the overview chapters on middle childhood and adolescence (1 and 12), major theories are presented that provide important perspectives on overall development, such as developmental-contextual theory. But in the content and application chapters, we have selected specific theories to illustrate a particular developmental area, such as Piaget's theory of cognitive development or Bowlby's theory of emotional attachment. At the end of each chapter, a table of theories is provided to help you review what you have read.

GOAL 3: TO APPRECIATE THE DIVERSE CONTEXTS OF MIDDLE CHILDHOOD

Each chapter concludes with a discussion of research in the cultural contexts of home, school, and community. The purpose of these sections is to locate the study of middle childhood in diverse contexts. We discuss family, peer, and neighborhood influences on middle childhood development, focusing on each chapter's specific area of development.

A METAPHOR FOR LEARNING

Throughout the text, we have utilized the metaphor of *travel* to characterize your journey as a student. The boxes labeled "Roadmap to Understanding" provide detailed extensions of the chapters' content. Throughout each chapter are "Guideposts for Working with School-Age Children" to stimulate your application of the basic research that you just read about. Interspersed, you will find "Stop and Reflect" questions that ask you to think about your own pathways and life experiences.

We wish you a successful trip through *Middle Childhood Development: A Contextual Approach*!

About the Authors

Mary Jo Zembar earned a Ph.D. in developmental psychology from the University of Houston. Professor and chair of psychology at Wittenberg University, Dr. Zembar teaches undergraduate courses in child and adolescent development, adult development and aging, and is the recipient of several teaching awards. Her research focuses on memory development and function in childhood and old age, and more recently she has carried out research on contexts of socialization in middle childhood. Dr. Zembar has published articles in such journals as *Personality and Individual Differences, Psychological Bulletin,* and *Journal of Experimental Child Psychology.* She also is coauthor of *Middle Childhood to Middle Adolescence: Development from Ages 8 to 18* (2007) published by Merrill/Prentice Hall. Along with her husband, she enjoys her two beautiful children who are in the throes of middle childhood.

    Libby Balter Blume earned a Ph.D. in human development from Texas Tech University. A certified family life educator and professor at the University of Detroit Mercy, she directs the developmental psychology and family life education program. Dr. Blume teaches undergraduate and graduate courses in child, adolescent, and lifespan human development, family relations, community development, visual communications, and women's studies. She has extensive experience as an art educator, preschool teacher, child development center director, and consultant to Head Start programs and to schools for gifted children from elementary to high school. Her research focuses on peer and family co-constructions of identity, ethnicity, and gender in middle childhood and adolescence. Dr. Blume has published articles in such journals as *Sex Education, Journal of Marriage and Family, Journal of Family Issues, Journal of Teaching in Marriage and Family, Family Relations,* and *Identity: An International Journal of Theory and Research* and is founding editor of the *Michigan Family Review.* She also is coauthor of *Middle Childhood to Middle Adolescence: Development from Ages 8 to 18* (2007) published by Merrill/Prentice Hall. When she is not teaching, writing, or editing, she enjoys spending time with her adult children and cooking gourmet meals with her husband for their friends and family.

Brief Contents

Contents

Chapter 5   **Cognitive Development in Middle Childhood**   **156**

Chapter 6   **Literacy, Intelligence, and Academic Achievement**   **190**

Middle Childhood Development

1

Middle Childhood
in Context

Tom McCarthy/PhotoEdit Inc.

Chapter Objectives

After reading this chapter, students will be able to:

▶ Define the period of middle childhood.

▶ Explain the reasons that students, researchers, educators, and service providers should study middle childhood.

▶ Discuss historical and contemporary portrayals of middle childhood.

▶ Name the developmental achievements of middle childhood.

▶ Identify the assumptions of ecological and contextual theories of human development.

▶ Describe the diverse contexts in which middle childhood development occurs.

Robyn, aged 8, arrives late to breakfast and plops down at the kitchen table with a thud, quickly pouring milk onto her cold cereal. Her 12-year-old sister Rachel and her 5-year-old sister Emily are almost finished eating. Hurrying to pack the girls' lunches before she is late for work again, their mother looks up. "How are you today, Robyn?" Robyn shrugs and replies, "I'd be lots better if I didn't have to go to that boring after-school program with Emily!" Rachel asks, "Why, don't you like it?" Robyn frowns. "None of my friends go there. They all say it's for little kids." *"I'm not little!" chimes in Emily. "Little enough!" snaps Robyn. "Why can't I go to swimming practice or dance classes like Rachel? I want to do something* important *after school, not just* play!"

DEFINING THE MIDDLE CHILDHOOD YEARS

Middle childhood is the developmental period between ages 6 and 12. As child developmentalists, however, we usually define middle childhood using indicators of child growth and development, such as cognitive or social maturation, rather than chronological age. During middle childhood, school-age children are likely to be developing new skills as well as making new friends. For example, developmental psychologists have described a "5- to 7-year-old shift" in thinking ability that signals a child's readiness to engage in formal learning (Davis-Kean & Sandler, 2001; Sameroff & Haith, 1996; White, 1996).

In this book, we are treating middle childhood as a developmental stage in its own right as well as a transitional period leading to adolescence. Because new developmental abilities emerge that cause school-age children to appear qualitatively different from children who are either younger or older than they are—either physically (e.g., the growth spurt), cognitively (e.g., the shift to concrete logic), affectively (e.g., feelings of self–competence), or socially (e.g., increased importance of peers)—we consider middle childhood to be an important and unique developmental stage in the life span. Developmental scholars have summarized the nature of middle childhood as follows:

- Around age 6 or 7, new cognitive capacities emerge that enable school-age children to handle more complex intellectual problem-solving and more intimate friendships than in early childhood.

- By around age 12, greater self-regulation and the consolidation of problem-solving skills allow school-age children to extend their abilities to tasks requiring flexible, abstract thinking and the maintenance of social relationships.

- Middle childhood development, although characterized by individual differences in the rates of growth, more powerfully predicts adolescent behaviors and success than does early childhood development (Collins, 1984; see also Feinstein & Bynner, 2004; Magnuson, Duncan, & Kalil, 2006; and Obradović, van Dulmen, Yates, Carlson, & Egelund, 2006).

These statements address, respectively, how school-age children typically appear when they *begin* this period and when they *end* the period and what can be predicted about their *futures*. For example, research suggests that Robyn's involvement in extracurricular activities in middle childhood will lead to her positive adjustment in early and middle adolescence (McHale, Crouter, & Tucker, 2001; Ripke, Huston, & Casey, 2006).

Studies of middle childhood development come from many different sources—from medicine, psychology, education, anthropology, and sociology, to name just a few. Many of these fields define middle childhood *developmentally*. Health care providers, for example, describe middle childhood as the period after early childhood growth and development but before puberty. Many clinical psychologists characterize middle childhood as a latency period that precedes the intense sexual interest of adolescence. Most educators believe that middle childhood begins when a child exhibits a cognitive readiness to enter the primary grades. Often, late-elementary or middle-school students *themselves* feel "in-between" childhood and adolescence, as humorously depicted by the "betweenagers" in Figure 1.1.

Other disciplines define middle childhood *culturally*. Sociologists and anthropologists, for example, believe that society or culture determines the timing of both middle

FIGURE 1.1
Betweenagers

Luann and her best
friend Bernice
describe a common
frustration of late
middle childhood.

Source: From "Luann"
by Greg Evans, January
14, 1990. LUANN: ©
GEC Inc./Dist. by
United Feature Syndi-
cate, Inc.

childhood and adolescence, whereas historians are likely to think that *all* of childhood is a modern invention. From today's perspective, for example, after-school child care is necessary because we believe that school-age children are not yet mature enough to be left unsupervised, as in the case study of Emily and Robyn. Similarly, juvenile justice programs have been established because we believe that most children are not legally competent to stand trial as adults until age 16 (Steinberg & Cauffman, 2001).

In this text, we have adopted the following underlying assumptions about middle childhood development (see Collins, 1984, 2005; Huston & Ripke, 2006a; Prout, 2005; Stipek, 2005; Wyn & White, 1997):

- The period of middle childhood is not defined by biological age but rather by culture.
- The school-age child is an individual worthy of our attention, rather than a person to be marginalized as one who is merely on a path to adolescence.
- The study of middle childhood requires understanding the contexts in which normal development occurs and the dynamic interactions between persons and environments.
- The concept of transitions is useful for understanding changes in the lived experiences of school-age children, brought about by developmental tasks, such as puberty, or by social practices, such as changing from elementary to middle school.
- Children contribute to their own development as active agents in the world.
- Scholarship on middle childhood development relies on research from diverse disciplines, traditionally organized under rubrics other than *middle childhood*, such as *school-age children* or *early adolescents*.

STOP What other labels or descriptions have you heard to describe this age group?

REASONS TO STUDY MIDDLE CHILDHOOD

Developmental researchers from the related disciplines of psychology, child development, applied developmental science, family studies, and the health fields have emphasized the importance of the preadolescent period as a time of rapid growth and change. Understanding the developmental processes and contextual factors influencing middle childhood may provide answers to important basic questions about how children develop between ages 6 and 12. For example, as we learn more about the importance of protective factors—such as close relationships with significant adults—we find that school-agers who have a role model, teacher, or mentor are less likely to use drugs and alcohol, attempt suicide, engage in violence, or become sexually active during middle childhood (Huesmann, Dubow, Eron, & Boxer, 2006; Resnick et al. 1997; Werner & Smith, 2001).

Many professionals who work with children between ages 6 and 12—whether in after-school child care centers, out-of-school recreation centers, or extramural athletic programs—need information on normative development, that is, on what to expect from children this age. We know, for example, that they are industrious workers, engaged learners, and loyal friends. But as we learn even more about middle childhood development and the factors that affect resiliency in the face of risks such as poor neighborhoods, poverty, or family dysfunction, we will be able to design better programs to meet this group's developmental needs. For example, we have learned from researchers who evaluate prevention and intervention programs that to be successful community-based programs for at-risk children should be long-term and intensive rather than short-term and less engaging (Roth, Brooks-Gunn, Murray, & Foster, 1998). Applying the findings of basic developmental science may help practitioners design better services for 6- to 12-year-olds.

Adults raising children also want to know how best to enhance their children's success and development. For example, because families remain an important developmental influence even as school-age children expand their interest in peers, we know it is important for parents to remain connected with maturing early adolescents as they begin to seek more autonomy (Roth & Brooks-Gunn, 2000). Most research on middle childhood parenting informs us that although a parenting style that is democratic, firm, and loving is beneficial for both children and adolescents (Baumrind, 1971), more strict limit setting may be necessary for children living in dangerous neighborhoods (Sampson & Morenoff, 1997). Understanding the development of their school-age children and seeking ways to enhance their family and peer relationships may help parents and other caregivers improve the daily lives of children and families.

Legislators and policy makers often look for information on the effectiveness of youth intervention programs or prevention policies (see Huston, 2005). Many public policy makers rely on findings from multidisciplinary middle childhood studies regarding the different developmental pathways of low-risk and high-risk adolescents and the factors that may alter healthy and risky behaviors (Roth & Brooks-Gunn, 2000). For example, researchers in pediatrics, psychiatry, psychology, public health, family studies, sociology, and education contribute to an overall understanding of such issues as substance abuse or school violence (McCall & Groark, 2000). Increasingly, public policy recommendations recognize middle childhood and early adolescence as important periods in which children, themselves, are seen as assets rather than as liabilities to communities in which they live (Roth & Brooks-Gunn, 2000). Broadening their awareness of developmental outcomes in middle childhood may help policy makers and government agencies make better use of research findings in funding programs for school-age children.

Teachers, principals, and school board members frequently use research findings on the middle childhood years to create developmentally appropriate curricula for the middle-level grades. Teachers who work with late-elementary or middle-school children need to identify developmental transitions between middle childhood and adolescence, such as signs of early puberty or hypothetical thinking. In view of research indicating substantial declines in academic achievement and motivation between elementary and middle school (Eccles & Buchanan, 1996), many scholars believe that the middle grades are "the last, best time" to reach vulnerable youth before educational problems become chronic (*Growing Up,* 2001). More important, researchers studying middle-level education believe that the developmental needs of the learner should dictate the curricular, instructional, and structural practices of a school (Anfara, 2001).

Historical Context of Middle Childhood

Our current view of middle childhood is based on the emergence over time of the idea of childhood as a period of development that is somehow distinct from adulthood (see Boocock & Scott, 2005; Illick, 2002). According to histories of childhood, Western cultural views of childhood began in the Middle Ages, when children's lives were first seen as separate from the world of adults (Aries, 1960/1962; deMause, 1995). Medieval European cultures divided childhood into *infancy, puerility,* and *adolescence* (Aries, 1960/1962). In this sequence, infancy (*in fans* means "without language" in Latin) preceded childhood (*pueritia* means "childhood or boyhood" in Latin), which was followed by adolescence (*adolescere* means "to grow into maturity" in Latin). This concept of developmental stages persisted throughout the European Renaissance and Enlightenment periods of the 17th and 18th centuries. Nevertheless, few Western children were protected from harsh treatment by adults or guaranteed the right to an education (deMause, 1995).

By the 19th century, however, an emerging middle class in both Europe and America allowed children time to prepare for a productive adult life. Childhood was viewed as a period worthy of nurture and protection. Nevertheless, in both Europe and America, poor children and children from underrepresented groups did not enjoy the same privileges as the rest of the population (Trawick-Smith, 2006). For example, many children were required to work on farms or in factories as slaves or for extremely low wages rather than attend school. Although African American and American Indian children often did not have the social and economic advantages of most European American children, those cultures also regarded middle childhood as an important and cherished developmental period (Horn, 1993).

Today, in non-Western cultures childhood is often more highly valued than in Western societies. For example, in Asian cultures, Confucian teachings to value and respect children underlie a traditional emphasis on childhood education in countries such as China and Japan. In traditional African cultures, adults—especially mothers—exhibit a high degree of caring and concern for children. Historically, Latino cultures have stressed a commitment to sharing child-rearing among all community members. And most American Indians emphasize teaching children and adolescents to be competent and skillful in the ways of their tribe (Trawick-Smith, 2006).

Most early practices in America, however, expressed ambiguity about childhood and adolescence on the one hand and the following stage, known as *youth,* on the other (Aries, 1960/1962). Economic arrangements, such as apprenticeships that often began at age 7 or 8, obscured the boundary between childhood and adulthood. To a great extent, this confusion persists today, as demonstrated by the overlapping or conflicting age parameters used by different disciplines for the period of middle childhood (refer to Table 1.1). Inconsistent use of terms such as *school-age children, early adolescents, preteens,* and *youth* also makes it very difficult for educators,

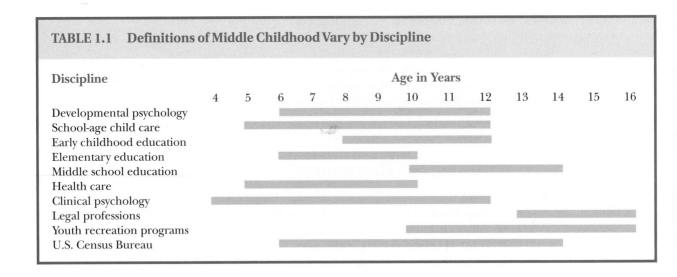

TABLE 1.1   Definitions of Middle Childhood Vary by Discipline

Discipline / Age in Years (4 5 6 7 8 9 10 11 12 13 14 15 16)

Developmental psychology
School-age child care
Early childhood education
Elementary education
Middle school education
Health care
Clinical psychology
Legal professions
Youth recreation programs
U.S. Census Bureau

researchers, parents, or service providers to know when they are referring to the same children. This problem is exacerbated when parents try to find suitable programs: Should they look at "youth" services if their child is only 10 years old?

STOP How would you have felt as a 10-year-old attending a youth program for teenagers?

Robyn, the middle child in her family, feels out of place in the after-school child care program attended by her younger sister Emily. She seems eager to engage in more varied out-of-school activities that could challenge her cognitive and physical skills beyond the classroom and would allow opportunities for more focused social interaction with friends.

Modern Contributions to Understanding Middle Childhood

At the turn of the 20th century, G. Stanley Hall, considered the first developmental psychologist by many scholars, reviewed the theoretical evidence for the concept that development extended beyond childhood into adolescence (Hall, 1904). Many developmental researchers, often Hall's students, carried out empirical studies of American children at different ages in an attempt to document the interaction of biological maturation, such as neurological development, and environmental experience, such as learning to read (Gesell & Ilg, 1943, 1946; Gesell, Ilg, & Ames, 1956). They accomplished this groundbreaking work by painstakingly assessing, interviewing, and observing children from infancy through adolescence. As a result, the first half of the 20th century was notable for the documentation of **normative**, or average, developmental abilities based on age across the years from birth through adolescence. By mid-century, the psychologist Arnold Gesell and his colleagues at the Yale Child Study Center had written a series of three books that fulfilled their goal of tracing "the course of development of normal youths in the concrete setting of their home, school, and community" (1956, p. xii).

Middle Childhood as a Developmental Period. Gesell documented the periods of infancy (birth to 2 years), preschool age (2 to 5 years), childhood (5 to 12 years), and adolescence (12 to 24 years) in three popular books published in the 1940s and

1950s. The first volume, *Infant and Child in the Culture of Today* (Gesell & Ilg, 1943), focused on early childhood (birth through age 5). The second and third volumes overlap the period presently called middle childhood: *The Child from Five to Ten* (Gesell & Ilg, 1946) and *Youth: The Years from Ten to Sixteen* (Gesell et al., 1956).

Gesell emphasized middle childhood as a distinct phase in the life span between early childhood and adolescence. He also believed that middle childhood is intermediate in both a maturational and a cultural sense. For example, cutting the first permanent tooth, a biological event, occurs around the time of school entrance, a sociological event. In fact, Gesell thought that middle childhood had been "slighted" by the educational system of his day, in which the curriculum was determined more by the institutional pressures of school and society than by the "psychology of development" (Gesell & Ilg, 1946). To understand how middle childhood came to be accepted as a stage of development, it is necessary to briefly examine what was occurring in American education in the early half of the 20th century.

In 1909, partly influenced by Hall's (1904) influential writings on development and partly as a response to overcrowding in the high schools of the era, the first junior high school was established to serve children in the seventh, eighth, and ninth grades. These "intermediate-school" models slowly began to replace the more common configuration of primary schools for grades 1 to 8 followed by secondary schools for grades 9 to 12. By the 1920s there were over 400 intermediate schools, and by the mid-1950s there were approximately 6,500 junior high schools in the United States (Wiles & Bondi, 2001). By this time, there also was an extensive educational literature on school-age children that described middle childhood as a unique developmental period called "preadolescence."

In the 1960s, a reform movement led by the humanistic educator William M. Alexander that focused on the needs of the student rather than the content of the curriculum resulted in the emergence of the modern middle school. These new schools started at even earlier ages than junior highs—at grade 5 or 6 (Manning & Bucher, 2000). The emergence of both junior high schools and middle schools was attributable to a desire to have high school academic subjects taught in earlier grades while emphasizing developmental differences in the ways that subject matter should be taught to less cognitively and socially mature students (Eichhorn, 1980; Wiles & Bondi, 2001).

In the 1970s, when most U.S. school systems were changing from junior highs to middle schools, the National Society for the Study of Education created a Committee on the Middle School Years to focus on ages 10 to 14 (Johnson, 1980). Noting the importance of the middle-school years, this committee recognized that the "preadolescent of eleven or twelve years is neither the ideal typical child of nine nor the archetypal adolescent of sixteen" (Lipsitz, 1980). Its major concern was the "fit" or "lack of fit" between social institutions, especially schools, and the developmental needs of school-age children (Lipsitz, 1980, p. 12).

In the 1980s, a panel of experts—assembled by the U.S. Committee on Child Development Research and Public Policy, the U.S. Commission on Behavioral and Social Sciences and Education, and the National Research Council—reviewed research on middle childhood and made recommendations for future research and public policy (Collins, 1984). The first task was to identify the age period commonly referred to as middle childhood: 6 to 12. Although the panel viewed any segmentation into age periods as somewhat arbitrary, they nevertheless felt that scholars had previously not been much concerned about the significance of changes in middle childhood. The members thought that by recognizing middle childhood as a separate developmental period, they would focus attention on school-age children's developmental characteristics and on the potential implications for teaching them (Collins, 1984, 2005; Huston & Ripke, 2006a).

The panel also sought to understand not only the development of children in middle childhood but also the **secular trends**, or variations across history in the average age when a given phenomenon occurs. For example, they soon realized that secular trends toward earlier puberty (than age 12) required consideration of more workable age groupings (e.g., preteens) for children whose physical, cognitive, and social characteristics were in transition (Collins, 1984). (Secular trends are discussed in detail in chapter 4.)

Middle Childhood as a Transition.   During the 1990s, scholars from many disciplines (including developmental psychology, human development, family science, education, social work, and others) began to reconceptualize middle childhood as a transitional period between early childhood and adolescence. Developmental researchers reviewed the scientific evidence for considering (a) childhood and adolescence as different stages of the life span and (b) the onset of early adolescence as a transitional period (Montemayor, Adams, & Gullotta, 1990). Their work was summarized in a book called *From Childhood to Adolescence: A Transitional Period?* After examining the similarities and differences between children and adolescents, most scholars have concluded that many developmental abilities emerge gradually rather than suddenly (Montemayor & Flannery, 1990). For example, the onset of puberty—as measured by hormone levels—begins earlier (around age 9 or 10!) than previously thought based on the appearance of observable secondary sexual characteristics, such as girls' breast development (Brooks-Gunn & Warren, 1989).

Today, many researchers identify developmental or social transitions, such as puberty, as events that bring about long-term psychological change (Graber, Brooks-Gunn, & Petersen, 1996). Other scholars, however, consider the study of transitions as a way to focus on how institutions, such as families or schools, structure the process of growing up (Wyn & White, 1997). Still others view transitions as opportunities to study how children may change their behaviors to fit a particular context, such as changing from elementary to middle school (Graber et al., 1996; Simmons & Blyth, 1987). Middle childhood transitions, however, depend on *both* age and generation; for example, children who are in the same grade level may experience similar educational and cultural trends. A few scholars have used a unique, though not popular, term to characterize the transitional nature of middle childhood: **tranescence,** defined as the stage of development that begins prior to the onset of puberty and extends through the early stages of adolescence (Eichhorn, 1966).

In considering the conditions necessary for successful navigation through the middle childhood years, psychologists, educators, and social policy experts increasingly have focused on predictors of adolescent outcomes. In 1994, building on the work of a previous research network on early childhood transitions, the MacArthur Foundation established a Task Force on Middle Childhood as well as an ongoing national research network. The MacArthur Network on Successful Pathways through Middle Childhood (1997) attempted to capture children's individual differences from the time they enter school until the early years of adolescence, as well as the diversity of influences and experiences of people of different ethnic, cultural, and economic backgrounds. In addition to school, the network's investigators examined

---

TABLE 1.2   Research Initiatives on Middle Childhood

The MacArthur Network on Successful Transitions through Middle Childhood has conducted cutting-edge research on middle childhood.

Project	Focus
MacArthur School Transition Study	Early intervention effects on school entry
The New Hope Child and Family Study	Work and family economics study
California Childhoods Project	Institutions, contexts, and pathways of development
Empirical Explorations of Pathways Through Middle Childhood	National longitudinal study of youth
Authority, Discipline, Compliance, and Autonomy in Middle Childhood	Historical essays on children's participation in institutions
Children of Immigrants	Ethnic identity and prejudice study
Task Force on "Race" and Ethnicity	Effects on developmental pathways
Ecocultural Interview Development	Daily routines and activities of middle childhood
Engagement with Institutions	How schools and communities engage children

Source: Detailed information on each project is available on the Web site: http://childhood.isr.umich.edu/index.html.

---

other contexts important to children, including family, community, economic resources, and culture, to address the following questions:

- What influences and experiences contribute to different outcomes for children during their first school years?
- How can the likelihood of successful outcomes be increased? (MacArthur Network on Successful Pathways through Middle Childhood, 2002).

See Table 1.2 for examples of ongoing research projects on middle childhood.

Today, when contemporary scholars meet to discuss research and share findings and methods of studying middle childhood, they often consider the implications of defining middle childhood as a period of preparation for adolescence along a path with many choices or "forks in the road." These alternative pathways may result in either risks or opportunities for school-age children. As summarized by one researcher, development "is about motion and momentum, about growing 'into' something, about making a transition, and about getting from one point to another" (Steinberg, 1995, p. 246). Thus, the current conceptualization of middle childhood development as a pathway, or developmental *trajectory,* reflects a movement away from describing developmental *periods* and toward explaining developmental *transitions* (e.g., Cooper, García Coll, Bartko, Davis, & Chatman, 2005; Huston & Ripke, 2006a; Weisner, 2005). Some contemporary middle childhood scholars envision the everyday activities of the school-age years—having breakfast, going to school, doing homework, hanging out with friends—as the "stepping-stones" children follow as they move along the pathway of development (Weisner, 2005).

In the latest publication of research from the MacArthur Network on Successful Pathways Through Middle Childhood (Huston & Ripke, 2006a), two overriding questions were addressed:

1. How do stability and change in middle childhood relate to developments in adolescence and adulthood?

Guideposts for Working with School-Age Children

- Children in middle childhood are often referred to as *school-age children, early adolescents, preteens,* or *youth.* Ask them which term best describes them and what they would like to be called.

- Familiarize yourself with developmental norms for the school-agers for whom you are responsible and carefully observe individual children to determine whether they are developing faster or slower than their age-mates.

- Determine what developmental transitions are facing the school-age children you work with by speaking with their parents or teachers.

- Talk with children to prepare them for what to expect as they face transitions, such as changing schools.

STOP When you were in middle childhood, what did you, your family, or your friends think that you were likely to "grow into"?

2. What do environmental contexts in middle childhood contribute to long-term developmental patterns?

The overall findings demonstrated that patterns of development during middle childhood often predicted later functioning over and above the contribution of early childhood development, with middle childhood development sometimes forecasting adulthood better than adolescence (Huston & Ripke, 2006b; see also Feinstein & Bynner, 2004).

MEANINGS OF CHILDHOOD IN POSTMODERN SOCIETIES

The idea that children's development in middle childhood represents a unique pattern of biological, social, and historical factors reflects an increasing emphasis on cultural relativism seen in many fields of study beginning in the late 20th century. You may have encountered this perspective in literature, philosophy, or the arts under the label of *postmodernism*. In historical terms, **postmodernity** refers to the idea that knowledge achieved through scientific research, sometimes called **logical positivism,** can no longer be regarded as universal and objective. A concept is **universal** when it has the same meaning, or exists in the same form, across different cultures. Postmodernists believe instead that all knowledge is partial and subjective. In this view, the meanings of childhood will vary from situation to situation and from culture to culture. Many postmodern academic approaches **deconstruct** the social discourse, or "read between the lines" of commonly held—but often unconscious—beliefs expressed in everyday conversations or routine actions, such as lunch times (e.g., Thorne, 2005). For example, understanding more fully contemporary usage of such terms as *middle childhood, the school-age years, early or preadolescence,* and *youth* requires deconstructing their meanings in the varied contexts of family, school, and community.

Do parents think there are unique challenges in middle childhood parenting? Do teachers believe that school-age children have special abilities, roles, and status in society? Do school-age children think of themselves as different from other age groups? Often, as we see in television portrayals of middle childhood, such as *Malcolm in the Middle* (Boomer, 2000), school-age children may feel powerless and dependent on others, whether in the family or school context. However, if we instead view middle childhood, youth, and adolescence as *social constructions* designed to control and limit children's access to power in society (Foucault, 1976/1978), the social function of childhood would become apparent.

The **social construction** of childhood refers to the ways in which the understandings of and expectations about children (and, later, adolescents) are passed on through society. For example, legally restricting child labor and mandating school attendance function together to limit youth's economic independence (Polakow Suransky, 1982). Families may also impose distance or curfew restrictions on children that limit their social interactions (O'Neil, 2002). In other words, the focus is not "on the inherent characteristics of young people themselves, but on the construction of youth through social processes (e.g., schooling, families or the labour market)" (Wyn & White, 1997, p. 9). In this view, the position individuals occupy in their social world (e.g., their age, gender, ethnicity, or social class) may interact with their exposure to material conditions (e.g., media, music, school environments, and youth subcultures) to socially construct the cultural life of middle childhood (Wyn & White, 1997; see also Prout, 2005).

Cultural Influences

Central to both positivist and postmodernist perspectives on development is the influence of culture: "Cultures make sense of the way people grow up" (Modell & Elder, 2002, p. 174). This view, called the **cultural ecology** of childhood, argues that children's participation in cultural activities is the major experience shaping development (Weisner, 1996, 2005). Through various social practices carried out in family, peer, and school contexts, children in middle childhood construct a sense of identity in relation to their families, their peer group, and the school culture.

In cultures whose primary goals for their children are other than individual achievement, children may be more often expected to assist with family and community survival (Weisner, 1998). For example, in some cultures, family life is often dependent on older children as important caregivers for younger siblings (Whiting & Edwards, 1992). When children are an important source of unpaid child care or family labor, the arbitrary separations between childhood, adolescence, and adulthood as unique developmental periods begin to blur (Montemayor, 2000).

Some cultures emphasize the difference between childhood and adulthood while others perceive development as continuous. In a classic ethnographic study, *Coming of Age in Samoa*, Margaret Mead (1928) found that the transition to adulthood was relatively smooth for Samoan adolescents because of their culture's structuring of adolescence as continuous with childhood as compared to Western societies (Côté, 2000a). Similarly, compared to the majority culture in the United States, many American Indian tribes do not expect children to be submissive to adults any more than adults are required to be submissive to each other (Broude, 1995).

Across ethnic groups in the United States, cultural constructions of middle childhood differ by family **ethnicity**, the sum total of ancestry and culture (McAdoo, 1999). Ethnicity is not so much a group characteristic as it is an encounter with a cultural difference that is perceived to influence social relations (Gjerde & Onishi, 2000). For example, African American and Hispanic children are often expected to take care of younger siblings. In fact, children of color frequently take on adult roles at an earlier age than do White children. In addition, youth who live on farms take on adult roles and responsibilities at an earlier age than do urban children; for example, Native American boys take on adult responsibilities of caring for family livestock (Montemayor, 2000). As a result, most scholars acknowledge that there are wide ethnic variations in individuals' behaviors that are based on the symbolic meanings attached to developmental processes in their societies (Cunningham & Spencer, 2000).

Anthropologists generally agree, however, that all cultures around the world draw some distinction among people on the basis of age, a phenomenon called **age grading**. At a minimum, most societies recognize differences between immature, mature, and elderly people (Broude, 1994). Although some form of age grouping is found in virtually all cultures, various ethnic groups may define middle childhood differently from others. As we have discussed in this chapter, Europeans and Americans commonly distinguish between infants, toddlers, schoolchildren, adolescents, young adults, middle-aged adults, and senior citizens. In many African cultures, males are classified into the categories of newly born infants, children on the lap, uninitiated boys, initiated bachelors, married men, elders, and retired elders (Broude, 1994).

When considering middle childhood as socially constructed, the idea that these age breakdowns may not be universal is important. A common fallacy is to think that children's development looks alike in different cultures (Chatterjee, Bailey, & Aronoff, 2001; Cole, 1996). Although humans, like most species, must necessarily experience biological immaturity, *childhood* is the manner in which a society understands and enacts that physical reality (Woodson, 1999). Anthropologists refer to taking an **emic** approach, one that acknowledges culturally specific variations, as contrasted with an **etic** approach, one that assumes similarity across cultures (Liddell, 2002). For example, cultural anthropologists have suggested that the concept of a middle childhood developmental transition toward more complex cognitive capacities and social skills may be more cultural (emic) than universal (etic) because it promotes the Western concept of individualized achievement in school (Weisner, 1998). The United Nations has stated (1986) that if "youth" is understood as an extension of childhood in some cultures but as the beginning of adulthood in others, then the concept is not universal. In the United States, for example, there are child labor laws to protect children from economic exploitation or developmentally inappropriate experiences. However, if we consider that—worldwide—50 million children under age 15 work in fields and factories (or fight in armed conflicts), childhood cannot be considered a protected status in all cultures (Wyn & White, 1997). A more balanced view of child labor is advocated by some scholars (e.g., McKechnie & Hobbs, 1999, 2002). "Work by children sometimes is viewed negatively, ideally to be replaced by a better alternative, namely, education. However, this either-or approach ignores the possibility of learning through work and assumes that all education is necessarily appropriate to all contexts" (McKechnie & Hobbs, 2002, p. 217). In this global view, the value of children's work is determined by the culture and family.

The meaning of being a school-age child depends on your experiences in a specific historical time and place (Närvänen & Näsman, 2004). For example, some authors have referred to children born in or after 1982 as the "millennial" generation because the first of this **cohort** (a group born in the same year) will have graduated from high school in or after the year 2000 (Howe & Strauss, 2000, Verhaagen, 2005). Yet there are many ways in which the experiences of a school-age child in the early 21st century may differ from those of "millennials," who were in middle childhood during the late 20th century—such as experiencing the 2001 terrorist attacks on the United States as an infant rather than as a young adult (see Gershoff & Aber, 2004a, 2004b). And although a generational event may affect all children, the experience of American children in immigrant families from Islamic countries may be quite different from that experienced by nonimmigrants. Arab American children, for example, may encounter prejudice and discrimination despite having been born in the United States.

Social position, racism, and segregation may also interact to create unique contexts and pathways for children of color and of immigrant families. Segregated school or neighborhood environments with limited resources may, at the same time, be supportive if they promote children's emotional and academic adjustment, helping them to manage the societal demands imposed by discrimination. Such contexts have been termed *adaptive* because they help children to navigate successful pathways through middle childhood (e.g., García Coll et al., 1996; García Coll & Szalacha, 2004; García Coll, Szalacha, & Palacios, 2005). Although increases in worldwide migration are a trend that is expected to increase over the next several decades (Prout, 2005), many school-age children reside in **transnational** families that maintain links to their countries of origin through regular travel to their homelands, visits from relatives who live abroad, or communications over the Internet with family and friends in their home countries (Blume & De Reus, 2007; Rumbaut, 2005).

Demographic Influences

Of the 32.9 million U.S. students in the grades below high school, 61% are identified as White (non-Hispanic), 19% as Hispanic, 16% as Black, and 4% as Asian and Pacific Islander and other races. Twenty percent have at least one foreign-born parent and 5% were born outside the United States. By 2020, the numbers of children of color are expected to increase dramatically, as seen in Figure 1.2. Between 2000 and 2004, the percentage of children who are non-Hispanic White declined slightly to 59% and is projected to decline to 53% by 2020. The percentage of the child population that is Hispanic increased from 9 to 19% between 1980 and 2004 and is expected to increase further, to 24%, by 2020. Non-Hispanic Asian and Pacific Islander children increased from 2 to 4% of the child population between 1980 and 2001; Asian-only children made up 4% of the child population in 2004 and are expected to increase to 5% of the

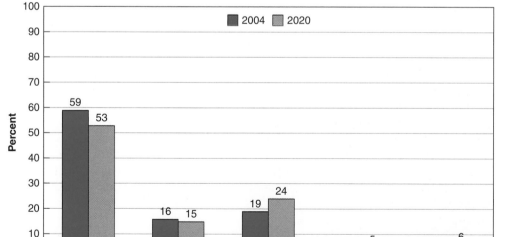

Percentage Distribution of Children Under Age 18 in the US, by Race and Ethnicity, 2004 and Projection, 2020

Note: Data reflect new race categories from the 2000 decennial census and only include those respondents who identified with a single race. Those who chose multiple races are included in 'all other races'. Other races also includes American Indians and Pacific Islanders. Those of Hispanic origin may be of any race.
Source: Data for 2020 projections. America's Children in Brief. Key National Indicators of Well-Being, 2004, Table POPI - Federal Interagency Forum on Child and Family Statistics, Washington, DC: U.S. Government Printing Office. Data for 2004. Child trends calculations of U.S. Census Bureau, Population Division, Population Estimates Program. "National estimates by demographic characteristics -single year of age, sex, race, and Hispanic Origin", Monthly Postcensal Resident Population, July 2003, July 2004. Available at http://www.census.gov/popest/datasets.html.

FIGURE 1.2
U.S. Ethnic Population of Children

The population of children of color in the United States is projected to increase dramatically by 2020.

Source: Child Trends. Child Trends Data Bank Indicator: Racial and Ethnic Composition of the Child Population. Retrieved from http://www.childtrendsdatabank.org/figures/60-Figure-2.gif. Copyright 2000 by Child Trends, Inc. Reprinted by permission.

population by 2020. The percentage of the child population that is non-Hispanic Black has stayed relatively constant, at about 15%, since 1980, where it is expected to remain in 2020 (Child Trends, 2005).

In 2000, the United States had only 3.3% of the world's children under age 15 but ranked sixth among the world's countries in contributing to the under-15 population. By contrast, the developing countries of India, Nigeria, Pakistan, Ethiopia, and Congo [Kinshasa] contributed approximately 60% of the growth in the world's population of children under age 15 during the last decade. By 2025, the United States is expected to have 15% more children, while the number of children globally will be just 3% larger than in 2000 (U.S. Bureau of the Census, 2001b). Nevertheless, because of generally lower birthrates in the United States compared to previous decades, children constitute a declining proportion of the U.S. population (Huston & Ripke, 2006a; Prout, 2005). In 2001, for example, the percentage of 6- to 11-year-olds in the United States was 8.5% of the population, compared to 9.1% in 1980 (Huston & Ripke, 2006a).

In the United States, elementary school enrollment is estimated at 16.8 million children in grades 1 through 4, and 16.1 million children in grades 5 through 8, comprising about 40% of the total school population (U.S. Bureau of the Census, 2001a, 2001b). These trends are important for understanding school-age children as a diverse group and for creating successful middle childhood programs. Increasingly, educators recognize that schools have the opportunity to structure the teaching and learning environment to allow for the emergence of multiple perspectives (Slattery, 1999).

Technological Influences

Diversity is also connected to technological innovations, particularly in terms of global media and communications technologies (Luke, 1999). For example, although school-age children may be exposed to gender and ethnic stereotypes from mass media such as television or video games, they often encounter counter-

A majority of today's school-age children have access to computers, either at home or school.

Krista Greco/Merrill

stereotypical portrayals in the media as well (Huesmann & Taylor, 2006; Wilson, 2004). Since passage of the Children's Television Act in 1990, television broadcasters have been required to provide multicultural educational and informational programs during the hours when children are likely to be in the viewing audience. Although most programming has been targeted at young children, longitudinal research with school-age viewers from grades 2 to 6 has documented that they learned prosocial and academic content from educational television programming. These effects were strongest for girls and for older children (Calvert & Kotler, 2003).

The contemporary school-age child from a middle-class family is more connected to global cultures than youth from previous generations (Howe & Strauss, 2000). In the year 2000, nearly two thirds (64.1%) of children in the United States aged 6 to 11 years had access to a computer at home and nearly one quarter (25%) had access to the Internet at home. Of all school-age children (6 to 17 years), 22% had access only at school, and only 10.4% had no access at all (U.S. Bureau of the Census, 2001c). Among 8- to 16-year-olds, 20% had a computer in their bedroom (of whom 54% had Internet access) (Wartella, Caplovitz, & Lee, 2004). In addition, a national random sample of American families revealed that 46% of 8- to 12-year-olds had a television in their bedrooms (Gentile & Walsh, 2002)! Despite such trends, in 2001, Internet use and computer access was lower in low-income than in high-income households, often termed the **digital divide** (Jennings & Wartella, 2004). In contrast to the 1990s, however, when boys were more likely to use computers and the Internet than girls were, overall computer and Internet use rates for boys and girls are now about the same (National Center for Education Statistics, 2003). Refer to Figure 1.3 for a comparison of children's use of computers in home and school settings.

Most studies of elementary and middle-school children have focused on the educational benefits of computer-based learning environments in the classroom and positive relationships between home and school learning in a computer-mediated environment (see Kafai, Fishman, Bruckman, & Rockman, 2002; Kafai & Sutton, 1999). "This group, supposedly 'the digital generation,' is claimed to represent the future, being 'in the vanguard'; yet it is also seen as vulnerable, at risk from new information and communication technologies (ICT)" (Livingstone, 2003, p. 148). Therefore, a discussion of postmodern influences on the social construction of youth would be incomplete without also considering **new media,**

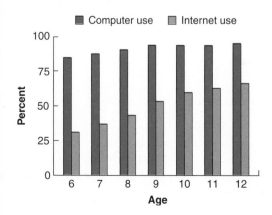

FIGURE 1.3

Computer and Internet Use of 6- to 12-Year-Olds

Between ages 6 and 12, computer use is fairly stable, but Internet use increases steadily.

Source: Adapted from *Computer and Internet use by children and adolescents in 2001: Statistical analysis report* (p. 5) by the National Center for Education Statistics, 2003. Washington, DC: U.S. Department of Education.

such as instant messaging, Web logs (blogs), and chat rooms; pagers, personal digital assistants (PDAs), and cell phones; video streaming, digital cameras, and high-definition television (HDTV); and digital video discs (DVDs), compact discs (CDs), and digital music players (MP3s, iPods). European researchers have found that new media have entered into the lives of children aged 6 to 16 through a gradual process of increasing access to and changing attitudes about new technologies (Krotz, 2001). A 3-year study of attitudes toward using computers, for example, revealed that most parents of 5- to 12-year olds see their primary value as an educational tool, whereas most children view computers as entertainment (Downs, 1999).

We know much more about children's use of computers, video games, and the Internet (e.g., Huston & Wright, 1997) than about their use of PDAs, cell phones, and wireless technologies (Jennings & Wartella, 2004; Wartella et al., 2004). Researchers who study the impact of *simultaneously* instant-messaging, e-mailing, and downloading homework assignments on children's and families' everyday lives have referred to the millennial generation as **Gen M**, as much for their ability to multitask as for their media use (Roberts, Foehr, & Rideout, 2005; Wallis, 2006; see also Lenhart, Rainie, & Lewis, 2001; Woodard & Gridina, 2000).

Through the influence of the Internet and satellite communications, a global youth culture is growing (Weisner, 2001). For example, researchers comparing families with school-age children to families with adolescents found that as children grow up, they increasingly use new media within a "community of users" (Caron & Caronia, 2001). (Social networking on the Internet will be discussed in chapter 10.)

By around age 10, school-age children show increased understanding of the technical and social complexities of the Internet, regardless of experience (Yan, 2005). Children are not only aware of historical change, such as new technologies, but they are also often part of that change (Modell & Elder, 2002). Newer nonsequential ways of accessing information, such as hypertext, have caused theorists to question developmental stage approaches to children's construction of knowledge (Luke, 1999). Let's see what that means in terms of our case study child, Robyn:

 STOP In what ways do you think your middle childhood was socially constructed?

When Robyn expresses interest in dance, what does she do? She doesn't want to go to the same dance studio as her older sister. In her after-school program that day, Robyn sits down at the computer, clicks on the icon for a Web browser, and logs on to the Internet. Robyn types "dance studios" into the search engine and finds four in her hometown!

Guideposts for Working with School-Age Children

- Because middle childhood is a social construction, talk with teachers, parents, and school-agers themselves to determine how they think about the "rules" of childhood.
- Conduct home visits or parent conferences to learn about cultural or ethnic values among diverse families when addressing their children's

developmental, psychological, or educational needs.

- Consider the pervasive influence of new media on school-age children by making sure that you design or select curricula that makes effective use of information and communications technology.

DEVELOPMENTAL MILESTONES IN MIDDLE CHILDHOOD

Now that we have defined middle childhood, you may be wondering "*What* is it that develops?" Recall that in this chapter we have described middle childhood both as a *stage* and as a *pathway* to future development. The metaphor of transition (i.e., the pathway) involves looking at markers (i.e., milestones) along the way in order to measure developmental progress. Developmental milestones in middle childhood can be classified into one of four broad **domains**—which provides the organizational framework for the remainder of this text. A developmental *domain* is an area of child or human development, such as physical, cognitive, affective, or social development. Refer to Figure 1.4 for a depiction of the four domains of middle childhood development.

1. *Physical Development.* In middle childhood, this domain includes biological and neurophysiological development, the refinement of perceptual and motor skills, and physical health, including nutrition and exercise. School-age children undergo rapid spurts in height and weight as well as improvement in athletic abilities. They begin the onset of puberty at varied ages, with 11 years the average age for girls and 13 years for boys, marked first by hormonal changes, followed by observable changes in physical appearance and behavior.

2. *Cognitive Development.* This domain includes intellectual and language development, reasoning abilities, and memory capacities. The middle years of childhood are characterized by a gradual increase in logical reasoning using concrete examples, increased awareness of memory and learning strategies, and the achievement and consolidation of important academic skills, such as reading, writing, and computing.

3. *Affective Development.* This domain includes personality, emotional development, motivation, and self-esteem. School-age children acquire personal competencies

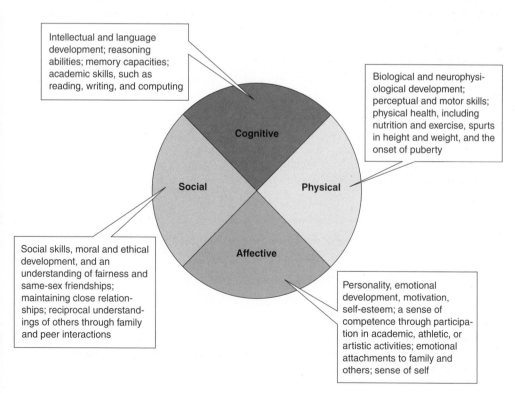

Intellectual and language development; reasoning abilities; memory capacities; academic skills, such as reading, writing, and computing

Biological and neurophysiological development; perceptual and motor skills; physical health, including nutrition and exercise, spurts in height and weight, and the onset of puberty

Social skills, moral and ethical development, and an understanding of fairness and same-sex friendships; maintaining close relationships; reciprocal understandings of others through family and peer interactions

Personality, emotional development, motivation, self-esteem; a sense of competence through participation in academic, athletic, or artistic activities; emotional attachments to family and others; sense of self

Cognitive

Social

Physical

Affective

FIGURE 1.4
Developmental Domains of Middle Childhood

Middle childhood is a distinct developmental period with normative changes occurring simultaneously in all domains.

through participation in academic, athletic, or artistic activities; emotional attachments to family members and others; and a deepening sense of who they are and what they can achieve through serious effort and commitment.

4. *Social Development.* This domain includes social skills and interpersonal understanding, moral and ethical development, and maintaining close relationships. Youth develop reciprocal understandings of others through family and peer interactions, deepening same-sex friendships, and seeking fairness in their family, school, and peer groups.

Individual children, however, are whole persons, living in the real world and developing as a totality rather than in separate functional domains of development (physical, cognitive, affective, social). Although a great deal of our knowledge about middle childhood comes from studies conducted on specific areas of development, our study of middle childhood takes a **holistic approach** to human development (Cairns, 2000; Magnusson, 1995, 2000). From a holistic point of view, biological, psychological, and social factors operate together to produce growth and change through reciprocal interaction with the environment, a process that starts at conception and goes on throughout the life span (Magnusson, 1995; Magnusson & Stattin, 2006). Box 1.1 describes the ways in which developmental principles should be reflected in school-age child care programs. By following these guidelines, parents and practitioners can apply their

BOX 1.1   Roadmap to Successful Practice
Developmental Implications of School-Age Child Care Programs

Aside from specific activities, there are general needs that all school-age children have, including opportunities (a) to be cooperative and responsible; (b) to be treated with dignity and respect; and (c) to be recognized for their individual styles of learning. In curriculum and programming, special attention should be given to:

1. Providing activities of high interest
2. Recognizing that there are many ways to learn
3. Letting children make choices about what they want to learn
4. Nurturing ways of knowing through guidance and encouragement
5. Creating an atmosphere of trust and honesty
6. Accepting children as they are—bold or timid, serious or "silly"
7. Providing opportunities for children's successes
8. Reinforcing children's achievements
9. Allowing time for spontaneous and natural play
10. Encouraging creative thinking and behavior
11. Taking into account what activities the children have been involved in during the day
12. Recognizing and planning for individual differences

People who plan out-of-school experiences need to emphasize alternatives and choices. No one plan is suitable to meet all needs.

Source: Based on "Themes and Issues in Middle Childhood" (pp. 51–52), by S. Lamorev, B. E. Robinson, B. H. Rowland, and M. Coleman, 1999, in *Latchkey Kids: Unlocking Doors for Children and their Families,* 2nd ed., Thousand Oaks, CA: Sage. Copyright 1999 by Sage Publications, Inc.

knowledge of child growth and development to a widespread context for middle childhood development.

THEORETICAL VIEWPOINTS

In this text, theories of development are integrated throughout the topical discussions of middle childhood, as shown in Table 1.3. In each chapter, you will read about the specific theories that exemplify particular domains of study, such as physical, cognitive, affective, or social development. However, because this text presents a contextual view of development, we first must examine two theories that are overarching in their scope: ecological theory and developmental-contextual theory. These two major **theoretical models** have guided a holistic approach to middle childhood.

TABLE 1.3   Summary Table of Developmental Theories

Chapter	Theories	Focus
1: Middle Childhood in Context	Ecological	The many embedded environments in which children develop over time—from the more immediate, such as family, school, and community, to the more remote, such as the broader society and culture
	Developmental-Contextual	Dynamic developmental and reciprocal relationship processes that occur between parents, children, and their social networks within the embedded contexts of ecological theory
2: Studying Middle Childhood	Purpose of Theories	To generate research questions and to provide a framework for organizing facts, interpreting data, and drawing conclusions
3: Physical Development in Middle Childhood	Behavior Genetics	Influence of genes and the environment on development through the analysis of shared and nonshared environments
	Biological	The study of such fields as behavioral neuroscience and how brain structure, function, and chemistry influence behavior
4: Puberty, Sexuality, and Health	Evolutionary Developmental	How selected genes helped our ancestors survive and reproduce, and how these same genes may influence our behavior and thinking
5: Cognitive Development In Middle Childhood	Cognitive Developmental	How children develop thought and problem-solving skills in direct interaction with the environment through the processes of assimilation and accommodation
	Sociocultural	Development of thought through language development and interacting with elders from one's culture
	Information Processing	How children process information by studying perception, memory, and knowledge and the factors that influence their development
6: Literacy, Intelligence and Academic Achievement	Psychometric	Using tests to assess individual and group differences among children's abilities; using the results to predict future performance and related abilities
7: Affective Development in Middle Childhood	Psychoanalytic	Process of individuation as the basis for personality development and establishing a sense of self

(continued)

TABLE 1.3   Summary Table of Developmental Theories (Continued)

Chapter	Theories	Focus
	Psychosocial	Period of industry vs. inferiority in which a major task is the acquisition of competence and the avoidance of failure
	Humanistic	Self-actualization and personal growth as well as the importance of positive regard from others
8: Relationships and Families	Attachment	Internal working models of early relationships in families as the basis of later close relationships, such as peer relations, friendships, and romantic partnerships
	Family Systems	Equilibrium among simultaneous interdependent subsystems, such as the parent-child, marital, or sibling systems
9: Social and Moral Development in Middle Childhood	Social Cognition	Observing models, examining the consequences of social behaviors, and predicting other people's motives in social interactions
	Social Perspective-Taking	Developmental stages of understanding and negotiating interpersonal relationships
	Moral Reasoning	Understanding of fairness, conventional morality, and concepts of care and justice
10: Friends, Play, and Peer Relations	Friendship Understanding	Developmental sequence of understanding the meaning and function of friendship
	Ethological	Social behavior and social status in peer relations and peer networks
11: Social Identities and Gender Development in Middle Childhood	Social Identity	Identification and belonging to social groups, such as gender and race/ethnicity, as well as explaining in-group and out-group attitudes
	Gender Schema	Gender beliefs reflected in the understanding of self and others and influencing children's behavior
12: Beyond Middle Childhood: Adolescence	Life Span	Development in relation to preceding and subsequent stages with a focus on both individual differences and developmental changes over time
	Life Course	Normative and nonnormative life events that are shaped by both historical events and adolescents' personal life histories

---

They do not focus on any one developmental domain, but rather describe and explain the interrelationships across time among many areas of development in the real world.

The Ecology of Human Development

The concept of interrelated systems in human development is epitomized by Urie Bronfenbrenner's ecological theory, which describes the complexity of human development, as well as the idea that the developing person is a biological system, interacting with other systems that are external to the individual. **Ecological theory** is important because it demonstrates the systemic interaction between the person and the environment, or ecology, at four different levels: the *microsystem,* the *mesosystem,* the *exosystem,* and the *macrosystem* (Bronfenbrenner, 1979; Bronfenbrenner & Crouter, 1983).

- The first of these levels, the **microsystem,** consists of interaction between the developing person and other individuals, such as parents. Thus, we may speak of the parent-child or the teacher-child systems, for example, as operating as microsystems.

- When two or more microsystems interact either indirectly, such as a parent-teacher conference in which parents and teachers interact together, or directly, such as when schoolchildren enter a new ecological setting like middle school, a **mesosystem** is operating.

- An **exosystem** refers to influences that are external to an individual child—such as the effect of parental employment—but which nevertheless affect children's development either directly, such as through school-age children's need for out-of-school supervision, or indirectly, such as through family income.

- Lastly, the **macrosystem** includes the broader cultural influences on development, such as ethnic or religious values.

Bronfenbrenner's (1979) ecological model is illustrated in Figure 1.5 using ever-widening circles of influence surrounding the child, who is pictured at the center. More recently, ecological theory has been reconceptualized using *time* as a defining feature:

- **Microtime** is used to analyze continuity within immediate episodes of children's behavior.

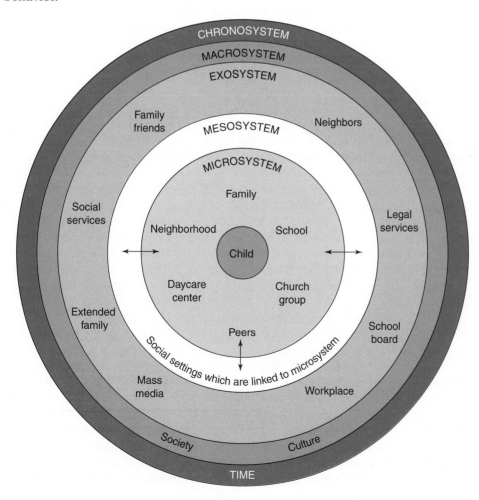

FIGURE 1.5
Bronfenbrenner's Bioecological Model

School-age children develop in the embedded contexts of families, communities, societies, and cultures.

Source: From Lerner, Richard. *Adolescence: Development, diversity, context, and application* (1st ed.) (p. 50). Copyright © 2002 by Pearson Education, Inc., Upper Saddle River, NJ. Adapted by permission of the publisher. Reprinted by permission.

- **Mesotime** is used to examine stability over longer periods of time—even years.
- **Macrotime** is used to interpret historical influences in the society over the life span of a person or a generation. (Bronfenbrenner & Morris, 2006)

In addition to emphasizing ecological contexts (the **bioecological model,** as it is now called), Bronfenbrenner and his colleagues have attempted to create a model that can be used to empirically test **proximal processes,** or mechanisms that mediate the interaction *over time* between genetics and the environment. Examples of such processes are parent-child activities, group or solitary play, reading, learning new skills, problem solving, performing complex tasks, and acquiring new knowledge (Bronfenbrenner & Ceci, 1994). These processes are a function of the characteristics of the developing person (e.g., middle childhood dispositions or abilities), the immediate or remote environmental context (e.g., home, school, or neighborhood), and the time periods in which the activity takes place (e.g., immediately, across days and weeks, or within and across generations) (Bronfenbrenner & Morris, 2006).

Recently, scholars have suggested that the boundaries between the ecological contexts are still too discrete. Rather than thinking of these developmental contexts as "levels" and describing the interaction among them, a more postmodern contextual approach would see these contexts as fluid rather than static. In such a revision of the ecological model, for example, researchers would no longer investigate only micro- or meso-level interactions and essentially ignore the other levels of the ecological "context." Instead, developmental scientists would engage in increasingly cross-level research that operationalizes a more truly multidirectional reciprocity (Prout, 2005), as discussed in the following section.

Developmental-Contextual Theory

Like bioecological theory, **developmental-contextual theory** also describes dynamic interactions between people and environments that occur simultaneously on many levels—biological, psychological, sociocultural, and historical (Riegel, 1976). In addition, developmental-contextual theory translates bioecological theory into a framework for applied research and practice (Ford & Lerner, 1992; Lerner, 2002a). For example, changes within one level of organization, such as developmental changes in the individual (e.g., *Robyn's interest in developing competence in swimming or dance*), are related to reciprocal changes in other levels, such as changes in patterns of family interaction (e.g., *she will no longer attend after-school care with her younger sister*) (Lerner, 1996). The case study of Robyn illustrates an important assumption of this theory: Stability or change in human development is dependent on person-context interactions (Lerner, 2002a; Magnusson & Stattin, 2006).

A key to understanding developmental-contextual theory is knowing that it describes a *dynamic* system (Lewis, 2000), from the micro level of the individual person (e.g., Robyn) to the macro level of the environment (e.g., her family, her friends, her after-school activities) (Magnusson & Stattin, 2006). In a developmental-contextual system, people are "fused" with their contexts across the life span such that "children function within and as part of, not just in relationship to, their contexts" (Ford & Lerner, 1992, p. 76). Developmental-contextual theory goes a step further than bioecological theory by enumerating varied contexts, specific people, and the relationships among them.

Developing individuals are embedded in a broader social network of school, work, or family relationships. In the developmental-contextual model depicted in Figure 1.6, both parent and child are whole persons, each developing in all domains

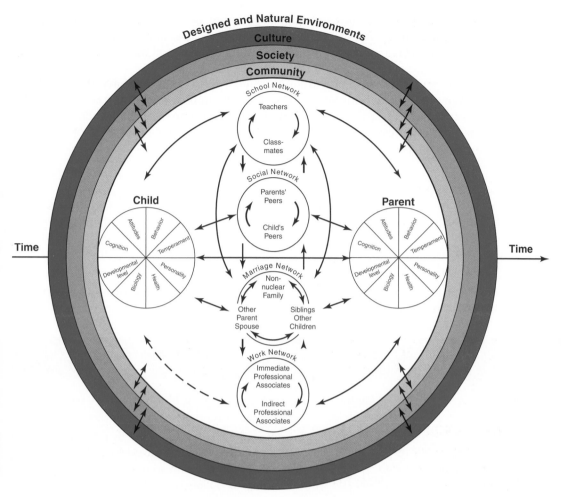

FIGURE 1.6
Lerner's Developmental Contextual Model

The developmental-contextual model illustrates how children's and parents' development are comprised of multiple, ongoing interactions among various social networks.

Source: From D. H. Ford and R. M. Lerner, *Developmental Systems Theory: An Integrative Approach* (p. 77). Copyright 1992 by Sage Publications, Inc. Reprinted by permission of the publisher.

of human development (represented as slices of a pie) while interacting in multiple environments. And, finally, all of these relations are continually changing across time. For example, families change from being made up of infants and young children to being made up of teenagers. Similarly, communities, societies, and cultures can also change over the course of time. Also, individuals and groups exist in a physical world that, of course, changes as well. Changes in any of these levels, therefore, may produce transformations in the other levels (Lerner, 2002b).

Another way to understand this dynamic process is to recognize that any developmental outcome is probabilistic—it will *probably* occur due to variations in the context or the timing of an interaction (Lerner, 2002b). Given that human development is the outcome of these ongoing exchanges between individual and environment, the essential process of development, called **probabilistic epigenesis**,

STOP Have you changed since middle childhood, and, if so, how are these changes interrelated?

involves *changing relations* between developing persons and changing contexts, whether the family studied over its life cycle, the classroom or lunchroom studied over the school year, or the community studied over several weeks, months, or years (Lerner, 1996).

Consistent with our contextual approach, ethnographers have theorized that these dynamic interactions are produced in a given historical time and place. In this view, particular trajectories of development may be shaped through **social practices,** defined as "organized activity that takes place in particular contexts of meaning" (Thorne, 2005, p. 85; see also Bourdieu, 1977).

> Take Robyn, for example: If she enrolls in dance classes instead of the after-school program, she will probably meet new friends, gain physical skills, and develop an appreciation of the arts—but only if she and her family choose dance over swim classes. For her to achieve a future dance career depends not only on her body type and talent but also on her persistence over time and on continued family, teacher, and peer support throughout her middle childhood and adolescence.

> Box 1.2 provides an example of longitudinal research on the benefits of extracurricular activities in middle childhood for adjustment in adolescence.

 Box 1.2   Roadmap to Understanding Theory and Research
Free Time Activities in Middle Childhood

The study *Free Time Activities in Middle Childhood: Links with Adjustment in Early Adolescence* (McHale, Crouter, & Tucker, 2001) used ecological theory to guide an investigation of the developmental significance of children's activities. Researchers assessed the links between how children spent their free time (in sports, hobbies, playing with toys and games, outdoor play, reading, television viewing, and hanging out) and their adjustment as they moved through middle childhood. As suggested by Bronfenbrenner's (1979) theory, across diverse ecologies the demands of children's daily activities offer important developmental opportunities. Researchers Susan McHale, Nan Crouter, and Corinna Tucker (2001) hypothesized that the different social contexts of children's free-time activities—whether children spend time with parents or in unsupervised settings with peers—would influence their later adjustment in early adolescence. The researchers (2001) cited several reasons why "middle childhood may be an important developmental period in which to study free-time use":

• Important individual and group differences may emerge in middle childhood. Although time use varies less in early childhood, by adolescence social class differences are more pronounced.

• Middle childhood is described by Erikson (1968) as a time of "industry" when children's attention is on becoming competent in a range of important skills.

• How children spend their time in middle childhood may have important implications for opportunities and choices later in adolescence when they have more chances to select their own "niches."

• American children spend more time than children from other countries on leisure activities—up to 50% of their waking hours. In addition, school-age children from lower socioeconomic backgrounds watch more television and spend more time playing outdoors (riding bikes, playing on playgrounds) than middle-class children, who spend more time reading or in organized sports.

• Studies of gender differences indicate that in the United States, boys and girls with similar amounts of free time spend it in different ways. Boys are more often involved in television

(continued)

Box 1.2   Roadmap to Understanding Theory and Research *(Continued)*
Free Time Activities in Middle Childhood

viewing or sports, while girls spend more time reading or doing hobbies.

According to the authors,

> . . . free-time activities may bring children into contact with peers and adults who share their interests; spending time in mutually enjoyable activities, in turn, may foster feelings of closeness and affiliation, with positive implications for psychological well-being. From a sociological perspective, time use matters because of both the nature *and* the social contexts of individuals' activities. (McHale, Crouter, & Tucker, 2001, p. 1766)

A second goal of the study was to explore whether the social contexts of activities (either with parents, unrelated adults, unsupervised peers, or alone) made a difference in later adjustment.

Method

Families with first-born boys (102) and first-born girls (96) were recruited for the study from rural and small school districts in a northeastern state. At the beginning of the study, the average age of the children was almost 11 years old, all but two adopted Asian children were White; and their families ranged from working- to upper-middle class. Ninety percent of mothers and all of the fathers were employed.

Two procedures were used for data collection in the study. First, an initial home interview and seven follow-up evening telephone interviews were conducted in which children and parents reported on (a) their daily activities outside of school and work (*hobbies, sports, reading, playing with toys and games, outdoor play, watching television,* or *hanging out*); (b) how long each activity lasted (*in minutes*); and (c) with whom they had engaged in that activity (*time with mother, time with father, time with peers with no adult present, time with nonparental adults,* and *time alone*). Second, several measures of the children's adjustment also were collected: (a) mothers rated their children's *conduct*; (b) children reported on their symptoms of *depression*; and (c) report cards were examined to determine school *grades*.

Results

The study revealed positive links between school-age children's free-time activities and their adjustment, suggesting that structured activities, such as hobbies and sports, are constructive ways for children to spend their time. In contrast to the positive implications of sports and hobbies, time spent playing outdoors and hanging out were linked to less-adaptive functioning, including both poorer grades and more behavior problems. Although reading was positively related to academic achievement, it was also associated with depression, perhaps because it is a solitary activity (McHale, Crouter, & Tucker, 2001).

The researchers also demonstrated that the nature of activities in middle childhood is related to differing opportunities for social ties. Some activities were done alone (e.g., *reading* and sometimes *hobbies*), some with unrelated adults (e.g., *hobbies* and *sports*), some with parents (e.g., *sports* and *TV*), and some with peers unsupervised by adults (e.g., *hanging out, playing outdoors*). Beyond these direct links between activities and social contexts, time spent with parents and adults was related to positive adjustment, whereas time spent alone and in unsupervised peer activities predicted adjustment problems. In the case of outdoor play and school grades, the results suggested that effects were different for girls and boys. Girls' adjustment was linked to time in particular social contexts, whereas boys' adjustment was explained by the nature of their activities (McHale, Crouter, & Tucker, 2001).

Conclusion

This study by McHale, Crouter, and Tucker (2001) exemplifies research conducted from an ecological perspective. In addition to examining factors at the *micro* level of analysis (e.g., children's grades, depression, and conduct), the authors also analyzed *mesosystem* relationships between the nature of the child's activities and differing social contexts (e.g., with parents, peers, unrelated adults, or alone). *Exosystem* considerations were reflected in controlling for such influences as parent employment, education, and socioeconomic status. Finally, while not explicitly addressed, the fact that the families in the study represented a very narrow sample of the rural northeastern United States may have underestimated *macrosystem* influences, such as ethnic or cultural differences, which might have been more significant if the study had included a more diverse group.

Guideposts for Working with School-Age Children

- Because middle childhood is not only an important developmental stage but also a transition to adolescence, use children's current abilities as a foundation for teaching future skills.

- Since home, school, and community are the primary contexts in which middle childhood development occurs, become familiar with these settings for the children you work with.

- Evaluate the ways that diverse contexts may affect children's performance, for example,

comparing their success on classroom tasks to their completion of homework assignments.

- Take a long view of growth and change over time by comparing children's current achievement of developmental or educational milestones to their performance over longer periods, such as the school year.

- Keep in mind how historical events, such as school desegregation, have shaped the contexts of middle childhood development over time.

CONTEXTS OF MIDDLE CHILDHOOD

Now that we have identified the age groupings, the developmental domains, and the theoretical assumptions that have been used to study school-age children, it is necessary to more closely examine the specific contexts of middle childhood, or *where* their development occurs. The multiple contexts that school-age children experience across middle childhood influence their development, and, like development, contexts are dynamic and changing (Crockett & Crouter, 1995; Sarampote, Bassett, & Winsler, 2004). After all, "human development is about children and families engaged in activities within a cultural and community context" Weisner, 2005, p. 1). In this chapter, our discussion of contexts describes the nature of developmental interactions between children and the people in the immediate setting (Silbereisen & Todt, 1994) rather than the diversity of family, school, or community contexts themselves. Specific findings related to these three contexts are discussed in more detail in the later chapters on the developmental domains.

Most important in our contextual approach is that contexts are seen as *resources* for development instead of mere settings in which development occurs. "In many nations, rethinking how diversity and contexts—economic, historical, political, cultural, and social—can be resources for children's pathways has moved to the top of the agenda for scholars, policymakers, and practitioners in school and community programs" (Cooper, García Coll, Bartko et al., 2005, p. 2). In this view, also referred to as an **ecocultural perspective,** developmental scholars no longer use demographic categories—such as ethnicity, gender, or social class—to make sense of children's experiences but rather examine how the meanings of their *lived* experiences may change across contexts, such as home, school, or community (e.g., Cooper, García Coll, Bartko et al., 2005). In other words, our focus is on what children *do* in the multiple contexts of home, school, and community (see Weisner, 2005).

Developmental researchers studying middle childhood have found that key contexts—family, school, peer group, and local neighborhood—help to shape both the opportunities and the risks to which children may be exposed (Crockett

BOX 1.3   Roadmap to Successful Practice
After-School Programs Promote Children's Development

In 1999, the National Research Council Board for Children, Youth, and Families and the Forum on Adolescence held a workshop for policy makers, researchers, and practitioners to examine research on (a) the developmental needs of children aged 5 to 14 and (b) the types of after-school programs that they need. The workshop participants discussed ways that after-school programs can be designed to provide school-age children with opportunities:

- To develop competence in a number of developmental domains
- To develop cross-cultural skills
- To learn from older youth and to mentor younger children
- To interact successfully with peers
- To establish close bonds with caring adults
- To contribute to their communities

The experts agreed that school-age children need a variety of skills to move successfully from middle childhood to adolescence. They also recognized that after-school programs may help children explore different areas of interest in which they can exercise their talents and achieve competence. Finally, they concluded that successful experiences in a wide range of out-of-school programs can give school-agers a positive sense of themselves and a healthy appreciation of others (Gootman, 2000).

In the past several years, there has been a dramatic increase in the level of state and federal funding for after-school programs. For example, the U.S. Department of Education funds the 21st Century Community Learning Center Program. The focus of this school-based program, authorized under Title X, Part I, of the Elementary and Secondary Education Act, is to provide learning opportunities for school-age children in supervised, drug-free environments in public school buildings. Other sources of funding for after-school programs have also been increasing, including the Safe Schools/Healthy Students Initiative (Gootman, 2000).

The National Research Council established the following recommendations to guide new after-school programming:

- Programs need to be designed to address age-related stages of development.
- Programs need to incorporate the kinds of activities that will build physical, cognitive, emotional, and social competencies.
- Programs need to incorporate academic experiences that will encourage a positive attitude toward learning.
- Programs need to address the challenges faced by school-age children in their daily lives.

& Crouter, 1995). For example, feeling unsafe on the way to and from school is a problem for children in rural as well as urban areas, for school-age children just starting their growth spurt, and for boys (Middle Start Initiative, 2002). One of the most difficult challenges for parents and teachers is to know when an individual child is developmentally ready for a given experience, such as walking home alone or attending after-school classes. Age alone does not tell us. Box 1.3 provides recommendations for developmentally appropriate after-school programs.

> *While Robyn is ready to join her older sister Rachel in attending dance classes, other girls of her same age may be too physically immature or emotionally undisciplined, and need a less structured activity in which to demonstrate their competencies—such as swimming or arts and crafts.*

Parent and child communication is an important component of family socialization.

Shirley Zeiberg/PH College

Families as Context

In middle childhood, families are an important developmental context for continuity and change; however, some aspects of family contexts may be more likely to change than others (Collins, 1990). For example, the family socioeconomic context—barring sudden unemployment or winning a lottery ticket—is more likely to stay stable across the childhood years from 4 to 13 than the school context, in which a normative transition to middle school is expected to occur around fifth or sixth grade (Crockett & Crouter, 1995). On the other hand, nonnormative events, such as family relocation, divorce, or remarriage, may also cause changes in context, such as moving to a new neighborhood or school district, which—taken together with expected transitions, such as puberty—may be particularly stressful in middle childhood or early adolescence (Crockett & Crouter, 1995).

Families are also an important context for socialization (e.g., Hofferth & Sandberg, 2001). Despite recent claims that peers overshadow parents in middle childhood (Harris, 1998), researchers have consistently documented that parents as supportive adults continue to be important in encouraging school-age children to engage in activities within safe boundaries (Middle Start Initiative, 2002). In addition, parents and siblings provide opportunities for understanding relationships (Collins, 1990). Through family relationships, school-age children learn to negotiate with others and adapt to others' individual differences and developmental needs (Baenen, 2002; Blume & Blume, 1997).

Schools as Context

Many schools in the 21st century, like the rest of U.S. society, are becoming increasingly diverse in terms of ethnicity, race, religion, and sexual preference, allowing school-age children more opportunities to enhance their cultural sensitivity and tolerance in the school context (Civil Rights Project, 2002; Cooper, García Coll, Thorne, & Orellana, 2005). A wide range of facilities, varied enrollments, and class sizes also characterizes school environments. Despite this diversity, however, most schools are age-segregated environments, especially when contrasted with mixed-age settings like families and neighborhoods (MacKinnon, Volling, & Lamb, 1994; McCarthy, 1972).

Across middle childhood, most American children are likely to move from a primary to a secondary school, whether from a K–6 primary school to a junior high for grades 7 to 9, or from a K–5 elementary school to a middle school for grades 6 to 8. This transition usually means a change from a small, neighborhood school with one group of classmates and only one teacher per grade to a larger school, farther from home, with many different classes and teachers (Jackson & Davis, 2000). In Michigan, for example, average enrollment per school more than doubles between the fifth and ninth grades (Middle Start Initiative, 2002).

Researchers studying school contexts have found that elementary and middle schools also differ in terms of both teacher-child and teacher-parent involvement (Eccles & Harold, 1993). Because they often have different teachers for each subject, children in middle schools have many more daily contacts with teachers than they did in elementary settings, but their parents are typically less involved. In *Turning Points 2000,* the most recent Task Force on the Education of Young Adolescents recommended not only involving families but also communities, recognizing that families and community contexts are inextricably linked (Davis, 2001).

Communities as Context

In middle childhood, school-age children increase their interactions with peers, usually with same-age and same-sex friends. Peer interactions in neighborhoods or nearby playgrounds are often school-age children's first community experiences. Although school-age children spend increasing amounts of time in out-of-school leisure activities, gender and social class distinctions shape their content (e.g., Morris & Kalil, 2006; Posner & Vandell, 1999). For example, middle-class 7- to 10-year-old boys typically spend more time in activities that enhance skill development while working-class boys spend more time in informal play, visiting relatives, or just "hanging out" (Lareau, 2000).

After-school programs for school-age children are usually based on involvement in activities.

Krista Greco/Merrill

Parents also tend to supervise school-age children more closely if they judge their neighborhood quality to be poor, thus limiting children's opportunities to develop social skills with peers (O'Neil, Parke, & McDowell, 2001). However, as children move through middle childhood and become increasingly involved in contexts outside the family, it becomes harder for parents to know all the details of their activities in the community (Crouter, Helms-Erikson, Updegraff, & McHale, 1999).

In the middle childhood period, many children also increase their familiarity with community organizations, such as Boys and Girls Clubs, Scouts, 4H, the YWCA or YMCA, Little League, and recreational programs (e.g., Lerner, Lerner, Almerigi, Theokas, & Phelps, 2005). For example, Boys and Girls Clubs of America operates over 2,850 neighborhood clubs serving 2,800,000 children, 71% of whom live in low-income areas (Anderson-Butcher, Newsome, & Ferrari, 2003; Roffman, Pagano, & Hirsch, 2001). Youth organizations, hobbies, and arts programs effectively encourage middle- and working-class school-agers to resist delinquent behaviors (Larson, 1994). In addition, as their social context expands, school-age children acquire a sense of belonging to a wider community than their immediate neighborhoods—called **social integration**—and develop positive relationships with peers and adults outside the family (Larson, 1994). See Box 1.4 for a model community effort to assess and provide after-school programs.

After-School Programs

As many as 6 million students participate in middle childhood after-school programs (U.S. Department of Education, 2000). Researchers suggest that children who attend such programs have increased achievement, better school attendance, and lower dropout rates (Fashola, 1998). Results of a study of seventh and eighth graders who attended an after-school program at least 3 days per week were happier, enjoyed activities more, and were less bored than when not attending (Dadisman, Vandell, & Pierce, 2002). Structured time also is related to a pattern of less risky future behavior in middle school and high school (Mancini & Huebner, 2004; Simpkins, Fredricks, Davis-Kean, & Eccles, 2006). Other researchers studying structured out-of-school involvement, such as taking dance classes, playing sports, or doing handicrafts, found that children's free-time choices influenced positive social-emotional development and school adjustment (Blume, 2001; Fredricks, Simpkins, & Eccles, 2005; McHale, Crouter, & Tucker, 1999; Morris & Kalil, 2006; Ripke, Huston, & Casey, 2006). Despite parental fears about overscheduling their school-agers, there is strong, consistent evidence that participation in organized activities during middle childhood is related to positive development (Mahoney, Harris, & Eccles, 2006).

Recently, the national 4-H Study of Positive Youth Development released its findings for fifth and sixth graders from 13 states. **Youth development** programs specifically promote positive adult-child relations, skill-building activities, and youth leadership and are characterized by an emphasis on the "Five C's" of competence, confidence, connection, character, and caring. Table 1.4 lists 40 middle childhood developmental strengths that are promoted by such programs. While only 13% of youth were not in any structured activities, most children surveyed were involved in more than one type of activity and their enrollments changed from grade to grade. Overall, sports and arts programs attracted the greatest numbers of participants and formal youth development programs, the least (Theokas, Lerner, Phelps, & Lerner, 2006). Youth development programs for adolescents are discussed in chapter 12.

Recognizing the critical role of community-level change in moving an out-of-school agenda, the Forum for Youth Investment began the Greater Resources for After-School Programming (GRASP) Project, with support from the Charles Stewart Mott Foundation. Through GRASP, the Forum partnered with four cities—Chicago, Kansas City, Little Rock, and Sacramento—to assess their current work in and deepen community discussions about out-of-school time. They addressed the following concerns:

- Opportunities are uneven across communities so that some young people have remarkably few choices.

- Programming drops off dramatically during the evening hours; weekend programs are in remarkably short supply.

- Only a small percentage of young people are enrolled in consistent, daily programs.

- Many providers are striving to provide well-balanced programming, focusing on a range of outcomes, but many of the largest programs take on a much narrower focus.

- Civic outcomes are consistently neglected, and the programs that do support them tend to be smaller and focused on older age groups.

A Case Study: Kansas City, Missouri

In keeping with national trends, 28 school-based programs are the primary providers of school-age child care in Kansas City. The overwhelming majority of children enrolled in school-based programs are elementary school age. Although nearly 27,000 children are being served, these programs are reaching less than 9% of the target population of 6- to 18-year-olds and less than 15% of the elementary children. Approximately 6% of school-age children and youth participate in voluntary, activity-based programs, such as Boys and Girls Clubs, Camp Fire USA, Boy Scouts, Girl Scouts, and city Parks and Recreation. The rest are served in smaller programs provided by child care centers, community-based groups, and faith-based organizations.

Among the school-based programs, all but one serve children aged 6 to 11; slightly less than half serve middle-schoolers aged 12 to 15; and only 7% serve youth over age 16. Although the activity-based programs enrolled only 8% of the population of school-age children in Kansas City, many families reported that they rely on such programs to create a network of out-of-school supervision for older children (Tolman, Pittman, Yohalem, Thomases, & Trammel, 2002).

Over 80% of all out-of-school programs in Kansas City identified care and supervision, socialization and recreation, and academics as primary outcomes. When asked to name the primary activities available to children and youth, Kansas City agencies named five areas with about equal priority: hobbies (52%), tutoring (51%), physical exercise (48%), academic enrichment (46%), and unstructured time (44%).

GRASP Project Conclusions

The following lessons and challenges emerged from the GRASP Projects in all four cities:

- Opportunities for learning and engagement happen in multiple places and programs found in communities (e.g., youth organizations, libraries, parks, homes, schools, faith institutions, city halls, community organizations, dance studios, workplaces)—places that are not only open and active in the hours immediately after school but also in the evenings, on weekends, and in the summers.

- Schools should be the anchor learning institution in a young person's life, but schools occupy less than a quarter of students' waking hours each year. In addition, they focus heavily on building strong academic skills—skills that are critical but not sufficient.

Developmentally, gaps exist that schools do not fill. Children and youth are looking for learning experiences across a range of areas from academic to social to civic (e.g., things to do, places to go, people to talk to). Many young people cannot find suitable experiences in or out of school.

Moving an Out-of-School Agenda (2002) concluded that creating the quality, quantity, and continuity of opportunities for young people from early childhood through the beginning of adulthood will require engaging in the following tasks:

1. Ensuring adequate coordination, collaboration, and networking among those working with young

(continued)

33

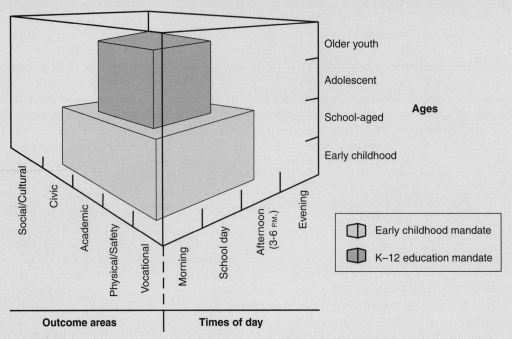

FIGURE 1.7

What Fills the Space?

Imagine the empty space. How is it filled in *your* community?

Source: From "Moving an Out-of-School Agenda: Lessons and Challenges Across Cities," by J. Tolman, K. Pittman, N. Yohalem, J. Thomases, and M. Trammel. Washington, DC: The Forum for Youth Investment. http://www.forumfyi.org/Files/GRASPpaper.pdf. Reprinted by permission.

people—within sectors, across sectors, and between organizations and community/family stakeholders

2. Building a stable, high-quality workforce through credentials, staff development, training, and compensation

3. Creating quality standards, assessments, and supports that result in effective organizations and programs

4. Developing the physical infrastructure (e.g., the transportation and physical space) that is the necessary context for accessible and quality out-of-school opportunities

5. Marshalling adequate funding streams (e.g., local, state and national, public and private) to guarantee stable and sufficient resources for programming

6. Building leadership and political will by engaging champions in the public and private

sectors, and at the highest levels of city government, to create and move an agenda

7. Ensuring consistent, meaningful youth engagement in decision making at the program, organization, and city levels

8. Building public will and constituency engagement in order to support stakeholder involvement, promote public commitment and awareness, and leverage meaningful action

9. Developing planning and visioning processes, structures, and products to build alignment, intentionality, and comprehensiveness within out-of-school programming

10. Strengthening mapping, monitoring, and research systems to collect, analyze, and disseminate information about programs, providers, funding, and young people

---

TABLE 1.4   40 Developmental Assets for Middle Childhood

Developmental assets help school-age children grow up healthy, caring, and responsible.

External Assets	**Support**	1. **Family support**—Family life provides high levels of love and support. 2. **Positive family communication**—Parent(s) and child communicate positively. Child feels comfortable seeking advice and counsel from parent(s). 3. **Other adult relationships**—Child receives support from adults other than her or his parent(s). 4. **Caring neighborhood**—Child experiences caring neighbors. 5. **Caring school climate**—Relationships with teachers and peers provide a caring, encouraging environment. 6. **Parent involvement in schooling**—Parent(s) are actively involved in helping the child succeed in school.
	Empowerment	7. **Community values youth**—Child feels valued and appreciated by adults in the community. 8. **Children as resources**—Child is included in decisions at home and in the community. 9. **Service to others**—Child has opportunities to help others in the community. 10. **Safety**—Child feels safe at home, at school, and in his or her neighborhood.
	Boundaries & Expectations	11. **Family boundaries**—Family has clear and consistent rules and consequences and monitors the child's whereabouts. 12. **School boundaries**—School provides clear rules and consequences. 13. **Neighborhood boundaries**—Neighbors take responsibility for monitoring the child's behavior. 14. **Adult role models**—Parent(s) and other adults in the child's family, as well as nonfamily adults, model positive, responsible behavior. 15. **Positive peer influence**—Child's closest friends model positive, responsible behavior. 16. **High expectations**—Parent(s) and teachers expect the child to do her or his best at school and in other activities.
	Constructive Use of Time	17. **Creative activities**—Child participates in music, art, drama, or creative writing two or more times per week. 18. **Child programs**—Child participates two or more times per week in cocurricular school activities or structured community programs for children. 19. **Religious community**—Child attends religious programs or services one or more times per week. 20. **Time at home**—Child spends some time most days both in high-quality interaction with parents and doing things at home other than watching TV or playing video games.
Internal Assets	**Commitment to Learning**	21. **Achievement motivation**—Child is motivated and strives to do well in school. 22. **Learning engagement**—Child is responsive, attentive, and actively engaged in learning at school and enjoys participating in learning activities outside of school. 23. **Homework**—Child usually hands in homework on time. 24. **Bonding to school**—Child cares about teachers and other adults at school. 25. **Reading for pleasure**—Child enjoys and engages in reading for fun most days of the week.
	Positive Values	26. **Caring**—Parent(s) tell the child it is important to help other people. 27. **Equality and social justice**—Parent(s) tell the child it is important to speak up for equal rights for all people. 28. **Integrity**—Parent(s) tell the child it is important to stand up for one's beliefs. 29. **Honesty**—Parent(s) tell the child it is important to tell the truth. 30. **Responsibility**—Parent(s) tell the child it is important to accept personal responsibility for behavior. 31. **Healthy lifestyle**—Parent(s) tell the child it is important to have good health habits and an understanding of healthy sexuality.

(continued)

TABLE 1.4   40 Developmental Assets for Middle Childhood (*continued*)

Internal Assets

Social Competencies	**32. Planning and decision making**—Child thinks about decisions and is usually happy with results of her or his decisions.
	33. Interpersonal competence—Child cares about and is affected by other people's feelings, enjoys making friends, and, when frustrated or angry, tries to calm her- or himself.
	34. Cultural competence—Child knows and is comfortable with people of different racial, ethnic, and cultural backgrounds and with her or his own cultural identity.
	35. Resistance skills—Child can stay away from people who are likely to get her or him in trouble and is able to say no to doing wrong or dangerous things.
	36. Peaceful conflict resolution—Child seeks to resolve conflict nonviolently.
Positive Identity	**37. Personal power**—Child feels he or she has some influence over things that happen in her or his life.
	38. Self-esteem—Child likes and is proud to be the person that he or she is.
	39. Sense of purpose—Child sometimes thinks about what life means and whether there is a purpose for her or his life.
	40. Positive view of personal future—Child is optimistic about her or his personal future.

Source: From "40 Developmental Assets™" by P. L. Benson, 2004, Minneapolis, MN: Search Institute^SM. Copyright © 2006 by Search Institute^SM, 615 First Ave. NE, Suite 125, Minneapolis, MN 55413, 800–888–7828, www.search-institute.org.

Recent research has revealed substantial variation in patterns over time of participation in out-of-school activities, such as sports. Key factors limiting involvement were parental under- and unemployment and timing of the transition to middle school or junior high, with a later transition being less likely to disrupt activity continuation (Pedersen, 2005). Research has also shown that patterns of parental encouragement and support for sports or music involvement have a cumulative positive effect on children's involvement and motivation (Fredricks et al., 2005).

STOP What out-of-school contexts did you experience during middle childhood and how did they change across ages 6 to 12?

At age 8, Robyn is already expressing to her mother an abiding interest in joining such activities to enhance her newly acquired sense of industriousness and her budding relationships with peers. As Robyn progresses from ages 8 to 12 she may be protected from risk by involvement in out-of-school activities—whether an after-school program, a sports program, a recreation center, or instruction in the performing or visual arts.

CHAPTER REVIEW

History of Middle Childhood

- Middle childhood is defined as ages 6 to 12, although different terms may be used to describe the middle childhood period and age groupings may vary by field.

- The history of childhood reveals that childhood as a distinct stage in the life span dates from medieval times, but the concept of childhood as a protected status is much more recent, beginning in the early 20th century. Only recently has society considered middle childhood to be a transitional pathway to adolescence.

- Middle childhood is socially constructed in several ways. In different generations, in diverse cultures and ethnicities, and in various socioeconomic groups, the meaning of middle childhood may vary widely.

Developmental Perspectives

- Middle childhood can be thought of as a distinct stage with its own developmental characteristics and abilities.
- Middle childhood can also be thought of as a transitional pathway to adolescence.

- Research on middle childhood is divided into four broad developmental domains: physical, cognitive, affective, and social.

Theoretical Perspectives

- Ecological theory of human development describes the multiple, overlapping environments in which children develop over time.

- Developmental–contextual theory describes multiple interrelationships among developmental domains, as well as dynamic interactions with the contexts in which children develop.

Contexts of Middle Childhood

- Family, school, and community contexts are linked.
- Contexts are resources for development instead of mere settings in which development occurs.
- Families, schools, peer groups, and communities help to shape both the opportunities and risks to which children may be exposed.

- Moving from an elementary to a middle-school environment may signal changes in peer group interactions, teacher-child relationships, and parent–teacher communication.

KEY TERMS

Age grading	Ecological theory	Mesosystem	Secular trends
Bioecological model	Emic	Mesotime	Social construction
Cohort	Ethnicity	Microsystem	Social integration
Cultural ecology	Etic	Microtime	Social practices
Deconstruct	Exosystem	Middle childhood	Theoretical models
Developmental-contextual theory	Gen M	New media	Tranescence
	Holistic approach	Normative	Transnational
Digital divide	Logical positivism	Postmodernity	Universal
Domains	Macrosystem	Probabilistic epigenesis	Youth development
Ecocultural perspective	Macrotime	Proximal processes	

SUGGESTED ACTIVITIES

1. Watch television programs, look at magazines, or read fiction that is directed at school-age children. How is this age group portrayed? Note the development of the characters or the subjects of articles. Compare what you find to the developmental domains described in the chapter. Are some developmental domains addressed more than others? How do the authors view middle childhood?

2. Talk with two or three school-age children about what they do before and after school. How long have they been involved in these activities? Are their siblings or friends also involved? What devel-

opmental contexts do they inhabit? Do you think that their experiences are typical of the out-of-school activities of middle childhood? Why or why not? What else could the community do to provide developmentally appropriate out-of-school activities for 6- to 12-year-olds?

3. Meet with the parent(s) of a school-age child. What are their developmental expectations for their child? How do they judge when their child is ready for a new experience? Do you think that their expectations are developmentally appropriate? Why or why not? Have they ever read advice books or attended classes for parents? If not, how did they learn about children's development? How do they think children in middle childhood are different from young children or ado-

lescents? What do they want for their children in the future?

4. Interview an elementary teacher and a middle-school teacher about the age groupings or grade levels in their schools. Describe their schools' organization or model (e.g., primary, middle, or junior high school). How are children grouped (e.g., by grade, by age, by ability)? When do children change schools (i.e., after what grade do they move from elementary to middle school or junior high)? How satisfied are the teachers with the current structure? How, if at all, would they change it? How has the educational system changed from when they were educated? Which model do they prefer? Why?

RECOMMENDED RESOURCES

Suggested Readings

Boocock, S. S., & Scott, K. A. (2005). *Kids in context: The sociological study of children and childhoods.* Lanham, MD: Rowman & Littlefield.

Campbell, P. (2000). Middle muddle. *The Horn Book, 76*(4), 483–487.

Gesell, A., & Ilg, F. L. (1946). *The child from five to ten.* New York: Harper.

Illick, J. E. (2002). *American childhoods.* Philadelphia, PA: University of Pennsylvania Press.

Lamorev, S., Robinson, B. E., Rowland, B. H., & Coleman, M. (1999). *Latchkey kids: Unlocking doors for children and their families* (2nd ed.). Thousand Oaks, CA: Sage.

Verhaagen, D. (2005). *Parenting the millenial generation: Guiding our children born between 1982 and 2000.* Westport, CT: Praeger.

Suggested Online Resources

From Baby Einstein to Leapfrog, from Doom to the Sims, from instant messaging to Internet chat rooms: Public interest in the role of interactive media in children's lives. http://www.srcd.org/Documents/Publications/SPR/spr18-4.pdf

The future of children: When school is out. http://www.futureofchildren.org/information2826/information_show.htm?doc_id=71875

Growing up: W. K. Kellogg Foundation 2001 annual report. http://www.wkkf.org/pubs/Pub3363.pdf

Out-of-school-time resources. http://www.forumfor youthinvestment.org/_portalcat.cfm?LID=B7F8CAC E-5A57-42F2-85C12AA02E13E438

When schools stay open late: National evaluation of the 21st century community learning centers. http://www.ed.gov/rschstat/eval/other/cclcfinalreport/index.html

Suggested Web Sites

After School Alliance. http://www.afterschoolalliance.org

Luann's Milestones. http://luannsroom.com/comics/luann/html/milestones.html

National Institute on Out-of-School Time. http://www.niost.org

National Middle School Association. http://www.nmsa.org

Successful Pathways through Middle Childhood. http://childhood.isr.umich.edu/index.html

Turning Points. http://www.turningpts.org/

Suggested Films and Videos

Best of The Wonder Years (1999). Delta Entertainment (70 minutes)

Billy Elliot (2000). Universal Pictures (1 hour, 51 minutes)

A history of after-school programs (2005). Magna Systems (30 minutes)

Mad hot ballroom (2005). Paramount Classics (1 hour, 50 minutes)

Program activities: Fostering the development of the school-age child (2005). Magna Systems (30 minutes)

School days (2003). Insight Media (30 minutes)

Setting the stage for school-age child care (2005). Magna Systems (30 minutes)

The child from seven to twelve (2001). Insight Media (20 minutes)

CHAPTER 2

Studying Middle Childhood

David Young-Wolff/PhotoEdit Inc.

_____

After reading this chapter, students will be able to:

▶ Understand the role that theory plays in generating research on middle childhood and organizing its findings.

▶ Describe three theoretical issues that are debated in the study of human development.

▶ Identify developmental research designs and the purpose, strengths, and limitations of each method.

▶ Summarize quantitative and qualitative data collection techniques.

▶ Communicate their own basic or applied research questions and the related ethical concerns associated with studying middle childhood.

Ten-year-old Takuya sits in his fifth-grade classroom anxiously watching the clock. He has only five minutes before the bell rings and releases him for lunch. Takuya and his family have just moved to this city, and he has had to make his way in a new community, neighborhood, and school. Takuya has had no problem adjusting to the academic challenges of his new school. As a matter of fact, he finds the demands of his teachers to be less rigorous than those at his old school. However, Takuya has had a tough time making friends and fitting into the cliques in school. It has been especially hard for him because he is more quiet and shy than most boys his age. Takuya has a difficult time going up to boys he doesn't know and making conversation. His 16-year-old brother, Naoki, is more outgoing and has made friends already with some boys he met working at his part-time job. The bell rings. Takuya gathers up his books and makes his way to the lunchroom, where he will probably eat lunch alone, again.

UNDERSTANDING DEVELOPMENT

As you observe the lunchroom scene, you may have a number of thoughts about Takuya's behavior: "*I wonder if some children are born to be more shy than others?*" or "*Takuya seems to be so quiet, he has probably been encouraged to act this way at home, in the classroom, or in his neighborhood.*" All of us have observations about school-age children that encourage us to think and speculate about the nature of children, how they develop, and what variables influence their behavior. These thoughts reflect our personal philosophy of human nature and child development (Lerner, 2002b). If you think that Takuya is shy because of inborn tendencies and that the environment has little influence on this trait, you are making an assumption that most human behavior and development are shaped by innate tendencies at birth and remain relatively stable across the life span. If, however, you walk away from the lunchroom thinking, "*I wonder who* taught *him to be so quiet and well-behaved?*" then you are suggesting that he has been encouraged to be so by his family or peers—an assumption that behavior is shaped largely by the environment in which children are raised. Each of these thoughts represents a general philosophy about the origins of human behavior and growth that you may not realize you hold. These implicit personal philosophies help us organize observations and make sense of the wide range of data we collect in our daily interactions with children. They also represent a specific theoretical viewpoint.

In developmental psychology, human development, and education, researchers studying middle childhood—as well as the practitioners who work with school-age children—rely on scientific **theories** to interpret children's development and behavior. A theory is a formal or informal attempt to describe or explain real phenomena, such as growth and change. A **developmental theory** describes changes within or among developmental domains or explains the course of development over time. Theories play a vital role in any scientific discipline. They give meaning to and provide a framework for facts, help us organize research questions and the information gathered from them, and help guide and direct future research (Miller, 2002).

STOP Do you often wonder what causes children to behave the way they do?

Theoretical Questions About Human Development

All developmental theories possess underlying assumptions about the nature of development (similar to thoughts you may have had about Takuya and Naoki as you read this chapter's case study). These assumptions can vary widely from one theory to another. Specific developmental theories are presented throughout the subsequent chapters of this book. This chapter introduces three theoretical issues that form the foundation for all developmental theories and continue to be prominent questions in most child development research (Lerner, 2002b; Miller, 2002). The study of human development raises questions about the progression of change over time (continuity–discontinuity), the influences of biology and the environment (nature–nurture), and the consistency of characteristics and behavior over one's lifetime (stability–instability).

Continuity or Discontinuity? This question asks whether development proceeds in a gradual, cumulative fashion (**continuity**) or in fits and starts, with periods of rapid development followed by periods of slower development (**discontinuity**). In developmental theories, the meaning of *continuity* is not unlike its common meaning: "something that has uninterrupted duration or continuation, especially without

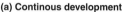

(a) Continous development

(b) Discontinous development

Infancy   Adulthood   Infancy   Adulthood

FIGURE 2.1
Continuity vs. Discontinuity

Panel (a) illustrates continuous development; panel (b) illustrates discontinuous development.

Source: From Berk, Laura E. *Child Development* (7th ed.) (p. 7). Published by Allyn & Bacon, Boston, MA. Copyright © 2006 by Pearson Education. Reprinted by permission of the publisher.

essential change" (Merriam-Webster, 2002). Therefore, if a developmental ability or behavior has continuity, we would expect it to gradually increase across developmental periods—the acquisition of motor skills, for example. Continuity may also represent the relationship between earlier forms of development and later ones. For example, the continuity of shyness during childhood does not mean that shyness increases per se, but rather that earlier levels of shyness are related to later ones. *Takuya's wariness of all adults in toddlerhood may manifest itself in his unwillingness to raise his hand in class in middle childhood.*

Other aspects of development, however, may be **discontinuous,** or emerge in *stages*. For example, school-age children typically show changes in problem-solving ability as they move from the logical reasoning stage of middle childhood to the abstract reasoning stage of adolescence. What all developmental *stage theories* have in common is an assumption of discontinuity, or changes in development that are not simply gradual but sudden leaps in level of performance. Figure 2.1 is a visual illustration of the different rates of development represented by these two viewpoints.

The best answer to this question is that *some* aspects of development, such as the increase in the size of our short-term memory, reflect more continuous change. Other aspects of development, such as problem solving, appear to develop in a more stagelike progression.

Nature or Nurture? This question asks whether development is influenced primarily by biological inheritance (**nature**) or environmental experiences (**nurture**). Those proposing that nature or biology dominates development point to genetic blueprints and biological predispositions (e.g., shy vs. outgoing) to explain children's development. Others argue that although genetic and biological predispositions may be important, children's environments and experiences (e.g., parenting styles, educational opportunities, sociocultural surroundings) play a greater role in shaping who a child becomes.

Using the case study, you could ask whether Takuya was born with shy tendencies or whether his family and peers encourage this reticent behavior.

Developmental scholars today agree that it is a combination of both biological and social factors that interact to determine development (Kagan, 2003; Ridley, 2003).

For example, researchers (Boyce & Ellis, 2005) have found that biological reactions to stress in middle childhood are influenced by both heredity (e.g., inheriting a neuro-chemistry that affects the nervous system's response to stress) and environment (e.g., childhood exposure to either protective or acutely stressful environments).

Stability or Instability?   This issue focuses on whether developmental character-istics are consistent over time and predictive of later development (**stability**) or sub-ject to change over time and context (**instability**). Theorists who suggest that certain aspects of development, such as shyness, are stable would predict that children will exhibit the same shy characteristics in adulthood. *They would argue that Takuya would grow up to be a shy and quiet man.* An alternative suggestion is that whether shy children will become shy adults depends on the experiences that they undergo during development. *Takuya may be required to take assertiveness training courses in his first job and may become less shy in adolescence.*

Evidence of stability in the personality of an individual across the years from early to middle childhood would be observed if a shy preschooler were to remain cautious of others in elementary school and still socially reserved in middle school. Furthermore, if personality traits were stable, it would *not* be developmentally appro-priate to think that children who have always seemed shy and reserved will ever be very outgoing. On the other hand, children's specific behaviors, such as aggression or withdrawal, may show instability over time as they try out varying strategies of cop-ing with the demands of the ever-widening contexts of childhood—from home to school and community.

[STOP] Do you think that your per-sonality has changed since you were a young child?

Linking Theory and Research

Theories and the research undertaken to investigate them are connected through either **deductive** or **inductive reasoning.** Using deductive reasoning, a researcher begins with a theory and then collects data to support or refute it. The majority of re-search studies are based on questions generated through deductive reasoning (Lerner, 2002b). One common deductive reasoning model is engaged in hypothesis testing. A **hypothesis** is a theoretical prediction, or statement, that has yet to be tested or supported. In hypothesis testing, if a theory suggests that environment largely influences behavior, then you might hypothesize that school-age children who watch violent sports on television (e.g., football, boxing) would behave more aggressively than children who do not watch violent sports on television. If the theory is accurate, then the findings of the study will support the hypothesis that environ-ment influences behavior.

A second way that research and theory are linked is through inductive reason-ing. Using inductive reasoning, a researcher begins with a research question or a general observation and collects data to gain an answer for immediate application or to generate a new theory, not necessarily to test the tenets of an existing theory. This reasoning style is more typical of practitioners and teachers who work with children on a day-to-day basis and who generate research questions out of neces-sity rather than for theoretical hypothesis testing. For example, a counselor in an after-school program observes fifth graders segregating into same-sex peer groups. She wants to know if this is "normal" or if she should try to intervene. Her research approach and her findings have immediate application to her question but are not related directly to a specific developmental theory about gender identity or peer affiliation.

Linking Research with Practice

Researchers, program providers, parents, policy makers, teachers, and students have in common the need to translate research into practice. **Basic research** in middle childhood development and adolescence begins with the study of normative development. However, **applied research** asks how this basic information is relevant to solving particular problems of practical significance. The integration of these two approaches—basic and applied—has been deemed a new model for the 21st century (Schwebel, Plumert, & Pick, 2000). This integrative model has three goals that are addressed in successive chapters of this book. First are the implications of basic research for applied issues. But a second, more challenging, goal is to examine how applied research studies are grounded in basic developmental theories. A third goal is to explore how you may conduct research of your own in the context of an applied problem facing you in the real world of the family, school, or community (Schwebel, Plumert, & Pick, 2000).

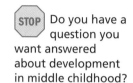 Do you have a question you want answered about development in middle childhood?

STUDYING CHANGE OVER TIME

The study of development involves understanding change over time. Three developmental approaches are designed specifically to assess age-related differences and change over time. (For a primer on other types of research designs, refer to the Appendix.)

Cross-Sectional Research Designs

The first approach, **cross-sectional studies,** assesses different age groups of children at the same point in time. For example, if you were interested in how strategies used in a memory task may change as children get older, you could administer a recall task to children who are 6, 8, 10, and 12 years old and ask them to rehearse aloud. By averaging the number of words rehearsed for each age group, you may find that as children get older, they rehearse more words together. Therefore, as children age, memory strategies become more complex. Figure 2.2 illustrates how this type of study is configured.

Cross-sectional studies are used frequently in developmental research because they are time- and cost-efficient. In addition, a well-designed cross-sectional study that includes an appropriate level and number of different age groups can accentuate

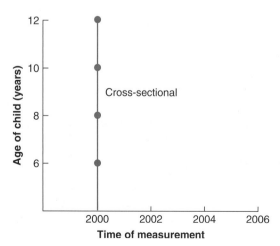

FIGURE 2.2
Cross-Sectional Design

Cross-sectional designs assess different-aged children at the same point in time.

developmental differences among cognitive and behavioral skills and, more specifically, identify *when* a skill emerges.

Limitations of Cross-Sectional Research. Cross-sectional designs are less able to identify *how* the change occurs (e.g., how does an individual child move from simple to complex rehearsal?) and the variables that may influence that change (e.g., practice at home or at school). In addition, because different age cohorts are used, it is difficult to rule out the possibility that the unique experiences of one age group have biased the results, called **cohort bias.** For example, all of the 10-year-olds in the study may have had a student teacher last year who specialized in teaching memory strategies to children. In such a case, the results might look as if rehearsal strategies are very sophisticated at 10 years of age and then become less so at 12! This finding would not be a reflection of the true pattern of memory strategy development, but rather an atypical developmental pattern due to a cohort effect.

Longitudinal Research Designs

The second approach to studying change over time is a **longitudinal study.** In a longitudinal study, one group of same-aged participants is studied at several different points in time. This design is illustrated in Figure 2.3.

These studies can take place over the course of several weeks or over many years. Because longitudinal studies follow the same child over time, changes in individual children can also be assessed. For example, if your research question asks *both* "To what extent are the memory strategies used by 8-year-olds different from those of 12-year-olds" *and* "How and when do they change?" a longitudinal design will best answer these questions. You could assess the memory strategies of a group of 8-year-olds, followed by similar assessments of the same group at 10 and 12 years of age. Not only could you observe potential differences between the memory strategies of the 8- and the 12-year-olds but you can also identify the evolution of memory strategies.

Longitudinal studies also allow for connections to be made between early experience and later development. For example, Emmy Werner (1989, 1993; Werner & Smith, 2001) was interested in how children's health status at birth and their early home environments affected later social and cognitive development. The findings of this landmark longitudinal study are described in Box 2.1.

FIGURE 2.3
Longitudinal Design

Longitudinal designs assess the same children over time to document developmental change.

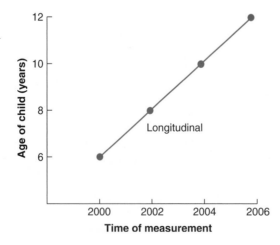

BOX 2.1 Roadmap to Understanding Theory and Research
A Longitudinal Design

The Kauai Longitudinal Study conducted by Emmy Werner and colleagues is considered a classic in longitudinal investigations for both its design features and research findings (Werner, 1989, 1993; Werner & Smith, 2001). The study had two principal goals: (1) to assess the long-term consequences of prenatal and perinatal stress; and (2) to document the effects of adverse early rearing conditions on children's physical, cognitive, and psychosocial development. To accomplish these goals, Werner chose to study all children born in 1955 on the Hawaiian island of Kauai. Werner explained that Kauai was chosen because its medical, public health, educational, and social services were comparable to a community of the same size on the U.S. mainland. (The island population was 45,000.) In addition, the population was known for its low mobility, its diversity of cultural influences, and its receptiveness to the goals of the research study.

In 1955, 693 infants were born on Kauai (i.e., they were considered a birth cohort). Their development was followed at ages 1, 2, 10, 18, 31 or 32, and 40 years. Physicians and public health nurses recorded complications during the prenatal period, labor, and the neonatal period. Nurses and social workers interviewed the mothers in the postpartum period and when the children were 1 and 10 years old; observations of parent-child interactions also were made at this time. Pediatricians and psychologists examined the children at 2 and 10 years of age and assessed their physical, intellectual, and social development. Any developmental delays, handicaps, or behavior problems were noted. Teachers evaluated the children's academic progress and school behavior. The research team administered a variety of aptitude, achievement, and personality tests in elementary grades and high school.

Information about the material, intellectual, and emotional aspects of family life was recorded, with special attention paid to stressful life events that disrupted the family unit (e.g., divorce, imprisonment, mental illness, drug and alcohol abuse). Interviews were conducted with the children when they were ages 18 and 31 or 32. The comprehensiveness of this database was nearly unprecedented!

Of the 698 children included in the study at birth, the majority, or two thirds, were born without complications and grew up in supportive home environments. Approximately one third of the children ($n = 201$) were identified as high-risk because they suffered some degree of perinatal stress, were born into poverty, and experienced some form of family distress. Two thirds of *these* children went on to develop serious learning or behavior problems by age 10 and had mental health problems, delinquency records, and/or teenage pregnancies by age 18.

One third of these high-risk children, however, *did not* develop learning or behavior problems and by age 18 appeared to have developed into competent and caring young adults. Werner was able to identify some of the factors that protected these children from developmental risk and supported their attempts to thrive in less than optimal home environments. She called them *resilient*.

As infants, these resilient children seemed to share an "easy" temperament, which made them easier to care for and thus more likely to elicit positive attention from family members and others. As toddlers, they were described as alert and autonomous and exhibited advanced communication, locomotion, and self-help skills. In elementary school, teachers reported that these children got along well

(continued)

> **BOX 2.1   Roadmap to Understanding Theory and Research** *(Continued)*
> *A Longitudinal Design*
>
> with their classmates, and by high school they exhibited a positive self-concept. All had the opportunity to establish a close bond with at least one caregiver during infancy, although for some of the children this relationship took place with someone other than a parent, such as a grandparent, older sibling, or baby-sitter. The resilient children sought further emotional support outside the home in the form of close friendships, extracurricular activities, and church involvement; during the interviews at 18, they believed that their lives had meaning.
>
> Because the design of the study allowed Werner to follow the same children forward through time, she was able to identify early those children "at-risk" and follow their developmental outcomes. From this continuity she determined that the negative impact of birth complications diminished over time and were overshadowed and mediated by child-rearing conditions. In addition, she identified protective factors that made some children resilient and develop into competent and caring young adults despite their biological and environmental risk factors.

Longitudinal studies can assist us in examining the stability of a characteristic or behavior. Does an inhibited toddler remain cautious into middle childhood? By employing a longitudinal design, Kagan and Saudino (2001) studied temperamental qualities in children from birth and suggested that if infants were "avoidant, affectively subdued, and remained proximal to a caregiver during initial encounters with an unfamiliar event [essentially shy]" (p. 111), they typically would show similar characteristics throughout the first decade of life (see also Kagan, Snidman, Kahn, & Towsley, 2007).

Finally, a longitudinal design allows us to explore how different factors may be related to one another over time. For example, what if we were to observe Takuya over the school year and find that he exhibits less shy behavior and has made friends with several boys who are more outgoing then he is? What we might ask is, "What factors influenced this change and in what way? Did his new friends encourage him to be more outgoing?" (i.e., friends mediate the change in behavior). Or, "Did his involvement in extracurricular activities give him the confidence he needed to become more outgoing toward others?" (i.e., individual characteristics lead to behavior change). By following groups of children like Takuya over time, a longitudinal design will allow you to examine the relationship among different variables and to identify which variables may predict change more reliably than others. Examples of current, ongoing longitudinal studies that include middle childhood development are listed in Table 2.1

Limitations of Longitudinal Research. Despite the many benefits of this research approach in the study of human development, not many longitudinal studies are conducted. They are costly and can take many years to complete. Research participants may also drop out of longitudinal studies, for a variety of reasons (e.g., moving away from the area, transferring to a different school, or disinterest). A loss of participants over time is referred to as **attrition.** Attrition can affect the results of a longitudinal study by reducing the total number of participants and thereby limiting the types of statistical analyses that can be performed. In addition, it may be precisely those characteristics that you had hoped to study that cause some participants to discontinue their participation!

TABLE 2.1 Current Longitudinal Studies That Include the Middle Childhood Years

Study Name	Description of Sample	Focus of Study
Beginning School Study (BSS)	Follows a sample of nearly 800 first graders in Baltimore, MD, since 1982	How social structure and psychological factors affect children's educational prospects
British Cohort Study (BCS70)	Follows approximately 17,000 individuals living in England, Scotland, and Wales who were born in one week in April 1970	Physical, educational, and social development through childhood, and includes economic development in adulthood
Columbia County Longitudinal Study	Includes all third-grade children and their parents living in Columbia County, NY, in 1960 until the present time	Individual and parental factors related to the development of aggression and other social behaviors
Colorado Adoption Project (CAP)	Studies birth and adoptive parents and their offspring since 1976	Examines both the genetic and environmental influences of intelligence, personality, and behavior
Dunedin Multidisciplinary Health and Development Study (DMHDS)	Follows 1037 children born between 1972–1973 in Dunedin, New Zealand	Studies how perinatal factors combine with familial and experiential factors to produce health and psychological outcomes
Early Childhood Longitudinal Program (ECLS)	Follows U.S. children from kindergarten (1998–1999) through the 8th grade (2007)	How family, school, community, and individual factors are associated with children's school experiences in kindergarten through middle school
Fels Longitudinal Study	Begun in 1927, includes U.S. participants from the prenatal period through old age	Physical growth and maturation along with body composition
Minnesota Longitudinal Study of Parents and Children	Has followed 267 U.S. first-time mothers and their children since 1975	Early social relationship experiences, risk and protective factors, and continuity and change
National Child Development Study (NCDS)	Follows a birth cohort born in England, Scotland, and Wales during one week in March 1958	Physical, educational, social, and economic development
Neighborhoods and Children: Project Human Development in Chicago Neighborhoods(PHDCN)	Has followed 6,500 U.S. children ranging in age from birth through age 18 for at least four years	The ways in which neighborhoods influence the lives and well-being of children
Panel Study of Income Dynamics (PSID)	Studies 8,000 U.S. families since 1968	Collects data on economic, health, and social behavior
School Transition Study (STS)	Begun in 1996, follows low-income children from kindergarten through fifth grade in three diverse cities in the U.S.	The impact of family, school, and community factors on the developmental pathways of low-income children
Simmons Longitudinal Study (SLS)	Follows U.S. children 5 years of age (1976) to young adulthood (present)	Examines behavioral, health, and family factors in preschool youth and their relationship to later academic performance and mental health adjustment
Study of Early Child Care and Youth Development (SECCYD)	Since 1991, follows children from birth through grade 9 at 10 locations around the U.S.	Examines how differences in child care experiences relate to children's social, emotional, intellectual, and language development and to their physical growth and health

Perhaps even more problematic is the often *selective* nature of attrition, meaning that certain types of participants may remain (e.g., people interested in learning about themselves or who appreciate the value of research) or may drop out of the study (e.g., people with low socioeconomic status or who are highly mobile). To conduct her longitudinal study, Werner (1989, 1993) chose the Hawaiian island of Kauai in part because of the population's low mobility; despite the common problem of attrition in longitudinal research, at the 18-year follow-up the researchers were able to locate 88% of the original cohort.

A final difficulty with longitudinal research involving tests (e.g., intelligence or personality assessments) is that the participants may become "test wise" after repeated exposures to the same measures. They might show improvement over time—not because of developmental change, but because of practice.

Longitudinal-Sequential Research Designs

The third approach, the **longitudinal-sequential study,** is a combination of cross-sectional and longitudinal approaches (Nesselroade & Baltes, 1974). In a longitudinal-sequential study, several different-aged groups of children are studied over a multiyear period (see Figure 2.4).

A longitudinal-sequential design capitalizes on the strengths of both cross-sectional and longitudinal studies while eliminating many of the disadvantages. For example, if the memory strategies of 6-, 8-, 10-, and 12-year-olds were measured in a cross-sectional study, you could observe age-related differences. If these same children were also assessed once a year over several years, this component of the research design would resemble a longitudinal study that could determine whether the rehearsal strategies of individual children changed over time. In this way, the effects of age and generation can be examined simultaneously as illustrated in Table 2.2.

FIGURE 2.4
Longitudinal-Sequential Design

A longitudinal-sequential design involves the study of different age groups of children over several different points in time.

Source: From Berk, Laura E. *Child Development* (3rd ed.). Published by Allyn and Bacon, Boston, MA. Copyright © 1994 by Pearson Education. Reprinted by permission of the publisher.

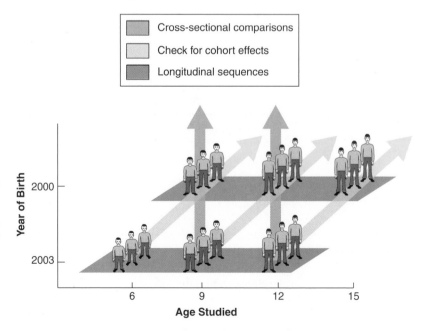

TABLE 2.2   Summary of the Strengths and Limitations of Three Developmental Designs

Developmental researchers most often use these designs in developmental research.

Design	Strengths	Limitations
Cross-sectional	• Assesses different age groups of children at the same time • Time and cost efficient • Can help identify norms for *when* a skill emerges	• Cannot identify *how* change occurs • Which variables most influence change and in what ways • Cohort effects
Longitudinal	• Assesses same-aged participants over several data points • Identifies *when* and *how* change occurs • Connections can be made between early experience and later development • How variables are related to one another	• Long and costly • Attrition • Participants may become "test-wise" • Cohort effects
Longitudinal-sequential	• Assesses different-aged groups of participants over several different points in time	• Requires more time than a cross-sectional study • Challenged by practice effects and attrition issues

---

These designs, however, continue to confront some of the same limitations as longitudinal studies. They still require repeated measures of the same children, take longer to complete than cross-sectional studies, and are vulnerable to attrition and practice effects.

Variable-Centered Versus Person-Centered Approaches

The research designs we have presented have been used for many years to study how one or more **variables,** or factors that vary across individuals in a study, may *cause* change to occur in another variable or group of variables, an approach referred to as the **variable-centered approach.** For example, to understand Takuya's shyness, research using a variable-centered approach would focus on which variables, such as late maturation or peer rejection, might contribute to or *cause* his shyness. More complex developmental theories, such as those presented in chapter 1, have moved away from variable-oriented models because they do not capture the complexity of development in all of its forms. The discipline of child development encourages the use of many of the same developmental research designs described in this chapter, but with the additional goal of describing *patterns* of individual development within multiple changing contexts.

In recent years, the study of development across the life span has become more person-centered (Magnusson, 2000). Researchers are increasingly studying the ways in which individuals contribute to their own development in the various contexts in which they find themselves (Lerner, 2002b). This **person-centered approach** permits the researcher to cluster together individuals who are functioning in similar ways and to follow their development over time (Bergman, Magnusson, & El-Khouri, 2003). For example, the person-centered approach would allow you to group Takuya with other children who have similar characteristics (e.g., Profile 1: minority ethnicity, English as a second language, late physical maturation, high shyness, poor peer relationships) compared to a group unlike him (e.g., Profile 2: majority ethnicity, native English speaker, on-time physical maturation, low shyness, good peer relationships). Then you could follow their development as they transition to high school, begin to date, make new friends, or engage in extracurricular activities in many changing contexts.

This approach may better answer the questions of (a) how these early characteristics (i.e., high shyness and poor peer status) might be related to later characteristics (i.e., compliance and loneliness), and (b) what variables might intercede to play a mediational role in development (e.g., involvement in extracurricular activities) (Mahoney, 2000). The person-centered approach allows for the assessment of multiple aspects of functioning simultaneously, takes a nonlinear approach to data analysis, and formulates the research in person terms. Person-centered research represents a theoretical shift in the study of human development that will likely affect not only the ways that research designs, data collection methods, and analytical techniques are selected but also the way research findings are reported in the future.

> **STOP** What are the personal characteristics that set you apart from your peers?

METHODS OF COLLECTING DATA

To answer research questions about middle childhood or to test hypotheses regarding school-age children, information needs to be collected systematically. The strategies used in this process are called *data collection techniques*. These techniques are not reserved for professional researchers only. A child care worker can utilize them in a day-care facility, a nurse in a pediatrician's office, a supervisor at a playground, or a counselor in high school. The challenge of data collection is to employ an appropriate assessment tool, which depends on a number of factors:

- Number of children to be studied
- Ages of children
- If siblings, parents, teachers, or peers will be assessed
- Whether the variables of interest are personal characteristics or behavioral indices
- The setting in which the study will take place
- The purpose of the research

For example, identifying factors that may precipitate violent outbursts by a single child in the classroom requires a data collection approach different from that used to survey a large group of school-aged children about the loss of extracurricular activities in their school district. Data collection techniques are generally divided into two distinct approaches: quantitative and qualitative.

Quantitative Data Collection

Quantitative data collection techniques collect data and information about the child in a way that allows the assigning of numbers to target behaviors. A score on a self-esteem questionnaire, the number of aggressive behaviors observed, or an intelligence quotient from an intelligence test are all examples of quantitative data.

Although using quantitative data makes traditional statistical analyses of the data easier, the original research question should dictate which technique is best suited to your research. For example, if the purpose of a research project is to understand the reading level of a group of fourth graders, or the memory capacities of

Standardized tests follow a uniform set of rules for administration, scoring, and interpretation.

Anthony Magnacca/Merrill

9-year-olds, or the number of hours middle-schoolers in the United States spend on homework compared to middle-schoolers in Japan, then it would make sense to use a quantitative data collection technique.

Standardized Measures. The easiest way to collect quantitative information about a child or group of children is to use scores from **standardized tests.** These tests are called *standardized* because the administration, scoring, and interpretation of the tests follow uniform procedures. Standardized tests have been shown to consistently evaluate individual abilities in specific domains. Examples of this type of data include an intelligence test, such as the *Wechsler Intelligence Scale for Children, Fourth Edition* (Wechsler, 2003), or an achievement test, such as the *Iowa Tests of Basic Skills* (Hoover, Dunbar, & Frisbie, 2001). Such tests follow specific rules for test taking, scoring, and interpreting scores.

All standardized tests produce a summary numeric score, which may provide useful comparative information about the child's social, emotional, or cognitive status. When standardized tests have been administered to hundreds or thousands of children to establish **norms,** or average performance standards for different-aged groups, they are called **norm-referenced tests.** Norm-referenced tests are useful because they provide a comparison, or "normative," group to which you compare your developmental data. **Criterion-referenced tests** are used often in educational settings and assess the performance of the student against some standard or set of standards.

There are different types of standardized measures, each assessing different competencies. For example, **aptitude tests** are used to *predict* performance, and **achievement tests** measure the skills the child has mastered. Standardized tests may provide us with information that is not easily observable, such as decision-making or hypothesis-testing abilities. Psychological tests that assess constructs such as self-esteem, social dissatisfaction, and peer relationships are often used in research to tell us something about the internal world of the child. It is important to understand the differences between the purposes of these tests so that the information can be used appropriately (Johnson & Johnson, 2002).

The primary advantage of using standardized tests is that measurement experts have previously examined and confirmed their **validity** (i.e., the test measures what it is supposed to measure) and **reliability** (i.e., the test performs consistently). When faced with a choice between using a published standardized test or creating your own, most experts recommend using an existing test. However, because of the proliferation of tests in the educational and mental health fields, many of these scores may already be noted in the school or medical records of the children you wish to study. The availability of such information may be helpful in understanding the hypothetical question you have posed.

The disadvantages of standardized tests are that many people may not have access to them and may lack training in administering them. An additional concern is that multiple-choice tests may not be a valid assessment of a child's skills. Therefore, **performance measures,** which measure children's ability to perform a given skill, should be used in conjunction with standardized paper-and-pencil tests. Performance measures typically assess motor and cognitive skills. They might require a child to walk a straight line with one foot in front of the other (motor skills) or put small blocks together to match a pattern (visual-spatial skills). However, performance measures only allow researchers to *infer* the cognitive steps taken to solve a performance task correctly. Finally, many researchers caution against relying too heavily on the use of a single score to make generalizations about a child's development. They recommend that test scores be used as only one piece of the total picture of a child's developmental profile.

> *Using a score from an introversion-extroversion scale may not capture the complexity of Takuya's social interactions during the first year in his new school.*

Systematic Observation.   There may be times when a hypothesis is best tested by observation—simply watching and listening to people. An **observational technique** involves the systematic collection and documentation of overt behavior; it is useful when the topic of study involves complex actions or interactions among a number of people (e.g., behavior of students between classes in middle school), behavior of which the participant may be unaware (e.g., reasons for self-consciousness), or transgressions (e.g., bullying). Observations can vary in structure and in information obtained. Again, the method chosen is based on the research question that needs to be answered.

Observing children in their natural environment requires **naturalistic** observational techniques. Many researchers feel that these techniques present the most accurate portrayal of the variables that influence development (Bronfenbrenner, 1979). The obvious advantage of this technique is that it allows the researcher to observe the child's behavior in a realistic setting, such as the playground. It is, however, problematic in that it is difficult for the observer to remain unobtrusive, and it is critical to do so to avoid biasing the child's behavior. Children may change their behavior if they feel they are being watched (especially by a strange adult!). Additionally, the researcher has no control over the setting, so the child of interest could disappear and there would be large blocks of time in which the target child is unobservable.

A potential solution to this problem is a **structured observation** of a child in a controlled setting, such as a laboratory classroom, school classroom, or home. A good example of how development can be studied using a structured observational technique is researchers' observations of the conversational styles of mothers in their homes with their 8- to 10-year-old daughters and with their 14- to 16-year-old daughters (Beaumont, 2000). The observers also coded the conversational styles of these same mothers at home in conversation with a friend. By observing these interactions in a structured situation in which they gave the participants a topic to discuss, the researchers were able to determine that mothers used a very different style when communicating with their friends than with their daughters. In addition, they found that daughters' and mothers' conversational styles differed (e.g., number of interruptions, amount of overlap). The researchers suggested that these differences explain some of the dissatisfaction and conflict that late school-agers and early adolescent girls have with their mothers.

Regardless of which observation technique is chosen, keeping a record of behavior is necessary. Record-keeping techniques require little or no training to use and are easy to employ in a variety of settings. The most inclusive type of record is a **specimen record,** in which the researcher records all observed behaviors over a specified period of time. This type of technique should be used if your research question is largely exploratory or if it is important to record the precursors and antecedents of the target behavior.

A specimen record would allow you to observe and record the series of events that led up to Takuya eating lunch alone (e.g., does he choose a seat away from others or avoid others' invitations to join them?), as well as how others responded to Takuya's lack of lunchroom companionship (e.g., does anyone approach him?).

Time sampling is the recording of observable behaviors every time they occur during a designated time period (e.g., for 15 minutes) or at designated time intervals (e.g., every 30 seconds for 15 minutes). The behavior and interval for observation are agreed upon prior to the start of the observation. For example, a group of researchers may create a list of social play behaviors that include both physical and verbal acts of friendship. Child A is observed for 15 minutes, and every time he engages in positive behavior its frequency and duration are recorded; child B is observed for the next 15 minutes and his positive behavior is recorded; child C's positive behavior is observed for the next 15 minutes; and then the order may be repeated. This technique records both the frequency *and* duration of a target behavior (or set of behaviors), thereby allowing a researcher (a) to see if the frequency of the behavior increases or decreases during a certain activity or time of day, and (b) to observe differences in the behavior's frequency and duration among the different children (see Figure 2.5).

Event sampling records how often a specific behavior occurs; it is used in research when a behavior is relatively infrequent. For example, a school counselor might notice Takuya sitting alone. Event sampling, where the frequency of his time spent alone is recorded over several weeks or months, could determine whether the behavior should be of concern and require intervention. The sample sheet in Figure 2.6 shows how time sampling can be applied to this chapter's case study.

Regardless of which of the various record-keeping methods is employed, the disadvantage of observational techniques is that the target behavior may occur infrequently, thus resulting in large amounts of time and energy spent by the observer with very little payoff by way of observation. In addition, all researchers are subject to bias in their observations. What one researcher may code as shyness, another may not. Typically, more than one observer should be used and some training given regarding the targeted behavior. For example, some discussion and consensus on what constitutes shyness might help decrease observer bias. Perhaps the greatest limitation of observational techniques is that a researcher can only infer the thought processes that led to the observable behavior.

Observer		Grade		Date	
Participant	10:00	10:15	10:30	11:00	TOTAL

FIGURE 2.5   Example of a Time Sampling Observation Form

Time sampling allows the observer to record behavior in segments of time and track patterns of behavior over time.

Observer		Grade		Date	
Participant	Raises Hand	Talks to Other Children	Interacts with Others	Talks to Adults	TOTAL

FIGURE 2.6   Event Sampling Observation Form

Event sampling allows the observer to record the frequency of a targeted behavior or group of behaviors.

Self-Report Techniques. **Self-report techniques** are defined as any method used to collect data in which the research participants report on their own feelings, abilities, attitudes, and behaviors or those of their siblings, parents, teachers, and peers. Questionnaires are a common self-report technique. Questionnaires may consist of structured items that may require a yes or no response, a response on a rating scale, or open-ended responses. The major advantage of questionnaires is that they allow for the collection of information from large groups of research participants in a relatively short period of time. They also tap into a person's attitudes and feelings, something not easily observed or reported by someone other than the subject.

Questionnaires are used often in research on middle childhood. For example, researchers used a homework questionnaire to find out whether student, family, and parenting style differences were related to the homework process and student outcomes (Cooper, Lindsay, & Nye, 2000). By using a questionnaire, they found that parents with students in higher grade levels reported giving students more homework autonomy, which in turn was found to be highly associated with higher standardized test scores, higher class grades, and more homework completed. Parental responses that reflected low homework autonomy (e.g., doing the assignment for their child, or helping so that it could get done faster) and poor elimination of distractions for their children (e.g., TV was always on) were related to their children's poorer school performance. A creative approach to collecting self-report data is presented in Box 2.2.

Despite the widespread use of questionnaires as a self-report technique, there are limitations to their usefulness when studying school-age children. Answers on questionnaires may be susceptible to a number of biases. An **honesty bias** is the tendency for children to present themselves in the best possible light. Children will be more honest if the responses make them look good, compared to those that make them look bad. For example, children would be less likely to answer honestly questions about theft or cheating than questions about friendships. Children between the ages of 6 and 12 also are vulnerable to **social desirability bias,** which is the need to please and seek approval from adults. This phenomenon may result in children's answering questions in the way they think you want them to respond, rather than in a way that provides a more accurate record of their own feelings and behaviors.

Siblings, parents, teachers, and peers can report on the targeted child as a way of checking the accuracy of the child's responses. However, if questions are retrospective, relying on a parent's or teacher's memory of the past, answers may reflect a **memory bias,** which is the tendency to underestimate or overestimate the abilities of a child.

Finally, the most challenging aspect of using questionnaires with this age group is the reading ability and comprehension required, which may affect participants' ability to understand and follow directions, to read and understand questionnaire items, or to interpret the questions correctly. If open-ended questions are used, then a child's writing skills may add an additional complication to the data collection technique. Because children's reading and writing skills can vary greatly, their responses may not be an accurate reflection of thought or feeling, but rather a reflection of what the child was capable of reading, understanding, or writing. For children ages 6 to 12, it is best to avoid these potential complications by either reading the questionnaire items to them or by changing the data collection procedure to an interview, which will be discussed in the following section on qualitative techniques. Observation methods and self-report techniques can yield more than quantitative information; however, data from these methods are typically numeric.

BOX 2.2   Roadmap to Understanding Theory and Research
Cultural and Contextual Influences on How Children in Middle Childhood Spend Their Time as Reflected in Self-Reports

From middle childhood to early adolescence, White suburban American children shift from spending more time with families to spending more time with peers, and increased conflict with parents parallels this shift (Larson, 2001; Rothbaum & Trommsdorff, 2007). This pattern has been described as a normative developmental task of Western adolescents as they attempt to establish a sense of autonomy and independence. Reed Larson and colleagues wondered, however, if the same shift occurred in urban African American youth from poor, working- and middle-class families (Larson, Richards, Sims, & Dworkin, 2001).

To study the settings in which fifth through eighth graders spent their days, Larson employed the Experience Sampling Method (ESM). Participants carried alarm watches, and each time they received a random signal they recorded (a) where they were, (b) with whom, and (c) what they were doing (i.e., self-reports).

The results from this ingenious self-report technique were compared to those from a sample of White suburban fifth through eighth graders studied with exactly the same procedures (Larson & Richards, 1989, 1991). As shown in Figure 2.7, urban African American children spent less time in school but no less time doing homework than White suburban children. They spent more time at home and with their families than their suburban counterparts, a pattern comparable to what is found in collectivist societies such as India (Verma & Sharma, 2006), and approximately the same amount of time in leisure activities. Larson et al. (2001) also found that the urban children reported higher rates of talking to family than the suburban children and that they spent less time than the suburban children in

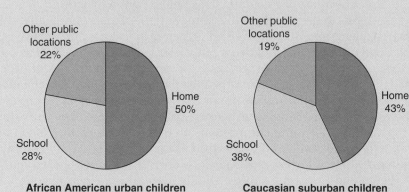

African American urban children   **Caucasian suburban children**

FIGURE 2.7
Where Children in Middle Childhood Spend Their Time

African American urban children spend more time at home than Caucasian suburban children. This pattern was consistent from fifth through eighth grade.

Source: Data are from "How urban African American young adolescents spend their time: Time budgets for locations, activities, and companionship," by R. Larson, M. H. Richards, B. Sims, & J. Dworkin, 2001, *American Journal of Community Psychology, 29,* pp. 565–597.

(continued)

BOX 2.2   Roadmap to Understanding Theory and Research *(Continued)*
Cultural and Contextual Influences on How Children in Middle
Childhood Spend Their Time as Reflected in Self-Reports

"outdoor public locations outside the immediate neighborhood" but more time at a relative's or neighbor's home. Perhaps most interesting is that for the urban children, time spent in each of these three major contexts did not change significantly from fifth to eighth grade.

This self-report technique provided interesting insight into the role that culture and context may play in influencing the social settings within which urban African American school-age children spend their time. The authors reported that the urban children exhibited patterns of time budgeting that reflected strong kinship ties (Hatchett & Jackson, 1993), stringent parental monitoring and control (Jarrett, 1995, 1997), and the perception of high-risk environments beyond the neighborhood. We need to continue to study *how* time spent in these contexts influences development in middle childhood.

Evaluating Quantitative Data

In order to draw conclusions from the quantitative data collected and apply it in an appropriate context, a number of questions may be asked to assess the quality of the data collection approach.

- Is the data collection technique reliable?
- Is the data collection technique valid?
- Is the data collection technique generalizable?

These questions should be asked not only of your own collection method but also of others' quantitative research findings. If the answers to these questions are affirmative, then you can feel *more* confident about the conclusions drawn. However, if the answer to any one of these questions is negative, then you have to acknowledge the limitations of the study.

Reliability. Is the data collection technique you use reliable? In other words, does the measure consistently yield similar results when given to the same research participants under similar circumstances? If a study is reliable, the measure used in a study will reflect similar scores from the same child over time and testing situation. One way to assess reliability is to readminister the same test to the same child after a short time interval (several months). This assessment of consistency is called **test-retest reliability.** Repeated performance on a test has been shown to vary as a function of time of day the test is administered or the gender of the test administrator, but performance should not vary so much that the findings for that child change significantly (Murphy & Davidshofer, 2001). For example, under normal circumstances, a child would not be categorized as having "normal" intelligence and then 6 months later receive a score on the same intelligence test that categorizes him as "educable mentally impaired."

If you are using an interview or observational technique, your observers should be recording and coding the same behavior in similar ways. A statistical check can be performed on the coding scores of the observers to see if they are coding similarly. The assessment of agreement is called **interrater reliability.** A researcher should report these reliabilities along with the results of the study so that others can evaluate the dependability of the findings. If, however, a readministered test were to yield a test score vastly different from the first, or two observers vary widely in how they are coding behavior, then the results of these data collection techniques would be regarded as unreliable and therefore suspect.

Validity. Is the technique valid? Validity is the extent to which the technique measures what it claims to measure. For example, if you are using a measure of rejection sensitivity, the instrument should assess sensitivity to rejection, not social avoidance or neuroticism. Likewise, a measure of tolerance for aggression should not measure dislike for the experimenter or experimental situation. The **predictive validity** of a measure refers to how accurately it predicts children's behaviors in the future or, perhaps, in other contexts. This type of validity is often of particular interest to developmentalists. For example, a finding that early aptitude in mathematics predicts good grades in math classes in middle school demonstrates predictive validity. A published test should report this information in its instruction booklet or manual. Also, if an interview or observational technique is used, the behavior being observed should meet the definitions for the construct in the research. For example, acts that count as physical and verbal aggression are clearly described in several published research articles and can be used in your own research (Crick, 1996; Tremblay, 2000). Even if the criteria or definitions of a certain set of behaviors are unclear, decisions about what you are interested in studying within your own research agenda need to be made prior to the commencement of your study (Johnson & Johnson, 2002).

Generalizability. One final question regarding the quality of the data collection approach is how **generalizable** the results are. Generalizability is the extent the findings of the study are applicable to other children or groups of children. This issue is common to several of the data collection techniques. If only a single child or group is tested, interviewed, or observed, the results cannot be applied beyond the research participants used in the study. If, however, the group of participants tested, interviewed, or observed includes a large number of persons with diverse racial, ethnic, economic, religious, and sexual-orientation backgrounds, then the results could be generalized to others. However, the goal of research is not always to generalize the results to others; it depends on the original research questions asked. It may be that the original hypothesis is best tested by a clinical interview with a small group of families, thereby limiting generalizability. However, if the results of a study are meant to apply to *all* 10-year-olds, then the participant population should be large and diverse. Information about the number and type of research participants in the study is typically included in the method section of a published study to allow the reader to draw conclusions about the generalizability of the findings.

A summary of the various quantitative data collection techniques can be found in Table 2.3.

The quantitative data collection techniques discussed in this section describe how researchers have collected information about the abilities and behaviors of school-age children. Recent textbooks on research methodology focus on these traditional methods exclusively (e.g., Greer & Mulhern, 2002). A reliance on quantitative data-gathering strategies has a long history in the social sciences, which have mimicked the natural sciences in reducing human behavior to a quantifiable unit of

TABLE 2.3   Summary of Quantitative Data Collection Techniques

Data collection techniques that typically yield numerical data, their suggested uses, and limitations.

Technique	Uses	Limitations
Self-Report Questionnaires	• Used with large number of participants • Assesses attitudes and feelings • Many data collected in a short period of time	• Subject to honesty bias, memory bias, and social desirability bias • Requires reading and writing competency
Systematic Observations	• Used with a small number of participants • Yields information about overt behavior in the child's natural environment • Useful to understand complex actions and interactions	• Behaviors may be influenced by observer presence • No control over experimental setting • Time-consuming and effortful • Subject to observer bias • Can only infer cognitions
Standardized Measures	• Used with large groups • Participants' scores can be compared to established norms • Reliability and validity can be established • Useful information in specific domains	• Limited test availability • Must be trained to administer • Cannot generalize from a single score • May not reflect developmental change

analysis (Fox, Porter, & Wokler, 1995). However, the complexity of human behavior does not lend itself easily to this type of reductionism (as might a chemical or biological phenomenon), and some researchers argue that the overuse of these techniques is restricting our view of developing children in all their complexities and contexts for growth (Galambos & Leadbeater, 2000). For this reason, a movement is taking place in the field of child development toward the increased use of qualitative data collection strategies (Camic, Rhodes, & Yardley, 2003; Hayes, 2000; Magee, 2002).

Qualitative Data Collection

Qualitative methods typically yield nonnumeric data that lead to a greater understanding of the participant. The data are summaries or descriptions of the development, and/or the factors that influence development, of an individual or groups of individuals. Most importantly, qualitative researchers study phenomena in their natural setting and attempt to make sense of the meanings that children bring to their world. Such data are not immediately ready for statistical analysis, but need some processing by the researcher. Qualitative researchers rely on the human researcher as instrument (rather than a pencil-and-paper test), respect the cultural and socio-historical "truths" told by their participants, and recognize their bias as "outsiders" and "interpreters" of experience (Merrick, 1999). Qualitative research may be conducted in many ways, but there are recurring features in the variety of approaches used (Miles & Huberman, 1994):

- Qualitative research is conducted through an intense and/or prolonged contact with a "field" or life situation.
- The researcher's role is to gain a "holistic" overview of the context under study.

- The researcher attempts to capture data "from the inside," and suspend preconceptions about the subject of interest.
- Researchers allow original responses to be maintained throughout the study.
- Most analysis is done with words.

Qualitative data collection techniques bring a rich analytical perspective to a research question that can be viewed as complementary to the more traditional quantitative techniques (Denzin & Lincoln, 2000; Ponterotto, 2005).

Interview Studies. An interview allows the researcher to pose questions to a person face-to-face. An advantage of this method is that it eliminates reading and writing skill requirements for the research participant, and the interviewer can answer any questions the interviewee may have about directions or specific items. An interview technique is particularly useful when researching populations in which English is a second language or when the researcher anticipates a need for flexibility in the generation of questions. Interviews can be conducted in different ways and can vary in structure and in the generalizability of the information obtained.

A **clinical interview method** is a flexible interview procedure that allows the interviewer to shape the order and type of questions asked to obtain the best reflection of the child's or parent's thinking. This technique involves modifications to questions based on the responses as well as multiple follow-up probes. Jean Piaget (1896–1980) was well known for using this technique to study cognitive development. After a child responded "yes" or "no" to a problem-solving question, Piaget proceeded to ask a series of questions that revealed the child's approach to his answer. The following conversation between Piaget and an 8-year-old illustrates the child's developing concept of age:

Question:	Have you siblings?
Answer:	I have two small brothers, Charles and Jean.
Question:	Who was born first?
Answer:	Me, then Charlie, and finally Jean.
Question:	When you are grown up, how old will you all be?
Answer:	I'll be the oldest, then Charlie and then Jean.
Question:	How much older will you be?
Answer:	The same as now.
Question:	Why?
Answer:	It's always the same. It all depends on when one was born.

For Piaget, the child's approach to the problem, not his final response, identified developmental differences in cognitive processing.

This flexible method allows an interviewer to gather in-depth information on a wide range of topics from a single interviewee. However, the questions developed during the interview are unlikely to be the same questions generated in an interview with another child, or by another interviewer, thereby making it difficult to generalize the findings to any other participant or population. Given the purposes of your research, this may not be a major concern. Another consideration is that most interviews will need to be transcribed and coded from audio or audiovi-

Patrick White/Merrill

A structured interview asks the same questions of all participants in the same way.

sual tapes, which might be very time-consuming if you have interviewed large numbers of children. One way to solve this problem is to use a more structured interview.

A **structured interview** asks the same questions of every person in the same way. This format assures that all interviewees are treated the same way and eliminates any researcher bias that may influence the direction of the interview. The design of the questions in a structured interview can also limit the length of response, thereby reducing the time spent transcribing the interview. Much valuable information and insight can be gathered by asking children and adolescents, parents, and teachers to comment on their lives and experiences. In one study, for example, researchers used a structured interview to determine which variables influenced girls to choose careers in science. Interviewers asked girls in grades 2, 5, 8, and 11 their feelings about science, science careers, peer and parental support, and how science is taught (Baker & Leary, 1995). Through this structured interview method, the researchers found that girls thought that women can and should do science and that they liked learning science in an interactive social context rather than in activities that encouraged independence and isolation, like reading, writing, and note-taking. Also, girls who chose science careers were attracted by the careers' potential to help others (e.g., medicine).

Structured interviews are also an integral part of focus groups, which generate and process qualitative data. Box 2.3 describes how focus groups operate.

Narrative studies. Many researchers recognize the limitations of traditional quantitative research methods, especially when studying experiences that are extremely difficult to speak about, such as difficult life transitions and trauma. At times, the best data collection method may be having the person tell a story about what transpired. **Narrative analysis,** or the analysis of stories, examines not only the content of the story but the *way* the story is told. This data collection technique focuses on how a person imposes order on experiences, the language that is used

Focus groups are a data collection technique that yields qualitative data. When a researcher is interested in learning about participants' perspectives, beliefs, and attitudes, focus groups are particularly fruitful. Focus groups involve children in the research process by inviting everyone in a target group to respond to a set of semistructured discussion questions. Observing the dynamics of the group interaction is as interesting and important a part of the process as the responses given. Focus groups are used frequently in applied settings such as health-related fields, psychological counseling, and education (Heary & Hennessy, 2002; Kennedy, Kools, & Krueger, 2001; Krueger & Casey, 2000).

A focus group approach was used to study how middle-school children experience and manage their asthma (Penza-Clyve, Mansell, & McQuaid, 2004). Thirty-six students (age range 9–15) participated in a series of interviews to discuss their health experiences with the interviewer and each other. Semistructured interview questions included:

- What are some of the annoying things about having asthma?
- What gets in the way of taking your regular inhalers?
- What advice would you give a kid with asthma who was having a hard time taking his or her medications regularly?

Analysis of the qualitative responses showed that most participants mentioned lack of motivation, remembering difficulties, and social barriers as reasons for not taking their medication.

> You can't just stop what you are doing with your friends, go home and take your inhalers and then go back to where your friends were, because they are not there anymore. (p. 193)

With the guidance of the interviewer, participants were also able to generate strategies to combat these problems. They suggested reward systems to increase motivation, enhancing memory by using more effective strategies such as notes and setting watches, and taking one's medication in private to avoid social embarrassment. One paradoxical finding was that although this age group complained that parental reminders to take their medication were annoying, they also reported parental prompts helped them adhere to their medication schedule.

Focus group methodology allows the participants to generate responses that are then used in a feedback loop to structure further questions. Responses to these questions assist in the identification of and potential solution to a problem, as was done in this study.

Some researchers have concerns about the suitability of this research methodology with school-age children (Morgan, 1996, 1997). However, others have argued that the format is well suited for young participants (Graue & Walsh, 1998; Horner, 2000) (for a review, see Morgan, Gibbs, Maxwell, & Britten, 2002).

Arguments Against Using Focus Groups	**Arguments for Using Focus Groups**
- Children this age may lack the cognitive competency to analyze and hypothesize about health issues.	- Research has shown this age group to be cognitively competent to utilize this format.
- Children in middle childhood may be unable to formulate responses to open-ended interview questions.	- When asked to describe specific events or activities, young persons give complete, descriptive responses.
- Not all topics of study are suitable for this discussion format.	- The format encourages children to talk to peers when they feel they cannot talk to adults.
- Peer hierarchies can dominate the flow of the discussion despite the best attempts of the interviewer to intervene.	- Participants feel empowered using the focus group format.
- Consensus building by majority can mute the voices of the minority.	- The group provides a safe haven for personal responses.
	- Children this age can gain support from peers who share their experiences.
	- Participants can learn from peers how they handle health issues.

to tell the story, and the cultural influences that are reflected in the story (Flick, 2002).

For example, Lyn Mikel Brown, Carol Gilligan, and their research team (1992) were engaged in a longitudinal study of girls (ages 7–18) to assess how their relational worlds and "voices" changed as they navigated through adolescence. After 3 years of structured interviews—asking carefully developed questions consistently and using standard procedures for analyzing interview data—the research team decided to abandon their research strategy. They felt that their well-designed questions no longer "seemed right" and "seemed to be cutting off girls' voices" (Brown & Gilligan, 1992, p. 18). Instead, they adopted a narrative approach to allow the girls to tell stories about when they felt "in relationship" and when they did not. Here is a story told by Noura about her anger when a teacher asks her to leave class for making a laughing noise:

> He could have just tried to ignore [my laughter], because we have to ignore a lot of things that a lot of our teachers do . . . like when they are really mean . . . not necessarily mean, but like we think of it as unfair, but I guess it really is fair in a way . . . It's his class and he can, or any teacher can just assign whatever they want, but I mean it seems unfair to us . . . I hate it . . . It makes me mad when they make you do like, I mean I guess it's good in the long run, but I don't know. (p. 121)

Consistent with the narrative format, Noura's story was analyzed for four components as she speaks of relationships: (a) Who is speaking? (b) In what body? (c) Telling what story about relationships—from whose perspective or from what vantage point? and (d) In what societal and cultural frameworks? Her telling of the story is noted for "speaking her feelings and then retracting them," for being "sure of her feelings and then uncertain" (p. 121). Her mixed response to what she perceives as unfair is compared to her ability to openly and confidently express anger 3 years previously at age 11.

Narratives were a rich source of data for this longitudinal study (Brown & Gilligan, 1992) that yielded important results about adolescent girls and their struggle to maintain their "voices" and sense of self. Narrative analysis has also been used to analyze stories about decisions to smoke (Baillie, Lovato, Johnson, & Kalaw, 2005), menarche (Teitelman, 2004), and gender and socioeconomic experiences of minorities (Mainess, Champion, & McCabe, 2002). Although it has provided another dimension to understanding these phenomena, narrative analysis also has limitations. It may not be useful with large numbers of participants, given the labor-intensiveness of the data collection, transcription, and analysis. And because of the importance of embedding the narrative in context, it is difficult to generalize the results from one participant's story to others', even from the same small sample.

STOP Do you have a story that captures or defines some aspect of your development?

Ethnography. The increasing need to understand the role that culture plays in the development of school-age children encourages us to look for techniques that disciplines like sociology and anthropology may use to study other societies and cultures. If your research question were to ask the extent to which cultural differences influence school-age children's view of homework, then **ethnography,** a technique borrowed from anthropology, might be useful. Ethnography is the study of a culture or social group, rather than of individuals, in order to understand the unique characteristics and values of the group and how they may influence the development of children (Creswell & Maietta, 2002; McCurdy, Spradley, & Shandy,

2005). Using a method called *participant observation*, the researcher lives with a group for several months or years and participates in their daily lives. Extensive field notes are taken and combined with observational data and interviews to present a detailed account of the unique values, attitudes, and behaviors of a culture or societal group.

For example, ethnographic data collection was used to explore how lunchtime at an elementary school serves to differentiate among children based on age, gender, racial ethnicity, and social class (Thorne, 2005). By spending over three years in the cafeteria of an elementary school with a diverse student body, the research team amassed extensive observations and field notes about the social world of these students. At this school, students who were identified as low income because they received a "free" or "reduced" lunch felt stigmatized. In addition, if a student brought lunch from home, the lunch items were examined by other students and offered clues not only to household income and patterns of consumption, but also to varied family cultures, child-rearing beliefs and practices, and ethnic food traditions. In addition to recording lunchtime food practices, ethnographers also observed how lunchtime afforded students a relatively free environment within which to interact with peers. With whom children sit and share food conveyed information to the researchers about peer hierarchies and how children negotiated differences during lunchtime.

The greatest advantage to using ethnography to study development is its ability to immerse observers in the culture so they can record the role that culture plays in the targeted area of development. A limitation is the bias an ethnographer's presence may introduce into the group. In addition, a clinical interview method or observational technique may introduce bias. The cultural perspective of the researcher may inadvertently influence the questions asked, the observations made, and the conclusions drawn. Finally, the findings from one culture or social group cannot be generalized (Hammersley, 1992).

Perhaps an ethnographic study of Takuya with his family, peers, and larger cultural community might yield interesting insights into his social skills, ability to deal with social exclusion, interactions with authority figures, and minority status within a majority culture.

Evaluating Qualitative Data

Qualitative data-gathering strategies have expanded our knowledge of how children develop within complex social networks and settings. They are not, however, immune to criticism. Some view qualitative research as too "relativistic," "loose," and subjective. Critics claim that there is no way to establish the validity or "truth value" of scientific claims or observations based on qualitative work (see Lincoln & Cannella, 2004). Those researchers who employ qualitative data collection techniques argue that the criteria by which we judge quantitative data do not, and *should* not, apply to qualitative research findings. So how should we judge the quality of this research process and its findings?

It is debatable whether the terms *validity* and *reliability* have a place in the evaluation of qualitative data (Guba & Lincoln, 2005). Typically, statistical analyses measure these criteria for various quantitative scores. If, however, your data collection methods provide no numbers, how can we be sure that you are measuring what you say you are (i.e., validity) and that your results will be consistent (i.e., reliability)? Because many researchers are trained to evaluate research findings using these criteria, qualitative researchers have provided the following comparable criteria or questions to employ with qualitative data (Lincoln & Guba, 2000; Morrow, 2005; Patton, 2002):

- Can I *depend* on the research process as well as the findings? (i.e., reliability)
- Was the research process and interpretation of data *credible*? (i.e., validity)
- Are the findings *transferable* to another individual, group, or context? (i.e., generalizability)

Dependability. This term refers to the rigor of the methodology used to collect data as well as takes into account the researcher's characteristics. Asking the following questions can assess the **dependability** of qualitative research:

- What types of data collection techniques were used? With whom? Under what arrangements?
- Who conducted this research and interpreted the data?
- What biases or preconceptions might the researchers have brought with them to the study?

The "dependability" of the study can be established by the researcher (a) disclosing his or her orientation; (b) engaging the material in an intensive and prolonged manner; (c) carrying out repeated observations; (d) checking the accuracy of specific items of data by using multiple sources (called **triangulation**); and (e) discussing the findings and process with colleagues and the participants in the study. If the data are collected and recorded in a careful and systematic manner and in a way that acknowledges the researcher's biases, then the findings of the study are dependable and likely to be found again in a similar research context.

Credibility. This criterion refers to the accuracy of the data collected and conclusions drawn. Readers of qualitative research can assess credibility by determining the adequacy of the researcher's understanding, interpretation, and representation of people's meanings. **Credibility** can be established by **referential adequacy**, which means comparing interpreted findings with the data and using consensus or researcher agreement to achieve interpretive conclusions. Also, references to theory and other empirical studies can help establish referential adequacy.

Transferability. **Transferability** is the ability to apply the findings of one qualitative research study to another. Qualitative researchers should provide a complete description of the process of their study, the data, and the interpretation of those data to enable the reader to make a decision about the transferability of findings from one individual or group to another. However, qualitative researchers believe that the strength of the qualitative method is its recognition of the subjectivity and reflexivity of the researchers and of the unique time and place associated with each study. A summary of the uses and limitations of qualitative data collection techniques can be found in Table 2.4.

TABLE 2.4 Summary of Qualitative Data Collection Techniques

Data collection techniques that typically yield verbal responses or descriptions and their suggested uses and limitations.

Technique	Uses	Limitations
Interviews	• Used with a small number of participants • Yields in-depth information • Requires no reading or writing competency	• Questions may vary • Difficult to generalize results • Relies on verbal ability • Subject to interviewer bias
Narrative Studies	• Used with a small number of participants • Useful for studying developmental transitions or trauma • Useful to understand the content of stories and *how* they are told	• Behavior may be influenced by observer • Data collection, transcription, and analysis are time-consuming and effortful • Researcher bias
Ethnography	• Used with large or small groups • Can observe the role of culture in development	• Ethnographer may influence group dynamics • Subject to observer bias • Difficult to generalize results

CONDUCTING YOUR OWN RESEARCH

After reading this chapter you might feel overwhelmed by the many choices researchers must make in order to study school-age children. However, becoming familiar with these data collection techniques allows you to link theoretical questions with practical application. Tables 2.3 and 2.4 can be used as guides to remind you of the common uses, strengths, and limitations of each technique. Remember, it is the theoretical question or hypothesis that best determines which data collection method should be used.

By presenting these data collection techniques one by one, we may have given the impression that choosing one excludes the others. Not so. Many researchers rely on a combination of these techniques to reach the best conclusions about development. For example, **case studies** are an accumulated record of a single child or group over time. Researchers using case studies may organize and summarize information obtained from a variety of measures, such as questionnaires, interviews, observations, and standardized or performance measures. For example, researchers studied a K–8 school that was unusually successful in producing achievement in students at high risk for academic failure. More specifically, 100% of the school's graduates successfully completed high school and college. To investigate which school variables were most related to this success, researchers used the following data collection strategies:

- Observations of teacher and student behavior in the classrooms
- Information gathered from briefings arranged by the school for the researchers
- Interviews with teachers, staff, students and parents
- Curricular documentation published by the school
- Artifacts of performance such as student homework, corrected papers, test scores, portfolios, and so on.

Researchers found that characteristics such as effective organizational and administrative structures; well-trained teachers who all share the same pedagogical philosophy;

small class sizes; and consistent delivery of research-based curriculum that focuses on reading, composition skills, and the conceptual understanding of math, science and social studies in an environment designed to motivate produced consistently successful students who had previously failed in other education environments (Pressley, Gaskins, Solic, & Collins, 2006).

Action Research

The desire of social scientists to conduct research with greater social relevance has resulted in the increased use of **action research** (Ungar & Teram, 2005). Action research is a methodological approach in which the researcher uses research findings to solve a practical problem or concern while, at the same time, generating critical knowledge about the issue. Action research has been practiced since the 1920s as a general strategy for institutional change. More recently, action research has been conducted in schools, family practice clinics, and neighborhood settings and has informed social policy makers about human development (Brydon-Miller, 1997, 2001; Ungar, 2001; 2004).

Action research does not have any prescribed methodology; its unique feature is that a study's focus and method may change as the research process unfolds. Most important, action researchers work collaboratively with research participants to shape the focus of the inquiry and to craft a solution to a mutually identified problem based on the study's findings.

Action research typically includes the following four steps, as illustrated in Figure 2.8:

1. Selecting an area of focus or inquiry
2. Collecting data and information
3. Analyzing and interpreting the data
4. Developing and implementing a plan for action

To apply the action research steps, you would begin with the identification of a question. For example, you might want to find out why a majority of your seventh-grade algebra students are not completing their homework. You construct a brief survey with items that ask the students to rate their level of agreement with a variety of possible explanations (e.g., not enough time due to extracurricular activities; don't understand the problems; not motivated). You also ask the students to answer open-ended questions that give them the opportunity to explain why their homework was not completed. Much to your surprise, you learn from your students that the book required for completing their homework was too heavy to take home on a regular basis. As a result, many students planned to finish their algebra assignment at school the next day, often unsuccessfully. You can now interpret the responses with your students and try several plans of action to increase the probability that homework is finished in the future.

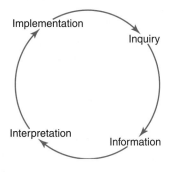

FIGURE 2.8

The Interactive Components of Action Research

This figure shows how the outcomes of action research influence the research process in a continuous feedback loop.

STOP Based on your personal experiences with school-age children, how would you involve them in asking a research question?

The preceding example followed the four suggested steps for action research. You identified a practical problem (unfinished homework) and collected data not only to identify the source of the problem but also to generate solutions with the participants in the study (the students). One of the advantages of action research is that it empowers practitioners working closely with school-age children to identify, explore, and "solve" their own specific research questions. However, it shares with many research methods vulnerability to experimenter bias. Remember that the biases of the person or persons asking the questions, collecting the information, performing analyses or interpreting, and planning a course of action may alter the direction and success of an action research project.

Program Evaluation

Many of you may be involved, currently or in the future, with a program that is designed to protect, help, and/or enhance the development of school-age children. At some point, either your own agency or program or an external funding source may want to know if your efforts are successful. The process of identifying the goals of your organization and assessing your success in meeting those objectives is **program evaluation**. The type of evaluation you undertake to assess your program depends on what you want to learn about the program. For example, if you are involved in a community recreation center and one of the center's goals is to provide a safe environment for children in the evening and on the weekends in order to reduce victimization rates, then your program evaluation should assess this component.

There are many ways to evaluate a program and many resources available to help you do so (Chen, 2005; Royse, Thyer, Padgett, & Logan, 2006). Asking the following questions is a good way to begin:

- Why is the evaluation being done?
- Who will receive the information from the evaluation?
- What kinds of information are needed to make the decision you or others need to make?
- From what sources should the information be collected?
- How can that information be collected? (For this step, you can utilize any number of the data collection techniques presented in this chapter.)
- What resources are available to collect the information?
- How should the outcome information be presented?

A thorough program evaluation can help you identify the strengths and weaknesses of your organization or program, assist you in increasing the efficiency and effectiveness of your services, and verify that you are doing what you think you are doing (McNamara, 1998).

Ethical Guidelines

When initiating research or evaluation with children and adolescents, ethical standards need to be followed. In any study, the needs of the children, their parents, and families must take priority over the advancement of science. It is imperative that you, as a potential researcher, know and adhere to ethical principles in your research. Ethical guidelines to protect the rights of children and parents who participate in research studies, listed in Table 2.5, have been adopted by the Society for Research in Child Development (SRCD).

TABLE 2.5 Ethical Standards for Research

1. *Nonharmful Procedures:* The investigator should use no research procedure that may harm the child either physically or psychologically.

2. *Informed Consent:* The investigator should inform the child of all features of the research that may affect his or her willingness to participate and should answer the child's questions in terms appropriate to the child's comprehension.

3. *Parental Consent:* The informed consent of parents or legal guardians should be obtained, preferably in writing.

4. *Additional Consent:* The informed consent of any persons, such as teachers for example, whose interaction with the child as the participant in the study, should also be obtained.

5. *Incentives:* Incentives to participate in a research project must be fair and must not unduly exceed the range of incentives that the child normally experiences.

6. *Deception:* If withholding information or deception is practiced, and there is reason to believe that the research participants have been negatively affected by it, adequate measures should be taken after the study to ensure the participants' understanding of the reasons for the deception.

7. *Anonymity:* To gain access to institutional records, the investigator should obtain permission from responsible authorities in charge of records. Anonymity of the information should be preserved and no information used other than that for which permission was obtained.

8. *Mutual Responsibilities:* From the beginning of each research investigation, there should be clear agreement between the investigator and the parents, guardians, or those who act *in loco parentis*, and the child, when appropriate, that defines the responsibilities of each.

9. *Jeopardy:* When, in the course of research, information comes to the investigator's attention that may jeopardize the child's well-being, the investigator has a responsibility to discuss the information with the parents or guardians and with those expert in the field in order that they may arrange the necessary assistance for the child.

10. *Unforeseen Consequences:* When research procedures result in undesirable consequences for the participant that were previously unforeseen, the investigator should immediately employ appropriate measures to correct these consequences.

11. *Confidentiality:* The investigator should keep in confidence all information obtained about research participants.

12. *Informing Participants:* Immediately after the data are collected, the investigator should clarify for the research participant any misconceptions that may have arisen and report general findings in terms appropriate to their understanding.

13. *Reporting Results:* Because the investigator's words may carry unintended weight with parents and children, caution should be exercised in reporting results, making evaluative statements, or giving advice.

14. *Implications of Findings:* Investigators should be mindful of the social, political, and human implications of their research and should be especially careful in the presentation of findings from the research.

15. *Scientific Misconduct:* Misconduct is defined as the fabrication or falsification of data, plagiarism, misrepresentation, or other practices that seriously deviate from those that are commonly accepted within the scientific community.

16. *Personal Misconduct:* Personal misconduct that results in a criminal conviction of a felony may be sufficient grounds for a member's expulsion from the Society.

Note: Fuller explanations of each guideline can be found at http://www.srcd.org/about.html#standards.

Source: From *Ethical standards for research with children* (Online) by the Society for Research in Child Development, 1990–1991. Available: http://www.srcd.org/about.html#standards. Reprinted by permission of Blackwell Publishing.

This chapter has provided you with an introduction to research designs and methods of collecting information about school-age children. Our hope is that as you develop questions about children with whom you work or the setting within which you work, you can employ some of these techniques to find answers. Even more important—regardless of whether you are a student, day care provider, or future teacher—this information may assist you in assessing the research methods used by others and thereby recognizing the strengths and limitations of developmental research.

CHAPTER REVIEW

Theoretical Issues

- Developmental theories describe change and the variables that affect that change. They also help organize our observations and guide our everyday interactions with school-aged children.

- A number of theoretical issues distinguish developmental theories from one another. Differences are based on whether children's skills develop in a continuous (i.e., gradual) or discontinuous (i.e., stagelike) pattern, how nature (e.g., biology) or nurture (e.g., environment) influences development, and whether characteristics of children remain stable or unstable across time and contexts.

- Theories are linked to research through either deductive or inductive reasoning. Research is linked to practice through both basic and applied research. Basic research informs professional practice with school-age children. Applied research is used to solve real-world problems facing children, their families, and teachers.

Developmental Research

- Cross-sectional studies assess children of different ages at the same point in time. These designs identify differences in a skill or ability between different-aged children and *when* a skill emerges or changes but are not able to identify *how* change occurs. Cohort effects may influence the developmental differences found in such studies.

- Longitudinal studies assess the same children over time. Because these designs follow the same children, *how* a skill or ability develops and *which* variables most influence the developmental process can be identified. Longitudinal studies also tell us something about how early experiences influence development later in life and the stability or instability of certain characteristics. Cohort effects, attrition, and research participants becoming "test-wise" need to be taken into consideration.

- Longitudinal-sequential studies combine cross-sectional and longitudinal designs by including several different cohorts and then following these groups over several years. These designs avoid many of the limitations of cross-sectional and longitudinal studies; however, not many sequential studies are conducted because of the time and costs involved.

Data Collection Techniques

- The type of data collection technique that researchers use depends on the question that needs answering. Quantitative data collection techniques include standardized measures, observations, and self-reports. Each of these data-gathering strategies has its strengths and limitations. Assessing the reliability, validity, and generalizability of each technique helps to determine the best use of the results.

- Qualitative data collection techniques typically yield nonnumeric data. Interviews, case studies, narrative studies, and ethnographies collect verbal information from the participants, and their content and "voice"

are interpreted to understand development. Assessing the dependability, credibility, and transferability of each technique aids in understanding how and to what extent the information from one particular study can be used.

Conducting Your Own Research

- One can make use of multiple data collection techniques when conducting research. Case studies are often derived by using several different methods.
- Action research combines data collection with a feedback loop so that the participants are continuously influencing the research question(s) being asked and the way the data are being collected.

- Program evaluation is a systematic process through which the goals of a program are identified and assessed. The outcomes of program evaluation can be used to improve the program by identifying its areas of strength and weakness.
- Researchers need to acquire informed consent, protect the identity of the participant, and treat any information obtained from the participant with confidentiality.

TABLE 2.6   Summary of Developmental Theories

Chapter	Theories	Focus
Studying Middle Childhood	Purpose of theories	To generate research questions and to provide a framework for organizing facts, interpreting data, and drawing conclusions

---

KEY TERMS

Achievement tests
Action research
Applied research
Aptitude tests
Attrition
Basic research
Case study
Clinical interview method
Cohort bias
Continuity
Credibility
Criterion-referenced tests
Cross-sectional study
Deductive reasoning
Dependability

Developmental theory
Discontinuity
Discontinuous
Ethnography
Event sampling
Generalizable
Honesty bias
Hypothesis
Inductive reasoning
Instability
Interrater reliability
Longitudinal-sequential
   study
Longitudinal study
Memory bias

Narrative analysis
Naturalistic
Nature
Norm-referenced tests
Norms
Nuture
Observational technique
Performance measures
Person-centered approach
Predictive validity
Program evaluation
Qualitative methods
Referential adequacy
Reliability
Self-report techniques

Social desirability bias
Specimen record
Stability
Standardized tests
Structured interview
Structured observation
Test-retest reliability
Theories
Time sampling
Transferability
Triangulation
Validity
Variable-centered
   approach
Variables

SUGGESTED ACTIVITIES

1. Observe any group of children between 6 to 12 years of age playing or interacting in their natural environment (e.g., playground, park, school, team practice). Record behaviors or characteristics you find interesting on the left side of the paper and on the right, write down your assumptions about the origins of those behaviors or characteristics. After you have recorded 8 to 10 observations, examine the list of assumptions on the right. Where do you think the majority of behaviors originate? Why? Do you have any information to support your assumptions?

2. Observing the same group of children, use the time sampling and event sampling sheets from this chapter (Figures 2.5 and 2.6) to record information about a target behavior (e.g., helping behavior, aggressive behavior, conflict resolution tactics). Which sampling sheet provided the best information about your target behavior? Why? What were the strengths and limitations of using observational techniques to understand the target behavior? Which data collection technique would you prefer to use?

3. Locate three recently published journal articles that use a cross-sectional, longitudinal, or longitudinal-sequential design. Ask yourself what research question was asked originally. Was the question answered by using the specific design? What design limitations did the authors of the article identify?

4. Ask several friends to share with you a story about their childhood that includes a common theme, such as getting into trouble at school, or their first romantic encounter, or an argument with their best friend. After collecting several stories, try to analyze components of the stories that may reflect something about the developmental status of the storyteller. Were common themes shared, and what can these themes tell us about how children develop in different contexts?

RECOMMENDED RESOURCES

Suggested Readings

Berg, B. L. (2007). *Qualitative research methods for the social sciences.* Boston: Allyn & Bacon.

Creasey, G. (2006). *Research methods in lifespan development.* Boston: Allyn & Bacon.

Haladyna, T. M. (2002). *Essentials of standardized achievement testing: Validity and accountability.* Boston: Allyn & Bacon.

Sagor, R. (2005). *The action research guidebook: A four-step process for educators and school teams.* Thousand Oaks, CA: Corwin Press.

Suggested Online Resources

Action Research (2006). http://carbon.cudenver.edu/~mryder/itc/act_res.html

Basic Guide to Program Evaluation (1999). http://www.mapnp.org/library/evaluatn/fnl_eval.html

The Qualitative Report (2006). http://www.nova.edu/ssss/QR/index.html

Suggested Web Sites

Database of Longitudinal Studies. http://www.nia.nih.gov/ResearchInformation/ScientificResources/LongitudinalStudies

Ethical Standards for Research with Children. http://www.srcd.org/ethicalstandards.html

Forum: Qualitative Social Research. http://www.qualitative-research.net/fqs/fqs-e/rubriken-e.htm

Research: Nonexperimental Methods. http://psy1.clarion.edu/mm/General/Methods/Methods.html

Suggested Films and Videos

Learning to observe. (2003). Insight Media. (Windows or Mac CD-ROM)

Observing child development. (2003). Prentice-Hall (Windows or Mac CD-ROM)

Qualitative research: Methods in the social sciences. (2006). Insight Media (20 minutes)

Research methods for the social sciences. (1995). Insight Media (33 minutes)

Survey savvy: Planning and conducting a successful survey. (2002). Insight Media (24 minutes)

3

Physical Development in Middle Childhood

Chapter Objectives

After reading this chapter, students will be able to:

▶ Define the theoretical assumptions and predictions of biological theories of development.

▶ Outline the developmental patterns of physical and brain maturation in middle childhood.

▶ Describe the general phases of motor skill acquisition in school-age children.

▶ Explain the importance of healthy levels of physical activity, exercise, and sports participation in middle childhood.

▶ Discuss the complexity of multiple contexts and their influence on physical well-being in middle childhood.

To complete the requirements for a class, you visit an after-school recreation program to determine what types of activities are appropriate and desirable for children in elementary through middle school. You notice that the younger children in grades K–2 are running, tumbling, singing, and coloring. The slightly older children in grades 3–5 are skipping, playing hopscotch and basketball, tossing beanbags, and playing card games. Children in grades 6–8 are bouncing on pogo sticks, playing air hockey and chess, and making braided friendship bracelets. You begin to reach some conclusions about age-appropriate activity, but you wonder, "Why these activities at these ages?"

MIDDLE CHILDHOOD BIOLOGICAL DEVELOPMENT

A casual observer of this case study might notice several developmental trends—or patterns—among the different-aged children. The younger children are engaged in activities that involve high levels of energy and gross motor movement. The slightly older group is engaged in activities that require finer motor skills, better coordination, and sustained attention. The oldest group is engaged in skills that require balance, quick responses, and thoughtful or careful planning. These group differences reflect the changes that occur in physical, motor, and brain development in school-age children. The many physical changes taking place during the middle childhood years require parents, educators, practitioners, and coaches to provide children with environmental support for optimal physical growth.

THEORETICAL VIEWPOINTS

In chapter 2, the *nature versus nurture* controversy was presented as one of several critical issues in developmental psychology. The general question raised was, "To what extent do genetics and biology shape who we become, compared to the contributions made by our environment?" A more specific question elicited by the case study in this chapter might be, "To what extent are the physical, cognitive, and motor skill differences of the children in the after-school program a product of genetic or environmental opportunities?" It is a difficult question to answer in theory; it is equally difficult to answer when applied to a specific domain. Because many experts believe that physical, brain, and motor development may be influenced *more* by "nature," we review several of these theoretical viewpoints. Other theoretical perspectives will be presented throughout the textbook and additional genetic/biological perspectives are presented in chapter 4.

Genetic Perspectives

A genetic theoretical viewpoint proposes that most development is determined by a child's genetic blueprint. In this view, children's height and bone length, motor milestones, and brain characteristics are largely determined by genetic codes passed down through the chromosomes of their parents, grandparents, great-grandparents, and so on. Although this theoretical viewpoint acknowledges the influence of the environment on development, the environmental role is small.

Theories espousing this view are supported by studies that have found many physical and cognitive similarities among individuals who are genetically similar, such as siblings (Plomin & Petrill, 1997; Scarr, 1997). Physical, intellectual, and personality characteristics that are similar among the most genetically related family members (e.g., identical twins) are thought to be genetically determined (Betancur, Leboyer, & Gillberg, 2002). Using this theoretical perspective, geneticists would explain size and motor skill differences between children in the case study as largely determined by a preprogrammed genetic plan. This supposition is supported, for example, by the finding that height is more similar in identical twins—differing by only about one third of an inch—than in fraternal twins who differ by $1\frac{1}{2}$ inches on average (Hauspie, Bergman, Bielicki, & Susanne, 1994).

A theoretical approach that emphasizes the role of genetic information is **behavioral genetics.** Behavioral genetics explains the observable variation in children's behavior and development by examining the relative contributions of genes and environmental factors (Plomin & Asbury, 2005). Behavioral geneticists use twin and adoption studies to demonstrate that *all* behavioral, intellectual, and personality traits are to some extent influenced by genetic predispositions (Turkheimer, 2000). The general methodology is to look for similarities and differences between identical and fraternal twins in order to determine which characteristics have a higher **heritability estimate,** or an estimate of the degree to which variation of a specific characteristic in a population is due to genetic factors (Plomin & Asbury, 2005). The estimate can range from 0.00 to 1.00, with higher heritability estimates indicating greater genetic influence. For example, height has been found to have an 80 to 95% heritability estimate. This means that 80 to 95% of the differences in height that exist among people can be explained by a programmed genetic code. Only 5 to 20% of the variation in height that you see among people today is influenced by environmental factors known to affect growth, such as diet, chronic illness, or early maturation.

Behavioral geneticists emphasize the role of genetics but do not ignore the role of the environment. They are interested in teasing out the effects of each on differences in development (Pike, 2002; Plomin & Asbury, 2005). For example, they recognize that genetically related children are typically raised in the same home by the same parents. Behavior geneticists acknowledge this influence, labeling this component **shared environments.** It is the environmental component (e.g., parenting, socioeconomic status, and schooling opportunities) that children share. Behavioral geneticists argue, however—and correctly so—that related siblings growing up in the same home may develop quite differently from one another (Plomin, 2004). They attribute this difference to **nonshared environments.** Nonshared environments include differential parental treatment due to birth order or gender, different teachers, different peer relationships, or extracurricular activities. Behavior geneticists argue that the effects of nonshared environments appear to be *greater* than those of shared environments (Plomin, 2004). In other words, biological siblings growing up in the same home are more likely to be *different* than they are similar. What makes them similar is largely genetic, followed by a smaller contribution of

Nonshared environments contribute to the differences between siblings raised in the same home.

Elizabeth Creus/Elizabeth Creus Photography

shared environmental experiences. What contributes to their differences is their nonshared experiences.

> *Behavior geneticists would predict that siblings in the after-school program are more likely to be similar in height than nonrelated peers. This height similarity would be attributed to genetic inheritance. Differences in height among siblings are not only due to genetics but also to nonshared environmental factors, such as one sibling who eats very poorly when the other does not.*

Critics of behavioral genetics say that in most of the studies cited as support for a *nature* position, genetics and environment are correlated (Maccoby, 2000). For example, athletic parents not only contribute their genes to their offspring but also typically provide a very active and stimulating environment for their children. Other critics cite the documented effectiveness of intervention programs. Children from disadvantaged backgrounds can be provided with improved nutrition and safe, structured opportunities to exercise, and an improvement in skeletal and muscular health is realized (Marcus et al., 2000).

Biological Perspectives

Biological theories, like genetic theories, also recognize the important role that heredity may play in determining development. Biological perspectives, however, place greater emphasis on biological structures and children's functioning. In biologically based theories, developmental patterns are studied and explained by examining hormonal functioning, brain maturation, the chemical makeup of the brain, and other physiological measures.

> *For example, a biological psychologist might explain the differences in size among same-aged children in the after-school program by differences in growth hormone levels or body metabolism.*

A specific example of an area within psychology that uses this biological perspective is **behavioral neuroscience.** Behavioral neuroscience is the study of the relationship between brain and behavior. Due to recent breakthroughs in biomedical technology, researchers can watch the brain function as a child engages in a variety of tasks. Using this technique, a direct connection may be observed between brain activity and overt behavior. This perspective emphasizes the role that biological growth and brain functioning may play in determining the behavioral differences or similarities observed among children.

The Interaction of Nature and Nurture

Although both the genetic and biological theoretical perspectives described above emphasize the role of nature in development, they also recognize the role of the environment, or nurture. All developmental theories tend to vary in the degree to which contributions are attributed to nature and to nurture. The most contemporary approach to understanding the nature-nurture debate is that *both* genetic predispositions *and* environmental experiences shape the development of children. The question posed now is "How?" (Gottesman & Hanson, 2005). There are several ways that genetic information may interact with the environment to influence development.

Maturation. The process whereby genes largely guide development over time is called **maturation.** A child's increase in height from birth to early adulthood is an example of a maturational process. This pattern of development is relatively universal for all children, driven by a biologically controlled release of growth hormones and interrupted only by extreme environmental interference, such as malnutrition or chronic illness.

Reaction Range. **Reaction ranges** explain how children differ in their responses to either the same environment or different environments (Goldsmith & Gottesman, 1996). How children respond depends both on their genetic makeup and on the quality of the environment. Figure 3.1 illustrates the genetically determined ranges of height for two different children and how the environment (e.g., prenatal exposure to alcohol or a healthy diet) may influence *where* each child may fall within the range of reaction.

Reaction ranges help us to understand how genetically similar children can differ in the way their genetic makeup responds to different life circumstances. It also accounts for how two children with extremely different genetic backgrounds can respond differently to the same environment. Remember the resilient children from the island of Kauai described in chapter 2?

Niche-Picking. The tendency for children to choose environments that are consistent with their inherited tendencies is referred to as **niche-picking** (Crosnoe & Muller, 2004; Scarr & McCartney, 1983). For example, shy children may gravitate toward activities or hobbies, such as chess or reading, that are solitary or quiet. Their choice of environment may encourage, or reinforce, their innately shy tendencies that—in turn—may reinforce their choice of activity, and so on. This concept suggests not only how intricately woven genetics and socialization processes are in the development of children but also how genetic predispositions may actually influence the types of environments to which children are exposed.

> STOP Do you resemble your biological parents in height? If not, what factors might have contributed to this difference?

Niche-picking also suggests that the *way* nature interacts with nurture may change across time. Genes interact with the environment to shape development in a variety of ways. As we discuss the research on physical, brain, and motor skill development in this chapter, we will continue to focus on the ways in which a child's genetic makeup—together with unique experiences—influence physical development.

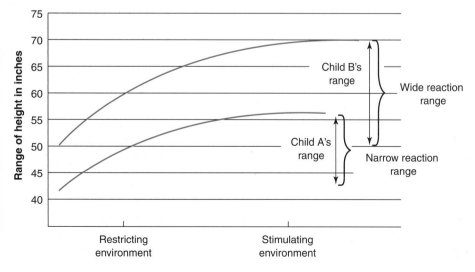

FIGURE 3.1

Reaction Ranges for Physical Growth

Each child's genetic inheritance determines the upper and lower limits of physical growth. The quality of the environment influences children's growth within this range.

Source: From *Child and Adolescent Development for Educators* (p. 67), by J. L. Meece, 2002, New York: McGraw-Hill. Copyright 2002 by McGraw-Hill. Adapted by permission of the publisher.

PHYSICAL DEVELOPMENT

Physical development most often refers to gains in height and weight. During middle childhood physical transformations also occur in facial structure, body proportion, bone growth, and fat and muscle tissue distribution. These physical changes that are driven by genetic, biological, and environmental factors transform childlike body shapes into more mature physical forms.

Changes in Body Size

The most notable difference among the children from the case study at the beginning of this chapter is the variation in their size. The general pattern of physical development between the ages of 6 and 12 is one of steady **growth.** Growth refers specifically to proportional changes in size. Children in middle childhood typically gain 2 to 3 inches in height and 4 to 6 pounds in weight per year (Tanner, 1990). This steady increase in body size is illustrated in Figure 3.2, where growth data are represented as **distance curves.**

Distance curves plot cumulative height and weight for a sample of children over time. The curve compares children's progress toward eventual adult maturity. Notice the similarity in patterns of growth from birth for boys and girls. In the height curve, note that the girls' curve crosses the boys' at age 10 and, for the next three years, girls

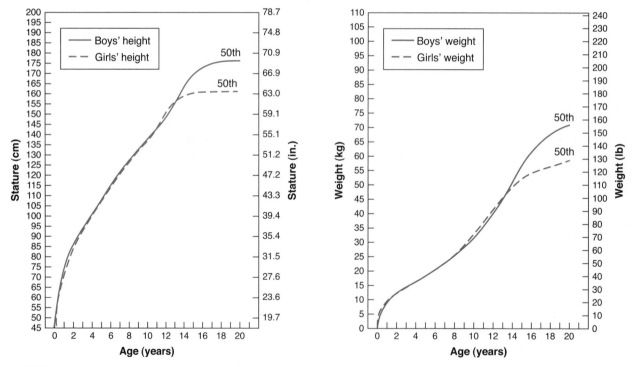

FIGURE 3.2
Distance Curves for Height and Weight

These growth curves show the gradual increase in height and weight that takes place over middle childhood.

Source: Based on data from the National Center for Health Statistics in collaboration with the National Center for Chronic Disease Prevention and Health Promotion 2000. http://www.cdc.gov/nchs/about/major/nhanes/growthcharts/clinicalcharts.htm.

are, on average, taller than boys. Similarly, the girls' weight curve crosses the boys' curve at 11 years and the girls are, on average, heavier than boys for the next several years. This change documents girls' earlier entry into pubertal maturation by approximately two years. After age 13, when boys begin pubertal maturation, they surpass girls in both height and weight.

Parents and health care providers typically pay the closest attention to an individual child's growth patterns. Many of us can visit the house in which we grew up and identify a marker showing that our height increased over time. Parents and health care providers are also often first to detect that children may be beginning to fall above or below the norms for their height or weight. In the majority of cases, there is no cause for alarm. Experts emphasize the need to treat these normative data as just that: an *average* height or weight for a given chronological age. Many children grow at different rates and follow different growth trajectories. Growth rates can vary based on genetic histories, ethnic background, illness, and other factors. For example, children from North America, northern Europe, and Africa tend to be taller than children from Asia and South America. Within the United States, African American children are on average taller than Caucasian, Asian, and Hispanic children.

Typically a pediatrician creates a growth chart for an individual child and plots his or her increases or decreases in height and weight over time. Comparisons are then made not only to the national averages but, more importantly, also to the child's growth history. Although it may have been correct for the observer in the chapter case study to assume that the larger children were the oldest, such an observation may not prove to be true for all children.

Recognizing that growth may occur at different rates, when might there be a cause for concern? A generally accepted rule of thumb is that if a child's height or weight falls below the 10th percentile, the cause should be investigated. When, based on national averages, 90% of same-aged children in a sample weigh more than a targeted child, or if height falls above the 90th percentile, further examination is warranted. Box 3.1 examines the health and psychosocial consequences to children who are short in stature.

 BOX 3.1   Roadmap to Understanding Theory and Research
The Psychosocial and Cognitive Consequences of Being Short

Children who are considered **short of stature (SS)** are at or below the third percentile in height compared to the height of same-aged peers. An additional characteristic of SS children is that there is no known organic cause for their shortness. They are not deficient in growth hormones, nor do they have a history of severe malnutrition or **failure to thrive,** a condition whereby infants show delays in growth due to a lack of attention or stimulation.

For many years, parents and physicians assumed that SS children would experience poor psychosocial functioning. Studies showed that SS children experienced poorer self-concepts and low self-esteem, exhibited fewer prosocial behaviors, exhibited more behavior problems, had difficulty with peer relationships, and generally felt uncomfortable about themselves especially in social settings (for a review see Voss, 2001).

These were appropriate conclusions to draw given the populations that were studied. Children in these studies had more difficulty with parents and peers or performed more poorly in school and, as a result, sought the advice of physicians

(continued)

BOX 3.1   Roadmap to Understanding Theory and Research *(Continued)*
The Psychosocial and Cognitive Consequences of Being Short

and psychologists for a remedy. Using participants from this clinical sample created a psychological profile of SS children that may not have applied to *all* SS children—just to those seeking professional help. In addition, there was no information to suggest that their height was the source of their problems! Even studies that used clinical samples did not show consistent or pervasive psychosocial problems in SS children when compared to normal-height children (Skuse, Gilmour, Tian, & Hindmarsh, 1994; von Busschbach et al., 1999; Zimet et al., 1995).

Using a clinical population, Sandberg and colleagues (1999) asked parents and SS children to report on social competencies (e.g., issues related to growth problems and height), internalizing behaviors (e.g., anxiety, depression), and externalizing behaviors (e.g., aggressive, uncontrolled behavior). Parents reported that their children experienced more teasing about their height, but there was little evidence that the teasing manifested itself in any significant internalizing behavior. Parents also reported that SS children were treated as younger than their chronological age, and this "juvenilized" treatment corresponded to reports of increased externalizing behavior. For SS children who had a younger sibling who was taller, the disparity produced enough stress to be related to lower feelings of self-competency and increased behavior problems; however, no other psychosocial factors showed a significant difference between SS and normal-height children. The most telling finding of the study was that parental reports about their children's psychosocial factors and behaviors were significantly more pessimistic than reports by the SS children. In other words, parents *thought* that their children were more affected by their height than the children themselves reported.

In a more recent study, children from a general population were asked to cast their peers in various roles for a class play (Sandberg, Bukowski, Fung, & Noll, 2004). The roles were accompanied by descriptions such as "good leader" and "has many friends" as well as "is very shy" and "doesn't join in." SS children were just as likely to be cast in a leadership role and fit the description "has many friends" as their taller peers.

More consistent findings emerge, however, when cognitive and academic outcomes are measured. Short-stature children have significantly poorer reading and math skills and poorer overall cognitive functioning and display underachievement in school (Sandberg et al., 1998), and these deficiencies are exacerbated by socioeconomically disadvantaged backgrounds (Dowdney, Skuse, Morris, & Pickles, 1998). These studies confirm the long-term cognitive outcomes for these children but have not yet begun to address the causal links between factors that cause short stature and cognitive deficits.

Height and weight data collected from children in the late 1800s has shown that children today—in almost all regions of the world—are taller and heavier. This pattern is referred to as a secular trend in growth (Tanner, 1990). Children raised in average economic conditions have increased in height approximately 2 centimeters (cm) each decade since the beginning of the 20th century. Reasons offered for this trend are multiple, complex, and include both genetic and environmental components. An evolutionary explanation for the secular change asserts that "tallness" genes are being selected over "shortness" genes (Tanner, 1978). Alternatively, environmental explanations may include improved prenatal care, immunizations, hygiene and sanitation, better nutrition, and less illness.

A related outcome to this growth trend is that girls and boys appear to be entering their second growth spurt associated with puberty earlier than ever before. Recent public health research indicates that some girls between 8 and 10 years of age are displaying early stages of pubertal maturation (Herman-Giddens et al., 1997). Earlier maturation has critical implications for social and emotional development as well as for how peers, parents, and teachers react to the maturing youth. These growth trends and their psychological consequences will be described in chapter 4.

Changes in Body Proportions

Although the most common childhood assessments of physical growth are height and weight, other parts of the body change in proportion. Ten-year-olds are not simply "bigger infants"; they have increased in size *and* changed in proportion. The child does not grow "all of a piece" but rather "differentially in all of his parts and systems" (Krogman, 1972, p. 60). **Stature,** or total height, is made up of head and neck length, trunk length, and leg length. The changing linear contributions of each body part can be seen in Figure 3.3, which shows that as children move through middle childhood, all three areas increase in their contributions to total stature. Boys' and girls' growth patterns are similar until puberty, when girls surpass boys, showing slightly greater growth in all three areas. After puberty, boys catch up and may even surpass girls' growth patterns.

The pattern of change in these separate body components illustrates two growth principles: *cephalocaudal* and *proximodistal* development. **Cephalocaudal**

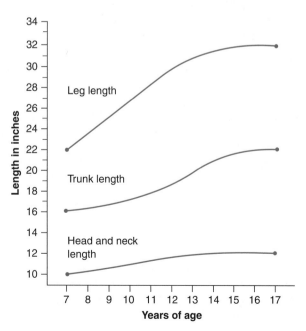

FIGURE 3.3

Changes Over Time in the Head and Neck, Trunk, and Legs

During middle childhood, leg length increases more rapidly, followed by the trunk and then the head and neck.

Source: Based on data from "Length of Head and Neck, Trunk, and Lower Extremities of Iowa City Children, Aged 7–17 Years," by H. V. Meredith, 1939, *Child Development, 10,* 129–144.

FIGURE 3.4
Changes in Body
Proportions from
the Prenatal Period
to Adulthood

At birth, the head
accounts for approxi-
mately 25% of an
infant's total stature.
This proportion
changes as the child
grows.

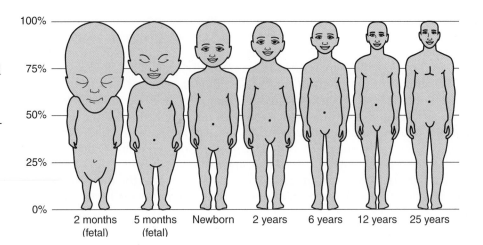

development is growth that proceeds from head to toe. For example, during prenatal and (most of) postnatal development, the head and neck areas develop first
and more quickly than the trunk, followed by the legs and feet. In contrast, **proximodistal** development proceeds from the inside out, with internal organs developing before the third layer of skin, limbs, hands, feet, fingers, and toes. For example,
in infancy, the head accounts for a greater proportion of total body stature than in
middle childhood or adolescence, when the trunk and limbs begin to grow propor-
tionately (see Figure 3.4).

In addition, as girls and boys begin their pubertal growth spurts, proximodistal
development reverses, so that hands and feet, followed by arms and legs, develop
more quickly than trunk, head, and neck areas (Wheeler, 1991). This explains the
long-legged, gangly look of prepubescent children who are often described as "all
arms and legs." For example, an average 10-year-old girl's foot size is 90% of its
eventual adult size. So it is possible for a mother to have a 12-year-old daughter with
the *same* shoe size. The daughter's feet, however, will not continue to grow. After the
peak growth spurt, proximodistal development reverses again, and the trunk and
head areas will catch up. This rapid growth of hands, feet, and limbs not only contributes to a disproportioned body in the latter years of middle childhood but also
causes more tripping, dropping of objects, and general all-around clumsiness as
prepubescent children grow accustomed to functioning with their quickly growing
appendages.

Finally, the jaws, teeth, and face also grow throughout middle childhood into
adolescence. The first set of teeth, commonly known as "baby teeth," begins to fall
out at 6 or 7 years of age. These 20 baby teeth are replaced by 32 permanent teeth
that begin to "erupt" around 6 to 7 years of age, with some of the molars coming in as
late as 10 to 12 years of age. The emergence of new teeth has implications for jaw
growth, as the jawbone must grow to accommodate more and larger teeth. In fact,
the correspondence between jawbone growth and tooth eruption may determine
who will need braces to align their permanent teeth and who will not.

A larger and more angular jaw line characterizes facial growth as children move
from early childhood to adolescence. Although the face grows wider from cheekbone
to cheekbone, it grows even longer from lengthening forehead to angular chin. Lastly
and most dramatically, the face increases in depth, literally growing forward in relation to the skull. This pattern of facial growth may explain the loss of the round faces

that characterize most young children, giving way to a sharper, more defined, and distinctive facial profile.

> *The oldest children in the after-school program have longer legs and trunks in relationship to their heads. Their faces are more angular, and they have all their permanent teeth.*

Skeletal Development

The bones of the body start out as soft, cartilage tissue but harden over time, a process called **ossification.** This hardening process continues until late adolescence; however, the onset and rate of ossification are different for various bones as well as for individuals. Because many of the bones in school-age children have only partially ossified, they are more pliable and less susceptible to breaks—an advantage considering the strain highly active children place on their bones.

Bones grow from special areas called **epiphyses,** or growth plates. A long bone, such as those in the limbs, will develop epiphyses at both ends, and over time the cartilage cells in the growth plates will harden, thus fusing the main bone shaft with the epiphysis at each end (see Figure 3.5). When this fusion takes place, further growth is no longer possible (Tanner, 1978).

Infancy and puberty are the two periods of greatest bone growth, with girls experiencing a steeper rise in bone density compared to boys as they enter puberty (McKay, Bailey, Mirwald, Davison, & Faulkner, 1998). Boys catch up as they enter puberty, with up to 90% of adult bone deposited by the end of adolescence for both boys and girls (Lypaczewski, Lappe, & Stubby, 2002).

Calcium is important for the growth of bones. A deficiency of calcium, usually due to poor diet, may cause **demineralization.** Demineralized bones are weaker, more brittle, and susceptible to breaks. Poor calcium intake during the growing years has been associated with a higher incidence of stress fractures in late adolescence and with osteoporosis later in life (Nowson, 2006).

STOP Think about your school pictures from kindergarten and sixth grade. What were the most notable changes that took place in your face?

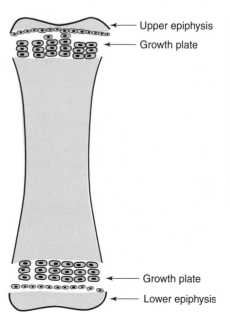

FIGURE 3.5

Limb Bone with Upper and Lower Epiphyses and Growth Plates

This diagram of a bone limb with underdeveloped growth plates at the top and bottom characterizes bone growth in middle childhood.

Upper epiphysis
Growth plate

Growth plate
Lower epiphysis

The high phosphorus content in soft drinks affects the retention of calcium and the formation of new bone by reducing the concentration of calcium in the blood, which in turn causes a release of calcium from bone. In addition, anabolic steroid use may, among many other potential side effects, cause the epiphyses to close prematurely, thus stunting bone growth and affecting eventual adult height (Jenkins & Reaburn, 2000).

The greatest threat to bone mineralization, however, is inactivity (Janz, 2002). Exercise increases bone width and mineralization, producing stronger bones and lessening susceptibility to injury (Welch & Weaver, 2005). Intervention programs that attempt to increase the physical activity of children aged 6 to 14 or that supplement the diets of children with calcium do indeed increase bone mass in children and adolescents (French, Fulkerson, & Story, 2000).

Body Fat Levels and Muscle Mass

Height and weight measures provide us with several important indices of growth. Measuring body fat and muscle mass provides additional indicators of a child's health and nutritional background. A heavy child may be large-boned, heavily muscled, or overweight.

Body Fat Levels. The amount of body fat, or **adipose tissue,** can be measured in *skinfolds,* a pinch of skin and fat measured to the nearest millimeter (mm) by a **skinfold caliper.** Skinfold measurements are usually taken at several different sites on the body. Figure 3.6 shows that there is a slight decrease in adipose tissue after age 4. At approximately age 7 for girls and age 8 for boys, there is a gradual increase in fat tissue, referred to as the **adiposity rebound,** which continues at a slightly higher rate throughout adolescence.

FIGURE 3.6

Developmental Changes in Fat Distribution for Boys and Girls

Trunk and extremity skinfold measures show an increase in subcutaneous fat for girls and a decrease for boys, particularly following puberty.

Source: From "Subcutaneous Fat Distribution During Growth" (p. 70) by R. Malina and C. Bouchard (1988) in C. Bouchard and F. E. Johnston (Eds.), *Fat Distribution During Growth and Later Health Outcomes.* New York: Liss. Copyright © 1988 by Alan R. Liss. Reprinted by permission of Wiley-Liss, Inc., a subsidiary of John Wiley & Sons, Inc.

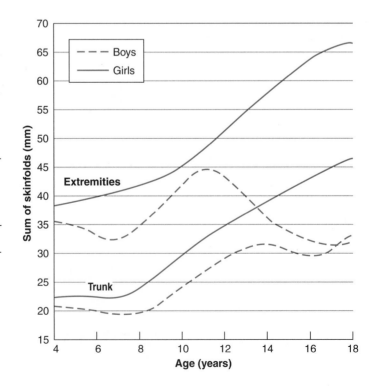

Another method used to measure body fat is the **body mass index** or **BMI.** BMI is a number that shows body weight adjusted for height. BMI is both gender and age specific and shows a pattern of development similar to skinfolds. BMI decreases during the preschool years and then increases into adulthood.

Before puberty, fat content is highly correlated with weight in both girls and boys. After puberty, muscle mass is more highly correlated with weight in boys. Girls consistently have greater skinfold totals than boys, and after age 12 this difference becomes more pronounced. By the end of the growth spurt in adolescence, fat accounts for 16% of total body weight in boys and 27% of total body weight in girls. As a result of the increase in adipose tissue after age 7, we find that physical activity and a balanced diet are important in maintaining body weight for both sexes, but particularly for girls. The number of children in middle childhood who are overweight or obese has increased in the United States over the past several decades (National Center for Health Statistics, 2004). The health and psychological consequences of this trend are discussed later in the chapter.

In the after-school recreational program differences in body fat among children were readily observable. Some children were overweight and others were quite thin.

Muscle Mass. We are born with most of the muscle fibers we are ever going to have. During the course of normal development, there is a large increase in muscle length and breadth with age. An increase in muscle size, called **hypertrophy,** results from both genetic and environmental factors. Muscle development appears to proceed along a normal maturational course consistent with bone growth and is a prerequisite to certain motor abilities. Systematic physical activity, however, enhances muscle composition. Physically active children have a higher proportion of muscle mass to body fat.

Boys and girls appear to be equal in tasks that require muscle movement until puberty. As boys enter puberty, the release of the hormone testosterone promotes the growth of muscle and subsequently widens the gender difference in muscle mass between males and females. Since muscle mass is harder to measure than body fat levels, measures of strength are often used to reflect muscle growth. Figure 3.7 shows age increases and gender differences in leg and arm strength.

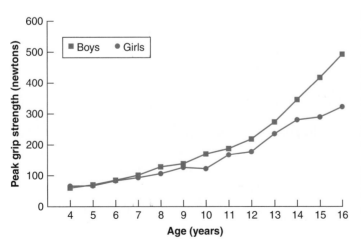

FIGURE 3.7

Strength Differences Between Males and Females

Boys and girls show a steady increase in arm strength throughout middle childhood and adolescence. Gender differences in strength increase as males go through puberty.

Source: Data from "Norms for Grip Strength in Children Aged 4–16 Years," by C. Hager-Ross, & B. Rosblad, 2002, *Acta Paediatrica, 91,* pp. 620–621.

A popular myth is that weight training should not begin until puberty because testosterone production is responsible for the increase in muscle mass in boys. This myth includes the warning that not only will premature weight lifting fail to produce any muscle gain but also it may interfere with normal growth. This myth is only partially supported by research. Lifting *maximum* weights in middle childhood will not produce the significant muscle gain that is typically sought. In addition, using incorrect lifting techniques to lift maximum weights can cause serious and sometimes permanent injury to immature tendons, ligaments, and bones (Mazur, Ketman, & Risser, 1993). However, other research shows that resistance training (i.e., *low* weight at high repetitions) in prepubescent boys and girls can produce increases in muscle mass and strength (Falk & Eliakim, 2003; Guy & Michell, 2001).

Contributions of Genetics, Biology, and Environment

Physical and skeletal growth is a maturational process that reflects a strong genetic component. Growth hormones are released according to a genetically encoded timetable, and only dramatic differences in environments will influence this development. Both body fat and muscle mass have some genetic predispositions as well (Czerwinski et al., 2007). However, these areas of growth also can be shaped by pubertal maturation, diet, sedentary or active lifestyles, and activity opportunities. Despite the parameters set by genetics, parents, teachers, and practitioners play an important role in physical maturation.

The children in the case study display the developmental differences outlined in this section. The older children are typically larger, better proportioned, and stronger than the younger children. This difference in size and strength is reflected in the activities in which they engage. The older children, for example, are able to shoot a heavy basketball over their heads while the younger children do not engage in play activities that require size or strength.

BRAIN DEVELOPMENT

Over the past decade, studies documenting developmental changes in brain structure and function have proliferated. An increase in our understanding of brain development is due largely to technological improvements in assessment. Modern brain-imaging techniques allow closer examination of brain tissue as well as identi-

Guideposts for Working with School-Age Children

- Because children grow at different rates and proportions, have children track their growth by keeping personal height charts. Calculate the average height of the group or different subgroups to emphasize this point.

- Since there may be psychosocial consequences to extreme statuses in height and weight, encourage children to be tolerant of those different in size.

- Provide ample opportunities for physical activity to promote bone growth and to regulate weight gain.

- Design activities so that children of all sizes can feel physically competent by varying the skills required.

- Try to make physical activity fun!

fication of which parts of the brain are called into action during various cognitive, emotional, and motor tasks. The majority of this research has focused on brain development during the prenatal and infancy periods because of the presumption that these periods are ones of tremendous growth and change. Neurological developmental phenomena begin before birth and continue to change during middle childhood. This early childhood research has direct implications for understanding brain maturation between the ages of 6 and 12.

Neuronal Development

One of the most significant developments in the brain during prenatal and early postnatal development is an increase in **neurons.** Neurons are nerve cells in the brain and spinal cord that transmit and receive information throughout the nervous system. Each neuron has a rounded body, called the **soma,** and two types of branched fibers: **dendrites,** which receive impulses, and an **axon,** which sends impulses through its terminals. Neurons are not physically connected to one another; instead, a tiny gap, or **synapse,** exists between neurons.

As illustrated in Figure 3.8, chemicals called **neurotransmitters** are released into the gap, thus completing the transmission of a neural impulse from one neuron to another. Sending and receiving neural impulses are the means by which communication takes place in the brain. This communication occurs between individual neurons, groups of neurons, and ultimately, brain structures.

The rate at which neurons develop prenatally is astounding. Before birth neurons are being generated in the brain at a rate of more than 250,000 per minute!

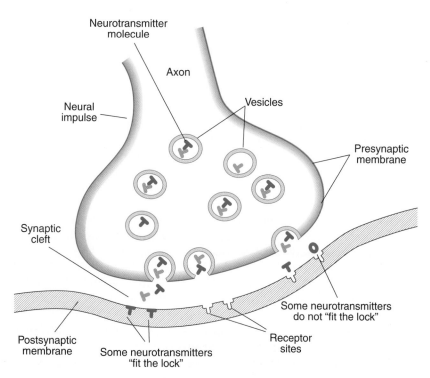

FIGURE 3.8
Synaptic Transmission

A neurotransmitter is released and floats across the "synaptic cleft," where it binds to the receptor sites on the receiving dendrite and the process begins anew.

Source: From *Psychology: Core Concepts,* 4/e, (p. 54), by P. G. Zimbardo, A. L. Weber, & R. L. Johnson, 2003. Boston: Allyn & Bacon. Copyright © 2003 by Pearson Education. Reprinted by permission of the publisher.

FIGURE 3.9
The Four Lobes of
the Brain

Neuronal connec-
tions develop first in
the occipital lobe, fol-
lowed by the parietal,
frontal, and then the
temporal lobes.

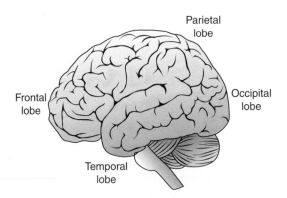

This calculation contributes to current estimates that at birth the human brain pos-
sesses approximately 10 billion neurons. One particularly interesting aspect of neural development is that during the prenatal period, the brain *overproduces* neurons,
possibly by a factor of 2 (Kolb, 1989). A process called **programmed cell death,** however, eliminates the extra cells. Recent research shows that the postnatal cell loss is
a function of an infant's experiences (Klintsova & Greenough, 1999). In infancy, if
neural pathways are stimulated, such as in the visual cortex from visual stimulation,
these neurons are more likely to entrench themselves and to survive within the neuronal network. Neurons that are not stimulated die off at high rates.

Neurons in the **cerebral cortex** are commonly referred to as "gray matter" because the tissue from the cerebral cortex turns a gray color when placed in alcohol or
other preservatives. The cerebral cortex is a layer of nerve cells $\frac{1}{32}$ to $\frac{1}{8}$ inch thick at the
outer edge of the brain. The growth of gray matter has been shown to increase after
birth until approximately early adolescence, followed by a gradual decrease (Gogate,
Giedd, Janson, & Rapoport, 2001). However, increases in gray matter differ regionally,
with peak volumes in the frontal and parietal areas around age 12 and peak volumes
of gray matter in the temporal area at age 18. These areas are identified in Figure 3.9.

Synaptogenesis. The second most significant aspect of brain development is an increase in the number of dendritic branches per neuron, a process called
synaptogenesis. This dendritic branching results in complex "webs" or "networks of
neurons" that represent an increase in connections between neurons and, consequently, greater communication among different and more distant structures of the
brain.

As in neuronal production, there appears to be an overproduction of synaptic
connections as well. This synaptic overproduction occurs in two waves: right before
birth and during early adolescence (Andersen, 2003). The role of postnatal experience in enhancing dendritic branching is similar in enhancing neuronal growth.
Neurons in networks receiving stimulation from the environment have been shown
to maintain and increase their connections. However, neurons that are not stimulated lose their connective fibers, a process known as **synaptic pruning.** A slight decrease in gray matter reported during middle childhood and middle adolescence
most likely reflects evidence of severe pruning of neuronal networks following
the waves of overproduction. Evidence of this pruning can be seen in Figure 3.10,
where the adolescent brain shows fewer dendritic branches than that of the younger
child. This pattern suggests that children during middle childhood and adolescence

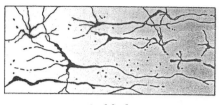

At birth

(A)

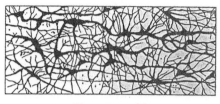

Six years old

(B)

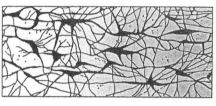

Fourteen years old

(C)

FIGURE 3.10

Changes in Dendritic Branching in the Cerebral Cortex

The brain of a 6-year-old shows increased "weblike" neuronal connections. However, the 14-year-old's brain shows less webbing as a result of synaptic pruning.

Source: From *The Postnatal Development of the Human Cerebral Cortex*, Vols. I–VIII, by Jesse LeRoy Conel, Cambridge, MA: Harvard University Press. Copyright © 1939, 1975 by the President and Fellows of Harvard College. Adapted and reprinted by permission of the publisher.

have fewer neurons and dendritic connections with which to work. Technically this is true, but what actually results from cell loss and pruning is a more integrated and differentiated brain. In other words, during middle childhood and adolescence, the brain becomes a leaner, meaner, learning machine! Synaptic pruning is also reflected in the finding that *overall brain size* shows little change between the ages of 4 and 18 (Giedd et al., 1999). The cognitive advantages school-age children show over infants are a result of a more refined, specialized, and connected brain—not simply one with more neurons.

Myelination. The third significant aspect of brain development is an increase in the **myelination** of axons. Myelination is the process whereby **glial cells** form an insulating sheath around the axons of neurons (Li & Noseworthy, 2002). Half of the brain's volume is made up of glial cells, which do not carry messages but rather serve to support and nourish neurons. Glial cells coat the axons of neurons with a fatty substance called **myelin.** The process of myelination serves to speed up neural impulses, as shown in Figure 3.11.

Studies show that myelination increases steadily with age (Giedd et al., 1999). An even more interesting finding is that some structures in the brain show earlier myelination than others (Gogate et al., 2001). For example, axons in the brain stem as well as axons in the major nerves running to the face, limbs, trunk, and organs all receive their myelin sheaths before birth or during infancy. Brain structures such as these

FIGURE 3.11
Effect of Myelination on Neural Impulses

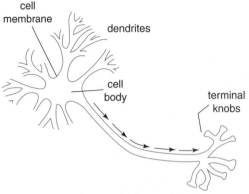

When the axon is unmyelinated, the neural impulse must travel the whole length of the axon.

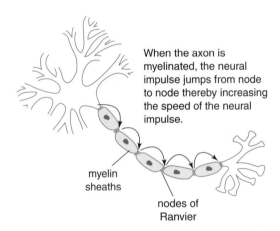

When the axon is myelinated, the neural impulse jumps from node to node thereby increasing the speed of the neural impulse.

are critical for survival and thus myelinate very soon after birth, whereas other structures—such as the **corpus callosum, limbic system,** and **frontal cortex** that are responsible for more complex human functioning—continue to myelinate through middle childhood into adolescence and early adulthood (see Figure 3.12 for the location of these structures).

Fiber Tracts.   The last significant change that characterizes brain development in middle childhood is the maturation of **fiber tracts.** Fiber tracts are bundles of axons largely responsible for passing neural impulses from one region of the brain to the other. Over time, the axons in these pathways become myelinated and, because of the density of the fatty covered axons, this tissue is referred to as "white matter." White matter shows a linear increase over childhood and adolescence and serves as connections between various areas of the brain (Lenroot & Giedd, 2006; Watts, Liston, Niogi, & Ulug, 2003).

Neuronal production, synaptic pruning, myelinated axons, and better communication between distant regions of the brain as a result of fiber tract maturation characterize the middle childhood years. These changes in brain structure appear to be related to changes in how 6- to 12-year-old children think, feel, and act.

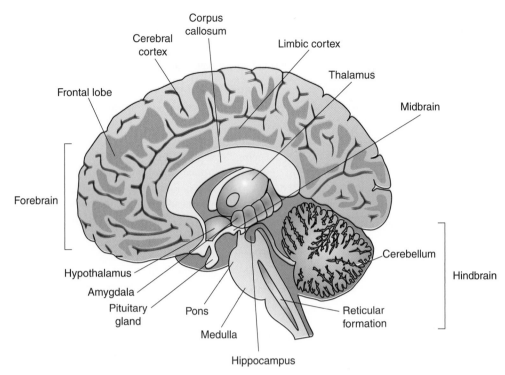

FIGURE 3.12

Brain Structures That Myelinate and Are Related to Changes in Function and Behavior

Structures of the brain myelinate at different times throughout early development.

Related Changes in Function

Some recent studies have shown that rather than a steady increase of myelination with age, there are growth spurts or periods within brain development. These growth spurts have documented high rates of programmed cell death and synaptic pruning in conjunction with higher levels of brain metabolism and myelination (Chugani, 1994). They appear to correspond in time to significant shifts in the perceptual-motor, cognitive, and emotional functioning of school-age children (Casey, Giedd, & Thomas, 2000; van Baal, Boomsma, & de Geus, 2001). For example, researchers have shown a growth spurt in the cerebellum between ages 4 and 6 that corresponds to improved coordination and balance in school-age children (Paus et al., 1999). Table 3.1 provides a more extensive list of how the heavily pruned and myelinated structures of the brain may coincide with patterns of pronounced perceptual, cognitive, and motor development during the same time period.

> *These neurological advancements are reflected in the tasks that engage children in the after-school program. The older children exhibit better coordination (e.g., skipping, hopscotch, and balancing on the pogo stick). They are able to concentrate on games that require focus and attention (e.g., card playing), and they exhibit more planful and purposeful behavior (e.g. chess).*

Contributions of Genetics, Biology, and Environment

Just what are the contributions of genetics and the environment to the development of the brain? Emerging consensus from research is that genetic effects may largely determine synaptic growth (Changeux & Dehaene, 1989; Chen & Tonegawa, 1997).

TABLE 3.1   Myelinated Brain Structures and Parallel Cognitive and Behavioral Functioning

This table shows the progress of myelination with age and the relationship between myelinated brain structures and function.

Brain Structure	Age of Myelination	Related Function
Brain stem, thalamus, cerebellum	First several months of life	The control of vital signs, sensations, reflexes
Visual cortex	2 to 4 months	Vision, forming three-dimensional images
Some areas of the cerebellum and cerebral cortex	3 months	Seeing, hearing, and sensing touch, certain reflexes disappear, involuntary jerking subsides
Some areas of the cerebellum and midbrain region	2 years	More complex motor control, such as walking, running, and manipulating objects; improved balance
Auditory cortex	5 to 11 years	Late stages of speech development and sensory-motor integration
Reticular formation	Around 10 years	Improved attention
Left temporal lobe	4 to 10 years	Increased proficiency in speaking, understanding, reading and writing language; multiple languages are learned most easily during this time
Right parietal lobe	6 to 12 years	Spatial perception, right-left orientation, spatial cognition
Corpus callosum	5 to 18 years	Increased speed of neural transmission between hemispheres, motor coordination, selective attention, skills that require holistic processing, such as reading; some aspects of creativity and difficult cognitive tasks
Frontal lobe	Throughout early adulthood	Logic, planning, reasoning, motivation, organizing, self-reflection
Hippocampus	Throughout life	Memorizing and recalling information

During synaptic pruning, however, genetic effects interact with environmental effects to determine which connections will be maintained or eliminated (Klintsova & Greenough, 1999). For example, a child who wears a patch over one eye beyond age 10 may never regain vision in that eye because the visual cortex will prune away the synapses necessary to process information from the eye. In this example, the child's *genetic predisposition* called for neuronal production and dendritic branching in the visual cortex, which is responsible for the sense of sight. However, the child's restrictive *environment* (i.e., the eye patch) resulted in the pruning of these unstimulated synaptic connections during middle childhood, and hence, the permanent loss of sight in one eye (Lewis & Maurer, 2005).

It appears that although human genetics provide the foundation for neuronal production, dendritic branching, and pruning, stimulation from a child's environment has an effect on how the brain continues to develop into early adulthood. Box 3.2 provides research findings on how child abuse and neglect affect the development of the brain. The effects of abuse are worse if they occur prior to adolescence (Teicher et al., 2003). This finding and others suggest that brain development may possess **critical periods,** or periods of vulnerability, during which development may be interfered with and permanent changes result (Maurer, 2005).

BOX 3.2   Roadmap to Understanding Theory and Research
The Effects of Child Abuse and Neglect on Brain Development

In this chapter you have learned that brain growth and maturation are influenced by the interaction of genes and experience. You've also learned about changes that take place in the brain under "normal" developmental conditions. What happens to the brain when a child is deprived of sufficient amounts of sensory and cognitive stimulation as well as nurturance and care? In 2003, 3 million cases of child abuse were reported to authorities; fewer than 1 million were substantiated, but the real incidence number is probably higher than either of these figures (Children's Bureau, 2005). How do child abuse and neglect affect brain development?

The answers to these questions are being investigated in a new subfield of child psychiatry called **developmental traumatology,** the systematic study of the psychobiological impact of chronic interpersonal violence on the child (De Bellis et al., 1999; De Bellis, 2005). It merges information from developmental psychopathology, developmental neuroscience, and stress and trauma research.

Child maltreatment affects the brain either *indirectly* through the stress response system elicited by the abuse or more *directly* through **experience-expectant processes** (Greenough & Black, 1992). Experience-expected processes are those that are genetically programmed to receive stimulation necessary for survival (e.g., neurons in the visual cortex of a human *expect* to receive stimulation in order that vision sensory areas can develop).

Indirect Effects

Stress is defined as an experience that produces a negative emotional reaction, including fear and a sense of loss of control. When an animal or human experiences stress, a physiological coping response is triggered. This response involves the hormonal system, the sympathetic nervous system, the neurotransmitter system, and the immune system. Physiological changes, such as increased heart rate, blood pressure, and the secretion of adrenaline, generally prepare your body to fight or flee impending danger. This response is very adaptive and serves humans, and other animals, well when threatened. Deleterious effects of the stress response system emerge when the system is called into action too often and for long durations.

Children who have been abused or neglected experience physiological stress responses at much greater frequencies and levels than nonabused children (Glaser, 2000). Specifically, elevated levels of **catecholamines** and **cortisol,** hormones that are released in response to stress, may alter brain development by:

1. Accelerating the loss of neurons (i.e., higher-than-normal programmed cell death) (De Bellis, Keshavan, & Harenski, 2001)

2. Delaying myelination (Dunlop, Archer, Quinlivan, Beazley, & Newnham, 1997)

3. Interfering with normal synaptic pruning (Todd, 1992)

Direct Effects

Based on assumptions from the experience-expectant model (Greenough & Black, 1992), some brain researchers have proposed that, during sensitive periods

(continued)

Box 3.2   Roadmap to Understanding Theory and Research *(Continued)*
The Effects of Child Abuse and Neglect on Brain Development

of brain development, maltreated children may be denied the stimulation or input necessary for neuronal proliferation and/or dendritic pruning. This lack of input thus results in the delay or absence of certain skills.

Whether the brain is affected indirectly through the stress response system or more directly by understimulation, studies have shown that maltreated children differ from nonmaltreated children in brain structure (De Bellis & Keshavan, 2003; De Bellis et al., 1999; Teicher et al., 2003). Maltreated children have:

- Smaller intracranial and cerebral volumes
- A smaller corpus callosum
- Limbic system dysfunction
- Larger ventricles (see Figure 3.13)

Maltreated children show different cognitive and emotional functioning (Bolger & Patterson, 2001; Margolin & Gordis, 2000), such as:

- Poor planning and organizational skills
- More attention to distraction
- Low IQ and reading ability
- Poor grades in school
- Language deficits
- Poor emotional self-regulation
- Low levels of empathy and sympathy
- Poor self-concept and low self-esteem
- Poor peer relationships

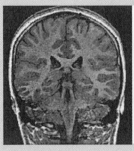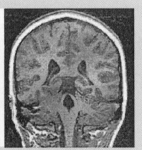

FIGURE 3.13

Effects of Traumatic Stress on the Brain

The brain on the right is that of a maltreated 11-year-old male. Larger "spaces" or ventricles in the middle of the brain translate into less brain tissue.

Source: From "Developmental Traumatology Part II: Brain Development" (p. 1277), by M. D. DeBellis, M. S. Keshavan, D. B. Clark, B. J. Casey, J. N. Giedd, et al., 1999, *Biological Psychiatry, 45,* 1271–1284. Copyright 1999 by the Society of Biological Psychiatry. Reprinted by permission of Elsevier.

(continued)

Box 3.2   Roadmap to Understanding Theory and Research *(Continued)*
The Effects of Child Abuse and Neglect on Brain Development

Maltreated children also are at higher risk of developing psychopathology (Cicchetti & Toth, 1998; Kaplan, Pelcovitz, & Labruna, 1999; Teicher et al., 2003).

Although children who have been abused and neglected share many of the characteristics mentioned here, it is difficult to draw causal links among abuse, changes in brain morphology, and functional or behavioral deficits. The lists of cognitive, emotional, and mental health outcomes for abused children can also result from living in a chronically stressful and impoverished environment with little stimulation or proper nutrition. The outcomes can also be linked to prenatal exposure to **teratogens** (i.e., factors that cause malformations in the fetus, such as postnatal exposure to lead) or to mental illness. More research needs to be carried out in order to distinguish between the different types of abuse (e.g., physical, sexual, emotional, and neglect), their specific effects on the brain, and later cognitive, emotional, and pathological outcomes that may be traced to abuse.

Other researchers, however, argue that very few critical periods can be identified in brain development (Thompson & Nelson, 2001). One explanation for the lack of critical periods is that children's brains possess **plasticity.** Plasticity is defined as the ability of neurons adjacent to damaged tissue to change their structure in order to support new and different tasks (Kolb, Gibb, & Robinson, 2003; Kolb & Whishaw, 1998). Research shows that if brain injury occurs early in life, many of the capabilities are recovered fully. If, however, damage occurs after adolescence when most of the pruning has taken place, recovery is often partial at best.

Another explanation is that much of brain development occurs over long periods of time, which eliminates the possibility of specific critical periods. One example of a critical period, given earlier, involving the visual system demonstrates that lack of visual stimulation to a patched eye will permanently change the neurological structures that control vision in that eye. However, the visual cortex develops very early and early interference in this system tends to show more long-term effects (Huttenlocher & Dabholkar, 1997). Most of the other areas of the brain take a much longer time to mature and therefore do not seem to possess such narrow developmental windows. For example, recent research shows that in the hippocampus, which is responsible for memory functioning, the formation of new neurons continues throughout one's lifetime (Tanapat, Hastings, & Gould, 2001). This extended developmental period, illustrated in Figure 3.14, argues against specific critical periods in brain development.

Some researchers refer to vulnerable periods of development as **sensitive periods** rather than as critical periods (Johnson, 2005). Sensitive periods represent points during development in which certain kinds of experiences are *especially important* to optimal development. In this chapter, we have identified several periods during brain development after synaptogenesis occurs when environmental stimulation is critical for the maintenance of synapses and dendritic branching. Poor stimulation does not *prevent* synaptic connections or dendritic branching from occurring, but

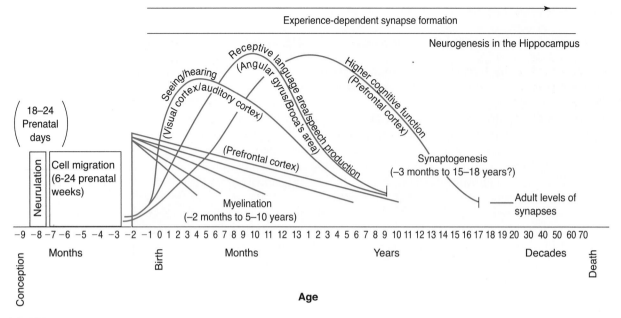

FIGURE 3.14

Developmental Course of Human Brain Development

This graph illustrates the waves of neuronal production followed by synaptic pruning and myelination that occur in brain structures throughout development.

Source: From "Developmental Science and the Media" by R. A. Thompson & C. A. Nelson, 2001, *American Psychologist, 56,* p. 8. Copyright 2001 by the American Psychological Association, Inc. Reprinted by permission of the author.

high levels of stimulation during these sensitive periods optimize neuronal growth that enhances brain development.

Both genetic inheritance *and* environmental experience play a critical role in brain development. Parents, teachers, and practitioners can exert a positive influence both directly and indirectly on the neuronal development of children.

Guideposts for Working with School-Age Children

- Provide safe, healthy, and stimulating environments for children of all ages.

- To encourage growth in different parts of the brain, expose children to a variety of experiences, such as music, visual and performing arts, languages, verbal information, literature, oral histories, tactile experiences, and symbol manipulation, such as mathematics.

- Expose children to new material at their own pace and according to individual progress, because neurological functioning may dictate different rates of learning among children.

- Because environmental conditions that introduce stress, malnutrition, abuse, neglect, and poverty into children's lives can have sustained effects on brain development, support local, state, and federal initiatives that attempt to eliminate these risk factors from children's lives.

MOTOR SKILL DEVELOPMENT

The development of children's motor behavior begins with simple reflexes and ends with very complex coordinated motor skills. Keep in mind that the motor behaviors we discuss in this section are based on the physical developmental patterns presented in earlier sections. These skills also adhere to the principles of cephalocaudal and proximodistal development, with motor control of the head and neck area developing earlier than that of trunk and limbs. Figure 3.15 displays four stages of motor development that proceed from very rudimentary movements to those that are much more specialized.

> *The children in the chapter case study display developmental differences in motor skills similar to the ones presented in the pyramid. The older children are using skills that are more refined and require greater dexterity, such as striking the puck in air hockey and braiding bracelets. Many of the younger children find these skills quite challenging.*

STOP What physical activities did you engage in during your school-age years?

Gross and Fine Motor Skills

Although the rate of physical growth slows somewhat during this period, **gross motor skills,** or skills that use large muscle groups, continue to improve. During middle childhood, increases in gross motor skills such as agility, flexibility, force, and balance are related to comparable improvements in the motor tasks that first emerged during early childhood, such as running, jumping, throwing, and balancing.

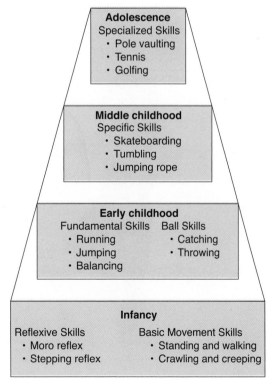

FIGURE 3.15

Phases of Motor Skill Development

This pyramid suggests that children build on earlier foundations of rudimentary motor skills to develop more specific and specialized skills over time.

Source: Based on *Growth and Development: The Child and Physical Activity* (p. 32), by L. D. Zaichowsky, L. B. Zaichowsky, & T. J. Martinek, 1980. St. Louis: C. V. Mosby. Copyright 1980 by the C. V. Mosby Company. Adapted by permission of the authors.

Developmental patterns of specific motor movements are refined and integrated during the school years:

1. *Running.* As children mature motorically they develop into more proficient runners. Their trunk rotation increases to allow for a longer stride and better arm-leg opposition. The longer stride encourages greater push-off from the back leg and thus increases running speed (Haywood & Getchell, 2001).

2. *Jumping.* Children's vertical jumping ability increases linearly between the ages of 7 and 11. Boys and girls also increase standing broad jump performance by 3 to 5 inches per year. Children accomplish this by engaging in a deeper preparatory crouch, extending both legs at liftoff, extending arms overhead in midjump, and flexing knees and torso forward for a two-footed landing.

3. *Throwing.* Boys and girls improve more than 100% in throwing accuracy and distance between the ages of 7 and 11 (Roberton & Konczak, 2001; Yan & Jevas, 2004). This skill is accomplished by shifting one's weight to the back foot, rotating the trunk back, stepping forward while extending the throwing arm fully, and rotating the trunk forward. In general, boys throw harder and more accurately than girls. This gender difference persists even with increased throwing practice and experience for girls (Runion, Langendorfer, & Roberton, 2003).

4. *Balancing.* This ability is measured by asking children to stand on one foot or walk a narrow beam. Because children's center of gravity moves lower in the body as a function of the physical development of trunk and limbs, their balance improves after ages 6 or 7. At 5 years of age, the center of gravity is near the belly button, while at 13, it is horizontal to the top of the hip. This development makes it easier for older children to balance in an upright position and facilitates the refinement of other skills (Loovis & Butterfield, 2000).

Because school-age children have increasing opportunities to participate in different activities, their motor skills become more *specific* and *integrated*. For example,

A lower center of gravity in school-age children improves balance.

Steve Gordon © Dorling Kindersley

during middle childhood, children convert their running and jumping skills to basketball playing and jumping rope; strength and flexibility, to gymnastics; throwing and catching skills, to baseball; and balance, strength, and coordination, to skating and hockey.

Recall from our chapter case study that an increasing specificity of motor skills is observed in the children enrolled in the after-school program. The older children engage in tasks that require greater accuracy (e.g., bean bag tossing), balance (e.g., hopscotch) and coordination (e.g., air hockey).

In addition to gross motor skill development, children show improvement in **fine motor skills.** Fine motor skills usually involve controlled and precise use of the hands and fingers and, with age, produce better coordination and dexterity. Skills using fine motor movements, such as piano playing, sewing, braiding, and hand-writing, all show improvement during middle childhood. Studies show that girls tend to have more advanced fine motor skills, but it is difficult to know if this is a true difference in skill or a preference for or practice of the activity.

Perceptual-Motor Skills

Perceptual-motor skills are abilities that require extensive integration between the sensory system (e.g., vision, hearing, taste, touch, smell) and the motor system. Although perceptual processes may develop somewhat independently of motor abilities, we cannot perform most motor skills without sensory perception (Cratty, 1986). As children get older, they are better able to process complex sensory information, which, in turn, allows them to have better motor control over skills such as catching, throwing, and hitting. Four major changes typically occur in perceptual-motor abilities between early childhood and middle childhood:

1. *A shift in the dominant sensory system occurs.* Young children's predominant reliance on touch and taste shifts to a reliance on visual information and influences school-age children's motor abilities.

2. *Intrasensory communication increases.* School-age children use information coming in from multiple senses, rather than just one, to regulate their motor behavior. For example, using information from eyes, ears, *and* hands makes older children better ball hitters.

3. *Discrimination among the senses improves.* Older children achieve finer distinctions among sensory information. For example, as school-age children are running to catch a pop-up ball, they make a distinction between visual information and tactile cues and choose the one that provides them with the most accurate information—thus catching the ball.

4. *Perception of body awareness develops.* The development of **laterality,** the ability to distinguish between two sides of the body, develops quite early in most children. However, **lateral awareness,** the correct labeling of the two sides of the body, is not well developed until age 7. **Lateral dominance** is a developed preference for the use of the left or right hand, the left or right foot, and the left or right eye. Studies show that 90% of children have an established hand preference by age 5 (Ozturk et al., 1999). However, the data also show that hand preference may take longer to develop in some children than in others, resulting in a debate over the origins of handedness (i.e., genetic or learned) (Annett, 1999; Provins, 1997).

Such changes reflect the relationship between improved perception and better-coordinated motor skills. For example, between ages 6 and 11, children exhibit more

STOP Do the physical activities you recall from your middle childhood reflect development of your motor abilities?

Guideposts for Working with School-Age Children

- Because children of the same age may differ widely in their skill and coordination ability, make a variety of activities available that require different skill levels.

- Provide a variety of motor activities for children to try. This broad exposure may encourage the development of different interests in the future.

- Allow children in middle childhood opportunities to practice and refine skills

such as throwing, catching, balancing, and kicking.

- Because boys' and girls' interests and ability to learn the same skills are highest during middle childhood, encourage both sexes to try a range of activities.

- Try to minimize competition by finding creative ways to choose teams and by encouraging teamwork so that children of all motor skill levels can feel good about their abilities.

accurate perceptions of moving objects and thus can more accurately judge the flight path of a ball (Lefebvre & Reid, 1998).

PHYSICAL WELL-BEING

Most school-age children engage in high levels of physical activity, as seen in the opening case study. **Physical activity** is usually defined as taking place any time the child is not asleep or completely sedentary (Macdonald, Ziviani, & Abbott, 2006). This definition includes lower-level movement activities (e.g., eating, attending school, completing homework, or playing a musical instrument) and higher-level movement activities (e.g., playing on the playground or at a park, as well as participating in organized sports practices or competitions). Research findings show that levels of physical activity increase from infancy, peak in middle childhood, and begin to decrease during middle adolescence (Eaton, McKeen, & Campbell, 2001). This pattern of activity may surprise you because most people assume that 2- or 3-year-olds are the most active. However, when researchers strapped motion recorders on the wrists and ankles of participants aged 6 weeks to 52 years, they found that children between the ages of 7 and 9 were the most active, as seen in Figure 3.16 (Eaton et al., 2001). This

FIGURE 3.16
Arm and Leg Movements per Hour by Age

Children appear to be most active during the middle childhood years.

Source: From "The Waxing and Waning of Movement: Implications for Psychological Development," by W. O. Eaton, N. A. McKeen, & D. W. Campbell, 2001, *Developmental Review, 21,* p. 205. Copyright 2001 by Academic Press. Reprinted by permission of Elsevier.

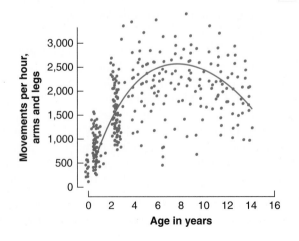

peak of activity occurred later in childhood than others have suggested (Pellegrini & Smith, 1998) and consequently elicits several interesting questions about the function of physical activity. These findings also have direct implications for how we parent and teach these highly active youth as well as how we may diagnose psychopathology, such as attention deficit hyperactivity disorder (ADHD).

Functions of Physical Activity

Researchers have found an inverted U-curved distribution for physical activity, indicating that activity is highest in middle childhood. This curve suggests a sensitive period in development during which motor activity alters brain development. Children's motor activity peaks at exactly the same time the cerebellum, which is responsible for the control of gross and fine motor movement, is pruning unstimulated synapses and dendrites (Byers, 1998). Researchers have proposed that because most children obtain rudimentary gross motor skills in early childhood, middle childhood is the period in which they seek practice and subsequent refinement of motor skills. In addition, in middle childhood, children may ultimately show mastery of a skill, thus contributing to their sense of self-competency and self-esteem. In other words, being physically active may be one domain in which a child excels (Rose, Larkin, & Berger, 1997).

Physical activity also increases bone mineralization, lowers blood pressure, and may help regulate weight (Heelan et al., 2005). Finally, researchers believe that high levels of physical play behavior, such as **rough-and-tumble play,** encourage social competency—especially among boys—and support the formation of hierarchical peer groups (Pellegrini & Smith, 1998). Rough-and-tumble play looks like fighting but involves chasing, wrestling, and restraining moves where no real conflict is involved. It is a form of play that assists boys in developing a leadership "pecking order" and, once established, may lead to *less* aggression and group conflict.

> *You notice gender differences in the types of activities in which boys and girls engage in the after-school program. In their game of chase, the boys have to be reminded to lower their voices and not play "so rough." The girls play separately from the boys and play games in which they take turns and accommodate each other's skill levels.*

Relationship Between Physical Activity and Other Developmental Domains. Children's high activity levels may reflect a more concrete and experiential way of learning about the world (Bjorklund, 1997). For example, children in middle childhood may be capable of some abstract thought but may still be relying on interactions with tangible objects to facilitate their thinking.

High levels of movement in children may be their way of exploring the world in a physical way. Other researchers have suggested that physical movement may be involved in emotional expression. School-age children are more reliant on physical means of expressing emotions, such as arm-flailing temper tantrums, fighting, or running away from a scolding parent, than are adolescents. A decline in overall physical activity after middle childhood is often paralleled by an increase in sophisticated means of emotional expression (e.g., arguing) and regulation (Eaton et al., 2001).

Factors That Influence Levels of Physical Activity. Research clearly shows that physical activity level is influenced by gender: Boys are more active than girls (Eaton et al., 2001). In addition, a decline in physical activity during adolescence is more pronounced for females than males (Beighle & Pangrazi, 2006; Thompson, Baxter-Jones, & Mirwald, 2003). Children who are overweight or obese are less likely to be physically active, with parental activity a major influence on children's activity level (Hancox, Milne, & Poulton, 2004). Children of active mothers are twice as likely to be active compared to children of inactive mothers. This level increases threefold if fathers are active. If both parents are active, children are six times more likely to be active (Aarnio, Winter, Kujala, & Kaprio, 1997). Socioeconomic status is also moderately associated with activity level (Frenn & Malin, 2003; Guillaume, Lapidus, Bjorntorp, & Lambert, 1997). This relationship manifests itself in the safety of and opportunity to engage in physical activity outside of school.

Implications of These Findings for Parents, Educators, and Practitioners. A peak in movement at 8 years does not correspond well with the expectations often placed on children by parents and teachers. Parents typically expect children of this age to be "old enough to control their behavior," especially if child care experts have given parents the impression that things will improve after the "terrible twos." Adults need to be discouraged from criticizing their school-age children for too high levels of activity and need to provide for them appropriate outlets for this normal expenditure of energy. Teachers need to be made aware of the normative activity levels of this age group and of research findings that recess breaks during elementary school seem to produce more on-task behavior and less fidgeting (Pellegrini & Bohn, 2005). Recess or other outlets for high levels of motor activity may facilitate school performance (Pelligrini & Bjorklund, 1997). Therefore, teachers should find ways to incorporate movement in many of their lesson plans for children throughout the middle childhood years. Finally, practitioners should be aware that middle childhood is the developmental period in which the greatest number of diagnoses is made for attention deficit hyperactivity disorder (ADHD) (Brownwell & Yogendran, 2001). Two of the symptoms of this disorder are rapid shifts in attention and high activity level, both of which are in evidence in "normal" groups of 7- to 9-year-olds. Although many diagnoses are valid, researchers have found that childhood hyperactivity is not a predictor of any other pathology in childhood or beyond, suggesting that high levels of activity are more normative than pathological (Nagin & Tremblay, 1999).

Exercise

A subcategory of physical activity is **exercise.** The most distinguishable characteristics of exercise are that it is planned, structured, repetitive, purposeful, and requires moderate to high levels of activity (Livingstone, Robson, Wallace, & McKinley, 2003). The National Association for Sport and Physical Education (NASPE) has issued specific activity guidelines for elementary school-age children. NASPE recommends that children engage in some form of moderate to high physical activity (i.e., exercise) for 30 to 60 minutes almost every day of the week (Corbin & Pangrazi, 2000). Children who meet or exceed these minimums have stronger and healthier cardiovascular systems, lower blood pressure, more favorable blood lipid profiles, stronger bones, and less body fat (Witzke & Snow, 2000).

Despite these well-supported health benefits, less than 50% of children and adolescents meet these minimal standards (NASPE, 1998). In addition, a significantly smaller proportion of girls than boys exercise sufficiently (Stone, McKenzie, Welk, & Booth, 1998). School-age children who do not meet the minimum activity goals are at higher risk for becoming overweight, experiencing elevated blood pressure, being diagnosed with type 2 diabetes (i.e., diabetes mellitus), or having one or more risk factors for cardiovascular disease or osteoporosis. Studies have also shown that when these health risk factors are identified in middle childhood they tend to carry over into adolescence and adulthood (Li et al., 2003; McGill & McMahan, 2003).

Clearly, finding ways to increase children's daily and weekly exercise opportunities should become a priority for parents, teachers, and practitioners. Conferences such as the one sponsored by the Centers for Disease Control and Prevention, *Guidelines for School and Community Programs to Promote Lifelong Physical Activity Among Young People* (1997), suggest focusing on the infrastructures in schools and communities to promote healthy physical activity patterns. Intervention programs that target children, their schools, and communities have been successful in increasing children's level of exercise in school but have been less successful with influencing exercise outside of school (Sallis et al., 1997).

You observed that the children in the after-school program who are most overweight are also the least physically active.

Sports Participation

As children enter middle childhood, they spend less time in unstructured free play and more time in structured activities, such as school- or church-sponsored activities and organized sports practices or competitions. In the last decade, the United States has seen a dramatic rise in the number of children involved in organized sports, especially girls. More than 20 million children, between 6 and 12 years of age,

A variety of physical and psychological benefits result from sports participation in middle childhood.

David Young-Wolff/PhotoEdit Inc.

participate in some type of organized sport (Landers-Potts & Grant, 1999). Despite the increase in the number of children involved, not all children participate to the same extent. For example, as girls move into adolescence, their participation typically declines. Low-income children spend less time in organized sports than middle-class children, often due to the expenses involved.

A variety of physical and psychological benefits may result from sports participation. The multiple physical benefits of systematic exercise outlined in the previous section of this chapter also apply to children who participate in organized sports. In addition, individual athletes (e.g., swimmers, runners, or skiers) learn the value of practice, self-discipline, and time and effort commitments. They also may gain feelings of competency and self-worth, have higher levels of self-esteem, and report enjoying themselves (Pugh, Wolff, DeFrancesco, Gilley, & Heitman, 2000). Participating in a sport increases skill building and, in many peer groups, is a characteristic of popularity. As a member of a team (e.g., soccer, baseball, football)—in addition to the advantages gained from individual participation—children learn about cooperation, perspective taking, and the benefits of teamwork. They also have opportunities to spend time with friends or to make new friends (Ewing, Gano-Overway, Branta, & Seefeldt, 2002). Studies show that if children enjoy their participation, they are much more likely to stay involved and to continue this activity for longer periods of time—sometimes into adulthood (Perkins, Jacobs, Barber, & Eccles, 2004; Thompson, Humbert, & Mirwald, 2003).

Disadvantages of participating in organized sports include acute injuries or—less often—permanent injuries to vulnerable bones and joints (Maffulli, Baxter-Jones, & Grieve, 2005). Some developmentalists worry that time spent in organized sports may reduce the amount of time spent in unstructured free play, which encourages imagination and self-motivation. Others suggest that participation in organized sports encourages a mindset of competition and winning. A survey of 10,000 youth athletes found that children stopped playing a sport due to lack of interest, lack of fun, poor coaching, and an overemphasis on winning. Their main sources of stress were criticisms (i.e., "being yelled at") from coaches, parents, fans, and teammates, and performing poorly in competition (Ewing & Seefeldt, 1989; for a review of stress in sports see Scanlan, Babkes, & Scanlan, 2005). The National Association for Sport and Physical Education (NASPE) has made recommendations for how after-school sports can better meet the developmental needs of children in middle childhood. These can be seen in Box 3.3.

STOP If you participated in an organized sport growing up, did you experience any positive or negative outcomes? What were the costs and benefits?

Childhood Injuries

Unintentional injuries are defined as bodily harm that results from *accidental* causes such as falls, motor vehicle accidents, drowning, electrocution, suffocation. Unintentional injuries are the leading cause of death for children ages 5–14. More than 5.5 million children from this age group also suffer nonfatal injuries requiring emergency room care (Burt & Fingerhut, 1998; CDC, 2004). Injuries requiring medical attention, or resulting in restricted activity, affect more than 20 million children and cost $17 billion annually for medical care (Danesco, Miller, & Spicer, 2000).

To reduce the incidence of future unintentional injuries, researchers focus on factors that identify which children are more likely to experience injury based on past statistics. Both internal and external variables place some children more at risk than others. Variables that contribute to increased injury rates in children include:

Box 3.3   Roadmap to Successful Practice
Recommendations for After-School Sports in Middle Schools

Many children discontinue physical activities and organized sports in middle childhood because of the increased level of competition, commitment, and stress that seems to accompany these sports. The Middle and Secondary School Physical Education Council (MASSPEC) makes the following recommendations for how after-school sports should be structured in middle school.

1. **The most appropriate practice for middle-school sport and physical activity programs is to provide a comprehensive array of after-school programs to meet the diverse experiences, interests and ability levels of students.**

   These programs must always be based on the needs of middle-school students and should include intramurals, activity clubs (e.g., sport, dance, exercise), special events, and open gym days/nights. Such programs should take precedence over interscholastic sports competition.

   The activities offered through after-school programs should include those introduced in middle-school physical education classes as well as novel programming concepts that may capture the interests of diverse groups of middle-school students. All students should be encouraged to participate in such after-school programs regardless of their ability and prior experience with organized sports. The primary purposes of these programs are to provide opportunities for students to:

   * Improve self-esteem and feelings of competence through positive interactions with their peers and adults
   * Acquire new skills and refine those previously learned
   * Learn to function effectively as members of a team or group
   * Improve personal health and fitness levels
   * Have fun and enjoy physical activity

2. **If middle schools decide to offer interscholastic sport programs, they should be progressively phased in. For example, the types of after-school programs listed above should be the only ones available to sixth graders.**

   This policy has several benefits for middle-school students including:

   * Providing a "transitional experience" so they become accustomed to staying after school to participate with classmates
   * Introducing them to sports that they might have been previously unfamiliar with
   * Bolstering confidence and self-esteem by letting students experience equitable competition and developmentally appropriate activities
   * Allowing them to participate in an environment that is less structured and less demanding than typically found in interscholastic sports

3. **The types of interscholastic sports offered to middle school students should be carefully considered.**

   Sports that encourage students to concentrate on personal improvement (e.g., track and field, swimming, etc.), accommodate large numbers of participants, and are inherently safe should take precedence over contact sports or sports that require extensive amounts of equipment or space.

(continued)

Box 3.3   Roadmap to Successful Practice *(Continued)*
Recommendations for After-School Sports in Middle Schools

4. If interscholastic sports are offered at the middle-school level, they must address the unique characteristics of middle-school students.

Therefore, playing rules, equipment, field dimensions, and so on must be modified to accommodate the ability levels and capacities of the participants. Middle-school athletic programs must not attempt to imitate those conducted at the high school level. Safety and developmental appropriateness must be the primary concerns. In addition, middle-school athletic programs should have skill refinements, basic tactics, and effective team membership as their primary goals instead of winning or entertaining spectators.

5. All students who want to participate and are willing to make the commitment necessary for team membership should be allowed to participate in interscholastic sports at the middle school.

An exclusive interscholastic program (cutting) has no place at the middle school because it contradicts the very tenets on which the middle school was founded. A variety of policies can be implemented to overcome any and all obstacles related to achieving this goal.

6. Even if interscholastic sports are offered at the middle school, the after-school programs listed in the first recommendation should continue to be offered since they are more consistent with the overall philosophy of the middle school.

Source: From "Co-Curricular Physical Activity and Sport Programs for Middle School Students," a position paper of the Middle and Secondary School Physical Education Council and The National Association for Sport and Physical Education, Reston, VA, 2002. Available from http://www.aahperd.org/naspe/pdf_files/pos_papers/coCurricular.pdf.

- Individual variables (e.g., age, gender, temperament, race/ethnicity)
- Behavioral variables (e.g., antisocial or conduct disorders)
- Risk-taking behavior (e.g., not wearing helmets or using seatbelts)
- Caregiver behaviors (e.g., level of parental supervision)
- Economic variables (e.g., income)
- Environmental variables (e.g., streets, playgrounds, neighborhoods)
- Sociocultural variables (e.g., crime rates, overcrowding) (Sleet & Mercy, 2003)

By identifying the individual and ecological characteristics of children who experience higher rates of injury, safety prevention programs can target populations who exhibit greater need.

Injury patterns appear to change over the life course and are closely related to developmental stage (Dahlberg & Potter, 2001). For example, there are high rates of injury in children ages 1–4, followed by a slight drop for children ages 5–9, then a sharp rise in injuries in children ages 10–14 that continues through adolescence and early adulthood. The increase in unintentional injuries, particularly in children ages 10–14 may, in part, be a result of children's increased exposure to activities and environments outside the home. During this time in children's lives, safety monitoring shifts from a reliance on parents/guardians in the home to reliance on self and others (e.g., peers, teachers, coaches).

Studies that examine car-pedestrian and car-bicycle collisions, in particular, find that immature perceptual and cognitive skills may also be putting children at greater risk for these injuries (Connelly, Conaglen, Parsonson, & Isler, 1998; Plumert, Kearney, & Cremer, 2004). For example, to safely cross a street with moving traffic, children must accurately judge the size of the gap between 2 cars in relation to the time it will take them to cross the road. When a "pretend road" was set up parallel to an actual road, children, ages 5–9 years, were asked to watch the cars on the actual road and cross the pretend road when they thought they could safely get to the other side. The younger children in the study picked gaps that were too short. They would have been hit on 6% of their crossings if they had been on the actual road. Approximately 75% of 5-year-olds made at least one road-crossing error and only 58% of 9-year-olds did so. These findings suggest that although 9-year-olds are better than 5-year-olds at making moving-car judgments, children in middle childhood still misjudge their ability to walk through traffic gaps safely.

In another study, researchers asked 5–12-year-old-children to stand at a roadside and indicate the last possible moment they could safely cross (Connelly et al., 1998). The researchers varied the car speeds throughout the study. Overall, the older children selected safe crossing gaps 92% of the time, whereas 5-year-olds selected safe gap crossings only 66% of the time. It was notable that the older children based their judgments more on distance away from the car rather than on the speed of the approaching vehicle. These results imply that children in middle childhood would make more crossing errors when cars are traveling faster than normal on a given roadway.

Finally, a study that used an interactive bicycling simulator demonstrated that children ages 10- and 12-years-old left far less time to spare between themselves and a vehicle approaching an intersection. When compared to adults in this study, children took longer in getting started on their bicycles and took longer to approach the roadway, thus underestimating their cycling abilities in their crossing calculations (Plumert et al., 2004).

These findings are consistent with other applied developmental research showing that children in middle childhood, when compared to adolescents or adults, have more difficulty judging how long it would take a moving vehicle to cross a line (Caird & Hancock, 1994), overestimate their physical abilities (e.g., starting their bikes), and generally have more difficulty coordinating their own physical movements with that of moving objects (Pitcairn & Edlmann, 2000; Schwebel & Plumert, 1999).

It appears that developmental changes in coordinating motor movements with visual information occur as children gain experience with specific tasks (Savelsbergh & van der Kamp, 2000). In other words, the more guidance and practice children have in crossing streets with adults who point out key variables, such as starting across the road before the first car clears, will assist children as they perform the same tasks on their own. This information is useful to professionals who design injury prevention strategies and to parents and teachers who want to reduce unintentional injuries in children of all ages.

Guideposts for Working with School-Age Children

- Incorporate many opportunities for physical movement in your interactions with school-age children.

- Provide opportunities for free play, because it is just as important for children in middle childhood as for younger children.

- Encourage all children to exercise every day within the range of their physical abilities.

- Assess children's developmental readiness to participate in organized sports and try to match their physical, social, and cognitive maturity with appropriate sports activities.

- Assist children in tasks that require perception-cognition coordination, such as ball catching and crossing a busy street, both on foot and on bicycle.

DEVELOPMENT IN CONTEXT

Chapter 1 emphasized the importance of examining the development of children within multiple contexts: family, school and community. How children influence—and are influenced by—these contexts often produces variations in physical development and behavior.

School-age children in the after-school recreation program differ in physical appearance and skill level, in part, as a result of differences among familial and cultural activity levels, opportunities to practice motor activities, and environmental stimulation that influences brain development.

Family Contexts

Children's physical growth may be affected by the genetic history of their parents as well as by how well families provide proper nutrition, medical care, and safe and stable homes for their children. Homeless children, for example, have been found to suffer from high levels of stress that ultimately affect their health and school performance (Parrish, 2004). Similarly, exposing children to violence in the home may affect neurological development by modifying children's arousal levels and ability to react appropriately to stress, elevating levels of neurotransmitters and hormones that affect growth and the timing of puberty, especially in girls, and negatively impacting cognitive development and academic achievement (El-Sheikh, Harger, & Whitson, 2001; Margolin & Gordis, 2000).

Children's motor coordination and skill level are affected by the opportunities provided by parents. More specifically, parents influence children's activity choices, such as sports participation, by providing (or not) the means to experience these activities. These might include participating in the activity with the child, buying athletic equipment, and providing or arranging children's transportation to and from the athletic event (Fredricks et al., 2005). Also, children who are White, from the Northeast and Midwest, from intact families, and whose parents have higher educational levels were more likely to participate in organized sports. Children who come from families with an older brother also participate in sports more, presumably because they are influenced by the participation of their older siblings (Hofferth & Sandberg, 2001; Videon, 2002).

Because parents are responsible for monitoring the amount of time children spend watching television, they can reduce the time spent on this activity and encourage children to engage in more cognitively stimulating activities such as reading. An enriched environment is necessary for optimal brain development. Parents greatly influence the types of physical, intellectual, and motoric experiences children have in middle childhood that ultimately affect development.

School Contexts

Schools should play a major role in facilitating the physical and motor growth of children. Teachers can provide children with the opportunity to experience new and different ways to move and use their bodies. Teachers also should recognize the different physical and motor competencies of children and provide opportunities so that children at all skill levels can experience success. Recess and physical activity during the school day is essential for optimal learning and fitness. Opportunities within the school day are especially important for children who may not be active outside of school due to financial constraints, limited parental involvement or supervision, or poor play area availability or safety. However, schools vary in the types and quality of play areas they offer students. As shown in Box 3.4, different types of playgrounds facilitate different skills in school-age children (Barbour, 1999).

BOX 3.4　Roadmap to Successful Practice
Playground Design and Children's Play Behavior

Barbour (1999) carried out an observational study that showed how different play equipment and configurations on school playgrounds can encourage different types of physical activity among children. The type and placement of equipment are listed in Figure 3.17. This study compared the play behavior of children who attended Schools A and B. The researchers found that children who played at School A's playground demonstrated less variety in their play, exhibited less extensive sand play of shorter duration, played soccer as the only game with rules, and played hide-and-seek less often because of fewer places to hide. In School A there was much less **cooperative play,** or play in which children orient toward a common goal, and less **sociodramatic play,** or pretend play with other children. Children also were more likely to run into one another as a result of cramped space, and there was greater competition for the equip-

ment because it had to be shared with all other kindergarten through grade 8 children at the school.

In contrast, children who played at School B showed a greater variety of play. They showed more extensive and longer sand play that involved construction (e.g., buildings and bridges); engaged in more cooperative and sociodramatic play; played soccer, football, Frisbee, and hide-and-seek; and also engaged in playground maintenance (e.g., raked the sand beneath the swings). They were less likely to run into one another, and there was less competition for equipment and toys because the older children in the school had their own playground with more age-appropriate equipment. This study illustrated that one group of children were afforded greater play options than the other. The type of play encouraged by the configuration of School B facilitates cognition and enhances social skills, and the benefits translated into the classroom (Bergen & Mauer, 2000).

(continued)

BOX 3.4 Roadmap to Successful Practice *(Continued)*
Playground Design and Children's Play Behavior

School A	School B
Equipment	**Equipment**
playstructure (built of wood)	playstructure (built of various materials)
narrow platforms	wide platforms
fireman's pole	fireman's pole
clatter bridge	clatter bridge
3 steel jungle gyms	2 tunnels
8-foot double slide	chain ladder
6 strap-seat swings	tire raft
2 seesaws	overhead ladder
overhead ladder	rings
uneven bars	parallel bars
soccer ball (on occasion)	2 slides
	spiral climber
	tic-tac-toe board
	dramatic play features (e.g., steering wheel, window)
	wheeled vehicle path
	storage shed
	tricycles, wagons
	various loose parts (e.g., building blocks, wooden planks, tires, plastic spools, pails, tools, containers, chairs, dramatic play props, sports equipment)
	canopied sand play area surrounded by benches
	2 play houses
	car (built of tires and posts)
	water play table
	4 raised, open-ended barrels
	3 strap-seat swings
	2 tire swings
	seesaw
	garden area
	picnic table
Spatial Configuration	**Spatial Configuration**
equipment scattered	equipment clustered
mainly isolated pieces of equipment (except wooden superstructure)	linkages of equipment
space crowded	space not crowded
adjacent field for group games	central open area for group games

FIGURE 3.17
Playground Design and Physical Competence

School A provides less equipment in a nonoptimal play space. School B provides a greater variety of equipment in a better-planned and larger play space that facilitates the quality of play interactions among children.

Source: From "The Impact of Playground Design on the Play Behaviors of Children with Differing Levels of Physical Competence," by A. C. Barbour, 1999, *Early Childhood Research Quarterly, 14,* p. 79. Copyright 1999 by Elsevier Science, Inc. Reprinted by permission of the publisher.

Several school districts are trying to encourage greater physical activity among their students by encouraging students who live less than one mile from school to walk, rather than be driven. To increase safety for children who walk, schools have developed partnerships with surrounding neighborhood associations to ensure that walkways exist and are kept safe and clear, in addition to creating "safe homes" where children can go if they feel threatened. For example, in a high-crime neighborhood in Chicago, a "walking school bus" program was initiated. Parents walked with their children to school and picked up additional children along the route (Chicago Department of Transportation, 1999). This program not only increased activity for both children and parents but also decreased crime in the neighborhoods (Kennedy, Washburn, & Martinez, 1998).

Intervention programs designed to increase physical activity in school-aged children have found that the groups who show the greatest increase in physical activity were provided an educational component along with the physical activity opportunities (Economos, 2001). Teachers should continue to teach children about the value of eating well and the benefits of lifelong exercise.

Community Contexts

Communities vary in the support they provide for optimal physical, brain, and motor development in children. The most direct influence that communities have on development is through the resources made available to children and families. Resources vary in quantity and quality based on the earning power of the people who live in a given community. Children who are raised in low-income communities typically have access to fewer or poorer quality resources. For example, school-age children who live in low-income neighborhoods may be less likely to have access to proper medical care, proper nutrition, quality after-school care, parks, and playgrounds (Duncan & Brooks-Gunn, 2000; Leventhal & Brooks-Gunn, 2003a). All of these features could adversely affect the physical and motor development of the child, as well as general health.

In addition, poor neighborhoods are often characterized by social disorganization and violence. Studies have found that parents in high-risk neighborhoods manage their children's free time either by keeping them at home (and out of danger) or by enrolling them in structured centers, thereby eliminating the possibility of their children participating in sports or other organized after-school activities (Furstenberg, Cook, Eccles, Elder, & Sameroff, 1999). Children who grow up in self-perceived dangerous neighborhoods also may experience more stress and more stress-related symptomology (Xue, Leventhal, Brooks-Gunn, & Earls, 2005). Researchers have found that these children have a much more pessimistic view of life, report a lessened ability to control their well-being, and tend to do more poorly in school (Garbarino, Hammond, Mercy, & Yung, 2004).

Children from some low-income families may be exposed less often to inside (e.g., reading books) and outside (e.g., trips to the library, museums, nature centers) learning opportunities that might facilitate brain development (Bradley & Corwyn, 2002). Children from low-income families also tend to go to poorer-quality schools that have fewer resources to offer to both low- and high-competency children. Researchers have reported that poor children were more likely to repeat a grade in school or to drop out, have a learning disability, or obtain lower grades in school (Duncan & Brooks-Gunn, 2000; McLoyd, 1998).

Homes, schools, and neighborhoods influence the physical growth and biological maturation of children. These different contexts, in turn, elicit and support different development at varying rates for each child. We need to continue to study children's growth within these multiple settings so that we might understand the multiple pathways and definitions of eventual adult health and well-being.

CHAPTER REVIEW

Theoretical Perspectives

- Theoretical perspectives vary widely in their emphasis on the genetic or biological origins of development.
- The contribution of genetics is emphasized by the viewpoint of behavioral genetics.
- Behavior neuroscience is an example of a biologically based approach to understanding the relationship between brain and behavior.
- Reaction ranges and niche-picking are ways in which genetic predispositions and biological processes interact with the environment to influence physical, cognitive, and motor development.

Physical Development

- Physical growth, typically measured by height and weight, increases gradually in middle childhood until the growth spurt associated with puberty in early adolescence.
- Girls begin to grow sooner and more quickly than boys. Once boys begin pubertal growth, they catch up and surpass girls in height and weight.
- Skeletal growth and a gradual increase in body fat and muscle tissue continue throughout middle childhood.
- Gender differences emerge and increase significantly during puberty. Females possess more body fat during middle childhood than males, who have slightly greater muscle mass.
- Although much of this development is maturational, environmental factors such as diet and physical activity can influence the dimensions of this growth.

Brain Maturation

- Neuronal loss, dendritic pruning, increased myelination, and increased communication among the brain regions characterize brain development in middle childhood.
- Structural changes loosely correspond to motoric and cognitive changes in middle childhood, such as improved gross and fine motor coordination; improved speaking, writing, and reading skills; increased attentional capacity; more logical and abstract thought; and the appearance of planning and reasoning skills.
- A well-coordinated interaction between genetically based neuronal changes and environmental influences shapes brain growth and function during middle childhood.

Motor Skill Development

- Between the ages of 6 and 12, motor skills become more integrated, specialized, and refined, encouraged by both brain development and opportunities presented to the child for motor movement.
- Gender differences in motor skill and coordination are minimal during this developmental period, with those skills that show differences (e.g., throwing) tending to originate more from cultural biases than physical capabilities.
- Perceptual-motor skills that require an integration of perceptual skills and motor abilities result from better brain integration and practice.
- Improvements in perceptual-motor skills are reflected in the child's increased ability to hit or catch a ball, dodge a ball, jump rope, or throw darts.

Physical Well-Being

- Children's involvement in physical activity, structured exercise, or organized sports participation has a positive impact on physical, skeletal, motor, and cognitive development.
- Unintentional injuries in middle childhood may be the result of increased involvement in high-risk activities both inside and outside the home as well as immature perceptual-motor coordination.
- Families, schools, and communities play a role in the type and degree of physical activity opportunities afforded to children.

Contexts for Development

- Multiple contexts within which a child grows can influence and be influenced by the child.
- Families make genetic contributions to physical growth and brain maturation and influence development by providing safe home environments as well as opportunities for children to practice motor skills, engage in physical activity, and influence exercise levels.
- Playgrounds, recess periods, physical education classes, extracurricular athletic programs, and after-school programs serve as valuable venues for the development of skills and as safe, structured environments for physical activity.
- Schools can capitalize on the cognitive windows of opportunity provided by brain growth as well as provide constant exposure to materials and instruction to enhance brain development through middle childhood.
- Communities differ in their abilities to provide resources for optimal physical and cognitive growth, such as the quality and quantity of early health care and nutrition; enrichment opportunities, such as museums and libraries; and activity environs, such as safe parks, playgrounds, athletic facilities, and community centers.

TABLE 3.2   Summary of Developmental Theories

Chapter	Theories	Focus
3: Physical Development in Middle Childhood	Behavior Genetics	Influence of genes and the environment on development through the analysis of shared and nonshared environments
	Biological	The study of such fields as behavioral neuroscience and how brain structure, function, and chemistry influence behavior

---

KEY TERMS

Adipose rebound	Dendritic branching	Hypertrophy	Proximodistal
Adipose tissue	Developmental	Lateral awareness	Reaction ranges
Amygdala	traumatology	Lateral dominance	Rough-and-tumble play
Axon	Distance curve	Laterality	Sensitive period
Behavioral genetics	Epiphyses	Limbic system	Shared environments
Behavioral neuroscience	Exercise	Maturation	Short of stature (SS)
Body mass index (BMI)	Experience-expectant	Myelin	Skinfold caliper
Catecholamines	processes	Myelination	Sociodramatic play
Cephalocaudal	Failure to thrive	Neurons	Soma
Cerebral cortex	Fiber tracts	Neurotransmitters	Stature
Cooperative play	Fine motor skills	Niche-picking	Stress
Corpus callosum	Frontal cortex	Nonshared environments	Synapse
Cortisol	Glial cells	Ossification	Synaptic pruning
Critical period	Gross motor skills	Physical activity	Synaptogenesis
Demineralization	Growth	Plasticity	Teratogens
Dendrites	Heritability estimates	Programmed cell death	Unintentional injuries

Suggested Activities

1. Collect pictures of children from birth to age 2, around age 6 or 7, and between 10 to 12 years of age. Identify the similarities among facial features in the infant pictures. Mix up the pictures and have everyone try to match the pictures with their adult classmates. At 6 or 7, the pictures should show increased facial structure, tooth loss, and hair color that is closer to adult coloring. At 10 or 12, the jawline should be more defined; nose, ears, and forehead are disproportionately large; and eyeglasses may be needed. The photographs at this age can be more easily matched with classmates.

2. Observe a group of children between the ages of 6 and 12 and identify differences and similarities in their physical appearance (e.g., height and weight, body shape). How does their appearance relate to their motoric abilities? Does their physical size enhance or detract from their ability to engage in both gross and fine motor skills? How so?

3. Survey parents of children between the ages of 6 and 12. Ask them about the number of hours per day their school-age child spends in stationary activities versus physical activities. Identify specifically the number of hours they spend in school, on homework, watching television, and practicing or playing a sport. Average the hours across a week or month and create a pie chart that represents different physical and sedentary activity segments of school-age children's lives. Are there age or gender differences?

Recommended Resources

Suggested Readings

Biehl, M. C., Park, M. J., Brindis, C. D., Pantell, R. H., & Irwin, C. E., Jr. (2002). *Building a strong foundation: Creating a health agenda for the middle childhood years.* San Francisco, CA: University of California, San Francisco School of Medicine, Public Policy and Education Center for Middle Childhood and Adolescent Health.

Cheatum, B. A., & Hammond, A. A. (2000). *Physical activities for improving children's learning and behavior: A guide to sensory motor development.* Champaign, IL: Human Kinetics.

Diamond, M., & Hopson, J. (1998). *Magic trees of the mind: How to nurture your child's intelligence, creativity, and healthy emotions from birth through adolescence.* New York: Penguin Putnam.

Jenkins, D., & Reaburn, P. (2000). *Guiding the young athlete: All you need to know.* St. Leonards, NSW: Allen & Unwin.

Suggested Online Resources

Brain Development from the Neuroscience for Kids Web site at the University of Washington (1996–2006). http://faculty.washington.edu/chudler/introb.html

Exercise and Physical Activity Recommendations from the American Heart Association (2006). http://www.americanheart.org/presenter.jhtml?identifier=4596

The Health of America's Middle Childhood Population (2002). http://policy.ucsf.edu/pubpdfs/PC%20MC%20Mono.pdf

Institute for the Study of Youth Sports (2006). http://edweb3.educ.msu.edu/ysi/

2000 CDC Growth Charts: United States. http://www.cdc.gov/growthcharts/

Suggested Web Sites

American Academy of Pediatrics.
http://www.aap.org

Children's Nutrition Research Center.
http://www.bcm.tmc.edu/cnrc/

Guidelines for School and Community Programs to Promote Lifelong Physical Activity Among Young People.
http://www.phppo.cdc.gov/cdcRecommends/showarticle.asp?a_artid=M0046823&TopNum=50&CallPg=Adv

National Health and Nutrition Examination Survey.
http://www.cdc.gov/nchs/nhanes.htm

Teaching Youngsters How to Be Good Sports.
http://www.youth-sports.com/related.html

Suggested Films and Videos

The brain: Effects of childhood trauma. (2002). Magna Systems (29 minutes)

Middle childhood: Physical growth and development. (1997). Magna Systems (28 minutes)

Mystery of twins. (1997). Insight Media (26 minutes)

Nature and nurture: Heredity and environment. (2003). Insight Media (30 minutes)

Physical growth and motor development. (1991). Concept Media (19 minutes)

Right from birth: The wonders of the brain. (2001). Insight Media (15 minutes)

The secret life of the brain. (2002). Insight Media (Series of five 60-minute programs)

Puberty, Sexuality, and Health

Corbis RF

Chapter Objectives

After reading this chapter, students will be able to:

▶ Understand the process of puberty and the variables that influence pubertal development.

▶ Identify the sexual changes occurring in this age group.

▶ Recognize the important roles played by diet, sleep, and health-related choices in middle childhood.

▶ Explain the contributions of family, school, and community contexts to pubertal and sexual maturation in middle childhood.

As you arrive at the local pool one summer day, you notice that a group of middle-school students is enjoying a day of swimming. As you continue to observe these students, you notice that they come in all shapes and sizes. Some of the males are tall and lanky with apparent muscles and body hair, other males are shorter and smaller-muscled with no outward signs of maturity, and some are overweight. Several of the females are tall with developing breasts, while others are considerably shorter with no figure, and some look too thin and unhealthy. Several youth have paired off as couples, but most stay in same-sex groups with varying degrees of flirting between the sexes.

PUBERTAL AND SEXUAL MATURATION AND HEALTH

The case study introducing this chapter depicts the biological changes that occur between middle childhood and early adolescence. Dramatic changes in physical growth are accompanied by pubertal and sexual maturation. Significant gender differences in these areas emerge as well. Health-related issues such as diet, sleep patterns, and substance use may influence, and be influenced by, the transition to adolescence.

THEORETICAL VIEWPOINT

Chapter 3 presented a brief introduction to a genetics-based theoretical perspective (i.e., behavioral genetics) and its emphasis on the role of inherited traits in the development of children. **Evolutionary developmental theory,** another genetics-based perspective, provides a different explanation of development and is highlighted in this chapter (Geary, 2000; Geary & Bjorklund, 2000). This theory is based on Darwin's influential theory of evolution (Darwin, 1859). Darwin observed that animal and plant species appeared to be marvelously adapted to their environments. He hypothesized that this adaptation was a result of **natural selection,** a process whereby, over time, animals or plants that possess those characteristics or traits that best ensure the survival of the species pass them down to future generations. Which traits survive is genetically determined, but they also shape—and are shaped by—the organisms' immediate ecology. Evolutionary developmental theory studies current human development as a product of the evolutionary history of our species.

This theoretical perspective posits current predispositions or behaviors as having been adaptive for our ancestors millions of years ago. For example, the length of our current developmental period, or the time from infancy to reproduction, has increased considerably over time. Comparative studies suggest that this longer period before reproduction allows for humans to develop the physical, cognitive, and social competencies necessary to survive into adulthood and reproduce (Geary, 1998).

> *This lengthy developmental period is highlighted in the opening case study. The young people are clearly experiencing physical, social, and cognitive growth but many are years away from reproductive status.*

Evolutionary developmental psychology has been used more recently to explain the phenomenon of early sexual maturation in girls (see Box 4.1).

This perspective emphasizes genetic contributions and focuses our attention on the competencies of our ancestors that are currently shared by all humans (e.g., a propensity to create emotional attachments, communicate, and explore our environments). Critics claim that this theoretical perspective places too much emphasis on genetics and pays too little attention to environmental influences. Other critics argue that there is no way to test evolutionary hypotheses. Evolutionary developmental theory, however, provides us with provocative ideas about how our biological inheritance may influence our physical, social, and cognitive growth.

BIOLOGICAL MATURATION

One of the major developmental tasks that most children in middle childhood begin to experience is **puberty,** or the transition from infertility to fertility. Puberty involves biological and physiological changes that have social and cognitive consequences

BOX 4.1   Roadmap to Understanding Theory and Research
Application of Evolutionary Developmental Theory to Pubertal Timing

The evolutionary developmental model has been used to explain early pubertal development in girls (Belsky, Steinberg, & Draper, 1991; Ellis, 2005). The theory suggests that early child-rearing contexts influence the individual's reproductive strategy in a way that resembles what would have been adaptive as the human species evolved: that over the course of human history, females growing up in adverse environments (e.g., instability, scarce resources, stressful living arrangements) would increase the survival of the species more by reproducing early. The application of evolutionary developmental theory to contemporary developmental patterns would suggest that family composition (e.g., who lives in the home) and family processes (e.g., how well they get along) may influence the physiological mechanisms that initiate and control pubertal development and thus reproductive capabilities. Specifically, the theory would predict that girls who are exposed to unstable resources; father's absence in the first seven years; and negative, coercive, and nonsupportive family relationships will show accelerated pubertal maturation, early sexual activity, and unstable adult romantic relationships.

This prediction was examined in a longitudinal study to see if mood disorders in mothers, biological father absence, and stressful family relationships led to earlier maturation in girls (Ellis & Garber, 2000). Researchers found that a history of mood disorders in mothers predicted earlier pubertal timing in daughters, and this was mediated by biological father absence. These results support the evolutionary developmental model of pubertal timing by linking stressful early family environments to early puberty.

But what is the mechanism by which family environments prompt biological maturation? One possibility is that girls reared in homes without their biological fathers have an increased chance of being exposed to unrelated male figures such as stepfathers or mothers' boyfriends (Manning, 2002). Exposure to *pheromones*, or chemical molecules emitted by humans and other animals, from unrelated males can accelerate female pubertal development (Izard, 1990). The evolutionary developmental model would predict that girls who are exposed to stepfathers and mothers' dating partners should mature earlier than those who live with biological fathers only. This pattern was found in the same longitudinal study. The greater the duration of exposure to the unrelated father figures, the earlier the pubertal timing (Ellis & Garber, 2000).

Another study found that the quality of the father-daughter relationship was highly associated with age of menarche. Absence of a warm and positive father-daughter relationship rather than the presence of a negative, coercive relationship was associated with early puberty (Ellis, Bates, et al. 2003; Ellis, McFayden-Ketchum, Dodge, Pettit, & Bates, 1999).

A more recent study provides an alternative explanation for early puberty (Comings, Muhleman, Johnson, & MacMurray, 2002). The results of this study suggest that an X-linked gene predisposes fathers to behaviors that include family abandonment, which is passed to their daughters, causing early puberty, precocious sexuality, and behavior problems. These findings support a genetic explanation of the evolutionary developmental hypothesis regarding the association of early environmental stressors and later reproductive strategies.

Whether it is exposure to pheromones or a recessive gene, both explanations rely on the premise that early puberty in females is adaptive behavior and is an evolving response to the increasing exposure children have to cohabiting parents and unstable and stressful family environments and relationships.

for young people. The first of several major changes is sexual maturation, or the development of **secondary sex characteristics** (e.g., pubic hair, body hair, genital and breast development). The second is somatic growth, or changes in the size, shape, and composition of the body. Researchers are still uncertain about the factors that trigger pubertal change, but we know a fair amount about the process once it begins.

The Pubertal Process

Between the ages of 6 (for girls) and 9 (for boys) there is an increase in adrenal androgens, hormones produced by the adrenal gland. The rise in androgens is referred to as **adrenarche** and occurs prior to any outward signs of pubertal change. Several years later, gonadal hormones begin to increase around age 8 for girls and age 11 for boys. This hormonal increase is referred to as **gonadarche,** which is the increased hormonal production by the pituitary gland. Adrenarche, in conjunction with gonadarche, begins the process of sexual maturation. Gonadarche involves a brain structure (e.g., the hypothalamus), a glandular system (e.g., the pituitary gland), and the gonadal system (e.g., the ovaries in females and testes in males). Together, this system is called the hypothalamic-pituitary-gonadal axis (illustrated in Figure 4.1). Figure 4.1 shows the components within the axis and how each contributes to the process of puberty.

Beginning around age 8 in girls, the hypothalamus, which is located in the limbic system, or the midbrain (see Figure 3.12 in chapter 3), signals for the release of gonadotropin-releasing hormone (GnRH). GnRH encourages the pituitary gland, which is part of the endocrine system, to release **gonadotropins,** which stimulate the growth of the sex organs (the testicles in boys and the ovaries in girls). The most prevalent gonadotropins are follicle-stimulating hormone (FSH), which is produced in both males and females, and either lutenizing hormone (LH), produced by females, or interstitial cell-stimulating hormone (ICSH), produced by males. Released in pulsating patterns or bursts and at higher levels during sleep, these gonadotropins elicit an increase of estrogen production from the ovaries in females and androgens, specifically testosterone, from the testes in males. The increased production of these sex steroids causes the ova and sperm to mature in females and males, respectively. The now-mature sperm can fertilize a mature egg to result in a viable pregnancy (Wilson, 2003).

FIGURE 4.1
Hypothalamic-Pituitary-Gonadal System

The neurological and hormonal mechanisms that trigger the onset of puberty as well as the feedback loop that determines hormone production.

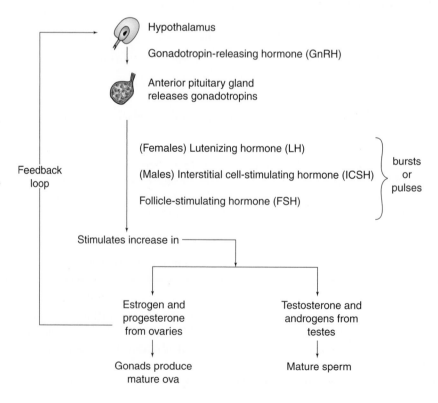

This maturational process involves a feedback loop whereby the levels of sex steroids are monitored by the hypothalamus (illustrated in Figure 4.1). During puberty, the hypothalamus becomes deaf to the signals being sent regarding the high levels of sex steroid production. An appropriate example would be a malfunctioning thermostat. If the thermostat kept registering the temperature in your house as too cold, your furnace would run longer and far more often than it should. This "deafness" or insensitivity of the hypothalamus during puberty contributes to the consistently high levels of sex steroid production during early adolescence. High hormone production is largely responsible for the somatic and maturational changes that result in the development of secondary sex characteristics.

Secondary Sex Characteristics

Hormonal changes take place several years before there are any visible signs of physical maturation. Although there is large variation among individuals in regard to the onset and course of development, there is a "typical" age of onset and set sequence for secondary sex characteristics (Brooks-Gunn & Reiter, 1990). Around age 8 in African-American girls and 9 to 10 years of age in Caucasian girls, breast budding occurs almost simultaneously with acceleration in height (Herman-Giddens, et al., 1997). Approximately 6 months later, pubic hair appears, and approximately $1\frac{1}{2}$ years after the onset of breast development, **menarche,** or the onset of menstruation, occurs. Table 4.1 presents the developmental sequence with variations in timing among subsets of girls, as we now understand it. Of note is that breast and height

---

TABLE 4.1   A Typical Sequence of Pubertal Changes

A list of secondary sex characteristics that represent biological changes undergone during puberty.

Female Characteristics	Age of First Appearance
Growth of breasts	8–13
Growth of pubic hair	8–14
Body growth	9.5–14.5 (average peak, 12)
Menarche	10–16.5 (average, 12.8)
Underarm hair	About 2 years after appearance of pubic hair
Increased output of oil- and sweat-producing glands (which may lead to acne)	About the same time as appearance of underarm hair

Male Characteristics	Age of First Appearance
Growth of testes, scrotal sac	10–13.5
Growth of pubic hair	10–15
Body growth	10.5–16 (average peak, 14)
Growth of penis, prostate gland, seminal vesicles	11–14.5 (average, 12.5)
Change in voice	About the same time as growth of penis
First ejaculation of semen	About 1 year after beginning of growth of penis
Facial and underarm hair	About 2 years after appearance of pubic hair
Increased output of oil- and sweat-producing glands (which may lead to acne)	About the same time as appearance of underarm hair

development as well as the emergence of pubic hair follows a stagelike progression (Marshall & Tanner, 1969). In females, the duration of pubertal development is 3 to 3.5 years but may be completed in as little as 2 years or take up to 5 to 6 years (Rogol, Roemmich, & Clark, 2002).

Boys typically begin pubertal development 1 to 2 years later than girls. The sequence of sexual maturation for boys begins at 11 to 12 years of age with testicular growth that in its third stage includes an increase in penis size. Testicular growth is generally followed by a growth spurt that is followed approximately 3 months later by the first appearance of pubic hair. The peak growth spurt for boys occurs between the ages of 13 and 14 years and corresponds to the occurrence of **semenarche,** or the first ejaculation.

Other changes for boys include voice deepening, a result of rapid vocal cord growth, which occurs around ages 14 to 15, and the growth of facial hair that begins on the upper lip and cheeks and then proceeds to the chin and neck. A complete list of pubertal changes for both boys and girls is provided in Table 4.1.

> *The middle-schoolers at the pool reflect different maturation rates for secondary sex characteristics in same-aged youth. Some of the girls exhibit breast development and tallness, and some of the boys show body hair and height.*

Somatic Growth

In addition to being responsible for sexual maturation, puberty also contributes to dramatic changes in body height, size, and proportion. Increased secretion of growth hormone, thyroid hormone, and sex steroids (e.g., estrogen and testosterone) is most responsible for these increases in growth.

Linear Growth (Height). The rate of linear growth slows during middle childhood and "dips" just before the growth spurt in early adolescence. Recent research that assesses growth at 6-month intervals in prepubescent girls and boys suggests that this growth spurt is made up of multiple smaller growth spurts over a 2- to 3-year period, rather than a single dramatic one (Bock, 2004). Girls and boys differ in the timing and magnitude of these growth spurts. Girls grow an average of 9.75 inches with a gain of 3.5 inches per year during their peak growth spurt at about age 12 (Marshall & Tanner, 1969). These patterns of growth can be seen in Figure 4.2. Skeletal maturity in African American girls is more advanced and the age of peak growth is earlier (Biro et al., 2001).

Boys grow an average of 10.92 inches with a peak growth spurt of 4 inches per year around age 14. The greater growth rate in males is largely accounted for by a greater increase in trunk length compared to girls (Tanner, 1986).

Body Weight and Composition. Body weight also increases dramatically during puberty. Girls' average weight gain peaks at 18.26 pounds per year around 12.5 years of age. By the end of the pubertal process, girls have gained an average of 24 pounds (Warren, 1983). Boys' peak weight gain is 19.8 pounds per year and occurs at 14 years of age (Barnes, 1975).

In addition to weight gain there is a change in the distribution of fat and muscle tissue in girls and boys (Grumbach & Styne, 1998). Before puberty begins, girls and boys have similar fat/muscle tissue ratios. During puberty, however, girls show an increase in fat tissue particularly in the breast, abdominal, and hip areas. Because this increase in fat tissue corresponds with menarche, it is believed that a certain amount

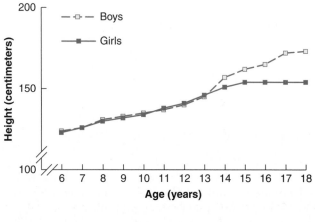

FIGURE 4.2
Average Heights and Weights from Ages 6 to 18

Patterns of height and weight gain for adolescent males and females.

Source: From *Guiding the Young Athlete: All You Need to Know* (pp. 2–3), by D. Jenkins & P. Reaburn, 2000, St. Leonards, Australia: Allen & Unwin. Copyright 2000 by Allen & Unwin. Reprinted by permission.

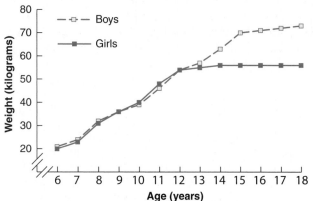

of body fat is necessary for the onset and maintenance of menstruation in girls (Berkey, Gardner, Frazier, & Colditz, 2000).

During puberty, boys gain bone and muscle tissue while simultaneously losing fat tissue. As adults, males have 150% of the lean body mass of the average female and twice the number of muscle cells (Cheek et al., 1974). This increase in muscle mass results in greater average strength in males compared to females in late adolescence. Boys also develop larger hearts and lungs relative to their size, a higher systolic blood pressure, a lower resting heart rate, and a greater capacity for carrying oxygen in the blood. These physiological changes probably contribute to the superior performance of males in athletic endeavors that require such capacities (e.g., weight-lifting, cross-country running).

Skeletal Size. The production of both estrogens and androgens promotes the deposition of bone mineral so that 90% of skeletal mass is present by age 18 in adolescents. In girls, bone mineral density increases significantly in the 3- to 4-year period after the onset of puberty. In boys, mineral density accrues over a longer period of time, 5 to 6 years.

Factors that may influence bone mineralization during puberty include adequate calcium intake, physical activity, and ethnic background. African American children, for example, have greater bone mineral density than do Caucasian and Hispanic children after age 5 (Rogol et al., 2002). In addition, adolescents with delayed puberty or those who are **amenorrheic** (i.e., without a menstrual cycle) fail to accumulate normal bone mineral density and may show reduced density, putting them at risk as adults for osteoporosis (Finkelstein et al., 1992).

> *Some of the girls at the pool are taller, heavier, and exhibit a more curvaceous figure (e.g., wider hips, narrow waist, larger breasts), while some of the boys are heavier and more muscular with broader chests and more narrow waists.*

Factors Influencing Pubertal Growth

Individuals vary in the timing of pubertal onset, its duration or "tempo," and its termination. In fact, very little is known about the "offset" mechanisms of puberty. There are a number of variables that may influence directly or indirectly when and how quickly one moves through puberty:

Genetics	Nutrition
Health and well-being	Metabolism
Physical activity and fitness	Gender
Socioeconomic conditions	Ethnicity
Exposure to environmental toxins	Hormonal levels
Family constellations	Social stressors

It is unlikely that any one of these variables alone will delay or accelerate pubertal growth. Rather, it is the interaction among several of these variables that may affect maturation in complex ways. For example, since the turn of the century, children in average economic conditions have increased in height approximately 1 to 2 cm per decade, a growth trend first discussed in chapter 3. Many sources report that this trend stabilized in industrialized countries in the mid-1900s. However, several recent comprehensive studies in the United States suggest that this secular growth trend is reoccurring (Freedman, Kettel Kahn, Serdula, Srinivasan, & Berenson, 2000; Herman-Giddens, Wang, & Koch, 2001). More specifically, in studies done on several U.S. populations, height gains were found to be significantly greater in 9- to 12-year-old children, with the largest height increases among African Americans and boys. The height gain was greater among younger adolescents compared to older adolescents, so the pattern points to earlier maturation rather than a difference in overall eventual adult height.

A similar secular trend has been observed in the onset of menstruation (Blythe & Rosenthal, 2000). Figure 4.3 shows a marked decrease in the age of menses as well as breast and pubic hair development over the last several decades. Most recently, a growth study in the Netherlands showed a 6-month decline in the age at menarche between 1955 and 1997 (Fredriks et al., 2000). Similarly, a U.S. study including both African American and Caucasian females showed that twice as many girls (in a 1992–1994 cohort) reached menarche before age 12 compared to girls from a 1978 to 1979 cohort (Wattigney, Srinivasan, Chen, Greenlund, & Berenson, 1999).

Many explanations have been offered for these historical trends, including the reduction of growth-retarding illnesses and family size as well as changes in child labor, diets, housing, personal hygiene, health habits, medical care, exposure to sex steroids, and/or environmental estrogens.

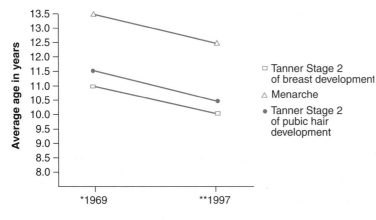

FIGURE 4.3
Secular Trend in Pubertal Maturation

The mean age of pubertal maturation including breast and pubic hair development and menarche has decreased over the last several decades.

*Marshall & Tanner (1969) studied 192 British Caucasian girls.

**Herman-Giddens et al. (1997) studied 17,000 American girls (data reported for Caucasian girls only).

Overnutrition or obesity, which is on the rise in this country, has been linked consistently to the precocious development of secondary sex characteristics (Wattigney et al., 1999; Adair & Gordon-Larsen, 2001). Recent findings suggest that obese children show higher levels of the hormone **leptin,** which is responsible for signaling to the brain information about sufficient fat stores (Clayton & Trueman, 2000). Leptin may spark the brain-hormone cycle; however, it is unclear whether leptin *causes* puberty or is merely present at higher levels when puberty begins. To further complicate matters, obesity is linked to early maturation in *females only* and early-maturing males in fact are thinner (Wang, 2002). More research is needed to understand how increased storage fat prompts early puberty.

At the pool, you observe that many of the girls who show the greatest evidence of breast development are also the ones who possess the greatest amounts of body fat.

Psychosocial Consequences of Pubertal Timing

Once the process of puberty begins, how do school-age children adjust psychologically to the rapid development of their bodies? The answer to this question is, "it depends."

Pubertal changes, such as sexual maturation and somatic growth, may take place at different rates among individuals.

Research tells us that, among other individual and environmental factors, adjustment to puberty depends on

- The timing of puberty
- Gender
- Ethnicity
- Simultaneous occurrence of other stressors
- Adjustment in middle childhood (Weichold, Silbereisen, & Schmitt-Rodermund, 2003)

The *early-maturation* or *early-timing* hypothesis identifies early maturation as the best predictor of adjustment to puberty (Brooks-Gunn, Petersen, & Eichorn, 1985; Caspi & Moffitt, 1991). Specifically, girls who mature *early* have the most difficulty adjusting to pubertal change because early physical changes are not accompanied by similar cognitive, social, and emotional changes. Thus early-maturing females are ill equipped to cope with the different expectations placed on them.

Researchers have found that when compared to same-aged peers, early-maturing girls experience significantly higher levels of psychological distress and are more vulnerable to prior psychological problems, deviant peer pressures, and fathers' hostile feelings (Ge, Conger, & Elder, 1996). Early-maturing girls are least satisfied with their height and weight, have poorer body image, and reported eating problems (Stice, Presnell, & Bearman, 2001). Early-maturing girls also engage more in drinking, smoking, and sexual activity (Magnusson, Stattin, & Allen, 1985; Wilson et al., 1994). These patterns of behavior apply to African American females as well as early-maturing females in many other countries (see Table 4.2).

It had long been thought that there was very little psychosocial risk associated with being an early-maturing male (Jones & Bayley, 1950; Mussen & Jones, 1957). In fact, the thinking was that it was advantageous for males to mature early because they were viewed as more desirable by females and were more admired by their peers. Recent research, however, shows psychosocial adjustment problems similar to those of females (Ge, Conger, & Elder, 2001). Early-maturing males manifest more hostile feelings and internalizing symptomology (e.g., anxiety) than on-time and late-maturing males. In addition, early-maturing males are more likely to engage in delinquent behavior, drug and alcohol use, and sexual activity and to experience greater depression (for a review, see Huddleston & Ge, 2003). These findings hold true for African Americans, Mexican Americans, and many other males from around the world (see Table 4.2)(Cota-Robles, Neiss, & Rowe, 2002).

Although there appears to be less psychosocial risk for girls associated with maturing later, in part because they are better prepared for puberty (Brooks-Gunn & Warren, 1989), this is less true for boys. Late-maturing boys have higher incidences of psychopathology and depressed mood, poorer body image, and lower self-esteem (Graber, Lewisohn, Seeley, & Brooks-Gunn, 1997; Siegel, Yancy, Aneshensel, & Schuler, 1999). These findings support an alternative hypothesis called the *maturational-deviance* hypothesis, which posits that children who are off-time (either early *or* late) will show greater adjustment problems.

Research findings support *both* hypotheses, and studies continue to be carried out to clarify whether early maturers or both early *and* late maturers exhibit higher risk behavior and emotional distress. As consistent as some of these patterns of adjustment are, researchers recognize that they do not hold true for *all* children and

STOP Did you experience pubertal development at the same time as your peers?

TABLE 4.2   Summary of Pubertal Maturation Status and Associated Outcomes in Diverse Populations

Country	Gender	Maturational Status	Outcomes
Hong Kong	Females and males	Early	• Earlier reported dating and sexual intercourse in males (Lam, Shi, Ho, Stewart, & Fan, 2002)
Finland	Females and males	Early	• More substance use • More friends who also engage in substance use (Dick, Rose, Pulkkinen, & Kaprio, 2001)
Germany	Females and males	Early	• Higher frequency of cigarette smoking and alcohol use (Wiesner & Ittel, 2002)
Jamaica	Females	Early	• Earlier sexual intercourse (Wyatt, Durvasula, Guthrie, LeFrance, & Forge, 1999)
Mexico	Females and males	Early	• Increased depressive symptoms in females (Benjet & Hernandez-Guzman, 2002)
The Netherlands	Females and males	Early and late	• Early-maturing females showed an increase in withdrawn and delinquent behavior • Late females showed increased social problems • Early-maturing males showed a decrease in social and attention problems • Late males showed increased attention problems (Laitinen-Krispijn, Van der Ende, Hazebroek-Kampschreur, & Verhulst, 1999)
Norway	Females and males	Early and late	• Early-maturing females showed poorer body image and negative self-evaluations • Late-maturing males showed greater negative self-evaluations (Alsaker, 1992)
Scotland	Females	Early	• Lower ratings of body image • Lower self-esteem (Williams & Currie, 2000)
Slovakia	Females	Early	• Greater adjustment problems with parents and teachers • More externalizing problems (Ruiselova, 1998)
Sweden	Females	Early	• Earlier sexual intercourse (Andersson-Ellstrom, Forssman, & Milsom, 1996)
	Males	Early and late	• Higher alcohol use • Greater alcoholism for late maturers (Andersson & Magnusson, 1990)
United States Caucasian	Females	Early	• Higher levels of psychological distress • More vulnerable to prior psychological problems, deviant peers, fathers' hostile feelings (Ge, Conger, & Elder, 1996)
	Males	Early	• More externalized hostile feelings • More internalized distress symptoms (Ge, Conger, & Elder, 2001)
	Females and males	Early	• More substance abuse (Tschann et al., 1994)

(continued)

TABLE 4.2   Summary of Pubertal Maturation Status and Associated Outcomes in Diverse Populations *(Continued)*

Country	Gender	Maturational Status	Outcomes
Caucasian African American Mexican American	Males	Early	• Higher levels of both violent and nonviolent delinquent behavior (Cota-Robles, Neiss, & Rowe, 2002)
African American	Females and males	Early	• Early-maturing boys and girls showed greater depressive symptomology • No difference in male depression (Ge et al., 2003)

that there are likely to be complex interactions of factors that determine the specific pathway followed.

Relationships Between Puberty and Function

The implicit assumption of the previous section is that pubertal change *causes* distress in maturing children or encourages them to engage in more high-risk behavior. The direct link between puberty and behavior is, unfortunately, not as simple as it might appear. The driving force behind puberty seems to be hormone production, and hormones often get blamed for the stress and unpredictability of young adolescent behavior. Hormones are both directly *and* indirectly responsible for some of the psychosocial consequences presented in Table 4.2.

Two models explain how children may be affected by biological change (Petersen & Taylor, 1980). The **direct-effects model** proposes a direct connection between physiological change and psychological adaptation. For example, research shows a relatively direct link between higher levels of testosterone and an increased readiness to respond with aggression to provocation (Olweus, Mattsson, Schalling, & Low, 1988).

In the **indirect-effects model,** on the other hand, the link between biological change and psychological adjustment or behavior is influenced by both **mediator** and/or **moderator variables**. Mediating variables could be internalized psychological factors, such as fantasies, beliefs, attitudes, or concerns. For example, a male may act

Guideposts for Working with School-Age Children

• Remember that a growth spurt will mark the beginning of puberty for girls and occurs later in the sequence for boys.

• Recognize the role that environmental factors such as poverty, diet, and stress may play in the timing and adjustment to biological change.

• Help middle-schoolers understand the various rates of development and what is "within the norm."

• Adjust your expectations of children in middle childhood because their cognitive, social, and emotional development may not be commensurate with their physical development.

• Be aware that some children may have more difficulty adjusting to these biological changes and may be in need of professional help.

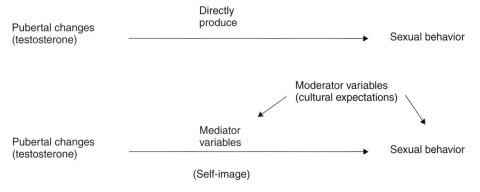

FIGURE 4.4
Two Models of the Relationship Between Pubertal Maturation and Psychological Development

The top figure represents a direct-effects model; the bottom figure, an indirect-effects model.

Source: Based on "The Biological Approach to Adolescence: Biological Change and Psychological Adaptation" (pp. 133–134), by Anne C. Peterson & Brandon Taylor, in J. Adelson (Ed.), *Handbook of Adolescent Psychology* (pp. 117–155). New York: Wiley, 1980. Copyright © 1980 by John Wiley and Sons. Reprinted by permission of the publisher.

aggressively because he has a fantasy about maintaining a masculine image. The fantasy is the mediating variable that contributes to the aggressive behavior. Moderator variables are outside of the individual. They could be such things as sociocultural contexts or socialization practices. A cultural expectation of masculinity that includes aggression would be a moderator variable that could contribute to the young child's self-image, and consequently, behavior.

Each model, shown in Figure 4.4, provides a framework to understand the relationship between biological changes and psychosocial adjustment in this rapid period of development.

SEXUALITY

The previous section described the many changes associated with puberty during adolescence. The biological and hormonal changes associated with puberty, however, occur gradually beginning in middle childhood. Because pubertal maturation is a process, *some* biological changes occur in *all* school-age children as they approach adolescence. During middle childhood, *more* changes may be present in *some* children (e.g., early maturers) than others. Sexuality in adolescence, like puberty, does not develop overnight. Sexuality is a process of development that begins in middle childhood, largely through sexual arousal and fantasy, and manifests itself in sexual behavior during adolescence.

Puberty and Sexuality

What is the relationship between pubertal change and sexuality? At the beginning of this chapter we discussed how the process of puberty encourages the release of specific hormones that are primarily responsible for the development of secondary sex characteristics and for the emergence of reproductive capabilities. There is research that suggests a direct link between increases in hormone levels and increases in sexual arousal and behavior. Several studies have shown that around age 10, as children begin to experience adrenarche, defined as an increase in androgens, they experience memorable sexual attraction for the first time (Herdt & McClintock, 2000; McClintock & Herdt, 1996). This finding holds true for both males and females and for children who report same-sex attraction (Herdt & Boxer, 1993). In addition, researchers have found that adolescent boys who demonstrate higher levels of testosterone also report higher levels of sexual activity (i.e., coitus) (Halpern, Udry, Campbell, & Suchindran, 1993).

The relationship between pubertal change and sexuality may not only be hormonal but may also include how the child and others respond to changes in secondary sex characteristics. For example, higher levels of androgens in adolescent females were *not* related to higher rates of sexual behavior, but rather were predictive of their anticipation of future sexual involvement. The best predictor of coital behavior in these girls was whether their friends were sexually active or at least supportive of sexual experimentation (Udry, Talbert, & Morris, 1986). More recent research continues to support a mediated model between puberty and sexual behavior (Udry & Campbell, 1994; Halpern, Udry, & Suchindran, 1997). In other words, hormones may enhance feelings of sexual arousal in children and adolescents but how they act on those feelings is very much determined by multiple internal and external variables (see Figure 4.4 earlier in the chapter).

The more mature-looking boys and girls at the pool are constantly flirting with one another and trying to get the attention of the opposite sex. There are a number of identifiable "couples" who engage in varying degrees of physical contact with one another.

Noncoital Behavior

During middle childhood, children have a range of sexual experiences that typically follow a **sexual continuum**. On one end of the continuum are experiences that include sexual arousal and self-exploration and/or stimulation. These behaviors do not involve a partner nor do they involve intercourse; they are labeled **noncoital**. These experiences represent the early sexual experiences of most children in middle childhood. They are followed by noncoital behaviors with a partner that are engaged in by fewer children in middle childhood and end with intercourse, usually in adolescence.

Sexual Desire.   Children around ages 9 and 10 report increased "feelings of arousal" or "sexual desires." Boys seem to become aware of their sexual interests and impulses several years earlier than girls do, and boys report more frequent sexual arousal (several times a day) than girls (once a week). Boys also report their sexual arousal to be more intense and distracting than do girls (Knoth, Boyd, & Singer, 1988; Savin-Williams & Diamond, 2000).

Masturbation.   **Masturbation** is defined as self-stimulation to the point of arousal (Bancroft, Herbenick, & Reynolds, 2003). Very little is known about the prevalence of masturbation in children under age 13. It has been suggested that our lack of sexual behavior data from this age group reflects society's ambivalence regarding the manifestations of sexuality in school-age children and the reluctance to acknowledge sexuality as a developmental process rather than a set of behaviors that commence in adolescence (Savin-Williams & Diamond, 2004). Limited available data suggest that boys and girls engage in a variety of solitary sexual behaviors. For example, 78% of college students retrospectively reported masturbating before 12 years of age (Bancroft et al., 2003). As children moved into adolescence, 32% of boys and 26% of girls in a sample of eighth to tenth graders reported bringing themselves to orgasm (Udry, 1988).

Adolescent males masturbate two times as often as females, and it is usually their earliest sexual experience. Females usually experience sexual contact with another person before they masturbate (Hyde & Jaffe, 2000). The prevalence of self-stimulation suggests that it is a "normative" aspect of sexual development both in middle childhood and adolescents. However, masturbation is still perceived as "taboo" in the United States and other countries, such as Finland, Sweden, Estonia, and Russia (Kontula & Haavio-Mannila, 2002). It appears that parents rarely talk to their children about masturbation as a normal sexual outlet and that it is perceived by teens to be less desirable than sex with a partner. As the result of a study comparing young adult males' reports of their own adolescent masturbation practices to self-reports collected when they were teens, researchers suggest that most studies underestimate the percentage who masturbate by as much as one-third (Halpern, Udry, Suchindran, & Campbell, 2000).

Noncoital Behavior with a Partner

Children in middle childhood may engage in interactive sexual activities that involve other children, such as talking about sex, kissing, hugging, watching or reading pornography, "humping" or simulating intercourse, or touching another's genitals.

Genital Contact. In a retrospective study using first-year college students, participants were asked to report on noncoital sexual activity with a peer prior to puberty. Twenty-nine percent of females and 33% of males reported direct genital contact with another child while in elementary school. Few participants reported being coerced, and both the thrill of doing something "forbidden" and curiosity were commonly cited reasons for having engaged in this behavior during this time period (Reynolds, Herbenick, & Bancroft, 2003).

Oral Sex. Researchers define oral sex as any oral/genital contact. In one study, 9% of females and 16% of males reported oral sexual behavior prior to high school (Reynolds et al., 2003). National survey data from children in late middle childhood and adolescence suggest that overall rates of reported oral sex have increased over the past decade.

These noncoital behaviors appear to be part of a pattern of developing sexuality for some children during middle childhood. Researchers are beginning to explore what relationship, if any, these early noncoital activities might have to later sexual behavior. For example, one study found that the earlier children participate in noncoital sexual activity, the earlier they participate in coitus (Bauserman & Davis, 1996). Another study found that especially for girls, self-reported noncoital contact with a partner during middle childhood predicted earlier sexual intercourse in adolescence (Reynolds et al., 2003).

Sexual Intercourse

Sexual intercourse, or **coitus,** is the behavior used most often to report on the status of children's and adolescents' sexual behavior. It is only one behavior along a sexual continuum, but because of the potential long-term consequences of intercourse (e.g., pregnancy), it is the most often-reported index. Nationwide, 6.2% of students had intercourse for the first time prior to age 13. More male (8.8%) than female (3.7%) youth reported early intercourse. These data vary according to gender, race, and ethnicity (CDC, 2005). As shown in Table 4.3, young Black adolescent males engage in intercourse at a much higher rate before the age of 13 (16.5%) than Hispanic youth (7.3%), or White youth (4%).

TABLE 4.3	Percentage of Youth Who Had Sexual Intercourse for the First Time Before Age 13	
Sex	Race/Ethnicity	Percent
Female	White	2.9%
	Black	7.1%
	Hispanic	3.6%
Male	White	5.0%
	Black	26.8%
	Hispanic	11.1%

Source: Data are from the *Youth Risk Behavior Survey,* 2005, Healthy Youth Web site, National Centers for Disease Control and Prevention and Health Promotion. Available from http://www.cdc.gov/healthyyouth/index/htm.

Children who report intercourse prior to age 13 tend to report more sex partners, partners who differ from their age more than 2 years (older or younger), and tend to overestimate the degree of sexual experience their friends have (Kinsman, Romer, Furstenberg, & Schwartz, 1998; Kupek, 2001; Leitenberg & Saltzman, 2000). In addition, 22% of females who reported having intercourse before age 15 stated that the intercourse was nonvoluntary (Abma, Driscoll, & Moore, 1998).

Why do some children initiate sexual intercourse earlier than others? Who delays their **sexual debut,** or first-time intercourse, and who abstains? These questions are of interest to parents, teachers, practitioners, and health care professionals who want to understand the individual and contextual variables that promote sexual debuts. The answer is determined by the complex interaction of biological, psychological, and sociocultural factors that exert both direct and indirect pressure on the adolescent (Crockett, Raffaelli, & Moilanen, 2003). Variables such as early maturation, substance use, having a history of sexual abuse, and having friends who view sexual behavior as acceptable are linked to the initiation of sexual intercourse. Having educational plans, good grades, high religiosity, family support, and parental supervision and communication are linked to the delay of sexual intercourse (Kirby, 2001; Miller, Benson, and Galbraith, 2001). It is unlikely, however, that any single variable can be identified as the sole determiner of sexual behavior. Rather, these variables are most likely to aggregate into a profile that is predictive of sexual debut or delay.

STOP When was your sexual debut and what were the circumstances surrounding the event?

Contraceptive Use

Children's understanding of contraception as well as their motivation to use it is determined not only by individual characteristics (e.g., gender, race, cognitive level) but also by how their friends, families, teachers, and society at large perceive its use and effectiveness (Lagana, 1999). We know that the rates of contraceptive use are increasing for adolescents; however, we do not know very much about the rates of contraceptive use in children under age 13. Researchers who have tried to understand which adolescents are least likely to use contraceptives have found that children under 13 are less likely to use contraceptives or use them consistently (Kirby, 2001).

Reasons given by the 37% of adolescents who report not using contraceptives, or not using them consistently, may apply to children in middle childhood as well. They are:

- Unavailability (i.e., they were unprepared)
- Being prepared (i.e., carrying a condom) might send the wrong message
- Too costly
- Uncomfortable (i.e., condoms reduce sensations and feelings of pleasure)
- No use of contraception is a sign of trust and fidelity in a sexual relationship

Understanding the reasons why school-age children and adolescents do not use contraceptives is important because those who do not use effective contraception consistently have a 90% chance of pregnancy within a year (Alan Guttmacher Institute, 1998). In addition to an unplanned pregnancy, nonuse or ineffective use of contraceptives may result in contracting a **sexually transmitted disease (STD)** that may have long-term consequences for the young person.

HIV/AIDS

Human immunodeficiency virus, or **HIV**, interferes with the body's ability to fight off viruses and bacteria that cause disease. Individuals who are infected by HIV get sick easily and have trouble getting well and usually die of an infection or cancer that the body would otherwise resist. The virus and the infection itself are known as HIV. The term **AIDS** stands for **acquired immunodeficiency syndrome** and is used to represent the later stages of an HIV infection. HIV can be transmitted during pregnancy, birth, breast-feeding, blood transfusions, sexual contact, and drug use. During 2004, there were an estimated 48 new diagnoses of AIDS in children younger than 13 years of age in the United States (Rhodes, 2005). Reported rates for children in other countries are alarmingly high. During 2005, 700,000 new cases of HIV were diagnosed in children (under the age of 15) around the world (UNAIDS/WHO, 2006). More than 80% of these new infections occurred in sub-Saharan Africa with as many as 90% acquiring the infection from their mothers through pregnancy, birth, or breast-feeding. As of 2005, approximately 2.3 million children were living with HIV.

The HIV/AIDS epidemic has contributed to rising child mortality rates and reductions in life expectancies, and has already orphaned a generation of children. By 2003, 15 million children under the age of 15 had been orphaned due to AIDS (UNAIDS/UNICEF & USAID, 2004; UNICEF, 2005). Research shows that the loss of either or both parents puts the child in a developmentally vulnerable position. Children who are orphaned as a result of AIDS are less physically healthy, more likely to fail in school and/or withdraw early, and more likely to become street children, victims of sexual abuse, and engage in high-risk behavior, such as unprotected sex or drug abuse (Andrews, Skinner, & Zuma, 2006).

Because most children with HIV are infected through mother-to-child transmission, prevention programs target the treatment of the mother and newborn with antiviral drugs developed specifically to fight AIDS. This approach has met with success and reduced the number of children infected with HIV in the United States (Albrecht et al., 2006). However, for children in middle childhood who may be at risk of contracting HIV through unprotected sex or drug use, AIDS awareness programs have been developed. These programs are often combined with sex-education and/or pregnancy prevention programs in schools and focus on educating children about

HIV/AIDS and how it is transmitted, and on reducing high-risk behavior such as unprotected sex and drug use.

SEX EDUCATION

Sex education classes in late elementary school typically provide students with information related to the biology of the reproductive system. The focus of these classes is on preparing children for somatic changes related to puberty (e.g., breast and genital development, menarche). Many practitioners feel, however, that a biological focus leaves children in middle childhood ill-prepared to deal with increased feelings of sexual arousal as well as opportunities to act on these feelings. Researchers who study the effective elements of successful comprehensive sexuality education programs find that they begin in late middle childhood (e.g., grades 5 and 6), and in addition to providing information on the biology of puberty these programs:

- Promote parental involvement and communication with regard to information, values, and beliefs that stress the effectiveness of abstinence.
- Provide support for increased parental monitoring and supervision.
- Teach children strategies for refusing sexual advances.
- Encourage assertiveness and teach social-problem solving skills.
- Focus on reducing the amount of time spent in situations of sexual possibility and delay sexual debut.
- Are sensitive to the cultural needs of the community.

Despite the fact that more than 70% of parents surveyed agree that schools should teach sex education, some school officials and parents worry that talking to children in middle childhood about sex and contraceptives implicitly condones sexual activity. They further argue that teaching children to abstain should be the focus of sex education classes.

Research consistently finds that communication with children and adolescents about sex and contraceptives does *not* increase sexual activity or encourage earlier sexual debut, but rather encourages the delay of sexual debut by approximately 1.5 years and increases the percentage of youth who report using condoms (Schuster, Bell, Berry, & Kanouse, 1998; Sellers, McGraw, & McKinlay, 1994). Another finding is that sex education programs that teach about and encourage abstinence are most effective with those youth who have not yet had intercourse (Aten, Siegel, Enaharo, &

Guideposts for Working with School-Age Children

- Engage in honest communication with school-age children about abstinence, sexual behavior, and contraception.
- Teach children how to negotiate sexual encounters and how to openly communicate with sexual partners about contraceptive use and HIV/AIDS.

- Encourage parents to talk to their children about sexual urges, fantasies, masturbation, petting, and intercourse because those who do, have children who delay their sexual debut.
- Try to engage children in academic and extracurricular activities because those who are engaged in school delay sexual activity longer than those who are not.

Auinger, 2002). For some populations (e.g., Black urban youth), this means providing abstinence training sooner (fifth or sixth grade) rather than later (Johnson, 2002).

HEALTH-RELATED CHOICES

During middle childhood, independent decision-making skills regarding self-care and health-risk behaviors develop. Children listen to and observe family members, peers, the media, and their culture to form their own beliefs about health and fitness. Healthy and unhealthy choices are more self-generated during this stage and, as a result, are also more vulnerable to prevention and intervention programs. Understanding how school-age children think about their health, health behavior, and the consequences of such behavior is necessary for professionals to design effective educational interventions.

Nutritional Needs and Dietary Behavior

Because school-age children are still growing, their nutritional intake is important. During middle childhood, energy intake (i.e., calories) must be sufficiently high to meet both growth *and* physical activity demands. Active children should aim to consume between 55 and 60% of their energy intake in the form of carbohydrates, less than 30% in the form of fats, and between 12 and 15% in the form of proteins. Protein is necessary for body growth, and thus protein requirements for children and adolescents are higher than for adults.

It is often difficult for active children to reach minimum nutritional goals by consuming three large meals a day. Consequently, it is suggested that children be provided four or five smaller meals a day with healthy snacks in between to provide sufficient energy.

Small amounts of vitamins and minerals are needed as well to maintain health. To ensure that children are receiving the necessary vitamins and minerals, it is best to encourage a well-balanced diet, rather than vitamin supplementation.

In 2001, just under half a million children in the United States reported living in a household with repeated hunger and insecure food sources, although this number is much higher in developing countries (Federal Interagency Forum on Child and Family Statistics, 2003). Nutritional deficiencies have direct implications for children's learning and behavior in school (Lozoff, Jimenez, Hagen, Mollen, & Wolf, 2000). Early nutritional deficiencies in infancy can inhibit critical growth in the brain and can affect long-term cognitive abilities (Brown & Pollitt, 1996). Daily deficiencies in school-age children can cause lethargy, poor concentration, greater susceptibility to illness, moodiness, and poor psychomotor skills. Supplemental breakfast and lunch programs provided to children from low socioeconomic households have been shown to improve overall health, energy levels, attendance, and subsequent academic performance (Grantham-McGregor, Ani, & Fernald, 2001; Shemilt et al., 2004).

Obesity, Dieting, and Body Satisfaction.   When the intake of calories exceeds total energy expenditure, weight gain results. Excessive weight gain can lead to **obesity,** which is defined as weighing more than 20% over one's ideal weight based on height, sex, and body composition. Several decades ago, a section on obesity, dieting, and body image would probably not have been included in this textbook—most certainly not in a section describing the development of school-age children. Unfortunately, the prevalence of obesity among young children has increased significantly in recent years

(Heinberg, Thompson, & Matson, 2001). Results from the 2003–2004 *National Health and Nutrition Examination Survey* indicate that the percentage of overweight children in middle childhood (ages 6–11) increased from 11% to 19% between 1988–1994 and 2003–2004 (Ogden et al., 2006). The prevalence rates are higher for Blacks and Hispanics than they are for Whites and Asians and are inextricably tied to socioeconomic status. Figure 4.5 shows the increase in obesity over the past few decades and illustrates gender and race differences. The origins of obesity have been traced to genetics, sedentary lifestyles, increased television viewing, and high-fat diets as well as socioeconomic status (Chambers, Hewitt, Schmitz, Corley, & Fulker, 2001; Drewnowski, 2004; Must & Tybor, 2005).

Obesity has a strong developmental component, with obesity in childhood predictive of obesity later in life. Both physical and psychological consequences may result from being overweight or obese. Children who are obese are at risk for hypertension, respiratory disease, Type 2 diabetes, and orthopedic disorders (Hill & Pomeroy, 2001). Heavier weight has also been associated with lower self-esteem and exclusion from peer groups (Zametkin, Zoon, Klein, & Munson, 2004). Psychosocial problems may include persistent teasing, which may produce body-image problems and eating disturbances (Gardner, Stark, Friedman, & Jackson, 2000; Heinberg, 1996).

The most overweight children in the program often are not included in group games and are the target of teasing.

FIGURE 4.5
Percentage of Children Who Are Overweight by Gender, Race, and Hispanic Origin

Since 1976 there has been an increase in the percentage of children who are overweight in every category of race and gender.

Source: From Centers for Disease Control and Prevention, National Center for Health Statistics, National Health and Nutrition Examination Survey.

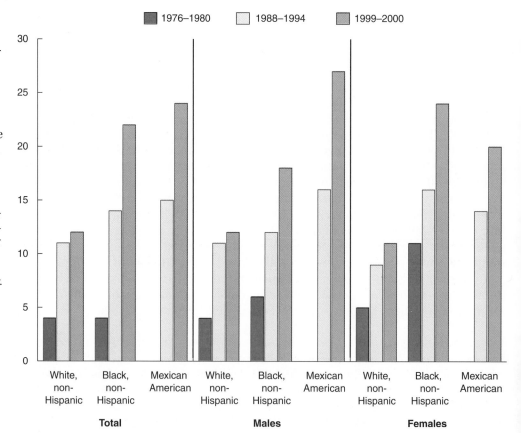

There are long-term health risks associated with obesity in middle childhood.

Obesity may also increase body dissatisfaction. For example, researchers surveyed 8- to 10-year-olds and found that 55% of the girls and 35% of the boys were dissatisfied with their size (Wood, Becker, & Thompson, 1996). Girls typically want to be thinner, while boys desire to be larger and more muscular (Smolak, Levine, & Thompson, 2001). In addition, European American girls generally have greater body dissatisfaction than African American girls. Body dissatisfaction can lead school-age children (and adolescents) to engage in caloric-reducing behavior such as dieting or hyperexercise.

Researchers surveyed more than 16,000 9- to 14-year-old boys and girls and found that only 20% of the 9-year-old girls were trying to lose weight compared to 44% of the 14-year-old girls (Field et al., 1999). In the study, girls were more likely to exercise than to diet, but information on body fat, muscle, and physical activity presented in this chapter and in chapter 3 would suggest that a reduced balanced diet *in addition to* increased exercise is critical for weight loss in girls. Of the 9-year-old boys in this study, 17% were trying to lose weight while 19% of the 14-year-olds were. They also were more likely to use exercise to control their weight. Information from this text would predict that increased exercise is sufficient for weight loss in boys.

Body dissatisfaction and dieting may be influenced by factors such as comparing oneself to media standards, peers, parents' weight attitudes and behaviors, sexual abuse, and early puberty maturation (Muir, Wertheim, & Paxton, 1999; Vander Wal & Thelen, 2001).

While observing in the recreation program, you are surprised to overhear a group of 10-year-old girls talking about who has the best shape.

Research findings have indicated that many school-age children are struggling with a weight problem that may affect their health as well as how they feel about themselves. Even when children are not obese, they often desire their bodies to be different. Parents, educators, and practitioners need to be aware that body dissatisfaction, dieting, and obesity are no longer problems that are relegated to developing adolescents. We need to be knowledgeable about the determinants of weight and body size and the importance of physical activity and exercise, and we need to impart this knowledge to school-age children.

- Offer school-age children more frequent, smaller, and healthier meals.
- Teach school-age children about the determinants of weight and body shape and the importance of exercise and how these are related to their current and future health.
- Provide children with opportunities to develop healthy cooking and eating habits and to view adults as positive role models for healthy diet and exercise.

STOP   Were you satisfied with your body shape in middle childhood?

Disordered Eating Behavior

Toward the end of middle childhood, individuals experience increased awareness of **body image**, or how they think and feel about their bodies. A preoccupation with body image and size may be further exacerbated by school transitions and the simultaneous occurrence of puberty and associated social and academic pressures (Levine, Smolak, Moodey, Shuman, & Hessen, 1994). Research illustrates that body and weight dissatisfaction occurs as early as third grade; is greater in European American than in African American children, females than males, and those with a heterosexual orientation; and increases over time, peaking around eighth or ninth grade (Thompson, Rafiroiu, & Sargent, 2003). These patterns of body dissatisfaction also tend to occur in other affluent countries, such as Hong Kong, Australia, and Sweden (Lam et al., 2002; Lunner et al., 2000).

Body dissatisfaction and weight concerns can lead to unhealthy dieting behaviors, which in turn may promote the development of disordered eating in school-age children and adolescents (Killen et al., 1996). Studies of middle-school students have reported that between 30 and 55% have dieted at some time (Shisslack et al., 1998) and that, among females, about one-third of normal dieters progress to other problem dieting behaviors (Shisslack, Crago, & Estes, 1995). Problem dieting behavior includes fasting or skipping meals, the use of diet pills, vomiting or using laxatives, smoking cigarettes, or binge eating (Croll, Neumark-Sztainer, Story, & Ireland, 2002; Neumark-Sztainer, Story, Falkner, Beuhring, & Resnick, 1999). These unhealthy dieting behaviors are far more prevalent among adolescents than children in middle childhood and often go unaddressed because of the varied unmonitored settings within which teenagers consume food. In addition, most unhealthy dieting patterns fall below the criteria for diagnosable eating disorders and may not be viewed as problematic.

Health consequences result from both disturbed eating patterns and eating disorders. Health problems associated with disturbed eating patterns are delayed sexual maturation, menstrual irregularity, constipation, weakness, irritability, sleep problems, and poor concentration (Story & Alton, 1996). Health consequences for eating disorders, however, presented in Box 4.2, are much more severe.

Different body weights are evident at the pool. There are several girls who look very, very thin, and you don't see them eat anything all day. There are also several boys who have excess weight around their midsection and snack continuously on junk food.

BOX 4.2   Roadmap to Understanding Theory and Research
The Symptomology and Health Consequences of Eating Disorders

It has been said that eating disorders are better understood as dieting disorders and that the emergence of eating disorders in early adolescence is closely related to poor body image and weight dissatisfaction in young teens (Thompson & Smolak, 2001). The most prevalent eating disorders are **anorexia nervosa (AN), bulimia nervosa (BN),** and **binge-eating disorder (BED).**

The prevalence rate of AN in adolescents ranges from 0.1% to 1%, with a greater incidence among girls than boys (a gender ratio of 10 to 1; Bulik, 2002). The mean age of onset for AN is 17, with peaks at 14 and 18 (American Psychiatric Association, 2000). Following are the *DSM-IV* diagnostic criteria for AN (APA, 2000, p. 589):

- Refusal to maintain a body weight at or above a minimally normal weight for age and height

- Intense fear of gaining weight or becoming fat even though underweight

- Disturbance in the way in which one's body weight or shape is experienced, undue influence of body weight or shape on self-evaluation, or denial of the seriousness of the current low body weight

- In postmenarcheal females, amenorrhea (i.e., the absence of at least three consecutive menstrual cycles)

Related health consequences for those diagnosed with AN are:

- Thinning hair
- Dry, flaking skin
- Constipation
- Downy growth of body hair (**lanugo**)
- Low blood pressure
- Passing out, dizziness, weakness
- Heightened sensory experiences
- High cholesterol levels
- Low chloride levels
- Severe electrolyte imbalances leading to heart attacks
- Kidney failure

- Low body temperature (hypothermia)
- Delayed bone growth and future osteoporosis

Bulimia nervosa is found in approximately 1% of the population. Like anorexia, BN is more common in females, with a female to male gender ratio of 33:1. The peak onset for BN is between 15 and 19 years of age. *DSM-IV* (2000, p. 594) diagnostic criteria are:

- Recurrent episodes of binge eating. An episode of binge eating is characterized by the following:

  Eating within any two-hour period an amount of food that is definitely larger than most people would eat during a similar period of time

  A sense of lack of control over eating during the episode

- Recurrent inappropriate compensatory behavior to prevent weight gain, such as self-induced vomiting, misuse of laxatives, diuretics, enemas, or other medications; fasting; or excessive exercise

- The binge eating and inappropriate compensatory behaviors both occur, on average, at least twice a week for three months. Self-evaluation is unduly influenced by body shape and weight. The disturbance does not occur exclusively during episodes of AN.

Health-related consequences resulting from prolonged BN are:

- Gastrointestinal disorders
- Anemia
- Tooth damage and gum disease
- Chronic sore throat
- Difficulties in breathing/swallowing
- **Hypokalemia** (abnormally low potassium concentration)
- Electrolyte imbalance
- General ill health/constant physical problems
- Possible rupture of heart or esophagus
- Dehydration
- Irregular heart rhythms

(continued)

BOX 4.2   Roadmap to Understanding Theory and Research *(Continued)*
The Symptomology and Health Consequences of Eating Disorders

A more recently proposed diagnostic category is binge-eating disorder, differentiated from BN by its lack of a purging component. Population-based studies suggest that between 0.7% and 3% of individuals report binge eating at least once per month. Binge eating is relatively equivalent between genders, and there are few differences across races and ethnic groups, with a slightly higher incidence in lower socioeconomic groups. One major health risk for this disorder is obesity and all its health-related consequences (see this chapter and chapter 3).

Although eating disorders occur most often in Caucasian female populations, recent research suggests that adolescent males are experiencing increasing pressure to adhere to an ideal muscular body type that may lead to purging as well as dietary supplement abuse and steroid use (Cohane & Pope, 2001; Dunn et al., 2001; Garry, Morrissey, & Whetstone, 2003; McCabe & Ricciardelli, 2003). In addition, recent studies that include large numbers of minority females are finding that in some subsamples, minority females are manifesting disordered eating and eating disorders at rates similar to those found in Caucasian populations (Striegel-Moore et al., 2000; Walcott, Pratt, & Patel, 2003).

Eating disorders may be caused by a variety of influences, including such factors as comparing one's self to media ideals or peers, internalizing unrealistic media images of attractiveness, being teased about one's appearance, modeling peers' or parents' weight practices or attitudes, sexual abuse or harassment, and early pubertal maturation (Shisslak & Crago, 2001; Vander Wal & Thelen, 2001).

Sleep

Sleep is a critical human function that serves to promote neurological development in infants as well as cognitive and emotional development in school-age children and adolescents. Research shows that sleep and waking behaviors change from infancy to adolescence, with a decrease in total sleep duration. Whereas infants sleep on average 14.2 hours at 6 months of age, 16-year-olds sleep an average of 8.1 hours (Iglowstein, Jenni, Molinari, & Largo, 2003; Ohayon, Carskadon, Guilleminault, & Vitiello, 2004). More specifically, children in middle childhood (sixth grade), when compared to younger children (second grade), go to sleep later, have more irregular sleep-wake schedules, and experience more weekend catch-up and shorter sleep periods—all of which results in less-than-optimal sleep (Sadeh, Raviv, & Gruber, 2000).

The delayed onset of sleep has both a physiological and a sociocultural explanation. First, researchers have identified that the **circadian cycle**, which is responsible for sleep/wake cycles in humans and other animals, shifts during middle childhood and the onset of puberty. The shift involves releasing **melatonin**, a sleep-inducing hormone, later in the evening so that children in middle childhood don't "feel sleepy" until later in the night (around 9:30 P.M.). In addition, studies show that older school-age children may voluntarily stay up later as a result of extracurricular activities, academic pressures (e.g., homework), and social activities (Wolfson et al., 1995). They also increase TV-watching, computer and Internet use, and ingest more caffeine products before bedtime, all of which can lead to delayed sleep (Owens, Stahl, Patton, Reddy, & Crouch, 2006). Taken together, these findings suggest that later sleep onsets for older school-age children are a function of both biological and psychosocial change.

During the school year, a later sleep onset paired with an earlier wake time may result in insufficient amounts of sleep for many children during the week. Children in this age group *need* 10 to 11 hours of sleep per night to report feeling "rested," but most get an average of 9.5 hours of sleep or less, largely due to a set wake-up time (Iglowstein et al., 2003). Consequences of sleep deprivation that are a source of concern for parents, teachers, practitioners, and health care workers include:

- Increased daytime sleepiness
- Poorer concentration and ability to focus attention
- Poorer school performance
- Increased moodiness and mood disorders
- Increased impulsivity and aggression
- Higher use of products with caffeine (Dahl & Lewin, 2002; Owens et al., 2006)

In a study that examined attitudes toward and beliefs about sleep in a sample of children from fifth to ninth grade, results showed that students perceived the need for sleep as one of the top three important health behaviors (the other two were exercise and not smoking) and recognized in themselves the outcomes of inadequate sleep in a number of domains (e.g., school athletics, social life). They also reported that they would welcome adult guidance (e.g., from doctors, teachers, coaches) regarding better sleep habits and their benefits (Owens et al., 2006). These results suggest that school-age children can comprehend—and are open to—information about the importance of sleep. Educational programming, such as the Web-based sleep education program "Garfield Star Sleeper Campaign," has been developed for school-aged children to deliver these messages.

Substance Use

National statistics show that substance use and abuse is a much greater threat to the health of adolescents than to that of children in middle childhood. The use of substances like alcohol and tobacco develops very rapidly during early adolescence. However, research suggests that the most persistent drug use and abuse *begins* in middle childhood and, therefore, warrants understanding of the factors that predict such use during these years.

Alcohol. We have very reliable data on the use of alcohol by adolescents who are in grades 9 through 12 as a result of several national surveys (e.g., *Monitoring the Future*, a survey sponsored by the National Institute on Drug Abuse, and the *Youth Risk Behavior Survey*, sponsored by the Centers for Disease Control). We do not, however, have the same national data on alcohol use in children ages 6 to 12. A series of studies, however, examined substance use (both alcohol and tobacco) in approximately 2500 students from grades 6 to 9 who attended seven middle schools in Maryland. Students were studied over multiple years to understand not only the prevalence of alcohol and tobacco use in sixth graders and older students but also the factors that predict early onset and increased use of substances in this age group (Simons-Morton, 2004; Simons-Morton, Haynie, Crump, Saylor, Eitel, & Yu, 1999; Simons-Morton, Haynie, Saylor, Crump, & Chen, 2005). In this sample, 6.5% of sixth graders and 19.6% of eighth graders reported drinking in the past 30 days (Simons-Morton et al., 1999). These figures can be compared to 58% of twelfth graders from a national sample who reported using alcohol in the past month (Johnston, O'Malley, Bachman, & Schulenberg, 2006).

Studies have shown that early drinking behavior (e.g., in sixth grade) can lead to a longer period of increased risk in adolescence and is associated with later alcohol and drug abuse (Grant, 1997) and delinquent and problem behavior (Dawkins, 1997). Factors that predict which children are more likely to initiate early alcohol use are having friends who drink and engage in antisocial behavior, having high expectations about drinking, and having parents who won't disapprove or don't monitor drinking behavior (Donovan, 2004; Simons-Morton, 2004). Childhood personality factors, such as impulsivity and a lack of control flexibility, as well as childhood aggression may help to identify which children might be at risk for the early onset of drinking (Lochman, Wells, & Murray, 2007; Wong et al., 2006).

Factors associated with early alcohol use include poorer physical and mental health, low grades in school, low educational aspirations, and engagement in antisocial behavior/delinquency (Perkins & Borden, 2003). Health and psychological consequences of long-term alcohol misuse are liver disease, cancer, cardiovascular disease, and neurological damage as well as psychiatric problems, such as depression, anxiety, and antisocial personality disorder (Naimi et al., 2003; Sher, 2006).

Because early alcohol use has such long-term consequences for both the individual and society at large, a range of prevention programs have been designed to deter children in middle childhood from drinking. One such program is *The Coping Power Program,* designed to identify aggressive children in elementary school (Lochman et al., 2007). Over an 18-month period, practitioners work intensively with both children and parents to reduce aggressive behavior. The program focuses on improving the child's social competence and ability to get along with other children, self-regulation and impulse control, school engagement and academic success, and improving parental interactions and interventions. Results have shown that this program produces significant preventative effects in children's substance use by improving factors presumed to mediate substance use. Children who were involved in the prevention program had lower levels of substance use compared to children who were not in the program (Lochman & Wells, 2004). The success of this program indicates that supporting positive skills in school-age children is one approach to keeping them on a path to healthy development.

Cigarette Smoking. The initiation of smoking appears to occur between grades 7 and 9, and nearly all first use occurs by age 18 [U.S. Department of Health and Human Services (USDHHS), 1994]. A consistent finding among national surveys is that the younger the age at which teens begin to smoke regularly, the more regular and heavier the use and the more likely they are to be nicotine dependent in adulthood (Chassin, Presson, Pitts, & Sherman, 2000). A series of studies that included middle-schoolers found that 7% of sixth graders reported smoking in the past 30 days compared to 20% of eighth graders and 23% of twelfth graders (Faulkner, Farrelly & Hersey, 2000; Johnston et al., 2006; Simons-Morton et al., 1999).

Overall smoking rates for adolescents have declined since peaking in 1996. Declines in smoking rates in all age groups are attributed to the increased cost of cigarettes, the prohibition of adolescent-targeted advertising, more prevalent antismoking messages, and increased negative public images of tobacco companies (Emery et al., 2005; Myers & MacPherson, 2004).

The health risks of smoking include increased respiratory infections, lessened lung capacity, and permanent lung damage (USDHHS, 1994). Recent research also shows that early initiation of smoking retards physical development (e.g., height, weight, and body mass index) in adolescent girls (Stice & Martinez, 2005). Perhaps the greater health risks occur over a longer period of time. Nearly one third of young people who take up smoking in middle childhood and adolescence will eventually die of a smoking-related illness (Gilpin, Choi, Berry, & Pierce, 1999).

Research shows that the time interval between first use (experimentation) and regular use is quite variable, with an average length of several years (USDHHS, 1994). This finding suggests that there is a small window following first use in which smoking can be either encouraged or discouraged. Factors associated with the increased likelihood of regular cigarette use are accessibility, affordability, peer and parental smoking, academic difficulty, school misbehavior (e.g., skipped classes, truancy, suspensions), and peer encouragement of such misbehaviors (Abroms, Simons-Morton, Haynie, & Chen, 2005; Bryant, Schulenberg, Bachman, O'Malley, & Johnston, 2000; Bryant, Schulenberg, O'Malley, Bachman, & Johnston, 2003). Early experience with nonusing peers, parents who convey nonuse messages and monitor time spent with deviant peers, successful school achievement, high levels of motivation, and commitment to school are protective factors against increased cigarette use over time (Bryant et al., 2003).

At one point you notice a small group of boys and girls gathered around a lounge chair at the pool, smoking cigarettes. Most of the children in this group were smoking, but several were merely observing.

Children and teens who smoke regularly resemble adults in that they report frequent attempts to quit smoking and experience nicotine withdrawal when nicotine abstinent (Colby, Tiffany, Shiffman, & Niaura, 2000). In a review of 17 cessation programs for adolescents, 10 were found to be effective, but with only a 12% success rate. This finding means that it is as difficult for adolescents who are regular smokers to quit smoking as it is for adults (Sussman, Lichtman, Ritt, & Pallonen, 1999). The key lies in prevention, and the most successful prevention programs begin early (grade 6) and are interactive. They teach young teens refusal skills (i.e., how to say "no"), use peer leaders, and emphasize that fewer adolescents actually smoke than teens frequently believe (Tobler et al., 2000). It also appears that recent antitobacco media campaigns may be effective when paired with the prevention components mentioned above (Pechman, 1997).

As reviewed in this chapter, the risks associated with smoking are severe. Children in middle childhood, however, may also face exposure to cigarettes in a less-than-voluntary capacity: exposure to secondhand smoke. The health consequences related to this exposure are presented in Box 4.3.

Other Drugs. Alcohol and tobacco are the drugs of choice for children in middle childhood. Marijuana and inhalants are the next most frequently used drugs. National surveys show that 6.6% of eighth graders have used marijuana in the last 30 days (Johnston et al., 2006). Patterns of marijuana use are similar to patterns of alcohol and tobacco use in that early initiation is a significant predictor of future problems, such as school failure, deviancy, poor physical and mental health in adulthood, and the use of other substances (Ellickson, D'Amico, Collins, & Klein, 2005; Kandel & Chen, 2000).

Children in middle childhood are at risk from secondhand smoke.

David Young-Wolff/Getty Images Inc.—Stone Allstock

BOX 4.3   Roadmap to Successful Practice
The Health Effects of Involuntary Exposure to Tobacco Smoke in School-Age Children

In 1986, Dr. C. Everett Koop released the first Surgeon General's report concluding that exposure to secondhand smoke caused disease in nonsmokers (U.S. Department of Health and Human Services, 1986). Twenty years later, a second report confirms earlier findings and documents new adverse effects of secondhand smoke on children and adults (U.S. Department of Health and Human Services, 2006).

The largest producer of secondhand smoke is cigarettes, followed by pipes and then cigars. *Secondhand smoke* refers to a nonsmoker's inhalation of both the smoke exhaled by the smoker, and the "sidestream" smoke that is released by the smoldering cigarette. Secondhand smoke resembles the smoke inhaled by the smoker in that it contains many chemicals (e.g., formaldehyde, cyanide, carbon monoxide, ammonia, and nico-

tine) that are known carcinogens. Although adults have experienced a decline in exposure to secondhand smoke as a result of smoking restrictions in the workplace and public spaces, children continue to be exposed to secondhand smoke in the home. Among children younger than 18 years of age, an estimated 22% are exposed to secondhand smoke, also referred to as *involuntary smoking*.

The amount of smoke to which children are exposed varies according to the number of smokers and the rate at which they are smoking, the size of the space in which the smoking takes place, and the rate of air exchange between smoke-filled air and uncontaminated air. These variables also can affect the health effects of secondhand smoke on schoolagers. As children get older, the effects of secondhand smoke decrease.

(continued)

BOX 4.3   Roadmap to Successful Practice *(Continued)*
The Health Effects of Involuntary Exposure to Tobacco Smoke
in School-Age Children

Based on several decades of sound scientific research, the Surgeon General's 2006 report presents the following causal relationships between:

- Parental smoking and coughing, phlegm, wheezing, and breathlessness in school-age children

- Parental smoking and ever having asthma in childhood

- Secondhand smoke exposure and the onset of wheeze illnesses in childhood

- Secondhand smoke and the onset of asthma in childhood

- Maternal smoking during pregnancy and adverse effects on lung function across childhood

The report also cites previous research that demonstrates improvement in respiratory symptoms in children whose parents have stopped smoking (O'Connell & Logan, 1974).

Finally, the report suggests that separating smokers from nonsmokers within the same air space, cleaning the air, and ventilating buildings may reduce—but not eliminate—the exposure of children and adults to secondhand smoke. The scientific evidence indicates that there is no risk-free level of exposure to secondhand smoke. Only by the elimination of indoor smoking can we fully protect children from the inhalation of secondhand smoke.

Raising Healthy Children is an example of a successful intervention program that targeted children in grades 1 and 2 and their families. The program focused on enhancing developmentally appropriate protective factors in the children's lives to reduce alcohol, tobacco, and marijuana use in grades 6 to 10. The intervention provided the children with opportunities for involvement with positive role models (e.g., family members and teachers who did not use substances); focused on the student's academic, cognitive, and social skills; gave positive reinforcement for prosocial involvement; and delivered clear standards about substance use. Although this program was unable to prevent use in all children, it was effective in reducing the frequency of alcohol and marijuana use during adolescence (Brown, Catalano, Fleming, Haggerty, & Abbott, 2005).

Inhalants are gases or fumes that can be inhaled from solvents (e.g., spray paint, gasoline, glue) for the purpose of getting high. These drugs appear to be more accessible, easily administered, and affordable to young children and, therefore, are used and abused with more frequency in middle childhood than in later adolescence. In a national sample of eighth graders, 4.2% reported using inhalants in the past 30 days, compared to only 2% of high school seniors (Johnston et al., 2006). (Note that the prevalence rate for both marijuana and inhalants are from samples of older students than those reported for alcohol and tobacco use.) Data from a single state demonstrated that inhalant use begins around the same time as tobacco (11.9 years), much earlier than the use of alcohol (12.8 years) and marijuana (13.8 years) (Mosher, Rotolo, Phillips, Krupski, & Stark, 2004).

Early use of inhalants is associated with long-term use of other drugs, (Wu, Schlenger, & Ringwalt, 2005) as well as a risk of becoming dependent on inhalants or other drugs (Wu, Pilowsky, & Schlenger, 2004). Although not technically referred to as a "gateway drug," the pattern of use very much suggests that early inhalant use leads to other drug use in later adolescence. Delinquency and mental health problems are also associated with inhalant use (Wu et al., 2004). Inhalant users are at risk for serious pulmonary, cardiac, and blood toxicity. In addition, they are at risk of suffering not only metabolic abnormalities but also permanent neurological damage (Kolecki & Shih, 2004).

Guideposts for Working with School-Age Children

- Because a well-balanced diet is important, teach children about proper nutrition and eating habits, model good eating habits, and provide nutritious snacks and meals.

- Try to send constant messages about the value of a "normal" body shape because children in middle childhood may be hypercritical of their bodies. Along with other factors, a poor body image may manifest itself in eating disturbances or disorders.

- Encourage children to get as much sleep as possible within the parameters of their academic and social lives.

- Be aware that most children and adolescents will try smoking cigarettes and drinking alcohol at least once; encourage good parental monitoring with strong nonuse messages.

- Remember that there is a short period between first use and regular use (approximately 2 years) when comprehensive prevention is the most effective.

STOP What factors influenced your decision to use or not use substances?

Inhalant use is difficult to treat, in part, because chronic users represent a very troubled subgroup of children. Educating youth about the specific risks of inhalants seems to be the key to decreasing use.

DEVELOPMENT IN CONTEXT

Children in middle childhood begin to take more responsibility for their health choices. They are more cognitively capable of comprehending the relationship between health behaviors and consequences; they can observe the effects of certain behaviors such as dieting, drug use, and obtaining sufficient amounts of sleep in themselves and in their peers; and they begin to form health habits that they will carry with them into the future. Understanding what children know about specific health issues, what they are willing to learn, and factors that predict health outcomes, will assist all of us in providing children with the support they need to make the right choices.

The biological development of older children and the health choices they make are, in large part, a function of the contexts within which they live. Health-related behaviors are influenced by and consequently influence ecological niches. The familial, educational, and community contexts of school-age children help shape the developmental trajectories of their biological maturation and health.

Family Context

Puberty may appear to be a phenomenon largely determined by genetics and biology, but as Box 4.1 illustrated, the family environment may affect the timing of pubertal maturation in girls. Research has shown that the absence of a biological father and the presence of an unrelated male, in addition to the absence of a warm and positive family connection, may accelerate girls' pubertal development. Early maturation and greater levels of family conflict have been associated with earlier sexual debut in African American youth as well (McBride, Paikoff, & Holmbeck, 2003).

Research also shows that living with both parents protects against early sexual debut, as does having good teen-parent communication, close parental monitoring, and strong parental attachment—particularly for African American and Hispanic youth (Crosby & Miller, 2002; Karofsky, Zeng, & Kosorock, 2001). Mothers are more likely than fathers to communicate with their children about sex-related topics, and mothers have more influence on the age of sexual debut of their daughters than their sons, as well as greater impact on age of sexual debut than condom use (Averett, Rees, & Argys, 2002; McNeely et al., 2002).

Parents can influence the health of their children by making healthy foods available, modeling good eating habits, or possessing positive attitudes and behaviors about eating. Research that examined household, parent, and child contributions to obesity showed that parents of obese children did not recognize the importance of their role in shaping their children's nutritional patterns. Parents of obese children were more likely to agree with statements such as "It doesn't matter which foods my child eats. As long as they eat enough, they will grow properly"; and "[My child] is old enough to take care of feeding him/herself." They also seemed less cognizant of the relationship between physical activity and related health and weight issues. The results of the study suggested that any effort to curb childhood obesity should include improving parent knowledge of child nutrition (Gable & Lutz, 2000).

Familial conflict has been shown to affect the quality of sleep in middle childhood. For example, studies have shown that increased marital conflict is associated with disruptions in the quality and quantity of 8- and 9-year-old children's sleep and increased sleepiness during the day. Researchers have suggested that exposure to marital conflict may influence children's biological regulatory processes, such as sleep (El-Sheikh, Buckhalt, Mize, & Acebo, 2006).

Parents may play a role in the initiation of smoking in middle childhood as well. When family factors were examined for their influence on daily smoking initiation in 10- and 11-year-olds, for example, researchers found that parental smoking contributed to the onset of daily smoking in their children—even if parents practiced good family management, were against teen tobacco use, and did not involve their children in their own tobacco use. To reduce risks for smoking initiation in children ages 10 and 11, these findings suggest that parents stop or reduce their *own* smoking (Hill, Hawkins, Catalano, Abbott, & Guo, 2005).

STOP What role (if any) did your parent(s) play in your health choices?

School Context

School transitions may influence how well females adjust to puberty. One study found that when girls experienced multiple stressors, such as puberty and dating, while they were transitioning to a middle school, their self-esteem declined precipitously (Simmons & Blyth, 1987). School was no longer an "arena of comfort" and they were particularly vulnerable to stress and its related outcomes. **Arenas of comfort** are contexts in which individuals can relax and rejuvenate so that stressful changes in another arena can be managed. Supportive schools can serve that role or, in the case of early-maturing girls, add to the stress (Call & Mortimer, 2001). Doing poorly in school and being disengaged from the academic environment *precedes* substance abuse, delinquency, and dropping out (Bryant et al., 2003). However, research shows that engagement in school as well as achievement is a protective factor against substance abuse and delinquency.

Schools also educate youth about pubertal changes, sexuality, HIV/AIDS, and contraceptive use. Forty-three of the 50 states now mandate that schools provide students with information about HIV/AIDS and its prevention. Approximately 88% of all high school students report being taught about HIV/AIDS infection in school (CDC, 2003).

In 2004, a federal child-nutrition law was passed requiring every school district that receives federal school-meal funds to establish a local "wellness policy" by the first day of the 2006–2007 school year. The law encourages the involvement of students and parents to help formulate policies to address nutrition education and physical activity goals, nutrition standards, and other school-based activities that serve to promote and reinforce wellness messages.

Community Context

The effects of the surrounding neighborhood on children's development often manifest themselves in socioeconomic opportunities or in the traditions of racial/ethnic groups. For example, one study assessed the neighborhood context in which children lived to help explain why members of racial/ethnic minorities or youths of lower SES were more likely to develop high-risk cardiovascular behaviors. The researchers found that youth who resided in neighborhoods characterized by low income, high levels of poverty, low education, low housing values, and more blue-collar workers were more likely to have poorer dietary habits. This was particularly true for females and African Americans. Lower SES also predicted higher smoking rates in Caucasian males and reduced physical activity for Hispanics. Neighborhood characteristics such as the unavailability of nutritious and low-cost foods, access to cigarettes, and lack of opportunities to exercise in safe locations put minority and poor youth at risk for cardiovascular disease (Lee & Cubbin, 2002).

The sense of organization and safety that children feel about their neighborhoods also has an impact on the health choices they make. In a study that assessed middle-school students' current alcohol, tobacco, and marijuana use, researchers also assessed students' perceptions of neighborhood disorder and students' sense of hope. Results showed that students who perceived their neighborhoods to be disordered and who had a low sense of hope showed the highest rates of substance use (Wilson, Syme, Boyce, Battistich, & Selvin, 2005). These findings argue for community support in creating safer neighborhood environments to assist in the prevention of substance use.

CHAPTER REVIEW

Biological Maturation and Health Behaviors

- Puberty promotes changes in height and weight, body composition, secondary sex characteristics, and sexual maturation.
- Sexual maturation in children includes sexual arousal, desires, self-stimulation, and noncoital and coital activity.

- Physical changes elicit accompanying changes in nutritional needs, exercise requirements, and sleep patterns.
- Children's cognitive and social contexts may encourage disturbed eating patterns and substance use/abuse.
- Individual, familial, school, and community variables influence puberty and healthy or high-risk health practices.

Theoretical Viewpoint

- Evolutionary developmental theory is a genetics-based theoretical perspective that emphasizes the adaptive features of our ancestors.

- Current genetic traits may have originated in previous eras while simultaneously adapting to present environmental demands.

Biological Maturation

- Puberty is a maturational process prompted by neurological and hormonal changes.
- Pubertal change includes the development of secondary sex characteristics and somatic growth (e.g., height and weight).
- Numerous factors such as genetics, nutrition, health, and some environmental factors influence pubertal growth.

- Pubertal change requires psychosocial adjustment. Some children (e.g., early-maturing girls and boys and late-maturing boys) have more difficulty adapting to pubertal change than those who mature on time or girls who mature later.
- Pubertal maturation may have both direct and indirect effects on how children think, feel, and act.

Sexuality

- Hormonal secretions that promote puberty are associated with increased sexual arousal. Sexual behavior may be influenced by hormones in boys but is mediated by social norms in girls.
- Children in middle childhood engage in more self-stimulation and noncoital behavior than coital behavior.

- Prevention programs designed for school-age children should include not sex education, but also some instruction in social problem-solving, refusal skills, and information about abstinence.

Related Health and Development Issues

- Children require multiple small meals during the day, and sufficient nutrition is critical for cognitive and emotional well-being.
- Children in middle childhood exhibit heightened sensitivity to body shape that may be a precursor to eating disturbances or disorders that are maladaptive and dangerous to their health.
- Appropriate amounts of sleep promote healthy emotional and cognitive functioning. As children move

through middle childhood they grow tired later in the evening and need to sleep later in the morning. Early school start times prevent this pattern, and sleep deficits result.
- Although the prevalence rate is low for children who use substances in middle childhood, those who do initiate use early are at higher risk for a constellation of high-risk behaviors (e.g., addiction, antisocial behavior, multiple substance use, etc.).

Development in Context

- Families pass along genetic information that may influence puberty. In addition, familial configurations and dynamics may influence the timing and tempo of maturation.
- Having open communication and warm and positive relationships with families serve as protective factors against drug use, high-risk sexual behavior, and unplanned pregnancies.
- Parents play a critical role in their children's eating habits, exercise, and smoking behavior.

- The transition between and structure of schools may act as an additional stressor for children who are experiencing puberty, especially girls. Schools also play a vital role in educating students about abstinence, HIV/AIDS, sexual behavior, and contraceptive use.
- Communities provide children and their families with differential opportunities to engage in healthy or unhealthy behaviors. The prospects of succeeding in a community are powerful predictors of abstinence, delayed sexual activity, and nondrug use.

TABLE 4.4 Summary of Developmental Theories		
Chapter	Theories	Focus
8. Puberty, Sexuality, and Health	Evolutionary, Developmental	How selected genes helped our ancestors survive and reproduce, and how these same genes may influence our behavior and thinking

KEY TERMS

Acquired immunodeficiency syndrome (AIDS)
Adrenarche
Amenorrheic
Anorexia nervosa (AN)
Arenas of comfort
Binge-eating disorder (BED)
Body image

Bulimia nervosa (BN)
Circadian cycle
Coitus
Direct-effects model
Evolutionary developmental theory
Gonadotropins
Gonardarche
Human immunodeficiency virus (HIV)

Hypokalemia
Indirect-effects model
Lanugo
Leptin
Masturbation
Melatonin
Mediator variables
Menarche
Moderator variables
Natural selection

Noncoital behavior
Obesity
Puberty
Secondary sex characteristics
Sexual continuum
Sexual debut
Sexually transmitted disease (STD)
Semenarche

SUGGESTED ACTIVITIES

1. Visit a school, recreational facility, or mall where you can observe the different maturation rates of school-age children. How do they differ in height, weight, body shape, and observable secondary sex characteristics? What gender and/or racial/ethnic differences do you see? How does the level of maturation seem to affect how they behave and how others behave towards them?

2. Ask children ages 6–12 to chart their sleep-wake cycles for approximately 10 days. Have them record their bedtime, whether this is regulated by parents and/or enforced, activities they engage in before bedtime, number of times they wake during the night, quality of sleep, waking time, level of difficulty waking, level of fatigue during the day. You could compare the sleep-wake cycles of younger and older children as well as their week and weekend sleep patterns.

3. Using the information from the chapter, design an effective sex education program for middle school students. What content would be included? What teaching techniques might be most effective? How might gender, race/ethnicity, or socioeconomic status influence the design of the program? What other components should be included or addressed? You could also design an HIV/AIDS prevention program addressing the same questions.

RECOMMENDED RESOURCES

Suggested Readings

Bancroft, J. (Ed.) (2003). *Sexual development in childhood.* Bloomington, IN: Indiana University Press.

Maine, M. (2000). *Body wars: Making peace with women's bodies: An activist's guide.* Carlsbad, CA: Gurze.

Worell, J., & Goodheart, C. D. (Eds.) (2006). *Handbook of girls' and women's psychological health.* New York: Oxford University Press.

Suggested Online Resources

The Health Consequences of Involuntary Exposure to Tobacco Smoke: A Report of the Surgeon General (2006). http://www.cdc.gov/tobacco

HIV/AIDS Surveillance Report (2006). http://www.cdc.gov/hiv/topics/surveillance/basic.htm

Sex Education and Teenage Sexuality Fact Sheet http://www.socwomen.org/socactivism/TeenSexFact.pdf

Suggested Web Sites

Dietary Guidelines for Americans 2005.
    http://www.healthierus.gov/dietaryguidelines/
Girls, Incorporated.
    http://www.girlsinc.org
Healthy People 2010.
    http://www.cdc.gov/nchs/hphome.htm

National Center on Sleep Disorders Research.
    http://www.nhlbi.nih.gov/sleep
National Clearinghouse for Alcohol and Drug Information.
    http://ncadi.samhsa.gov/

Suggested Films and Videos

Animated neuroscience and the action of nicotine, cocaine, and marijuana in the brain (1998). Films for the Humanities & Sciences (25 minutes)

Biology of sex and gender (2003). Insight Media (30 minutes)

Eating disorders: Causes, symptoms, and treatment (2002). Insight Media (22 minutes)

Messing with heads: Marijuana and mental illness (2005). Films for the Humanities & Sciences (46 minutes)

5

Cognitive Development in Middle Childhood

EyeWire Collection/Getty Images - Photodisc

Chapter Objectives

After reading this chapter, students will be able to:

▶ Define cognitive development in middle childhood.

▶ Identify three theoretical approaches to cognitive development.

▶ Understand how each theoretical perspective explains the cognitive development of school-age children.

▶ Explain the contributions of family, school, and community contexts to cognitive development in middle childhood.

Nine-year-old Anya's older brother Alexandr, age 13, wants her to play chess with him. He participates in an informal chess club at the local high school and is always looking for ways to practice his game. "Anya, wanna play chess?" "No," she responds, "I'm not very good. You always beat me." Alexandr asks, "How do you expect to get better if you don't practice? Come on, I'll help you." Alexandr is true to his word. He reminds Anya what the names of all the pieces are and how they move. He also reminds her of the rules and how someone wins. Anya tries her best, but it takes her a long time to decide how to move her pieces; sometimes she does so incorrectly and she forgets to play defensively. Alexandr, on the other hand, is able to see the game as it unfolds across the entire board. He ascertains what the pros and cons of a move might be very quickly, and then he decides on the best move. He is able to think several moves ahead and plays both defensively and offensively.

COGNITION IN MIDDLE CHILDHOOD

Cognition is a categorical term that represents thinking, reasoning abilities, memory skills, decision making, problem solving, and other aspects of intellectual functioning. The middle years of childhood are characterized by a gradual increase in logical thought, an improvement in memory and learning strategies, and the ability to learn through dialogue with others. The case study of Anya and Alexandr, for example, illustrates cognitive differences among different-aged youth. Cognitive changes occurring in middle childhood, as well as practice and familiarity with both formal and informal experiences, moderate the development of cognitive skills. Finally, family, school, community, and culture play important roles in the development of school-aged children's intellectual lives.

THEORETICAL VIEWPOINTS

In this chapter three different theoretical perspectives are presented to explain the cognitive competencies that emerge in middle childhood, how they are different from the cognitive competencies of preschool children and adolescents, and how they develop over time. They are Piaget's cognitive developmental theory, Vygotsky's sociocultural theory, and the information-processing perspective. Although each theoretical perspective is presented separately, they should be viewed as complementary to one another. Together, all three theories provide us with a better understanding of how 8- to 12-year-old children think.

These theories also are offered as contemporary alternatives to a theoretical viewpoint that dominated psychology through the better part of the 20th century: **behaviorism**. Behaviorists argued that the environment influenced developmental change and that development occurred through principles of learning. From a behaviorist's perspective, children's learning is largely determined by paired associations with environmental events (i.e., **classical conditioning**) and/or influenced by the rewards and punishment that follow behavior (i.e., **operant conditioning**). Observation supports the notion that children develop paired associations (e.g., a child may wince after the appearance of lightning because of previous experience with the thunder that follows). There is also research evidence that external rewards and punishments influence children's behavior.

> *For example, verbal praise after making a good move in chess may encourage Anya to continue this behavior in the future.*

Much of what we learned from this theoretical perspective is still widely applied in the fields of education and clinical and counseling psychology. For example, a system of rewards that is used to change children's study habits employs principles of learning theory. But learning theorists could not offer insight into the internal mechanisms that promote cognitive advancement or explain the cognitive connections children make on their own without influence from the outside world. The field needed theoretical perspectives that better reflect the rich and complex inner worlds of school-age children and adolescents. The following theoretical frameworks meet those needs.

Piaget's Cognitive Developmental Theory

Jean Piaget (1896–1980) created a theory that explains how children come to understand the world and create internal cognitive concepts about the world through their direct experiences and interactions with the environment. Piaget thought that children constructed knowledge through their interactions with the environment (e.g., running their fingers through water) that resulted in internal cognitive change. Therefore, his theory is referred to as a **constructivist view** of cognitive development.

Developmental Components of the Theory. A fundamental concept in Piaget's theory is a **schema**, or a mental structure by which children organize their world. A schema can be simplistically thought of as a concept or category. Another helpful analogy might be a file folder that helps children organize and differentiate incoming information. **Adaptation** is the process by which children build schemata (the plural of *schema)* through direct interaction with the environment. Piaget called the mechanisms by which schemata increase and change *assimilation* and *accommodation.*

Assimilation represents the process by which an already existing schema is applied to the external world and helps the child to incorporate new information. For example, when confronted with a new version of checkers (e.g., Chinese checkers), Anya assimilates by playing the game according to the old rules of checkers with some minor modifications. The existing schema of how to play checkers provides her with the fundamental knowledge of or experience necessary for playing this new version; and thus assimilation occurs with a successful outcome. However, this existing file folder (i.e., schema) would *not* be useful to adapt to playing the game of chess. The existing schema would need to be drastically modified.

Changing or creating a new schema to better fit new information or experience is called **accommodation**. Learning to play chess would require accommodation of game-playing strategies. Learning the difference between the rules of checkers and chess reflects accommodation. Accommodation has occurred by either changing the existing file folder of "games" to include checkers *and* chess or creating a new file folder for chess. By constantly assimilating and accommodating schemata, the child grows and develops cognitively.

The rates at which assimilation and accommodation are used vary over the course of development. When a child is not changing much, assimilation is predominantly used because the existing schemata are sufficient to make sense of the world. If, however, a child is going through a rapid period of development, assimilation may not be enough, and *cognitive disequilibrium* occurs. **Cognitive disequilibrium** represents an imbalance of developmental mechanisms, and accommodation is necessary for new schemata to be created to handle the new information. The constant cycles between cognitive equilibrium (when the information is assimilated easily) and cognitive disequilibrium (when accommodation is required) is called **equilibration** and, simply put, is Piaget's theoretical explanation for *how* and *why* a child learns.

Piaget's Stages of Cognitive Development. The method Piaget used to learn about children's thinking is called the clinical interview process, which was explained in chapter 2. He watched how children solved a problem or asked them questions about what caused things to happen (e.g., "How does the sun rise?"). Then, he followed up their original answers with a series of probe questions so that he could understand the nature and process of their thinking (Gardner, Kornhaber, & Wake, 1996).

As Piaget interviewed more children of all ages and as his own children grew older, he began to see distinct and qualitative differences in the ways in which different-aged children interacted with and learned about the world. From these observations he proposed four stages through which children progress as they develop cognitively (Piaget, 1963, 1977).

- **Sensorimotor Stage** (ages 0–2). Children predominantly learn and act upon the world through their senses and motor abilities.
- **Preoperational Stage** (ages 2–7). Children learn about and act upon the world through symbols and language. They rely on their perceptions and how things appear to them.
- **Concrete Operational Stage** (ages 7–11). Children develop the ability to apply logical thought to concrete problems.
- **Formal Operational Stage** (ages 11–15 years or older). Preadolescents and adolescents are able to apply logic to all types of problems including abstract ones.

Piaget suggested that these stages are **universal** and **invariant**: They apply to children everywhere, and cognitive development proceeds through these stages in order. No stage can be skipped or missed, because each follows the previous one in a specific order. Although there are many interesting dimensions to both the sensorimotor and preoperational stages, this chapter focuses on the school-age child in the concrete operational stage.

The Concrete Operational Child

The period of middle childhood defined in this textbook (6 to 12 years of age) consists of school-age children transitioning from preoperational thought to concrete thought and then preparing to move on to formal operational thinking. This pattern of development reflects the change from a dependency in early childhood on rigid, self-centered, or **egocentric thought** that relies heavily on how things appear from the child's perspective to a dependency on *operations*. The term **operation** refers to an internalized mental action that follows logical rules. School-age children tend to develop internalized representations about *concrete* objects, such as things that can be seen, felt, or experienced. Thus, concrete operational thinkers are usually characterized by the tangible logic of their thinking. During formal operational thinking, on the other hand, internal representations are based on more abstract concepts.

Conservation. One of the major accomplishments of the concrete operational period is the ability to **conserve**. **Conservation** is the ability to understand that the amount or quantity of an object remains the same despite an outward change in appearance. For example, if you were to take a ball of clay and roll it into a long, thin shape, a 10-year-old child would understand that it is still the same amount of clay. Likewise, if you took two glasses with equal amounts of water, poured one in a tall cylinder and the other in a low, flat dish, an 11-year-old child would claim that the amount of water is equivalent—despite the difference in appearance. Table 5.1 provides a series of tasks that Piaget developed to illustrate the progression through which school-age children develop conservation.

One interesting note is that children do not seem to grasp the concept of conservation uniformly. The application of conservation principles to different types of problems usually follows a sequence (Piaget & Inhelder, 1969):

Conservation of number	Ages 5–6
Substance (mass)	Ages 7–8
Area	Ages 7–8

TABLE 5.1   Examples of Piagetian Conservation Tasks

Piagetian conservation tasks assess children's problem-solving approaches. The understanding of conservation typically follows this sequence of tasks.

Conservation Task	Original Presentation	Transformation

Number

Are there the same number of pennies in each row?

Now are there the same number of pennies in each row, or does one row have more?

Length

Is each of these sticks just as long as the other?

Now are the two sticks each equally as long, or is one longer?

Liquid

Is there the same amount of water in each glass?

Now, Is there the same amount of water in each glass, or does one have more?

Mass

Is there the same amount of clay in each ball?

Now does each piece have the same amount of clay, or does one have more?

Area

Do each of these two cows have the same amount of grass to eat?

Now does each cow have the same amount of grass to eat, or does one cow have more?

Weight

Do each of these two balls of clay weigh the same amount?

Now (without placing them back on the scale to confirm what is correct for the child) do the two pieces of clay weigh the same, or does one weigh more?

Volume

Does the water level rise equally in each glass when the two balls of clay are dropped in the water?

Now (after one piece of clay is removed from the water and reshaped) will the water levels rise equally, or will one rise more?

Liquid	Ages 7–8
Weight	Ages 9–10
Volume	Ages 11–12

The ability to conserve is promoted by the development of several separate abilities. The first is **decentration,** or the ability to consider more than one feature of an object at a time. Most 5-year-olds have difficulty taking more than one dimension into consideration when approaching a problem. For example, in a water conservation task, preoperational children will typically answer that the *taller* cylinder has more water. They are taking into account only one dimension (i.e., height) and ignoring others (e.g., width or depth). A concrete operational child, however, typically can take more than one dimension into account at the same time.

Notice that Alexandr is much better at thinking about offensive and defensive moves when moving his chess pieces than Anya, who is exhibiting decentration, but not as expertly as her older brother.

Decentration contributes not only to the development of conservation but also to a child's social competence. When a child recognizes that there are multiple sides to an argument, or multiple viewpoints to an issue, a greater sense of one's role in relationship to others results (Bonino & Cattelino, 1999). Decentration also can be observed in children's emerging comprehension that words can have more than one meaning, as explained in Box 5.1.

BOX 5.1   Roadmap to Understanding Theory and Research
A Developing Sense of Humor

In middle childhood, advances in cognition are reflected and influenced by children's use and understanding of language. As school-age children begin to utilize multiple perspectives to solve conservation tasks, so too do they use and understand language in multiple ways. For example, learning homonyms requires children to comprehend that words that sound the same, *pair* and *pear*, may be spelled differently and have different meanings. They also learn to appreciate that the same word may have multiple meanings, such as the words *cool* or *neat*. *Cool* can be used to express a temperature, "It's cool outside," or satisfaction, "That bike is so cool!" (Berk, 2003). This more sophisticated understanding of double meanings allows 8- to 10-year-olds to comprehend metaphors, such as "thin as a rail" or "cute as a button" (Nippold, Taylor, & Baker, 1996). Children as young as 8 are also able to recognize some forms of irony as well as exaggerated forms of sarcasm (Creusere, 2000; Pexman, Glenwright, Krol, & James, 2005).

Advanced uses and comprehension of language are also reflected in a child's changing sense of humor. Preschoolers and early elementary schoolchildren laugh at incongruencies such as a male calling a female "a boy," or a donkey wearing a lion's mane (McGhee, 1976). Children from ages 6 to 12 are delighted by jokes, puns, and riddles that play off the double meaning of words and phrases such as

"Is your refrigerator running?

"Yes."

"Then you better catch it!"

or

"Knock, knock."

"Who's there?"

(continued)

BOX 5.1   Roadmap to Understanding Theory and Research *(Continued)*
A Developing Sense of Humor

"Boo."

"Boo who?"

"Why ya cryin?"

This recognition and appreciation for multiple interpretations of word meaning in middle childhood might also explain the popularity of particular children's literature such as the stories of Amelia Bedelia, the scatter-brained housekeeper who misinterprets most of her housekeeping instructions. When told to draw the drapes when the sun comes in, she sits down and draws a picture of them rather than closing them. When told to dress the chicken for dinner, she dresses the chicken in suspenders and booties rather than herbs and spices.

Consider this passage from *Charlie and the Chocolate Factory*, another favorite story of this age group:

Grandpa Joe lifted Charlie up so that he could get a better view, and looking in, Charlie saw a long table, and on the table there were rows and rows of small white square-shaped candies. The candies looked very much like square sugar lumps—except that each of them had a funny little pink face painted on one side. . . .

"There you are!" cried Mr. Wonka. "Square candies that look round!" "They don't look round to me," said Mike Teavee. "They look square," said Veruca Salt. "They look completely square." "But they *are* square," said Mr. Wonka. "I never said they weren't." "You said they were *round*!" said Veruca Salt. "I never said anything of the sort," said Mr. Wonka. "I said they *looked* round." "But they *don't* look round!" said Veruca Salt. "They look square!". . .

[Mr. Wonka] took a key from his pocket, and unlocked the door, and flung it open . . . and suddenly . . . at the sound of the door opening, all the rows and rows of little square candies looked quickly round to see who was coming in. The tiny faces actually turned toward the door and stared at Mr. Wonka. "There you are!" he cried triumphantly. "They're looking round! There's no argument about it! They are square candies that look round!" (pp. 113–114)

Source: Excerpt from *Charlie and the Chocolate Factory* by Roald Dahl. Text and illustrations copyright © 1964, renewed 1992 by Roald Dahl Nominee Limited. Used by permission of Alfred A. Knopf, an imprint of Random House Children's Books, a division of Random House, Inc.

Another concept that contributes to the development of conservation is **reversibility**. Children capable of reversible thought can follow a line of reasoning back to where it started. In the event of a water conservation task, a concrete operational child might follow the line of reasoning that if you poured the water back into the original glasses the amount of liquid would be the same. Her answer would be correct based on reversible thinking.

Finally, understanding **transformation**, or paying attention to the means by which one state is changed to another, allows conservation to develop. Concrete operational thinkers are capable of integrating a series of events into a whole with a beginning and endpoint compared to preoperational thinkers who tend to focus on a single point in time. A good illustration of this thinking is reflected in the following task. Take a pencil and hold it upright. Now let it fall. Ask a child to choose between the figures illustrated in Figure 5.1 that represent what just happened.

Preoperational thinkers will focus on the beginning and end states and consistently choose Panel A; concrete operational thinkers will attend to the transformation of the pencil from its vertical to horizontal position and most likely choose Panel B. The choice of Panel B represents an understanding that a relationship exists between the beginning and end states and the successive steps in between.

The gradual development of decentration, reversibility, and transformation contribute to the development of conservation, the precursor to logical thought in

FIGURE 5.1

A Transformation Task

Children younger than 7 tend to pay most attention to static states, or what the object looks like at the beginning or end of a task. Children in concrete operations begin to attend to the transformations an object undergoes.

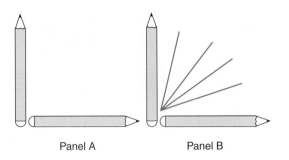

Panel A   Panel B

school-age children. Piaget thought that conservation gave a certain stability to the physical world and also made it possible for children to learn and understand mathematical operations such as multiplying, dividing, ordering (i.e., greater than, less than), and substituting (i.e., one thing equals another).

Classification. To classify is the ability to place objects that are alike in the same class or category. A simple classification task would present a child with the following array of objects: one large red triangle, one large blue circle, one small red circle, and one small blue triangle. The child is asked to sort the objects into groups or to "put the objects together that belong together." A preoperational thinker might focus on a single dimension (an example of centration) and put the triangles together and the circles together. This is one way in which these objects "fit together." When asked if there is another way to group them, many young preoperational children would respond, "No." A concrete operational thinker, however, would group according to shape, then size, and then color.

In addition to understanding that objects possess multiple attributes that fit together with other objects, Piaget described concrete operational thinkers as being able to comprehend that there can be a hierarchy of groupings, which he called **hierarchical classification**. Children in the concrete operational stage begin to understand that smaller groups can be subsets of larger groups. For example, in a **class inclusion** task that assesses classification skills, Piaget would present a child with 18 brown wooden beads and 2 white wooden beads and ask the child, "Are there more brown wooden beads or wooden beads?" Concrete operational thinkers seem to recognize that brown wooden beads *and* white wooden beads belong to the larger class of wooden beads. Younger preoperational thinkers usually focus on the larger number and respond (incorrectly), "Brown wooden beads" (see Figure 5.2).

Understanding hierarchical classification assists in the understanding of numerical and mathematical concepts (e.g., subsets) as well as phenomena in the natural sciences where classifying plants and animals, natural elements, and types of rocks helps us organize and make sense of our physical world.

FIGURE 5.2

A Class Inclusion (Classification) Task

Successful completion of a classification task requires an understanding that both brown and white wooden beads belong to the larger group, wooden beads.

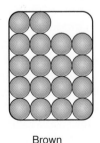   +   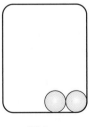   =   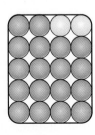

Brown   +   White   =   Wooden

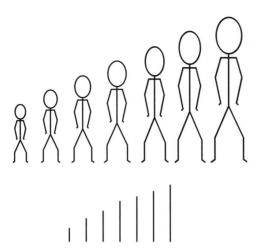

FIGURE 5.3
A Seriation Task Using Dolls or Sticks

In a seriation task a child is asked to put the dolls or sticks in order from the tallest to the shortest.

Finally, the tendency of school-age children to collect things is both a reflection of as well as practice in classification schemes. Collecting stamps, baseball cards, rocks, autographs, and American Girl dolls, for example, provides the school-age child with many opportunities to sort, group, and reorganize objects that share common attributes.

Seriation. Another logical operation of concrete thought is **seriation**, or the ability to mentally arrange elements according to increasing or decreasing size. When provided with different-sized sticks and asked to put them in order from the tallest to the shortest, preoperational thinkers usually can correctly identify the tallest and shortest, but have difficulty ordering the sticks in between (see Figure 5.3). Correct ordering of the sticks in a seriation task requires an understanding that stick A has a relationship to stick B (i.e., taller) *but also* and *at the same time* a relationship to stick C (i.e., taller or shorter).

The schema to understand seriation is created during the concrete operational period. The acquisition of decentration promotes comprehension of a series. Learning about seriation is similar to learning about conservation in that it emerges at different ages in the following sequence:

Seriation of length	Ages 7–8
Seriation of weight	Ages 9–10
Seriation of volume	Ages 11–12

Seriation is also demonstrated in school-age children's ability to order a series of events, such as the four seasons, or the order of holidays throughout the year.

Causality. Preschool children tend to believe that if two events occur together, one caused the other. During one of Piaget's interviews, for example, a young child reported that she causes the sun to rise by waking up in the morning (Piaget & Inhelder, 1969). These two events are paired together in her mind in a causal relationship. Children aged 7 to 11 tend to understand cause and effect more accurately. The implications of this cognitive development are that school-aged children are more curious about the origins of physical phenomena and may ask many questions that begin with "Why?" and "How come?" The science curriculum for this age group can be broadened to include experimentation (e.g., science fair projects) because experiments are of interest to this age group, and multiple causal connections can be explored and better understood.

In addition, more accurate reasoning about causality promotes social interactions. Concrete operational thinkers can now make the distinction between accidental versus intentional behavior and its consequences. This differentiation may influence the nature of a relationship between friends and peers, discussed further in chapter 10.

Seven- to eight-year-old children begin to accommodate their schemata so that logical or practical thought begins to dominate over perception of how things appear. They show gradual mastery over conservation tasks by employing decentration and reversible thought and by taking transformations into account. Their ability to understand hierarchical classification, seriation, and causality promotes a more realistic understanding of mathematics, history, and social studies. These cognitive advancements also apply to their view of themselves in the world and their relationships with others. Children in middle childhood, however, learn best when concepts are made more concrete or embedded within concrete contexts. Box 5.2 illustrates how teachers can make assignments more concrete.

STOP If you ever participated in a science fair, how old were you and what types of cognitive skills did you employ?

Basis of Cognitive Development

Piaget proposed that the basis on which one develops cognitively is influenced by *both* biological maturation *and* environmental stimulation. Normal physical maturation of the brain and central nervous system as well as motor development are essential for cognitive development to occur. Healthy neurological development, development of the senses, and the progression of motor skills are necessary for children to act on their environment, thereby making changes to their internal schemata. Equally influential, however, are the opportunities presented by one's surroundings. Children need to have the opportunity to experience and interact with their world and, as they mature, to explore and experiment with objects and people in their environment. Optimal cognitive development results from healthy brain and motor development coupled with opportunities to explore the world.

Think about how Anya's chess-playing experiences with her brother may influence the development of the cognitive skills required to play this game.

Piaget did not think that children should be pushed academically before they are cognitively ready to master concepts on their own. Attempts to teach preoperational children conservation skills, or concrete operational children formal operational skills, have not been successful (for a review, see Wadsworth, 1996). Piaget suggested that changes in schemata necessary for higher-order thinking come about only after considerable assimilation and accommodation of experiences and that premature direct instruction has little long-lasting effect. He also did not think that children need expensive or elaborate toys to facilitate learning. Rather, children learn through interacting with common objects found in their world, such as arranging sticks or shells or collecting dried leaves and reeds.

The Role of Culture

What role might culture play in the development of schemata, and how might it affect progress through the four stages of Piaget's theory? Research carried out with children from different cultural backgrounds shows differential progress through these stages (for a review, see Rogoff, 2003). Participation in formal schooling, for example, seems to facilitate logical problem-solving skills (Morrison, McMahon,

BOX 5.2   Roadmap to Successful Practice
Making School Assignments More Concrete

Piaget proposed that children during the middle childhood years learned more easily if concepts were presented more concretely (Piaget & Inhelder, 1969). What does it mean to make concepts more concrete? The following ideas were taken from a list compiled by a middle-school teacher under the heading of "active learning." Incorporating movement into his pedagogy and content, he has made the learning process more tangible, sensory-based, easily linked to past experience, and memorable; in other words, more concrete.

- With colored chalk, draw a huge interior diagram of the heart on the school parking lot or a sidewalk. Let the students walk through the diagram as you demonstrate how blood flows from the body into the heart through the chambers and valves, to the lungs, back to the heart, then out to the body again. They can narrate the process while walking or race to different sections by traveling the way the blood does. They can hold different-colored cards to represent oxygenated and unoxygenated blood. They can do crazy dances in the lung area to simulate the oxygen–carbon dioxide exchange.

- Encourage students to represent concepts and terms artistically. They can draw science cycles, dramatically portray atomic interactions, and sculpt with clay while describing the stages of the writing process.

- In science you can ask students to portray the earth, the moon, and the sun in a darkened room with a single light source, watching the changing shadow patterns on the students' bodies as they rotate and revolve.

- In English classes, adopt Victor Borge's idea of each punctuation mark representing a particular noise. A whistle, clap, or howl can substitute for commas, question marks, and quotation marks, respectively. Ask students to read dialogue between two characters aloud and, every time they come to a punctuation mark, to make the representative noises.

Source: From *Meet Me in the Middle: Becoming an Accomplished Middle-Level Teacher* (pp. 44–48) by Rick Wormeli, Copyright © 2001, with permission of Stenhouse Publishers.

Griffith, & Frazier, 1996). Studies have found that children who do not attend school, such as the Hausa of Nigeria, show delayed conservation skills and do not show mastery of conservation (e.g., number, length, and liquid) until age 11 or 12 (Fahrmeier, 1978). Others, such as Mongolian nomads, never demonstrate mastery of tasks from Piaget's final formal operational stage (Cole, 1990). Practice using reversible and transformational thought may account for these differences. For example, school activities and curricula appear to encourage the ordering of objects and learning about multiple ways that objects are related to one another. Children not exposed to these structured tasks may show delayed or absent reasoning skills on traditional conservation tasks.

However, cross-cultural research also has identified the nature of the task as equally predictive of children's performance. Children with little or no formal schooling did less well than schooled peers on Piaget's tasks *when they were presented in a traditional format*. On the other hand, when the tasks were embedded in a more familiar context, operational skills appeared *even in children with little formal education*. Six- to nine-year-old Brazilian street vendors who spent most of their time selling candy on the streets were presented with the following class inclusion task:

> For you to get more money, is it better to sell me the mint chewing gum or [all] the chewing gum? Why?

Using this more familiar and practical class inclusion task, the street vendors showed *greater* classification skills than more formally educated middle-class Brazilian children their same age (Ceci & Roazzi, 1994). Formal educational opportunities as well as familiarity and practice with the task may explain the variability children show in their cognitive skills throughout their middle childhood years.

Culture influences cognitive development in the opportunities it affords children in their everyday lives. For example, young Brazilian street vendors exhibit high-speed mathematical calculations. Mexican children who participate with their families in making pottery show conservation of quantity skills at a very young age (Price-Williams, Gordon, & Ramirez, 1969). Advanced spatial maps are developed by aboriginal youth in Australia, and Mayan children remember complex weaving patterns (Levinson, 1997; Maynard & Greenfield, 2003). These findings suggest that culture influences the everyday tasks in which children engage and consequently manifests its influence in the *types* of cognitive skills that emerge first and develop more quickly.

> *Anya and Alexandr's parents are immigrants from Russia, a country with a rich tradition in chess playing. Both parents are skilled players and play with their children often. Their cultural background influences Anya and Alexandr by giving them more opportunities to play this particular game and, for Anya, by having an older brother to tutor her.*

Piaget's theory has its critics. Some researchers believe that the clinical interview method is too flexible and does not provide consistency in the probe questions asked and, therefore, in the children's responses. Others argue that the problem-solving tasks he created are too unfamiliar to children and thus underestimate their cognitive abilities. Critics also point out that the proposed mechanisms of cognitive development such as equilibration, assimilation, and accommodation cannot be measured (for a review, see Feldman, 2003). Perhaps the most important criticism of all is that the problem-solving skills Piaget assessed should not be used as the standard of cognitive achievement. Children from immigrant cultures within the United States and from other countries may excel at other cognitive skills that are more adaptive to their environment (Mistry & Saraswathi, 2003).

Despite these criticisms, Piaget has provided us with a unique way of looking at cognitive development and a comprehensive theory that accurately describes differences in the ways that Western-schooled children think and learn about the world. His assessment about how cognition develops has direct implications for educational practice and has been incorporated into classrooms all over the world (Vergnaud, 1996). For example, Piagetian educators present material to children when they are "cognitively ready." In doing so, they allow students' current level of thinking to let them know when school-age children are ready to assimilate new

Guideposts for Working with School-Age Children

- Develop as many "hands-on" and experiential learning opportunities as possible because children learn best when they are active participants in the process.
- Spend more time on one theme or unit as opposed to introducing a new theme often to allow for optimal exploration and self-discovery by the students.

- Because children's cognitive skills may be influenced by their cultural experiences, try to capitalize on those experiences and make them part of the instruction.
- Evaluate children's learning and educational progress against their own performance.

material into their present cognitive structures. In other words, children's learning should never be rushed or hurried just to move on to a new unit. Practitioners who are sensitive to individual differences in rates of learning are also applying Piagetian theory. Because building on earlier schemata is essential to successful later learning, individualized instruction for each child or instruction in small groups with same-skilled children is optimal.

SOCIOCULTURAL PERSPECTIVE

Although Piaget's theory of cognitive development is taught widely and is perhaps more well known, there are alternative and complementary ways to think about how children learn and the factors that facilitate this development. Lev Vygotsky (1896–1934), a Russian psychologist, offered a different view of cognitive development. Whereas Piaget observed children constructing knowledge independently, Vygotsky believed that cognitive development was inextricably tied to the child's social and contextual environment. In other words, children's cognitive growth is constructed out of their interactions with others as well as the roles and expectations that are assigned to them in a given context.

> *For example, a 9-year-old girl like Anya who is taught to play chess through the mentoring of siblings, peers, and parents learns that this is an age-appropriate expectation of her culture and a desirable skill for her to develop.*

This sociocultural perspective would "observe the changing participation of children in sociocultural activity rather than aim to understand what pieces of knowledge or skill they have already 'acquired'" (Rogoff, 1996, p. 284). The units of analysis in this perspective are what the child says and does, how others respond to the child, and how these dynamics may change over time.

Developmental Components of the Theory

Vygotsky proposed that children's interactions with others in a social setting and their developing use of language or numbers create thought (Blanck, 1992). He suggested several ways that both the social context and others in that context specifically contribute to the development of knowledge.

According to Vygotsky, guidance from an older peer facilitates learning.

Anthony Magnacca/Merrill

Zone of Proximal Development. First, he defined the **zone of proximal development (ZPD)** as a range of skills or tasks that include on one end what a child can do easily alone and at the other what a child can do with assistance from another. Each child approaches a task with her own "zone of readiness" and learns from her interactions with others. Consider the following example from the chess-playing case study at the beginning of the chapter:

> *Alexandr watches Anya move her bishop incorrectly. "No, Anya," he says, "the bishop can only move diagonally," and he physically shows her the directions this piece can move. Later in the game, Anya puts her hand on her bishop and repeats to herself what Alexandr has told her, "only diagonally," and proceeds to move the piece correctly.*

Vygotsky's theory proposes that children take the dialogue from these interactions and convert it into **private speech**, or self-guiding speech, and use this speech to organize their own thoughts and behaviors (Vygotsky, 1988).

A zone of proximal development requires guidance or collaboration with a peer, an older sibling, a parent, teacher, or elder. These others can facilitate cognitive development by prompting, providing clues, modeling, explaining, questioning, discussing, encouraging, and holding the child's attention. Cognitive development occurs when a child is provided with a challenge just beyond her current competency level and then is assisted in her success by another. That assistance is internalized and becomes a part of the competency with which the child approaches another task. For example, research with Mexican American and African American children shows that students learn more in school when involved in group projects and cooperative learning assignments than when working alone (Landrine, 1995).

Scaffolding. Another method that is used intuitively by parents and teachers to assist children in their zones of proximal development is called *scaffolding*. **Scaffolding** refers to decreasing the amount of direct instruction provided to the child over the course of a single learning session.

> *In the chapter case study, as the game advances, Alexandr reduces the number of verbal corrections he gives Anya and eventually stops showing her how the pieces*

STOP Under what circumstances (e.g., a difficult task, an embarrassing situation) are you helped by using private speech (i.e., talking to yourself)?

move. (Alexandr sensed that Anya needed more explicit intervention at the beginning of the game and less as the game progressed.)

Research has shown that children who are exposed to effective scaffolding are more successful when asked to master the task on their own (Mattanah, Pratt, Cowan, & Cowan, 2005; McNeill, Lizotte, Krajcik, & Marx, 2006). Box 5.3 illustrates how scaffolding can be used in reading instruction.

Scaffolding tends to rely on verbal as well as physical instruction and describes well the transmission of knowledge that occurs when a child is performing a task or solving a problem. However, it also has been demonstrated that many children learn within informal contexts, such as when they observe a skilled adult perform a task without direct instruction. This type of learning is more accurately referred to as

 BOX 5.3   Roadmap to Successful Practice
Enhancing Reading Comprehension with Reciprocal Teaching

Reciprocal teaching is an interactive teaching technique designed to improve reading comprehension in children (Latendresse, 2004; Palinscar & Brown, 1984). It is based on the Vygotskian principles of zones of proximal development and scaffolding and requires the teacher and a small group of students (e.g., between two and four) to engage in a cooperative dialogue to enhance the understanding of a passage of text using four strategies:

1. Questioning
2. Summarizing
3. Clarifying
4. Predicting

Once the group has read a passage, the dialogue leader (at first the teacher, later a student) begins by asking questions about it. Students offer answers, raise additional questions, and in case of disagreement about content, reread the text. Next, the leader summarizes the passage, and students discuss the summary and clarify ideas that are unfamiliar to any group members. Finally, the leader encourages students to predict future content based on prior knowledge and clues in the text narrative. The four strategies ensure that students will link new information to previously acquired knowledge, explain their ideas, use what they have learned to acquire new knowledge, and keep their interaction goal oriented.

This exercise creates a zone of proximal development by providing the students with a passage of text that is just above their comprehension level. With the teacher's guidance, the students gain access to the necessary information to facilitate understanding. The teacher also exhibits scaffolding by first asking, explaining, and modeling the four strategies listed above and then gradually decreasing involvement and thereby making the students assume more responsibility for their learning.

Research shows that children from the primary through middle-school grades who experience reciprocal teaching show impressive gains in reading comprehension (Hashey & Connors, 2003; Lederer, 2000).

Learning occurs indirectly through the observation of skilled adults engaging in everyday tasks.

David W. Hamilton/Getty Images, Inc.

guided participation. Early observation gives way to guided participation until mastery of an everyday task is complete. A Mayan girl begins to learn to weave by watching her mother and other adult women weave on a loom. At age 5 she weaves leaves on a play loom, at age 7 she weaves with help from her mother, and by age 9 she weaves alone (Rogoff, 1990). Guided participation extends Vygotsky's notion of learning from structured and explicit learning situations (e.g., schools) to informal everyday contexts.

Basis of Cognitive Development

Vygotsky and other socioculturalists see biology and environment as intertwined and as forces that coconstruct development. Vygotsky suggested that one's biological predispositions—gender, temperament, or mental retardation—may be viewed and valued by one's culture differentially. For example, being a boy or girl, having a difficult or easy temperament, or having special needs influences how you interact with the world and how others respond to that interaction. Although socioculturalists acknowledge the role of biology in development, they tend to focus more on articulating and assessing the cultural forces that shape cognition.

The Role of Culture

Vygotsky's theory did not propose stages of cognitive development, nor did it summarize what 6- to 12-year-olds can or cannot cognitively accomplish. The absence of both universal stages and a summary of competencies reflects the very focus of this theory. There *are no* universal stages and competencies because children's learning is created by their individual sociocultural histories and interactional contexts. One's culture does not merely contribute *to* development. Rather, it *is* the context that is necessary for development to take place.

For example, in the United States, it is not until around age 10 that parents report feeling comfortable leaving their children to take care of themselves or younger children (Rogoff, 1996). By contrast, in San Pedro, located in the highlands of Guatemala, 3- to 5-year-old children are responsible for taking care of 1-year-old siblings. The difference in caretaking abilities between U.S. and Guatemalan children seems to emerge from differential sociocultural experiences and expectations. These 3- to 5-year-olds have grown up observing other children caring for younger siblings (i.e., guided participation) and most likely experiencing care by an older sibling themselves (i.e., scaffolding).

In addition, it is against Mayan cultural norms to force someone to cooperate against their will. San Pedro children treat their infant siblings with respect and autonomy and willingly subordinate their wishes to those of the infant. The result of this cultural experience is that children who care for younger children show less cognitive **egocentrism** and learn to become a cooperative and interdependent member of the community (Gaskins, 1999; Rogoff, 1996). This theoretical perspective places great emphasis on the role of culture as it is transmitted and embodied by siblings, parents, teachers, and elders in the community.

Critics of Vygotsky's theoretical perspective point to the vagueness of some of his developmental concepts. For example, the zone of proximal development, defined broadly, focuses our attention on the "readiness" of children to learn certain tasks with or without the assistance of others. But Vygotsky never suggests *what types* of mental representations are formed by these social interactions and *how* they are formed.

We also do not get a sense of how cognitive development influences the way children progress through the zone of proximal development. How do children's newly developed cognitions influence the way they interact with their environment? Finally, unlike Piaget, Vygotsky did not leave a legacy of tasks that allow us to see development clearly in children.

Vygotsky did, however, redirect our focus to several critical aspects of cognitive development. His proposal that language and social interaction are tools that help develop thought has spurred much research in this area. His emphasis on culture and context helps us understand the cultural variation we see in cognitive skills and correctly predicts multiple pathways of cognitive development (Guberman, 1999; Miller, 2002; Rogoff, 2003).

 What role did older siblings, friends, relatives, and other adults play in your learning and what did you learn from them?

 Guideposts for Working with School-Age Children

- Because siblings, parents, and teachers play an important role in children's cognitive development, involve them and others in all levels of instruction whenever possible.

- Include same-age or older peers in the learning process through peer tutoring or collaborative learning environments.

- Try to present tasks to children that are just above their competency level and that they can accomplish with help to increase children's joy and excitement in a challenge.

- Utilize scaffolding by providing children with modeling or clues so that you can gradually withdraw your support and they may begin to carry out the activity independently.

- Contextualize learning skills so that children see the connection between the skill and how it applies to their everyday lives.

- Focus assessments not on what children have learned but on what they can do with help to determine their readiness, or zone of proximal development.

Many of these practical suggestions are incorporated in the pedagogical philosophy of Maria Montessori. Although Maria Montessori's writings preceded the published works of both Piaget and Vygotsky, many of their theoretical assumptions about cognitive development are reflected in her teaching methods and educational philosophy, as presented in Box 5.4.

BOX 5.4   Roadmap to Successful Practice
The Montessori Approach

There are more than 4,000 Montessori schools throughout the United States. Each Montessori school builds on the educational legacy of Dr. Maria Montessori, who founded the first school in 1907. In Montessori schools throughout the world, children develop the habits and skills of lifelong learning. Guided by teachers trained to observe and identify children's unique learning capabilities, children learn in educational partnership with their teachers. Try to identify the components of the "Montessori Way" that reflect the theoretical ideas and suggestions of either Piaget, Vygotsky, or both.

1. *A Child-Centered Environment.* The focus of activity in the Montessori setting is on children learning, not on teachers teaching. Generally, students will work individually or in small, self-selected groups. There will be very few whole-group lessons.

2. *A Responsive Prepared Environment.* The environment should be designed to meet the needs, interests, abilities, and development of the children in the class. The educators should design and adapt the environment with this community of children in mind, rapidly modifying the selection of educational materials available, the physical layout, and the tone of the class to best fit the ever-changing needs of the children.

3. *A Focus on Individual Progress and Development.* Within a Montessori environment, children progress at their own pace, moving on to the next step in each area of learning as they are each ready to do so. Although the child lives within a larger community of children, each student is viewed as a universe of one.

4. *Hands-on Learning.* In a Montessori learning environment, students rarely learn from texts or workbooks. In all cases, direct, personal, hands-on contact with either real things under study or with concrete learning materials that bring abstract concepts to life allow children to learn with much deeper understanding.

5. *Spontaneous Activity.* It is natural for children to talk, move, touch things, and explore the world around them. Any true Montessori environment encourages children to move about freely, within reasonable limits of appropriate behavior. Much of the time the children select work that has been presented to them individually and that captures their interest and attention, although the Montessori educator also strives to draw their attention and capture their interest in new challenges and areas of inquiry. And even within this atmosphere of spontaneous activity, students do eventually have to master the basic skills of their culture, even if initially they would prefer to avoid them.

6. *Active Learning.* In Montessori learning environments, children not only select their own work from the choices presented to them but also continue to work with tasks, returning to continue their work over many weeks or months, until finally the work is so easy for them that they can demonstrate it to younger children. This is one of many ways that Montessori educators use to confirm that students have reached mastery of each skill.

7. *Self-Motivated Activity.* One of Montessori's key concepts is the idea that children are

(continued)

BOX 5.4   Roadmap to Successful Practice *(Continued)*
The Montessori Approach

driven by their desire to become independent and competent beings in the world, to learn new things and master new skills. For this reason, outside rewards to create external motivation are both unnecessary and can potentially lead to passive adults who are dependent on others for everything from their self-image to permission to follow their dreams. In the process of making independent choices and exploring concepts largely on their own, Montessori children construct their own sense of individual identity and personal judgment of right and wrong.

8. *Freedom within Limits.* Montessori children enjoy considerable freedom of movement and choice; however, their freedom always

exists within carefully defined limits on the range of their behavior. They are free to do anything appropriate to the ground rules of the community but are redirected promptly and firmly if they cross over the line.

9. *Self-Disciplined Learning.* In Montessori programs, children do not work for grades or external rewards, nor do they simply complete assignments given them by their Montessori educators. Children learn because they are interested in things and because all children share a desire to become competent and independent human beings.

Source: From *Twenty Best Practices of an Authentic Montessori School.* Retrieved from http://www.montessori.org. Copyright 2006 by the Montessori Foundation. Adapted by permission of the author.

INFORMATION-PROCESSING PERSPECTIVE IN MIDDLE CHILDHOOD

This theoretical perspective has emerged as a result of the rise of modern technology, most specifically the computer. When computer scientists began to create computer programs that took in information, matched it with existing information, analyzed, manipulated, transformed, and stored information, it appeared to some cognitive psychologists that this might be how humans process information as well. In the late 1960s a model was designed to simulate how humans think and learn (Shiffrin & Atkinson, 1969) (see Figure 5.4).

In the first stage, called the **sensory register**, individuals take in information from the outside world and hold it for a very short period of time (e.g., milliseconds). For

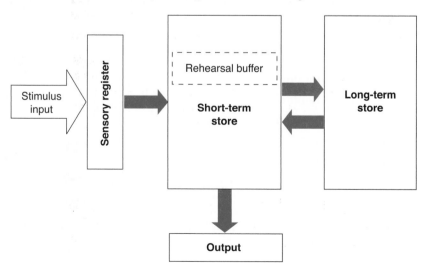

FIGURE 5.4
Information-Processing Model

A flowchart of the memory system.

Source: Based on "Storage and Retrieval Processes in Long-Term Memory," by Richard M. Shiffrin & Richard C. Atkinson, 1969, *Psychological Review, 76,* pp. 179–193. Copyright © 1969 by the American Psychological Association. Adapted by permission of the author.

example, your experience of reading this page might register in this first stage as black words on a white page, the weight of the book in your hands, the movement of your eyes across the page, and the sound of music in another room. The purpose of this phase of processing is to hold information in storage until attention is paid to certain elements of the experience. If attention is directed to the words on the page, for example, then this information is **encoded**, or transformed into a representation, and transferred to the second stage, called your **short-term memory**.

In the second stage, the new information is held for a longer period of time (e.g., 20–30 seconds) so that decisions about what to do with it can be made. You have to work quickly, though, because this store is very limited in capacity and information is very vulnerable to loss or interference. If you are motivated to retain the information from the page, then more processing of the information should occur (e.g., you might reread some parts of a paragraph or take notes on a section or practice memorizing an italicized word). As a result of processing this information more deeply, it will be transferred to **long-term store** (LTS).

Long-term store, the third stage in information processing, is unlimited in capacity, and the information stored lasts for a very long time. Information in long-term store, like the words on this page, gets stored along with similar information and is permanently ready for you to retrieve at a later date. When you are ready to use the information, it is called back to the short-term memory and is displayed as output in the form of a correct answer, idea, or behavior.

The focus of this perspective is on how information is encoded, manipulated, transformed, memorized, retrieved, and used in cognitive processing. It uses the computer as a metaphor for the human mind to help reduce, compartmentalize, and analyze the cognitive components that contribute to the process of learning.

Developmental Components of the Theory

The model shown in Figure 5.4 is based on how adults might process information. It does not suggest how cognitive processes develop over time or what influences their development or how children might process information differently from adults. Over the past few decades, developmental psychologists have focused their research on these developmental questions and have identified the following seven components as responsible for the increased cognitive processing exhibited by school-age children, adolescents, and adults (Schneider & Bjorklund, 2003):

1. Increased short-term store capacity
2. Faster speed of processing
3. Improved attentional focus
4. Improved mnemonic strategies
5. Increase in knowledge base
6. Greater automaticity
7. Greater metacognition

Short-Term Store (STS) Capacity. You read in the previous section that the short-term store is limited in capacity, or in the amount of information that it can hold. Capacity is usually measured by a **digit span task**, where a child must repeat, in exact order, a series of rapidly presented digits that increases in number of digits at every trial. Studies have shown that capacity increases with age. The memory span of 2-year-olds is about two items, 5-year-olds about four items, 7-year-olds about five items, 9-year-olds about six items, and the average span of adults is about seven items (Dempster, 1981). The greater the capacity of the STS, the more information it can hold to be manipulated and transferred to long-term store (LTS).

Speed of Processing. The amount of time it takes for children to encode the information that comes into their STS, transfer it to LTS, and retrieve information from LTS decreases with age (Luna, Garver, Urban, Lazar, & Sweeney, 2004). This means that as most children get older they process information faster. The advantage of greater speed of processing is that it gets information from STS to LTS faster, thus clearing space for more information to enter STS, increasing processing capacity (for a review, see Kail, 1995). These age differences are in part explained by maturational factors, such as myelination of neuronal axons (see chapter 3), and in part by experience with the tasks and material (Schneider & Bjorklund, 2003).

> *Notice how quickly Alexandr moves his chess pieces and how much longer it takes Anya to evaluate the board, calculate the consequences of her next move, and make her decision.*

Attention. **Selective attention** is the ability to ignore irrelevant stimuli or distractions and focus on just those aspects of a situation that are relevant to achieving the goals of the task. Researchers presented different-aged children with a stream of numbers on a computer screen and asked them to push a button whenever they saw a particular sequence of numbers (e.g., 1, 3, 9). Older children between 6 and 9 years of age showed markedly superior selective attention when compared to younger children (Lin, Hsiao, & Chen, 1999).

Selective attention develops as a result of **cognitive inhibition,** or the ability to ignore both internal and external distraction (e.g., irrelevant thought, behaviors, impulses). Gains in cognitive inhibition occur from early to middle childhood and into adolescence. The development of the frontal lobes is responsible for controlling irrelevant information and unwanted impulses. Studies have also found that damage to the frontal lobes increases distractibility in both children and adults (Dempster, 1995). By clearing the STS of irrelevant information, cognitive inhibition increases cognitive capacity in the same way as speed of processing does by freeing up more STS to apply to the task at hand.

Mnemonic Strategies. **Mnemonic strategies** are any strategies that aid in remembering. The most common mnemonic techniques used by school-aged children are **rehearsal**, repeating the to-be-remembered items, and **organization**, putting together words or objects that go together.

Rehearsal is typically studied by presenting the child with a list of related or unrelated items, one at a time, and asking them to "say aloud anything that is going on in your head to help you remember them." Children 5 years of age or younger tend not to rehearse at all. Six- to seven-year-olds engage in **passive rehearsal**, or single-item rehearsal (e.g., dog, dog, dog), and children in middle childhood begin to transition between passive and **active rehearsal**, or multi-item rehearsal (e.g., dog, cat, fish, dog, cat, fish) also known as **cumulative rehearsal** (Guttentag, Ornstein, & Siemens, 1987; Ornstein, Naus, & Liberty, 1975).

To study mnemonic organization, children are presented with a randomly ordered list of categorizable pictures or words printed on cards (e.g., animals, fruits, pieces of clothing, body parts). They are told to "sort the cards in any way that will help you remember them later." Children 5 years of age and younger tend to sort the cards randomly or in the order the cards were handed to them. Around ages 6 and 7, children begin to sort together items that are highly associated with one another (e.g., dog, cat, fish and apple, pear, orange). Eight- to eleven-year-old children consistently cluster highly associated items together and also less closely associated items together (e.g., dog, cat, goat, deer) (Bjorklund & de Marchena, 1984; Schneider, 1986). The developmental progression of these and other mnemonic strategies is shown in Table 5.2.

Research has shown a link between the effective use of a strategy and improved memory performance. Those children who use more active rehearsal or categorical sorting remember more words than those children who use passive rehearsal or very little grouping in their organizational strategies (Carr & Schneider, 1991; Cox et al., 1989).

A recent model of strategy development suggests that strategies do not develop one at a time in a unilinear way. Rather, as children develop they generate a variety of strategies, make a decision to use one or several strategies, and then modify their strategy choice the next time. Sometimes the strategy improves their performance,

TABLE 5.2   Approximate Ages by Which Most Children Spontaneously Display Various Memory Strategies Effectively for Children in Schooled Cultures[1]

Children develop better organizational and retrieval strategies during middle childhood as well the ability to apply more focused attention to a task.

	6–7 years	8–10 years	11–14 years
Single-item rehearsal	X		
Cumulative rehearsal			X
Organization with highly associated items	X		
Organization with less highly associated items		X	
Effective allocation of study time		X	
Retrieval strategies		X	
Elaboration[2]			X
Strategies for remembering complex text[2]			X

[1]Younger children than listed often display effective strategies when prompted.

[2]These strategies may not be displayed until later and many adults fail to use these strategies effectively.

Source: From "Memory and Knowledge Development" by W. Schneider & D. Bjorklund, 2003, in J. Valsiner & K. Connolly (Eds.), *Handbook of Developmental Psychology* (p. 378). Thousand Oaks, CA: Sage. Copyright 2003 by Jaan Valsiner and Kevin Connolly. Reprinted by permission of Sage Publications, Inc.

but sometimes—especially the first few times they try out a new strategy—it does not. Gradually the strategy that results in the best performance over time wins out (Siegler, 1996).

It appears that effective spontaneous strategy use develops from a number of different factors. An increase in STS capacity frees up space for more items to be rehearsed or grouped together, and increased speed of processing frees up cognitive capacity to be applied to more complex strategy use (Case, Kurland, & Goldberg, 1982). In addition, research has shown that both parents and teachers play a critical role in the development and use of mnemonic strategies. Parents and teachers are both explicit (e.g., they provide the phrase "Every Good Boy Does Fine" to remember a musical scale) and implicit (e.g., the parent organizes her grocery list by store aisle) in their memory instruction (Bjorklund, 2000; Moely, Santulli, & Obach, 1995).

Children who receive mnemonic advice tend to use strategies more and are better memorizers compared to those who receive little guidance. Practice with a task and familiarity with the materials also aids in strategy use. For example, children who memorize a list of spelling words every week during the school year have more strategy practice than children who do not engage in this academic exercise. They also may be more successful in their memory performance if they practice spelling words in familiar English (for English-speaking children) than if the words were presented in an unfamiliar language.

STOP When was the last time you had to remember something and what did you do to remember it?

Knowledge Base. A **knowledge base** is what children have stored in their long-term memory (LTS). It is their representation of world knowledge that is usually highly organized, with strong connections among items that are related. As children reach middle childhood, they have more experiences than younger children, gain more knowledge about the world, and increase the amount and richness of their knowledge bases. Research has shown that children who are more familiar with the to-be-remembered information (i.e., those who have richer and more extensive knowledge bases) recall that information better and typically implement mnemonic strategies faster and more effectively, producing better memory performance (i.e., better test scores). This developmental difference is not all that surprising, but what happens on memory tasks when the tables are turned and the *younger* child is the one who knows *more*? In a study, children who were advanced chess players (i.e., chess experts) were asked to memorize a series of chess positions on a chessboard. Their memory performance was compared to college-age chess novices (i.e., college students who knew very little about the game of chess). The younger children remembered more chess positions than the college students (Chi, 1978)! This and other studies point to the important role that knowledge base plays in improving cognitive performance by increasing the speed and ease with which information is moved and retrieved from LTS (Bjorklund & Schneider, 1996; Schneider, Bjorklund, & Maier-Bruckner, 1996).

Alexandr has a full repertoire of opening and closing moves from past playing experience from which to draw. He relies automatically on his past knowledge. Most of the positions on the chessboard are new to Anya, and she is just beginning to add to her knowledge base of chess positions and movements. Comparing new moves to what she knows takes effort, as does committing new moves to memory.

Cognitive Efficiency. When children are confronted with a new learning task, such as memorizing the capitals of the 50 states, they may spend considerable effort simply coming up with memory strategies to learn so much information. Consequently, their strategies may take so much mental effort that they have little attentional capacity left over to apply to remembering many of the capitals. As children gain practice on cognitive tasks, their performance becomes more **automatic**, or requires less attentional capacity, and therefore more attention can be applied to the to-be-learned material. This *automaticity*, or increased cognitive efficiency, takes place over time, with both practice and sufficient motivation (Guttentag, 1995). This is another explanation for why older children perform better on cognitive tasks than younger children. School-age children are able to implement cognitive strategies more automatically, thus leaving more room in STS for performing the learning task (i.e., transferring information into LTS) (Case, 1992).

> *With practice, the effort it takes Anya to recall moves and strategies will become more automatic, allowing her to focus on other aspects of the game.*

Metacognition. As children approach middle childhood they show improved **metacognitive skills**, or a more sophisticated understanding of how their mind and the minds of others works. They are more likely to describe the mind as an active, constructive agent that selects and transforms information (Flavell, 2000). This more mature understanding of the mind reflects an increase in **metamemory**, or a specific knowledge about what memory is, how it works, and what factors influence its functioning (Flavell, Miller, & Miller, 2002). Research has shown that older children are more aware that the type of cognitive task and the difficulty of the to-be-learned materials determines how much effort they need to put into the task as well as what their predicted success might be. For example, when compared to 6- to 7-year olds, 11-year-olds were more likely to report that memorizing pairs of opposites (e.g., boy, girl) would be easier than memorizing pairs of unrelated words (e.g. Mary, walk) (Kreutzer, Leonard, & Flavell, 1975).

Older children also more accurately estimate their memory abilities (e.g., how many words out of 100 could you remember if you were able to study them only once?). They allocate their study time appropriately (e.g., more study time needed for more difficult material) and realize that recall of gist is easier than verbatim memory and that sets of categorized items are easier to recall than sets of noncategorized items (O'Sullivan, 1996; Schneider, 1998). They are also much better at monitoring their cognitive progress, referred to as **self-monitoring**, and determining when the material has been learned sufficiently (Ringel & Springer, 1980).

In general, children's metamemory knowledge increases with age and is correlated with age-related improvements in memory behavior (Schneider & Lockl, 2002; Schneider & Pressley, 1997). Metamemorial knowledge may in part develop from a child's successes and failures in remembering but also from direct encouragement from parents and teachers. For example, a parent may ask a child to help create a way to remember a permission slip that is due the next day and then discuss why the method worked or didn't work. Contemporary memory strategy training programs usually include some metamemory component that teaches children to assess their performance when using different types of cognitive strategies and to attribute their relative performance to these various strategies (Schneider & Pressley, 1997).

STOP Were you taught explicitly how to remember? If so, what suggestions were provided you?

CHAPTER 5 Cognitive Development in Middle Childhood

Basis of Cognitive Development

The information-processing perspective recognizes the contributions of both nature and nurture. Biological brain maturation increases brain capacity, myelination of neuronal axons increases the speed of processing, and frontal lobe development may influence the development of selective attention and cognitive inhibition that improve the child's ability to focus on the task at hand and ignore distracting stimuli. Equally important are the practice opportunities provided by a child's home and educational environments. Explicit and implicit memory instruction from peers, parents, and teachers facilitates mnemonic strategy development and increases metamemorial knowledge. Informal practice, such as playing memory games, may encourage the automatization of strategies, and knowledge acquisition from a child's environment may improve cognitive performance. Box 5.5 provides an example of how neurological and environmental factors interact in children who have attentional processing disorders.

The Role of Culture

Children educated in an American school system typically exhibit the cognitive competencies defined by the information-processing perspective. When information-processing tasks, such as the ones described in the previous section, are administered to children from different cultural and educational backgrounds, differences in abilities are noted. For example, Chinese children show greater short-term memory capacity for numbers because the terms for the digits 1 to 9 are shorter in Chinese and can be articulated more rapidly, thereby allowing more numbers to be rehearsed together (Chen & Stevenson, 1988).

Nine-year-old children from Guatemala remember the placement of more objects (out of a total of 40) than American 9-year-olds who tried to rehearse the objects in a list. The experience that these Guatemalan children have had with spatial memory in producing complex weaving designs proved useful in this memory task (Rogoff & Waddell, 1982). The mathematical calculating abilities of 6- to 9-year-old Brazilian candy vendors based on need and practical experience exceed the calculating ability of their American counterparts (Saxe, 1988). The experience and expectations of one's culture has a significant influence on the types of memory and problem-solving skills required and produced by children of all ages.

The computer metaphor provides the information-processing perspective with some of its strengths, but this model fails to communicate the different ways children may learn in different contexts. For example, although information processors acknowledge the contributions of the environment, the model fails to articulate how that give-and-take interaction occurs. The model also does not explain well the development of creativity and imagination, or thinking "outside the box," and it does not outline how human factors such as motivation and emotional arousal enhance or interfere with cognitive processing.

However, the information-processing approach provides us with an accurate portrayal of the complexity of thought. It also breaks down the complexity of cognition into its components and shows developmental differences in these components as well as what influences their development. The approach proposes very specific mechanisms of development and offers rigorous and precise methods to assess cognitive development. This has allowed very specific applications to be made to educational settings.

BOX 5.5   Roadmap to Understanding Theory and Research
The Relationship Between ADHD, School Performance, and Reading Comprehension

ADHD is **attention deficit disorder** with **hyperactivity** (American Psychiatric Association, 2000). It is estimated that approximately 1 to 5% of children have ADHD, with boys diagnosed three to nine times more often than girls. The main characteristic of this disorder is the inability of children to inhibit their behavior. This inability manifests itself in impulsivity, poor attention, an inability to complete a task or adhere to rules of social conduct, and, for many children, overactivity (Barkley, 2000).

It should come as no surprise that in a school setting that requires children to sit still, attend, listen, obey, inhibit impulsive behavior, cooperate, organize actions, and follow through on instructions, children with ADHD do poorly. They seem to have at least two main problems with academic work: (1) They are not getting as much done as non-ADHD children, and so have lower grades and are retained more often. Approximately one third of these children will be retained in at least one grade before reaching high school, and ADHD children are more likely than their classmates to drop out of school or be suspended. (2) Their ability levels are also somewhat below those of children without ADHD and may decline over time. Children with ADHD are more likely to have learning disabilities (LDs), with 20 to 25% of them having a reading disorder (Barkley, 2000).

How, specifically, does ADHD affect children's information-processing capabilities and therefore academic performance? Research has found that ADHD is associated with deficits in sustained attention and "executive functioning," which enables a school-aged child to engage successfully in independent, purposive, self-serving behavior. Executive functioning includes nonverbal working memory, internalization of speech, self-monitoring, and self-regulation (Barkley, 1998; Perugini, Harvey, Lovejoy, Sandstrom, & Webb, 2000). Researchers have also found that when asked to generate a list of words all beginning with the same letter, children with ADHD show a delay in the first 15 seconds of the task. This delay reflects insufficient automating skills for processing verbal information (Hurks et

al., 2004). Children with ADHD also show poorer story recall (Lorch et al., 2004).

Interventions at home and in the classroom tend to focus on space and time management. For example, parents might ensure that their child has a quiet place to study with minimal distraction. Teachers might provide the child with shorter blocks of instruction and frequent opportunities to engage in physical activity. These modifications in the learning environment are helpful, but recent research suggests that parents and teachers could play a more critical role in the learning process.

A series of studies examined children's story comprehension (Lorch et al., 2004; Lorch et al., 1999; Lorch, Eastham, Milich, & Lemberger, 2004; Lorch, Milich, & Sanchez, 1998). A story comprehension task was chosen because successful comprehension requires multiple cognitive skills: the strategic allocation of attention; the selection, encoding, and interpretation of important information; the retrieval of relevant background information; the generation of inferences; and the monitoring of comprehension. In one study (Figure 5.5), 7- to 11-year-old children listened to one of two folktales on audiotape and recalled the story both before and after studying a written version for up to 10 minutes. Non-ADHD children recalled more causal connectors, or themes that moved the story along, than ADHD children. In addition, there was no difference in studying time between the two groups. These findings showed that study time alone does not improve story comprehension for children with ADHD. These children experience difficulty extracting and encoding the main events and then constructing a coherent story from memory, not simply slower processing.

Based on these findings, one practical intervention strategy would be to assist the child in pulling out the connected or causal events of a story and putting them into a more memorable form. For example, parents or teachers might ask why certain events occurred in the story or have the children predict what might come next based

(continued)

BOX 5.5   Roadmap to Understanding Theory and Research *(Continued)*
The Relationship Between ADHD, School Performance, and Reading Comprehension

on prior events. The researchers suggest that the story comprehension task they used approximates some of the academic requirements of a classroom, such as listening to directions, stories, or lectures. This connecting ability is critical when children in grade 4 and higher are required to read chapters of texts or lengthy books, extract the main ideas, and connect the information together to be remembered at a later time. More direct intervention techniques like the one suggested here might prove to be more beneficial for children with ADHD.

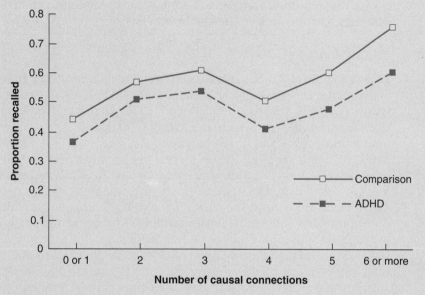

FIGURE 5.5

Proportion of Events Recalled as a Function of Diagnostic Group and Number of Causal Connections

Children with ADHD recall fewer causal connections when listening to a story, compared to non-ADHD children.

Source: Copyright © 2004 from "Story Comprehension and the Impact of Studying on Recall in Children with Attention Deficit Hyperactivity Disorder," by E. P. Lorch et al., *Journal of Clinical Child and Adolescent Psychology, 33,* p. 511. Reproduced by permission of Tylor & Francis Group, LLC., http://www.taylorandfrancis.com.

 Guideposts for Working with School-Age Children

- Because selective attention improves with age, help younger school-age children avoid distractions by providing them with quiet work and study environments at home and school.

- Help children focus attention on the relevant information by asking questions about the main ideas of a story or having them outline the steps of their solution to a math problem.

- Use instructional activities that will capture and hold children's interest by incorporating physical activity into the lesson or by using examples or materials that are currently popular (e.g., movies, video games).

- Discuss with children how one might remember better and let them share their strategies with one another. Be explicit about what mnemonic strategies are and how and why they work.

- Help children to set their learning goals and monitor their progress towards those goals.

DEVELOPMENT IN CONTEXT

All three theoretical perspectives presented in this chapter recognize, to varying degrees, the role that the environment plays in the intellectual functioning and growth of children. As developmental scientists examine the everyday experiences of children, they have realized that children's cognition develops—not in a vacuum—but in social contexts rich with opportunities for active observation, modeling, and dialogue with others (Gauvain, 2001; Rogoff, Paradise, Mejia Arauz, Correa-Chavez, & Angelillo, 2003). Research shows that cognitive development is shaped by the social learning opportunities—or lack thereof—provided by parents, teachers, schools, neighborhoods, communities, and cultures. And, in turn, children's cognitive status influences how they respond to or are treated by others.

Family Context

During middle childhood, parents are still largely responsible for influencing which activities the child engages in as well as the child's level of participation in these activities (Gauvain & Savage, 1995; Rogoff, 1998). To this end, parents shape the cognitive opportunities to which the child is exposed. An example of how family interaction shapes the development of a cognitive skill is the study of **planning skills**. Planning skills are the deliberate organization of a sequence of actions oriented toward achieving a specific goal (Gauvain, 1999). For example, planning skills are required to complete homework within a designated period of time, or to retrieve water successfully from the community well. Throughout middle childhood, children show good conceptual understanding of planning and when it is needed. They are capable of planning longer sequences of steps, are able to use knowledge of familiar events to plan flexibly, and consider more alternatives and correct their planning errors more readily during execution (Hudson & Fivush, 1991). Research suggests that social interaction is an important context for the development of planning skills. Children learn about the process of planning as they coordinate plans with others; however, the content of what is planned, the overall goals of planning, and the opportunity for practice reflect the values and goals of the family.

For example, one study asked 7- to 10-year-old schoolchildren to report on their involvement in planning activities during nonschool hours (Gauvain & Huard, 1999). Children were asked about the nature and extent of their after-school activities, along with who was responsible (child, parent, or both) for planning these activities. Results indicated that children's responsibility for planning their own after-school activities increased with age. For many children however, there was little free time after school to plan, either on their own or with peers, because their time was filled with adult-determined and planned obligations. Children with full schedules, largely determined by adults, reported feeling more stress during the day than children with more free time (Guavain & Huard, 1999).

In sum, during middle childhood, school-age children have opportunities to develop planning skills in the family context, but these opportunities are affected in important ways by the cultural values and practices held by the family.

School Context

How might the experience of formal schooling affect and be affected by the development of cognitive skills? Earlier in this chapter we discussed how schooled and nonschooled children performed differently on formal cognitive tasks. This difference was largely due to familiarity with the task materials and experience with the task. How might the structural or pedagogical characteristics of a formal classroom shape the development of a cognitive skill? We know that, for example, when teachers are explicit in their learning strategy instruction and offer specific strategies to try, children are not only more likely to exhibit these strategic skills, but show improved learning benefits in the classroom as well (Moely, Hart, Leal, Santulli, Rao et al., 1992).

Teachers who use collaborative problem-solving techniques in the later elementary school grades find that specific cognitive skills are required and enhanced through this process. In one study, pairs of 10- to 11-year-old children worked on a computer task that involved scientific reasoning (Teasley, 1995). They were to figure out how a spaceship moved and discover the function or purpose of an unlabeled computer key. The results showed that the amount of task-related talk in which the children engaged was related to success on the task. When the dialogue between the two children was examined, researchers found that children benefited from having to examine and consider the thoughts of their partner. Additional research shows that problem-solving with a peer is made even more effective if feedback is provided by the teacher (Ellis, Klahr, & Siegler, 1993).

Community Context

As was described in chapter 1, children in middle childhood are coming of age during a technology-rich period in our cultural history. Most children in the United States have access to television, and many have access to computers, either in the school or at home. Much has been written about the physical and social effects of increased time spent with this technology (Huston & Wright, 1997). How might the increased exposure to television watching, Internet use, and video games influence cognitive development?

In a national study, researchers asked children under 12 and their parents to report on the titles of television programs, videotapes, and electronic games that the children viewed and the time spent on each. Results showed that children, ages 9–12, spent an average of 14 hours per week viewing television (Subrahmanyam, Greenfield, Kraut, & Gross, 2001). Girls watched more educational programming and boys watched significantly more noneducational programming such as cartoons (Wright et al., 2001). Available evidence shows that educational television programs developed for middle childhood audiences are successful in improving viewers' problem-solving abilities (Hall, Esty, & Fisch, 1990) and science knowledge (Clifford, Gunter, & McAleer, 1995). For example, results of two studies on the effectiveness of *Cro*, a Saturday-morning cartoon about science and technology aimed at 6- to 11-year-olds, indicated that watching *Cro* increased children's understanding of technology, especially for girls (see Fisch, 1998 for a review).

Time spent viewing noneducational television, however, is negatively related to academic achievement. In other words, the more time spent watching noneducational television in middle childhood, the lower are grades, IQ, and achievement test scores (Anderson, Huston, Schmitt, Linebarger, & Wright, 2001).

Children between 2 and 17 years in homes with computers spent approximately 1 hour, 37 minutes a day on computers (Stanger & Gridina, 1999). Computer use was divided between the Internet and computer games. Research shows that the Internet is used mostly to help with schoolwork, for communication purposes, and for fun, such as looking up information on interests and hobbies, and downloading music. Boys and girls who are between the ages of 8 and 13 use the Internet equally for educational purposes. African American children use the Internet less often than do White children. This finding may be related to children's socioeconominc status and their access to computers. A recent study examining the use of the Internet in low-income families showed that academic achievement, as measured by grades, and standardized test scores of reading achievement increased as a result of increased use of Internet resources (Jackson et al., 2006).

In a national sample of children in middle childhood, boys spent 6.25 hours and girls 4.41 hours a week playing video games. Research shows that playing video games contributes to the development of cognitive skills, specifically to visual skills (Subrahmanyam, Kraut, Greenfield, & Gross, 2000). For example, computer games are designed to shift the balance of information processing, from verbal to visual. Playing action games that involve rapid movement, imagery, required interaction responses, and multiple activities occurring simultaneously improves visual skills, such as spatial representation, iconic skills, and divided visual attention, all components of visual intelligence (De Lisi & Wolford, 2002; Subrahmanyam et al., 2001).

Although video games may enhance children's ability to mentally rotate objects or keep track of events at multiple locations, children may not have the cognitive capacity to multitask as well as they think they do. When children think they are instant messaging friends, listening to music, and doing homework all at once, they are not. Their brains are not processing all of this stimulation simultaneously, but sequentially. In other words, they are switching attention from one task to the other. Neuroscience studies tell us that the part of the brain responsible for switching attention from one task to another is the prefrontal cortex (right behind the eyes). This part of the brain is not fully developed until late adolescence, which explains why children do not multitask as well as adults. When they try to multitask, they make more errors and take longer to get each task accomplished than if they had completed them sequentially (Dreher & Grafman, 2003; Rubinstein, Meyer, & Evans, 2001).

Cognitive skills do not develop independently from the contexts within which children develop. Family interactions, school environments, and one's cultural tools influence the types of cognitive skills that develop, how well they develop, and the timing of their development in school-age children.

When children multi-task, they make more errors and take longer to complete the task.

David Young-Wolff/PhotoEdit Inc.

CHAPTER REVIEW

Piaget's Theoretical Perspective

- According to Piaget's theory of cognitive development, children learn by experiencing cognitive disequilibrium. Through the processes of assimilation and accommodation children add to schemata to enhance their understanding of the world.

- Children in middle childhood are in Piaget's stage of concrete operational thought that spans ages 7 to 11.

- Concrete operational thinkers are able to conserve because they can decentrate and can engage in reversible and transformational thinking. They can also understand hierarchical classification, seriation, time and space, and causality. Their thought is logical and based on concrete objects and experiences.

- Piaget's theory of cognitive development recognizes the equal contribution of biology and environment in the development of cognition. Piaget's theory best describes the development of problem-solving skills in a Western educational setting.

Sociocultural Perspective

- Vygotsky's theory of cognitive development proposes that cognition arises out of children's interactions with their environments and the expectations of their cultural contexts.

- Through zones of proximal development, scaffolding, and guided participation children are active participants in the learning process.

- Vygotsky's theory places much greater emphasis on the role of culture in a child's learning and is particularly useful as we gain more knowledge about the diversity of development.

Information-Processing Perspective

- The information-processing model uses the computer as a metaphor for learning and examines the role of attention and memory in how children process information.

- Children in middle childhood have increased short-term memory capacity. They process information more quickly, exhibit improved attention, and use more sophisticated mnemonic strategies. Their knowledge base is more extensive, their skills become more automatic, and they have greater metacognitive understanding. All of these components add together for a more efficient, quicker and sophisticated learner.

- The information-processing approach recognizes equal contributions from nature and nurture, with children's cultural experiences influencing the type and rate of skill development.

Development in Context

- The contributions of families in the cognitive lives of children manifest themselves in the cognitive opportunities they afford them. The development of planning skills, for example, is based on children's observations of their parent's planning skills, direct and indirect guidance by parents, and focus on the values on which parents place a high priority.

- The structure and pedagogical philosophies of a school may have a direct impact on which cognitive skills are emphasized and thereby identified as most critical for success in that culture.

- Exposure to electronic and digital environments appears to be shaping the cognitive skills of those children who engage in their use.

TABLE 5.3   Summary of Developmental Theories

Chapter	Theories	Focus
4: Cognitive Development in Middle Childhood	Cognitive Developmental	How children develop thought and problem-solving skills in direct interaction with the environment through the processes of assimilation and accommodation
	Sociocultural	Development of thought through language development and interacting with elders from one's culture
	Information Processing	Children process information through perception, memory, and knowledge and the factors that influence their development

KEY TERMS

Accommodation
Active rehearsal
Adaptation
ADHD
Assimilation
Automatic
Behaviorism
Classical conditioning
Class inclusion
Cognitive disequilibrium
Cognitive inhibition
Concrete operational stage
Conservation
Conserve

Constructivist view
Cumulative rehearsal
Decentration
Digit span task
Egocentric thought
Egocentrism
Encoded
Equilibration
Formal operational stage
Guided participation
Hierarchical classification
Invariant
Knowledge base
Long-term store

Metacognition
Metacognitive skills
Metamemory
Mnemonic strategies
Operant conditioning
Operation
Organization
Passive rehearsal
Planning skills
Preoperational stage
Private speech
Reciprocal teaching
Rehearsal
Reversibility

Scaffolding
Schema
Selective attention
Self-monitoring
Sensorimotor stage
Sensory register
Seriation
Short-term memory
Transformation
Universal
Zone of proximal development (ZPD)

SUGGESTED ACTIVITIES

1. Conduct several conservation tasks with children of different ages. Table 5.1 provides you with an outline of several conservation tasks.

2. Observe children in a classroom, social gathering (e.g., Girl Scouts or Boy Scouts), after-school activity, athletic practice or event, a church service or church-related event, or at home. Record examples of scaffolding and guided participation. What is being learned? Who is teaching, who is learning, and what is the interactive process, if any?

3. On a set of index cards make two lists. One list should consist of the picture and printed word of 16 common items (e.g., ball, cup, shoe). The other list should con-

sist of the picture and printed word of 16 common items that belong to four separate groups (e.g., four fruits, four pieces of clothing, four modes of transportation, and four tools). Using these two lists, monitor the types of rehearsal and organizational strategies different-aged children use as they try to remember the lists of unassociated and then associated items.

4. Ask different-aged children the following metamemory questions: "How many words out of 100 could you remember if you could study them only once?" "How would you remember to bring your skates to school tomorrow?" These questions assess a child's metacognitive skills.

RECOMMENDED RESOURCES

Suggested Readings

Berk, L. E. (2001). *Awakening children's minds: How parents and teachers can make a difference.* New York: Oxford University Press.

DuPaul, G. J., & Stoner, G. (2003). *ADHD in the schools: Assessment and intervention strategies* (2nd ed.). New York: Guilford.

Lillard, A. S. (2005). *Montessori: The science behind the genius.* New York: Oxford University Press.

Rogoff, B. (2003). *The cultural nature of human development.* New York: Oxford University Press.

Wadsworth, B. J. (1996). *Piaget's theory of cognitive and affective development: Foundations of constructivism* (5th ed.). White Plains, NY: Longman.

Suggested Online Resources

Attention Deficit Hyperactivity Disorder. (2006). http://www.nimh.nih.gov/publicat/adhd.cfm

Bergen, D. (2004). *Play's Role in Brain Development.* http://www.acei.org/brainspeaks.pdf

Streaming Video of Piagetian Tasks http://www.soe.jcu.edu.au/subjects/ed1481/movies/

Suggested Web Sites

Annenberg Public Policy Center . http://www.annenbergpublicpolicycenter.org/05_media_developing_child/media_developing_child.htm

Building the Field of Digital Media and Learning. http://www.digitallearning.macfound.org/site/c.enJLKQNlFiG/b.2029199/k.BFC9/Home.htm

The Montessori Foundation. http://www.montessori.org

National Institute on Media and the Family. http://www.mediafamily.org/facts/index.shtml

Suggested Films and Videos

Concrete operations. With David Elkind, Ph.D. (1993). Davidson Films (25 minutes)

Maria Montessori: Her life and legacy. (2004). Davidson Films (35 minutes)

Piaget's developmental theory: An overview. (1989). Davidson Films (25 minutes)

Scaffolding self-regulated learning in primary classrooms. With Elena Bodrova, Ph.D. and Deborah Leong, Ph.D. (1996). Davidson Films (35 minutes)

Vygotsky's developmental theory: An introduction. (1994). Davidson Films (28 minutes

The wonder years, episode 25: "Math class." (1989). New World Entertainment

6

Literacy, Intelligence, and Academic Achievement

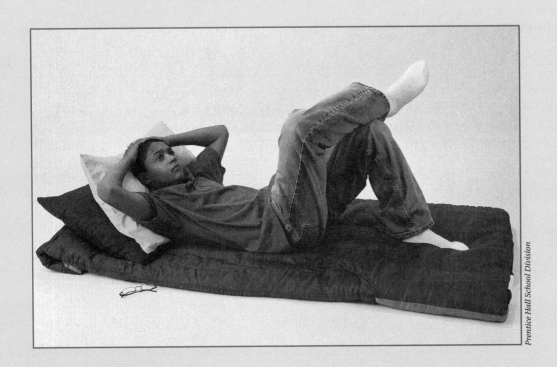

Prentice Hall School Division

After reading this chapter, students will be able to:

▶ Translate how changes in cognition throughout middle childhood are reflected in language development, reading, writing, mathematical skills, and scientific reasoning.

▶ Define a psychometric approach to intellectual functioning in middle childhood.

▶ Identify the constructs of creativity and its relationship to intelligence and other attributes.

▶ Understand the variables related to academic achievement in school-age children.

▶ Discuss the contributions of family, school, and community contexts to the development of language and literacy skills, intelligence, creativity, and academic achievement.

It is 10:00 A.M. Saturday morning and 12-year-old Kevin is lying in bed wondering how he did on his California Achievement Test (CAT). He felt pretty good about his performance on the math items, but he thought the reading comprehension sections were really difficult. He knows that good scores are desirable and will please his parents, but he worries because he typically does not do as well on these tests as his older sister did. He has to work very hard in school to achieve good grades, and he doesn't find school all that interesting or relevant. Kevin is very good with his hands and tools and thinks he might like to be a carpenter or designer.

APPLIED COGNITION IN ACADEMIC CONTEXTS

Although cognitive theories provide us with explanations of *how* cognition might develop, it is less clear how cognitive development is related to language acquisition or to learning specific skills in an academic setting. Cognitive changes in school-age children contribute to, and are reflected by, change in children's language, literacy, and mathematical skills during middle childhood. These skills define "intelligence" in our culture, and their development predicts how well school-age children perform in school and on national achievement tests.

Language Development

The foundation of language development is established during the preschool and early elementary school years. School-age children, however, continue to refine their language skills in several domains. For example, their understanding of word meaning, or **semantic** development, continues throughout middle childhood. A first grader may know the meaning of 8,000 to 14,000 words, but a high-schooler knows 80,000 words (Owens, 1996). These numbers are equivalent to the acquisition of 6,200 words per year between first grade and graduating from high school. The understanding that words have multiple meanings also increases. This more complex understanding of word use may be attributed, in part, to cognitive development.

With the advancement of cognition children become better communicators and possess a more sophisticated sense of humor. A related advancement is that school-age children also begin to comprehend the use of idioms, such as "Who let the cat out of the bag?" Research shows that the comprehension of multiple word use, idioms, and forms of sarcasm may not occur until adolescence (Bloom, 1998). Semantic development in middle childhood seems to rely heavily on the context of the conversation and children's ability to figure out the meaning of a word or phrase by what another person intended to say, rather than a literal interpretation of word choice (Baumann, Font, Edwards, & Boland, 2005; Cain, Oakhill, & Elbro, 2003).

Syntax development, or grammatical understanding and construction, expands during middle childhood. Children begin to understand the difference between active and passive voice (O'Grady, 1997). If given a toy car and truck and asked to show the experimenter "the car hit the truck" and "the car was hit by the truck," a 10-year-old is more likely than a 6-year-old to play out the scene of both statements correctly. The older child will listen to the meaning of the statements rather than automatically link the action of the verb to the nearest noun. Older children also begin to understand and use more sophisticated syntactical rules, such as the correct use of subject-verb and noun-pronoun agreement, correct uses of *that* and *which* to introduce subordinate clauses, and the proper use of punctuation such as colons and semicolons. During middle childhood, children also begin to learn how to use the articles *a* and *the* correctly as well as understand connectives, such as *but, although, yet, however,* and *unless* (Vion & Colas, 2004).

Middle childhood is also the period in which children improve on the **pragmatics** of language, or the social etiquette of language. For example, school-age children become better at maintaining and contributing to a conversation by asking questions and adding information. Between ages 5 and 9, children become better at **shading,** or changing the topic during a conversation. They do so more gradually and tactfully than younger children. This results from an increasing awareness of the needs of the listener. As children move through middle childhood they become more aware of when they are misunderstood and do a better job of clarifying their meaning by changing or adding words to their sentences (Ninio & Snow, 1996).

Compared to preschool and early elementary schoolchildren, children from 6 to 12 years of age are more effective communicators, use more complex grammatical constructions, and are more aware of their role as a listener and communicator within multiple contexts. Greater diversity among language skills in older children results largely from environmental factors. Children with larger vocabularies, more complex grammar, and social language manners have been shown to come from homes with two parents and parents with higher educational backgrounds and income levels. They also converse with their parents more often and have more positive speech interactions with them (Hoff & Tian, 2005; Weigel, Martin, & Bennett, 2005). The differences in language development influenced by these factors are evident by kindergarten and remain stable through adolescence (Farkas & Beron, 2004).

One's cultural background has been shown to influence language development as well. In the development of pragmatics, for example, American children often argue with their older siblings and sometimes speak to them with disrespect. In contrast, children from Japan are expected to speak to elders, which includes older siblings, with respect at all times. In Western societies children are expected to speak up and ask questions when they have them. But Mexican American and Southeast Asian communities, as well as some African American communities from the Southeast, teach children to engage in conversation with an adult only when the adult initiates the conversation (Grant & Gomez, 2001). Thus, vocabulary, grammar use, and pragmatics are influenced by the language culture that surrounds the child. Children's language development will affect their ability to learn in school and converse with others (Craig & Washington, 2004; Gonzalez, 2005).

Reading

Just as in language development, much of the foundation for reading has been laid prior to preschool, during preschool, and in the early elementary grades (K–3). Identifying letters and matching letters with individual sounds, knowing what a word is, and interpreting spaces and punctuation are the earliest building blocks for reading skills. By third grade, children engage in rapid word recognition (made easier by increased vocabularies) and are capable of self-monitoring their reading comprehension (Howes, 2003).

In the United States, fourth grade is considered a critical point in the elementary school experience. Grade 4 is the year in which the linguistic, cognitive, and conceptual demands of reading increase substantially. These greater demands emerge largely as a result of the increased reliance on textbooks as the main instructional tool. There are also greater expectations for independent reading and writing; more unfamiliar, specialized, and technical vocabulary; more complex syntax in textbooks; increased requirements for **inferencing,** or drawing conclusions from existing information; and using prior knowledge to "figure things out." It is also the point at which children who had been previously successful begin to experience reading difficulties, perhaps because of these increased demands (Allington & Johnston, 2002). Fourth grade has been described as a transitional year in which reading shifts from learning to read to reading to learn (Chall, 1983; Ely, 1997).

For some children, their developing cognition prepares them to deal with increased demands on their intellectual competencies. For example, increases in selective attention and speed of processing, which occur with age and practice, allow for more rapid decoding and word recognition (Beers, 2003). These two processes are critical for the development of reading skills and comprehension. Problems with decoding and/or word recognition are a possible source of poor reading ability as suggested in Box 6.1.

BOX 6.1   Roadmap to Understanding Theory and Research
The Acquisition of Reading and Its Relationship to Later Reading Disabilities

Skilled readers are able to derive meaning from printed text accurately and efficiently. Research has shown that in doing so, they fluidly coordinate many component skills, each of which has been sharpened through instruction and experience over many years. Figure 6.1 illustrates the major "strands" that are woven together during the course of becoming a skilled reader. It is customary to consider separately the strands involved in rec-ognizing individual printed words from those involved in comprehending the meaning of the string of words that have been identified, even though those two processes operate (and develop) interactively rather than independently (Committee on the Prevention of Reading Difficulties in Young Children, 1998).

There are a number of hypotheses as to what is responsible for poor reading skills; however, many

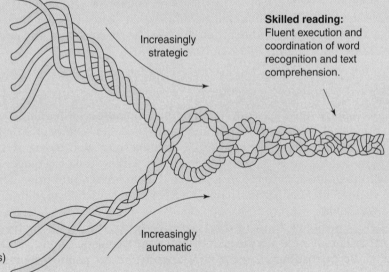

FIGURE 6.1

Illustration of the Many Strands That Are Woven Together in Skilled Reading

The ability to read requires the mastery of word recognition and language comprehension. Poor reading skills can result in difficulty with any number of strands.

Source: From "Connecting Early Language and Literacy to Later Reading (Dis)Abilities: Evidence, Theory, and Practice," by Hollis S. Scarborough, in Susan B. Neuman & David K. Dickinson (Eds.), 2001, *Handbook of Early Literacy Research,* Vol. 1 (p. 98). New York: Guilford. Copyright © 2001 by The Guilford Press. Reprinted by permission of the publisher.

(continued)

> **BOX 6.1   Roadmap to Understanding Theory and Research** *(Continued)*
> *The Acquisition of Reading and Its Relationship to Later Reading Disabilities*
>
> children who have trouble learning to read in the early school years stumble in mastering the "word recognition" strands. They need to understand that a printed letter represents the smallest meaningful speech element, or **phoneme.** Grasping this alphabetic principle will be difficult if a child does not yet appreciate that spoken words consist of phonemes. Without this "phonemic awareness" the child cannot truly understand what letters stand for (Liberman, 1973).
>
> Recognizing printed words further requires that one learn and apply the many correspondences between particular letters and phonemes, so that the pronunciation of a printed word can be figured out (i.e., decoded) and then matched to stored information about spoken words in one's mental lexicon to enable one to recognize the identity of the printed word. Phonological decoding is the most reliable guide to word recognition.
>
> Finally, skilled reading requires that the processes involved in word recognition become so well practiced that they can proceed extremely quickly and almost effortlessly, freeing up the reader's cognitive resources for comprehension processes.
>
> Although most reading disabilities are associated with deficits in phonemic awareness, decod-
>
> ing, and sight recognition of printed words, reading skill can also be seriously impeded by weaknesses in the "comprehension" strands, particularly beyond second grade when reading materials become more complex. Even if the pronunciations of all the letter strings in a passage are correctly decoded, the text will not be well comprehended if the child (1) does not know the words in their spoken form, (2) cannot parse the syntactic and semantic relationships among the words, or (3) lacks critical background knowledge or inferential skills to interpret the text appropriately and "read between the lines." Note that in such instances, "reading comprehension" deficits are essentially oral language limitations.
>
> A daunting fact about reading (dis)abilities is that differences among schoolchildren in their levels of reading achievement show strong stability over time, despite remedial efforts usually undertaken to strengthen the skills of lower achievers (Scarborough, 1998). Only about 5–10% of children who read satisfactorily in the primary grades ever stumble later, and 65–75% of children designated as reading disabled early on continue to read poorly throughout their school careers (and beyond).

Increases in short-term capacity allow for greater verbal memory. Increases in knowledge base, or available schemata, facilitate the use of old or familiar knowledge to make sense of new knowledge. For example, children who exhibit good reading comprehension skills display extensive background knowledge of the world, a wide vocabulary, and a familiarity with the semantic and syntactic structure of the English language (Snow, Burns, & Griffin, 1998). Practice in strategy use comes in handy as children initially use conscious strategies to understand and use text, which then become more automatic (Burns, Griffin, & Snow, 1999). An increase in metacognitive skills (as described in chapter 5) is reflected in children's increased awareness of what they know and don't know, or what they comprehend or don't comprehend, from their reading.

The shift from preoperational thought to concrete operational thought results in children being less egocentric (i.e., focusing on one's own perspective) and therefore more capable of understanding the viewpoint of the author, which might be different from their own or one with which they disagree. School-age children also demonstrate the ability to recognize different writing conventions that are used to achieve different purposes via text (e.g., humor, explanation, dialogue) (Lyon, 1999). They can incorporate this understanding into their writing as well.

Changes in cognitive development between the ages of 6 and 12 allow for the average reader to

- Read and learn from all variety of texts, including both fiction and nonfiction.
- Monitor their own comprehension, summarize main points, and discuss details of text.
- Expand their understanding of concepts and ideas by making inferences and using additional print resources.
- Build a connection between existing knowledge and learn something new from material presented in print.

STOP How did your reading ability in middle childhood help or hinder your academic progress?

Writing

The skill of writing develops in a very similar way to reading and within the same developmental time frame. Young children (ages 2 and 3) in the early phases of the preoperational stage of cognitive development begin to recognize and use a letter to represent a sound, a string of sounds to represent words, and words to represent people, objects, and ideas. They begin to write—as well as their fine motor skills will allow—somewhere between the ages of 3 and 5. Parents and preschool staff should not be concerned with teaching children how to write but rather with providing young children many opportunities to draw, to write, and to use writing implements.

With time, practice, encouragement, and opportunity, children in the early elementary school grades (ages 5 to 7) are able to hold the writing implements more correctly, which gives them better control over the mechanics of writing. They tend to write more often and construct longer pieces of written work. At this developmental level, the act of writing takes up so much attentional capacity that misspelled words, no spacing or punctuation, and poor cohesion of thought often accompany early writing efforts. Because these technical writing errors are understandable from a developmental perspective, avoid criticism and instead focus on providing support and encouragement for the act of writing itself as an attempt at a new form of communication in early childhood. Greater attention to technical errors is more appropriate for children in middle childhood (Puckett & Black, 2001).

During the middle childhood years, children gain the capacity to pay more attention to what they are writing and how they are writing, so that technical features such as spelling, spacing, punctuation, and coherence improve. Greater attentional capacity also allows them to focus a piece of writing, maintain a constant point of view, and carry a story through to the middle and the end. Constructing a complete and coherent story makes cognitive demands on long-term memory and sequencing abilities, which children in middle childhood are better able to meet. Their more complex and expansive knowledge base enables them to generate more ideas from which to write and access larger vocabularies. In addition, greater metacognitive skills encourage constant monitoring of what is written, as exemplified by more rereading and editing.

As children progress toward the concrete operational stage of thought, they begin to decentrate (i.e., take multiple dimensions into account) and are able to produce written work in both print and cursive letters (around ages 6 and 7). As concrete operational thinkers, children understand and appreciate other perspectives (i.e., become less egocentric) and are able to modify their writing for particular audiences. They can also take multiple perspectives into consideration. Writing assignments that encourage them to compare and contrast several viewpoints, critique a single perspective, or provide an alternative viewpoint are appropriate for this age group. The multiple topics about which children write also reflect a move away from stories written about themselves (e.g., egocentrism) or events that have occurred (i.e., concrete experiences) to more abstract or imaginary stories (e.g., formal operational thought).

During middle childhood some children begin to show preferences for writing compared to other academic skills as well as specific strengths in certain genres, such as poetry or science fiction. In addition, children in this age group begin to recognize and appreciate writing as a process. Varied writing opportunities that may encourage and support writing in middle childhood include autobiographies, fortunes, songs, bumper stickers, scripts, cereal boxes, epithets, and travel brochures (for a more extensive list see Wormeli, 2001, p. 120).

Mathematical Operations

In the preschool years, children begin counting by reciting the number words in sequence (e.g., *one, two, three, four, five*). This **rote counting** helps them to develop a sense of number. They learn that numbers come before or after each other and that numbers are smaller or larger than one another. They learn that one counting word corresponds with each object they count (i.e., one-to-one correspondence), and they also develop a sense of sequence and pattern (Franke, 2003). Counting, sequencing, and detecting patterns are often considered the basis of the elementary school curriculum. Comprehension of these concepts is necessary to support students in developing the skills and understanding necessary to operate on numbers and to solve a variety of mathematical problems that are introduced in the early elementary school grades, such as addition and subtraction.

Multiplication, division, fractions, decimals, ratios, and geometry are some of the mathematical concepts and operations typically introduced during middle childhood. A number of developmental changes described in the previous sections may help explain why children in middle childhood might be cognitively "ready" to address these mathematical skills and concepts. For example, Piaget researched extensively how children develop the concept of number. A developmental pattern he observed was that as children exhibit decentration they can begin to generate multiple ways to solve a mathematical problem. For example, $9 \times 2 = 18$, but so does 3×6; and you can solve the addition problem $9 + 4$ by adding 4 units to 9 or knowing that $10 + 4$ is 14 and taking away 1.

Children who showed an understanding of seriation demonstrated a more sophisticated understanding of mathematical concepts. They were able to assimilate not only that one number can be larger than another but also that it can—at the same time—be smaller than another number. Seriation allows for a comprehension of number lines as well as greater- and/or less-than problems. Understanding reversibility allows a child to appreciate the relationship between addition and subtraction. Taking two apples out of a basket after adding two reverses or "undoes" the first operation. The same understanding of reversibility can be applied to multiplication and division.

Perhaps the most significant cognitive advancement toward understanding mathematical concepts is the ability to conserve number. If children begin with two equivalent quantities (i.e., numbers) and can comprehend that the quantity of 5 does not change when one group is spread out or bunched together, then they have begun to understand the invariance of numbers in the environment. With such knowledge, school-age children can better predict relationships between numbers and quantities.

Learning more demanding mathematical concepts also requires some memorization. Even though math educators argue that understanding is more important than rote memorization, students still need to memorize rules that can be applied to a variety of problems. Usually, school-age children either intentionally or unintentionally memorize their multiplication tables, as well as other mathematical "facts" or "rules." Over time and with practice, children also tend to invent their own strategies to facilitate learning mathematical concepts and operations (Ernest, 2000; Mabbott & Bisanz, 2003). Once certain operations become automatized, attentional capacity becomes available to apply to the remainder of the problem. Learning how to identify the greatest common factor in the numerator and denominator of a fraction, for example, would be much easier if you could focus your attention on what those common factors are, rather than struggle to determine which factors go into either the numerator or the denominator.

Finally, mathematical concepts are learned best if they can be linked to something that is familiar or known to the child. In other words, if the concepts can be linked to previously learned math concepts or embedded in practical problems that make sense to children, they will be able to assimilate the information more easily. Using other terms, one's knowledge base can and will facilitate the decoding and storage of this new information.

Although the developmental progressions described in this chapter are relatively universal, individual differences in learning rates and styles are often observed among school-age children. During the past decade in particular, researchers have determined that if the task is made more familiar, children will typically exhibit cognitive abilities, such as decentration, multiple-perspective taking, strategy generation,

Mathematical concepts are best learned if they are linked to familiar terms or applied to practical problems.

© Ellen B. Senisi

> ### Guideposts for Working with School-Age Children
>
> - Engage children in conversation often. Ask them questions, answer their questions, and correct improper grammar and vocabulary use by repeating what was said correctly.
> - Encourage reading in all forms. Read to children and have them read to you and to each other. Provide them access to appropriate reading-level materials.
> - Provide opportunities for children to write— about anything! Help them to appreciate writing
>
> as one form of communication by encouraging them to write letters to loved ones or long-distance pen pals.
> - Show children that mathematics is an integral part of their lives by having them count change, calculate discounts at the grocery store, tell time, or engage in any number of common everyday tasks that involve numerical understanding and calculation.

and even mathematical skills, at a much earlier age than Piaget predicted (Siegler, 1996). Despite the appearance of these skills in highly supportive environments, however, there is a tendency for children to approach the world in the patterns outlined earlier.

The patterns of skill development portrayed in this chapter describe "average" learners who share a common cultural background with their teacher, class, school, and curriculum material. Much of how children learn and what they learn can also be traced to their parents' educational values, the pedagogical practices of their teachers, their classroom environments, and the support they receive from their schools and communities.

THEORETICAL VIEWPOINT

Both Piaget's theory of cognitive development and the information-processing perspective explain in theoretical terms how intellectual growth occurs and how older children are "smarter" than younger children. They explain patterns of cognitive development based on research conducted with thousands of different-aged children (refer to chapter 5). There is another approach, however, that focuses on individual differences in cognitive abilities: the *psychometric approach*.

The focus of a **psychometric approach** is on identifying the cognitive strengths and weaknesses of individuals and/or groups of individuals. It emphasizes the development of tests to assess these intellectual skills and uses the results to make predictions about children's future performance potential.

In the opening case study, Kevin has been engaged in a psychometric approach to education: achievement testing. His test scores will provide him, his parents, and teachers with information about his cognitive strengths and weaknesses. His performance also will be compared to a national same-aged cohort (and his sister!).

Perhaps the most well-known contribution of psychometrics is the development and widespread use of intelligence tests. However, there is a long and controversial history in this country about what constitutes intelligence, how it should be measured, and how the scores from intelligence tests should be used. A brief summary of this history will be helpful in providing a context for understanding where we are today in the testing movement.

Theories of Intelligence

Charles Spearman was responsible for developing one of the earliest theories of intelligence, in 1904. He proposed a two-factor theory of intelligence that included a global mental ability called *g* that represented general intelligence and was highly correlated with academic achievement. He also identified *s* as an ability specific to the particular test. One conclusion derived from this model was that since specific factors (*s*) were unique to individual tests, any individual test differences were due solely to individual differences in general intelligence, or *g*. Spearman's concept of *g* is traditionally associated with the representation of intelligence as a single global factor.

E. L. Thorndike and later L. L. Thurstone argued that although most cognitive tests of *g* correlated positively with one another (which supported the concept of a global *g*), individual factors within the tests were more highly related to one another. For example, items that assessed reading comprehension and verbal analogies were more highly related to each other than reading comprehension and adding fractions. Using a statistical technique called **factor analysis** that identifies groups of related items in a test, Thurstone (1938) proposed seven group factors, or **primary mental abilities,** that make up intelligence:

1. *Verbal Comprehension.* Vocabulary, reading comprehension, and verbal analogies
2. *Word Fluency.* Ability to quickly generate and manipulate a large number of words with specific characteristics, as in anagrams or rhyming tests
3. *Number.* Ability to quickly and accurately carry out mathematical operations
4. *Space.* Spatial visualizations as well as ability to mentally transform spatial figures
5. *Associative Memory.* Rote memory
6. *Perceptual Speed.* Quickness in perceiving visual details, anomalies, and similarities
7. *Reasoning.* Skill in a variety of inductive, deductive, and arithmetic reasoning tasks

The foundation of this theory is that intelligence is made up of multiple independent dimensions. The implication is that two adolescents with similar *g* could actually differ dramatically in their cognitive strengths and weaknesses. Thurstone thought, therefore, that any intelligence test should include assessment of all seven primary abilities. There have been additional theories of intelligence put forth in the ensuing years, but most contemporary theories derive from the Spearman/Thorndike–Thurstone traditions (e.g., Garlick, 2002; Jensen, 1998).

STOP In your opinion, what are the characteristics of someone who demonstrates intelligence?

Measures of Intelligence

Alfred Binet and Theodore Simon, commissioned by the French government to devise a test that would differentiate between children who could not learn because of low ability and those who would not learn because of poor motivation, created the first intelligence test in 1905 (Thorndike, 2005). Binet did not really have a theory of mental ability, but he thought that intelligence could be best expressed in and assessed by complex cognitive tasks. The first intelligence test consisted of items that assessed memory, knowledge, and reasoning skills arranged in a sequence of increasing difficulty and grouped into age levels, or when the "average" child could accomplish them. This first test has undergone numerous revisions and is now known as the *Stanford-Binet Intelligence Scale, Fifth Edition* (Roid, 2003).

Currently, the most widely used intelligence tests are the Wechsler Scales. Designed by David Wechsler (1939), a clinical psychologist who used the test to help identify cognitive strengths and weaknesses in his clients and assist in diagnoses, the tests were based on his definition of intelligence as "the aggregate or global capacity of the individual to act purposefully, to think rationally, and to deal effectively with his environment" (p. 3). Because the test seemed to be a valid measure of general intelligence, its use expanded to other populations.

There are three separate Wechsler scales:

- *Wechsler Preschool and Primary Scale of Intelligence–Third Edition* (WPPSI-III) (Wechsler, 2002)
- *Wechsler Intelligence Scale for Children–Fourth Edition* (WISC-IV) (Wechsler, 2003)
- *Wechsler Adult Intelligence Scale–Third Edition* (WAIS-III) (Wechsler, 1997)

The WISC-IV is designed for use with children and adolescents ages 6 to 16 years 11 months and will be the focus of this section. Following are sample items from several of the 10 core subtests:

- *Similarities.* In what way are wool and cotton alike?
- *Vocabulary.* What does *corrupt* mean?
- *Comprehension.* Why do people buy fire insurance?
- *Digit span.* I am going to say some numbers. Listen carefully and when I am through, say the numbers right after me: 7 3 4 1 8 6.
- *Coding.* In the top row, each figure is shown with a number. Fill in the number that goes with each figure in the second row. (See Figure 6.2.)
- *Matrix Reasoning.* For each item the child looks at an incomplete matrix and selects the missing portion from five response options.
- *Picture Concepts.* The child identifies objects that share some common property.

Some of the items in this test require children to arrange materials rather than talk with the test administrator. This procedure allows non-English-speaking children, as well as youth with speech or language disorders, to demonstrate their intellectual capabilities. Some professionals find the division between verbal and performance

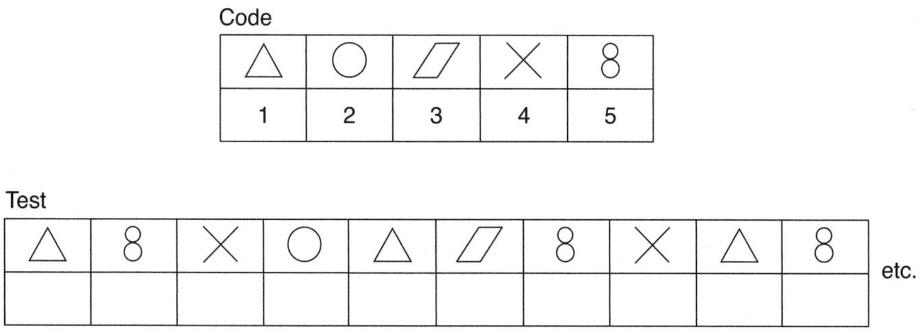

FIGURE 6.2
Sample Coding Task

This sample task, similar to items on the WISC, requires test takers to fill in the bottom row with the appropriate numbers deduced from the code.

items very useful for assessment purposes (Hildebrand & Ledbetter, 2001). The items make up four index scores—*Verbal Comprehension, Perceptual Organization, Freedom from Distractibility,* and *Processing Speed*—that are combined to give an overall ability score. When the four index scores are added together, they produce a total ability score, or **intelligence quotient (IQ).** On the Wechsler scales, the mean total IQ is set at 100 with a standard deviation of 15. Most other major intelligence tests have set the same mean so it is easy to compare the IQ score from one intelligence test to another.

How to Interpret an IQ Score. An IQ score represents how far the child's raw score (number of items answered correctly) differs from the typical performance of same-aged individuals. To develop norms for the WISC-IV (for more on norm-based tests, see chapter 2), thousands of children and adolescents were given the test; their performance created a bell-shaped curve, as shown in Figure 6.3. The highest point of the curve represents the average performance of a particular age group and accounts for the scores of the largest number of children. Children who are represented to the right of the highest point answered more items correctly, and children who are represented to the left of the highest point answered fewer items correctly. The bell-shaped, or **normal curve,** has at its center the mean, or average, score on this intelligence test (100) and a **standard deviation** of 15, which shows how spread out the scores are from the mean. Figure 6.3 also displays the intellectual labels that are applied to the various ranges of scores. An IQ of 100 can be interpreted to mean that a child scored higher than 50% of children who took this test and is in the "average" range.

The Stability of IQ. **Stability** refers to the consistency of performance over time. In other words, is an IQ score achieved at age 10 related to IQ at age 20? Research on the stability of IQ shows that the older the individual is at the first test-taking session, the better that score predicts IQ at later points in time. Correlations between IQ scores achieved after age 6 and those taken later are quite high (e.g., .70s–.80s). IQ scores obtained during preschool are less predictive of later

FIGURE 6.3

Percentage of Individuals and Intelligence Classifications at Different Points from the Mean IQ of 100

The normal curve shows that the majority of people fall within one standard deviation of the mean. Most people achieve an IQ between 85 and 115.

Source: From *Psychological Testing and Assessment* (4th ed.) by R. J. Cohen & M. E. Swerdik, 1999, Mountain View, CA: Mayfield. Copyright 1999 by the McGraw-Hill Companies. Reprinted by permission.

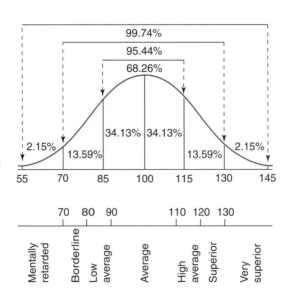

scores (Humphreys & Davey, 1988). In addition, less time between test-taking sessions produces stronger relationships between IQ scores. IQ tests taken several years apart yield IQ scores that are more similar than those from tests taken 20 years apart.

The Relationship of Intelligence to Academic Achievement and Occupation

Researchers have found that IQ scores are related to a number of variables that we value highly in our society. For example, a high score on an intelligence test is related to higher academic achievement (Jensen, 1998). Research also shows that IQ is positively correlated with achievement test scores, higher grade-point averages (GPAs), and adult education attainment (McCall, Evahn, & Kratzer, 1992).

In addition, numerous studies have demonstrated that IQ is significantly related to job performance and job complexity (Gottfredson, 1997). Figure 6.4 depicts the mean *g* scores (comparable to IQ) for different occupations. The bars represent the range of *g* scores for approximately two-thirds of persons in that occupation (Ree & Earles, 1992). There is also a relationship between *g* and both income and job prestige (Nyborg & Jensen, 2001). Clearly, high scores on intelligence tests are related to greater success in academics and job-related performance.

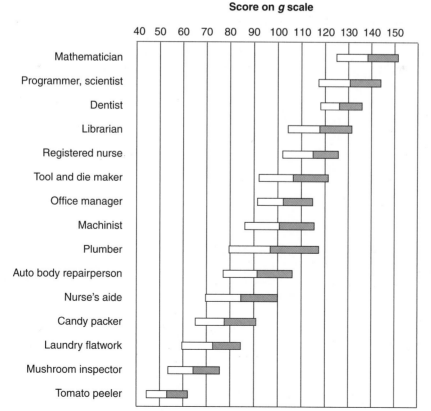

FIGURE 6.4
Mean General Intelligence Scores (g scores) on the General Aptitude Test Battery for Selected Occupations

The bars represent the range of *g* scores for different occupations.

Source: From *Measurement and Evaluation in Psychology and Education*, 7th ed. (p. 282) by R. M. Thorndike, 2005, Upper Saddle River, NJ: Pearson Education, Inc. Copyright © 2005 by Pearson Education, Inc. Reprinted by permission of Pearson Education, Inc., Upper Saddle River, NJ.

Factors That Influence Intelligence Scores

The originators of intelligence tests believed that they were assessing general intellectual competency that predicted success in life. Research has revealed, however, other factors not related to ability that may influence children's performance on intelligence tests.

Socioeconomic Status (SES). Children who are raised in poverty are severely limited in their intellectual potential by their environment (Turkheimer, Haley, Waldron, D'Onofrio, & Gottesman, 2003). For example, children who come from low-income homes score as much as 15 to 20 points below their middle-class peers (Neisser et al., 1996). The reasons suggested are that poor children may lack the material (e.g., books, music lessons, computers) and familial support (e.g., help from parents on homework, engagement in school-related activities) that promote intellectual development. Low-income children are also more likely to live in neighborhoods that lack extracurricular opportunities (e.g., parks, recreational facilities) and contain poor-quality schools. Furthermore, adoption studies using a behavior-genetic framework have shown that when low-income children are adopted into middle-class families, their IQ scores rise.

Ethnicity. African American youth score, on average, 15 points below Caucasian youth. Hispanic youth fall midway between these two groups, and Asian Americans score slightly higher than Caucasians (Ceci, Rosenblum, & Kumpf, 1998). Much of this pattern may be explained by the large percentage of African American youth who live in poverty—42%, compared to 22% of all American children. Some studies that equalize SES, however, have shown differences in IQ scores, with Caucasians scoring higher than African Americans (Jensen & Reynolds, 1982).

These findings are not controversial in themselves; it is how they have been interpreted that has raised the concern of many social scientists. Controversies have stemmed from the claims some researchers have made about the origins of intelligence. They have suggested that intelligence is largely biologically determined and therefore not amenable to improvement (Jensen, 2001). Opponents of this view argue that scores on intelligence tests can be influenced by many nonintellectual factors, such as years of schooling, SES, and familiarity with the culture for which the test was written. Researchers have in fact shown that when any one of these factors is manipulated, IQ changes (Barnett & Camilli, 2002; Grissmer, Williamson, Kirby, & Berends, 1998).

Alternative Views of Intelligence

Some researchers are dissatisfied with our nation's heavy reliance on intelligence tests and the subsequent use of these tests for educational and occupational prognoses. Consequently, several alternatives to the traditional views of intelligence and assessment have been introduced.

Multiple Intelligences. Howard Gardner (1983, 1999, 2004) proposed a theory of **multiple intelligences** that takes into account more than just the higher-order cognitive abilities that make up *g*. He believed that people can be "intelligent" in many different ways and consequently proposed nine basic forms of intelligence:

1. *Linguistic.* The ability to use language well (e.g., journalists and lawyers)

2. *Spatial.* The ability to reason well about spatial relations (e.g., architects and surgeons)

3. *Musical.* The ability to compose and understand music (e.g., audio engineers and musicians)

4. *Logical-Mathematical.* The ability to manipulate abstract symbols (e.g., scientists and computer programmers)

5. *Bodily-Kinesthetic.* The ability to plan and understand sequences of movements (e.g., dancers and athletes)

6. *Intrapersonal.* The ability to understand oneself (e.g., clergy and psychologists)

7. *Interpersonal.* The ability to understand other people and social interactions (e.g., politicians and teachers)

8. *Naturalist.* The ability to observe carefully (e.g., forest rangers and biologists)

9. *Existential.* The ability to address "the big questions" about existence (e.g., philosophers and theologians) (Gardner, 1999)

These separate classifications are not meant to suggest that individuals excel in only one domain, but rather that these abilities work together to allow people to solve a range of problems and learn what they need to adapt to their environment.

Gardner's theory holds wide appeal because it resonates with people who may know someone who is not "book-smart" but "street-wise." It values the talents of someone who may have dropped out of high school but can reconstruct a car engine in very little time. It lends equal weight to a form of practical intelligence that guides people to act purposefully, think rationally, and deal effectively with their environment—ideas not dissimilar from Wechsler's definition of intelligence.

Kevin may possess high levels of spatial intelligence rather than linguistic intelligence.

Triarchic Model of Intelligence. Sternberg (1985, 2003a) has also developed a theory of multiple intelligences. His theory is labeled the **triarchic model of intelligence** because he proposes three distinct types of intelligence:

- *Componential.* The ability to learn to write clearly, calculate and reason about math, and understand literature
- *Experiential.* The ability to formulate novel solutions to problems
- *Contextual.* The ability how to do things related to one's sociocultural background

Componential or analytical intelligence is what is tested with traditional intelligence tests. Experiential or creative intelligence facilitates creative solutions to problems or the development of novel products. Contextual or practical intelligence is largely distinct from analytical intelligence but also highly correlated to job performance (Sternberg et al., 2000).

Using the terminology of this theoretical model, Kevin shows high levels of experiential intelligence and possibly contextual experience rather than componential intelligence.

Sternberg defined successful intelligence as the "ability to succeed according to what one values in life, within one's sociocultural context" (Sternberg, 2003a, p. 400). This definition broadens the scope of what it means to be intelligent and

Contextual or practical intelligence is highly valued in many different communities and cultures.

Laima Druskis/PH College

 STOP Do you know someone who is very creative or skilled with his hands but does not do well on standard intelligence measures?

opens the door to the possibility that there is more to intelligence than *g*. His argument was based on studies that explored what is considered "intelligent" in other countries. Cross-cultural studies have shown that those individuals who score high in practical intelligence are usually considered most intelligent. In rural Kenya, for example, practical knowledge regarding use of natural herbal medicines is valued highly and correlates negatively with tests of intelligence as well as math achievement (Sternberg et al., 2001). In another study, 261 adolescents who lived in rural and semiurban Yup'ik Alaskan communities were administered tests that assessed academic intelligence and practical intelligence (e.g., knowledge of fish preparation, weather, hunting, and herb and berry gathering). Urban Yup'ik youth outperformed rural Yup'ik on tests of componential intelligence. But rural Yup'ik scored higher than their urban counterparts on tests of practical intelligence, and both Yup'ik youth and adults rated the value of practical skills more highly (Grigorenko et al., 2004). Results such as these strengthen the argument for multiple means of assessing intelligence with sensitivity to cultural experience. The advantage of this

Guideposts for Working with School-Age Children

- To help put children's test scores in context, make sure you understand what information is being reported (e.g., general ability score, IQ).

- Help parents, educators, practitioners, and children understand what is being measured and what the limitations of the tests are.

- Limit your reliance on intelligence tests, because factors such as socioeconomic status and ethnicity can influence performance on any test of cognitive abilities.

- Encourage children to develop their intelligence in as many different areas as possible, such as music or athletics.

- Value practical intellectual skills and recognize their relationship to future job success.

approach is that we learn more about the role intelligence plays in the everyday lives of diverse children.

CREATIVITY IN MIDDLE CHILDHOOD

The theories of Gardner and Sternberg challenge the long-held unidimensional view of intelligence. Analytical thinking—what is largely measured by intelligence tests—represents only one aspect of thinking and predicts success in life in a very narrow way. Possessing practical or creative ways of thinking may make one equally successful in life; however, these abilities are not regularly assessed by tests or valued very highly by schools.

In 1950, Guilford's Presidential Address to the American Psychological Association implored the academic community to study a neglected human attribute: creativity. Since that time, scholars have defined and measured creativity in multiple ways (Sternberg & Lubart, 1999). A current working definition of **creativity** is thinking that is novel and that produces ideas or outcomes that are of value to the individual and/or society (Sternberg, 1999).

Creativity is measured largely by using tasks that assess **divergent thinking.** Divergent thinking is called for when individuals have to produce multiple responses and no one answer is correct. A popular measure of divergent thinking is the *Torrance Tests of Creative Thinking* (Torrance, 1974), which assesses creativity by having children generate questions about a scene, construct a picture using colored shapes, and generate unusual uses for a common object. This is in contrast to **convergent thinking,** which is called for when individuals are presented with novel problems that have a single best answer. Researchers have studied the development of divergent thinking skills across the lifespan to obtain an understanding of how creativity develops in childhood and its stability or continuity across the same time period.

Developmental Trends in Creativity

Longitudinal studies that follow children across their early and middle childhood years find that creativity (as measured by divergent thinking) increases substantially in early childhood until around ages 5 to 6. This peak is followed by a slow decline until age 9, known as the fourth-grade slump, followed by a gradual increase to ninth grade and beyond (Claxton, Pannells, & Rhoads, 2005). Different longitudinal studies find the peaks and slumps to occur at slightly different ages, but there is general agreement that creativity follows a U-shaped trajectory throughout childhood (Smith & Carlsson, 1990; Torrance, 1967). It is possible that as children enter a formal educational setting, either their creativity is discouraged or much of their attentional energy is spent on convergent thinking that leaves little time and effort to engage in creative acts (Gardner, 1982).

Several longitudinal studies that assessed creativity in adolescence found that those students who displayed creative abilities in high school became creative adults who were successful in fields related to their teenage interests. These studies also found that adolescents' extracurricular creative activities rather than in-class performance were most predictive of later adult creativeness (Milgram & Hong, 1999; Perleth & Heller, 1994).

A Developmental Approach to Creativity

Researchers also are interested in identifying the cognitive, personality, motivational, and contextual factors that describe and influence creative children. How do these children differ from noncreative thinkers, and what aspects of their environment support the development and expression of their creativity? Creativity is best thought of as multidimensional and influenced by a number of internal and external factors throughout childhood (Feldman, 1999; Sternberg & Lubart, 1996).

Cognitive Processes. Many creative adults who engaged in their domain of creative talent (e.g., painting, music, mathematics) during childhood moved through mastering that domain in astonishing speed. Creative children are often several stages or levels above their same-age peers in the development of domain-specific cognition (Ward, Smith, & Finke, 1999). Also, children who are high in creativity are often very intelligent and show high cognitive flexibility.

Socioemotional Processes. Children who frequently engage in make-believe or pretend play in their preschool years tend to show higher levels of imaginative and creative thought as older children and adults (Singer & Brink, 2003). Pretend play appears to foster insight abilities and divergent thinking, both of which are related to creativity in middle childhood (Russ, 2003). Relatedly, when a sample of fourth-graders was asked about current imaginary playmates, 52% reported having them. These children also scored higher on several measures of creativity. It was more common for girls to have imaginary playmates, and creativity was related to how developed the playmates were and the number of imaginary companions (Hoff, 2005).

More creative children and adults tend to reflect openness to experiences, impulsivity, aesthetic sensitivity, independence, introversion, and a high level of energy and commitment to their creative talent (for a review, see Feist, 1999). A few studies show that highly creative individuals have some difficulty establishing and maintaining intimate social relationships, in part because of their preoccupation with creating (Gardner, 1993).

Family. The development of creativity does not appear to reside solely within the child. The immediate and extended family supports childhood creativity by providing a stable and child-centered environment. These families value independence over conformity, exhibit more unconventional parenting styles, and are open to varied expressions of thoughts and feelings (Bloom, 1985; Robinson & Noble, 1991). Families shape the trajectory of creativity development in children by providing resources and opportunities as well as encouragement and support.

Education. Schools *can* and *should* provide the training and preparation necessary for children to expand their creativity. It is not always evident that they do, however. In many areas of creativity (e.g., music, art, physics), much preparation and mastery of content and skills is needed prior to true creative activity. Many creative adults speak fondly of teachers and mentors who guided their development during the school-age years (Goldsmith, 1990). Interview data suggest, however, that the rigid formality of the school curriculum stifled children's creativity and forced them to find creative outlets elsewhere (Gardner, 1993). In a recent study, questionnaires were administered to elementary school teachers to assess their conceptions of creativity and creative students. Teachers were found to possess inaccurate concepts regarding what constitutes creativity and admitted to problems with the classroom behaviors demonstrated by creative students (Aljughaiman & Mowrer-Reynolds, 2005). Research shows that Western schools tend to value only a single way of being intelligent, that which requires memory and analytical skills. Currently, most of our schools do not nurture and reward students who are high in creativity (Sternberg, 2003b).

Characteristics of the Domain and Field. For many creative individuals, the state of the domain within which they excel sets the stage for their creativity. Domains change with time, and some fields are more open to creative contributions at different points in time than others (Csikszentmihalyi, 1990; Gruber & Davis, 1988). The example often cited is that Einstein's theory of relativity had such an impact on the scientific community at that time in part because the field was ready for his revolutionary ideas. The field of physics was open to his creativity. Today, Einstein's ideas about relativity would not address the needs of modern-day physics and would be viewed as far less creative.

Sociocultural/Contextual Aspects. Qualities of the society within which creative activities take place and the culture in which that society is embedded predicts the probability of developing creativity in its young people. How creativity is rewarded and reinforced within a society predicts the ways in which children of that society will seek out or be given opportunities for creative endeavors (Lubart, 1999). For example, in a society that does not allow girls to play musical instruments, little musical creativity in females is likely to be realized.

Historical Trends. Many aspects of creativity are a function of time, place, and circumstances of one's birth. The kinds of opportunities for developing children's creative talents are constrained and channeled by the historical time within which they live. Creative solutions to oil dependency, or a cure for AIDS, may result more out of necessity or a specific historical event than anything having to do with the creative individual.

Taken together, these components represent the internal and external forces that may encourage some children to develop and exhibit their creativity at various times in their lives or in the history of humankind.

The Relationship Between Creativity and Intelligence

In many cases, highly creative children are also highly intelligent. This begs the question: Is creativity a subcomponent of intelligence or a distinct construct? The relationship between creativity and intelligence has been studied extensively. The conventional view is that intelligence and creativity may overlap in some respects, but not in others (for a review, see Sternberg & O'Hara, 1999). In other words, highly intelligent children are likely to be more creative than are people with lower intelligence, but high intelligence is neither necessary nor sufficient for creativity (Nickerson, 1999).

Sternberg's triarchic theory of intelligence, presented earlier in the chapter, posits that intelligence is made up of not only analytical skills but also of practical and creative skills. When researchers systematically examined the relationship between these three components, they found creative intelligence to be distinctly different from practical and analytical intelligence. Performance and ability in one component cannot be predicted from the others; the highest correlation achieved between creativity and either analytical or practical intelligence is .40 (Sternberg, 2003b). Sternberg argues that teachers should be made aware that creativity is not part of general intelligence, and that teaching for creative thinking in schools can improve children's academic performance.

> *Kevin may show real creative promise, but unfortunately, his form of creativity is not measured on achievement tests.*

Creativity Across Cultures

The conception of creativity, the domains of the creative process (e.g., art, music, science, literature), and the extent to which creativity is nurtured varies across cultures (Lubart, 1999). For example, in Western societies creativity is thought of as the ability to produce an outcome that is novel and valued. This "product orientation" is supported in the way creativity is measured: Children are given a task in which they are asked to generate a product or solution. In Eastern cultures, the conception of creativity is less focused on innovative products. Instead, creativity involves a state of personal fulfillment, a connection to another realm, or the experience of inner peace (Kuo, 1996). In Hinduism, for example, creativity is seen as spiritual or religious expression, not as a novel solution (Sherr, 1982).

Cultures also differ in how they transmit messages to their youth regarding the value of creativity, the ways in which schools encourage its development, and its place in society (Amabile, 1982, 1983, 1996). For example, in China and Japan, children are encouraged to adhere to group standards and are motivated to find a way to fit in with others (Niu & Sternberg, 2003). In Chinese and Japanese schools, teachers rarely, if ever, recognize a student who shows exceptional creative talent. This cultural transmission, in turn, affects the level of creativity in that culture's young children (Stevenson, 1998).

The Origins of Creativity

Where does creativity come from? Are some children born with special gifts and talents that they express throughout their lives, or can creativity be nurtured? Some creativity scholars purport that certain aspects of creative thinking must be genetically prescribed or driven by specific physiological states, such as cortical arousal, cognitive disinhibition and reactivity, and a high need for stimulation (for a review, see Martindale, 1999).

Others think that creativity can be taught—or at least encouraged—and should be rewarded by teachers (Niu & Sternberg, 2003; Sternberg & Williams, 1996). For example, students can be asked to create novel products, such as a new type of doorknob; to write stories from a choice of titles; or to produce artwork to illustrate a concept (Sternberg, 2003b). Results from teaching creative thinking skills to middle- and high-school students are that they not only improve in creative thinking, but overall academic performance improves as well (Sternberg & Williams, 1996). Box 6.2 describes how teachers can "teach to creativity."

BOX 6.2   Roadmap to Successful Practice
Teaching for Creativity

A creative individual often visualizes how "the old" can be used, thought of, or transformed in a new way. People refer to this as "thinking outside the box." For many of us, creative thinking seems beyond our abilities. We think of it as a cognitive gift bestowed upon one at birth. Robert Sternberg and colleagues disagree profoundly with these sentiments. After a decade of research, Sternberg believes that creative thinking skills can be learned and has developed a program for teaching them (Sternberg & Williams, 1996).

In one such "teaching" study, his research team had 86 fourth graders take a pretest on insightful thinking. Then some of the children received their regular school instruction and others were taught how to use insight skills to solve a problem. On a posttest of their insight skills, children who were taught how to solve problems using insight showed greater gains from pretest to posttest than those children who were exposed to the regular curriculum (Davidson & Sternberg, 1984).

Sternberg also believes that creativity is not just a matter of thinking in a certain way, but rather it is an attitude toward life (Sternberg & Lubart, 1995, 1996). In other words, creative adults have *decided* to be creative. Adults can use several strategies to support children in making these same creative decisions (Sternberg, 2000). Here are 12 ways to enhance creative thinking

1. *Redefine Problems.* Prod children to see a problem in a different way.

2. *Analyze Your Own Ideas.* Encourage children to critique their own ideas.

3. *Sell Your Ideas.* Because most creative ideas challenge the status quo, encourage children to "sell" their idea to their audience.

4. *Accept That Knowledge Is a Double-Edged Sword.* Knowledge is valuable for creativity;

too much knowledge could impede creativity. Tell children that their flexible views of the world can be paired with an adult's "expert" knowledge to create together.

5. *Surmount Obstacles.* Be supportive of creative children when they meet the obstacles society puts in their path.

6. *Take Sensible Risks.* Our educational system rewards students who play it safe. Creative children tend to take risks. Teachers and parents need to encourage such risk taking.

7. *Be Willing to Grow.* Encourage children to move beyond their first creative enterprise. There is a lifetime of creating ahead of them.

8. *Believe in Yourself.* When children's creativity gets a poor reception, encourage them to believe in their talent.

9. *Tolerate Ambiguity.* Provide ways for students to tolerate creative ambiguity that is likely to occur during the development phase.

10. *Find What You Love to Do and Do It.* Children are at their most creative when they are doing what they love to do.

11. *Allow Time.* Don't rush children. Creative activities require time, reflection, and revision.

12. *Allow Mistakes.* Avoid criticism. If children become afraid to make mistakes, they will be less creative.

Source: From *Creative Thinking in the Classroom* by R. J. Sternberg, 2003, *Scandinavian Journal of Educational Research, 47,* pp. 325–338.

Guideposts for Working with School-Age Children

- • Recognize that divergent thinking is as valuable as convergent thinking and can be enhanced with practice.
- • Encourage children to "brainstorm" about a whole range of problems or issues.
- • Encourage children to use analogies and metaphors when they are generating solutions to a problem.

- • Support children's creativity by providing them time, space, and encouragement to pursue their interests.
- • Help creative children balance their creative impulses with required school tasks.

ACADEMIC ACHIEVEMENT IN MIDDLE CHILDHOOD

This chapter focuses on the many ways our society assesses cognitive development in school-age children. The ability to read, write, and perform mathematical calculations, an IQ score that reflects a range of cognitive skills, and creative problem-solving are indices of academic success or achievement. Developing literacy skills and performing well in school is vital to the future success of children in our technology-rich society. It appears, however, that during middle childhood children begin to become challenged by and/or bored with school and may become disengaged. When researchers have examined academic achievement indicators, such as grades, literacy rates, attendance, graduation, and school engagement, they find that not all school-age children achieve at the same rates. Extensive research has begun to elucidate the factors that may contribute to these differences in academic achievement.

Gender and Academic Achievement

Most studies show that, on average, girls do better in school than boys. Girls get higher grades and complete high school at a higher rate compared to boys (Jacobs, 2002). Standardized achievement tests also show that females are better at spelling and perform better on tests of literacy, writing, and general knowledge (National Center for Education Statistics, 2003). An international aptitude test administered to fourth graders in 35 countries, for example, showed that females outscored males on reading literacy in every country. Although there were no differences between boys and girls in fourth grade on mathematics, boys began to perform better than girls on science tests in fourth grade (International Association for the Evaluation of Education Achievement, n.d.). Girls continue to exhibit higher verbal ability throughout high school, but they begin to lose ground to boys after fourth grade on tests of both mathematical and science ability. These gender differences in math and science achievement have implications for girls' future careers and have been a source of concern for educators everywhere.

> *These findings match the pattern found in Kevin and his sister. Kevin's older sister performed better than he did on achievement tests, but Kevin found the math sections of the test easier than the verbal sections.*

During the past decade, there has been a concerted effort to find out why there is a shortage of women in the science, math, engineering, and technical fields (AAUW,

1992). In 1995, 22% of America's scientists and engineers were women, compared to half of the social scientists. Women who do pursue careers in science, engineering, and mathematics most often choose fields in the biological sciences, where they represent 40% of the workforce, with smaller percentages found in mathematics or computer science (33%), the physical sciences (22%), and engineering (9%) (National Science Board, 1998).

Part of the explanation can be traced to gender differences in the cognitive abilities of middle-school students. In late elementary school, females outperform males on several verbal skills tasks: verbal reasoning, verbal fluency, comprehension, and understanding logical relations (Hedges & Nowell, 1995). Males, on the other hand, outperform females on spatial skills tasks such as mental rotation, spatial perception, and spatial visualization (Voyer, Voyer, & Bryden, 1995) (examples of these tasks are presented in Figure 6.5). Males also perform better on mathematical achievement tests than females. However, gender differences do not apply to all aspects of mathematical skill. Males and females do equally well in basic math knowledge, and girls actually have better computational skills. Performance in mathematical reasoning and geometry shows the greatest difference (Fennema, Sowder, & Carpenter, 1999). Males also display greater confidence in their math

Mental rotation
Choose the responses that show the standard in a different orientation.

 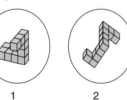

Spatial perception
Pick the tilted bottle that has a horizontal water line.

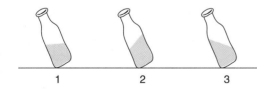

Spatial visualization
Find the figure embedded in the complex shape below.

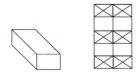

FIGURE 6.5
Types of Spatial Tasks

Examples of visual-spatial tasks on which boys typically outperform girls.

Source: From "Emergence and Characterization of Sex Differences in Spatial Ability: A Meta-Analysis," by M. C. Linn & A. C. Petersen, 1985, *Child Development, 56,* pp. 1482, 1483, 1485. Copyright 1985 by the Society for Research in Child Development, Inc. Reprinted by permission of the society.

TABLE 6.1 Cognitive Tasks That Usually Show Sex Differences	
Women Score Higher	**Men Score Higher**
Tasks that require rapid access to and use of phonological, semantic, and other information in long-term memory	Tasks that require transformations to visual working memory
Knowledge areas of literature and foreign languages	General knowledge
Production and comprehension of complex prose	Tests of fluid reasoning (especially in math and science)
Fine motor tasks	Motor tasks that involve aiming
Perceptual speed	Tasks that involve moving objects
Decoding nonverbal communication	
Perceptual thresholds (in multiple modalities)	
Higher grades in school (all or most subjects)	
Speech articulation	

Source: Based on "Sex Differences in Intelligence: Implications for Education" (p. 1102) by D. F. Halpern, *American Psychologist, 52* (10), 1091–1102, 1997. Copyright by the American Psychological Association. Reprinted by permission of the author.

skills, which is a strong predictor of math performance (Casey, Nuttall, & Pezaris, 2001). Table 6.1 provides a more extensive list of gender differences in cognitive abilities.

The poorer mathematical reasoning skills exhibited by many female adolescents have several educational implications. Beginning at age 12, girls begin to like math and science less and to like language arts and social studies more than do boys (Kahle & Lakes, 2003; Sadker & Sadker, 1994). They also do not expect to do as well in these subjects and attribute their failures to lack of ability (Eccles, Barber, Jozefowicz, Malenchuk, & Vida, 1999). By high school, girls self-select out of higher-level, "academic-track" math and science courses, such as calculus and chemistry. One of the long-term consequences of these choices is that girls lack the prerequisite high school math and science courses necessary to pursue certain majors in college (e.g., engineering, computer science). Consequently, the number of women who pursue advanced degrees in these fields is significantly reduced (Halpern, 2004).

Some researchers, on the one hand, argue that the gender gap in mathematics is biologically driven. Selected research shows that prenatal hormones circulating in the brain encourage differential development in the hemispheres of male and female fetuses (Berenbaum, Korman, & Leveroni, 1995). Others believe intelligence has its roots in genetics (Plomin, 2000; see chapter 3 for a review of behavioral genetics). There is evidence, however, that sociocultural factors may influence girls' attitudes toward math and science. For example, parents tend to view math as more important for sons and language arts and social studies as more important for daughters (Andre, Whigham, Hendrickson, & Chambers, 1999). Parents are more likely to encourage their sons to take advanced high school courses in chemistry, mathematics, and physics and have higher expectations for their success (Wigfield, Battle, Keller, & Eccles, 2002).

Teacher characteristics and the classroom environment also have been identified as contributors to this gender gap. Seventh and eighth graders attending math and science camps identified a math or science teacher as "a person who has made math, science, or engineering interesting" for them (Gilbert, 1996, p. 491). Unfortunately, many females report being passed over in classroom discussions, not encouraged by the teacher, and made to feel stupid (Sadker & Sadker, 1994). Classroom environments can be made to feel more "girl-friendly" by incorporating

- Low levels of competition, public drill, and practice
- High levels of teacher attention
- Hands-on activities
- Female role models
- Same-sex cooperative learning communities
- Nonsexist books and materials (Evans, Whigham, & Wang, 1995)

Fortunately, sex differences in mathematical reasoning have begun to decline, and females' enrollments are up in math and science courses (Campbell, Hombo, & Mazzeo, 2000; Freeman, 2004). Programs designed to interest girls in math and science and that demonstrate how this knowledge will allow them to help others appear to be working.

STOP How encouraged or discouraged you were by parents, peers, and teachers to pursue science in middle childhood?

Diverse Groups and Academic Achievement

School-age children who are poor, belong to minority groups, and live in urban areas do not perform as well in school as children who are wealthier, of majority status, and live in the suburbs. What is the relationship between poverty, ethnicity, urban living, and academic achievement? The answer is a complicated one, but several factors have been identified by researchers.

The public school population in urban cities tends to have higher percentages of poor and minority students than suburban school populations (U.S. Census, 2000).

Anthony Magnacca/Merrill

Traditional science classes are intimidating and uninspiring for many girls. Small groups, a female teacher, and lessons about helping people through science may attract girls to science classes.

FIGURE 6.6

Student Characteristics of Large Urban Schools Versus National Statistics

Students who attend large, urban schools are more likely than students nationally to be nonwhite, eligible for the free-lunch program, and English-language learners.

Source: From "Poverty and Student Achievement: A Hopeful Review," by J. Hannaway, in J. Flood & P. A. Anders (Eds.), 2005, *Literacy Development of Students in Urban Schools: Research and Policy* (p. 6). Newark, DE: International Reading Association. Copyright © 2005 by The International Reading Association. Reprinted by permission of the publisher.

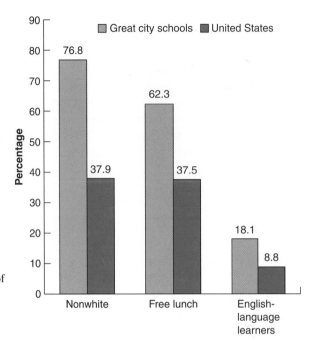

For example, students who attend a school that is part of the Council of Great City Schools (a coalition of 60 of the largest urban school districts in the country) are more likely than students nationally to be nonwhite, eligible for free-lunch subsidy, and English-language learners (see Figure 6.6). Another relevant statistic is that 40% of urban students attend high-poverty schools. How does poverty affect academic achievement in school-age children?

Research shows that children from poor households may have fewer direct learning experiences at home. Because their parents may be working longer hours, for example, the children may be read to less often, conversed with less often, and not provided the same academic support during their early school years that parents from higher income homes are shown to provide (Lee & Burkham, 2002). Children from poor households are also less likely to have academic out-of-school experiences compared to students from well-to-do homes. Studies also have shown that although poor children make great strides during the academic school year, they may experience a learning loss over the summer. Compared to lower-SES children, school-agers from higher SES homes may have more opportunities to travel, go to camp, and engage in other activities that promote learning during summer vacations (Cooper, Nye, Charlton, & Lindsay, 1996; Entwisle, Alexander, & Olson, 2001). Differences in a number of critical school factors, such as class sizes, teacher quality, resources, peer influence, and school climate may also disadvantage poor children who attend high-poverty schools (Hauser-Cram, Erickson Warfield, Stadler, & Sirin, 2006). All of these factors directly and indirectly affect the academic performance of children from poor or language-minority, urban homes.

The patterns mentioned here are based on large groups of children and do not specify the different trajectories of academic achievement that smaller groups of children may follow. For example, studies of immigrant children show very different patterns of academic performance throughout their school years, despite their low socioeconomic status (Ruiz-de-Velasco, Fix, & Clewell, 2000; Suarez-Orozco &

Suarez-Orozco, 2001). One study followed two groups of children (first graders and fourth graders) for three years to examine the development of their academic attitudes and behaviors during middle childhood (García Coll, Szalacha, & Palacios, 2005). Children were chosen from Dominican, Portuguese, and Cambodian immigrant families. In general, all children reported very positive academic aspirations, expectations, and attitudes throughout the three years. Most of the children were engaged in school, performing well, and were on positive academic pathways. Such findings suggest that family obligation may be a major motivator for the academic achievement exhibited by children of immigrant communities (Fuligni, Alvarez, Bachman, & Ruble, 2005).

School Engagement and Academic Achievement

School engagement is a multidimensional construct that includes students' cognitive investment, willingness to participate, and the emotional appeal of school (Blumenfeld et al., 2005). Each one of these cognitive, behavioral, and emotional components is related to academic performance and has been linked to early school withdrawal.

Research has shown that students who report being more engaged in school attain higher academic achievement (National Research Council and Institute of Medicine, 2003). There also appears to be a bidirectional relationship between engagement and academic achievement. The more engaged the students, the more they learn; and the more that is learned, the better they feel about themselves and school, increasing their level of engagement, and so on (Hauser-Cram et al., 2006).

A two-year study of school engagement in middle childhood included over 600 students between grades 3 through 5 drawn from four urban schools with large numbers of Latino and African American students (Blumenfeld et al., 2005). Very small percentages of the students from these school districts met the state competency standards for reading or math. Although overall engagement was moderately high, examiners were able to identify six patterns of engagement over a two-year period. Students who were less engaged were more likely to be boys, from the higher grades, and doing very poorly academically. These less-engaged students also had less favorable perceptions of their school environments, including low teacher and peer support, poor work norms, and challenging tasks. One recommendation for resource-limited schools is to identify those students who are least engaged and direct resources towards them.

> *Kevin did not feel very engaged in school despite performing relatively well. His attitude about the relevance of school is not very positive.*

Culture and Academic Achievement

The cultural values that are shared with school-age children may have an impact on the attitudes and motivation they apply in a school setting. An example of how culture may influence academic achievement—both directly and indirectly—is reflected in differences in science and mathematics performances on international skills tests among children in the United States, Japan, and China (Mathematics Achievement, 1996; Stevenson, Lee, & Stigler, 1986). The best-performing U.S. fifth graders (from Minnesota) scored lower on the mathematics test than the worst-performing Japanese classrooms and all but one of the Chinese classrooms.

Studies attempting to identify the cultural influences that contribute to these differences have isolated factors in both the home and school environments. For example, American children spend about half as much classroom time in academic activities as children in Japan and China. Teachers in the United States spend a much smaller proportion of their time imparting information than do Japanese or Chinese teachers (e.g., American teachers spend more time giving directions). Teachers in the United States also focus more of their instruction on skills and basic computation and less on higher-order conceptual thinking and problem solving. In addition, both the school day and year is much shorter in the United States, and American children spend less time on homework than Japanese or Chinese students (Chen, Lee, & Stevenson, 1996; Larson, 2001).

Researchers have also found differences in the values and communities that surround academic achievement and group relations, particularly in Japan (Shapiro & Azuma, 2004). Japanese attitudes toward achievement emphasize that success comes from hard work. In class, Japanese teachers focus on the children's engagement in their work rather than on discipline. Japanese teachers also delegate more classroom responsibility to children and support the development of peer groups as part of the learning environment. For example, classmates serve as resources in examining mathematical concepts. Teachers typically examine a few problems in depth rather than cover many problems superficially. Often, children's errors are used as learning tools for the entire class (Stevenson & Lee, 1990).

What makes the achievement of Japanese children so surprising to educators in the United States is that during early childhood, Japanese parents and teachers emphasize social development much more than cognitive development (Abe & Izard, 1999). For example, Japanese parents emphasize empathy for others, and Japanese kindergartners spend four times as much time in free play as kindergartners in the United States. Japanese elementary schools also emphasize children's supporting each other and working together, not grades or test scores. Perhaps this attention to sociability allows children in elementary school to develop a sense of community in the classroom and encourages them to focus their attention on the subjects being taught (Lewis, 1995).

Kevin's cultural surroundings make him aware of the value of good test scores. He has an accurate sense of his parent's expectations about his performance as well as an understanding that his promotion to the next grade may be achievement-test based.

Guideposts for Working with School-Age Children

- Be sensitive to children's stereotypical gender expectations about their cognitive strengths and weaknesses.
- Reinforce children when they succeed in a cognitive task about which they feel anxious (e.g., girls using mathematics).
- Provide children with engaging intellectual opportunities after school, on the weekends, and especially during the summer.
- Communicate explicit educational expectations to keep children engaged in school.
- Attend to children's physical and mental health needs. These need to be taken care of so that children can learn.

DEVELOPMENT IN CONTEXT

Middle childhood is often a critical point in students' educational trajectories. Individual and environmental factors come together to influence children's engagement with, and commitment to, education and the application of their cognitive gifts. This chapter has provided many examples of how families, schools, and communities provide a context for the development of literacy skills, intelligence, creativity, and academic achievement in school-age children. This section elaborates on those contextual features and how they affect children's pathways to academic success.

Family Contexts

How well children perform academically is based, in part, on their cognitive abilities, motivation, and engagement in school. Decades of research show, however, that parental interest and involvement in their children's school life is also related to school achievement (Van Voorhis, 2000; Weiss, Dearing, Mayer, Kreider, & McCartney, 2005). Studies have illustrated that parental involvement is most effective when parents support their children's academic achievement at home in the following ways:

- *Managing and Organizing Time.* Parents of successful students actively help them organize their daily and weekly schedules and check to see if they are following their routines. Regular routines at home are also related to better school performance (Taylor, 1996).

- *Involvement with Homework.* Making certain that homework is completed, discussing the specifics of assignments and papers, explaining the assignments, checking accuracy, and actively helping children complete assignments are all related to children's academic performance (Cooper, Jackson, & Nye, 2001).

- *Discussing School Matters.* Children whose parents converse regularly with them about school experiences, both good and bad, perform better academically (Ho & Willms, 1996; Steinberg, 1996).

- *Literacy and Reading at Home.* There is a strong relationship between literacy activities and opportunities in the home (e.g., silent reading time, numerous printed material) and school performance (Gauvain, Savage, & McCollum, 2000).

Unfortunately, parental involvement in children's schooling occurs less often in working-class families and families in which mothers work full time (Muller & Kerbow, 1993). Also, parents with more formal education are more likely to be involved in their children's schooling than parents with less education (Useem, 1992). Box 6.3 provides examples of ways that parents and students can get more help with homework.

More important than family demographics, however, is parents' and teachers' perceptions of the roles they should play in their children's education. If they believe that their involvement can affect their children's education, parents tend to be more engaged in schools and at home (Hoover-Dempsey, Walker, Jones, & Reed, 2002; Sheldon, 2002). Research also shows that when teachers and schools reach out to families and make them feel comfortable and capable of promoting their children's education, parents are likely to become more involved in helping their children succeed in school (Giles, 2005; Van Voorhis, 2000). Improved reading and math achievement, student attendance, and perceptions of the school climate by students and parents reflect this greater success (Haynes, Emmons, & Woodruff, 1998; Sheldon, 2003).

STOP How did your family members support your educational experience?

BOX 6.3   Roadmap to Successful Practice
Homework Help for Students and Parents

For the student who can't remember a homework assignment or is having difficulty with geometry, and for parents who may not be confident that their child does not have homework for the second week in a row, help is here. Schoolnotes.com is a free online service that, if adopted by the teacher, offers multiple services to students and their parents. Students can:

- E-mail their teacher to seek clarification.
- Get a list of suggested Web sites for student research.
- Utilize electronic flashcards.
- Review their homework assignments.
- Finish copying notes and other material from the chalkboard.
- Receive recognition from teachers for their effort and success.

Parents can:

- E-mail the teacher with questions.

- Review the homework assignments posted for their child.
- Understand better the goals and expectations of the teacher.

There are several advantages to this three-way communication system. First, it allows parents to more directly understand the academic expectations, thereby providing them with more information with which to assist their child. Second, teachers and parents can hold students more accountable for their learning. Third, if students miss school, this service provides an immediate opportunity for them to learn what they have missed and need to make up. The greatest disadvantage of this service is the need for Internet access and computer skills, neither of which is distributed equally across the population.

Source: Excerpted from *Meet Me in the Middle: Becoming an Accomplished Middle-Level Teacher* (pp. 172–173) by Rick Wormeli. Copyright © 2001, with permission of Stenhouse Publishers.

School Contexts

The transition from elementary school to middle school, discussed in chapter 1, is an important developmental context. Students experience a dramatic shift in context as they move from an educational environment that is reportedly more familiar, friendly, safe, and secure to one that is larger, more unfamiliar, and aloof. The following list describes six ways in which elementary schools typically differ from middle schools (Eccles et al., 1993). Middle schools are characterized by

1. A greater emphasis on teacher control and discipline and fewer opportunities for student decision making, choice, and self-management
2. Less personal and positive teacher-student relationships
3. An increase in practices such as whole-class task organization, between-classroom ability grouping, and public evaluation of the correctness of work
4. Teachers who feel less effective as teachers, especially with low-ability students
5. Classwork that requires lower-level cognitive skills than does classwork at the elementary level
6. Teachers who appear to use a higher standard in judging students' competence and in grading students' performance

Unfortunately, the structural, curricular, pedagogical, and personnel changes that take place in middle school do not match well with the developmental needs of a middle-school child. This mismatch may well lead to decreased motivation, less interest in curricula, and lower self-esteem (Eccles et al., 1993; Erkut, Marx, Fields, & Sing, 1999; Pianta, Stuhlman, & Hamre, 2002).

In their report, *Turning Points: Preparing American Youth for the Twenty-First Century*, the Carnegie Council on Adolescent Development (1989) recognized the mismatch and made several recommendations for middle schools:

- Develop smaller "communities" or "houses" to lessen the impersonal nature of large middle schools.
- Lower student-to-counselor ratios from several hundred–to-1 to 10-to-1.
- Involve parents and community leaders in schools.
- Develop curricula that produce students who are literate, understand the sciences, and have a sense of health, ethics, and citizenship.
- Have teachers team-teach in more flexibly designed curriculum blocks that integrate several disciplines, instead of presenting students with disconnected, rigidly separated, 50-minute segments.
- Boost students' health and fitness with more in-school programs and help students who need public health care get it.

These recommendations have begun to be implemented in nearly 100 schools in 15 states. Results have shown significant improvements in reading, math, and language arts achievement (Carnegie Council on Adolescent Development, 1995).

Community Contexts

Communities can support literacy development, creativity, and academic achievement in school-age children in both direct, and indirect ways. Communities directly influence children's literacy development, for example, by providing public libraries with programming for school-age children, or by establishing literacy support services for children and adults. A more indirect way might be to assist in the elimination of barriers to literacy development. For example, research shows that children who are at highest risk for academic failure are also the unhealthiest (Center for Mental Health in Schools, 1999). Factors that are linked to poor literacy development, such as poverty, urban living, and minority status, are the same ones that are associated with poor physical and mental health. Poor physical and mental health become barriers for literacy development and subsequent academic achievement. Table 6.2 presents health and social welfare factors that may influence literacy development. Because many of these factors are interrelated, many children will experience multiple risk factors.

Intervention programs, in the form of "full-service community schools," are designed to address health and social welfare barriers to literacy development. Community schools may vary in the specific services they provide, but most of them share several common elements. In community schools, the school building is the base of operation. Schools partner with outside agencies to provide medical and mental health services to the students and their families. Students and their families have access to on-site health and mental health care, dental care, group and individual counseling, and case management. The school building is open extended hours: afternoons, evenings, weekends, year round. Community schools typically have a parent resource center and after-school programs, and the school curriculum follows the *Turning Points* recommendations (presented in the previous section) (Dryfoos, 2005).

The Coalition for Community Schools has recently published *Making the Difference* (Blank, Melaville, & Shah, 2003), a report that synthesizes research conducted

TABLE 6.2	Health and Social Welfare Factors That Influence Literacy Development	
Health Barriers		**Psychological and Behavioral Barriers**
Asthma		Stress
Overweight		Lack of motivation
Dental problems		Impact of abuse
Nutritional deficiency/hunger		Attention deficit disorder
Chronic diseases		Substance abuse
Juvenile diabetes		Unprotected sexual activity
Cerebral palsy		**Family Problems**
Lead poisoning		Poverty
Learning Disabilities		Lack of health insurance
Mental retardation		Homelessness
Speech, hearing problems		Conflict/violence
Dyslexia		Parental substance abuse
Dyslexia		Parental substance abuse

Source: From "The Effects of Health and Social Welfare Factors on Literacy Development in Urban Schools," by J. Dryfoos, in J. Flood & P. A. Anders (Eds.), 2005, *Literacy Development of Students in Urban Schools: Research and Policy* (p. 37). Newark, DE: International Reading Association. Copyright 2005 by The International Reading Association. Reprinted by permission of the publisher.

on the effectiveness of community schools. Findings from 20 outcome studies showed the following results for the students:

- Improved grades in school courses and/or scores in proficiency testing
- Improved attendance
- Reduced behavioral or discipline problems and/or suspensions/expulsions
- Greater classroom cooperation, completion of homework and assignments, adherence to school rules and positive attitude
- Increased promotions and on-time graduations

These are very positive educational outcomes for school-age children and their families. The effectiveness of these interventions shows the interrelatedness between physical health, mental health, and emotional well-being with the development of literacy skills, school engagement, and academic achievement.

CHAPTER REVIEW

Applied Cognition in Academic Contexts

- Literacy development is the practical application of cognitive advances.
- One's general cognitive abilities can be assessed by intelligence and/or achievement tests.
- Creativity is distinct from intelligence and represents another form of applied cognition.
- Academic achievement is our society's measure of cognitive development.

Theoretical Viewpoint

- The psychometric approach to intelligence focuses on individual and group differences in cognitive abilities. The emphasis of this approach is on creating tests that produce an outcome of intelligence.
- The first intelligence test, created by Binet and Simon in 1905, discriminated between low-achieving students in the French educational system. The current intelligence tests, Stanford-Binet-V, and the WISC-IV, provide an IQ score that compares an adolescent's cognitive performance with same-aged peers.

- Children's intelligence remains relatively stable over their lifetime, is highly related to achievement test scores, and is predictive of job performance and success.
- One major criticism of the use of intelligence tests is their cultural bias in that both socioeconomic status and ethnicity can influence test performance.
- Two alternative views of intelligence are Gardner's theory of multiple intelligences and Sternberg's triarchic model of intelligence.

Creativity

- Creativity is thinking that is novel and that produces ideas or outcomes that are of value to the individual and/or society.
- Creativity peaks in early childhood, declines during middle childhood and then increases during adolescence. Levels of creativity in childhood are related to adult levels of creativity.

- Models of creativity show it to be influenced by a variety of familial, educational, and sociohistorical factors.
- There is a moderate relationship between creativity and intelligence, and its origins appear to be both biological and socially prescribed.

Academic Achievement

- Girls tend to perform better on verbal-oriented achievement tests in middle childhood, whereas boys perform better on math and science achievement tests.
- School-agers who live in low-income, urban, minority cities attend school with high-poverty rates and perform more poorly on achievement tests.

- Children who are highly engaged in school achieve higher academic outcomes.
- Children who come from cultural backgrounds that emphasize educational attainment but also transmit a sense of family obligation do well in school despite their low-income status.

Development in Context

- Parents can play a unique role in the academic lives of their children. Their contributions are most effective when they help their children organize their time and schedules, assist them in their homework and discuss school-related matters with their children on a regular basis.
- The perceived academic and personal support of a school in middle childhood can affect the motivation

and ability for children to succeed at the middle-school level.
- Community schools that provide full health and mental health services for children and families indirectly influence literacy development in children.

TABLE 6.3 Summary of Developmental Theories

Chapter	Theories	Focus
6: Literacy, Intelligence, and Academic Achievement	Psychometric approach	Using tests to assess individual and group differences among children's abilities; using the results to predict future performance and related abilities

KEY TERMS

Analytical reasoning	Intelligence quotient (IQ)	Psychometric approach	Standard deviation
Convergent thinking	Multiple intelligences	Rote counting	Syntax
Creativity	Normal curve	School engagement	Triarchic model of
Divergent thinking	Phoneme	Semantic	intelligence
Factor analysis	Pragmatics	Shading	
Inferencing	Primary mental abilities	Stability	

SUGGESTED ACTIVITIES

1. Interview a fourth-grade teacher. Ask the teacher how children's learning changes in fourth grade. What percentage of the class enters fourth grade with adequate reading skills? What happens to those whose skills are less than adequate? What other changes does the teacher see in writing and mathematical competency?

2. Discuss whether several of Gardner's intelligences (e.g., interpersonal intelligence) or Sternberg's practical intelligence should be considered intelligence. Why or why not?

3. Read the autobiography or biography of several creative individuals. How do they describe their childhood? When did they or others first notice their creative talent? Was it encouraged in school or valued by their society/culture?

4. Find out what your local school district is doing to help all children achieve academically.

RECOMMENDED RESOURCES

Suggested Readings

Beers, K. (2003). *When kids can't read, what teachers can do: A guide for teachers, 6–12.* Portsmouth, NH: Heineman.

Gardner, H. (1983). *Frames of mind: The theory of multiple intelligences.* New York: Basic.

Gardner, H. (1993). *Creating minds: An anatomy of creativity seen through lives of Freud, Einstein, Picasso, Stravinsky, Eliot, Graham, and Gandhi.* New York: Basic.

O'Reilly, P., Penn, E. M., & deMarrais, K. (Eds.) (2001). *Educating young adolescent girls.* Mahwah, NJ: Erlbaum.

Suggested Online Resources

Before it's too late: A Report to the Nation from the National Commission on Mathematics and Science Teaching for the 21st Century. http://www.ed.gov/inits/Math/glenn/report.pdf

Children's Literature (2006). http://www.scils.rutgers.edu/~kvander/ChildrenLit/index.html

Girls in science, girls in research (2004). http://www.uky.edu/PR/News/040305_girls_in_science.html

Suggested Web Sites

Cognitive Growth and Education.
     http://www.ncrel.org/sdrs/areas/at0cont.htm
The Council of Great City Schools.
     http://www.cgcs.org
An Intelligence Test.
     http://iqtest.com

International Children's Digital Library.
     http://www.icdlbooks.org/
International Reading Association.
     http://www.reading.org/
National Forum to Accelerate Middle Grades Reform.
     http://www.mgforum.org

Suggested Films and Videos

Enhancing social and cognitive growth in children: intellectual growth and achievement. (1994). Insight Media (27 minutes)

Intelligence. (2001). RMI Media (30 minutes)

Intelligence and creativity. (2001). Insight Media (30 minutes)

Setting the stage for school-age care. (2005). Magna Systems (30 minutes)

The 21st century classroom: Beyond standards and testing (2002). Insight Media (80 minutes)

7

Affective Development in Middle Childhood

Chapter Objectives

After reading this chapter, students will be able to:

▶ Define affective development in middle childhood.

▶ Summarize theories of middle childhood personality development.

▶ Describe school-age children's achievement of self-competence, self-esteem, and self-efficacy.

▶ Discuss current research on emotional understanding, temperament, and coping in school-age children.

▶ Explain the contributions of family, school, and community contexts to affective development in middle childhood.

Justin is the best video game player in the fifth grade. He plays every spare moment, even when he is supposed to be doing his homework. In fact, his mother is concerned that he spends too much time playing computer games. When he and his friends get together at the neighborhood arcade, the group of boys take turns, trying hard to beat Justin's best score. While they are playing, they talk about their day, their activities, and their accomplishments. "I scored three points more'n you!" "I got to the next level [of the game]!" No matter where they are—at the arcade, at school, or at one another's houses—Justin and his friends try to outperform each other.

MIDDLE CHILDHOOD AFFECTIVE DEVELOPMENT

Affective development in middle childhood includes personality, emotional development, motivation, and self-esteem. School-age children acquire personal competencies through participation in academic, athletic, or artistic activities; emotional self-regulation; and a deepening sense of who they are and what they can achieve through serious effort and commitment. Middle childhood is a period of intense acquisition of physical and cognitive abilities and the application of these newly learned skills to concrete problems school-age children encounter in the real world.

In this chapter, we explore more deeply the nature of school-age children's competencies, motivations, and commitments. Children between ages 6 and 12 often may seem obsessed with one task while never completing another. They may seem unfeeling or uncaring when interacting with friends or family, yet show immeasurable empathy when thinking about feelings or emotions in particular situations. Often, they act like young children. At other times, they may seem emotionally mature beyond their years. Why are school-age children so self-absorbed, so intense, and usually so confident? To answer these questions, we must turn to theories of personality and motivation.

> *Our case study child Justin's perceptual-motor skills are exceptional. He could be great at sports like soccer or hockey. Justin just doesn't seem to care about anything except video games!*

THEORETICAL VIEWPOINTS

Personality psychology is the study of individual differences among people. Theories of personality offer us several alternative explanations for differences in personal characteristics, such as temperament, motivation, or self-esteem, to name just a few. Because the overarching perspective of this text is contextual, however, our task is to ask how personality differences in middle childhood interact with the demands of the school-age child's environment to result in dynamic and adaptive development.

> *For example, Justin's personal desire to build his skills on computer games bumps up against his family's demands for emotional availability. His sisters always seem to bother him when he's trying to concentrate. When he tells his sisters to go away, they complain to his father that he's being mean. How do personality theorists explain such interactions?*

Two compatible theoretical approaches to the study of personality are **psychodynamic theories** and **humanistic theories**. What these two approaches have in common is a focus on the individual person—that is, on the *self.*

Personality Perspectives

Personality psychology has its origin in the psychoanalytic theory of Sigmund Freud. Freud (1959) developed a theory of human personality development based on biological drives and instincts—specifically, *pleasure.* In Freudian theory, the "self" resides in three major personality systems: the *id, ego,* and *superego.* The **id** represents the inner world of subjective experience (e.g., *Justin's enjoyment of video games*). The **ego**, or rational mind, represents the part of the personality that interacts with objective reality and struggles against the pleasure-seeking drives of the id

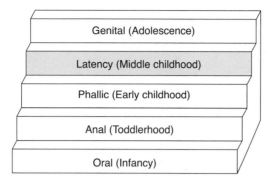

FIGURE 7.1
Freud's
Psychosexual Stages

Freud's developmental stage theory characterizes middle childhood as a calm period when children show little or no sexual interest.

to maintain self-control (e.g., *Justin's need to balance video-gaming with other activities*). The self is also constantly reminded by the **superego**, or conscience, to resist the pleasure-seeking drives of the id and to strive toward an **ego ideal**, or perfect self (e.g., *Justin's drive to record the highest score*). Through clinical work with adult patients over many years, Freud constructed a developmental stage theory, shown in Figure 7.1, that describes the gradual unfolding of personality from infancy through adulthood, driven by the gratification of pleasure.

In Freud's developmental approach, infants fulfill their pleasure-seeking needs by nursing or sucking (oral stage); toddlers achieve emotional satisfaction by acquiring control over biological functions, such as toileting (anal stage); and preschoolers enjoy discovering and exploring their own bodies, often sexually through masturbation, or using scatological (i.e., bathroom) humor (phallic stage). In middle childhood, however, Freud believed that the child's sexual jealousy becomes dormant (**latency stage**). According to Freudian theory, the latency-age child does not show sexual interest again until puberty. Recently, however, researchers of school-age children's curiosity about sexuality and attention to sexualized content in society and the media have refuted Freud's proposed period of latency (see Strasburger & Wilson, 2002).

Many contemporary scholars have criticized Freud's psychosexual approach. For example, Freud described a period in early childhood in which young children "fall in love" with their opposite-sex parent to the point of jealousy or fear of the other (same-sex) parent, called the Oedipal complex, named for Oedipus, a character from Greek mythology who killed his father and married his mother (or for girls, called the Electra complex after Agamemnon's daughter who revenged her father's murder by killing her mother). Cognitive developmental psychologists have offered an alternative explanation for the child's resolution of the Oedipal crisis by citing the preoperational child's emerging conservation abilities (described in chapter 5). The post-Oedipal child can now reason that since age and social roles (such as mother/son) are related, a little boy will never grow old enough to marry his mother (Watson & Fischer, 1980)! In addition, feminist psychoanalytic theorists have questioned the validity of the Oedipal/Electra crisis, claiming that girls as well as boys must develop and maintain a close emotional attachment to a nurturing parent (usually female) in order to assure the "reproduction of mothering" in successive generations (see Chodorow, 1999). (Attachment theory will be fully discussed in chapter 8.)

Psychosocial Theory. Erik Erikson, a child psychoanalyst, revised and expanded Freud's theory to better account for the influence of society and culture on personality. In Erikson's (1950, 1968) *psychosocial* approach, the support and guidance of significant others influence the possible outcomes of normative developmental crises

FIGURE 7.2
Erikson's
Psychosocial Stages

Erikson's
developmental stage
theory characterizes
middle childhood as
a time of
industriousness.

Source: From *The Young
Child: Development from
Prebirth through Age
Eight,* 4th ed. (p. 256), by
Margaret B. Puckett &
Janet K. Black, 2005,
Upper Saddle River, NJ:
Merrill/Prentice Hall.
Adapted by permission
of the publisher.
Reprinted by permission.

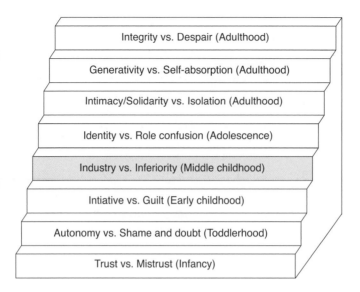

that occur at each of eight stages of the life span (see Figure 7.2). Erikson (1950) considered the primary psychosocial task of infancy to be the development of *basic
trust*, or the belief that others will care for you. For toddlers, the normative task is
to develop *autonomy*, or a sense of yourself as a separate individual, as in learning to
walk without assistance. And in early childhood, the psychosocial challenge is to
develop *initiative*, or a sense of curiosity, typically through play and experimentation
with toys and other common materials.

In each of the psychosocial stages, if the individual is not provided adequate support
for the appropriate tasks, a crisis may occur. For example, infants may develop a *mistrust*
of others if they are ignored when crying, fearful, or hungry. Toddlers may experience
shame or doubt in their ability to act independently of their caregivers, especially if they
are criticized during their immature attempts at self-care (e.g., using the toilet).
Preschoolers may experience *guilt* if their initiatives are criticized for not meeting adult
standards (e.g., drawing a picture or dressing themselves).

In middle childhood, the school-age child's primary psychosocial task is to acquire
a **sense of industry**, or the ability to work on a skill or project and to follow through
over an extended period of time (e.g., art or science projects). However, school-age
children who are not provided adequate encouragement for their "industriousness"
may develop a sense of inferiority—especially if they were to try new skills or plans
without adequate instruction or support, or if they were ridiculed for their failures
(Erikson, 1950). A sense of industry *and* appropriate guidance from others are required
to acquire the basic skills needed both in the wider culture and in school settings, such
as reading, writing, and computing. In fact, most school-age children seem to focus the
majority of their time and attention on the acquisition of skills and the development of
competence.

> *Recall our case study child, Justin. He really enjoys playing computer games. And
> he knows that he is good at it !*

The industry stage in middle childhood contributes to an emerging sense of
identity. But first, we need to understand the development of the school-age child's
sense of self.

Humanistic Perspectives

Personality theories that focus on the development of a positive sense of self are often termed **humanistic**. Humanistic theorists draw our attention to the basic human needs of individuals and to their emotional well-being. In contrast to psychodynamic theories that explain connections between the past and present (e.g., Freud) or the person and others (e.g., Erikson), humanistic theories focus on the person's current inner experiences. Among many other approaches, humanistic psychology includes theories of **self-actualization** and **person-centered experience**.

Self-Actualization Theory. Abraham Maslow is often considered the founder of humanistic psychology. His book *Toward a Psychology of Being* (1962) outlined self-actualization theory. He proposed that all people try to satisfy five basic human needs:

1. Physiological needs
2. Needs for safety and security
3. Needs for love and belonging
4. Need for self-esteem
5. Need for self-actualization

Maslow (1962) theorized that these requirements form a **hierarchy of needs**, from physiological and safety needs that are essential for physical survival to those needs that are essential for psychological health, such as love, belonging, and self-esteem. Figure 7.3 depicts Maslow's hierarchy as a pyramid. This hierarchy of needs, according

FIGURE 7.3
Maslow's Hierarchy of Needs

A sense of self-esteem, competence, and belonging are basic human needs according to Maslow.

to Maslow, leads ultimately to **self-actualization**, or the drive to be your best and fulfill your potential.

Because they focus primarily on the individual, self-actualization approaches have been criticized for ignoring the social context of the larger environment or community (see Prochaska & Norcross, 2002). In his later writings, however, Maslow (1971) revised the hierarchy by adding a higher need beyond self-actualization: **self-transcendence**, or a drive toward life experiences that go beyond your personal goals and connect you with others or with universal human experience. Maslow (1971) called these transcendent "ways of being" **peak experiences**. During peak experiences, the person is totally absorbed—emotionally and intellectually—in an activity. Maslow believed that children are naturally capable of peak experiences, which occur frequently in the school-age years.

> *Justin's computer gaming is an example of just such a peak experience. When Justin is "in the zone" he sometimes forgets to eat and doesn't even hear his mother calling him to the table for dinner!*

The task of education, according to Maslow, is to cultivate self-actualization: "Even the difficult tasks of learning to read and subtract and multiply, which are necessary in an industrialized society, can be enhanced and made joyful" (1971, p. 188). These activities then become self-validating. Self-actualization theory was applied to education by Rogers in his book *Freedom to Learn* (1969) (see Box 7.1).

Person-Centered Theory. According to Maslow's contemporary Carl Rogers, children are born with an innate capacity to experience the world. Although their reality is shaped in part by the environment (*in Justin's case by the virtual world of*

 BOX 7.1   Roadmap to Successful Practice
Freedom to Learn

In the beginning of his book on education, Carl Rogers (1969) quoted a diary sent to him by an elementary teacher. The sixth-grade teacher had decided to try a new unstructured approach. She began by telling the class that they were going to experiment: The students could do anything they wanted, or nothing at all! Most children became so interested in what they were doing that they did not even go out to recess. By the end of the term, the students were described as having developed their own standards of behavior and living up to them. The teacher wrote, "I cannot explain exactly what happened, but it seems to me, that when their self-concept changed, when they discovered they can, they did!" (p. 22).

Rogers (1969) compared this teacher's classroom experiment to the tenets of a therapeutic encounter group: relatively unstructured and providing a climate of maximum freedom for personal expression, exploration of feelings, and interpersonal communication. Rogers's therapeutic goal was to promote optimal personal growth. In *Freedom to Learn,* he proposed a humanistic model for education, stressing that schools should encourage children to be dependable, realistic, self-enhancing, socialized, creative, unpredictable, and ever-developing.

Source: Based on *Freedom to Learn* by C. R. Rogers, 1969, Columbus, OH: Charles E. Merrill. Copyright © 1969 by Charles E Merrill Publishing Co.

his game!), Rogers (1961) believed that individuals respond not to an "objective" reality, but to the world as they *experience* it, an approach also called **phenomenological**. Person-centered psychologists, like Maslow and Rogers, assert that individuals positively value those experiences that they perceive as life-enhancing and negatively value those experiences that may limit personal growth (Prochaska & Norcross, 2002). These opportunities are called *self*-experiences in Rogerian theory.

In middle childhood, growth-enhancing opportunities often involve the development of skills and abilities that allow school-agers to succeed in a particular culture, what Erikson (1968) called *a sense of industry.* As school-age children acquire (or "own" in Rogerian terms) positive self-experiences, they begin to develop what Rogers called **positive self-regard,** or acceptance of themselves. School-age children also come to value those experiences that afford them opportunities for positive regard from others, such as parents, teachers, or peers. Taken together, these internalized notions of what is valued by self and others are called **conditions of worth.** (*Certainly, Justin's peers admire his computer skills.*)

Developmental psychologists have examined various aspects of self-worth in middle childhood as well as the motivation of school-age children toward self-actualization and competence. Practitioners have also applied Rogerian techniques to support children's affective development, using techniques described in Box 7.2.

STOP When you were in middle childhood, who regarded you highly? Why? How did you know?

BOX 7.2   Roadmap to Successful Practice
Rogerian Techniques

Rogerians believe that children internalize positive regard from significant others when they receive support, acceptance, and approval (Marion, 1999). In 1962, Thomas Gordon, a Rogerian therapist, developed a program of child guidance based on Carl Rogers's theory, called *Parent Effectiveness Training* (PET), and later a variation called *Teacher Effectiveness Training* (TET). Other similar guidance programs include *Systematic Training for Effective Parenting* (STEP), developed by Don Dinkmeyer and Gary McKay (1989).

These programs are designed to teach adults to identify the course of a problem before deciding how to deal with it. If the child, rather than the adult, owns the problem, the adult may ask, "You seem to have a problem. Do you need my help?" Active listening is a strategy that an adult trained in the Rogerian framework would use. For example, if a child were to say, "I hate school!" an active listener would say, "It sounds as if you are upset about going to school." With this kind of feedback, the listener can be sure of what the child meant to say. Active listening involves simply reflecting the child's message and communicating acceptance of the child's feelings without judging or offering advice.

On the other hand, sending "I messages" is a communication strategy that you can use when you, the adult (not the child), own a problem. "I messages" are clear declarative statements that do not accuse the child of causing the adult's feeling: "I feel frustrated when you play video games instead of doing your homework" or "I'm really proud of your hard work on this science project" (Marion, 1999, p. 265). Table 7.1 provides a list of terms that can be used to express a wide range of positive and negative feelings.

(continued)

BOX 7.2   **Roadmap to Successful Practice** *(Continued)*
Rogerian Techniques

TABLE 7.1   **Semantic Differential of Emotions**

These opposing emotion terms can be useful to help school-age children identify their feelings in an "I message."

Negative	. . . "I feel . . ." . . .	Positive
Sad		Happy
Angry		Glad
Scared		Brave
Ashamed		Proud
Anxious		Relaxed
Distrustful		Trusting
Worried		Confident
Disappointed		Satisfied
Calm		Excited
Confused		Sure
Hated		Loved
Disliked		Liked
Rejected		Accepted

Source: Based on *Guidance of Young Children* (pp. 260–265) by M. Marion, 1999, Columbus, OH: Merrill. Copyright © 1999 by Charles E. Merrill Publishing Co.

DEVELOPMENT OF SELF-UNDERSTANDING IN MIDDLE CHILDHOOD

Many related terms have been used by developmental, clinical, and personality psychologists to describe individuals' understanding and evaluation of themselves (for a recent review, see Jacobs, Bleeker, & Constantino, 2003). *Self-concept, self-competence, self-worth,* and *self-esteem* are the psychological constructs most typically employed in research and practice with school-age children—but they are not interchangeable! *Self-concept* and *self-competence* are cognitive constructions. **Self-concept** comprises your *knowledge* of who you are, and **self-competence** refers to what you can do. On the other hand, *self-worth* and *self-esteem* are affective terms. **Self-worth** is the *feeling* that you are valued for yourself as an individual person, reflecting the Rogerian notion of positive regard discussed in the previous section. More often, in educational or counseling settings, such self-evaluations are referred to as **self-esteem**.

These two approaches to describing the *self* (i.e., cognitive and affective) are derived from a distinction originally made by the 19th-century psychologist and philosopher William James (for a review of self-representations in children, see Harter, 2006). James (1890) distinguished between two fundamental aspects of the self: **the "I"** and **the "me."** The "*I*" refers to a subjective awareness of yourself as a person, sometimes referred to as the *self as subject or agent.* The "*me*" refers to facts that

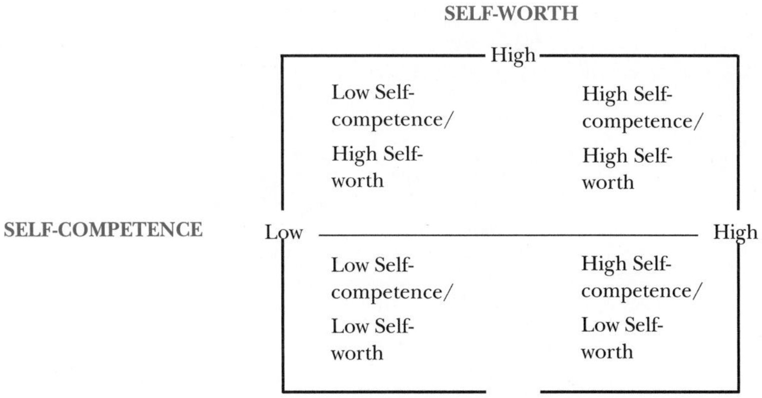

SELF-WORTH

FIGURE 7.4
Self-Esteem Matrix

Self-esteem is based on school-age children's self-evaluations of their competencies and worthiness to significant others.

Low Self-competence/ High Self-worth	High Self-competence/ High Self-worth
Low Self-competence/ Low Self-worth	High Self-competence/ Low Self-worth

SELF-COMPETENCE   Low ————————————— High

are objectively known about you, sometimes called the *self as object*. For James, a person must first construct an "I-self" in infancy, who then, throughout childhood and adulthood, constructs the "me-self" (for historical reviews, see Harter, 1992, 1999). These dual aspects of the self were subsequently elaborated by sociologists like Charles Cooley (1902) and George Herbert Mead (1934), who described a "looking-glass self," the idea that you see yourself as others see you (cf. Harter, Stocker, & Robinson, 1996). Thus, the middle childhood period involves both the cognitive construction of self-concept, based on knowledge of your own skills and abilities (i.e., self-competence), and the affective construction of self-esteem, based on the internalization of positive regard from others (i.e., self-worth). See Figure 7.4 for a graphic example of how *competence* and *worthiness* intersect to form a matrix of meaning for individuals.

Justin, for example, knows he's skilled at video games and receives admiration from his friends, leading to his positive sense of self-worth.

Self-Concept

Developmentally, self-concept progresses from the recognition in early childhood of concrete, observable characteristics (e.g., "I have red shoes") and overt abilities or activities (e.g., "I'm a good runner") to more of a focus in middle childhood on inner, psychological characteristics (e.g., "I'm a competitive person) and comparisons to others (e.g., "I scored more than you") (Harter, 1998). A common approach to the study of person concepts is to ask children for open-ended descriptions of themselves or others (Ruble & Dweck, 1995). In these studies, researchers have found that at age 8, there seems to be a change in school-age children's evaluation of enduring personal features rather than immediate behaviors (e.g., Lively & Bromley, 1973; Peevers & Secord, 1973). Studies using hypothetical stories about target children who are, for example, *generous* or *athletic* have also found that children over age 7 were more likely to predict future behavior based on stable personality traits than were younger children, who more often based their evaluations on whether or not they liked the person or valued their behavior in the immediate context (Alvarez, Ruble, & Bolger, 2001; Ruble & Dweck, 1995).

Self-Competence. The school-age years, beginning around ages 7 or 8, seem to be a "sensitive period" in self-concepts about competence (Ruble, 1987). A popular

School-age children begin to reflect on how they are distinct from others.

Shirley Zeiberg/PH College

measure of self-perception is called the "What I am Like" scale that includes the following components of self-concept (Harter, 1982, 1985):

- Physical appearance
- Social acceptance
- Scholastic competence
- Athletic competence
- Behavioral conduct

Refer to Table 7.2 for sample items from this measure of self-competence. Researchers have consistently found that school-age children can successfully differentiate among these five areas.

Recent results of a longitudinal-sequential study of two cohorts of children from elementary school through high school revealed strong, positive increases in self-competence ratings between grades 3 and 6 for both girls and boys in the domains of scholastic competence, social acceptance, and athletic competence (Cole et al., 2001). However, in the domains of physical appearance (for both sexes, but especially for girls) and behavioral conduct (for both sexes, but more so for boys), self-ratings declined during middle childhood (Cole et al., 2001). In addition, behavior genetic researchers studying children from 10 to 18 have suggested that the stability of perceived scholastic and athletic competence as well as physical appearance and general self-worth may be genetically influenced (McGuire et al., 1999). (Behavior genetics was discussed in chapter 3.)

In middle childhood, a major advance in thinking about one's own skills is the ability to generalize across the competency domains. Note that school-age children's understanding of *multidimensional* self-concepts (i.e., constructed across several competency domains) can be explained by the shift to concrete operations, as was described by Piaget (and discussed in chapter 5). During middle childhood, school-age children acquire the cognitive conservation abilities that allow them to recognize a stable self despite differing self-presentations (i.e., transformations) in varied academic or social contexts. Neo-Piagetians (e.g., Fischer, Shaver, & Carnochan, 1990) and information-processing theorists (e.g., Case, 1991) have similarly explained the acquisition of other higher-order generalizations, such as emotional dispositions and personality traits.

TABLE 7.2   Sample Items from the "*What I Am Like*" Scale

This self-report instrument is used to assess school-age children's sense of self-competence.

Really True For Me	Sort of True For Me		BUT		Sort of True For Me	Really True For Me
		Some students feel that they are good at their schoolwork	BUT	Other students worry about whether they can do the schoolwork assigned them		
		Some students find it hard to make friends	BUT	For other students it's pretty easy		
		Some students do very well at all kinds of sports	BUT	Others don't feel that they are very good when it comes to sports		
		Some students aren't sure their teacher likes them	BUT	Other students are pretty sure their teacher likes them		
		Some students wish they looked different	BUT	Other students like the way they look		
		Some students feel that they are just as smart as other students their age	BUT	Other students aren't so sure and wonder if they are as smart		
		Some students have a lot of friends	BUT	Other students don't have very many friends		
		Some students wish they could be a lot better at sports	BUT	Other students feel they are good enough at sports		
		Some students feel that there are a lot of things about themselves that they would change if they could	BUT	Other students would like to stay pretty much the same		
		Some students are pretty sure of themselves	BUT	Other students are not very sure of themselves		
		Some students feel good about the way they act	BUT	Other students wish they acted differently		
		Some students think that maybe they are not a very good person	BUT	Other students are pretty sure that they are a good person		
		Some students are very happy being the way they are	BUT	Other students wish they were different		
		Some students aren't very happy with the way they do a lot of things	BUT	Other students think the way they do things is fine		
		Some students are usually sure that what they are doing is the right thing	BUT	Other students aren't so sure whether or not what they are doing is the right thing		

Source: From *The Self-Perception Profile for Children* by S. Harter. Unpublished manual, Denver, CO, 1985. Copyright © 1985 by Susan Harter. Reprinted by permission.

In the chapter case, for example, Justin is confident and self-assured, whether he is playing video games, doing classroom assignments, or just talking to his friends.

In these cognitive conceptualizations, a second major advance of middle childhood is the coordination of self-concept features into a representational *system* of the self. For example, the school-age child may construct the self-concept "smart" based on successful performance in both English and math or, conversely, "dumb" based on poor performance. The school-age child also has increasing tolerance for contradictory self-representations, sometimes called "bidimensional thought" (Case, 1991; Jacobs et al., 2003). For instance, a child who does well in language and social studies but receives low grades in math and science could construct a self-concept of "good at some things, bad at others," leading to both positive *and* negative self-evaluations (Harter, 1998, 2006). The extent to which these labels may become internalized as **personality traits**, that is, as stable characteristics of the person, depends in part on the support and feedback provided by others. A balanced view of self, in which both positive and negative attributes are acknowledged, is fostered by comparing one's skills and abilities to those of others.

A third major advance in middle childhood is the ability of school-age children to compare themselves to others, called **social comparison** (Harter, 1998; for a review, see Frey & Ruble, 1990). In middle childhood, comparisons to peers become particularly salient as a means for the self-assessment of personal competence, compared to *temporal* comparisons (i.e., "how I am performing now compared to when I was younger") or to age norms (i.e., "what kids my age should be able to do") (Damon & Hart, 1988; Harter, 2006; Jacobs et al., 2003). Often, school-age children boast to others about their accomplishments (*remember Justin?*) with social comparisons leading to the "positive self-evaluations that typically persist at this age level" (Harter, 1998, p. 570). Consistent with Rogers' (1961) humanistic theory of positive regard from others, school-age children—like all humans—value affirming feedback from others.

By about 7 or 8, children spontaneously compare peers' performance to their own, although at first their perceptions may seem unrelated to normative judgments of competence by adults! As school-age children mature, the accuracy of their self-evaluations increases due to their increasing ability to incorporate environmental information and to make realistic social comparisons (Novick, Cauce, & Grove, 1998). For example, agreement between children's self-evaluations and teacher evaluations of their cognitive competencies, such as reading or math ability, increases between the third and sixth grades (Shirk & Renouf, 1992). Overall, self-competence ratings become increasingly correlated with the appraisals of others (Phillips & Zimmerman, 1990).

By the end of middle childhood, however, children are keenly aware of both the positive *and* negative consequences of overtly comparing themselves to others; older children are more likely than younger children to perceive such behavior as "showing off." Nevertheless, researchers have found that older children do not abandon their use of social comparison; they simply become more covert, using visual attention, such as watching or glancing, rather than direct questioning. This finding suggests that "children may learn that subtle comparison yields positive [affective] consequences while avoiding negative [social] consequences produced by more detectable forms of comparison" (Pomerantz, Ruble, Frey, & Greulich, 1995, p. 736).

STOP What areas of competence did you excel in as a child? Did you compare yourself to your friends?

Guideposts for Working with School-Age Children

- Help children to identify their skills in a variety of competence domains by talking about what they're good at.

- Because school-age children may hold both positive and negative self-concepts at the same time, support children by accepting their strengths and their limitations.

- Help children to realize that overt social comparisons may lead to negative interactions with peers by suggesting strategies that may help them to be more subtle, such as complimenting others' achievements.

- Encourage children to strive for self-competence rather than always comparing themselves to others.

Self-Esteem

During middle childhood, school-age children readily construct affective judgments about their competencies, which is made possible by their ability to form a multidimensional self-concept and to engage in social comparisons. Taken together, these self-evaluations contribute to a sense of **self-esteem**, or how they feel about themselves. By around age 8, children experience an important developmental shift in the relation between self-perceptions and behavior (Davis-Kean & Sandler, 2001). Assessing feelings of self-esteem is the most common way for researchers to measure positive or negative affect in school-age children (Anderson, 1992).

Self-Worth. In research with both late-elementary and middle-school children, looking good (i.e., physical appearance) and being well liked (i.e., social acceptance) were most highly related to **self-worth**, or liking oneself (Harter, 1987). In addition, when researchers examined the relationship between peer approval and self-worth in sixth to eighth graders, they found support for the idea that peer approval may *precede* self-worth (Harter et al., 1996). Despite their increasing self-competence, *how* school-age children think others see them and *how much* they are accepted are still important. (Peer relations in middle childhood are discussed in chapter 10.)

By middle childhood, most children have established a sense of their own *global* self-worth, or how much they are valued *as a person* (Harter, 2006). When researchers compared the degree to which self-worth is related to the five competency areas rated by elementary-age and middle-grades students on the "What I Am Like" scale, physical appearance was the area most highly related to self-worth for both age groups. Social acceptance, however, was more highly related for children in grades 6 to 8 than for elementary-age children. By comparison, preschool children can discriminate among four domains of competence (physical competence, cognitive competence, maternal acceptance, and social acceptance) but perceptions of their competencies do *not* include an overall sense of self-worth (Harter & Pike, 1984; Harter, 1996a).

These findings generally support Erikson's psychosocial theory that in middle childhood developing a sense of industry (vs. inferiority) is related to the development of competence. However, "the salience of competence as a developmental issue is at once both a source of self-esteem and a potential threat to one's self-worth. Thus, a task in middle childhood involves coordination of one's sense of self-worth with one's emerging sense of competence" (Shirk & Renouf, 1992, p. 56). For example, when researchers compared school-age children's perceptions of their *competence* in different domains with their ratings of the *importance* of these factors, they found that all of the competency domains contributed to children's overall evaluation of their self-worth, but to differing degrees. Figure 7.5 illustrates how the discrepancies

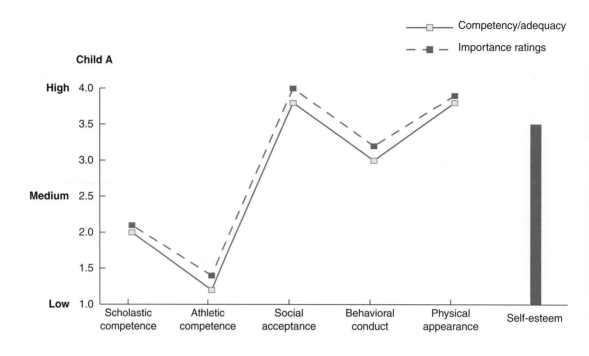

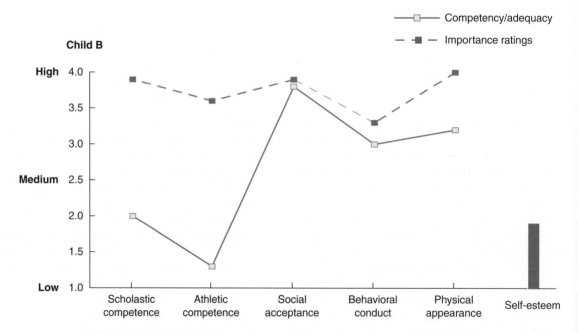

FIGURE 7.5

Importance Ratings of Competence as Predictors of Self-Esteem

Self-esteem is higher in a child (top graph) for whom competency judgments and importance ratings are closely related than a child for whom there is a greater discrepancy (bottom graph).

Source: From "Visions of Self: Beyond the Me in the Mirror," by S. Harter, 1992, in S. Harter, J. S. Eccles, & L. L. Carstensen (Eds.), *Nebraska Symposium on Motivation: Vol. 40. Developmental perspectives on motivation* (p. 108). Lincoln, NB. Copyright © 1992 University of Nebraska Press. Reprinted by permission of the publisher.

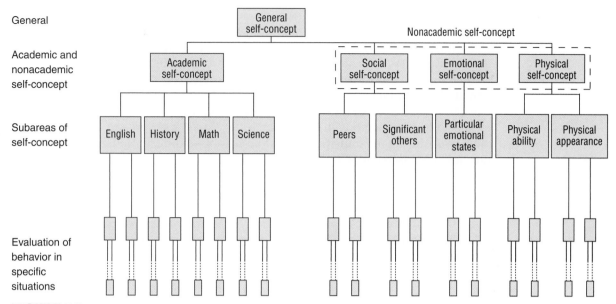

FIGURE 7.6
Self-Worth Hierarchy

Overall self-concept is composed of separate areas in a hierarchy from general to specific.

Source: From "Theoretical Perspectives on the Self-Concept," by H. W. Marsh & J. Hattie, 1996, in
B. A. Bracken (Ed.), *Handbook of self-concept: Developmental, social, and clinical considerations* (p. 54).
New York: Wiley. Copyright © 1996 by John Wiley and Sons. Reprinted by permission of the publisher.

between competency ratings and importance ratings predicted self-esteem for two
children with similar domain-specific self-competence profiles *but very different levels of global self-worth* (Harter, 1992).

Overall, researchers on self-competence have found considerable support for a
hierarchical model (not unlike Maslow's hierarchy of needs) in which general self-
concept is placed at the apex of an organizational chart with the competence domains nested underneath according to the importance an individual child may
place on particular domains, as shown in Figure 7.6 (Harter, 1996b; see also Eccles-
Parsons et al., 1983, and Marsh & Hattie, 1996). Because individual acts of competence occur in a socially constructed world, children—like adults—evaluate their
accomplishments in terms of social standards for what is valued or "worthy"
(Mruk, 1995).

Although some researchers have found that domain-specific ratings, such as academic competence, drop sharply during the transition between elementary and
junior high or middle school (e.g., Simmons & Blyth, 1987), other researchers have
found that the high self-esteem typically found in early childhood levels off in middle childhood. Still others have found that domain-specific self-evaluations may yet
change as individual children change interests and activities during the school-age
years (Jacobs et al., 2003). For example, in a study of individual differences in sixth-,
seventh-, and eighth-grade children's ratings of perceived competence *after* the middle school transition, researchers found that about 50% of the children were stable
over seven months in their self-competency ratings in the academic domain, while
the other 50% of students either increased or decreased in their self-evaluations of
academic competence (Harter, Whitesell, & Kowalski, 1992).

STOP Did your
parents,
teachers, or friends
value your perform-
ance in certain
school subjects or
extracurricular
activities more than
in others?

The focus of most middle childhood school transition research has been on the systematic effects that changes in the educational environment have on school-age children (Harter et al., 1992). In most school districts, a shift to junior high or middle school is associated with an increase in whole-group instruction, between-classroom ability grouping, and public evaluation of the correctness of work; changes such as these are likely to increase social comparison, concerns about evaluation, and competitiveness (Eccles, 1992; Entwisle, Alexander, & Olson, 2006). Researchers have found that the strain associated with both changes in the peer group and the demands of school work during the transition to middle school—although moderated by support from close friends, parents, and teachers—was related to lower feelings of competence and self-worth (Fenzel, 2000).

In addition, a large-scale longitudinal study of school-age children in family and school contexts found that junior high teachers also felt less effective, especially for low-ability students (Eccles, 1992). Figure 7.7 illustrates these effects on low-ability students' self-ratings of math competence. "High-to-high" students had a teacher who was rated as highly effective in both sixth and seventh grades; "high-to-low" students had a highly effective teacher in sixth grade but a teacher rated as less effective in seventh; "low-to-high" students had a less effective teacher in sixth but a highly effective teacher in seventh grade; and "low-to-low" students had teachers rated as less effective in both grades.

Ideal Self. One plausible explanation for such differing perceptions of their competence is that most school-agers can also create representations of what they may

FIGURE 7.7

Expectations for Math Performance

Low-ability students expect to do worse across the transition to junior high school when they rate their teachers as less effective.

Source: From "School and Family Effects on the Ontogeny of Children's Interests, Self-Perceptions, and Activity Choices," by J. Eccles, 1992, in S. Harter, J. S. Eccles, & L. L. Carstensen (Eds.), *Nebraska Symposium on Motivation: Vol. 40. Developmental perspectives on motivation* (pp. 188–189). Lincoln, NB. Copyright © 1992 University of Nebraska. Reprinted by permission.

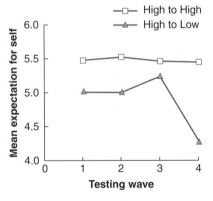

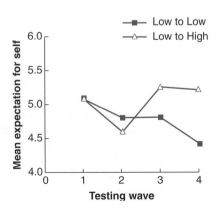

BOX 7.3   Roadmap to Successful Practice
Teachers' Support for Competence

Teachers establish an overall context for competence by:

1. *Employing Different Activity Structures in the Classroom.* Students working in small groups, in contrast to those working individually or in a whole-class activity, are more likely to seek assistance from other students as well as the teacher. During small-group activities, students work collaboratively with others, reducing the potential for social comparison.

2. *Fostering Help-Seeking Behaviors.* In classrooms that foster conversation, discussion, and inquiry, students feel free to seek help for tasks. With increased competence, children become more accurate in monitoring their knowledge states, more attuned to when help is necessary, and better at formulating questions when they encounter difficulties.

3. *Establishing Patterns of Discourse That Facilitate Intrinsic Motivation.* Teachers who provide feedback that focuses on specific strengths and weaknesses in performance rather than global assessments or normative grading tend to maximize intrinsic motivation and, as a result, support students' continued effort following failure.

4. *Helping to Socialize Students' Expectancies for Success.* Teachers who respond to requests for help with hints and contingent instruction, rather than direct and controlling answers, help students learn that problems and uncertainties can be tolerated—and perhaps even shared and transformed into intellectual challenges. Demonstrating to children that they deserve answers to their questions arguably helps children with a personal sense of empowerment.

Source: Based on "What do I need to do to succeed . . . when I don't understand what I'm doing!?: Developmental influences on students' adaptive help-seeking" (pp. 293–295) by R. S. Newman, in A. Wigfield & J. S. Eccles (Eds.), *The development of achievement motivation*, 2002, San Diego, CA: Academic. Copyright © 2002 by Academic Press.

want to be, or feel that they *should* be, comprising an **ideal self** (Harter, 1998, 2006). The contrast between children's **real self** (i.e., how they perceive themselves to be, in actuality) and their ideal self (likely fostered by social comparisons) may lead to negative self-evaluations, especially if children experience repeated social or academic failures (Harter, 1998; see also Pomerantz & Ruble, 1997; Pomerantz & Saxon, 2001). The disparity between children's real and ideal selves is lower in middle childhood than in adolescence, however, presumably because school-age children are not yet abstract, hypothetical thinkers (Higgins, 1991).

Box 7.3 describes classroom strategies that teachers can use to support school-age children's sense of self-competence and self-worth. Interestingly, when sixth and seventh graders were asked (in small focus groups) to invent a program to enhance self-esteem for other students, they described activity-based (rather than didactic) programs individualized to the developmental level of the participants. They also stressed using locations and resources in the surrounding community that included older students, role models, and teachers (DuBois, Lockerd, Reach, & Parra, 2003).

Guideposts for Working with School-Age Children

- Support their need to look good and be well liked because these are the most important contributors to school-age children's self-esteem.
- Compliment children's efforts because a competency domain that is highly valued by parents, teachers, or peers contributes more to overall self-worth than other skills.
- School-age children may need emotional support from parents and teachers because their positive self-evaluations often weaken across school transitions, especially to middle school or junior high school.
- Support children's changing goals by fostering the acquisition of new skills.
- Provide performance feedback to individual children rather than group evaluations or ability comparisons.

Self-Efficacy

According to personality psychologists, all people have an innate drive toward mastery over the environment, referred to as **effectance motivation** (White, 1959) or **self-efficacy**, the belief in your own ability to solve a problem or accomplish a task (Bandura, 1981, 1990, 1994). Self-efficacy includes perceived abilities that are demonstrated in achievement behaviors in various school subjects (Schunk & Pajares, 2002). Recently, researchers found that elementary-school children's self-perceptions about their Internet skills matched their feelings of self-efficacy in other content areas, such as reading (Hinson, DiStefano, & Daniel, 2004).

Self-efficacy has been linked to choice of tasks, effort and persistence, and achievement. Individuals' perceived self-efficacy is related to four determinants:

1. *Previous Performance.* Succeeding leads to a stronger sense of personal efficacy.
2. *Vicarious Learning.* Watching models succeed or fail on similar tasks teaches the task.
3. *Verbal Encouragement by Others.* Parents, teachers, or peers are the primary influences in middle childhood.
4. *Emotional Reactions.* Anxiety or worry may lead to a lower sense of self-efficacy (Bandura, 1994; see also Eccles, Wigfield, & Scheifele, 1998).

Much prior research has suggested that children's conception of their *own* ability tends to be more predictive of their achievement than are their conceptions of *others'* abilities (Pomerantz & Saxon, 2001). Recall that older children are able to make comparisons based on *ability,* such as "I'm smart"; younger children make comparisons based on a specific performance, such as "I won" (e.g., Ruble, Eisenberg, & Higgins, 1994). In several studies designed to distinguish the multiple dimensions of school-age children's conceptions of their own competence, researchers have found that whether or not ability is thought of as stable over time may affect self-evaluations in middle childhood. Thinking of ability as stable is typically associated with placing importance on being *competent* (Pomerantz & Ruble, 1997; Pomerantz & Saxon, 2001). In addition, stability may be thought of in two ways:

1. *Stable to External Forces* (e.g., teacher evaluations or peer comparisons)
2. *Stable to Internal Forces* (e.g., trying hard or feeling competent) (Pomerantz & Saxon, 2001)

From fourth to sixth grades, children increasingly view ability as stable to external forces but decreasingly view it as stable to internal forces, meaning that their own abilities are more often defined by *others*. In addition, these school-agers are likely to perceive their failures as a negative predictor of their future performance and to experience lower feelings of self-efficacy (Pomerantz & Saxon, 2001).

Although children think of ability as stable at about 7 to 9 years of age, conceptions of ability as *capacity* do not emerge until about 11 to 13 years (Pomerantz & Ruble, 1997). Not surprisingly, children who think of ability as capacity seem to incorporate external feedback more readily, such as teacher evaluations, probably because they believe that they can acquire new abilities; they have *capacity*.

> *Consider Justin, a fourth grader. He clearly thinks of his ability as constant, and that translates into a high level of perceived competence. Justin also receives positive regard from peers for his skill at progressing through the levels of the game easily. But at age 10, he is just beginning to conceive of his computer ability as capacity. What would this newly emergent understanding afford? If Justin were to believe in his own capacity, he might be more likely to incorporate suggestions from others or to utilize the embedded hints that were programmed into the game, because he would believe that he could improve his score!*

Research on academic achievement in middle childhood has demonstrated that when children believe that their ability is due to a fixed trait (e.g., intelligence), they tend to be more vulnerable in the face of difficulty or challenge because they may see failures as an indictment of their intelligence. In contrast, children who think that their ability is due to a capacity for learning tend to persevere despite failure experiences because they believe that the goal of learning is to increase their mastery (see Henderson & Dweck, 1990). In this manner, children's expectancies regarding their future performance may mediate their level of motivation for certain tasks, as shown in Table 7.3.

TABLE 7.3   The Motivational Process Model

Whether school-age children think that their ability is fixed or changing has been shown to influence their goal orientation, confidence, and achievement.

Theory of Intelligence	Goal Orientation	Confidence in Ability	Achievement Behavior
Stable • Intelligence is fixed	Performance • To gain positive evaluation of competence	If high →	Mastery oriented • Seek challenge • High persistence
		If low →	Helpless • Avoid challenge • Low persistence
Capacity • Intelligence is malleable	Learning • To increase competence	If low or high →	Mastery oriented • Seek challenge • High persistence

Source: Based on "Motivation and Achievement" by V. L. Henderson & C. S. Dweck, in S. Feldman & G. R. Elliott (Eds.), *At the threshold: The developing adolescent* (p. 310), 1990, Cambridge, MA: Harvard University Press. Copyright © 1990 by the President and Fellows of Harvard College. Adapted by permission.

Achievement Motivation. Heightened feelings of self-efficacy occur when an activity or task is seen as *intrinsically motivating.* **Intrinsic motivation** concerns the performance of activities for their own sake, in contrast to **extrinsic motivation**, in which activities are performed for an external reward. *Academic* instrinsic motivation involves enjoyment of school learning characterized by the following criteria:

- Mastery orientation
- Curiosity
- Persistence
- Task autonomy
- Seeking of challenge
- Desire for novelty (adapted from Gottfried, Fleming, & Gottfried, 2001)

Providing choices in curriculum assignments and projects, encouraging greater autonomy in classroom activities and homework, and decreasing extrinsic motivational practices, such as working for a grade rather than for the fun of learning, have been suggested as ways to increase school-agers' intrinsic motivation (Gottfried, Fleming, & Gottfried, 2001). Examples of such teaching strategies are provided in Figure 7.8. In a longitudinal study of reading, math, science, and social studies, researchers found that academic intrinsic motivation at ages 9, 10, 13, and 16 predicted school-age children's academic motivation at subsequent ages in all domains (Eccles, et al., 1998).

Intrinsically motivated activities are inherently pleasurable and offer the school-age child opportunities for what Rogers (1980) called "self-experiences" or Maslow (1987) called "peak experiences." Researchers who have studied school-age children's engagement in such activities have called them *"flow experiences"* (Csikszentmihalyi & Rathunde, 1992). **Flow** is characterized by

STOP Have you ever become so engaged in what you were doing that you lost track of time and place?

- Being immersed in an activity
- Merging actions and awareness (nothing else matters!)
- Focusing attention on a limited stimulus field
- Lacking self-consciousness
- Feeling in control of the environment and your actions

Box 7.4 illustrates the nature of a flow activity. Flow researchers have stressed that such activities must occur in a context of *self*-evaluation, rather than being driven by a concern with evaluation by others. For example, the discovery of problems that have the potential for creative solutions, such as a scientific question, is partly driven by an interest in the subject matter and partly by the intrinsic reward of finding a solution! These two factors have been integrated into a theory of motivation called **self-determination** (Deci & Ryan, 1985). Self-determination involves the degree to which school-age children experience themselves as autonomous, that is, as having choices as opposed to feeling pressured (Grolnick, Gurland, Jacob, & Decourcey, 2002). Self-determination theory also suggests that a basic need for competence is the major reason why people seek out optimal stimulation and challenging experiences (Eccles, et al., 1998).

Self-determination theory may help to explain why Justin seeks out computer games to challenge his personal sense of efficacy. When he is playing, Justin appears to be in

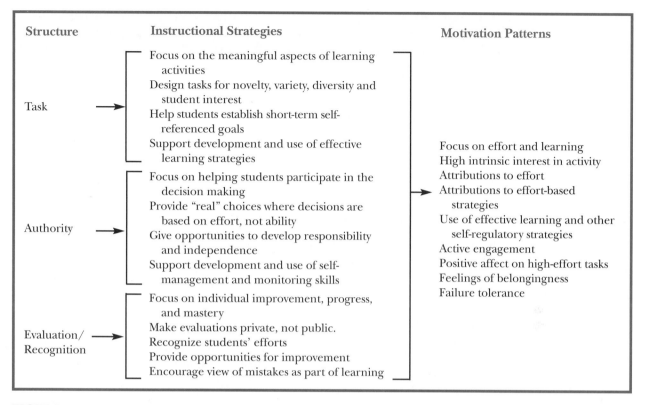

Structure	Instructional Strategies	Motivation Patterns
Task	Focus on the meaningful aspects of learning activities Design tasks for novelty, variety, diversity and student interest Help students establish short-term self-referenced goals Support development and use of effective learning strategies	
Authority	Focus on helping students participate in the decision making Provide "real" choices where decisions are based on effort, not ability Give opportunities to develop responsibility and independence Support development and use of self-management and monitoring skills	Focus on effort and learning High intrinsic interest in activity Attributions to effort Attributions to effort-based strategies Use of effective learning and other self-regulatory strategies Active engagement Positive affect on high-effort tasks Feelings of belongingness Failure tolerance
Evaluation/ Recognition	Focus on individual improvement, progress, and mastery Make evaluations private, not public. Recognize students' efforts Provide opportunities for improvement Encourage view of mistakes as part of learning	

FIGURE 7.8
Instructional Strategies and Student Motivation

The instructional strategies teachers employ to teach a task, provide support, or evaluate students' work can influence school-age children's motivation.

Source: From "Motivation to Succeed" by J. Eccles, A. Wigfield, & U. Schiefele in N. Eisenberg (Ed.), *Handbook of child psychology, Vol. 3: Social, emotional, and personality development* (p. 1065), 1998, New York: Wiley. Copyright © 1998 by John Wiley and Sons. Reprinted by permission of the publisher.

Children who are immersed in challenging activities are usually intrinsically motivated.

David Young-Wolff/PhotoEdit Inc.

BOX 7.4   Roadmap to Understanding Theory and Research
The Psychology of Flow

In research conducted by Mihalyi Csikszentmihalyi (1990), flow experiences provided participants with a sense of discovery and creativity, pushed them to higher levels of performance, and led to altered states of consciousness. According to Csikszentmihalyi, flow transforms the self by making it more complex. Using the example of a tennis match, Figure 7.9 illustrates two theoretically important dimensions of flow experiences: challenges and skills, represented on the two axes of the diagram. The letter A represents a boy who is learning to play tennis. The diagram shows him at four different points in time:

- A_1 When he starts playing and has practically no skills, he will probably be in flow if he just hits the ball over the net.

- A_2 After a while, if he keeps practicing and his skills improve, he will grow bored just batting the ball over the net and will no longer feel in flow.

- A_3 If he meets a more practiced opponent, he may feel anxiety concerning his poor performance and be out of flow.

- A_4 If he improves his skills as a way to regain flow, he will have achieved a more complex experience than A_1 because it involves greater challenges and demands greater skill.

This final state (A_4), although complex and enjoyable, does not represent a stable situation. As he keeps playing at that level, either he will become bored by a lack of challenge or he will become anxious and frustrated by his relatively low ability. Flow theory predicts that the motivation to enjoy himself again will push him to get back into the flow channel, but now at a level of complexity even higher than A_4. According to Csikszentmihalyi (1990), this dynamic feature explains why flow activities lead to growth and discovery.

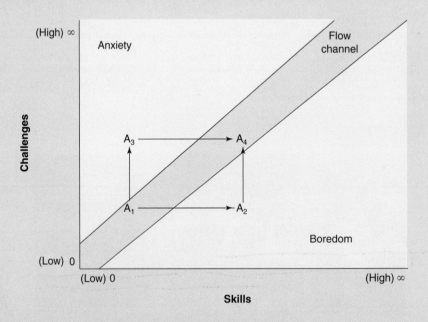

FIGURE 7.9
Creative Flow

Flow experiences intensify as optimal challenges and the skills to meet those challenges increase.

Source: From *Flow: The Psychology of Optimal Experience* (p. 74) by M. Csikszentmihalyi, 1990, New York: Harper & Row. Copyright © 1990 by Mihalyi Csikszentmihalyi. Reprinted by permission of Harper Collins Publishers.

a state of "flow." He doesn't hear his mother calling. He doesn't care if his sister is waiting. Why? Flow happens because the video game provides a perfect opportunity for action that matches Justin's abilities.

Sometimes, however, *synergistic* extrinsic motivators, or extrinsic motivation "in the service of intrinsic motivation" may help to support a sense of competence or involvement with a particular task (e.g., teaching the skills necessary for solving a problem in a specific domain, or daily charting of a child's progress)(Collins & Amabile, 1999; see also Deci & Ryan, 1985). For example, helping children to develop short-term goals has been found to promote self-efficacy and intrinsic interest (Schunk & Pajares, 2002). A study of school-age children's interest in self-evaluative information about their math performance is described in Box 7.5.

 BOX 7.5   Roadmap to Understanding Theory and Research
A Laboratory Study of Self-Evaluative Information Seeking

Diane Ruble and her colleagues hypothesized that changes in the meaning of performance and ability should lead to increased self-evaluation during the early school-age years. For children receiving relatively negative feedback, however, an approach-avoidance conflict is likely to emerge, such that low-ability children would show less interest in evaluative feedback than high-ability children. To test these predictions, children 7, 8, and 9 years of age (classified as high, medium, and low in math ability) performed a series of arithmetic tasks, on which they were given ambiguous information to look at during "rest" periods:

1. *Social Comparison Information.* Folders containing the outcomes on the same tasks of other children their age.
2. *Autonomous Evaluation Information.* Folders containing information on their own performance on previous tests and the answer keys.
3. *Control Condition.* The room also contained age-appropriate toys.

Consistent with predictions, children low in ability showed the *least* interest in obtaining information relevant to their performance. Overall, interest in obtaining self-evaluative information increased with age, as expected, but the relative "avoidance" of the low-ability children was generally consistent across ages. Low-ability children preferred social to autonomous information at ages 9 and 11. At 7, however, they showed equal interest (lack of interest?) in both. For high-ability children, interest in social comparison information remained relatively constant across age, whereas interest in autonomous evaluation increased dramatically. Medium-ability children preferred social to autonomous evaluation folders at all age levels, with little change in evaluation interest across age.

Although the researchers could only speculate about the meaning of these trends, the findings were consistent with their predictions that information seeking would increase with age and that high- and low-ability children would show differential interest. A self-evaluation of high ability apparently allowed older children to shift toward emphasizing mastery rather than self-assessment goals, a shift with major implications for subsequent performance and self-esteem.

Source: Based on "The Acquisition of Self-Knowledge: A Self-Socialization Perspective" (pp. 255–256) by D. Ruble in N. Eisenberg (Ed.), *Contemporary topics in developmental psychology* 1987, New York: Wiley. Copyright © 1987 by John Wiley & Sons.

Guideposts for Working with School-Age Children

- Help children to recall their previous performance of a task when attempting it again and to analyze what they might do differently next time.
- Encourage children to think about their capacity for learning rather than about their ability as unchanging by reminding them of a past success.
- Because children's expectations of success or failure affect their motivation for the task, praise the effort rather than the outcome.

- Provide activities that are intrinsically motivating, such as art and music, and discourage working only for extrinsic rewards, such as grades.
- Stimulate flow experiences by allowing school-age children to work independently and to become immersed in activities that are engaging and challenging.

Not accidentally, video games are designed to keep track of players' progress and chart the highest scores.

Longitudinal research with children from grades 6 to 8 has also shown that increases in students' self-evaluations of their academic competence predicts *increases* in intrinsic motivation, while decreases in perceived competence predicts *declines* in intrinsic motivation. Students who show no change in perceived academic competence also show little change in their motivational orientation (Harter et al., 1992). In addition, feeling positive toward school is associated with intrinsic motivation *but not with extrinsic motivation.*

Specific anxiety about school performance, on the other hand, is related to extrinsic motivation but not to intrinsic motivation. These findings suggest that an extrinsic orientation may be accompanied by pressure to perform and thus lead to feelings of anxiety, whereas an intrinsic orientation may lead to liking school (see Harter et al., 1992; Isen, 2000). Generally, academic intrinsic motivation decreases slightly across the years from middle to high school. Similar findings have been reported for both American and European students, especially in the curriculum areas of science and math (Eccles et al., 1998).

EMOTIONAL DEVELOPMENT AND TEMPERAMENT

How do feelings, such as anxiety or pleasure, either hinder or support school-age children's growing sense of self-competence and self-worth? Emotion theorists have defined the concept of **emotional competence** as "readiness to establish, maintain, or change the relation between the person and the environment on matters of significance to that person" (Saarni, 1998, p. 238). This action-oriented definition varies from most definitions of emotional development because it does not refer to inner feelings (e.g., happy or sad), outer emotional expressions (e.g., laughing or crying), internal affective states (e.g., calm or nervous), or cognitive abilities (e.g., emotional intelligence). Instead, *emotion is described as a person-environment transaction* whereby emotional meaning is socially constructed in each interaction. Such an approach fits best with the contextual framework of this text.

Emotional competence refers to how children and adults understand emotions in the context of the social demands placed on them (Saarni, 1990, 2000, 2001a; Halberstadt, Dunsmore, & Denham, 2001). This approach to emotional development has been termed a *functionalist approach* to emotion in that it focuses on the function of emotion in human experience (Campos, Mumme, Kermoian, & Campos, 1994). As an example of functionalism, it also relates to our previous discussion of self-efficacy (see Saarni, 2001b); school-age children need to have the capacity and skills to regulate their own emotional experience as well as to respond to others.

In middle childhood, emotional competence involves the ability of school-age children to understand their own emotional states, to correctly interpret their affective experiences with others, and to control their emotions. This complex task of emotional self-regulation involves managing negative feelings, such as anxiety or frustration, and focusing on positive goals. For example, emotion-regulating skills allow school-age children to manage their emotions by seeking out rewarding experiences and avoiding unpleasant ones (Salovey, Bedell, Detweiler, & Mayer, 2000). In self-psychology, such self-control behaviors are commonly referred to as successful coping skills. In the school-age years, a variety of emotional coping strategies emerge:

- *Redefining a Situation.* Thinking "it's just a story" when listening to a sad account
- *Altering an Emotional Reaction.* Thinking happy thoughts in a sad situation
- *Dissociating Emotional Expression from Emotional Experience.* Expressing an emotion to others that is different from how you really feel
- *Relating Self-Regulation to Goals.* Thinking about the potential benefits of self-control versus the potential costs of losing control
- *Attributing Intent to Emotion.* Thinking "I shouldn't be mad at my little brother; he didn't mean it" (adapted from Thompson, 1998)

Emotional Intelligence

Emotion has been studied from a variety of theoretical frameworks (e.g., Fox, 1994). Psychoanalytic theorists have viewed emotions as instinctual physiological drives, such as fear, pleasure, or anger. Developmental psychologists have described emotion based on human infants' ability to discriminate among facial expressions of emotion, such as frowning or smiling. Cognitive psychologists have described emotion as the interpretation of affective experiences, such as feeling upset and deciding whether you are experiencing anger or sadness. Evolutionary psychologists have theorized that emotional behavior is an adaptive mechanism that serves to motivate all action, as in "fight or flight" decisions. Neuropsychological researchers have identified the areas of the brain that control emotions, such as the *amygdala*, and have proposed that emotions are neural events. Recently, social psychologists have proposed that individuals differ in how skilled they are at perceiving, understanding, and utilizing emotion information, called "emotional intelligence." The emotional intelligence framework is specified in Table 7.4.

Emotional intelligence is "the ability to perceive and express emotions, to understand and use them, and to manage emotions so as to foster personal growth" (Salovey et al., 2000, p. 504). Researchers have operationally defined emotional intelligence by the specific competencies it encompasses, including:

- Ability to perceive, appraise, and express emotions accurately
- Ability to access and generate feelings when they facilitate understanding

---

TABLE 7.4   The Emotional Intelligence Framework

Emotional intelligence in middle childhood develops gradually as school-age children begin to understand and manage complex and conflicting emotions.

Perception, appraisal, and expression of emotion

- Ability to identify emotion in one's physical and psychological states.
- Ability to identify emotion in other people and objects.
- Ability to express emotions accurately, and to express needs related to those feelings.
- Ability to discriminate between accurate and inaccurate, or honest and dishonest, expressions of feelings.

Emotional facilitation of thinking

- Ability to redirect and prioritize one's thinking based on the feelings associated with objects, events, and other people.
- Ability to generate or emulate vivid emotions to facilitate judgments and memories concerning feelings.
- Ability to capitalize on mood swings to take multiple points of view; ability to integrate these mood-induced perspectives.
- Ability to use emotional states to facilitate problem solving and creativity.

Understanding and analyzing emotional information: employing emotional knowledge

- Ability to understand how different emotions are related.
- Ability to perceive the causes and consequences of feelings.
- Ability to interpret complex feelings, such as emotional blends and contradictory feeling states.
- Ability to understand and predict likely transitions between emotions.

Regulation of emotion

- Ability to be open to feelings, both those that are pleasant and those that are unpleasant.
- Ability to monitor and reflect on emotions.
- Ability to engage, prolong, or detach from an emotional state, depending upon its judged informativeness or utility.
- Ability to manage emotion in oneself and others.

Source: From "Emotional Development, Emotional Intelligence" by Peter Salovey, 1997, New York: Basic Books. Copyright © 1997 by Peter Salovey and David J. Sluyter. Reprinted by permission of Basic Books, a member of Perseus Books Group.

- Ability to understand affect-laden information and make use of emotional knowledge
- Ability to regulate emotions to promote intellectual growth and well-being

How many of these competencies are present by middle childhood? To answer this question requires a description of the development of emotional understanding in the school-age years.

By middle childhood, children are able to reflect on their own emotional experiences and those of others. They readily understand that their cognitive appraisal of emotional states is important in determining how they feel about people or events. For example, although children under age 7 can describe how their parents might be proud or ashamed of their actions, not until about age 8 can children understand

School-age children are able to reflect on their own emotional experiences.

Silver Burdett Ginn

that they can be proud or ashamed of *themselves*, even in the absence of adult observation or feedback (Harter & Whitesell, 1989). They also believe that emotions are strongest immediately after an emotion-eliciting situation, and that they become weaker with time (Saarni, Mumme, & Campos, 1998; see also Saarni, Campos, Camras, & Witherington, 2006).

In addition, several studies have shown that school-age children understand that they can conceal their genuine feelings and instead display false emotional reactions, for example, pretending you like a gift so as not to hurt your grandfather's feelings (Saarni et al., 1998). Researchers have consistently found that school-agers between ages 9 and 12, compared to younger children, can understand multiple, sometimes conflicting, emotions. For example, school-age children can be *happy* and *sad* at the same time when thinking about a divorce situation ("I'm glad I get to live with my dad, but I'm sad about not being able to live with mom too"). However, not until age 12 can children think simultaneously about opposing emotions toward the same target ("I love my dad, even though I'm mad at him right now") (Whitesell & Harter, 1989). Children's book authors routinely focus on such middle childhood emotional conflict, as discussed in Box 7.6.

If the conflicting emotions are not equally *intense* or if the emotions are very *dissimilar*, however, children may experience conflict (Whitesell & Harter, 1989). For example, depression has been described by early adolescents as a mixture of sadness and anger. Researchers have found that emotions produce the greatest conflict (a) when a negative emotion is either equal to or more intense than a positive emotion *and* (b) when the two emotions are quite different, or even opposites (Harter & Whitesell, 1989).

> *For example, imagine that our case study child Justin is proud of himself for winning his game and simultaneously angry with his best friend for not congratulating him.*

By the end of middle childhood, children are also better able to appreciate the psychological complexity of emotional experiences. For example, by age 11 they are more likely to attribute emotional arousal to internal causes rather than to external events. This emergent emotional understanding allows school-age children to predict the emotions of others without needing to observe facial or verbal cues, such as

Box 7.6   Roadmap to Successful Practice
Ramona and Her Father by *Beverly Cleary*

In an intriguing essay, Carolyn Saarni (1990) discusses a favorite children's book for middle childhood readers, *Ramona and Her Father* by Beverly Cleary (1977). When 8-year-old Ramona came home from school, no one was waiting for her. She pounded on the back door, and no one answered. She rang the front doorbell, but still no one came. The book's narrative describes her mixed emotions when her father finally arrived:

- Maybe her father was angry with her
- Maybe he had gone away because she tried to make him stop smoking
- Maybe he was worried about being out of work
- Maybe she had made him so angry he did not love her anymore

In her essay, Saarni (1990) points out Ramona's own emotional state (fear), the attributions she makes about her father's emotional condition (anger), personal information (unemployment), and her own relationship with him (love). When Mr. Quimby finally appeared, Ramona was simultaneously relieved, glad to see him, and angry. Saarni suggests that books such as the *Ramona* series can assist young readers to comprehend the emotional roller coaster that school-age children often experience by mirroring the internal processes they go through as they develop emotional competence.

Source: Based on "Emotional competence: How emotions and relationships become integrated" (pp. 115–182) by C. Saarni in R. A. Thompson (Ed.), *Socioemotional development: Nebraska symposium on motivation, 1990,* Lincoln, NB: University of Nebraska Press. Copyright © 1990 by the University of Nebraska.

inferring how others may feel in competitive or conflictual situations even if they were not present (Thompson, 1998; see also Lightfoot & Bullock, 1990).

Consider that even if he had not seen Justin reach a difficult level of the video game, his friend could have inferred that Justin is pleased with himself.

Temperament

As children mature during middle childhood, they are better able to discern the emotional experience of others by combining situational cues with information about the

Guideposts for Working with School-Age Children

- Notice when children experience intense feelings of pride or shame about their own behavior or performance and be supportive.
- Accept that children may not wish to reveal their true feelings to you or to others, and do not pressure them.

- Help children recognize when they are experiencing simultaneous, conflicting emotions by using reflective listening.
- Model emotional competence by talking with children about your feelings using "I-messages."

target person's past experiences or their characteristic emotional reactions, often called *temperament* (Saarni et al., 1998). **Temperament** refers to a person's characteristic behavioral style based on individual differences in personality. People differ in the ways that they respond to people, tasks, and events. These predispositions in how they react to outside stimuli are usually quite stable across the life span and are generally considered a personality influence on the ability for self-regulation (Bates, 2000; Goldsmith, 1993). In middle childhood, temperament characteristics may include:

- Activity level
- Approach/extraversion
- Attention
- Fear
- Flexibility/adaptability
- High intensity pleasure
- Irritability
- Negative emotionality
- Positive mood
- Regularity of daily habits
- Shyness
- Task orientation/persistence (adapted from Capaldi & Rothbart, 1992 and Rothbart & Bates, 1998)

Temperament researchers have found that African American and European American 10- to 14-year-old boys were rated higher than girls on positive mood and activity level. On the other hand, girls were rated higher than boys on attention (Kim, Brody, & Murry, 2003). Other researchers have reported positive relationships between specific temperament characteristics (e.g., positive mood, approach, flexibility, task orientation, persistence, and regularity) and school-age children's self-reported competence (Windle et al., 1986). Figure 7.10 illustrates how individual temperament characteristics form three behavioral tendencies in adolescence. These categories of temperament have been used to assess (a) how adaptable and

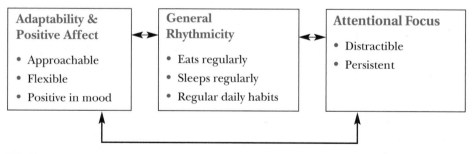

FIGURE 7.10

Dimensions of Temperament

Adolescents vary from high to low on these three interrelated dimensions of temperament.

Source: Based on "Revised Dimensions of Temperament Survey (DOTS-R): Simultaneous group confirmatory factor analysis for adolescent gender groups" by M. Windle, 1992, in *Psychological Assessment, 4,* 2, 231. Copyright © 1992 by the American Psychological Association.

FIGURE 7.11

A Conceptual Model of Temperament as Related to Emotion

Differences in temperament influence school-age children's motivations, self-regulation, and actions in the real-world environment.

Source: From "Temperament as an Emotion Construct: Theoretical and Practical Issues" by J. E. Bates, in M. Lewis, & J. M. Haviland-Jones (Eds.), *Handbook of emotions,* 2nd ed. (p. 386), 2000, New York: Guilford. Copyright © 2000 by Guilford Press. Reprinted by permission of the publisher.

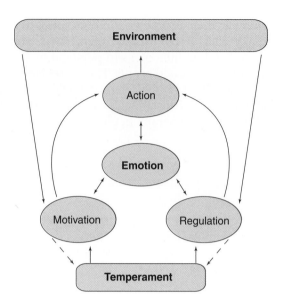

positive teens are; (b) how regular they are in their habits; and (c) how focused they are (Windle, 1992).

Temperament and Emotions. Affective temperamental dispositions, such as a tendency to be easily angered, constitute individual differences in **emotionality** (Bates, 2000). Although school-age children may vary somewhat their reactions in various social contexts, such as the home or the classroom, researchers have found that overall they may possess a particular adjustment style that is predictable from certain aspects of temperament. For example, positive emotionality predicts higher well-being and social competence (Lengua, 2003). In addition, temperament traits measured in early childhood, such as negative emotionality, predicted more behavior problems in the school-age years (Bates, 2000; see also Menzulis, Hyde, & Abramson, 2003). Figure 7.11 illustrates a conceptual model of how temperament is related to emotion: The environment affects motivation and self-regulation, which in turn influence the child's emotions and subsequent actions.

> *Justin's temperamental characteristics of low distractibility and high task persistence positively influence his motivation to play video games and his ability to regulate his emotional reactions while he is engaged. In turn, he experiences emotional satisfaction or pleasure, which then leads to the action of pursuing his goal of mastery over the game.*

Temperament and Self-Regulation. Temperament is a useful construct for thinking about how school-age children develop different styles of coping with environmental demands (Saarni et al., 1998). When researchers examine *how* children respond emotionally to other people or events, they usually measure the intensity of their response, the level of their emotional arousal, the duration of their response, and their overall emotional tone. These measures comprise an estimate of emotionality, which is often used to infer temperament's influence on emotional experience (Saarni et al., 1998). For example, if a child typically responds with *high* emotionality, we can then examine how this temperamental trait may influence

Guideposts for Working with School-Age Children

- Notice children's characteristic ways of responding to other people or events and provide them with the space and time they need to adjust.

- Provide suggestions to children for coping strategies that minimize negative emotions and

avoid behavior problems, such as giving them choices of activities, work schedules, and partners.

- Encourage self-control by helping children think through the outcomes of their past responses to stressful situations.

coping ability in different social situations. Individual differences in children's emotional competence, however, may influence their perceptions of emotional experiences or interactions with others. For example, a 10-year-old said about the loss of her allowance, "I wouldn't let my anger show, because my father doesn't like that and he would yell at me. That would only make things worse" (Meerum Terwogt & Olthof, 1992, p. 228).

Although temperamental traits are sometimes seen as innate characteristics that are stable across childhood, successful outcomes also depend on developmental processes, such as increasing self-control, in varying social contexts (Rothbart & Bates, 1998). The benefits of self-control are most evident in studies of individual differences, which have found that higher self-control is related to better grades and greater social acceptance (Twenge & Baumeister, 2002). For example, in a study of children in grades 3 to 5, self-regulation predicted more active coping and lower adjustment problems (Lengua & Long, 2002).

 STOP How is your typical emotional response today similar to the coping style you remember using in middle childhood?

CONTEXTS FOR AFFECTIVE DEVELOPMENT

By middle childhood, most school-age children have formed beliefs about their own self-efficacy and self-control, in part based on their developing self-competence and on positive regard from others. Family, school, and community contexts, therefore, are important influences on affective development in middle childhood, especially on school-age children's emotional competence.

Family Contexts

School-age children's emotional competence is related to parents' feelings of self-efficacy (Coleman & Karraker, 2000; Grusec & Mammone, 1995). If parents think that their children are behaving appropriately, the adults are more likely to experience feelings of success in child-rearing, or high *parenting* self-efficacy. On the other hand, if parents think that their children's behavior is "out of control," they are more likely to feel unsuccessful as parents. Low self-efficacy parents often give difficult children inconsistent affective messages, for example, negative messages delivered in a teasing or joking style (Grusec & Mammone, 1995).

In addition, parents may make inferences, called **attributions,** about the causes of children's misbehavior, such as whether a behavior was intentional or accidental. The more intentional a negative behavior is seen to be, the more angry parents become. Such negative attributions may, in turn, influence parents' expectations about school-age children's future coping behaviors. If they view their children's behavior as intentional, parents are more likely to view problem behaviors as influenced by personality traits (internal attribution) than by environmental circumstances (external attribution) (for a review of parental attribution, see Grusec & Mammone, 1995).

Children's resistance to parental control has been shown to directly predict middle childhood behavior problems (Bates, 2000). When researchers examined the effects of family factors on fifth- and sixth-graders' self-control, they found that the quality of mother-child interactions and mothers' self-control were related to the self-control of the school-age children themselves, regardless of the number of parents or number of siblings in the home (Zauszneiwski, Chung, Chang, & Krafcik, 2002).

Many studies have demonstrated that school-age children's self-esteem is enhanced by parental practices that

- Offer acceptance, approval, affection, and involvement.
- Treat the child's interests and problems as meaningful.
- Give the child reasons for rules and enforce limits fairly.
- Encourage children to uphold high standards of behavior.
- Use noncoercive forms of discipline, such as denial of privileges.
- Take into account the child's opinions in decision making. (Baumrind, 1978; Coopersmith, 1967; Harter, 1996a)

Researchers have found that open communication between parents and children between ages 5 and 10 is related to lower levels of harsh discipline and higher levels of positive child adjustment in middle childhood (Criss, Shaw, & Ingoldsby, 2003). In addition, parenting that involves the granting of autonomy along with high levels of involvement and modest levels of structure from parents has also been associated with academic competence, general conduct, and positive psychosocial development in adolescence (Gray & Steinberg, 1999a). For African American, Asian American, and Latino American students, however, this style of parenting is not as strong a predictor of academic success and other positive outcomes as it is for European Americans (Chao, 2001; Steinberg, Dornbusch, & Brown, 1992). (Diversity in parenting styles is discussed in more detail in chapter 8.)

School Contexts

In middle childhood, school environments exert demands on children that make self-evaluation more salient and peer comparison more likely, especially during the transition from elementary to middle school or junior high. Because they become much better at understanding, evaluating, and integrating the feedback that they receive from teachers and peers, older school-age children become more accurate in their self-assessments, which may cause some to become more negative (Wigfield & Eccles, 2002). In addition, gender differences in competency beliefs are common in school contexts, particularly in gender-stereotyped domains, such as math and science. For example, even after controlling for differences in actual skills, researchers reported that boys held higher competency beliefs for math and sports than did girls, whereas girls rated themselves higher in reading, English, and social studies than did boys (Wigfield & Eccles, 2002). In the Michigan Study of Middle Childhood, mothers who believed that males are better at math than girls also rated sons as having more math talent than daughters compared to those mothers who thought that boys and girls were equally likely to be talented in math (Eccles, 1992).

When social and economic conditions are prejudicial, even students with confidence in their competence may find that no level of effort will bring about desired results (Schunk & Pajares, 2002). For example, studies of the academic achievement of African American students in the United States often focus on achievement differences with the majority population of European American children. Most studies, however, have not adequately separated differences due to racial/ethnic culture and those due to social class, despite the fact that approximately one third of African American and Latino youth, compared to one quarter of Asian youth and only 5% of European American youth, are enrolled in the 47 largest urban school districts in the country. In these schools, 28% of families live at the poverty level, and 58% are eligible for free or reduced-cost lunches (Eccles & Wigfield, 2002).

Many minority students are vulnerable to social stereotypes of low achievement to the extent that mixed messages about their academic potential may undermine their achievement motivation and school success (Eccles & Wigfield, 2002; see also Graham & Taylor, 2002). Given these statistics, many comparative studies may really be assessing differences in school context, not student ability. In a recent study of seventh- and eighth-grade African American students, the percentage of middle-class neighbors and perceived academic abilities were linked to children's educational values, which in turn were linked to school effort (Ceballo, McLoyd, & Toyokawa, 2004).

More recently, research has included new immigrant populations, who are often doing better than both White middle-class children and third- or fourth-generation members of the same national heritage. In schools where students are successful, teachers establish *contextual* learning goals, such as mastery-oriented learning, autonomy of students, and feedback individualized to each child's intellectual development. In these environments, students are energized by challenges, persevere when facing difficulties, and request task-relevant information when they need help. In contrast, in schools that emphasize *performance* goals, students more often stress getting good grades, get feedback based on comparisons with classmates, and ask for the correct answers—if they ask for help at all (Newman, 2002).

Effective teachers are those who promote the best "fit" between a student's personal learning goals and the classroom environment, such as individual, whole-class, and small-group activities that allow for different types of student-teacher interaction. Patterns of classroom discourse that potentially facilitate help-seeking skills, such as fostering discussion, conversation, and inquiry, have been found to maximize students' expectancies for success (Newman, 2002). For example, if girls were to refrain from asking questions in math class so as not to appear "dumb," they would put themselves at a disadvantage consistent with gender stereotypes!

In a large cross-cultural study of German, Russian, Swiss, Czech, and American children between ages 7 and 13, girls who outperformed boys had stronger beliefs than did boys in their own effort, in being lucky, and in getting their teacher's help—although they tended to discount their own talent (Stetsenko, Little, Gordeeva, Grasshof, & Oettingen, 2000). In terms of academic achievement, late-elementary and middle-school girls in mixed-sex schools may often feel caught between a desire to achieve and concern about appearing too competitive or unattractive by gender-stereotypic standards of femininity. Ideally, single-sex classes may improve girls' achievement in math and science, as discussed in chapter 6 (AAUW, 1992; Orenstein, 1994).

STOP How did the expectations between your school and home differ? Were your teachers from the same cultural, language, or ethnic group as you?

Community Contexts

From a contextual perspective, cultures influence affective development and the interpretation of emotion in particular settings. To examine the cultural context of affective development we must ask four important questions:

1. Are emotions universal?
2. Does emotional development look different in diverse cultural contexts?
3. What role do cultural beliefs play in understanding emotional expression?
4. How do societies construct meaning from emotional experience? (adapted from Saarni, 1998)

Although basic human emotional experiences remain very similar across cultures, cultural variation in terms of how emotions are *valued* is best illustrated by cross-cultural research. For example, Utku Eskimos teach that anger is *always* inappropriate and immature (Nussbaum, 2000). Cultural beliefs and norms may also help us to interpret the acceptability of individual characteristics, such as temperament, and the behaviors that are permissible or expected in a given culture. For example, shyness, defined as an anxious reaction to novel or stressful situations, has different meanings in American and Asian cultures (recall the case study of Takuya from chapter 2). Because assertiveness and competitiveness are often endorsed in our individualistic American culture, a shy child in the United States may be more disadvantaged than a shy child in China or Japan, where inhibited behavior is seen by the more collectivistic culture as supporting group efforts (Rubin, 1998).

Cross-cultural studies also provide pertinent information about how children may develop emotionally in response to adults' repetition of the cultural discourse on child-rearing. For example, the appropriateness of emotional arousal (e.g., "we don't laugh out loud in church"), the degree of caregiver responsiveness to emotional distress (e.g., "you'll go to your room if you don't stop crying"), and norms for the regulation of emotion (e.g., "big kids don't have temper tantrums") may all affect children's opportunities to learn to cope successfully with emotion (Thompson, 1990).

Cultural competence is defined as respecting and responding positively to differences between groups and individuals of diverse backgrounds and traditions (Huebner & Mancini, 2003). People from diverse cultures are likely to respond affectively in different ways both to the world around them and to their own feelings, because they must ultimately make use of the vocabulary of emotions that the culture makes available (Hewitt, 1998). Cultural competence can be fostered by providing school-age children with opportunities for interracial and intercultural interactions. When youth do not live in culturally diverse neighborhoods, cultural competence may be encouraged by identifying the following resources (see Huebner & Mancini, 2003):

- Community-based activities or volunteer projects in other parts of the community
- Church services in ethnically diverse neighborhoods
- Exchange programs with youth from other countries
- Pen pals or Internet buddies from other places

CHAPTER REVIEW

Affective Development

- Affective development is a domain of middle childhood development that includes self-understanding, emotional development, self-control, and motivation.
- School-age children acquire personal competencies through participation in academic, athletic, or artistic activities.

- School-agers apply their skills to concrete problems they encounter in the real world.

Theoretical Viewpoints

- Erikson believed that in middle childhood, the school-age child's primary psychosocial task is to acquire a sense of industry, or the ability to work on a skill or project and to follow through over an extended period of time. The opposite of a sense of industry is a sense of inferiority.
- Maslow believed that school-age children have an innate need to feel *self-actualized*, to do their best and fulfill their potential.

- Rogers believed that school-age children come to value those experiences that afford them opportunities for positive regard from others, such as parents, teachers, or peers. Taken together, these internalized notions of what is valued are called *conditions of worth*.

Self-Understanding

- Developmentally, self-concept progresses from a focus on concrete, observable characteristics, overt abilities, or activities to more of a focus on inner, psychological characteristics.
- School-age children can successfully differentiate among multi-dimensional components of *self-competence* (e.g., athletic, academic, social, behavioral, and physical appearance).
- During middle childhood, school-age children readily construct affective judgments about their competencies, made possible by the ability to conceive of a mul-

tidimensional self-concept and to engage in social comparisons. Taken together, these self-evaluations contribute to their sense of *self-esteem*, or how they feel about themselves.
- Most school-agers can also create representations of what they may *want* to be, or feel that they *should* be, comprising their *ideal* selves.
- Positive self-evaluations of academic competence in middle childhood predict *increases* in school-age children's intrinsic motivation which, in turn, may positively influence their academic achievement.

Emotion and Temperament

- Emotional competence refers to how school-age children understand emotions in the context of the social demands placed on them.
- In middle childhood, emotional competence involves the ability of school-age children to understand their own emotional states, to correctly interpret their affective experiences with others, and to control their emotions.
- By the end of middle childhood, school-age children are also better able to appreciate the psychological

complexity of emotional experiences, such as having two conflicting feelings or purposely displaying false emotions.
- *Temperament*, or a person's characteristic behavioral style based on individual differences in personality, is sometimes seen as stable across childhood but may also be affected by development in middle childhood, such as increases in self-control.

Affective Development in Context

- Parents can enhance school-age children's academic motivation by providing them with an intellectually stimulating home environment and offering support for homework and school projects.

- Effective teachers promote the best "fit" between a student's temperament and the classroom environment.

- Cultural competence can be fostered by providing school-age children with opportunities for interracial and intercultural interactions.

TABLE 7.5   Summary of Developmental Theories

Chapter	Theory	Focus
7: Affective Development in Middle Childhood	Psychoanalytic	Process of individuation as the basis for personality development and establishing a sense of self
	Psychosocial	Period of industry vs. inferiority in which a major task is the acquisition of competence and the avoidance of failure
	Humanistic	Self-actualization and personal growth as well as the importance of positive regard from others

---

KEY TERMS

Achievement motivation	Extrinsic motivation	Personality traits	Self-efficacy
Attributions	Flow experiences	Person-centered theory	Self-esteem
Conditions of worth	Hierarchy of needs	Phenomenological	Self-transcendence
Cultural competence	Humanistic theories	Positive self-regard	Self-worth
Effectance motivation	I, Me	Psychodynamic theories	Sense of industry
Ego	Id	Real self	Social comparison
Ego ideal	Ideal self	Self-actualization	Superego
Emotional competence	Intrinsic motivation	Self-competence	Temperament
Emotional intelligence	Latency stage	Self-concept	
Emotionality	Peak experiences	Self-determination theory	

SUGGESTED ACTIVITIES

1. Visit a recreation center or playground and observe a group of school-age children. Describe the activities you see that could be characterized as helping to develop their sense of competence.

2. Interview a middle-school teacher about the school curriculum. How does he or she evaluate the students? Do students usually work alone or in groups? Ask about possible effects of social comparison on academic motivation. What does the teacher do to enhance students' intrinsic motivation?

3. Interview a school-age child about his or her sense of self-competence. In what domains (e.g., athletic, academic, social, emotional, cultural) does the child feel most effective? Ask if those areas are important to significant others, such as parents, teachers, or peers.

4. Analyze your own family-of-origin experiences. What cultural messages did you receive from family members or significant others that increased or diminished your sense of self-worth?

RECOMMENDED RESOURCES

Suggested Readings

Csikszentmihalyi, M. (1990). *Flow: The psychology of optimal experience.* New York: Harper and Row.

Goleman, D. (1995). *Emotional intelligence: Why it can matter more than IQ.* New York: Bantam.

Hewitt, J. P. (1998). *The myth of self-esteem: Finding happiness and solving problems in America.* New York: St. Martin's.

Orenstein, P. (1994). *SchoolGirls: Young women, self-esteem and the confidence gap.* New York: Anchor.

Rogers, C. R. (1969). *Freedom to learn.* Columbus, OH: Merrill.

Suggested Online Resources

Bright Futures Family Tip Sheets: Middle Childhood (2001). http://www.brightfutures.org/TipSheets/pdf/mc_color.pdf

The Effects of Reward Systems on Academic Performance (2001). http://www.nmsa.org/Publications/MiddleSchoolJournal/Articles/September2001/Article10/tabid/410/Default.aspx

The Importance of Emotional Intelligence during Transition into Middle School (2002). http://www.nmsa.org/Publications/MiddleSchoolJournal/Articles/January2002/Article10/tabid/411/Default.aspx

Promoting Involvement of Recent Immigrant Families in Their Children's Education. http://www.gse.harvard.edu/hfrp/projects/fine/resources/research/golan.html

Suggested Web Sites

Active Listening: A Communication Tool. http://edis.ifas.ufl.edu/BODY_HE361

Family Involvement Network of Educators. http://www.gse.harvard.edu/hfrp/projects/fine.html

Media Awareness Network. http://www.media-awareness.ca/english/parents/video_games/concerns/violence_videogames.cfm

Suggested Films and Videos

Boys, girls, and games (2001). ACCESS (29 minutes)

Constructing the self (2003). Films for the Humanities and Sciences (53 minutes)

Emotional intelligence (1997). Films for the Humanities and Sciences (29 minutes)

Erik H. Erikson: A life's work (1991). Davidson Films (38 minutes)

Flow (2003). Insight Media (55 minutes)

Social and emotional development (2000). Films for the Humanities and Sciences (29 minutes)

The Wonder Years, episode 13: "Coda" (1989). New World Entertainment (21 minutes)

Relationships and Families

8

Robert Brenner/PhotoEdit Inc.

Chapter Objectives

After reading this chapter, students will be able to:

▶ Define close relationships in middle childhood.

▶ Summarize attachment and family systems theories.

▶ Describe current research on parent-child and sibling interaction in middle childhood.

▶ Discuss the influences of family diversity on school-age children.

▶ Explain the contributions of family, school, and community to close relationships in middle childhood.

They seemed like a perfectly normal family, 10-year-old Jon thought: two parents, him, and a bossy teenage sister. That is, until Dad moved out. Jon suspected something was wrong even before his parents sat down together and told them about the divorce—all that yelling and arguing! Jon thinks that his recent behavior may have had something to do with his parents' conflict and worries that he may lose his father's love. Jon just hopes he will still be able to spend time with his father— maybe even go to live with him. You can't divorce your children, can you? Most of all, Jon wishes that everything could just go back to the way it was before his parents separated.

Family Relations in Middle Childhood

Attachments in middle childhood, as in infancy and early childhood, are largely based on the interactions of school-age children with their families. Although interactions with family members may become more distant as peer relations intensify (Collins & Repinski, 1994), most of the research on family relations in middle childhood is based on the study of parent-child and sibling relationships. (Peer relationships and friendships are the focus of chapter 10.) In this chapter, we define *family relations* as enduring ties or connections between family members, composed of frequent interdependent action sequences that occur across diverse settings and tasks (cf. Brown, Feiring, & Furman, 1999; Kelley et al., 1983).

Theoretical Viewpoints

Various theories have guided the existing research on family relations in middle childhood, primarily attachment theories and family systems theories. Both of these theoretical perspectives assume the relationship *itself* adds a new dimension to each interaction—whether it is among siblings, between parents and children, or with other relatives. In this regard, our focus is not on the individual child, as in chapter 7, but on the characteristics of close relationships and on family systems networks.

Attachment Perspectives

Theories of attachment have been important in the study of relationship development since the mid-20th century. Growing out of psychoanalytic theory's emphasis on the importance of early relationships—especially the mother-infant bond—attachment theories have been used to describe relationship histories across the life span, from infancy to adulthood (e.g., Ainsworth & Bell, 1970; Bartholomew & Horowitz, 1991; Bowlby, 1988; Elicker, Englund, & Sroufe, 1992; Hazan & Shaver, 1987; Kerns & Richardson, 2005; Lewis, Feiring, & Rosenthal, 2000; Main, Kaplan, & Cassidy, 1985; Thompson, 1999; Weinfeld, Sroufe, & Egeland, 2000). However, while psychoanalysis focused primarily on the development of *individuals*, attachment theory focuses on the development of *relationships* (Fonagy, 1999).

Stages of Attachment. John Bowlby (1969, 1973) described a developmental sequence of attachment relationships in the first 3 years of life. These phases of early attachment are described in Table 8.1. For Bowlby and other psychoanalysts (e.g., Mahler, Pine, & Bergman, 1975) the goal of attachment is to move from a totally dependent relationship with an attachment figure in infancy to a more interdependent partnership. By age 3, young children are likely to have formed an enduring emotional attachment to at least one, if not more, caregivers. Recently, developmental theorists have also described the phases as they apply to the development of attachments in middle childhood, shown in the right-hand column of Table 8.1. In this developmental sequence, middle childhood attachment behaviors are seen as a "supervision partnership" (Waters & Cummings, 2000) in which children cooperate with parents to achieve goals of both exploration and security. For example, children may cooperate with parents' supervision of their activities—using the home as a place to play, seeking parents' help when stressed or upset by

---

TABLE 8.1 Phases of Attachment

Bowlby's phases of infant attachment are reflected in normative changes in parent and peer attachment in middle childhood.

Attachment Phase	Infancy and Early Childhood	Middle Childhood
1. Pre-attachment	8 to 12 weeks • Orienting to people • Crying, cooing, smiling • Reaching toward others	• Spends time with certain people • Seeks friendships
2. Attachment-in-the-making	3 to 6–7 months • Discriminates primary caregivers • Social smiling • Babbling with familiar others	• Confides in parents, siblings, or friends • Smiles, giggles, tells jokes • Talks on the phone or text-messages
3. Clear-cut attachment	6 months to 2–3 years • Crawls, walks • Explores environment using attachment figure as a secure base • Stranger anxiety begins about 10 months	• Feels more bold in their exploration if a close friend or favorite teacher is nearby • Turns to family, friends, or teachers for reassurance
4. Goal-corrected partnership	2–3 years and older • Communicates with words • Able to consider intentions of caregivers • Less distress at separation with secure attachment	• Expresses concern over separations from family or close friends (e.g., divorce or moving to another city) • Seeks psychological, not physical, availability • Withdrawing when needs cannot be met

Source: Based on "Ontogeny of Attachment in Middle Childhood: Conceptualization of Normative Changes" by O. Mayseless. In K. A. Kerns and R. A. Richardson (Eds.), *Attachment in Middle Childhood* (pp. 1–23), 2005. New York: Guilford Press.

school or social problems, or disclosing information about their lives (Raikes & Thompson, 2005).

Bowlby was influenced by **ethology,** or the study of animal behavior, such as research on imprinting, or following behavior, in goslings (e.g., Lorenz, 1970) and comfort-seeking behaviors in infant monkeys separated from their mothers at birth (e.g., Harlow & Harlow, 1962). Bowlby theorized that proximity-seeking behaviors in animals may serve a similar function in humans. For example, all children turn to their parents for security, but in middle childhood and adolescence, they also seek proximity to their peers for a safe haven from distress (e.g., Nickerson & Nagle, 2005). By middle childhood, however, attachment goals are often met by peers and friends in a quest for social connections to others beyond their families (Furman & Wehner, 1994; see also Mikulincer & Selinger, 2001).

Life-span research has documented that four types of attachment behaviors apply to middle childhood as well as to infancy, as illustrated in Table 8.2 (Bowlby, 1988). From this perspective, the responsiveness of a school-age child's attachment figure can provide a sense of security that is highly adaptive, similar to Erikson's sense of "basic trust" in others (described in chapter 7). On the other hand, unresponsiveness may

TABLE 8.2 Goals of Attachment		
Attachment behaviors may fulfill any of four functions.		
System	**Description**	**Middle Childhood Example**
Attachment	Behaviors that maintain proximity to an attachment figure	Checking in with their parents; staying near to a close friend
Affiliative	Behaviors that ensure social relatedness to an attachment figure	Smiling, sitting or walking together, or holding hands
Caretaking	Behaviors that elicit care from an attachment figure	Seeking comfort from family or friends when distressed
Reproductive	Behaviors that promote sexual attachments	Flirting, hugging, or kissing

result in a sense of "mistrust" of others, described by attachment researchers as anxious attachment, or insecurity.

In the case of Jon, his insecurity is demonstrated by the worry that he might not see his father very often after his parents divorce.

Categories of Attachment. Researchers who have studied infants in stressful situations have found that they may experience a range of attachment, from secure to insecure (Ainsworth, Bell, & Stayton, 1971). During a sequence of short-term separations and reunions alternating between their mother and a stranger in a laboratory playroom, called the *Strange Situation,* researchers classified children into four attachment groups (Ainsworth, Blehar, Waters, & Wall, 1978; Main & Solomon, 1990):

A. *Anxious-Avoidant.* Explores readily; little visible distress when left alone; looks away and actively avoids parents upon reunion.

B. *Secure.* Uses mother as a secure base for exploration; shows signs of missing parent during separations; greets parent positively upon reunion.

C. *Anxious-Resistant.* Visibly distressed upon entering playroom; fails to explore; is distressed during separation; shows angry rejection or ambivalence upon reunion.

D. *Disorganized.* Does not show a clear-cut attachment strategy; appears confused, disoriented.

With older children, adolescents, and adults, self-report methods of assessing attachment security have proven equally useful for determining attachment classifications (for reviews of measures, see Bartholomew & Horowitz, 1991; Kerns, Schlegelmilch, Morgan, & Abraham, 2005; Kerns, Tomich, Aspelmeier, & Contreras, 2000; Solomon & George, 1999). For example, school-age children have successfully characterized their own sense of security or anxiety by using paper-and-pencil measures based on Harter's "How I See Myself" scale described in chapter 7: "Your family moves to a new neighborhood. Some kids would want to explore their new neighborhood a little on their own, but other kids would stay home unless their mother could go with them. Which is more like you?" (Kerns, Klepac, & Cole, 1996, p. 1326; see also Finnegan, Hodges, & Perry, 1996). Another self-report measure, The People in My Life (PIML) scale, has also been used successfully with fifth and sixth graders (Ridenour, Greenberg, & Cook, 2006). Other middle childhood researchers have observed and coded children's doll play (Granot & Mayesless, 2001; Main et al., 1885), asked children to complete stories about separation (Oppenheim & Waters, 1995), interviewed children about their attachments to parents (Kerns et al., 2005), or asked children to draw pictures of their families and coded them for indications of the attachment categories (Fury, Carlson, & Sroufe, 1997). Table 8.3 provides a list of attachment measures for use with school-age children.

Generally, researchers have found that the secure (group B) and insecure groups (groups A and C) are replicable with school-age children (group D is not classifiable, by definition). "Once the attachment bonds are stabilized during infancy and early childhood, they tend to persist in subsequent years, especially in stable child-rearing

TABLE 8.3 Attachment Measures for 6- to 12-Year-Olds	
Measure	**Description**
Identification of attachment figures	
Important People Interview	Interview to obtain attachment hierarchy and hierarchy violations
Attachment Figure Interview	Interview to identify primary and secondary attachment figures
Perceptions of attachment quality	
Security Scale	Questionnaire assessing dimension of security for mother-child and father-child relationship
Avoidant and Preoccupied Scales	Questionnaire assessing Avoidant and Preoccupied attachment styles (as dimensions)
Narrative discourse measures	
Doll Story Completion Task	Story-stem interview to access four attachment patterns (rating and classifications): Secure, Avoidant, Ambivalent, Disorganized
Separation Anxiety Test	Picture-based interview that classifies children into three groups: Secure (Autonomous), Dismissing (Avoidant), Enmeshed (Ambivalent)
Attachment Interview for Childhood and Adolescence	Interview regarding childhood relationships, with scoring that classifies children into four groups: Secure, Dismissing, Preoccupied, Unresolved
Friends and Family Interview	Interview regarding self and childhood close relationships with scoring for narrative coherence and secure-base availability of parents
Analysis of drawings	
Family Drawing	Child's drawing of family that is scored for attachment category (Secure, Avoidant, Resistant) and for ratings that reflect the child's representation of self and attachment figure

Source: From "Assessing Attachment in Middle Childhood" by K. A. Kerns, A. Schlegelmilch, T. A. Morgan, and M. M. Abraham. In K. A. Kerns and R. A. Richardson (Eds.), *Attachment in Middle Childhood* (p. 51), 2005. New York: Guilford Press. Reprinted by permission.

environments (Bowlby, 1988), although they may undergo transformations and reintegration during later years" (Ammaniti, Speranza, & Fedele, 2005, p. 119).

For example, Jon's secure attachment to his mother is likely to influence his sustained reliance on her as his primary attachment figure.

Recall, however, that attachment is not generally considered a personality *trait* that is stable, but rather is seen as a feature of a particular *relationship*. Therefore, it is important to remember that a secure or insecure attachment classification applies *only* to the relationship being studied at *that time* (e.g., a parent-child relationship). If *every* relationship can potentially be classified as either *secure* or *insecure*, however, how can attachment theory contribute to our overall understanding of family relations in middle childhood?

Working Models of Attachment. Bowlby (1969) theorized that our early attachments to parents or other caregivers would form the basis of all future relationships through the mechanism of an **internal working model**, or the mental representation of *all* relationships. The working model formulation states that our earliest attachments may influence our social relationships—from early childhood peer interactions to middle childhood friendships to adolescent romantic partnerships (for a review, see Bretherton & Munholland, 1999). From this perspective, then, school-age children continue to be affected by early attachment relations to others, called "social objects." For example, children who are securely attached to parents during the middle childhood years have shown greater social skills, academic competence, and positive school behavior; have more reciprocated and supportive friendships; and are more popular with their peers (Booth-LaForce, Rubin, Rose-Krasnor, & Burgess, 2005; Coleman, 2003; Granot & Mayseless, 2001; Jacobsen & Hofmann, 1997; Kerns et al., 1996).

Over the years since Bowlby first proposed attachment theory, many developmental researchers have tested the "working model" hypothesis through longitudinal studies (e.g., Ammaniti et al., 2005; Bohlin, Hagekull, & Rydell, 2000; Elicker et al., 1992; Freitag, Belsky, Grossmann, Grossmann, & Scheuerer-Englisch, 1996; Lewis et al., 2000; Weinfield et al., 2000; for reviews, see Kerns & Richardson, 2005 and Thompson, 1999). Taken together, these varied research studies lend strong support for Bowlby's hypothesis that an internal working model of relationships guides close relationships during middle childhood. For example, in a longitudinal study of attachment from 12 months through 11 years of age, most school-age children who had at least one sibling changed from insecure to secure. Other studies, however, have found that the birth of a sibling has a negative effect on attachment (Ammaniti et al., 2005). (Sibling relationships will be discussed later in the chapter.)

Some researchers have also recently suggested that middle childhood may be the period when children begin to integrate their working models into an **attachment style,** or consistent way of relating to others (Mayseless, 2005). Although discrete attachment behaviors, such as crying or clinging, are displayed in the preschool years, in middle childhood they become more organized and sophisticated, such as withdrawing or not communicating. In middle childhood, for example, school-age children are more able to:

- Reason using concrete representations of people, objects, and events.
- Employ planning strategies and adopt goals for their own behavior.

- Monitor their own mental processes.
- Acquire new information and use it in problem-solving. (adapted from Mayseless, 2005)

For example, when 11-year-olds were asked about their thoughts, feelings, and experiences with friends, parents, and siblings, both boys and girls were able to tell coherent and integrated stories about their views of themselves and their relationships (Steele & Steele, 2005). Because of these increasing cognitive capacities, examining attachment styles in middle childhood is mainly focused on the meaning of attachment behavior and the purpose it serves rather than on the behaviors themselves (Mayseless, 2005). Therefore, studying attachment in middle childhood necessitates a systems perspective.

STOP With whom did you have a secure attachment in middle childhood?

Family Systems Perspectives

Systems thinking developed as a 20th-century movement intended to integrate all scientific knowledge. Its founders believed that the same mathematical principles could be applied to understanding living and nonliving systems, including biological environments and electronic circuits (von Bertalanffy, 1975). This perspective began to be applied to family relationships in the late 1960s (White & Klein, 2002), and the tradition has continued to evolve with attention to language and culture as even larger systems (Robinson, 1999). Box 8.1, for example, applies a **family systems** analysis to children's use of the Internet.

 BOX 8.1   Roadmap to Understanding Theory and Research
Technology and Family Systems Theory

In a review of research on the effects of new communications technologies on families, Nancy Jennings and Ellen Wartella (2004) applied family systems thinking to the parental regulation of digital media technology. This type of analysis involves seeing families as interactional systems that are embedded in larger systems of communication, such as the Internet. The review examined three subsystems in families—the spouse, parental, and sibling subsystems—and the outside influences on these subsystems and the family as a whole.

The Spousal Subsystem

Most research has focused on how husbands or wives as individuals use computer technology differently based on gender. For example, women are more likely than men to report that e-mail has strengthened family communication and connectedness and that they use it regularly to sustain relationships with their extended family. The little research that has examined the effects of computers on the spousal

relationship seems to indicate that computers in the home may have a negative impact on marital relations. For example, fathers' home computing time—especially if they were in user groups or clubs—was related to increased conflict with their wives over the amount of time they spent on the computer. On the other hand, in their parenting role as fathers, they spent more time with their children. Fathers are more likely to play video games or work with the computer with children than are mothers.

The Parental Subsystem

Parent-child interactions with school-age children at the computer are similar to interactions when parents and children are reading books together. For example, they often ask questions, use repetitions, and replay games that children have mastered. By adolescence, computers have even increased some family interactions, such as planning outings or vacations, shopping for gifts for family members, or getting in touch with parents of their children's friends.

(continued)

BOX 8.1   Roadmap to Understanding Theory and Research *(Continued)*
Technology and Family Systems Theory

As computers and the Internet have been integrated into homes, parental attitudes have also changed, becoming more ambivalent. Although 70 to 80% of parents are hopeful about the benefits of computer technology for their children's development and education, over 75% are also concerned that their children might release personal information and view sexual material on the Internet. Six areas of concern have been identified by researchers and practitioners:

- Distribution of pornography
- Sexual predators
- Misinformation
- Loss of privacy
- Unscrupulous vendors
- Social isolation and behavior disorders

Most parental concerns revolve around the fear that they cannot control what their children see or do on the Web. Nevertheless, most parents are more tolerant of their children's computer use than of television.

Parents generally have different rules for children on the basis of gender and age. Parents have greater concerns about girls' Internet use and impose more restrictions on both boys and girls as they approach adolescence. However, the more children use a particular medium—even the telephone—the more parents try to control its use! The fact that parental regulation shifts as children's media use shifts is particularly important because children are often early adopters of new technologies.

The Sibling Subsystem

Most research on children's computing has focused on them as individual users, not as players in the social context. However, research on video and computer games indicates that siblings often play together, with cooperative play often replaced by sibling rivalry as their skills increase at differing rates. In addition, if video game systems are in children's bedrooms, they are twice as likely to be in boys' rooms as in girls' rooms. Boys with brothers and no sisters reported playing by themselves about half the time and with family about 20% of the time. In contrast, girls with sisters but no brothers played alone only 8% of the time and with family over half the time. Girls, however, use the Internet as much as boys—only differently. Girls use computers for schoolwork, e-mail, chat rooms, and instant messaging (IM), whereas boys use it more for entertainment.

Jennings and Wartella (2004) concluded that many gaps exist in the description of how families interact when they use technology together. They suggest using systems theory to theorize and study how families use and are influenced by the new technologies. In addition, they recommend a greater attempt to apply theory to practice to answer research questions such as "what roles media play in the maintenance of family relationships, in the socialization of children, and in the ways families themselves are engaged in life outside the home" (p. 606).

Source: Based on "Technology and the Family" by Nancy Jennings and Ellen Wartella. In A. Vangelisti (Ed.), *Handbook of Family Communication* (pp. 593–608), 2004. Mahwah, NJ: Erlbaum.

The basic principle of systems theory is wholeness: All of the elements of a system are interrelated and cannot be fully understood as individual parts. Applied to families and peer networks, this theory identifies elements such as individuals, sibling groups, and friendships as subsystems that influence—and are influenced by—each other. Likewise, families can be seen as part of a larger system where they interact with other systems, such as culture, schools, employers, and other families—not unlike Bronfenbrenner's ecological model.

In the chapter case, for example, Jon imagines what he'll do and say to his classmates about the divorce. He thinks that it's definitely going to be uncomfortable: All his friends will ask where his dad is.

System Levels. The various subsystems, each of them a part of larger systems, may be thought of as **system levels** (Blume, 2006). Each system level creates a different perspective with its own emphases. At the level of a household, some of the most important processes relate to emotion, power and control, caretaking, and economic survival. At larger system levels, processes such as beliefs and expectations are evident (Walsh, 1998). Within a family, subsystems develop their own systemic patterns. For example, in middle childhood, sibling subsystems are often characterized by competitiveness or conflict as well as by emotional support. Such subsystems may either generate stress or may provide a buffer to help children cope with personal and family-level challenges. Larger systems, such as middle childhood friendship networks, also can be sources of support.

> *Jon feels better about his parents' divorce once he has talked with his friends about their families. He hadn't realized how many of their parents were divorced, and he heard many encouraging stories.*

Equilibrium. Systemic processes are assumed to follow patterns. When changes occur, systems detect those changes through feedback loops and often respond by trying to restore familiar patterns. In the process of changing, systems must balance change and stability, or maintain **equilibrium** (Keeney & Ross, 1985). If, for example, the family has been organized into a caregiving system while nursing a relative through a prolonged illness, systems theories predict that some other family member could replace the patient as a focus for family concern when he or she dies or becomes well again. Although family patterns can take many forms, one of the most recognizable is a sequence in which a particular kind of event seems to be followed by a predictable response. Disrupting familiar sequences can lead to different outcomes (Madanes, 1981).

When scholars refer to a "systemic" family characteristic, they may mean that a family tends to handle the same process consistently. Family therapists have termed this type of consistency **family rules**—unwritten and unspoken sets of assumptions about what interactions are expected (Blume, 2006). Any such consistency, of course, is only temporary, because family systems must adapt over time in response to changing membership and to changes in larger systems (Minuchin, 1974).

Boundaries. Systems are defined by **boundaries** that separate their elements from one another and from outside influences (Minuchin, 1974; Walsh, 1998). For a household, the family boundary traditionally has been thought of in terms of physical protection and movement: walls, doors, and windows serve as barriers (e.g., Lennard & Lennard, 1977). But boundaries also exist in family rules. "You mustn't play with older children" is a boundary. Family boundaries are needed to preserve the family's values and its resources, protecting family members from harm.

Boundaries typically change over time (McGoldrick & Carter, 2003). After the early childhood years, when firm boundaries are more typical, families of school-age children often conclude that they have to become more flexible. Their children's friends and their parents, teachers, or coaches, for example, may make demands on their time and energy or seek to influence family beliefs and traditions. To the extent that a family excludes these influences, school-age children may be isolated and miss out on important sources of socialization in middle childhood (Combrinck-Graham, 1985). Other families may conclude that their boundaries need to become more solid because their school-age children lack clear guidance and support. For

FIGURE 8.1

Binuclear Family System Model

Ahrons (1994) used the model of a binuclear family system to convince divorced parents that their decisions had real impact on each other.

Source: From "Organization, Planning Decision Making, and Action," by Thomas W. Blume, 2006, in *Becoming a Family Counselor: A Bridge to Family Therapy Theory and Practice* (p. 160). New York: Wiley. Copyright © 2006 by John Wiley and Sons, Inc. Reprinted by permission.

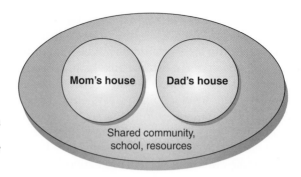

example, in families where no adult is available for after-school supervision, parents of school-age children commonly become more concerned about their family boundaries as the risk of involvement with drugs, sex, and violence become more apparent (Blume, 2006).

In recent decades, electronic communication (e.g., television, cell phones, Internet) has redefined the concept of family boundaries so that parents' emphasis is less on physical movement and more on movement of information. To the extent that children's technological skills often exceed those of their parents, maintaining these information boundaries represents a new challenge for family systems (Wang, Bianchi, & Raley, 2005).

Family boundaries also may change several times during middle childhood for reasons unrelated to individual development. New siblings may arrive, older siblings may establish their own households, grandparents or other relatives may die or remarry. Furthermore, parents' primary relationships can change. Single parents can find partners, and married parents can divorce. Each of these changes calls for establishing new system rules. For example, family therapists have described a **binuclear family system** model (Ahrons, 1994), illustrated in Figure 8.1, that helps divorcing parents recognize the continuing interconnectedness of their lives and provides guidance on handling the complexities of new stepfamily relationships (Emery, 1994).

In the chapter case, Jon's parents can work toward creating a shared family boundary for their two households that provides a sense of belonging as he moves between them.

Triangles. Within family systems, one of the most often-observed and most powerful configurations is the triangle. **Triangles** are formed when two individuals or other subsystems develop a stable pattern involving communication, support, or distraction provided by a third subsystem (Bowen, 1978). Many children are triangled at birth when a parent or other caregiver becomes more attentive to a new infant, gaining emotional support from this interaction while their adult relationships become less important.

School-age children in triangles often report feeling that they cannot please both sides. For example, a school-age child triangled between two adults—such as a single parent and a grandparent or two divorcing parents—may become the only pathway through which they communicate. In addition, several triangles may exist at the same time, of course, creating complex networks of competing loyalties and communication challenges. In middle childhood, triangles are likely to include peers, parents, grandparents, and siblings.

Many family therapists see contemporary families as contexts for development in which the behavior of children can be seen as an adaptation to the system. "Each event provokes an adaptation in participants which reflects their perception of the event, and this response defines the context in which others are responding, so that no behaviour can usefully be seen in isolation" (Stratton, 2003, p. 335).

Think about Jon's reluctance to risk asking his mom if he can move in with his father. Her initial reaction to his mentioning to her that he'd like to live with his dad someday has already been pretty negative, so he is unlikely to say more.

> **STOP** How did your relationship with your parents influence other members of your family?

Family Interaction in Middle Childhood

Our first relationships are usually family relationships. From an attachment theory perspective, families—particularly parent and sibling interactions—will likely influence school-age children's relationships with their peers. From a family systems view, however, interpreting the quality of a relationship between any two people also requires examining the forces that contribute to and emerge from their interactions (Cowan, Powell, & Cowan, 1998). The development of positive parent-child relationships, appropriate and consistent discipline, and supervision and monitoring of children's activities have been associated with lower probabilities of antisocial behavior in adolescence (Patterson & Fisher, 2002). To understand family interactions in middle childhood, we must consider the quality of relationships among parents, siblings, and extended family (Cowan et al., 1998; see also Updegraff, Madden-Derdich, Estrada, Sales, & Leonard, 2002).

Parent-Child Relationships

During middle childhood, parent-child relations become increasingly reciprocal, with parent-child interactions consisting less of caregiving or playing and more of supervising from a distance than in early childhood (McHale, Dariotis, & Kauh, 2003). For example, Table 8.4 provides tips for parental monitoring of children's Internet use. As a result of both individual child development and changing social expectations, parent-child relations in middle childhood involve:

- Increased cognitive abilities for solving concrete problems
- Greater physical and social knowledge
- More involvement with peers and contexts outside the family
- Increased emphasis on school adjustment and academic achievement
- Greater capacity for self-regulation and social responsibility (adapted from Peterson, Madden-Derdich, & Leonard, 2000)

Although individual child characteristics have been associated with the later development of problem behavior, "children who are at risk for persistent antisocial behavior by middle childhood have already experienced initial but powerful social interactional learning in the family setting" (Smith, Sprengelmeyer, & Moore, 2004, p. 240). For example, school-age children's problem behavior can elicit more negative behavior from their own parents—as well as other children's parents. In other words, the relationship between children's behavior and parenting behavior is a complex bidirectional process (Smith et al., 2004; see also Stafford, 2004).

TABLE 8.4 Monitoring Children's Use of Computers

DOs	DON'Ts
Let your kids be your guide, but talk to them about how to use technologies safely and wisely. See for yourself what it's all about: • Get on IM. • Download an MP3 music file. • Play a video game. • Create a MySpace account.	Believe the younger generation is on the road to perdition: • Don't be a disapproving elder. • Don't have a pious attitude. • Don't make uninformed pronouncements.
Set limits, monitor content, and teach "techno-manners" for everyone: • Restrict cell phones at the dinner table. • Stop playing video games while someone is talking to you. • Notice when family members come home even if you're online.	Let the human moments disappear because of your own addiction to screens: • Don't be a screen-sucker. • Don't watch too much television. • Don't fail to monitor your own online behavior.
Search for what's positive and innovative in the ways your children are using and adapting to new technologies: • Look for the good. • Imagine how it could be used to enhance relationships and learning.	Let technology steal your kids from you: • Don't forget to enjoy your children. • Don't avoid face-to-face conversations. • Don't skip dinner with the family.
Take time to hang out with your kids. Spend time together doing mundane, nontechnological things: • Wash the car. • Play Ping-Pong. • Debate politics. • Take them out for ice cream (no cell phones or iPods allowed).	

Source: Based on "The Multitasking Generation: Tips for Parents" (pp. 50–51), in *Time Magazine, 167* (13), March 27, 2006.

Recently, parenting research has been sharply criticized for assuming that parenting practices *cause* developmental outcomes even though most studies have been correlational (Kerr, Stattin, Biesecker, & Ferrer-Wreder, 2003). (Refer to chapter 2 for a discussion of research designs.) As an alternative, parenting scholars have proposed a systems approach to conceptualizing communication processes within families. In this model, illustrated in Figure 8.2, communication patterns are seen as bidirectional, meaning that parenting behaviors, such as support or criticism, can evoke emotional reactions in their children, which in turn influence how children respond to parents (Kerr et al., 2003).

This systems model applied to Jon's family would suggest that his feelings about his parents will become an important link in a chain of events involving his disclosing feelings to them about the divorce—leading ultimately to an ongoing pattern of open communication and trust.

Parenting Styles. Most research on parenting in middle childhood has focused on the concept of **parenting styles,** or ways that parents guide their children's behavior (e.g., Baumrind, 1971). Some researchers have proposed that parenting style is best

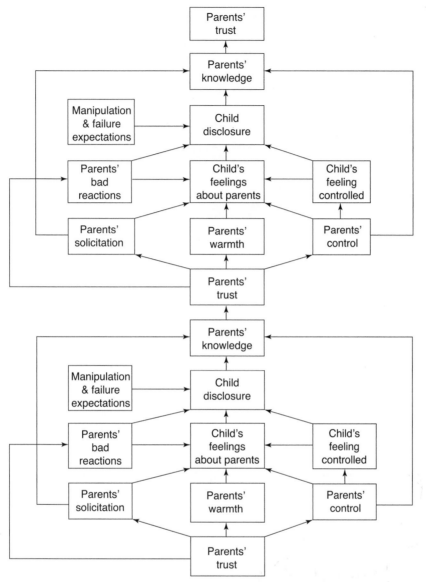

FIGURE 8.2
A Systems Model of Family Communication

This bidirectional model of ongoing communication and control processes within families describes parent-child interactions and the feelings they evoke.

Source: From "Relationships with Parents and Peers in Adolescence," by Margaret Kerr, Hakan Stattin, Gretchen Biesecker, & Laura Ferrer-Wreder, 2003. In R. M. Lerner & M. A. Easterbrook (Eds.), *Handbook of psychology: Developmental psychology, Vol. 6: Emotion and personality development in childhood* (p. 409). New York: Wiley. Copyright © 2003 by John Wiley and Sons. Reprinted by permission of the publisher.

conceptualized as a context that moderates the influence of specific parenting practices on the child (Darling & Steinberg, 1993). In this model, parenting *practices* have been studied separately from parenting styles. **Parenting practices** refers to the goal-directed parenting behaviors that parents engage in to socialize their children. Parenting styles, on the other hand, refers to the emotional climate that parents create, such as warm or controlling (Darling & Steinberg, 1993).

As illustrated in Figure 8.3, parenting styles may vary from **authoritative** (i.e., high levels of control and warmth) to **authoritarian** (i.e., controlling but low in warmth) to **permissive** (i.e., warm but low in control) to **uninvolved** (i.e., neither warm nor controlling). Most research demonstrates that authoritative parenting is associated with positive psychosocial outcomes (Baumrind, 1971, 1978). Generally, research on the influence of parenting styles in middle childhood and adolescence indicates that authoritative parents raise children who achieve more in school, score

FIGURE 8.3
Parenting Styles
Matrix

Parenting styles are
conceptualized along
two dimensions:
Warmth and Control.

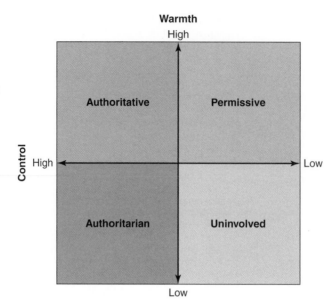

higher on self-esteem, report less depression and anxiety, and are less likely to
engage in problem behavior (Baumrind, 1991; Gray & Steinberg, 1999; Steinberg,
2001). In addition, authoritative parenting in middle childhood and secure attachment are positively related. Children in grades 4 to 6 whose parents were warm and
involved and who monitored their behavior while still granting them psychological
autonomy were more likely to score high on attachment security (Karavasilis, Doyle,
& Markiewicz, 2003).

Developmental scholars have also suggested that authoritative parenting provides an emotional context for later adjustment (Darling & Steinberg, 1993). For example, researchers who examined differences in parenting styles across teenagers'
friendship networks have found that adolescents whose *friends* described their

Authoritative parent-
ing promotes self-
reliance and positive
outcomes in middle
childhood.

Mary Kate Denny/PhotoEdit Inc.

own parents as authoritative have higher academic competence and report lower levels of delinquency and substance use. In addition, boys whose friends described their parents as authoritative report lower levels of peer conformity and are less likely to engage in misbehavior at school. Among girls, higher levels of authoritative parenting by friends' parents is related to higher scores on measures of work orientation, self-reliance, and self-esteem and lower levels of depression or anxiety. These results suggest that the quality of parenting available in friends' homes is also an important, although indirect, influence (Fletcher, Darling, Steinberg, & Dornbusch, 1995).

Positive benefits of authoritative parenting have consistently been reported from all racial/ethnic groups and nationalities (Steinberg, 2001). In fact, when researchers have more closely examined *which* aspects of authoritative parenting contribute to positive outcomes, parental involvement and support were positively related to psychosocial development, whereas behavioral control, although reducing behavior problems, was negatively related to emotional well-being (Gray & Steinberg, 1999). Similarly, parents' reports of more support and monitoring and less harsh punishment were related to psychological adjustment, better grades, and fewer behavior problems for school-age children, irrespective of parents' race, ethnicity, family structure, education, income, or gender (Amato & Fowler, 2002).

Nonetheless, parenting styles research has been criticized because most research has been with middle-class European Americans. The few studies of ethnic-minority families suggest that African American and Chinese American children may be *less* negatively affected by authoritarian parenting than European Americans (for a recent review, see Grolnick, 2003). These findings are consistent with our contextual view of development, in which the cultural and ecological contexts of parenting makes a difference. For example, African American parents may employ parenting practices (more control, less autonomy) that appear authoritarian by middle-class, European American standards because of the risks present in the urban neighborhoods in which many African American families live (Taylor, 2000).

Differential Parenting. Developmental psychologists assert that it is not reasonable to expect that a given behavior or style of parenting would have the same effect on every child. Different parenting strategies or degrees of effort may be required to bring about the same outcome in different children—even within the same family (Collins, Maccoby, Steinberg, Hetherington, & Bornstein, 2000; Conger & Conger, 1994). **Differential parenting** results when parents treat siblings differently from one another. Recent studies of parent–child interaction have investigated two aspects of differential parental treatment. "*Differential positivity* refers to one child in the family receiving more positive affect, engagement, and involvement from the parent than another child in the family. *Differential negativity* refers to the parent directing more affectively negative behavior toward one child than toward another" (Jenkins, Rasbash, & O'Conner, 2003, p. 99). Not surprisingly, school-age children experience greater well-being and self-esteem when they perceive the differential treatment to be *fair* (Kowal, Kramer, Krill, & Crick, 2002).

Recall from chapter 3 that behavior geneticists assume that the shared environment, such as parenting practices, affects children in similar ways whereas the nonshared environment consists of unique influences on children's development, such as child characteristics. Many behavior-genetic researchers who investigate the differential treatment of siblings have suggested that parenting is part of the shared

Guideposts for Working with School-Age Children

- Foster attachment bonds between adults and children by showing mutual respect and affection.

- Recognize that school-age children can reflect on their own behavior and encourage them to ask themselves what they should do or not do.

- Set limits and rules carefully, always giving school-age children explanations and reasons for your decisions.

- When children in a family or other group, such as a classroom, are given differing privileges or responsibilities, provide them with your rationale for *not* treating them the same.

environment, because parents usually report that they treat their children similarly in terms of knowledge of their activities, attempts to control their behavior, and successes in controlling them. However, children often report that their parents treat them differently from their siblings (Reiss, Neiderhiser, Hetherington, & Plomin, 2000).

In our chapter case study, Jon's parents may treat him and Janel differently after the divorce, based on the different characteristics of their two children.

Recently behavior-genetic theorists have concluded that "at any point in time, measures of the nonshared environment reflect—in all likelihood—a bidirectional effect: the influences of parents, siblings, peers and others on the developing child and the continuing impact on that child of family and friends" (Reiss et al., 2000, p. 164). Such a view is consistent with family systems theory in which all changes in a system affect everyone. For example, in a large nationally representative study of Canadian children between ages 4 and 11 years, researchers found that stressful family environments, such as marital dissatisfaction, large family size, single parenthood, and low SES, were associated with more differential parenting than could be explained by the characteristics of individual children. The researchers suggest that the *differences* in how parents treat their children are attributable to aspects of family life *shared* by siblings (Jenkins et al., 2003).

Sibling Relationships

Sibling interaction is a relatively new focus in the study of middle childhood close relationships (McGuire, Manke, Eftekhari, & Dunn, 2000). As with parenting research, most sibling research has been guided primarily by attachment and family systems theories (see Hetherington, 1994). As a normative component of many family systems, the sibling subsystem has many features in common with other relationships. For example, like parent-child relations, interactions between older and younger siblings are usually hierarchical because of differences in age and status (Stoneman & Brody, 1993). Although in some ways siblings are like peers, the nature and level of negativity between siblings is likely to differ from that of friends for two reasons (see McHale, Dariotis, & Kauh, 2003, for a review of sibling relationships in middle childhood):

- *Siblings are not usually the same age* (unless they are twins). Children more often assume a leader or follower role with siblings than their friends, who are more often age peers.

- *Sibling relationships are not voluntary.* Children are more likely to invest in maintaining harmony with their peers because they could lose their friendship.

Sibling researchers have identified three **sibling interaction styles**, based on the degree of siblings' positivity or negativity:

- *Harmonious.* Compassionate or caring sibling relationships
- *Typical.* Relationships that are characterized by ambivalence among siblings
- *Conflicted.* Sibling relationships that are hostile and/or alienated (adapted from Brody, Stoneman, & McCoy, 1994)

In middle childhood, sibling relationships are usually characterized by high levels of conflict. Sibling conflict often peaks in middle childhood (Cole & Kerns, 2001) and then decreases across adolescence when sibling relations tend to become more egalitarian (McGuire et al., 2000).

Reflect again on the family in our chapter case study. Jon thinks Janel is bossy, suggesting that sister and brother are probably "conflicted."

When school-age siblings were interviewed about the content of their disagreements, they most often mentioned fights over personal possessions or physical aggression as the reasons for conflict, not parental favoritism (McGuire et al., 2000). When parents exhibit high levels of conflict with each other, however, or when mothers are more negative with children, siblings are more negative with each other. In a large-scale British population survey, for example, siblings were more negative in two-parent than in single-parent households (Jenkins, Dunn, O'Connor, Rasbash, & Behnke, 2005). In another study, however, sibling negativity was highest in single-mother families when compared to children in intact marriages and stepfamilies. Full siblings were also more negative than half- or stepsiblings (Deater-Deckard, Dunn, & Lussier, 2002). From these studies, we cannot conclude that family structure *per se* is related to differences in sibling conflict.

Family researchers instead emphasize interdependency among the marital relationship, the general emotional climate of the family, and sibling characteristics. Siblings with less difficult temperaments, whose parents perceive their family relationships to be close, and whose fathers are generally positive in their interactions with them are more likely than siblings from other families to have less conflicted sibling relationships in late middle childhood (Brody et al., 1994). In addition, the more differentially two siblings are treated by their parents, the more negative sibling interactions are. In families with multiple sibling pairs, a moderate level of similarity has been found in siblings' negativity, suggesting that *processes* shared in families affect how sibling relationships develop (Jenkins, Dunn, et al., 2005). For example, ineffective parenting and sibling conflict measured in middle childhood interact to predict boys' antisocial behavior and children's emotional and peer adjustment in adolescence (Bank, Burraston, & Snyder, 2004; Stocker, Burwell, & Briggs, 2002).

Siblings and Gender. In middle childhood, children's perceptions of sibling relationships may also differ according to the gender composition of the sibling dyad (McHale et al., 1999). Male sibling dyads report lower levels of intimacy, caring, and conflict resolution than either male/female or female sibling dyads (Cole & Kerns, 2001). In a longitudinal study across middle childhood and early adolescence, older (first-born) siblings' gender-role attitudes, personality characteristics, and leisure activities predicted their younger (second-born) siblings' gender-role orientations two years later, independent of parental influences and children's own characteristics (McHale, Updegraff, Helms-Erikson, & Crouter, 2001).

On the other hand, with development, older siblings became *less* like their younger brothers or sisters, suggesting a process of distancing from their families. *(Janel, for example, has little in common with Jon.)* First-born siblings also may become more gender stereotyped between ages 10 and 12, called *gender intensification* (discussed in chapter 11). Overall, however, most girls are less traditional in terms of sex roles than boys, especially boys with younger sisters (McHale, Updegraff, et al., 2001). Moreover, having a brother or sister and belonging to a same- versus opposite-sex sibling dyad is likely to predict friendship experiences in adolescence. Although girls often learn control tactics from their brothers, which they apply to their friendships, boys are less likely to model the intimacy that characterizes their sisters' friendships. Furthermore, adolescents from mixed-sex sibling dyads are more likely to have friends with instrumental (masculine) qualities and who engage in masculine-stereotyped activities (Updegraff, McHale, & Crouter, 2000).

Parental involvement in children's sibling relationships is also related to the gender composition of the sibling dyad, with fathers spending more time with male-male dyads. However, mothers spend more time overall with siblings than fathers. In addition, mothers and fathers usually differ in their reactions to sibling conflict, with mothers using noninvolvement (e.g., telling them to work it out) and coaching (e.g., giving advice) more than fathers, who were more likely to step in and solve the problem (McHale, Updegraff, Tucker, & Crouter, 2000).

Sibling Caregiving. In many cultures, older siblings—especially girls—take care of younger children in the family, ranging from providing full basic care while a parent is away to entertaining them while a parent is present, but busy. Although not infre-

In many cultures, older girls take care of younger siblings.

Barnabas Kindersley © Dorling Kindersley

> **Guideposts for Working with School-Age Children**
>
> - Use authoritative parenting to encourage school-agers' autonomous decision making within reasonable limits.
> - Expect that parenting practices affect each child differently and modify your strategies based on the reactions of a particular child.
> - Ask children you work with the age and sex of their siblings, if any, and make visits to the home or neighborhood to observe sibling interaction whenever possible.
> - Encourage fathers to spend time in parenting activities with daughters as well as sons during middle childhood.

quent in industrialized countries like the United States, sibling caretaking is a primary form of child care in many agrarian societies. For example, the Kwara'ae of Melanesia reward their children for being good caretakers, and siblings are given a primary socialization role in families. Across all cultures, however, sibling care is unique because siblings are usually in the same age cohort relative to parents. Sibling caregiving, therefore, promotes interdependence and prosocial behavior within the family context (see Maynard, 2004).

STOP If you have siblings, what did you fight about and how did your parents typically react?

RESEARCH ON FAMILY DIVERSITY

From a contextual perspective on middle childhood, family interactions may vary as a result of both differences in family environment and in the larger culture in which families are embedded (McHale et al., 2003). In the 21st century, family composition is becoming increasingly diverse. For example, in 2000, almost 30% of all U.S. children and over 50% of African American children under age 18 were being raised in single-parent households. About 17% live with a biological parent and a stepparent. Nearly 4 million children live in homes maintained by their grandparents (Ihinger-Tallmam & Cooney, 2005). By 2010, almost 50% of children in the United States are expected to experience the divorce of their parents and to spend about 5 years in a single-parent family (Kurdek, 1994). Figure 8.4 illustrates the marital status of the United States population in 2000.

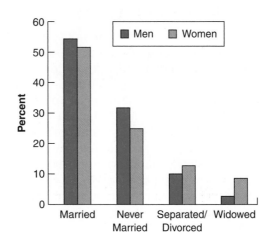

FIGURE 8.4
Marital Status of Parents in 2000

Source: Based on data from U.S. Census Bureau, Current Population reports, P20-537, "American Families and Living Arrangements." http://www.census.gov/prod/2001pubs/p20–537.pdf

Remember, however, that families—like middle childhood—are social constructions. Although most legal criteria for defining families rely on relationships defined by blood, marriage, or adoption, family relationships also exist along a biological-social continuum (see Holtzman, 2005). For example, when gay couples adopt children, in most jurisdictions only one individual is designated the adoptive parent while the partner's **coparental relationship** is socially—but not legally—defined (Holtzman, 2005). In such cases, the nonadoptive parent cannot sign school permission forms, medical releases, or—if the couple separates—have a legal right to parental visitation! Recently, however, some courts have ruled that unmarried heterosexual couples, gay or lesbian couples, elderly people and their caregivers, or coresident students constitute families (Lamanna & Riedmann, 2006).

Family communication scholars have described families as *discourse-dependent*, when they define *themselves* through social interaction (Galvin, 2005). In this view, consistent with both social construction and narrative family systems perspectives, language follows children's lived experiences. For example, how school-age children talk about families reveals their understanding of family relationships:

- *Labeling* (e.g., My "brother," "half-sister," "partner")
- *Explaining* (e.g., "How come your parents are Irish and you're Chinese?")
- *Legitimizing* (e.g., "Is she your *real* daughter?")
- *Defending* (e.g., "He is my father even if he didn't marry my mother.")

A qualitative study described how middle childhood girls interpreted family situation comedies on television. In talking about TV families in focus groups, the 9- to 13-year-olds compared their own families and the families of their friends to the families portrayed on television. Girls whose families were *not* like the ones on television thought the TV families were unrealistic. For example, one girl said that the sisters *she* knows do not get along as well as the siblings in the show *Sister, sister*. The girls also criticized the portrayal of parents in shows like *Home Improvement* as unlike real families. On the other hand, girls whose families were *like* those on television thought that TV families were realistic. In the focus group discussions, most of the girls dismissed families that were different from their own rather than accepting alternative family dynamics. These results suggest that any family portrayal that deviates from school-agers' lived experiences is likely to be criticized (Fingerson, 1999).

Families Living Together

Two-parent families are the norm in the United States. As recently as 2002, about 69% of children under age 18 lived with two married parents, although only 7% of married-couple families with children had a mother who did not work outside the home. Living in a two-parent household, however, does not necessarily mean that children live with their biological parents in an intact first marriage. For example, in a recent study, 88% of children lived with their biological parents (some unmarried), 7% with their biological mother and stepfather, 2% with their biological father and stepmother, and 1% with their adoptive mother and stepfather (Lamanna & Riedmann, 2006). **Cohabiting couples** (i.e., couples who live together in a romantic relationship but are not married) account for between 40 and 50% of births outside of marriage, up from about 30% ten years ago. Today, about 40% of all children are expected to spend some portion of their childhood living with cohabiting parents (Child Trends, 2006).

The Healthy Marriage Initiative of the U.S. Department of Health and Human Services promotes the strengthening of traditional families, citing research evidence that children fare better in two-parent than in single-parent families (Administration for Children and Families, 2006). However, despite a general consensus among family researchers that a healthy marriage can benefit both a couple and their children, scholars also question the idea that marriage *per se* will make a family immune to chronic economic and social stress (Smock, 2006). For example, when comparing two-parent families and single-parent families, about one-half of the difference in child outcomes is due to lower household income in families headed by a single mother (Child Trends, 2006). In addition, family researchers have consistently found that school-age children raised in so-called "nontraditional" families (e.g., divorced, single-parent, cohabiting, gay and lesbian, or adoptive families) typically have successful—or even enhanced—developmental outcomes (e.g., Amato & Fowler, 2002; Golombok, 2006; Hetherington, Stanley-Hagan, & Anderson, 1989; Kelly & Emery, 2003; Stacey & Davenport, 2002). "As we begin to understand the range of sizes, shapes, and colors that today's families come in, we find that the differences *within* family types are more important than the differences *between* them. No particular family form is doomed to fail" (Coontz, 1999, p. 6).

Single Parenting. One-quarter of all U.S. households are headed by single adults, with 28% of children under 18 living with a single parent. Of those, 23% live with their mothers, 5% with their fathers, and an additional 4% with another adult, such as a relative or foster parent (Lamanna & Riedman, 2006). Although a majority of children in the United States live in single-parent families as a result of divorce, just over 1 in 5 (23.3%) of never-married women in 2000 have had children—up from 18.1% in 1990. Interestingly, in roughly that same ten-year period, teen birthrates have come down by over 30%, the lowest in over 50 years (Seccombe & Warner, 2004). From these statistics, it is clear that adult women are increasingly making a choice to have children outside of marriage.

In the United States, the living arrangements of children in single-parent families vary greatly by race/ethnicity, as shown in Figure 8.5. Across all ethnic groups, however, more children live in single-mother than single-father families, largely due

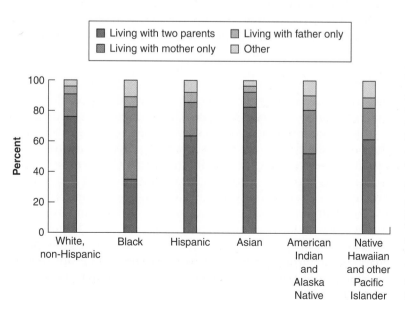

FIGURE 8.5
Living Arrangements of U.S. Children by Race/Ethnicity

Source: From "Living arrangements of children under 18 by race/ethnicity, 2000," in *Marriages and Families: Making Choices in a Diverse Society,* 9/e, (p. 476), by Mary Ann Lamanna and Agnes Riedmann, 2006. Belmont, CA: Wadsworth. Reprinted with permission of Wadsworth, a division of Thomson Learning: www.thomsonrights.com. Fax 800 730-2215.

to the fact that family courts are more likely to award custody of school-age children to mothers than to fathers following divorce. This trend is rapidly changing: The number of single fathers has increased by 500% from 393,000 in 1970 to 2 million in 2000 (compared to a 300% increase in single-mothers) (Seccombe & Warner, 2004)! In a revealing qualitative study of 10 African American single fathers who chose to parent full-time, several reasons to become a custodial father emerged from their narratives (Coles, 2002):

- Parenting is not a choice but a responsibility.
- Breaking the cycle of uninvolved fathers.
- Fulfilling a dream.
- Defeating racial and gender stereotypes.
- Having available resources.

Although most American men become single parents as the result of divorce, about one-third of custodial fathers have never been married.

Recent research on the distinctive contributions of mothers and fathers to development in middle childhood has been focused on the benefits of positive role models for both boys and girls: School-age children seem to adapt better in the custody of a same-sex parent. In father-custody families, boys are generally more mature, social, and independent; less demanding; and have higher self-esteem than girls. Girls in the custody of their fathers, on the other hand, have shown higher levels of aggression and less prosocial behavior than girls in mother-custody families (Hetherington et al., 1989).

Recall Jon's family. Even though his parents' divorce is not yet final, everyone assumes that both he and his sister Janel will live with their mother. But Jon wants to live with his dad!

Grandparenting. In 2000, about 8% (nearly 5.5 million) of American children lived in an **intergenerational** household with a grandparent, compared to 3% in 1970. Of those families with grandparents, about one-quarter, or 2.4 million, have sole responsibility for raising grandchildren (Lamanna & Riedmann, 2006). Grandparents raising their grandchildren, compared to other parents, tend to be less well educated, younger at the birth of their first child, single, African American, and female (Caputo, 2001). In addition, 19% of grandparent-headed households live below the poverty line and 33% lack health insurance, especially when grandparents are caring for their grandchildren informally (Grinwis, Smith, & Dannison, 2004; Hayslip & Kaminski, 2005). Some grandparents may have to reduce their work hours to care for their grandchildren, whereas others may need to return to work to have money to raise them.

Grandparents' reasons for taking on the parenting role vary from wanting to help their adult child in a time of crisis to being the only relative available. Grandparents sometimes serve as coparents with their adult children—as in the case of divorce—or as custodial parents—as in the case of parental drug abuse or illness. Most research on custodial grandparenting indicates that social support from friends, family, and the community is crucial to grandparents' physical and mental health and their ability to cope with the demands of parenting (Hayslip & Kaminski, 2005).

Researchers studying the parenting practices of grandparents have compared custodial grandparents to other parents. The two groups did not differ in their understanding of child development or their parenting behaviors, but grandparents were more likely to turn to their grandchildren for emotional support and less likely

---

TABLE 8.5   Common Problems of Children in Custodial Grandparent Families

Grandparents often face the dual challenges of meeting the needs of both their adult children and their grandchildren.

Problems of Adult Child	Behavior or Disorder of Minor Child	Possible Outcomes for Minor Child
Parental substance abuse	Fetal alcohol syndrome, ADD/ADHD, substance abuse, and pregnancy	Poor academic performance, grief and loss, embarrassment, anger, fear
Child abuse/neglect Teen unable to parent	Depression, anxiety, post-traumatic stress, other psychiatric disorder	Inadequate coping skills, poor social supports, suicide, fear, anger, grief and loss
Unemployment/divorce	Depression, anxiety, post-traumatic stress	Inadequate coping skills, self-blame or guilt, embarrassment
Death/AIDS/HIV	Depression, anxiety, post-traumatic stress	Shame and isolation, anger, grief and loss, embarrassment, fear
Imprisonment of parent(s)	Emotional/behavioral problems, post-traumatic stress	Shame and isolation, anger, grief and loss, embarrassment, fear

Source: From "Custodial grandparent families: Steps for developing responsive health care systems," by Barbara Grinwis, Andrea B. Smith, & Linda L. Dannison, 2004, *Michigan Family Review, 9*(1), 40. Reprinted by permission of the publisher.

to respond to their grandchildren's emotional needs (Hayslip & Kaminski, 2005). Grandparented children, however, often deal with many troubling and confusing emotions, such as grief over the dual losses of attachment figures in their lives: "Children in the care of grandparents have not only lost a parent but also have suffered the loss of their 'traditional' grandparent" (Grinwis et al., 2004, p. 39). Table 8.5 lists the most common emotional and behavioral problems of school-age children being cared for by grandparents and potential outcomes if they are left unaddressed.

Interventionists working with custodial grandparents recommend caregiver support groups and parenting training that includes topics on:

- Parenting styles and limit-setting
- Communication skills
- Advocacy and legal issues
- Drug use and sexuality
- Grief and loss of attachment security

Box 8.2 outlines 10 strategies for developing family-level interventions with custodial grandparents caring for school-age children.

Gay Parenting. **Gay families** include gay or lesbian partners who may have adopted children, conceived through donor insemination, or are raising their children from a previous heterosexual relationship. Children raised in gay and lesbian families commonly have ongoing contact with their nonresident parents (Berger, 2001). For example, in a longitudinal British study of lesbian households, children raised by lesbian mothers had more postseparation contact with their fathers than did children raised by heterosexual mothers (Tasker & Golombok, 1997). In addition, children often viewed their mother's female partner as an added member of their family constellation rather than as a competitor to their fathers. In contrast, children

BOX 8.2   Roadmap to Successful Practice
Steps for Developing Responsive Family Interventions with Custodial Grandparents

Providing a safe, nurturing, and healthy environment for both grandparents and grandchildren optimizes children's development and positively influences their chances for success, both individually and as a family unit (Smith, Dannison, & Vacha-Haase, 1998). Steps that practitioners can take to positively support custodial grandparent family members include:

1. *Identify grandparents who have taken on this parenting role.* Specifically define what role the grandparent is playing in caregiving as well as the role, if any, that the biological parent(s) fulfills. Don't assume that because the grandparent always brings the child to the office that she is doing the working mother a favor. Learn who is responsible for the child. Identify the legal relationships.

2. *Attend to needs specific to the grandparent.* Depression is common among custodial grandparents (Smith & Dannison, 2002). Custodial grandparents are unique among their peers and as a result often feel isolated and lonely, which increases their psychosocial problems. Screening by standardized assessment may be beneficial, but health care providers also need to attend to changes in mental status, cognition, and physical ability.

3. *Educate the custodial grandparent on realistic performance expectations and normal parenting skills.* Grandparents' lack of access to support and educational resources may lead them to maintain unrealistic demands for developmental skills beyond the abilities of the child. They may view corporal punishment as an appropriate standard and alienate the children they are attempting to nurture. Grandparents also may be excessively permissive out of a sense of guilt or misguided compassion. Either approach will be detrimental to grandchildren who are in need of guidance and security.

4. *Suggest involvement in available parenting or social support programs.* These services can help all members of custodial grandparent families overcome the difficulties they may

experience within the school, court, or social service systems. Other benefits are the potential availability of respite and opportunities to interact with others who are experiencing similar circumstances.

5. *Assist grandparents in advocating for services to meet the special needs of their grandchildren.* Many custodial grandchildren have specific physical, cognitive, or social needs that must be identified and treated. Provide grandparents with specific information about their grandchild's condition and instructions about how best to obtain services. Making this task as easy as possible—by providing grandparents with phone numbers, contact names, and established appointment times—will help grandparents take the first steps toward obtaining necessary services and/or treatment.

6. *Demonstrate concern regarding financial stability.* Anxiety about money creates a great deal of stress for many grandparents. Determine ways that medical costs, including prescribed medications, can be decreased. At the same time, determine if there are adequate financial resources to provide for basic needs including food, heat, and necessary clothing. Determine if grandchildren are eligible for state-provided programs, including Medicaid, WIC, school lunch programs, or other services, such as the National Family Caregiver Support Program (NFCSP).

7. *Provide nutrition education and develop exercise and personal wellness goals for both grandparents and grandchildren.* Reliance on outdated parenting practices may predispose grandparents to offer empty calorie foods, use food as a reward, and depend on the television as a babysitter. A dietary consultant may influence positive changes in the home. A simple, attainable exercise program can not only improve personal well-being but can also be used by both grandparent and grandchild for stress relief and a time of positive interaction.

(continued)

BOX 8.2   Roadmap to Successful Practice (Continued)
Steps for Developing Responsive Family Interventions with Custodial Grandparents

8. *Discuss immunization schedules, counseling, and well-child visits, which are proactive tenets of medicine.* Provide a resource list of area agencies that offer free immunizations and well-child checkups and organizations that offer counseling services at a reduced or sliding fee scale.

9. *Take time to discuss the importance of established routines for meals, sleep, and schoolwork.* Emphasize the necessity of boundaries and consistency for all children, but especially for children coming from chaotic past environments. Assist grandparents in developing a schedule for each day and also for each week. Planning fun times together on a regular basis (e.g., Tuesday is pancake dinner night; Friday afternoons is when we

go to the library) will enable grandchildren to establish a sense of family history and traditions that will enhance this new family relationship. Encourage consistency within the daily schedule.

10. *Affirm grandparents' commitment to raise their grandchild.* The task they are undertaking is daunting and they will receive little recognition or feedback for their efforts. Offer the support necessary to ensure their success and to enhance developmental outcomes for the children in their care.

Source: From "Custodial Grandparent Families: Steps for Developing Responsive Health Care Systems," by Barbara Grinwis, Andrea B. Smith, & Linda L. Dannison, 2004, *Michigan Family Review, 9*(1), 41–42. Adapted by permission of the publisher.

---

raised by single-parent or divorced heterosexual mothers often resisted their mothers' new male partners becoming father figures, especially if their biological fathers were still in contact with them (Golombok, MacCallum, Goodman, & Rutter, 2002; Hare & Richards, 1993).

Overall, the picture emerging from over two decades of research on children raised in lesbian and gay families confirms that the sexual orientation of parents is not a factor in child outcomes. For example, no differences have been found in children raised by lesbian mothers or gay fathers on measures of psychological adjustment compared to children raised by heterosexual parents (Stacey & Bilbarz, 2001; Stacey & Davenport, 2002; see also Golombok & Tasker, 1996). How children in lesbian-mother families feel about their mothers' relationships and their family identities also does not differ from children raised by heterosexual mothers (Tasker & Golombok, 1997). Box 8.3 provides concrete suggestions for talking with school-age children raised by gay or lesbian parents about their families.

Families Living Apart

Understanding that families are socially constructed is important to understanding the implications of separation and divorce, remarriage, and transnational parenting (i.e., residing for at least part of the year in a different country than one's children). A contextual definition of families requires us to consider any group of people with biological or social connections to be a family. Some families may reside together in a household, such as single-parent families or stepfamilies, but others, such as divorced families or transnational families, may live apart from each other in more than one geographic location.

Separation and Divorce. Researchers who have compared children living with two parents to children with divorced parents have reported behavior problems in divorced families (Clarke-Stewart & Brentano, 2006). For example, children whose

BOX 8.3 Roadmap to Successful Practice
Talking to Children About Families

As children become a part of the larger peer culture, children age 8 and older will be exposed to other people's judgments of their families. The earlier children are given appropriate information about their gay and lesbian families, the easier it will be for them to understand and appreciate them. The information that follows is intended to support parents in responding to their children's (spoken and unspoken) questions as they come to understand who they are in the context of their family and who their family is in the context of their community.

"Nobody talks about their parents."

Around age 7, some children no longer want or know how to talk about their families. This is especially true if their family is perceived to be "different." Children need others, including adults in authority, to bring up the topic of families and how they are the same or different for discussion within the peer group.

At this time, children also may need to be in charge of to whom they come out about their family. Children often share intimate details ("secrets") of their lives with only a few close friends. They will learn where, when, and with whom it is safe to talk about their lives. When this occurs, many parents feel that their child is rejecting them or is ashamed of their sexuality or gender identity. Most of this behavior, however, is typical. In fact, heterosexual parents may also experience a sense of rejection for other reasons.

While the child may choose to be less open, you as parents do not have to make the same choice. Children still need models of us as proud and respectful of ourselves and our relationships. Of course, the community in which you live impacts how comfortable you are with being out. You and your children should always be sure that you are not in danger if you are open about your sexual orientation or gender identity.

Offering opportunities to participate in activities within the gay and lesbian community is still important. However, we should anticipate that our children might make a choice to be less connected at this stage of development.

"Everyone uses 'gay' as an insult and the teachers don't say anything."

It is common for children in this age group to begin to call each other names like "gay," "faggot," "lezzy," and "dyke." Children recognize and are sensitive to attacks on people who are like the people in their families and communities. Our children often feel personally insulted when this name-calling occurs even if it was not directed at them or their family.

Parents can work with school systems to sensitize them to the impact of insulting language on their children. If this is not possible, parents can still talk to their children about their experiences and feelings and acknowledge how difficult this may be for them. Talking about the words, their meanings, and the ways in which they feel hurtful to us in our community helps children identify their own feelings related to this kind of name-calling. It is important to help children separate their personal response to the name-calling from the intent on the part of the aggressor. In all cases, hurtful name-calling is wrong and our children can be helped to understand this.

"Some kids asked me if my mom is a lesbian. I don't know what to do."

This can be a scary time for our children. They need us to give them strategies for responding to the questions or insults of other children. Some strategies that have worked for children in this age group include:

- *Giving direct responses such as, "Yes, she is."* Children have reported that this takes the power away from the child asking the question. If the child tries to keep it a secret, other children can use it to tease or bully him or her. If they are honest and matter-of-fact, the words may lose their power.

- *Making a joke in response.* Some children feel more comfortable redirecting the questions or insults using humor. This may help children by getting them the approval of their peer group. They also do not have to directly confirm or deny the comment.

(continued)

BOX 8.3   Roadmap to Successful Practice *(Continued)*
Talking to Children About Families

- ***Seeking help from adults.*** Children have gone to teachers or principals to ask for assistance in stopping harassment or educating their peers. Some children have held discussions in their classrooms about their families and why the words children use hurt their feelings. Not every child will feel safe doing this but some have used it effectively.

- ***Ignoring comments.*** Walking away from potentially inflammatory situations suits the personality of some children. They choose not to engage in discussions or confrontations. However, this may increase the teasing later on or cause them to worry about the next time it happens. These children may need additional help with strategies or may need their parents to communicate with the school.

- ***Finding a supportive group of friends.*** For all children, this is a time where having one or more close friends who can be trusted makes them feel safer. Allies are important. Parents can try to encourage children to find friends who will be accepting of their families. Children begin to seek out friends whom they perceive to be the same as themselves. Groups such as Children of Lesbians and Gays Everywhere (COLAGE) can offer local peer groups or a pen pal, so children have contact with others who have similar families and experiences.

Concluding Thoughts

As children grow in their knowledge and understanding of the world and issues of race, sexual orientation, relationships, gender identity and expression, their questions can become far more explicit. For example, they might ask:

- "Did you know you were gay before you met Ray?"

- "How did you choose the donor?"

- "Why did you go to China to adopt me?"

- "How did you decide to become a woman? Do you not like boys or men?"

Parents need to be careful not to read too much into their questions and use these as opportunities to educate their children about the full range of options available for creating families and expressing identity. The best way to teach about this is to tell your own personal story or stories of others you know. Read your child's cues for how much he or she can handle at each given moment. It is fine to offer some information and wait for them to come back for greater clarity or detail when they are ready.

Source: From "Talking to Children About Our Families" (pp. 1, 4–6) by Margie Brickley and Aimee Gelnaw, 2006. Washington, DC: Family Pride Coalition. Available from http://www.familyequality.org. Adapted by permission.

parents divorce are more prone to depression, antisocial behavior, impulsive/hyperactive behavior, low academic achievement, and behavioral difficulties in school than are children whose parents do not divorce (Child Trends, 2006). However, most psychological disturbances in girls living with their mothers have disappeared by two years after a divorce, whereas the same is not true for boys. In contrast to girls who live with single mothers and to children in nondivorced families, boys show more noncompliant and aggressive behavior—even two to three years postdivorce (Hetherington et al., 1989). Recent longitudinal studies of separated and divorced families, however, have found that such behavior problems often *preceded* a divorce—leading researchers to suggest that children's behavior may have contributed to divorce or that predivorce conflict could be a *cause* of children's adjustment problems (Cherlin et al., 1991; Reiss et al. 2000).

From a developmental perspective, school-age children are better able than preschool children to accurately assign responsibility for the divorce, to resolve loyalty conflicts, and to assess and cope with parents' volatile emotions. In early childhood, for example, children are more likely to blame themselves, fear abandonment, and misperceive parents' emotions, needs, and behaviors. However, considerable diversity exists in children's responses to their parents' marital transitions. Children with personality and behavior problems not only may be more vulnerable to the effects of their parents' divorce but also more likely to have parents who later divorce (Hetherington et al., 1989).

Conflict may indirectly impact the quality of parenting before, during, and after a divorce (Sun & Li, 2002). For example, in a nationally representative sample of over 2,500 married U.S. families with children between ages 2 and 11 years, parents' use of harsh discipline and low parental involvement partly explained a relationship between marital conflict and children's poor adjustment (Buehler & Gerard, 2002). Nevertheless, the effects of divorce on children may be less traumatic than the effects of living with marital conflict. Parental conflict has been linked to behavioral and emotional adjustment problems in both boys and girls (Amato, 2000; Amato & Booth, 1996, 2001; Amato & Keith, 1991; Kelly & Emery, 2003).

Family researchers have also suggested that when married parents have a poor-quality relationship, their children's ability to communicate within their own future marriages may be affected (Child Trends, 2006). For example, adult women who lived with only one parent as children were subject to an elevated risk of divorce themselves compared to children who grew up with both parents—even if their single parent remarried (Teachman, 2002). From an attachment theory standpoint, divorce may be particularly difficult for children and adolescents who are developmentally just beginning to explore working models of relationships (Hines, 1997).

> *Jonathan, Sr. and Joanna are equally relieved to be finally getting a divorce. They both knew that their marriage had been over for some time, but they stayed together "for the children." Finally, they realized that having unhappy parents made Jon and Janel miserable, too.*

It is very important to recognize, however, that "after three decades of research into family functioning in the marriage and after divorce, a general consensus has emerged in the social science community regarding the diversity of children's experiences with divorce, and the extent of risk that divorce creates. Coming from a divorced family does not, in itself, tell us much about the particular pathways and outcomes of these youngsters as they traverse adolescence and enter adulthood" (Kelly, 2003, p. 241). For example, approximately 75 to 80% of children do not have significant problems in adjustment. They enjoy intimate relationships, have not divorced, and are not depressed or anxious (Kelly, 2003).

Protective factors for children experiencing divorce are supportive relationships with same-sex parents prior to divorce (Videon, 2002) and continuing close relationships with their noncustodial parents—particularly fathers (Amato & Gilbreth, 1999; Kelly & Emery, 2003). When *both* parents engage in active, authoritative, competent parenting, adolescent boys from divorced families have no more delinquent behaviors than do those in married families (Kelly, 2003). School-age children and adolescents also are able to take advantage of support systems outside their immediate family, such as extended family, teacher, church, or peer networks (Hetherington et al., 1989). Refer to Box 8.4 for a discussion of ways to assist school-age children's divorce adjustment.

Remarriage and Stepfamilies. About 5 to 6% of school-age children live in stepfamilies. In the United States, the majority of divorced parents remarry and form stepfamilies within five years, adding new relationship stress to children's lives as they adjust to stepparents and/or stepsiblings (Kelly & Emery, 2003). In fact, research suggests that it may be harder to negotiate relationships in stepfamilies than in

---

BOX 8.4   Roadmap to Successful Practice
Intervention Programs for Divorce Adjustment

Joan Kelly and Robert Emery (2003) advocate a systems approach (including family systems and broader social and legal systems) to children's adjustment problems following divorce. They specifically recommend intervention programs that minimize parental conflict, promote authoritative and close relationships between children and both of their parents, enhance economic stability in the postdivorce family, and, when appropriate, help children have a voice in the interventions. Examples of program interventions currently available are parent education programs for parents and children, divorce mediation, collaborative lawyering, judicial settlement conferences, parenting coordinator or arbitration programs for chronically litigating parents, and family and group therapy for children and parents.

Of these types of programs, only mediation and divorce education have a consistent record of evaluation by researchers. For example, Emery has found that an average of 5 hours of custody mediation led to significant and positive effects on parent-child and parent-parent relationships 12 years later, including more sustained contact between fathers and children. Most divorce education programs for parents and children in the United States in the past decade, particularly those associated with family courts, are generally limited to one to two sessions in the court sector and four to six sessions in the community or schools. They are usually evaluated only with parent satisfaction questionnaires. However, evaluation studies of research-based programs designed to facilitate children's postdivorce adjustment have been found to be effective in educating parents and promoting changes in parenting behaviors associated with poor child outcomes.

Kelly and Emery encourage researchers to develop objective, reliable, and valid measures of the important struggles associated with divorce that might be apparent first in schools or clinical practice. They suggest that practitioners and educators should remember, however, that many painful memories expressed by young people from divorced families are not evidence of pathology. They conclude that the majority of findings show that most children do well following divorce. Furthermore, Kelly and Emery believe that public policies need to acknowledge that when divorce occurs, parents and legal systems designed to assist families can utilize research knowledge and skills to reduce the risks associated with divorce.

Source: Based on "Children's Adjustment Following Divorce: Risk and Resilience Perspectives," by Joan B. Kelly & Robert E. Emery, 2003, *Family Relations 52*, 4, 360. Copyright © 2003 by the National Council on Family Relations.

---

biological families. In a study of families with children between ages 4 and 17, children's behavior predicted an increase in marital conflict, particularly in stepfamilies. In addition, differences between siblings in exposure to conflict and the extent to which siblings were a source of argument increased more in stepfamilies than in biological families. Overall, boys were exposed to more conflict over time than were girls (Jenkins, Simpson, Dunn, Rasbash, & O'Connor, 2005).

Even under the best of circumstances, it typically takes about two to three years for new parent-child and sibling bonds to form, not unlike the early attachment sequence described by Bowlby! In addition, school-age children often experience multiple moves and school transitions as a result of becoming stepchildren (Child

Trends, 2006). Therefore, when compared to children living with married biological parents, stepchildren may receive lower grades and scores on achievement tests and demonstrate more behavioral problems (Coleman, Ganong, & Fine, 2000).

The following recommendations for family practitioners use a systems approach to work with stepfamilies (adapted from Pasley, Dollahite, & Ihinger-Tallman, 1993):

- *Discuss remarriage issues* (e.g., loyalty, role ambiguity, unrealistic expectations).
- *Focus early intervention on the spouses* (e.g., building a new parental coalition).
- *Teach skills to stepparents* (e.g., supporting the biological parent's role and new parenting skills).
- *Find ways to reduce jealousy* (e.g., sharing family histories and traditions with new stepfamily members).
- *Increase family flexibility* (e.g., facilitating adaptable roles and boundaries).
- *Reduce loyalty conflicts* (e.g., resisting biological parent-child coalitions and triangles).
- *Help family members resolve grief* (e.g., mourning loss of prior family or bonds with a noncustodial parent).

Clinical observations suggest that children often conceive of their families extending beyond one household. Most children, for example, make little distinction between biological grandparents and step-grandparents (Furstenberg, 1988). When asked to draw family pictures, however, some school-age children include stepsiblings and stepparents (or noncustodial birth parents) but others do not (Stafford, 2004). From a family systems perspective, "attention to both the marital and parental subsystems must be the focus of therapy with stepfamilies" (Pasley et al., 1993, p. 318).

Child Custody. A recent meta-analysis comparing joint custody arrangements with legal custody awarded to one parent included over 30 studies of postdivorce families (Bausermann, 2002). **Joint custody** is defined as either shared *physical* custody, with children spending about equal time with both parents, or shared *legal* custody, with the primary residence often remaining with one parent. Overall, joint-custodial parents report having fewer past and current conflicts with each other than sole-custody parents. In addition, children in joint custodial families do not differ from intact families. Joint-custody children have higher divorce adjustment, as well as general emotional and behavioral adjustment, better family relationships, and higher self-esteem than children in sole custody (Bausermann, 2002).

These findings suggest that one of the most difficult relationships for school-age children to navigate may be the often ambiguous relationship to a noncustodial parent. **Noncustodial parents** do not have physical or legal custody of their children—either because of legal custody decisions or because they are removed or voluntarily absent from their children. Results of studies provide mixed evidence on the benefits to school-age children and adolescents of differing levels and types of contact with nonresident parents. For example, it appears that the quality of the parent-child relationship rather than the frequency of interaction is important (for a recent review, see Stewart, 2003).

Today, it is increasingly rare for postdivorce parents to have no involvement with their children. The majority of parents engage in **parallel parenting** in which low conflict, low communication, and emotional disengagement between the ex-partners are the most typical features. Between 35 and 40% of mother-custody children have at least weekly contact with their fathers, particularly in the first several years after divorce, and between 25 and 30% of parents have a cooperative coparental relationship characterized by joint planning for the children, frequent communication, and coordination of activities and schedules (Kelly, 2003). Box 8.5 describes research on coparenting fathers one year after divorce.

Joanna and Jonathan are planning to ask the family court for joint custody. They have already begun talking about how they will coparent Jon and Janel after the divorce.

BOX 8.5   Roadmap to Understanding Theory and Research
Fathers' Involvement One Year after Divorce

In a study of families with children under 12 years, researchers examined fathers' involvement in coparenting during the first year following divorce (Madden-Derdich & Leonard, 2000). Using family systems theory as a framework, they expected that if family rules in fact regulate family interaction (e.g, who can be a member of the family), then family relationships are likely to be functional. However, during critical developmental transitions, such as marriage, birth of a child, divorce, and remarriage), the rules that regulate interaction must be redefined as family memberships and roles are changing.

In the case of noncustodial fathers, within one year of divorce many fathers report minimal parental interaction with their children. This study predicted that fathers with a clearly defined parental role would stay more involved. Four factors were hypothesized to predict noncustodial fathers' involvement as coparents:

• Fathers' satisfaction with their own parenting performance

• Support from their former spouse for coparenting

• Fathers' satisfaction with their father-child relationship(s)

• Conflicts with their former spouse over parenting issues

The first three predictors were hypothesized to have a positive effect on fathers' interaction, whereas conflict was hypothesized to have a negative impact.

A random sample of couples was selected from divorce court records in a large metropolitan area. Of the 62 eligible fathers, most were White and about one-third were college-educated. Their incomes ranged from $5,000 to more than $50,000, and their average age was 38.2 years. Fathers had an average of 2.3 children and had been married an average of 12 years. Data were collected by survey.

After controlling for legal custody arrangements (mother custody or joint custody), the most significant predictor of fathers' involvement was mothers' support of coparenting, followed by the fathers' feelings of satisfaction with his parenting role. Parenting satisfaction was positively related to their involvement in coparenting only for fathers who shared joint legal custody of their children. Contrary to hypotheses, conflict with their former spouse was not a significant deterrent of fathers' involvement in parenting. On the other hand, "this finding supports the systemically based belief that despite legal termination of the marriage, mothers continue to exert an influence over fathers' parental interaction" (Madden-Derdich & Leonard, 2000, p. 316).

Several explanations were suggested by the authors for their findings:

• ***Mothers' gatekeeping.*** Mothers retain control over physical custody in 90% of divorces, allowing them control over father-child contact.

• ***Fathers' role identity.*** For fathers with joint custody, parental roles are clearer.

Despite legal termination of a marriage, mothers continue to influence fathers' parental interaction. The difficult task faced by practitioners working with divorcing families is to acquire a clear understanding of the role that mothers play in the postdivorce identity of fathers. Both perceptions of the individual (i.e., fathers' satisfaction with their own parenting performance) and interpersonal factors (i.e., fathers' perception of parenting support from mothers) contribute to fathers' relationships with their children after a divorce. These results may be especially meaningful to noncustodial fathers who believe that they are good parents.

Source: Based on "Parental Role Identity and Fathers' Involvement in Coparental Interaction After Divorce: Fathers' Perspectives," by Debra Madden-Derdich and Stacie A. Leonard, 2000, *Family Relations, 49,* 311–318.

Transnational Families. In 2004, approximately 35 million people, or 12% of the U.S. population, were identified as foreign-born, with one out of five children currently living in an immigrant family. Many immigrant families often maintain family relations across borders, bridging their homeplaces of origin and settlement (Blume & De Reus, 2007). **Transnational families** occur when some members of the family are anchored in one place, but where family relationships transcend national boundaries (De Reus & Blume, 2008). For example, migrant laborers, nannies, domestic workers, or corporate managers may leave spouses or children in their countries of origin while seeking employment opportunities in the United States. Often, children in transnational families are left in the care of relatives but maintain long-distance relationships with nonresident parents via letters, e-mail, or phone calls.

Family therapists have suggested several questions to ask when working with transnational parents that encourage their flexible role-taking across time, for example:

- How do family members describe roles and responsibilities in their families?
- Does each person acknowledge how they and others have adapted to the loss of family members who were previously living together?
- Who else in the transnational family system might be a resource or need resources for the next adaptation to take place? (adapted from Turner & Simmons, 2006)

Immigrant families may also have school-age children who were too young at the time of immigration to remember their home countries or American-born children who have never visited their parents' countries of origin. As a result, many immigrant parents seek to transmit their culture by maintaining a continued connection with their places of origin. Recent research suggests that the maintenance of cultural traditions and the validation of ethnic identity serves as a protective factor from symptoms of depression and anxiety, poor educational achievement, and low personal satisfaction compared to rapid assimilation (Falicov, 2005).

Practitioners who work with new immigrant families recommend that parents and children together examine family photographs taken in both former and new countries of residence or retell family stories from before and after immigration as a way of preserving family narratives (e.g., Stone, Gomez, Hotzoglou, & Lipnitsky, 2005). From a family systems perspective, family stories are produced through social interaction to make sense of migration experiences (Anthias, 2002).

Guideposts for Working with School-Age Children

- Acknowledge family diversity, such as intergenerational families, adoptive families, gay or lesbian families, never-married or cohabiting families, divorced or separated families, and stepfamilies.
- Be ready to listen when children from separating or divorcing families talk about their parents' fighting, because it may affect their social adjustment and peer relations.

- Provide information to parents on conflict resolution strategies and, when appropriate, divorce adjustment programs and resources.
- Invite whole families to participate in school activities or events, not just children's biological or custodial parent(s).
- Explore ways to set up long-distance conference calls or Internet-assisted chats with transnational or nonresident parents.

RELATIONSHIP CONTEXTS IN MIDDLE CHILDHOOD

In this chapter, we have discussed the development of school-age children's family relationships. From our developmental-contextual perspective, we view the family, school, and community as the ecological contexts in which family relations are embedded. Thus, these three contexts each serve as an applied lens for examining specific relational issues in middle childhood: (a) visitation with grandparents following divorce; (b) teachers as contexts for secure attachments; and (c) neighborhood effects on parenting practices.

Family Contexts

Developmental scholars have suggested that continuities in attachment styles may depend on the stability of child-rearing environments over time (see Woodward, Fergusson, & Belsky, 2000). However, in some families, children may spend less time with extended family members, such as aunts, cousins, or grandparents, than others. For example, when families with two biological parents, stepparents, or a single mother were compared, children in stepfamilies had lower rates of contact with grandparents than the other two types of families. Associations between closeness to their maternal grandparents and children's socioemotional adjustment was found *only* for children living with both of their biological parents or with their mother and a stepfather, suggesting that the grandparental relationship is mediated through mothers.

Since 1986, grandparent visitation has been guaranteed by statute in all 50 states, although it is often challenged in family court by custodial parents. For example, a recent review of grandparent visitation cases revealed that in about one-quarter of cases, grandparents were awarded visitation after the death, divorce, or incapacity of their adult child. However, family courts decided about half of cases by protecting parents' rights to limit children's contact with their grandparents. Justices considered children's rights and child developmental concerns about equally in their interpretation of what is in "the best interests of the child" (Henderson, 2005).

Involved grandparents have frequent contact with their grandchildren.

Richard Lord/The Image Works

Like other family relationships, families construct their own meanings of what it means to be a grandparent (see Seccombe & Warner, 2004). For example, in a national study of **grandparenting styles**, three distinct patterns were noted (Cherlin & Furstenberg, 1992):

- *Companionate.* About 50% of grandparents enjoyed recreational activities, occasional overnight stays, and babysitting; relations with grandchildren were intimate, fun, and friendly.
- *Remote.* About 30% of grandparents had emotionally distant relationships, usually because they lived far from their grandchildren.
- *Involved.* About 15% of grandparents had more frequent interactions or were living with their grandchildren, sometimes as custodial grandparents.

Grandparenting styles also may differ by gender of grandparent, with women more often assuming caregiving responsibilities for their grandchildren (Seccombe & Warner, 2004). Family scholars studying ethnic-minority families in the United States have found similar patterns. In African American families, for example, grandmothers often have important responsibilities for child-rearing and for supporting children's primary parents (Hunter, 1997). The importance of relations with grandparents is "consistent with a family systems perspective in which a particular relationship is examined in the context of a network of family relationships" (Lussier, Deater-Deckard, Dunn, & Davies, 2002, p. 373).

School Contexts

Schools also serve as important contexts for the development of attachment relationships in middle childhood (e.g., Crosnoe, Johnson, & Elder, 2004; Zionts, 2005). A teacher, for example, who serves as a "secure base" for school-age children contributes to their positive school adjustment, particularly for children with disorganized attachment relationships with their primary caregivers or who have multiple risk factors for insecure attachment, such as poor parenting and neighborhood adversity. Such children are more likely than secure children to exhibit conduct disorders in school, poor social skills, and low academic achievement (Zionts, 2005).

On the other hand, children with a "teacher-as-secure-base" may exhibit improved peer relations, increased prosocial behaviors, and more mutual friendships (Zionts, 2005). Strong attachment bonds between teachers and adolescents have also been associated with higher academic achievement and with a lower likelihood of disciplinary problems, especially for girls (Crosnoe et al., 2004). Taken together, these findings support attachment theory's prediction that relationships with significant adults, such as teachers or mentors, serve an important developmental function for school-age children—especially those who may be at risk (see also Christenson & Sheridan, 2001).

Community Contexts

Parenting practices are given meaning by parents' perceptions of the particular settings in which their children interact. For example, researchers have found that African American mothers' perceptions of neighborhood safety and children's degree of access to the wider community have a significant impact on parenting practices.

The more mothers reported that neighborhoods were deteriorated, the more firmly they controlled their children's activities and behaviors (Taylor, 2000; see also Bowen, Bowen, & Cook, 2000). In addition, research on parents' limit-setting suggests that firm, strict parenting is likely to result in more *positive* outcomes for African American youth (Granic, Dishion, & Hollenstein, 2003).

In a nationally representative sample of two-parent families with children under age 13, Black children's fathers adopted an authoritarian model of parenting—exhibiting less engagement and less warmth but more control and responsibility than White children's fathers. Hispanic children's fathers exerted less control but also took more responsibility than White children's fathers, although they did not differ from White fathers in warmth. This research suggests that parenting attitudes are a major factor in racial/ethnic differences in parenting style, whereas economic factors strongly affect engagement and responsibility (Hofferth, 2003).

Although neighborhood residence may be a direct source of economic disparities among families with school-age children, neighborhood conditions also have an independent effect on children's physical, emotional, and educational outcomes (Leventhal & Brooks-Gunn, 2003b). Developmental science scholars have recently proposed three models for understanding how neighborhood context affects middle childhood development that include the following emphases:

- *Institutional resources* (e.g., libraries, parks, schools, museums, community centers, child care, health care, employment)
- *Relationships* (e.g., parenting practices, emotional availability, social networks, and supportive home environments)
- *Community norms* (e.g., informal systems of support, monitoring of public safety, and working together toward common goals)

These models were investigated in a unique social policy experiment called the "Moving to Opportunity" project. Children whose families moved from low-income neighborhoods to more moderate-income neighborhoods (compared to children whose families moved to poor or near-poor neighborhoods) demonstrated improved physical and emotional health, economic well-being, and educational achievement (Leventhal & Brooks-Gunn, 2003b).

CHAPTER REVIEW

Theoretical Viewpoints

- Close relationships are enduring ties or connections between people with frequent interdependent action sequences that occur across diverse settings and tasks.
- Attachment theory describes four behavioral systems that organize relationships (attachment, affiliation, caretaking, and sexual/reproductive systems).
- Attachments, which may be either secure or insecure, generate internal working models of relationships that guide future social interactions.

- Family systems theory asserts that families are composed of many simultaneously operating subsystems and can only be understood by viewing the entire system as a whole.
- Families maintain their equilibrium through mechanisms such as system rules.

Family Relationships

- Individual characteristics of children, their parents, and siblings influence family interactions.
- Sibling conflicts are most intense in middle childhood and decline in later adolescence.

- Authoritative parenting styles and secure attachments lead to positive psychosocial outcomes.
- Ongoing conflict between parents is more distressing to children than divorce or separation.

Family Diversity

- Contemporary school-age children live in diverse types of families (e.g., gay or lesbian, single-parent, intergenerational, or stepfamilies).
- Two-parent families are beneficial but are not the only family structure in which school-age children are successful.

- Grandparents provide varying levels of support to their adult children and grandchildren.

Relationship Development in Context

- Families are an important context for the development of intergenerational relationships.
- Schools provide opportunities for teachers to act as attachment figures.

- Neighborhood factors, such as poverty and safety concerns, affect parenting strategies and child outcomes.
- The effects of parenting styles on school-agers are sensitive to variations in culture.

TABLE 8.6   Summary of Developmental Theories

Chapter	Theories	Focus
8: Relationships and Families	Attachment	Internal working models of early relationships in families as the basis of later close relationships, such as peer relations, friendships, and romantic partnerships
	Family Systems	Equilibrium among simultaneous interdependent subsystems, such as the parent-child, marital, or sibling systems

---

KEY TERMS

Anxious-avoidant
Anxious-resistant
Attachment style
Authoritative parenting
Authoritarian parenting
Binuclear family system
Boundaries
Cohabiting couples

Coparental relationship
Differential parenting
Equilibrium
Ethology
Family rules
Family systems
Gay families
Grandparenting styles

Intergenerational
Internal working model
Joint custody
Noncustodial parents
Parallel parenting
Parenting styles
Parenting practices
Permissive parenting

Secure attachment
Sibling interaction styles
System levels
Transnational families
Triangles
Uninvolved parenting

SUGGESTED ACTIVITIES

1. Spend an hour at a shopping mall observing families with school-agers. Record an example of authoritative, authoritarian, and permissive parenting. What event or behavior precipitated each of the interventions and what reactions did each style elicit from the children?

2. Go to dinner with a family that has school-age children. Observe the parent to parent, parent-child, and sibling interactions. How did the various subsystems affect the conversation? Did you see examples of family rules or feedback loops?

3. Go to the library or newsstand and examine the variety of parenting magazines available. Is the focus on traditional or nontraditional families? Select one and look at the table of contents. Are there any articles appropriate for parenting in middle childhood?

4. Surf the Internet for Web sites on parenting and family relationships. How many address developmental issues of middle childhood? Is the advice developmentally appropriate?

5. Interview your own family members and construct a family tree (i.e., genogram). Go back as many generations as possible and include as many branches as you can. What have you learned about your family's history or diversity that you didn't know before?

RECOMMENDED RESOURCES

Suggested Readings

Bank, S. P., & Kahn, M. D. (2003). *The sibling bond.* New York: Basic.

Bray, J. H., & Kelly, J. (1999). *Stepfamilies.* New York: Broadway.

Christenson, S. L., & Sheridan, S. M. (2001). *Schools and families: Creating essential connections for learning.* New York: Guildford Press.

Clarke-Stewart, A., & Brentano, C. (2006). *Divorce: Causes and consequences.* New Haven, CT: Yale University Press.

Coontz, S. (1998). *The way we really are: Coming to terms with America's changing families.* New York: Basic.

Dowd, N. (2000). *Redefining fatherhood.* New York: New York University Press.

Drucker, J. (2001). *Lesbian and gay families speak out: Understanding the joys and challenges of diverse family life.* New York: Perseus.

Suggested Online Resources

Children in the Middle http://208.109.164.42/online/demo/

Divorce Source http://divorcesource.com

Talking to Children about Our Families http://www.familyequality.org/resources/publications/talking-toourchildren.pdf

Talking to Children about Divorce www.divorce-education.com

That's a Family! http://www.womedia.org/taf_clips.htm

Suggested Web Sites

American Association for Marriage and Family Therapy. http://aamft.org/index_nm.asp

Council on Contemporary Families. http://www.contemporaryfamilies.org

National Fatherhood Initiative. http://www.fatherhood.org

National Parenting Education Network. http://www.npen.org/

Parents and Families of Lesbians and Gays (PFLAG). http://www.pflag.org

Single-Parent Tips. http://www.singleparent-tips.com

Suggested Films and Videos

Diversity rules: The changing nature of families. (2001). Insight Media (25 minutes)

Family matters: Family types. (2005). Insight Media (30 minutes)

Family ties . . . Strengthening the family unit. (2000). Films for the Humanities and Sciences (23 minutes)

John Bowlby: Attachment theory across generations. (2007). Davidson Films (40 minutes)

Kramer v. Kramer. (1979). Columbia Pictures (105 minutes)

Surviving divorce. (2006). Films for the Humanities and Sciences (13 minutes)

9

Social and Moral Development in Middle Childhood

Jeff Greenberg/PhotoEdit Inc.

Chapter Objectives

After reading this chapter, students will be able to:

▶ Define social competence in middle childhood.

▶ Summarize theories of social cognition.

▶ Describe social perspective taking, moral, and religious reasoning in school-age children.

▶ Discuss current research on school-age children's prosocial and aggressive behavior.

▶ Explain the contributions of family, school, and community contexts to social development in middle childhood.

Alesha, age 11, is just settling into her new middle school. The first two months have been stressful—learning the new building, meeting new people, changing classes five times a day—but she has survived with the help of her friends from elementary school. She has just started to feel adventurous enough to meet some new people. Choir, last hour of the day, is one of the few places she goes without her two best friends, Jennifer and Kelly. There is one nice girl, Mandy, and within a few days they seem like old friends—they know about each other's secrets and most embarrassing moments—and Mandy invites Alesha over after school.

MIDDLE CHILDHOOD SOCIAL DEVELOPMENT

Building on an understanding of *self* (discussed in chapter 7), school-age children can move beyond themselves and on to relations with others. **Social development** in middle childhood includes acquiring social skills; increasing interpersonal understanding; refining concepts of friendship; and using moral reasoning to guide social interactions with family and peers. **Social competence** is defined as the ability to interact effectively with others, based in large part on school-agers' maturing emotional understanding and self-control.

School-age children's social and moral development allows relationships built during middle childhood to pave the way for adolescent dating experiences. How do children make friends and influence other people? Do school-age children really disregard their parents in favor of peers? Does peer pressure influence children's moral reasoning? Understanding these complex social interactions requires that we examine theories of social cognitive development and moral reasoning.

THEORETICAL VIEWPOINTS

The study of social development in middle childhood involves **social cognition**, or the understanding of others, such as friends or family. Social cognitive development also influences school-age behaviors, such as the imitation of peers. Social cognitive theories provide explanations of how social interactions (behaviors) help to construct our understandings of social relationships (cognitions). Specifically, the study of middle childhood social development utilizes three related social-cognitive approaches: social learning, social information processing, and social theories of mind.

Social Learning

Bandura's (1971) **social learning theory** states that we learn social skills and behaviors by observing the behavior of others. Also called "observational" learning, social learning offers a straightforward way to understand school-age children's readiness to copy the attitudes and actions of highly respected peers and positive (or sometimes negative) role models. Social learning theory draws heavily on the principles of behaviorist theory, especially reinforcement. However, in *social* learning theory, **vicarious reinforcement** is the cognitive process through which people of all ages formulate expectations about the desirability of certain behaviors by seeing the results of others' behaviors—even before any direct action is taken (Crain, 2000). In other words, children are reinforced by how they see others behaving and the subsequent social responses to those actions.

> *When Mandy invites Alesha over after school, the girls go upstairs to Mandy's bedroom. Alesha is completely surprised when Mandy pulls an aerosol can out of her dresser drawer. Alesha and her friends have always been antidrug, and she tries to stay away from the obvious drug users in the school. But Mandy seems like a really normal person, someone Alesha likes!*

Social learning theory takes into account a person's perceptions and cognitions of their own and others' behaviors and their positive or negative consequences. Social learning, therefore, goes far beyond a direct, linear connection between an environmental model (stimulus) and a person's behavior (response) as described by classical learning theory (Muuss, 1996). Social, or observational, learning is divided into four sequential processes:

- *Attention.* To imitate a model, individuals first have to pay attention to it. Models are attractive because they have status, power, or influence, such as media celebrities or older peers.
- *Retention.* Because individuals often imitate models some time after they have observed them, retention abilities allow them to remember the model's features and behaviors.
- *Motor Reproduction.* From observation alone, individuals can learn a behavior pattern, but to successfully copy it may require skill acquisition and practice.
- *Reinforcement.* If individuals successfully perform according to a model that they have observed, the behavior may be self-reinforcing. They may also be vicariously reinforced if the model's behavior has been positively rewarded by others.

In a more recent revision of his original theory, Bandura (1987) proposed a contextual model called **reciprocal determinism** that includes a bidirectional relationship among three interacting factors, as shown in Figure 9.1. In the revised theory, now known as **social *cognitive* theory**, to reflect the influence of people's own thoughts on their behavior, three determinants reciprocally affect each other:

- $E = Environment.$ The external, social environment that provides the stimulus for learning
- $B = Behavior.$ The learner's response to the environmental stimulus
- $P = Person.$ The personality, cognitive ability, motivation, and beliefs of the person

In recent explanations of social cognitive theory, Bandura (2001) has called attention to **agency**, or a person's ability to choose among several alternative courses of action: "Agency refers to acts done intentionally" (p. 6). In addition, people evaluate the effects of their actions on others.

Alesha, for example, ponders the possible result of rejecting Mandy's offer: losing a new friend, or rejecting her parents' values and disappointing them.

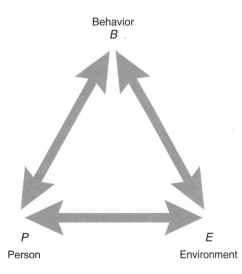

FIGURE 9.1
Reciprocal Determinism in Social Cognition

Social understanding in middle childhood is determined by mutual, ongoing interactions between school-age children, their social environment, and their interpretation of their own and others' behaviors.

STOP What did you learn from observing the behavior of other children during elementary or middle school?

This agentic perspective on social cognition, therefore, requires a further understanding of precisely *how* school-age children may make decisions about the appropriateness and desirability of certain social behaviors.

Social Information Processing

In recent years, ***social* information-processing** models of children's social behavior have emerged to describe the specific cognitive mechanisms school-age children use to process social information (for a review, see Crick & Dodge, 1994). From this perspective, when children are faced with a social situation, they engage in six mental steps as they make a decision how to act:

1. *Encoding of internal and external cues.* Selectively attending to filtered, personalized memories of similar situations (e.g., *the intent of a peer with whom the child is interacting, for example, Mandy*).

2. *Interpretation and mental representation of cues.* Analyzing the events that have occurred in the interaction and making an inference about the perspectives or intentions of others (e.g., *"She is lowering her voice; she seems secretive"*).

3. *Clarification of goals.* Selecting a desired outcome for the current situation (e.g., *"I want to be her friend"*).

4. *Construction of a response.* Accessing possible responses from memory or constructing novel ones and evaluating possible outcomes (e.g., *"I could ask her what's wrong so she'll see that I want to be her friend, or I could just wait and see what she does next"*).

5. *Response decision.* Selecting the response with the most positive outcome based on the degree of confidence (i.e., self-efficacy) they have in their own ability to enact the response (e.g., *"I don't want to embarrass her; I'll wait until she shares her secret with me"*).

6. *Behavior enactment.* Evaluating the peer's response and reenacting steps 1–5, if necessary, with different strategies (e.g., *"I'll continue playing as if nothing is wrong"*).

Often children engage in multiple social information-processing steps at the same time. For example, they may interpret cues while encoding them or consider the meaning of their partner's behavior while accessing other possible responses. Overall, however, the information-processing components, or six mental steps, of this problem-solving process have been predictive of children's social adjustment (Crick & Dodge, 1994). The model has also been used to teach school-age children successful ways to work together to influence social situations.

Describing the ways in which school-age children's mental processes are influenced by their interactions with others is a major contribution of social information-processing research. Social information-processing theorists have proposed that social experiences may lead to the generation of mental structures that are remembered in the form of social knowledge. These stored memories form a "database" that influences children's future processing of social cues, as diagrammed in Figure 9.2. In other words, children mentally represent social behavior and its outcomes, store these representations in memory as part of their general social knowledge, and use this information to guide their future actions with others (Crick & Dodge, 1994).

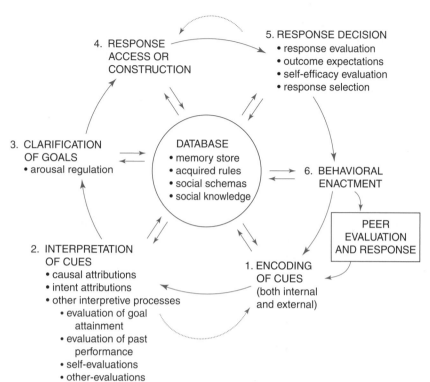

FIGURE 9.2
Social Information-Processing Model

School-age children go through six steps of information processing to make sense of peer interactions.

Source: From "A Review and Reformulation of Social Information-Processing Mechanisms in Children's Social Adjustment," by N. R. Crick and K. A. Dodge, 1994, *Psychological Bulletin, 115,* p. 76. Copyright © 1994 by the American Psychological Association. Reprinted by permission of the author.

This theoretical perspective on social cognition is also likely to lead to a better understanding of *how* children learn about themselves and others in a social context. During middle childhood, most children become increasingly capable of representing, organizing, and interpreting social information.

Alesha thinks to herself, "Only losers use drugs."

In essence, children create their own theories about people and how they may be likely to act in social situations, called *theories* of mind.

Social Theories of Mind

Recall that social cognition means knowing about people and how they act (Flavell & Miller, 1998; see also Shantz, 1983). Even very young children can "theorize" about others' mental states to predict and explain behavior, a process called **social theories of mind**. For example, beginning around age 4, a child may start to perceive that two people's conflicting representations of the same event caused them to behave differently (Flavell & Miller, 1998). Children's theories of mind help them to understand not only simple links between a psychological cause and a behavior but also a larger system of interconnections among the environment, behavior, and the person (recall Bandura's reciprocal determinism: $E \times B \times P$).

A theories-of-mind perspective contributes the idea that *children themselves* construct theories as they interact with others. For example, during middle childhood, children come to understand the reciprocal nature of friendship based on an emerging understanding that their friends can "think about each other's beliefs about each other." By adolescence, most children will come to understand that all such social knowledge is *situated* in the personal and sociocultural context of relationships (Flavell & Miller, 1998). This evidence has implications for both basic research (i.e., understanding how peers influence social development) and for applied research (i.e., helping children with poor peer relations) (Ladd, 1999). School-age children's development of social knowledge about others is also central to studies of social perspective-taking and moral reasoning.

SOCIAL AND MORAL UNDERSTANDING IN MIDDLE CHILDHOOD

School-age children's social interactions are an important developmental context for the growth of interpersonal understanding and of moral reasoning. Although these research foci each provide a slightly different "lens" to use in examining school-age social-cognitive understanding, together they can provide a clearer picture of middle childhood than when viewed separately. For example, how do developmental psychologists explain school-age children's struggles to understand the nature of interpersonal relationships and to recognize the perspective of others? How might such mental representations affect their ongoing moral conduct?

> *Why does Mandy believe that she can predict what Alesha will think (e.g., "getting high is cool") or do (e.g., agree to huff)? Mandy's theory could be based on social interactions with Alesha and memories of her past behavior, or it may be Mandy's own vicarious desire. Mandy decides to share her secret with Alesha.*

Interpersonal Understanding

Because understanding others is necessary for success in social interactions, the study of children's social perspective-taking ability has been a major focus in research on social development (Cillessen & Bellmore, 2002). **Social perspective-taking** involves a gradual, qualitative progression from egocentric thinking to an eventual understanding of mutual perspectives within a social system, such as a family or peer group (Durkin, 1995).

In research on social perspective-taking, children are typically asked to respond to a series of social dilemmas in which conflicting feelings may occur (Selman, 1980). For example, one dilemma involves a hypothetical child, Holly, who is confronted with an urgent choice between climbing a tree to save her friend's kitten and honoring a promise to her father not to climb trees. The children in the study were asked a series of social perspective-taking questions, such as "Does Holly know how her friend feels about the kitten?" and "How will Holly's father feel if he finds out that she climbed the tree?"

In early childhood, most interviewees focused on saving the kitten by climbing the tree and assumed that everyone would feel the same way; however, by middle childhood, most children could take other people's perspectives into account (i.e., the father's concern for Holly's safety as well as her friend's distress) and considered other solutions to the dilemma, such as calling the fire department (Selman, 1980).

Recall from chapter 5 that in early childhood the majority of children are *egocentric,* failing to distinguish between their own perspective and that of others. Between ages 6 and 8, however, most children begin to engage in *social informational role-taking.* For example, researchers have found that 6- and 7-year-olds may not take into account

---

TABLE 9.1   Stages of Social Perspective-Taking

School-age children can understand how they are seen by a friend but are just beginning to develop an understanding of how others might view their friendship.

Developmental Levels (Approximate Age of Emergence in Reflective Social Thought)	Levels of Social Perspective Taking Used to Analyze the Understanding of Interpersonal Issues
0: Preschool (ages three to five)	To understand my own perspective (first-person [egocentric] and physicalistic level)
1: Early elementary (ages six to seven)	To understand your perspective, distinct from mine (first-person and subjective level)
2: Upper elementary (ages eight to eleven)	To understand your view of my (subjective) perspective (second-person and reciprocal level)
3: Middle school (ages twelve to fourteen)	To understand her or his view of us (our perspective) (third-person and mutual level)
4: High school (ages fifteen to eighteen)	To understand my own perspective in the context of multiple perspectives (third-person and generalized other level)

Source: From Robert L. Selman, Table 2.1, "Overview of Social Perspective Taking: A Developmental Analysis." In *The Promotion of Social Awareness: Powerful Lessons from the Partnership of Developmental Theory and Classroom Practice* (p. 21). © 2003 Russell Sage Foundation, 112 East 64th Street, New York, NY 10021. Reprinted with permission.

---

others' perspectives, relying instead on their own subjective experiences (i.e., a first-person perspective). These children are aware that other people may have a view of events that differs from their own, but still can focus on only one perspective at a time.

By age 8, children begin to understand others' feelings and intentions, not just their own. Between ages 8 and 11, most children can put themselves in another's place and reflect on another's intentions and behaviors, called *reciprocal role-taking* (i.e., a second-person perspective). By around age 12, most school-agers can appreciate the fact that people differ in their views of the same experience. Between ages 12 and 14, however, children can also view themselves from the perspective of a third person, called *mutual role taking.* Nevertheless, until adolescence most children do not take into account the social conventions that govern behavior regardless of the partners' viewpoints in a particular situation, called *generalized-other role taking* (Selman, 1980, 2003). Refer to Table 9.1 for a chart of the levels of social perspective-taking used to understand interpersonal issues.

This developmental sequence also influences social behavior. Most researchers have found that children with more advanced role-taking skills are more socially skilled with peers and play more cooperatively. Others have found that training children in perspective-taking does not always lead to improved social relations (Durkin, 1995; Selman, 2003). In addition, researchers report that children may use role-taking in some situations but not in others (Damon, 1983; Selman, 2003). As a result, some developmental theorists have suggested that social perspective-taking may not be a general "ability" that children acquire but rather an "activity" they increasingly engage in as they mature (see Damon, 1983).

> *For example, in the case study, there may have been other discussions of shared intentions, negotiation of each other's perspectives, or evaluations of alternatives that led Mandy to predict Alesha's attitude toward using drugs.*

School-age children still need help from adults to negotiate successfully with others.

Valerie Schultz/Merrill

In social situations, children's perspective-taking must also be *coordinated* with the perspectives of others. In this context, successive levels of interpersonal understanding are applied to social interactions through a process that researchers have called **interpersonal negotiation** (Selman, 2003). Table 9.2 illustrates the conceptual relationships among interpersonal understanding, coordination, and negotiation, called the *interpersonal action framework*. In this developmental sequence, each step in the development of children's social perspective coordination broadens their social understanding as well as their strategies for negotiating interpersonal conflicts (Selman, 2003).

> *The interpersonal conflict that Alesha faces involves not only resolving the dilemma of accepting or rejecting an offer of inhalants at that moment but also of facing Mandy at school afterwards.*

In interpersonal negotiation research, children are asked to respond to hypothetical dilemmas called "risky incidents." For example, one incident involved Kathy, a 10-year-old girl, and her best friend, Becky. When Jeanette, a new girl in town, in-

---

TABLE 9.2   Stages of Interpersonal Action

School-age children's interpersonal negotiation strategies are linked to their level of social perspective taking.

Levels of Social Perspective Taking	Interpersonal Negotiation Strategies
0: Egocentric, undifferentiated	Physical force
1: Subjective, differentiated	Unilateral power
2: Reciprocal, self-reflective	Cooperative exchange
3: Mutual, third-person	Mutual compromise
4: Intimate, societal	Collaboration

Source: Based on *The Promotion of Social Awareness: Powerful Lessons from the Partnership of Developmental Theory and Classroom Practice* (p. 31) by R. L. Selman, 2003. New York: Russell Sage Foundation. Copyright 2003 Russell Sage Foundation.

vited Kathy to go to a show on the same afternoon that she had a date with Becky, Kathy was not sure what to do. Compared to the previously described "Holly dilemma," this story requires children to coordinate the differing perspectives in a social interaction and then to negotiate *with others* to avoid a conflict. In solving such a dilemma, children could negotiate solutions in which they might either

- Change their own goal.
- Change the goal of the other person.
- Find a mutually acceptable goal.

Possible actions at the lowest level of interpersonal negotiation, called *impulsive,* would include Kathy accepting Jeanette's invitation without thinking, or Becky breaking off her friendship with Kathy in an unreflective reaction. At the next level, called *unilateral,* Becky could order Kathy to "never do it again" or Kathy could simply comply: "I'll never do it again." In either case, the girls have not negotiated but rather given orders or obeyed orders unilaterally. At the next two levels, called *cooperative* and *compromise,* the girls could agree to take turns, "I'll go with Jeannette this Saturday, but next week I'll get my mom to take you and me to the movies" (Selman, 2003, p. 35). At the highest level, called *collaborative,* children together focus on what it may take to maintain their friendship in the future.

By middle childhood, most children can consider the "we-ness" of an interpersonal dilemma—in this case, the ongoing friendship between Kathy and Becky. Research on interpersonal negotiation strategies when children are engaged in actual social interaction, however, has revealed that school-age children's choice of one strategy over another is fluid and context-dependent (Selman, 2003). For example, Kathy may know that she *should* talk to Becky before deciding what to do, *but she may not.* Researchers have suggested that the choice of a strategy may be based on a personality factor, called **interpersonal orientation**: the characteristic tendency either to transform one's own behavior or to try to change the other person. Nevertheless, interpersonal orientation may depend, in part, on children's level of negotiation skill (Selman, 2003). Therefore, action researchers have developed intervention programs and classroom-based curricula to foster negotiation skills in school-age children, as described in Box 9.1 (Nakkula & Nikitopoulos, 2001).

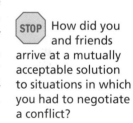 **STOP** How did you and friends arrive at a mutually acceptable solution to situations in which you had to negotiate a conflict?

 Guideposts for Working with School-Age Children

- Discuss youth fiction or feature films that present social perspectives that may be different from those of the children in your care.

- Foster discussion of conflicts that allows school-age children to disagree but still listen to one another's perspectives.

- Have students role-play social dilemmas in pairs or small groups to encourage the awareness of others' perspectives on issues.

- Help them think through the short-term and long-term consequences of their own social behaviors by reviewing what happened in prior social interactions.

- Minimize the stating of arbitrary rules for social behavior in favor of discussing particular social negotiation strategies in specific situations.

> ### BOX 9.1   Roadmap to Successful Practice
> *Program for Young Negotiators*
>
> *Young Negotiators* is a middle-school problem-solving and conflict-resolution curriculum of the *Program on Negotiation* at Harvard Law School designed to train middle-school students in principled negotiation. The curriculum guides its participants through 10 sequentially ordered modules. Each of the modules uses a combination of games, role plays, and class discussions to teach particular negotiation concepts, such as perceptions, empathy, negotiation interests versus positions, and collaboration versus competition. The overall program goal is to teach a "win-win" approach. In the beginning levels, students learn what negotiation is and why it is important. Then they learn to use specific negotiation techniques. In the final levels, students apply their negotiation skills to situations from their own lives (Nakkula & Nikitopoulos, 2001).
>
> In an evaluation study of the *Young Negotiators* curriculum in Argentina, early adolescents' negotiation scores improved by almost 5% on a measure of overall negotiation. These results exceeded changes found with the same measure in studies of the *Young Negotiators* curriculum when taught in other contexts, possibly because teachers in Argentina expressed a strong interest in being trained in the model and using it with their students. In addition, many of the
>
> school administrators stated that *Young Negotiators'* focus on problem solving and perspective-taking was consistent with the core mission of their schools (Nakkula & Nikitopoulos, 2001).
>
> Participants in the study also showed increases in their developmental level of interpersonal competence (Selman, 2003) that exceeded the degree of developmental growth that would be expected over a five-month period. In this social cognitive approach, the transition from late elementary school to middle and high school is marked by changes in perspective-taking, collaboration, and interpersonal negotiation skills.
>
> Although the *Young Negotiators* curriculum offers both perspective-taking and action-strategy exercises, students seem to prefer interactive role plays over reflective discussions. Based on these findings, teachers should think about balancing the curricular activities. In addition, teachers who incorporate the negotiation approach into their everyday instruction are likely to reinforce the messages presented through the formal training modules. In this sense, the *Program for Young Negotiators* can be considered an effective comprehensive approach to conflict resolution (Nakkula & Nikitopoulos, 2001).

Moral Reasoning

As school-age children mature, they become increasingly able to think about moral issues that may occur during social interactions. Not infrequently, social dilemmas—such as whether to rescue Holly's cat, whether to go out with Jeanette and leave Becky alone, or whether to use inhalants with Mandy—invoke choices between behaviors that could be considered either "right" or "wrong." Researchers on moral reasoning pioneered the use of hypothetical stories (like those used to assess social perspective-taking) that present children with questions about what course of action a fictional character should take (see Colby & Kohlberg, 1987a, 1987b). For example, one story recounts the moral dilemma of Heinz, who cannot afford to buy a drug that could save his wife's life. Should he steal it? How do school-age children resolve such moral or ethical dilemmas? To answer this important question, we must look again at the influential developmental theory of Jean Piaget.

According to Piaget's (1932/1965) cognitive developmental theory (introduced in chapter 5), preoperational children are **moral realists**. In early childhood, they consider the *consequences* of an action over and above the consideration of a person's *intentions*. For example, accidentally breaking 10 cups is usually seen by younger children as worse than intentionally breaking just 1. Young children may only under-stand a morality of "constraint" in which their moral behavior is controlled by the unilateral authority of adults or of powerful peers, such as bullies, rather than by mu-tual respect (Lapsley, 1996).

By the time children reach the concrete reasoning stage of middle childhood, however, most have become **moral relativists**. They now think that an intentional action is worse than an accidental behavior, regardless of the result. In addition, con-temporary theorists claim that school-age children do not just shift from one type of reasoning to another (Lapsley, 1996). Rather, there is a gradual developmental trend toward increasing integration of consequences and intentions with age (see Grueneich, 1982) such that by the end of middle childhood, school-agers have achieved what Piaget referred to as the morality of "cooperation."

In Piaget's view, the fundamental understanding of morality is transformed as children gain greater experience with peers (Lapsley, 1996; Youniss, 1980). Through cooperative exchanges with others, children learn that the rules guiding social life are not just arbitrary but rather are socially constructed, flexible arrangements with others. Some researchers have called this developmental domain an understanding of social conventions rather than of *morality* (Rest, Narvaez, Bebeau, & Thoma, 1999; Turiel, 1998, see also 2006). **Social conventions** are behaviors that are agreed upon by society but are not necessarily guided by moral obligations to others. Can school-age children *really* make moral decisions? In defining the moral domain, researchers have described four interrelated psychological processes (Rest et al., 1999):

1. *Moral judgment.* Judging which action would be justifiable as moral

2. *Moral sensitivity.* Being aware there is a moral problem when it exists; interpret-ing the situation; role-playing how various actions would affect others

3. *Moral motivation.* Committing to a moral course of action; valuing moral actions over other values; taking personal responsibility for moral outcomes

4. *Moral character.* Having courage; persisting in a moral task

Alesha thinks about making up an excuse so she can decline Mandy's offer without taking a moral stand on drug use. She could claim she had asthma or something, but she is afraid that it will end the new friendship. And if Mandy gets high, and still is a good student, maybe it isn't so bad after all?

Stages of Moral Judgment. Based on Piaget's stage approach to cognitive develop-ment as the acquisition of increasingly mature problem-solving strategies, Lawrence Kohlberg described six stages of **moral reasoning,** as seen in Table 9.3 (Colby, Kohlberg, & Gibbs, 1983). In the first stage, called *heteronomous* morality, children use a punishment and obedience orientation to make moral judgments based on adult rules for appropriate behavior and comply with social norms imposed by adults (e.g., avoiding punishment [*getting caught with drugs*]), similar to Piaget's morality of constraint. In the second stage, called *instrumental* morality, they use an individualistic orientation to satisfy their own needs by engaging in concrete ex-changes with others (e.g., sharing [*drugs*] to get something in return [*friendship*]). Both of these stages together comprise the **preconventional** level of moral reason-ing, typical of early childhood, in which many children are still egocentric.

By middle childhood, however, most children have moved into the second level of moral reasoning ability called **conventional**, composed of stages 3 and 4. School-age children in the third stage of moral reasoning, called *interpersonal* morality, can

TABLE 9.3   Moral Reasoning

Six stages of moral reasoning were proposed by Lawrence Kohlberg. By the end of middle childhood, most children can use conventional thinking that is based on conforming to others' expectations.

Ages	Level	Stage
5–8 years	I. Preconventional	1. Heteronomous morality
8–10 years		2. Instrumental morality
10–12 years	II. Conventional	3. Interpersonal morality
12–18 years		4. Social system morality
18–26 years	III. Postconventional	5. Social welfare morality
26+		6. Principled morality

understand the perspectives of others (as described by social role-taking) and make moral judgments based on shared expectations in a relationship or on obligations to others (e.g., pleasing an authority figure [*or peer*]), similar to Piaget's morality of co-operation. In the fourth stage, called *social system* morality, children are able to adopt the perspective of society and make judgments based on the good of the group (e.g., following the rules [*or social norms*]).

The final level of moral reasoning is called **postconventional** morality, comprised of stages 5 and 6. In the fifth stage, called *social welfare* morality, school-age children and adolescents begin to understand abstract moral values and the importance of human rights (e.g., treating people equally). The sixth stage—which researchers have rarely observed, even in adults—is called *principled* morality and requires that individuals use universal ethical principles to guide everyday decision making (e.g., promoting social justice).

Kohlberg's moral reasoning stages have been widely criticized for several reasons. First, it is not clear whether they are based on a process of coordinating conflicting perspectives (as suggested by the social role-taking sequence discussed earlier) or by an increasing ability to generate solutions to moral dilemmas by applying universal moral principles (Carpendale, 2000). Why is this distinction important? Our concern—and that of Kohlberg's critics—involves his belief that there is a moral ideal against which all people should be evaluated. From our developmental-contextual viewpoint, however, a universal approach to morality runs counter to the idea that in differing cultures there may be different norms for moral behavior, often called **ethical relativism** (Shweder, 1991).

A second major criticism of Kohlberg's moral reasoning stages is that both children and adults often perform better on the hypothetical moral dilemmas than they do in real life referred to as the *competence-performance distinction.*

> *Alesha knows that inhalant use is dangerous and that her parents would not approve of any involvement with peers who abuse drugs. But when faced with a situation in which drugs are offered by a familiar and trusted friend, she nevertheless may choose to try them.*

A stage approach does not necessarily imply consistency in reasoning across widely varying content (Carpendale, 2000). The empirical fact that an individual uses more than one stage to think about various moral issues may depend more on the *personal relevance* of the particular situation under discussion and on *caring about* the people involved.

A third criticism of Kohlberg's moral reasoning stages is that they were developed based on research *only* with men and boys. To remedy this significant limitation, Carol Gilligan (1977), a student of Kohlberg, conducted a study of women and girls.

Ethics of Care. Gilligan (1977, 1982) argued that Kohlberg's emphasis on justice ignored a uniquely feminine approach to moral reasoning: caring for others. She claimed that girls and women approach moral problems from the perspective of interpersonal ideals, whereas boys and men more often rely on a commitment to ideals of justice. Her research with girls and women did, in fact, demonstrate a gender bias in the scoring of moral dilemmas: Females were more likely than males to be scored at Kohlberg's stage 3 (interpersonal morality). However, Gilligan claimed that these scores did not mean that females are less mature than males in moral reasoning ability but rather that they more often base their moral decision making on a concern for others.

> From this perspective, Alesha might sniff the inhalant because she doesn't want to insult Mandy.

Based on her research with girls and women, Gilligan (1977) described three levels in females' moral reasoning, referred to as the **ethics of care**:

1. Being responsive to others and appreciating the importance of relationships
2. Caring for others, even if it may mean self-sacrifice
3. A sense of universal obligation for all people

Table 9.4 compares the ethics of care to a moral orientation based on justice, such as Kohlberg's stages of moral reasoning.

Not all moral reasoning research unequivocally supports the ethics of care, however (see Turiel, 1998). In research using stories about friendship considerations versus self-interests with 7- to 15-year-olds, both justice and care orientations

---

TABLE 9.4 Comparing Moral Orientations

Carol Gilligan proposed the ethics of care as an alternative to Kohlberg's focus on moral justice reasoning.

Moral Orientation	What Becomes a Problem	Resolution of a Conflict
Care	A morality of care rests on an understanding of relationships and a response to another in terms of that person's terms and contexts (e.g., not breaking trusts or severing ties between people)	Resolutions are sought that restore relationships or connections between people (e.g., ensuring the care of others or stopping hurt and suffering)
Justice	A morality of justice or fairness rests on understanding relationships as reciprocity between separate individuals (e.g., mediating conflicting claims with fairness as the goal)	Resolutions are sought that consider duties and obligations and adherence to one's values and principles (e.g., using an impartial, objective measure of choice that ensures fairness in arriving at a decision)

Source: Based on "Listening to Voices We Have Not Heard" (pp. 42–44) by N. P. Lyons in C. Gilligan, N. P. Lyons, & T. J. Hanmer (Eds.), *Making Connections: The Relational Worlds of Adolescent Girls at the Emma Willard School*, Cambridge, MA: Harvard University Press, 1990. Copyright 1990 by the President and Fellows of Harvard College.

became more interconnected (Keller & Edelstein, 1991). For example, researchers interviewed 10 boys and 10 girls from grades 1, 4, 7, and 10 in a study designed to compare "care" versus "justice" orientations (Walker, de Vries, & Trevethan, 1987). In thinking about real-life dilemmas, compared to hypothetical dilemmas, children who used a care orientation or a split orientation (care/justice) showed higher levels of moral reasoning. Neither girls nor boys used one orientation more than the other, however. In a similar test of the care orientation, no differences between boys and girls were reported for African American adolescents who were asked a hypothetical dilemma about leaving their grandmother's home to move with their mother to a northern city (Stack, 1990). Therefore, many researchers have concluded that the two moral orientations may not be gender typed (Lapsley, 1996). Furthermore, feminist ethicists have questioned the distinction between care and justice, claiming that it reinforces feminine stereotyping and creates a false dichotomy between a concern for justice and the well-being of others (Turiel, 1998; see also Okin, 1989).

Developmental researchers and educators recommend school-based programs to help students think about their relationships and the kinds of moral dilemmas they may face in school, such as being angry with friends, struggling for independence, and experiencing unfairness (Gilligan, Lyons, & Hanmer, 1990). In most secondary schools, successful educational interventions have involved minimizing competition, redefining responsibilities, listening to others, and making fair decisions (Gilligan et al., 1990; see also Gilligan & Brown, 1992, and Pipher, 1994).

Fairness. In middle childhood, concern about fairness—whether in the family, the classroom, or the peer group—is a common moral issue. Often the focus of such research is on **distributive justice** reasoning, or how children decide what is "fair." As in the other moral domains we have discussed, studies of children's thinking about distributive justice have utilized hypothetical stories about sharing to assess fairness decisions. One such sharing dilemma describes students who sold the drawings and paintings they made in class at the local fair and made a lot of money. The "fairness" dilemma asked how the students should split up the money (Damon, 1975). Children's responses were rated according to the following criteria:

- *Equality.* Everyone gets the same.
- *Merit.* Whoever makes the most or the best gets the most.
- *Equity.* The poorer or youngest child gets more than the others.
- *Self-interest.* Whoever wants the most should get it.
- *Behavioral or physical.* The best-behaved, the biggest child, or girls should get more. (adapted from Lapsley, 1996)

Their responses were then categorized into levels of distributive justice (fairness) reasoning (Damon, 1975).

By middle childhood, fairness reasoning is positively related to Piaget's stage of concrete operational thought: Most 8-year-olds can coordinate claims based on equality and merit (Damon, 1975). For example, in order to coordinate sharing with the idea that some people may deserve more, children need to be able to use conservation skills (i.e., compensate claims for equality with claims of merit). In addition, in order to assess each person's claim, children need perspective-taking skills. For example, self-reflective role-taking is necessary for Level 2-B positive justice reasoning when children consider claims for equality and reciprocity, such as "We can't give him more just because he's older!" (Lapsley, 1996).

By age 10, notions about reciprocity are usually consolidated into what some theorists call "moral necessity," resulting from moral reasoning that requires equal treatment (Nucci, 2001). However, between 10 and 12 years of age, children typically realize that fairness doesn't always mean equality. For example, children begin to realize that the "fairness" inherent in unequal treatment of older and younger siblings by parents may be based on a system of "equity" that often requires taking into account others' special needs or status (Nucci, 2001). Positive justice reasoning is therefore, not surprisingly, often associated with more successful social interactions. Using naturalistic observations, researchers have found that children with higher levels of positive justice reasoning not only are more socially competent *themselves* but also receive more positive interactions from their peers (for a review, see Lapsley, 1996). Table 9.5 provides a comparison of Kohlberg's stages of moral reasoning with school-age children's understanding of fairness.

As we discussed in chapter 7, teachers can encourage a social context where differences in ability or status are accepted, thereby modeling a sense of fairness based on equity rather than equality. For example, teachers who offer classroom help to less advanced children in a social climate free from ridicule also encourage respect among their peers. In addition, researchers on moral education recommend that teachers should refrain from creating and enforcing arbitrary or needless

TABLE 9.5   Comparing Justice and Fairness Reasoning

In middle childhood, justice *means* fairness, as shown in this comparison of Kohlberg's and Damon's sequences of moral reasoning.

Ages	Moral Justice Domain (Kohlberg)	Fairness Domain (Damon)
5–8	Stage 1: Rules are to be obeyed. One should avoid physical damage to persons and property. Inability to coordinate perspectives of self and others; thus, favoring the self is seen as right.	Recognition of prima facie obligations (e.g., not to hit and hurt others). However, beyond those basic requirements, fairness is prioritized in terms of self-interest.
8–10	Stage 2: Morality as instrumental exchange—"You scratch my back, I'll scratch yours." Act to meet one's own interests and needs and let others do the same. Rules followed only when in someone's interest.	Fairness is now coordinated with conceptions of "just" reciprocity defined primarily in terms of strict equality, with some beginning concerns for equity.
10–12	Stage 3: Being good means living up to what is expected by people around you and by one's role (e.g., good brother or sister). Fairness is the golden rule. One should be caring of others.	Fairness is seen as requiring more than strict equality. Concerns for equity (taking into account the special needs, situations, or contributions of others) are now coordinated with reciprocity in structuring moral decisions.

Source: Based on *Education in the Moral Domain* (pp. 83–85) by L. P. Nucci, Cambridge, UK: 2001. Copyright © 2001 by Cambridge University Press. Adapted with the permission of Cambridge University Press.

FIGURE 9.3
Domains of Moral Values

Moral values representing the overlap among social, religious, and cultural values are taught in character education programs.

Source: From "Can Good Character Be Taught?" by M. Murphy, in *Character Education in America's Blue Ribbon Schools: Best Practices for Meeting the Challenge* (p. 12), 2002, Lanham, MD: Scarecrow Press. Copyright © 2002 by Madonna M. Murphy. Reprinted by permission.

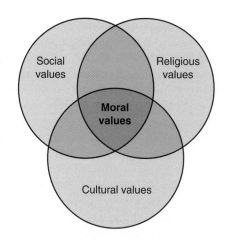

rules, especially in middle childhood and adolescence. For example, in one research focus group, fifth graders objected to "the need to raise one's hand to say something in class. . . . As one girl put it, 'We manage to be polite and talk at home without raising our hands, why can't we be expected to do that here?'" (Nucci, 2001, p. 164).

Character Education. Many schools have developed **character education** programs consisting of techniques for enhancing moral behavior (e.g., Huffman, 1994; Lapsley & Narvaez, 2006; Lickona, 1991; Murphy, 2002; Nucci, 2001). In general, such school-based programs have demonstrated decreases in disciplinary problems and absenteeism (Huffman, 1994). One character-building program for 8- to 12-year-olds, for example, stresses school-agers' industriousness and perseverance as well as the moral values of generosity, companionship, and social responsibility (Isaacs, 2001). **Moral values** are those values that all people "ought to" uphold no matter what their culture, society, or religion, such as kindness (Murphy, 2002), as illustrated by the Venn diagram in Figure 9.3. In this respect, then, character education programs are consistent with Kohlberg's belief in universal moral principles, discussed earlier. However, like Kohlberg's stages of moral reasoning, these programs have been criticized for ignoring differences in values among multiethnic children and their families.

STOP What family or school experiences taught you the values of your community?

Nevertheless, if parents and teachers are involved in developing the content of character education in their local areas, these programs can be effective in promoting a schoolwide focus on ethical behavior (Murphy, 2002). Figure 9.4 depicts a comprehensive model of character education used in the U.S. Department of Education's Elementary School Recognition Program, also called "Blue Ribbon Schools."

Researchers (Murphy, 2002) who have evaluated character education in the Blue Ribbon Schools determined that successful programs include:

- *A strong school mission.* Committing to developing students' sense of moral values
- *Participation by the entire community.* Collaborative decision making by principals, teachers, staff, students, and parents to determine the desired character qualities and the activities to foster them
- *High standards for academic performance.* Encouraging cooperative learning and interdisciplinary character-building themes across the curriculum

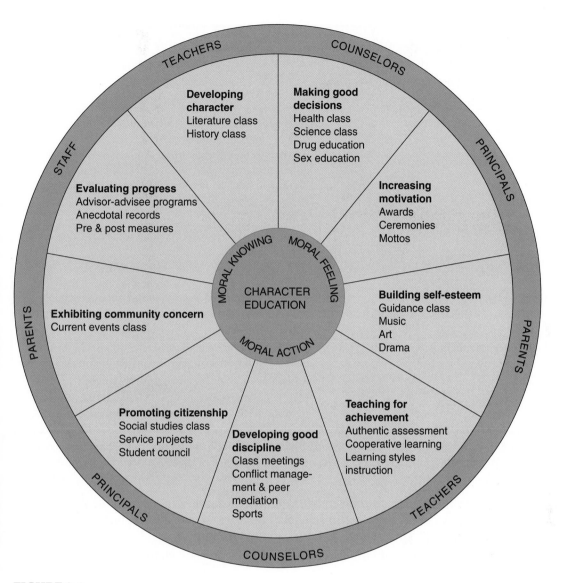

FIGURE 9.4
A Model for Character Education

This comprehensive model for character education developed for the U.S. Department of Education's Blue Ribbon Schools promotes moral knowing, moral feeling, and moral action.

Source: From "Can Good Character Be Taught?" by M. Murphy, 2002, in *Character Education in America's Blue Ribbon Schools: Best Practices for Meeting the Challenge* (p. 22), Lanham, MD: Scarecrow Press. Copyright © 2002 by Madonna M. Murphy. Reprinted by permission.

- *High standards for student behavior.* Creating a caring school climate that is safe, nurturing, drug-free, and involved in community and global affairs
- *A student recognition program.* Communicating, encouraging, and reinforcing the character qualities, attitudes, and behaviors that are valued by the school and community

TABLE 9.6 Types of Character Education	
Character education programs take many different forms.	
Type of Program	**Content**
Moral Reasoning/Cognitive Development	Discussion of moral dilemmas facilitates student development of moral reasoning
Moral Education/Virtue	Academic content (literature, history) used to teach about moral traditions in order to facilitate moral habits and internal moral qualities (virtues)
Life Skills Education	Practical skills, communication, and positive social attitudes (self-esteem) stressed
Service Learning	"Hands-on" experiences of community service integrated into curriculum
Citizenship Training/Civics Education	American civic values taught as a preparation for future citizenship
Caring Community	Caring relationships fostered in the class and school
Health Education/Drug, Pregnancy, and Violence Prevention	Program-oriented approach used to prevent unhealthy/antisocial behaviors
Conflict Resolution/Peer Mediation	Students trained to mediate peer conflicts as a means of developing constructive conflict resolution skills
Ethics/Moral Philosophy	Ethics or moral philosophy, explicitly taught
Religious Education	Character education taught in the context of a faith tradition justifying morality from a transcendent source

Source: From *A Primer for Evaluating a Character Education Initiative* (p. 3) by Martin W. Berkowitz, 1998, Washington, DC: The Character Education Partnership. Copyright © 1998, Character Education Partnership. Reprinted by permission.

- *Comprehensive character education.* Integrating character education into all subject areas (e.g., math, science, literature, social studies, health) and service areas (e.g., counseling, cafeteria, administration)
- *Schoolwide evaluation.* Assessing the success of character education in the school

The objectives of character education, however, can often be met by a wide variety of programs, as seen in Table 9.6. One popular example, a service learning approach, is more fully elaborated in Box 9.2.

Guideposts for Working with School-Age Children

- Implement character education approaches that help children develop an understanding of moral values.
- Foster discussion of values that allows school-age children the opportunity to listen to the moral reasoning of others.

- Discuss the fairness of parental or teacher rules.
- Encourage cooperation and caring rather than winning or losing by implementing cooperative learning and team activities.

BOX 9.2   Roadmap to Successful Practice
Moral Action Through Service Learning

In a book titled *Education in the Moral Domain,* Larry Nucci describes service learning as an organized effort designed to give students opportunities to engage in helpful behavior. He assumes that the formation of moral identity is enhanced when children and adolescents explore forms of moral action, such as service to others. Through service-learning programs, youth are supported in their explorations by people they trust and admire and feel that their actions genuinely contribute to the welfare of others. For service learning to have meaning for the young person, however, the activities must also be voluntary or have a significant element of choice (Nucci, 2001).

Children and adolescents benefit from opportunities to engage in community-service activities if they are provided a range of volunteer options. Such choices, according to Nucci, fit with their own sense of personal autonomy as well as their developing moral identities. For example, elementary schools may require service hours for graduation from the eighth grade but allow students a large choice of options through which to meet such community service. Service learning also need not be limited to extracurricular activities, such as a "buddy system" in which upper-grade students serve as tutors for lower-grade students.

Research examining service-learning programs has reported that students who have been involved in volunteer experiences, such as serving as a referee or coach for youth sports, helping with a community food-distribution program, or tutoring, were less likely than other adolescents to be involved in problem behaviors. Studies have also reported that early engagement in social organizations is associated with long-term engagement in positive social activities and can have a positive impact on inner-city youth whose daily lives may not provide environmental support for the construction or enactment of positive moral identities (Nucci, 2001).

RELIGION, FAITH, AND SPIRITUALITY IN MIDDLE CHILDHOOD

From a contextual perspective, moral development always takes place in multiple contexts. The family, for example, directly affects the child through the transmission of religious values, beliefs, and practices (Boyatzis, Dollahite, & Marks, 2005). *Religion, faith,* and *spirituality* are related systems of meaning through which children are exposed to moral issues and ethical behaviors. Developmental researchers, faith-based practitioners, and religious educators use different but related constructs to describe a person's religious development. Religion, or **religiosity**, typically includes organized religious practices or activities, such as attendance at religious services, performance of rituals, and membership in a church, temple, synagogue, or mosque; commitment to organizational beliefs or adherence to specific institutionally based belief systems; and integrating one's values or beliefs with one's behavior in daily life and personal worship or practices (e.g., prayer, scriptural reading, meditation) (Zinnbauer, Pargament, & Cole, 1997).

On the other hand, **faith** is defined as a way of finding shared meaning and purpose in life; an orientation of the person toward values and beliefs; and a capacity to acknowledge and commit to a higher power in a quest for the universal (Fowler, 1981, 1991). Similarly, **spirituality** is usually characterized as a personal and subjective feeling or experience of connectedness/relationship/oneness with a higher power or transcendent reality (e.g., God or Nature). Spirituality has also been described in terms of integrating one's values or beliefs with one's behavior in daily life; attaining a desirable inner affective state such as comfort, anxiety reduction, or security; and obtaining personal growth, actualization, mastery, or self-control

Religious practices give children opportunities to be connected to a higher power.

Eugene Gordon/PH College

(Zinnbauer et al., 1997). More recently, spirituality has been associated with a search for meaning or one's place in the world (Roehlkepartain, Benson, King, & Wagener, 2005). Increasingly, scholars emphasize developmental contexts, or how spirituality results from transactions between people and their environments, such as families, schools, peers, and communities (Lerner, Alberts, Anderson, & Dowling, 2005).

Developmental theorists, however, have cautioned against an artificial separation of constructs such as spirituality, faith, and religion, especially since worldwide data show that most people see themselves as both spiritual and religious (e.g., King & Boyatzis, 2004). Nevertheless, faith, spirituality, and religion have all been relatively neglected areas in developmental research (Benson, 2004; King & Boyatzis, 2004, Oser, Scarlett, & Bucher, 2006; Roehlkepartain et al., 2005).

Stages of Faith Development

An influential theory of faith development outlines a six-stage sequence through which individuals mature into believers in a higher power (Fowler, 1981, 1991). In early childhood, during the stage called *intuitive-projective*, young children are becoming self-aware and experience intuitive understandings of their existence in the world. Later, as children attain concrete operational thinking during the school-age years, they begin to adopt the stories, beliefs, and observances that symbolize their belonging to a community. In this stage, called *mythic-literal faith*, beliefs, moral rules, and obligations are absolute (recall the earlier discussion of moral reasoning in middle childhood).

In adolescence, teenagers begin to form a personal myth: "the myth of becoming one's own in identity and faith, incorporating one's past and anticipated future" (Fowler, 1981, p. 173). This stage, called *synthetic-conventional faith*, is a conformist period when teens are tuned in to the values and expectations of others. Although personal values and beliefs may be deeply felt, they are not fully examined until later adolescence when most people begin to develop an *individual-reflective faith*, taking responsibility for their own commitments and critically reflecting on their identity (self) and outlook (ideology) (Fowler, 1981). These stages describe a cognitive-developmental theory of faith understanding.

Stages of Religious Reasoning

Another stage approach describes how children's reasoning about religious concepts develops (Oser, 1991; Oser & Gmünder 1991). In this developmental sequence, children are asked to resolve ambiguities in hypothetical situations, called *contingencies* (similar to Kohlberg's dilemmas, discussed earlier) (Oser et al., 2006). For example, in one story a young man named Paul is in a plane about to crash. He promises God that if he survives, he will forego a promising career and serve humanity in a third world country. Paul survives. Children are then asked several questions about whether Paul should keep his promise to God, what will happen if he does not, and how he should think about surviving the crash (Oser et al., 2006).

At the beginning of middle childhood, at around age 6, school-age children typically say that "Paul has to keep his promise, otherwise God will give him a stomachache." However, by the end of middle childhood, at about age 12, school-agers usually say that "God helped Paul so now he has to do some good . . . or pray so that he won't be punished." Adolescents, on the other hand, are more likely to say that "whatever decision Paul makes, he will likely use his faith in God to act responsibly—because acting responsibly is really what is God's will" (Oser et al., 2006, p. 963). God does not punish people; God is much more mysterious (Oser & Gmünder, 1991). Table 9.7 provides a comparison of the stages of faith and the stages of religious judgment.

TABLE 9.7	Comparing Faith and Religious Reasoning	
Level	**Stages of Faith (Fowler)**	**Stages of Religious Reasoning (Oser & Gmünder)**
Infancy	**Primal:** Develop attachment and trust in one's caregivers.	
Early Childhood	**Intuitive-Projective:** Represent God as both threatening and protective, like caregivers.	**Religious Heteronomy:** God is understood as active in world affairs; people react to God's power.
Middle Childhood	**Mythic-Literal:** Express and explain faith through stories that are shared by family, community, or culture.	**Do et Des (Give So You May Receive):** God can be influenced through promises, prayers, and deeds.
Early Adolescence	**Synthetic-Conventional:** Identify with the worldview of consensually or conventionally sanctioned groups to which one belongs.	**Ego Autonomy:** Individuals are responsible for their own lives. God has a separate existence and hidden responsibility.
Late Adolescence	**Individualistic-Reflective:** Examine one's commitments, beliefs, and values and choose a faith tradition.	**Mediated Autonomy:** God has a Divine plan and one lives accordingly. Social [civic] engagement becomes a form of religious expression.

Source: Based on "Religious and Spiritual Development throughout the Life Span" (pp. 960–962) by Fritz K. Oser, George Scarlett, & Anton Bucher, in W. Damon (Series Ed.) & R. M. Lerner (Vol. Ed.), *Handbook of child psychology, Vol. 1: Theoretical models of human development* 6th ed., 2006, (pp. 942–998). New York: Wiley.

Like the stages of faith development, the stages of religious judgment reflect qualitatively different thinking with age. At the lower stages, the child thinks in either/or terms; either God intervenes—or not—but is seen as directly affecting people. At the middle stages, children see people as free to make choices, while acknowledging that God is doing the same, possibly in opposition to them. At higher stages, children see people's actions as unimportant compared to their intention to fulfill their faith in God and act responsibly toward others (Oser et al., 2006).

From a contextual perspective, "healthy development involves positive changes in the relation between a developing person—who is both able to contribute positively to self, family, and community and committed to doing so—and a community supporting the development of such citizens" (Lerner, Alberts et al., 2005, p. 62; see also King et al., 2005). For example, the relationship between spirituality and helping others in middle childhood was documented in a national study involving school-agers from 9 to 15 years of age (Lerner, Alberts et al., 2005). The factors (and sample items) most highly related to spirituality included the following items:

- *Orientation to do good work.* Imagine you saw a little kid fall and get hurt on the playground. Would you run over and try to help?
- *Orientation to help others.* How many hours did you give help to people outside your family with special needs during the last month without pay?

These items are also commonly referred to as prosocial or altruistic behaviors.

PROSOCIAL BEHAVIOR IN MIDDLE CHILDHOOD

In most studies of children's moral development, **prosocial behavior** is defined as "voluntary behavior intended to benefit another person" (Eisenberg & Fabes, 1998, p. 701; see also Eisenberg, Fabes, & Spinrad, 2006). A related term is **altruism**, or prosocial acts that are motivated by internal rewards, such as concern for others, rather than by the expectation of external rewards, such as parental or teacher approval. Like the other social-cognitive and moral reasoning abilities discussed in this chapter, prosocial reasoning is commonly assessed using hypothetical stories, and children are asked whether or not the protagonist should help the person in need (see Carlo, Hausmann, Christiansen, & Randall, 2003).

School-age children with prosocial tendencies differ from nonprosocial children. Prosocial behavior has been linked to stable individual differences in emotionality and self-regulation (Eisenberg et al., 1999). Prosocial children are typically **empathic** (i.e., they respond to others' emotional states). Specifically, prosocial children tend to be high in social skills (i.e., socially appropriate behavior and constructive coping behavior) and low in negative emotionality (discussed in chapter 7). A theoretical model of the relationship between emotion and self-regulation is provided in Table 9.8.

The empathy skills of school-age children can be enhanced by classroom activities such as role-playing and discussing alternative solutions to conflicts. For example, compared to control groups, children given empathy training subsequently showed significantly more cooperation, helping, and generosity (Mussen & Eisenberg, 2001; see Feshbach & Feshbach, 1982, 1983). Both school and peer success may also be enhanced by associations with prosocial models, as suggested by Bandura's social cognitive theory. Prosocial behavior (i.e., cooperating, helping, sharing, and consoling) assessed in third grade predicted academic achievement and social preferences in eighth grade, with

---

TABLE 9.8   Dispositions for Prosocial Behavior

School-agers who engage in prosocial behaviors tend to be high in self-regulation and low in negative emotionality.

Style of Regulation

Emotional Intensity	Highly Inhibited	Optimal Regulation	Under-Regulation
	(High inhibitory control; Low activational control; Underutilization of adaptive attentional, social communicative, and other mechanisms)	(Moderate use of inhibitory control: Relatively high use of activational control; Attentional and social communicative mechanism, planning, and problem-focused coping; Flexible use of self-regulatory mechanisms)	(Low in inhibition; Underutilization of adaptive attentional, activational control; Problem-focused mechanisms)
Moderately High	Inhibited; Expressive at a young age but learns to inhibit over expressions of emotion; Shy; Low to average social skills; Prone to reactive (emotion induced) withdrawal; Lack of flexibility in coping; Prone to anxiety, fear, and personal distress	Expressive; Interpersonally engaging; Sociable; Socially competent and popular; Constructive coping behaviors; Resilient; Prone to sympathy and spontaneous prosocial behavior; Prone to high levels of positive emotion	Uncontrolled, active behavior; Social or extroverted; Frequently controversial or rejected children (particularly boys); Nonconstructive ways of coping with emotion; Prone to reactive aggression; Low in prosocial behavior; Prone to personal distress, frustration, and negative affectivity
Moderately Low	Inhibited and passive; Highly controlled; Nonexpressive; Unsociable or introverted; Prone to proactive withdrawal; Low to average social skills and popularity; Lack of flexibility in coping; Somewhat flat affect	Placid; Average expressiveness; Sociable; Socially competent and popular; Constructive coping behaviors; Resilient; Moderately high in prosocial behavior and sympathy; Prone to positive emotion	Erratic behavior; Extroverted and sensation-seeking; Low to average popularity; Often nonconstructive coping; Prone to proactive aggression and manipulative behavior; Low in prosocial behavior and vicarious emotional responding

Source: From "The Relations of Children's Dispositional Prosocial Behavior to Emotionality, Regulation, and Social Functioning," by N. Eisenberg et al., *Child Development, 67,* 975. Copyright © 1996 by the Society for Research in Child Development. Adapted by permission of the society.

adolescents preferring to study or play with peers who share, console, and help others (Caprara, Barbaranelli, Pastorelli, Bandura, & Zimbardo, 2000).

Although many social behaviors fall under the general heading of "prosocial," when third- to sixth-grade children were asked what *they* thought was normative in their own peer groups (e.g., *"What do boys/girls do when they want to be nice to someone?"*), they responded with behaviors other than sharing, comforting, or acting altruistically, such as "*be friends*" or "*include them in our group*" (Greener & Crick, 1999; see also Thompson, Arora, & Sharp, 2002). For example, "*being included*" was the most frequent prosocial behavior cited by both boys and girls, especially for grades 3 and 4, probably because same-sex peer relationships and friendships become particularly important during the school-age years.

On the other hand, cross-sex interactions included more *sharing* and *caring*, especially for grade 6 when the prospect of dating became more salient. When the children were asked about prosocial behaviors toward the opposite sex (e.g., "*What do boys do when they want to be nice to girls?*"), two additional categories of responses were found: romantic behaviors (e.g., "*flirt*," "*ask them out on a date*," "*send love letters*") and negative behaviors (e.g., "*push*," "*pretend they hate them*," "*tease*") (Greener & Crick, 1999). Interestingly, many researchers have found that pushing, poking, and teasing are actually common courtship behaviors in middle childhood, rather than indicators of males' cross-sex aggression or sexual harassment (see Pellegrini, 2001).

Antisocial Behavior

Antisocial behavior is defined as actions "that inflict physical or mental harm or property loss or damage on others, and which may or may not constitute the breaking of criminal laws" (Coie & Dodge, 1998, p. 781). They typically include **aggressive behaviors**, or behaviors aimed at harming or injuring another person. In addition, it is helpful to our understanding of antisocial behaviors to consider aggression as distinct from other kinds of antisocial behavior, such as substance abuse or lying, based on the fact that aggressive behaviors (e.g., bullying or fighting) are usually both destructive and overt acts, as illustrated in Figure 9.5.

As early as middle childhood, antisocial children tend to associate with other antisocial or rejected peers. For example, the friends of antisocial boys tend to live in the same neighborhood block and to have met in unsupervised activities (Dishion, Andrews, & Crosby, 1995). According to the **differential-association hypothesis** of delinquent behavior, youth who spend time with delinquent friends are expected to commit delinquent acts themselves. Furthermore, delinquent friends are assumed to have greater influence if they have more positive relationships with their friends (Berndt, 2002; see also Fuligni, Eccles, Barber, & Clements, 2001). The influence of antisocial peers has been termed "deviancy training" (i.e., contingent positive reactions to rule-breaking discussions) and is associated with higher levels of adolescent violence (Dishion, McCord, & Poulin, 1999). Not all studies have supported this social learning hypothesis, however (Agnew, 1991). For example, it does *not* appear that antisocial children have deficits in interacting with their friends (Dishion et al., 1995). In fact, having just one close friend may have a moderating effect on antisocial behavior.

Kelly, Jennifer, and Alesha have a long-standing friendship based on shared prosocial activities. For example, last year they tutored elementary school students after school, which helped them overcome the temptation to hang out with an antisocial crowd.

Aggression. In middle childhood, aggressive behaviors typically involve fighting, threats of harm, bullying, gossiping, or teasing (Underwood, Galen, & Paquette, 2001; Underwood, 2003). Most middle childhood developmental researchers distinguish among three types of aggression (e.g., Crick, 1996):

1. *Physical aggression.* Using violence to hurt someone physically (e.g., hitting, pushing, assaulting)

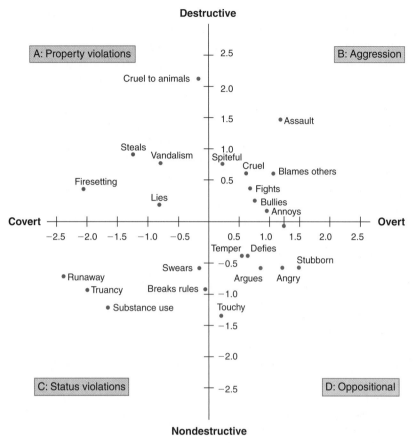

FIGURE 9.5
Dimensions of Antisocial Behavior

Antisocial behaviors can be classified into four categories based on parent and teacher ratings.

Source: Reprinted from *Clinical Psychology Review, 13,* by P. J. Frick, B. B. Lahey, & R. Loeber. "Oppositional defiant disorder and conduct disorder: A meta-analytic review of factor analyses and cross-validation in a clinic sample" (p. 327). Copyright © 1993, with permission from Elsevier.

2. *Verbal aggression.* Using words to hurt someone psychologically (e.g., insulting, teasing, name-calling)

3. *Relational aggression.* Using exclusion to ostracize someone socially (e.g., shunning, spreading rumors, gossiping)

Girls in elementary school use more verbal and relational aggression than boys (Crick, Bigbee, & Howes, 1996; Murray-Close, Ostrov, & Crick, 2007). They also report that they would say things like "We're going to be in a group and you're not going to be in it" or they would "Tell a lie about them that they didn't do" (Crick, 2007). As a group, boys appear to be significantly more physically aggressive than girls. However, many of these findings are based on peer or teacher self-reports and may reflect gender stereotyping rather than actual sex differences. In addition, when girls do engage in physical aggression, their behavior is often seen as more deviant by their peers and teachers than boys' aggression (see Underwood et al., 2001). For example, in a Canadian study of playground behavior, aggression was negatively related to likeability for girls but not for boys (Serbin, Marchessault, McAffer, Peters, & Schwartzman, 1993). Similarly, high levels of relational aggression in third grade predicted low friend preference in third grade, but only for girls (Zimmer-Genbeck, Geiger, & Crick, 2005).

In a person-centered study of popular boys in grades 4 to 6 (refer to chapter 2 for a discussion of person- vs. variable-centered approaches), peers saw *prosocial* boys as "models" (i.e., "cool, athletic, leaders, cooperative, studious, not shy, and nonaggressive"). On the other hand, they perceived the popular *antisocial* boys as "tough" (i.e., "cool, athletic, and aggressive"). "These findings suggest that highly aggressive boys can be among the most popular and socially connected in elementary classrooms" (Rodkin, Farmer, Pearl, & Van Acker, 2000, p. 14). In longitudinal research, both physical and verbal aggression (e.g., fighting, insulting, and hurting others) were related to third-graders' low school achievement and peer preferences, but they did not predict these outcomes in eighth grade (Caprara et al., 2000).

By middle childhood, most children refrain from physical aggression. Instead, they may use relational aggression to maintain a sense of belonging to their peer group or to test out various social norms (Underwood et al., 2001). As we saw in chapter 7, most school-agers can understand the nature of deception and false statements. For example, in a study of third to sixth graders, both boys and girls questioned the veracity of gossip (i.e., references to the personal qualities, behaviors, or affairs of others), although girls were more likely to attribute false gossip to jealousy than were boys (Kuttler, Parker, & LaGreca, 2002). Middle childhood girls are also significantly more likely than boys to recruit other girls to retaliate or "freeze out" their friends (Azmitia, Kamprath, & Linnet, 1998). Therefore, it should be no surprise that relationally aggressive children (often girls) also report significantly higher levels of loneliness, depression, and isolation compared to their nonaggressive peers (Crick & Grotpeter, 1995). Relationally aggressive dominant girls, however, are often perceived as popular by their peers, suggesting that leadership also may serve as a risk factor for antisocial behavior (Sippola, 2004; see also Underwood, 2003).

Bullying. An all-too-commmon form of aggression during middle childhood is **bullying**, or long-standing acts of physical, verbal, or relational aggression that are directed at a *particular* peer (Rubin, Bukowski, & Parker, 1998, see also 2006; Sharp & Smith, 1994). Estimated numbers of bullying victims range from 10 to 27% of the school-age population (Berger, 2007; Haddow, 2006; Hawkins, Pepler, & Craig, 2001; Ma, Stewin, & Mah, 2001; Sutton, Smith, & Swettenham, 1999a). Bullying may include *racial harassment*, based on membership in an ethnic or racial minority group, or *sexual harassment*, based on gender or sexual orientation. Although *homophobic* bullying (i.e., calling someone "gay") may be a way of labeling a heterosexual child "weak," when it is used against a sexual minority adolescent it is particularly hurtful and damaging (Poteat & Espelage, 2007; Thompson et al., 2002). Definitions of bullying also have recently been expanded to include "*cyber*bullying," or using the Internet to stalk or humiliate a peer by sending e-mail or posting online journals (also called weblogs, or "blogs" for short) to circulate rumors, photographs, or other slanderous material (Simmons, 2003).

When middle-school students were asked in individual interviews about bullying and victimization they described a wide range of behaviors, from physical aggression to verbal teasing to social exclusion. Sixth graders were most often the targets of name-calling and teasing, which usually decreased by eighth grade. Although age and ethnicity were frequently cited as risk factors for victimization by bullies, having less money, fewer fashionable clothes, wearing glasses, and being overweight also led to harassment (Espelage & Asidao, 2002). During middle childhood, the ability to infer stereotypes increases dramatically (Abrams, Rutland, & Cameron, 2003; McKown, 2004). In addition, school-age children's awareness of the widely held stereotypes of others also increases, especially among stigmatized groups, such as African Americans and Latinos (McKown & Weinstein, 2003).

Whether bullies are motivated by a lack of social perspective-taking ability, low self-esteem, deficits in information-processing ability, or a faulty theory-of-mind about others is a matter of continuing theoretical debate (Arsenio & Lemerise, 2001; Crick & Dodge,

STOP Were you ever bullied? How did parents, teachers, and peers respond to bullies or victims?

1999; O'Moore & Kirkham, 2001; Sutton, Smith, & Swettenham, 1999a, 1999b; Toblin, Schwartz, Gorman, & Aboudezzeddine, 2005). Each of these explanations has some empirical support, as does physical appearance, ethnicity and culture, and family or genetic factors (for a recent review, see Berger, 2007). For example, among fourth-grade boys, better perspective-taking ability was related to more severe antisocial behavior—perhaps because the bully knows what will "get" the other person (e.g., Sutton et al., 1999a).

In other studies, the processing of social information has successfully discriminated *proactive aggression*, which is similar to bullying, from **reactive aggression**, which occurs in the heat of the moment (e.g., Crick & Dodge, 1999). The model of proactive aggression assumes that there is usually an ulterior motive for aggressive behavior, such as appearing powerful to your peers. Such socially reinforced aggression does not need a precipitating event for it to occur, but may be prompted by temperamental dispositions of the bully (Thompson et al., 2002). For example, individual differences in empathy and emotional regulation have been suggested as an alternative explanation for bullying (Arsenio & Lemerise, 2001), as described in Box 9.3. Research on bullying suggests that bullies are characterized by weak impulse control, strong aggressive tendencies, and a high tolerance for aggression. Not

BOX 9.3   Roadmap to Understanding Theory and Research
An Experiment in Emotion Regulation

In a laboratory study, children were made angry by losing at a computer game while being taunted by a peer who was a "confederate" in the research (Underwood & Hurley, 1999). After the provocation but before a debriefing, the researchers asked the children a series of questions about what they felt like doing to the peer and why they did not show their true feelings. Responses reflected the extreme variability in strategies for emotion regulation during middle childhood:

- *"Keeping my mouth shut, and smiling back at him."*

- *"Teaching him a lesson, telling him how to do things to make people like him,"* but did not because he *"didn't feel like it."*

- *"I felt like hitting her,"* but did not because *"I knew it wouldn't help me win the game or anything."*

- *"I felt like I wanted to smack her,"* but did not *"because I am not here to fight."* This same girl told us that she usually hits people who provoke her.

- *"Just killing myself—I hate my sister when she is being sassy and naughty, that's when I feel like killing myself,"* but that he did not do this because *"I usually hit myself in the head or stop thinking about it or stop the game."*

- *"I felt like saying 'I am trying as hard as I can and please don't tease me,'"* but did not

because *"I thought I would be hurting her feelings."*

The researchers questioned why some children are able to be very strategic about controlling their emotions in a manner consistent with their social goals and why others are so disregulated. They acknowledged that emotion researchers and peer relations experts alike have agreed that emotions influence all aspects of social information processing and that emotions are regulated at many different levels. But they concluded that emotion regulation is complicated by the fact that emotional arousal is determined not only by various types of regulatory processes but also by individual differences in temperament, such as emotional intensity, as shown in the previous examples. The researchers suggest that given that children's interactions with peers can generate everything from extreme happiness to intense pain, examining children's developing emotion scripts for managing emotions with peers might provide insight into how and why emotions can energize or overwhelm us.

Source: Based on "Emotion Regulation in Peer Relationships During Middle Childhood," by M. K. Underwood & J. C. Hurley, in L. Balter & C. S. Tamis-LaMonda (Eds.), *Child Psychology: A Handbook of Contemporary Issues* (p. 255), 1999. Philadelphia: Psychology Press. Copyright 1999 by Psychology Press.

surprisingly, affiliating with an aggressive crowd decreases the likelihood that children will be victims of overt aggression (Prinstein & La Greca, 2002).

Frequently, bullies do not experience much resistance to their aggression (Rubin et al., 1998). Reluctance to intervene begins with children over the age of 8 or 9, possibly because younger children are less aware of peer group pressure (Thompson et al., 2002). See Box 9.4 for a sample checklist to screen for bullying victimization. Victims of bullies often have difficulty managing conflicts and lack self-confidence, self-esteem, and prosocial skills (Champion, Vernberg, & Shipman, 2003).

BOX 9.4 Roadmap to Successful Practice
Life in School Checklist

The *Life in School Checklist* can provide the following:

- A bullying index
- A comprehensive picture of "life in school"
- A means of identifying individuals who are likely to be victims of bullying

- Extra information of your own choice can be obtained by putting your own questions on the back page

Life in School Checklist

This checklist can be used to determine if school-age children were bullied in the past week.

I am a boy ☐   I am a girl ☐   Age ☐   Year ☐

During this week another pupil:	Not at all	Once	More than once		During this week another pupil:	Not at all	Once	More than once
1. Helped me with my homework				22.	Smiled at me			
2. Called me names				23.	Tried to get me into trouble			
3. Said something nice to me				24.	Helped me carry something			
4. Was nasty about my family				25.	Tried to hurt me			
5. Tried to kick me				26.	Helped me with my classwork			
6. Was very nice to me				27.	Made me do something I didn't want to			
7. Was unkind because I am different				28.	Talked about T.V. with me			
8. Gave me a present				29.	Took something off me			
9. Said they'd beat me up				30.	Shared something with me			
10. Gave me some money				31.	Was rude about the colour of my skin			
11. Tried to make me give them money				32.	Shouted at me			
12. Tried to frighten me				33.	Played a game with me			
13. Asked me a stupid question				34.	Tried to trip me up			
14. Lent me something				35.	Talked about things I like			
15. Stopped me playing a game				36.	Laughed at me horribly			
16. Was unkind about something I did				37.	Said they would tell on me			
17. Talked about clothes with me				38.	Tried to break something of mine			
18. Told me a joke				39.	Told a lie about me			
19. Told me a lie				40.	Tried to hit me			
20. Got a gang on me								
21. Tried to make me hurt other people								

Source: From "Measuring Bullying with the 'Life in School' Checklist" by T. Arora in D. Thompson, T. Arora, & S. Sharp, *Bullying: Effective Strategies for Long-Term Improvement* (pp. 184–189), 2002, London: Routledge Falmer. Copyright 2002 by David Thompson, Tiny Arora, & Sonia Sharp. Reprinted by permission.

(continued)

BOX 9.4   Roadmap to Successful Practice (*Continued*)
Life in School Checklist

Children are asked to report only on those events that happened during the past week because people's recall of events that happened more than a week ago is fairly poor, and estimates based on looking further back in time are therefore more unreliable. The index can be used for groups of students of around 40 or more, so it will also be possible to assess the effects that the strategies are having on different groups in the school. For groups smaller than 40, the index will not be sufficiently reliable to allow valid comparisons.

Based on the checklist designed for secondary schools, over half of both students and teachers see the following items as instances of bullying:

- *Item 5.* Tried to kick me
- *Item 9.* Threatened to hurt me
- *Item 11.* Demanded money from me
- *Item 25.* Tried to hurt me
- *Item 38.* Tried to break something of mine
- *Item 40.* Tried to hit me

Children who check these items under the "more than once" category are likely to see themselves as victims of bullying. If limited time is available for analysis and if the main interest is in bullying, then the responses to these items alone will give a quick impression of the extent of this occurring in a school.

Scoring the Bullying Index

- *Step 1.* For each of the six items, count the number of times that a check was placed under the category "more than once." Do this separately for each item (Items 5, 9, 11, 25, 38, and 40).
- *Step 2.* Divide the scores for each separate item by the number of checklists completed. Multiply by 100 to obtain the percentage of student responses under each item.
- *Step 3.* Add all six percentages.
- *Step 4.* Divide this number by 6.

The figure thus obtained is the Bullying Index (e.g., 7.12 or 8.03). The range of the index can vary a great deal from school to school.

The entire checklist can be used to obtain a more all-round picture of what happens in school during a period of one week. This is also useful for looking at a small group or for assessing how an individual student experiences contacts with other students in the school. In the case of groups, it will be possible to work out the percentages of the responses to each item on the checklist under the two different categories of "once" and "more than once." The main purpose of the index is to use it like a dipstick, at the beginning of an intervention and at later intervals in order to find out whether the antibullying strategies are having an effect.

A recent naturalistic study of bullying in grades 1 to 6 examined what happens when peers *did* intervene (about half the time) on behalf of the victim (Hawkins et al., 2001). Interventions directed toward the bully were likely to be aggressive, whereas interventions directed toward the victim or the dyad were nonaggressive. In addition, girls were more likely to intervene when the bully and victim were female and used mostly verbal assertions. Boys were more likely to intervene when the bully and victim were male and used verbal, physical, and a combination of the two types about equally. The majority of all peer interventions were effective in stopping the bullying (Hawkins et al., 2001).

Antibullying programs may be individual, family, or systems focused (Kerns & Prinz, 2002). Such programs in schools recommend teaching children conflict resolution skills, how to help victims, and when to seek adult help (Garrity, Jens, Porter, Sager, & Short-Camilli, 1995; Swearer & Doll, 2002). Other recommendations include promoting relationships between students and playground or lunchroom supervisors, raising teachers' awareness of bullying, and providing training for all the adults in identifying bullying incidents (Sharp & Smith, 1994; also see Scaglione & Scaglione, 2006). For example, one successful violence prevention

Guideposts for Working with School-Age Children

- Encourage prosocial reasoning by doing activities such as role-playing and discussing alternative ways of helping others in need.
- Help children to identify the various crowds in their school or neighborhood and to think about with whom they may feel either comfortable or challenged.
- Discuss the hurtfulness of stereotyping others based on their social group membership (e.g.,

ethnicity, race, gender, nationality, religion, or sexual orientation).
- Discourage gossiping, peer exclusion, and other forms of relational aggression.
- Suggest to children ways of identifying and responding to bullying.

program provided workshops for teachers, administrators, hall monitors, teaching assistants, the school secretary, nurse, and police officer on a curriculum in teaching prosocial skills and anger management (Casella & Burstyn, 2002). See Table 9.9 for a list of bullying prevention strategies. It is important, however, to rigorously evaluate studies of large-scale bullying prevention programs to ensure they are effective (Bauer, Lozano, & Rivara, 2007). In the event that a violent incident does occur, Box 9.5 reviews current guidelines for crisis responses to school violence from the American Academy of Experts in Traumatic Stress.

TABLE 9.9   Prevention of Bullying

Prevention Strategies

- Patrol "bullying hot spots."
- Find out who is often involved in bullying.
- Avoid labeling children.
- Watch out for lone students.
- Talk to students who are directly involved.
- Make it known that bullying won't be tolerated.

Responding to Aggression and Resolving Conflict

- Try to keep calm.
- Avoid rushing.
- Do not be seen to jump to conclusions.
- Listen well.
- Don't be sidetracked.
- Avoid sarcasm and direct personal criticism.
- Label the behavior and not the child.
- Don't make threats that can't or won't be carried out.
- Don't use severe threats at the very beginning.

- Avoid using teachers as a means of controlling children.
- Consider using a "time-out" tactic.
- Look for a "win-win" solution.
- Develop a hierarchy of sanctions.

Encourage Positive Behavior

- Adopt a "catch them being good" philosophy.
- Small rewards can be effective.
- Have the same reward system in the classroom as on the school grounds.
- Pass on information about good behavior.
- Remember individual differences.
- Respond to children's self-reports of good behavior.
- Introduce a student "things I am proud of" book.
- Set up student self-monitoring using a charting system.

Source: Based on "How to Prevent and Respond to Bullying Behavior in the Junior/Middle School Playground," by M. Boulton, in S. Sharp & P. K. Smith (Eds.), *Tackling Bullying in Your School: A Practical Handbook for Teachers* (pp. 122–130), 1994, London: Routledge. Copyright © 1994 by Sonia Sharp and Peter K. Smith.

BOX 9.5   Roadmap to Understanding Theory and Research
Crisis Responses to School Violence

What Is a Crisis?

A crisis is an event of limited duration that is typically unpredicted and overwhelming for those who experience it. This situation may be volatile in nature and, at times, may involve threat to the survival of an individual or groups of individuals. Moreover, a crisis state may result upon exposure to drastic and tragic change in an individual's environment. This alteration in the status quo is unwanted, frightening, and often renders a person with a sense of vulnerability and helplessness. Ultimately, with successful intervention, the equilibrium is restored between the environment and the individual's perception of their world as a safe and secure place. Examples of crises that can potentially have a large scale effect on the students, faculty, and administrators in a school building or district include: an accident involving a student or faculty member, a suicide or death of a student or faculty member, severe violence (e.g., gang fight), hostage taking, a fire at school, or a natural disaster (e.g., hurricane).

What Is Crisis Response?

Crisis response, as it pertains to the school environment, is a proactive, organized and well-thought-out plan to a crisis situation that has adversely affected many individuals in a school district, including students, faculty and administrators. The primary goals of crisis response are

- To prevent a chaotic situation from escalating into a potentially catastrophic one
- To help those affected by the crisis to return, as quickly as possible, to precrisis functioning
- To decrease the potential long-term effects of the crisis on functioning

Why a Crisis Response Plan?

Research conducted over the past 10 years has revealed that schools are increasingly more prone to crisis situations that adversely affect large numbers of students and faculty. The rise in adolescent suicide, increased assaults on teachers, high levels of substance abuse among students, and increased violence in the schools are some of the reasons cited.

Research has also indicated that today's school districts need to contend with reactions to new types of trauma/disasters. For example, hostage taking, sniper attacks, murders, terrorist activities and bomb scares were almost nonexistent in the schools 30 years ago, but today occur with greater frequency. Thus, it is strongly recommended that school districts need to be prepared for a crisis situation that can potentially affect the functioning of their students, faculty, and administrators.

Research has emerged over the past ten years supporting a proactive approach to a crisis, as opposed to one that is reactive in nature. Such an approach is much better in dealing effectively with a large-scale crisis situation. A reactive approach is spontaneous, and not fully thought out, planned, or practiced, and can result in the response that is less effective in meeting the immediate, and possibly the long-term needs of the students, faculty, and administrators. A proactive approach to a crisis is one that is organized, planned, and practiced and more likely results in a response that can have a dramatic effect on reducing the short and long-term consequences of the crisis on the individuals in a school district.

What Types of Behaviors/Reactions Can Teachers Expect from Their Students After a Crisis Situation Has Occurred?

The manner in which people react to crisis situations is dependent upon a number of variables including personal history, personality variables, severity and proximity of the event, level of social support, and the type and quality of intervention. While no two people respond to situations, including crisis situations, in exactly the same manner, the following are often seen as immediate reactions to a significant crisis:

- Shock, numbness
- Denial or inability to acknowledge the situation has occurred
- Dissociative behavior—appearing dazed, apathetic, expressing feelings of unreality
- Confusion

(continued)

BOX 9.5   Roadmap to Understanding Theory and Research *(Continued)*
Crisis Responses to School Violenc

- Disorganization
- Difficulty making decisions
- Suggestibility

It is important to note that most children will recover from the effects of a crisis with adequate support from family, friends, and school personnel. Their response to a crisis can be viewed as "a normal response to an abnormal situation."

Understanding the typical reactions of individuals exposed to a crisis situation is a critical step in identifying people who may be in need of further professional assistance. Several investigators have described age-appropriate reactions of individuals exposed to a traumatic event. Although there is heterogeneity in the reactions of individuals surrounding a crisis, most of these responses are expected reactions in middle childhood and subside in several weeks following the crisis.

- Sadness and crying
- School avoidance
- Physical complaints (e.g., headaches)
- Poor concentration
- Irritability
- Fear of personal harm
- Regressive behavior (clinging, whining)
- Nightmares

- Aggressive behavior at home or school
- Bed wetting
- Anxiety and fears
- Confusion
- Eating difficulty
- Withdrawal/social isolation
- Attention-seeking behavior

While the emotional effects of the crisis can be significant and can potentially influence functioning for weeks to months, most children will make a full recovery.

Conclusion

The immediacy and unpredictability of crisis situations often leave individuals with a sense of worry, vulnerability, and distrust. A school system is unique in that it brings together individuals of all ages and professionals from numerous disciplines. Effective response to a crisis capitalizes on the resources within the school environment. *A Crisis Response Team* that identifies and responds to a crisis in a unified and collaborative manner can alter the aftermath of a crisis.

Source: Excerpted from *"A Practical Guide for Crisis Response in Our Schools"* by The American Academy of Experts in Traumatic Stress, 1999, 368 Veterans Memorial Highway, Commack, New York 11725, http:/www.aaets.org. Reprinted by permission.

SOCIAL AND MORAL DEVELOPMENT IN CONTEXT

The contexts for peer interaction in middle childhood have changed since early childhood, from home and child care settings to a wider variety of social settings, such as being together at school, talking on the telephone, "hanging out" in the neighborhood, watching videos or listening to music, and sports (see Zarbatany, Hartmann, & Rankin, 1990). Each of these social contexts provides school-age children frequent opportunities to develop deeper understandings of others, increased moral and prosocial reasoning, and effective social skills.

Family Contexts

Discussions of parenting and family contexts inevitably raise the issue of values (Cowan et al., 1998). For example, there is little agreement on whether children should fight back when bullied or try to avoid aggression or retaliation. To think about how children

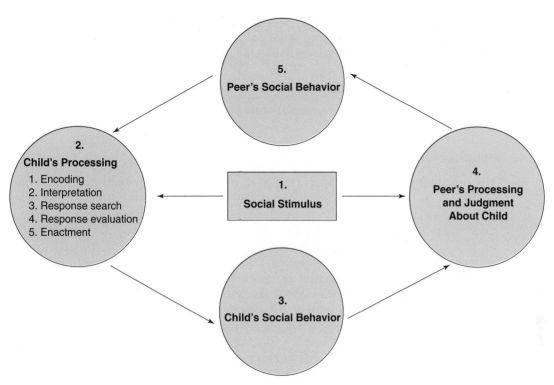

FIGURE 9.6

Social Decision-Making Model

In middle childhood peer interaction, a social stimulus, such as an argument, causes social information processing on the part of both children, resulting in both peers making judgments about each other and then acting accordingly.

Source: From "Social Competence in Children," by K. A. Dodge, G. S. Petit, C. L. McClasky, & M. M. Brown, 1987, *Monographs of the Society for Research in Child Development, 51 (2 Serial No. 213, 2).* Copyright © 1986 by the Society for Research in Child Development. Reprinted by permission of the society.

acquire values or standards of behavior in social contexts, such as family or peer contexts, requires "a more explicit interest in the agency of parents and children, that is, in the meanings they construct of each others' behavior, in their capacity for strategic action, and in their ability to behave 'as if' the other is also an agent" (Grusec, Goodnow, & Kuczynski, 2000, p. 205). Such approaches may include alerting school-age children to competing ways to view the world and helping them to hold "internal dialogues" with others—their parents, for example—as they face moral or social dilemmas (Grusec et al., 2000). Refer to Figure 9.6 for an illustration of this process of social decision making.

> *As Alesha is thinking about Mandy's offer to get high and contemplating the dilemma of doing inhalants or risking the new friendship, she engages in an "internal" conversation with her parents. She can hear her parents say, "Only losers do drugs," and thinks to herself, "But I'm not one of those kids!"*

Much research now also supports a link between parents' monitoring of their children's lives and less antisocial behavior (Amato & Fowler, 2002). For example, children in grades 6 to 9 (especially girls who are on their own after school) are more susceptible to peer pressure after school to engage in antisocial activity, such as stealing or vandalism (Steinberg, 1986). In addition, ineffective parenting predicted middle childhood boys' antisocial behavior and association with deviant peers at ages 12 to 16 (Bank et al., 2004).

Let's return to our chapter case one last time. Mandy and Alesha are unsupervised after coming home from school, giving them an opportunity for drug abuse.

School Contexts

The prevention of violence is a concern in most present-day schools, and the last decade in particular has seen a burgeoning of violence prevention programs in schools. As discussed earlier in this chapter, some bullying prevention programs address the whole school, meaning that they attempt to alter the school climate (see Christenson & Sheridan, 2001). A starting place for violence prevention may be to enhance students' sense of belonging, because middle school students who have engaged in violent behavior also experience disconnection from the school and teachers (Karcher, 2002). For example, an Internet survey that included school-age children and adolescents concluded that interventions are needed to increase the social competence and connectedness of alienated students (Thomas & Smith, 2004).

When researchers have more closely examined the effects of school-based interventions on school-age children's developmental trajectories toward violence, boys, lower-income students, and racial-minority children demonstrated higher initial levels of risk and increases in violence from ages 6 to 12. But even low-risk children (i.e., girls, higher-income students, and White children) caught up to the high-risk group by age 12. All of the children, however, were deflected from paths toward aggression and violence when their teachers taught a conflict resolution curriculum (Aber, Brown, & Jones, 2003).

Many school-based programs, therefore, focus on the remediation of students' negotiation skills. For example, a classroom-based violence prevention program called Project WIN (Working Out Integrated Negotiations) targeted fifth graders in a low-income community. The project taught cooperative attitudes in the classroom setting and included activities to increase liking, trust, and teamwork as well as activities to decrease anger, learn nonviolent alternatives to fighting, and learn about win-win outcomes. The intervention increased students' cooperative attitudes, anger management awareness, and understanding of negotiation strategies when compared to a control group (Roberts, White, & Yeomans, 2004).

Community Contexts

Although the primary social contexts in middle childhood are likely to be home and school, school-age children also frequently interact with people in their neighborhoods, with children who attend different schools, and with adults in the community (McWhirter, McWhirter, McWhirter, & McWhirter, 2007). A fruitful approach to studying community awareness is the study of school-age children's political understanding. For example, cognitive-developmental theorists have proposed stages of political development involved in the understanding of civic life, similar to the stages of moral reasoning discussed in this chapter. **Political development** is the understanding of community action and the social processes through which political commitments emerge (see Yates & Youniss, 1998). The issues are less about party affiliation and more about understanding society and power (Haste & Torney-Purta, 1992).

From this contextual perspective, children construct understandings of civil society through interaction with members of their communities (Lerner, Brentano, Dowling, & Anderson, 2002; Pace, 2003). Researchers have identified three ways that children are likely to learn about politics, usually called civics in the school curriculum:

1. *Observation.* Observing how people relate to them as an individual and as a community member
2. *Listening.* Listening to what other people are saying about politics and governments and relating it to what they see
3. *Personal Action.* Learning about politics by participating in civic activities (adapted from Jankowski, 1992)

The range of civic and community activities that youth participate in is often referred to as **civic engagement.** Civic engagement and service projects in their neighborhoods or churches help children to think about government and politics, not as distant institutions, but as forces that affect their own lives and communities (Flanagan & Van Horn, 2003). In addition, longitudinal research has clearly demonstrated that youth involvement in their communities is related to political identity and civic engagement in adulthood, especially when volunteerism was supported by their close friends and family. For example, children and adolescents' involvement in community service projects in an inner city sustained their social activism into adulthood (Yates & Youniss, 1998).

CHAPTER REVIEW

Social Development

- Social development in middle childhood includes increasing interpersonal understanding and using moral reasoning to guide social interactions.

- Social competence is defined as the ability to interact effectively with others.

Theoretical Viewpoints

- Social learning theory states that we learn social skills by observing others, using the processes of attention, retention, motor reproduction, and reinforcement.

- Social cognitive theory accounts for the reciprocal influences of the environment, the person, and his or her own behaviors on subsequent actions.

- Social information-processing theory describes the cognitive steps used to process social information, from initially encoding internal and external cues to finally enacting a behavior.

- Social theories of mind claim that we construct predictions about others' behaviors based on our understandings of their mental states.

Social Understanding

- Social role-taking involves a gradual increase in understanding the perspectives of others in social interactions.

- Interpersonal negotiation strategies for resolving social conflicts increase across middle childhood.

Moral Development

- Moral reasoning changes from compliance with authority to an increasing ability to reflect on social conventions, fairness, and the needs of others.
- Different but related stages of thinking about God describe school-agers' spirituality: faith and religious reasoning.
- Altruism and prosocial behavior is motivated by internal rewards, such as concern for others, rather than by the expectation of external rewards.

- Antisocial behaviors, such as aggression and bullying, often involve poor role-taking ability.
- In middle childhood, aggressive behavior is more often verbal or relational aggression than physical aggression.

Social Development in Context

- Peer relations supplement, but do not replace, family relations and the importance of parenting during middle childhood.
- Schools with a positive social climate among students, staff, and teachers are less prone to school violence and bullying.

- Children construct understandings of civil society through interaction with members of their communities and develop political awareness through civic engagement.

TABLE 9.10 Summary of Developmental Theories

Chapter	Theory	Focus
9: Social and Moral Development in Middle Childhood	Social Cognition	Observing models, examining the consequences of social behaviors, and predicting other people's motives in social interactions
	Social Perspective-Taking	Developmental stages of understanding and negotiating interpersonal relationships
	Moral Reasoning	Understanding of fairness, conventional morality, and concepts of care and justice

---

KEY TERMS

Agency
Aggressive behavior
Altruism
Antisocial behavior
Bullying
Character education
Civic engagement
Conventional level
Differential-association hypothesis
Distributive justice

Empathic
Ethical relativism
Ethics of care
Faith
Interpersonal orientation
Interpersonal negotiation
Moral realists
Moral reasoning levels
Moral relativists
Moral values
Political development

Postconventional morality
Preconventional level
Proactive aggression
Prosocial behavior
Reactive aggression
Reciprocal determinism
Religiosity
Social cognition
Social cognitive theory
Social competence
Social conventions

Social development
Social information processing
Social learning theory
Social perspective-taking
Social theories of mind
Spirituality
Vicarious reinforcement

SUGGESTED ACTIVITIES

1. Select a novel for young readers from the youth literature section of a library or bookstore. Describe the nature of the peer interactions, friendships, and moral dilemmas portrayed in the story.

2. Interview a school-age child about his or her friendships. Ask about the child's best friend, peer network (clique), and social group (crowd).

3. Read a school-ager's online diary (Web log, or "blog") at http://clubpenguin.com. Analyze the blog's content and related peer commentary for evidence of antisocial behavior (e.g., relational aggression, gossip) or prosocial behavior (e.g., support, friendship).

4. Play a card game, such as "Scruples for Children," that presents moral dilemmas for discussion or make up some ethical issues of your own. How would school-age children typically answer if they were conventional thinkers? How would they apply the positive justice principles of fairness to the situation?

RECOMMENDED RESOURCES

Suggested Readings

Gilligan, C. (1982). *In a different voice: Psychological theory and women's development.* Cambridge, MA: Harvard University Press.

Nucci, L. P. (2001). *Education in the moral domain.* Cambridge, UK: Cambridge University Press.

Scaglione, J., & Scaglione, A. M. (2006). *Bully-proofing children: A practical hands-on guide to stop bullying.* Lanham, MD: Rowman & Littlefield.

Selman, R. L. (2003). *The promotion of social awareness: Powerful lessons from the partnership of developmental theory and classroom practice.* New York: Russell Sage Foundation.

Simmons, R. (2002). *Odd girl out: The hidden culture of aggression in girls.* New York: Harcourt.

Suggested Online Resources

Bullying Resources: California Department of Education. http://www.cde.ca.gov/ls/ss/se/bullyres.asp

Olweus Bullying Prevention Program. http://Modelprograms.samhsa.gov/pdfs/model/Olweus%20Bully.pdf

Overlap Between Peer Networks and Friends and Its Implications. http://www.sonet.pdx.edu/PeerNetworks/GroupID/Overlap-Net&Frnds.htm

Stop Bullying Now. http://www.stopbullyingnow.hrsa.gov/index.asp?area=main

Teaching Social Awareness: An Interview with Robert Selman. http://gseweb.harvard.edu/news/features/selman02012003.html

Young People in Canada: Their Health and Well-Being. Chapter 4: The peer group. http://www.phac-aspc.gc.ca/dca-dea/publications/hbsc-2004/chapter_4_e.html

Suggested Web Sites

Association for Moral Education. http://www.amenetwork.org

Center for Spiritual Development in Childhood and Adolescence. http://www.spiritualdevelopmentcenter.org/Display.asp?Page=Ages7to9

Character Education Partnership. http://www.character.org

Office for Studies in Moral Development and Education. http://MoralEd.org.

Social Networks Research Group: Peer Networks. http://www.sonet.pdx.edu/PeerNetworks/index.htm

Sociometry in the Classroom: How to Do It. http://www.users.muohio.edu/shermalw/sociometryfiles/socio_introduction.htmlx

Suggested Films and Videos

Bandura's social cognitive theory: An introduction (2003). Insight Media (30 minutes)

Bully girls (2006). Films for the Humanities and Sciences (20 minutes)

Encouraging moral development in children (2006). Films for the Humanities and Sciences (14 minutes)

Let's get real (2005). New Day Films (35 minutes)

A society of children: Psychosocial development during the school years (2003). Insight Media (30 minutes)

Understanding and coping with bullies (2001). Magna Systems (20 minutes)

CHAPTER 10

Friends, Play, and Peer Relations

Peter Buckley/PH College

After reading this chapter, students will be able to:

▶ Define social provisions in school-age peer relations.

▶ Describe theoretical approaches to studying friendship and peer relations.

▶ Discuss the influences of peer networks on middle childhood play and peer interaction.

▶ Summarize research on social skills in middle childhood.

▶ Explain the contributions of family, school, and community contexts to peer relations in middle childhood.

Seven-year-old José and his two other buddies are playing in the neighborhood after school as they always do. They are playing an imaginary game in which they are the only survivors on earth and are hiding from the space aliens. José and his friends have been playing this game for weeks. They notice a new boy named Emilio hanging around, secretly watching them. José wants to call him over but isn't sure his friends will welcome this new kid into their group. José is uncertain about what to do.

SCHOOL-AGE PEER RELATIONS

As we discussed in chapter 9, a positive climate for social and moral growth is one that fosters successful peer interaction (Nucci, 2001). By definition, school-age **peers** are similar in age, gender, and social status. For example, 30% of a child's social interactions in middle childhood involve same-age peers, compared to 10% in early childhood (Rubin, Bukowski, & Parker, 1998). Some scholars have recently suggested that during middle childhood, a "group of peers" becomes a "peer group" (Rubin, Coplan, Chen, Buskirk, & Wojslawlowski, 2005). School-age children's behavior in the peer group has also proven to be a stable indicator of their **social competence,** defined as the ability to interact effectively with others (Hartup, 1996; Zeller, Vannatta, Schaffer, & Noll, 2003). Furthermore, children's concerns about acceptance in the peer group often rise during middle childhood.

Not surprisingly, many peer relations researchers focus on the study of friendships among school-age children (for reviews, see Rubin et al., 2005 and Rubin et al., 1998). **Friends,** unlike mere acquaintances, are children who interact over time, developing a lasting bond of mutual attachment and trust. Friendship processes have consistently been linked to social developmental outcomes, also called **social provisions**. In a classic text called *The Interpersonal Theory of Psychiatry,* Harry Stack Sullivan (1953/1981) argued that friends fulfill social needs, called **communal needs,** such as companionship, acceptance, and intimacy (Buhrmester, 1996). In many ways, this formulation is similar to Maslow's need for belonging (described in chapter 7). Furthermore, communal needs can be distinguished from other human needs:

- *Communal needs*. Interpersonal needs for affection, nurturance, enjoyment, support, companionship, intimacy, and sexual fulfillment
- *Survival needs*. Physical needs for safety, food, shelter, and health
- *Agentic needs*. Individual needs for competency, achievement, status, power, approval, autonomy, identity and self-esteem (see Buhrmester, 1996)

The social concerns of school-age children often focus on the communal needs of acceptance by peers and the avoidance of peer rejection.

> *José and his friends have been playing space invaders for weeks. His immense satisfaction while interacting with his friends displays his ongoing needs for both companionship and identity.*

THEORETICAL VIEWPOINTS

The development of peer interaction in middle childhood has been explained by researchers employing two very different—but complementary—theoretical approaches. On the one hand, social-cognitive researchers have described school-age children's interactions with friends using a cognitive-developmental sequence of friendship understanding similar to the stages of interpersonal understanding discussed in chapter 9. On the other hand, peer interaction researchers have adopted ethological approaches to describe school-age children's group interactions. Recall from chapter 8 that **ethological theory** was developed by animal behaviorists to describe group relations based on observed behaviors, such as attachment and separation. In the case of peer relations research, however, the primary interest of researchers has been social hierarchies in peer contexts, such as schools or playgrounds.

Friendship Understanding

Middle childhood brings about marked changes in the understanding of friendship. In early childhood, friendship is usually associated with sharing a current activity, whereas in middle childhood children begin to recognize that friendships can last over time (Parker & Seal, 1996). Sullivan (1953/1981) referred to friends in the middle childhood years between ages 8 and 10 as **chums.** "Chumships" are reciprocal relationships, with school-age children sharing secrets and trusting each other not to reveal them. In addition, school-age chums usually indicate an increasing appreciation of each other's feelings and intentions, brought about by advances in their social perspective-taking ability (Rubin et al., 1998).

Friendship stages in middle childhood have been found to parallel the stages of social understanding (discussed in chapter 9). Contemporary researchers have typically investigated school-age children's friendship concepts by asking them what they expect from a best friend. Many school-age children have best friends and are satisfied with those friendships (Parker & Asher, 1993).

Children who are *social-informational* perspective takers and *unilateral* negotiators will likely think of friendships as *one-way*, that is, they may think about what a friend could do for them, or vice versa, but not what they reciprocally could do for each other (Selman, 1980). In the hypothetical story about Holly from chapter 9, for example, it is likely that a child who understood friendship as one-way would suggest that Kathy take the "better" offer. (*In the chapter case, Jose would probably ignore Emilio if his chums voiced their disapproval.*) Some researchers have termed this period a "reward-cost" stage, in which children around 7 or 8 believe that friends are rewarding to be with compared to nonfriends (Bigelow, 1977; see also Rubin et al., 1998).

By ages 10 or 11, however, most school-age children demonstrate "normative" friendships, in which they recognize that friends are supposed to be loyal to each other (Bigelow, 1977; Bigelow & LaGaipa, 1995). Recall that these children are likely to be *self-reflective* perspective takers and *cooperative* or *compromising* negotiators. They conceptualize friendships as *reciprocal*, although it is still highly unlikely that these relationships will survive difficult arguments or negative events (Selman, 1980). For this reason, school-agers have often been called "fair-weather" friends because their relationships may not weather stormy periods (Rubin et al., 1998). In addition, when boys in one study terminated a friendship because of conflict, the typical length of time for working it through and renewing the friendship was one day, but for girls it took about two weeks. One explanation for this sex difference is that triads are more common in the friendships of school-age girls than boys, causing one member of the group to feel left out (Azmitia et al., 1998).

> *For example, José and his friends are not likely to sustain their game once Emilio joins in, but will recover quickly and resume their former activity.*

By the end of middle childhood, most children are capable of *mutual* role-taking and *collaborative* negotiation, as we described in chapter 9. Friends at this "empathic" stage expect each other to provide companionship, help, protection, and support, making active attempts to understand each other (Azmitia et al., 1998; Bigelow & LaGaipa, 1995). For them, friendships are becoming *intimate*, characterized by an enduring sense of trust in each other. For example, between third and sixth grades, the expectation that friends would keep secrets rose from 25% to 72% among girls, although boys had no such similar expectation until the end of sixth grade (Azmitia et al., 1998).

TABLE 10.1   Comparing Friendship and Peer Relations

In middle childhood, maturing peer relations depend on children's developing understanding of friendship.

Stage	Peer Relations	Friendship
Stage 0	Physical connections	Momentary physical interaction
Stage 1	Unilateral relations	One-way assistance
Stage 2	Bilateral partnerships	Fair-weather cooperation
Stage 3	Homogenous community	Intimate and mutual sharing
Stage 4	Pluralistic organization	Autonomous interdependence

Source: Based on "Four Domains, Five Stages: A Summary Portrait of Interpersonal Understanding," by R. S. Selman. In *The Growth of Interpersonal Understanding: Developmental and Clinical Implications* (pp. 136–147), 1980. New York: Academic.

These maturing notions of friendship translate into social interaction with peers during middle childhood. In addition, peer acceptance influences school-age friendships, as seen in Table 10.1. The quality of middle childhood friendships is related to positive self-regard, higher involvement in school, and perceiving more support from classmates as well as sociability and leadership. Friends have also been found to protect school-age children against the negative social outcomes typically associated with shyness (Rubin et al., 2004).

In early adolescence, the ability to form close friendships becomes increasingly important (Buhrmester, 1990; see also Furman & Shaffer, 2003; Collins & Repinski, 1994). **Close friendships** are defined not only as emotionally close but also as having a mutual impact on each other (e.g., Berscheid, Snyder, & Omoto, 1989). Closeness between friends is commonly measured as the

- Frequency of social interactions
- Diversity of social interactions
- Influence of social interactions

Closeness, however, seems to be more important to girls than to boys. For example, when describing friendships, girls are more likely to mention mutual support and self-disclosure, whereas boys more often refer to joint activities and companionship (Feiring, 1993). Although girls become intimate with friends earlier in adolescence than boys, we also know that same-sex friendships are equally important to boys as girls (Roy, Benenson, & Lilly, 2000). In addition, close, cross-sex friendships may increase as early adolescents become more interested in heterosexual dating (Buhrmester, 1990).

STOP Did you have a best friend in middle childhood?

Ethological Approaches

During middle childhood, some children seem to have many friends and others only a few. The study of peer relations from an ethological perspective requires observing children's interactions in groups as well as asking children to report on their friendship choices. In addition, peer relations researchers typically describe children's social interactions in terms of social status, such as being popular.

Popularity. A central concern of many—if not all—school-agers is *popularity.* **Popularity** (also called *social status)* has been operationally defined by a majority of peer interaction researchers as the number of individuals who name an individual target child as "liked" or "disliked" or as a "friend" or "best friend" (Newcomb, Bukowski, & Pattee, 1993). Children with the most "liked" nominations are considered **popular,** whereas those with the most "disliked" nominations are considered **rejected.** Children with few or no nominations are often termed **neglected.** Children are considered **controversial** if they are both nominated frequently by some *and* actively disliked by others.

Boys' social status tends to be based on social dominance, athletic ability, coolness, and toughness, whereas girls' status depends more on family background, socioecomomic status, and physical appearance (McHale et al., 2003). Generally, school-age children with diverse social status classifications differ in behavior and characteristics (Newcomb et al., 1993; Wentzel, 2003):

- *Popular children.* Tend to exhibit higher levels of positive social behavior and cognitive ability and lower levels of aggression and withdrawal than average children
- *Rejected children.* Tend to exhibit just the opposite pattern—either more aggressive (i.e., *aggressive-rejected*) or more withdrawn (i.e., *aggressive-withdrawn*) and as a result less sociable and cognitively skilled than average children
- *Neglected children.* Tend to exhibit less social interaction and disruptive behavior but more withdrawal than average children
- *Controversial children.* Tend to be less compliant and more aggressive than average children

Peer Acceptance. In addition to totaling the number of friendship nominations a particular child may receive, researchers may examine the nominations to see if they are reciprocal. Peer relations researchers often distinguish **peer acceptance** (i.e., the number of "liked" ratings children receive) from friendship (i.e., the number of reciprocated "friend" choices) (Asher, Parker, & Walker, 1996). The concept of peer acceptance differs from friendship because it refers to children's relationships within a *group* rather than the quality of children's *dyadic* relationships with individual peers. For example, peer relations researchers sometimes observe classroom or playground social interactions and chart peer relationships based on frequencies of actual contacts between acquaintances (i.e., peers children "know" but with whom they have no close reciprocated ties) (Ladd & Kochenderfer, 1996). Either method (i.e., ratings or observations) is called a **sociometric** classification of group acceptance and can be summarized in a visual diagram called a *sociogram,* shown in Figure 10.1.

Peer acceptance may influence friendships by determining the amount of choice that children have in friends (Azmitia et al., 1998). Recall that in the transition to middle school, peer group sizes may increase as children attend several different classes in a typical day. For both boys and girls, the anticipated transition produced feelings of anxiety (Pratt & George, 2005). When patterns of attraction to peers were examined across the transition to middle school, researchers found that attractions to aggressive peers and to children who stand out in the peer group increase with age, especially attraction to aggressive boys among girls (Bukowski, Sippola, & Newcomb, 2000).

Girls experience less stability in the number of reciprocated friendships across the school transition than do boys, although they have similar numbers of friends overall. Girls also are more likely than boys to form *new* reciprocated friendships

FIGURE 10.1
Sociogram

This sociogram of best friend choices in middle childhood models the reciprocal best friend choices of four girls (shaded circles) as well as a mixed-sex peer network with a popular boy named Nathan at the center.

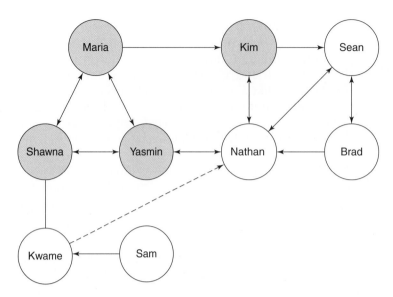

with previously unfamiliar peers, especially if they had attended relatively small elementary schools (Hardy, Bukowski, & Sippola, 2002). In other words, girls may experience more *changes* in friends than boys after the middle school transition.

In a recent study, sixth-grade sociometric status ("liked-most" and "liked-least" scores) predicted eighth-grade school adjustment (Wentzel, 2003). Although the number and stability of friendships do not always contribute to adjustment in the transition to middle school, having supportive friends predicts increasing popularity (Berndt, 1989). A classroom activity called the "Class Play" is described in Box 10.1.

 BOX 10.1   Roadmap to Understanding Theory and Research
The Revised Class Play

Using a procedure called the *Revised Class Play*, designed to measure peers' behavioral reputation ("*What is this child like?*"), elementary, middle, and high school students were asked to cast their classmates into 30 roles (half reflecting positive attributes, half negative) in a hypothetical play. Both boys and girls categorized their peers according to four types of behaviors:

- Leadership behaviors
- Prosocial behaviors
- Aggressive-disruptive behaviors
- Sensitive-isolated behaviors

Both middle-school children and adolescents perceived leadership and prosocial behaviors as positive, and aggressive-disruptive and sensitive-isolated behaviors as negative. However, compared to elementary-age children, they also saw aggressive-disruptive behaviors as positively related to *leadership*. In middle school, the researchers suggested, a peer with a "bad reputation" would be likely to become a leader in the peer group (Zeller et al., 2003).

This technique has proven useful for determining school-agers' reputations in their peer groups.

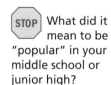

STOP What did it mean to be "popular" in your middle school or junior high?

> *José's group of friends are the "cool" kids in their neighborhood and are looked up to by most of the other children their age or younger.*

PEER INTERACTION IN MIDDLE CHILDHOOD

Peer groups, like other organizations, have distinctive structures. In size, they average about 5 or 6 members (Rubin et al., 2005). In a peer group's organization, some members are central while others are marginal, for example. In a study of fourth, fifth, and sixth graders, peers' positions in the organization of same-sex peer groups were significantly related to their social status. Peer group members who were marginal in the peer-group organization were more likely to be rejected and friendless, whereas those in a central position were likely to be popular and have at least one friend (Lease & Axelrod, 2001). Recall that rejected children are also more likely to be the victims of bullying. Furthermore, rejected children on the margins of the group are often perceived by their peers as "different" in their social behavior (i.e., more odd, inattentive, excluded, shy, or anxious) compared to rejected peers who are less marginal (Lease, McFall, & Viken, 2003).

Peer Networks

Researchers studying the formation of peer groups have defined a **clique** as a small group of close friends (for an ethnographic study of peer networks, see Adler & Adler, 1998). Generally, girls' friendship networks are smaller (i.e., more *intensive*) than boys' networks (i.e., more *extensive*). Longitudinal research, however, has shown that boys' friendship networks are more likely to become interconnected over time compared to girls' (Ladd, 1999). Interestingly, the size and density of adolescent's networks has been related to their parents' friendship

A small group of friends that deliberately excludes non-members is called a clique.

Anthony Magnacca/Merrill

networks—especially mothers'—perhaps due to the influence of social learning (Parke & Buriel, 1998).

Based on the principles of social learning theory, peer and friendship networks are likely to form because of three factors (Hartup, 1996):

1. *Socio-demographics.* Children are likely to come into proximity because of age, socioeconomic status, ethnicity, etc.

2. *Social selection.* Children construct relationships with others who are similar to themselves or to whom they are attracted.

3. *Mutual socialization.* Children become increasingly similar to their friends as they interact.

Unlike interaction-based cliques that are composed of friendship networks, **crowds** are reputation-based groups of children who are not necessarily friends but who share similar values, attitudes, and behaviors, such as "jocks" or "brains" (Prinstein & La Greca, 2002; see also Brown, Eicher, & Petrie, 1986). Peer crowds serve an important relational function when children enter a new school and interact with increasing numbers of peers. The crowd system may act as a social guide to help school-age children maintain peer relationships, meet possible friends, and—eventually—choose romantic partners.

José is already in a clique that includes his two friends. They all dress alike, like the same sports teams, and play the same video games.

Social Networking. Due to the recent popularity of social networking sites on the Internet, such as Club Penguin, school-agers' peer networks have expanded to include children who have not necessarily met face-to-face. Club Penguin is a Web site similar to those for adults and teens, such as MySpace, Friendster, and Facebook, but with stricter rules. It was developed by three Canadian fathers as an advertisement-free site with a system for eliminating bad language, bullies, and possible predators (Neary, 2007).

Some researchers have characterized children's use of online diaries as an effective way for caring adults to gain access to children's own accounts of their lives by studying the self-presentations they create for their peers in a Web community (Moinian, 2006). In addition, positive feedback from online peers on the personal Web profiles of school-agers enhances their social self-esteem and well-being (Valkenburg, Peter, & Schouten, 2006). However, because school-age children are likely to share their personal information with strangers in online forums or blogs, it is important for parents and school personnel to monitor children's online peer behavior (Millard, 2006; Aftab, 2000). For example, Box 10.2 describes the Child Online Protection Act, enacted by the U.S. Congress in 1998 to protect children from Internet predators.

Most school-age children already know many rules for online safety, such as never giving out your name, address, phone number, school, and parent's name or not lying about your age so you can go to a site on the Internet (Aftab, 2000). Refer to Box 10.3 for a sample agreement to use the Internet safely that school-age children can sign.

Such measures seem particularly important as Internet use becomes more widespread. For example, middle-class seventh graders report instant-messaging (IMing) 2 to 3 friends daily. The most common topics were friends (58%), gossip (51%), and boyfriend/girlfriend "stuff" (50%). Ninety-two percent said that their reason for IMing

BOX 10.2   Roadmap to Successful Practice
The Child Online Protection Act

In October 1998 Congress enacted the Child Online Protection Act and established the Commission on Online Child Protection to study methods to help reduce access by minors to certain sexually explicit material, defined in the statute as harmful to minors. Congress directed the commission to evaluate the accessibility, cost, and effectiveness of protective technologies and methods, as well as their possible effects on privacy, First Amendment values, and law enforcement. The commission studied a wide range of child-protective technologies and methods, including:

- Filtering and blocking services
- Labeling and rating systems
- Age verification efforts
- A new top-level domain for harmful-to-minors material
- "Greenspaces" containing only child-appropriate materials
- Internet monitoring and time-limiting technologies
- Acceptable use policies and family contracts
- Online resources providing access to protective technologies and methods
- Increased prosecution against illegal online material

The commission concluded that the most effective means of protecting children from harmful content on the Internet includes aggressive efforts toward public education, consumer empowerment, increased resources for enforcement of existing laws, and greater use of existing technologies. Witness after witness testified that protection of children online requires more education, more technologies, heightened public awareness of existing technologies, and better enforcement of existing laws.

Government at all levels and the Internet community must unite to provide broadly available education resources to families and caregivers. Voluntary methods and technologies to protect children must be developed, tested, evaluated, and made readily available. Coupled with information to make these methods understandable and useful, these voluntary approaches provide powerful technologies for families. As we move forward, it is also important that technologies to protect children reflect next-generation Internet systems and the convergence of old and new media. Finally, it is imperative that government allocate increased resources to law enforcement at the federal, state, and local level for training, staffing, and equipment so that existing laws against child pornography and obscenity are more effectively enforced.

The Internet's global nature presents law enforcement with an additional concern, because a substantial amount of obscene material, child pornography, and harmful-to-minors material originates abroad. While issues of extradition, need for legal assistance from foreign law enforcement, and conflict of law issues make prosecution difficult, these problems have been addressed previously in the narcotics, fraud, and intellectual property areas. U.S. leadership in this area may lead to models of international cooperation.

Source: Adapted from "U.S. Commission on Online Child Protection (COPA) (2000)." *Report to Congress, October 21, 2001.* Washington, DC: COCP.

was "to hang out with a friend" (Gross, Juvonen, & Gable, 2002). Refer to Figure 10.2 for a comparison of the ways 12-year-old boys and girls spend their time online.

Same-Sex Networks. Typically, the peer groups of school-age children are segregated by sex. Girls usually place a priority on interpersonal connections (i.e., communal needs), whereas boys place a higher priority on status concerns (i.e., agentic needs) (see Maccoby, 1990, 1998). For example, in a study of friendship quality, girls reported more frequent intimate and supportive interactions with female friends than boys did with male friends (Buhrmester, 1996). In other studies, boys were more

BOX 10.3   Roadmap to Successful Practice
My Agreement about Using the Internet

MY AGREEMENT ABOUT USING THE INTERNET

I want to use our computer and the Internet. I know that there are certain rules about what I should do online. I agree to follow these rules and my parents agree to help me follow these rules:

1. I will not give my name, address, telephone number, school, or my parents' names, address, or telephone number, to anyone I meet on the computer.

2. I understand that some people online pretend to be someone else. Sometimes they pretend to be kids, when they're really grown ups. I will tell my parents about people I meet online. I will also tell my parents before I answer any e-mails I get from or send e-mails to new people I meet online.

3. I will not buy or order anything online without asking my parents or give out any credit card information.

4. I will not fill out any form online that asks me for any information about myself or my family without asking my parents first.

5. I will not get into arguments or fights online. If someone tries to start an argument or fight with me, I won't answer him or her and will tell my parents.

6. If I see something I do not like or that I know my parents don't want me to see, I will click on the "back" button or log off.

7. If I see people doing things or saying things to other kids online I know they're not supposed to do or say, I'll tell my parents.

8. I won't keep online secrets from my parents.

9. If someone sends me any pictures or any e-mails using bad language, I will tell my parents.

10. If someone asks me to do something I am not supposed to do, I will tell my parents.

11. I will not call anyone I met online, in person, unless my parents say it's okay.

12. I will never meet in person anyone I met online, unless my parents say it's okay.

13. I will never send anything to anyone I met online, unless my parents say it's okay.

14. If anyone I met online sends me anything, I will tell my parents.

15. I will not use something I found online and pretend it's mine.

16. I won't say bad things about people online, and I will practice good Netiquette.

17. I won't use bad language online.

18. I know that my parents want to make sure I'm safe online, and I will listen to them when they ask me not to do something.

19. I will help teach my parents more about computers and the Internet.

20. I will practice safe computing, and check for viruses whenever I borrow a disk from someone or download something from the Internet.

I promise to follow these rules (signed by the child).

I promise to help my child follow these rules and not to over react if my child tells me about bad things in cyberspace (signed by parent).

Source: From "Parenting Online: My Agreement About Using the Internet" (http://wirekids.org/parents/parentingonline/agreement.html). Copyright © 2007 by Parry Aftab. This is used with the permission of Dr. Parry Aftab, Executive Director of WiredSafety.org. For permission to duplicate this material, contact permissions@aftab.com or Parry Aftab, directly, at Parry@Aftab.com.

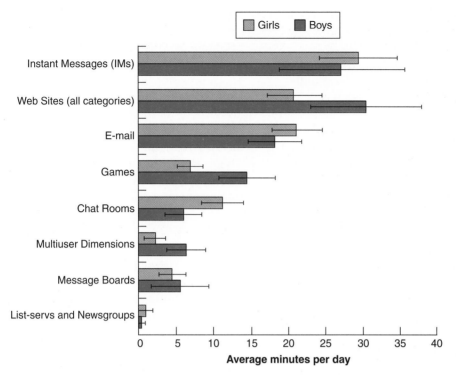

FIGURE 10.2
Social Networking
Activities on the
Internet

Instant messaging,
e-mailing, and social
networking Web sites
are new media for
communicating with
friends by late middle
childhood.

Source: From "Internet
use and well-being in
adolescence" (p. 83) by
Elisheva F. Gross, Janna
Juvonen, & Shelley L.
Gable, 2002, *Journal of
Social Issues, 58,* 75–90.
Reprinted by permission.

likely than girls to express anger towards well-liked peers, perhaps due to concerns about competition. Girls were more likely to judge a friend's misdeeds in terms of how these behaviors would affect their relationship (see Ladd, 1999).

Such sex differences are likely due to differential gender socialization experiences in family, school, and community contexts. For example, in a study of school-age children's social networks on a school playground, ethnographic observers found that sex-typed play (i.e., all-boy or all-girl) interacted with stereotypical behaviors related to other social categories, such as age, race, and social class. Girls' and boys' hairstyles and clothing, for instance, amplified differences between male and female peer groups (Thorne, A., 1993; Thorne, B., 1997a). In addition, the greater social prestige of early pubertal maturation for boys versus girls reproduced the dynamics of male dominance on the playground (Thorne, 1997b). Socially unskilled children who are rejected by their same-sex peers, however, may be more likely to seek opposite-sex friends.

José and his friends have little or no interaction with girls at this age.

Cross-Sex Networks. Cross-sex interactions are often an extension of peer networks in middle childhood rather than the more intimate relationships characteristic of adolescents. For example, middle-school heterosexual dating (or "going together") usually consists of peer groups going out together and is often a combination of male and female cliques (Pellegrini, 2001). Keep in mind, however, that although children may *begin* to explore dating they still may belong to small friendship groups (i.e., *cliques*) and larger social groups (i.e., *crowds*). Crowds serve the function of defining those peers with whom children share a group identity. For example, by providing a system for categorizing unknown peers, crowds allow middle-school children to anticipate the type of relationship that might develop with a person in a

Guideposts for Working with School-Age Children

- Provide opportunities for school-agers to reflect on the nature of friendship by reading youth literature and discussing themes such as support, loyalty, and trust.

- Frequently reassign students to different groups for classroom projects so that they can become better acquainted with less familiar peers.

- Praise children for befriending students who may differ from themselves or who interact on the margins of their friendship network or peer group.

- Encourage boys and girls to appreciate the social provisions of cross-sex peer groups by pointing out the strengths of fulfilling their needs both for individual agency and for communion with others.

- Because both same-sex and cross-sex friendships increase in middle childhood, expect that dating may occur in the context of early adolescent crowds.

STOP Did you or any of your friends "go steady" in middle childhood?

particular crowd, such as "trendies" or "grits" (Brown, Mory, & Kinney, 1994). Often, potential dating partners will be members of the crowd.

Just because school-age children are not dating, however, does not imply that they are not engaged in romantic activity, such as flirting or kissing (Connolly, Craig, Goldberg, & Pepler, 2004). For example, in a recent study, researchers found that, in the transition from same-sex friendships to dating, heterosexual teenagers typically join mixed-sex groups in which they begin to pair off. In this sense, mixed-sex affiliative and early dating stages may coexist rather than be sequential (Connolly et al., 2004).

PLAY AND SOCIAL SKILLS IN MIDDLE CHILDHOOD

Recall that *social competence* is the ability to interact effectively with others. In studying children's social competence, most researchers and practitioners have focused on how positive social relationships are linked to acquiring the skills necessary for effective social interaction, such as maintaining friendships and playing together (e.g., Chan, Ramey, Ramey, & Schmitt, 2000).

Middle Childhood Play

The play of 6- to 12-year-olds is typically spontaneous, intrinsically motivated, and characterized by active engagement (see Manning, 1998, for a review). Middle childhood play often involves active experimentation that challenges school-age children's increasing cognitive abilities, such as testing scientific phenomena. Common indoor activities—such as board games, word games, computer simulation or role-playing games, and video games—almost always require greater logical reasoning and memory skills than were present in early childhood. Similarly, middle childhood outdoor play activities—such as in-line skating, rope-skipping, and skateboarding—provide more difficult physical challenges for school-agers than is appropriate for young children. When play is free from external pressures, it benefits children's self-development in the same way as do flow experiences, discussed in chapter 7 (Rathunde & Csikszentmihalyi, 2006).

His neighborhood provides a perfect setting for José and his friends to exercise their cognitive and motor skills and act out their fantasies.

In most industrialized countries, hobbies and sports are also important middle childhood play activities (Fredricks et al., 2005; McHale, Crouter, et al., 2001). In the school-age years, typical hobbies are collecting, arts and crafts, computer-gaming, model-building, or playing a musical instrument. In addition, school-age children also may make a hobby of learning sports statistics, jokes, or trivia as a means of entertaining their friends or families (Davies, 2004).

Cross-Cultural Play. Ethnographic researchers have found that socioeconomic status and gender affect the type and amount of play observed across cultures (Manning, 1998). A child from a more affluent society, for example, may play as a leisure activity, such as engaging in sports or hobbies, whereas a child from a less affluent society might engage in play activities related to work or survival, as in the herding games played by boys in Kenya. The influence of such contextual factors on the play of middle childhood in six cultures and the United States has been extensively studied by anthropologists and is discussed in Box 10.4 (Edwards, 2000). By middle childhood, age and gender segregation in play is common in some cultures but not others (Best, 2004).

In 1990, the International Play Association (IPA) published a Declaration on the Child's Right to Play to supplement Article 31 of the 1989 United Nations Convention on the Rights of the Child (for a history, see Guddemi, Jambor, & Moore, 1998). Refer to Table 10.2 for the list of children's rights to play. School-age children should be guaranteed opportunities to engage in play and develop social relationships with peers, irrespective of gender, culture, or social class (IPA, 1990).

Social Play and Games. From a peer relations perspective, middle childhood play is likely to be characterized by differing levels of social interaction than at earlier ages (Parten, 1933). Compared to early childhood, when play was more often **parallel** (i.e., playing alongside others, but still individually) or **associative** (i.e., playing in a loosely organized group, with much coming and going), school-age children increasingly engage in **cooperative play** (i.e., playing together in a structured game or fantasy with assigned roles) (see Table 10.3). Although the cooperative level of social participation most often describes the *group* play of school-age children, **solitary** play (i.e., playing alone) can also be observed at any age (Pellegrini & Smith, 2003).

School-age children's cooperative play with peers often involves structured games with rules.

Anthony Magnacca/Merrill

BOX 10.4   Roadmap to Understanding Theory and Research
Play in Six Cultures

Carolyn Pope Edwards (2000) conducted a qualitative and quantitative reanalysis of the Six Cultures study and its sequel, the Children of Different Worlds project on children's play, collected in the 1950s (Whiting, B. 1963; Whiting, B. & Edwards, 1973, 1988; Whiting, B. & Whiting, 1975). The cultures were (1) Nyansongo, Kenya; (2) Juxtlahuaca, Mexico; (3) Tarong, Phillipines; (4) Taira, Okinawa; (5) Khalapur, India; and (6) a small town in the United States. A count was performed of children aged 3 to 10 in each community sample scored as engaging in creative-constructive play, fantasy play, role play, and games with rules.

Children in many communities participated in subsistence activities and child care in ways that promoted their responsibility and nurturance but still allowed time for play with peers and siblings (often, they combined moments and episodes of fun, entertainment, and constructive problem solving into their work). Children also had less exposure to novelty and stimulation coming from media and recreational and educational institutions than today and less access to the products, by-products, and waste products of the industrial world. Only in Orchard Town, New England, did children in the 1950s already have a plethora of games, art materials, and toys, as well as tools, scraps, and trash so useful to use and combine with natural materials in constructing toys and creating imaginative narratives.

As a result of these contextual factors, children's play showed much variability across the sample communities. Games with rules, for example, were more prevalent in the three complex communities where parents were part of classed societies with economic role specialization and hierarchy (Orchard Town, Khalapur, and Taira) and in Tarong, with its nucleated living arrangements. . . . Because competitive games thrive best with peer groups rather than mixed ages, they were most often seen on the school playgrounds rather than backyards. . . .

Gender segregation was the grand rule of social interaction during middle childhood (ages 6 to 10). Boys and girls segregated into same-gender

peer groups whenever there were enough children available and especially did so when they had already divided themselves into age-homogeneous groupings. After age 6, schooling was a factor that allowed boys and girls in most communities access to peers. The three communities with the highest percentages of same-gender interaction were Taira and Juxtlahuaca, where children played in public areas and the streets, and Nyansongo, where boys went off together to herd cattle (combining work with play) in the fields. . . .

During middle childhood, boys reduced contact and interaction with their mothers and other adult females and were observed at greater distances from home than were girls. The highest levels of distant-from-home observations in the study were found in the 6- to 10-year-olds from the denser settlements of Orchard Town, Taira, and Khalapur, where school-aged children (only the boys in Khalapur) had freedom to wander to play. . . .

Children in all communities, this review suggests, seemed to have an appetite for self-expression, peer collaboration, exploration, rehearsal, imagination, and problem solving. Their outlets were socially mediated and took many varieties of play and work, with not necessarily clear boundary lines dividing them. Both play and work allowed children to build their repertoires of skills and schemes and to exercise and extend their knowledge and control over their environments.

Cultural norms and opportunities determined the degree to which play was stimulated by the physical and social environments. Key factors included whether adults considered play a good use of children's time or just an annoyance, whether adults preferred to conservatively preserve tradition or instead to instigate innovation, and whether the environment provided easy access to models and materials for creative and constructive play.

Source: Based on "Children's Play in Cross-Cultural Perspective: A New Look at the *Six Cultures Study*" by Carolyn Pope Edwards, 2000, in *Cross-Cultural Research, 34*(4), 318–338. Copyright © 2000 by Sage Publications, Inc.

TABLE 10.2   Children's Right to Play

Article 31 of the United Nations Convention on the Rights of the Child, 1989, states:

1. That every child has the right to rest and leisure, to engage in play and recreational activities appropriate to the age of the child and to participate freely in cultural life and the arts.
2. That member governments shall respect and promote the right of the child to participate fully in cultural and artistic life and shall encourage the provision of appropriate and equal opportunities for cultural, artistic, recreational and leisure activity.

Declaration of the Child's Right to Play:

- Children are the foundation of the world's future.
- Children have played at all times throughout history and in all cultures.
- Play, along with the basic needs of nutrition, health, shelter and education, is vital to develop the potential of all children.
- Play is communication and expression, combining thought and action; it gives satisfaction and a feeling of achievement.
- Play is instinctive, voluntary and spontaneous.
- Plays helps children develop physically, mentally, emotionally, and socially.
- Play is a means of learning to live, not a mere passing of time.

Source: Adapted from "IPA Declaration of the Child's Right to Play" by the International Association for the Child's Right to Play. Retrieved August 20, 2006, from http://www.ipaworld.org/ipa_declaration.html.

Piaget (1962/1952) proposed that cognitive advances during middle childhood allow school-age children to successfully play **games with rules,** such as sports or video and board games, compared to younger children who typically engage in more **functional, constructive,** and **symbolic play** than school-agers (see Smilansky, 1968), also described in Table 10.3. When 10-year-old American boys engaged in symbolic fantasy play with action figures, for example, they made up elaborate "rules

---

TABLE 10.3   Levels of Children's Play

Each social play stage can be nested in each of the cognitive play stages. School-age children can engage in Games with Rules—such as video games—whether by themselves (solitary play), alongside others at an arcade (parallel play), against several players in a multiple user domain (MUD) on the Internet (associative play), or with a friend on their home game system (cooperative play).

Social Play	Cognitive Play
Solitary	**Functional**
• Plays alone	• Manipulates toys
• Watches others playing	• Explores how things work
Parallel	**Constructive**
• Plays alongside others	• Combines materials or objects
Associative	**Symbolic**
• Plays in a loosely organized group	• Pretends or acts out stories
Cooperative	**Games with Rules**
• Plays together with common goals	• Follows rules and assigned roles

of engagement." Games with rules allow school-age children to interact with peers in a structured activity as well as assess their status in the peer group (Davies, 2004).

Games with rules may occur outdoors as well as indoors, for example, games of tag, hopscotch, or hula-hoop contests. Team sports, such as baseball or soccer, and individual sports, such as tennis or swimming, typify middle childhood outdoor games with rules. But even unstructured associative play in the outdoors can become rule-bound, as in the following example:

> . . . at a family picnic, a group of cousins, girls and boys, ranging in age from 8 to 12 were taking turns swinging out on a rope and dropping into a river. Gradually, they suggested specific ways of doing this, and a competition evolved, with more and more elaborate tasks being proposed. They had to turn around on the rope and face the bank before dropping into the water; or skim the water with their feet before letting go; or grasp their knees after letting go, to cannonball into the water. Implicitly, they seemed impelled to introduce structure, competition, and consequently defined skills into what had begun as spontaneous play. (Davies, 2004, pp. 357–358)

José and his buddies almost always play together, making up increasingly challenging rules for their favorite outdoor game, kickball.

Computer Games. Today, many education scholars call computer-gaming "the new electronic playground" (Kafai, 1998; Seiter, 2004). Computer and video games not only allow school-age children ample opportunities to follow well-defined rules for play but also appeal to them to uncover rules that are unknown at the beginning of a game. In many games, for example, the rules change as a player progresses to the next level of the game, requiring school-age children to employ cognitive skills such as trial and error, pattern generalization, and hypothesis-testing. In this regard, computing is viewed as a constructive activity: "The process of game construction represented for Piaget the ultimate efforts by children to master their environment by creating external representations of the world" (Kafai, 1998, p. 95; see also Sefton-Green & Buckingham, 1996). Recently, computing has been described as fostering positive child development: "developing technological fluency enables youth to see themselves as competent learners of skills and knowledge that are highly valued by modern society. . . . Learners can use technologies to express their sense of self, as well as explore their identity, through behaviors in the context of a community of practice" (Bers, 2006, p. 201).

Although many adults may think of gaming only as a solitary play activity, computer and video games are becoming increasingly cooperative. For example, players can interact with other game players in "multiple user domains" (MUDs) or "massively multiplayer online role-playing games" (MMORPGs) on networked computers, the Internet, or mobile media, such as cell phones. Extremely popular with boys, MMORPGs are always "on" and are referred to as *pervasive* learning games (Thomas, 2006). By constructing rules for team play, school-age children "practice effective communication, work out compromises, and develop trust. These enhanced social skills allow children to see others' perspectives and allow them to realize the benefits of playing socially and cooperatively" (Manning, 1998, p. 157). A three-year study of an after-school computer laboratory program for children ages 8 to 11 revealed that children used the Internet to *play* (Seiter, 2004). For example, school-age users of Club Penguin, described earlier, can make animated penguins wander through a snowy virtual world, playing games and winning "coins," which allows them to buy and furnish their own igloos—much like the popular adult game of *The Sims*™ (Neary, 2007). In Zora, another multiuser virtual environment designed for school-agers, children can design and inhabit a virtual

---

Guideposts for Working with School-Age Children

- Give school-age children adequate unstructured time for spontaneous play indoors and outdoors, such as recess in both elementary and middle schools.

- Recognize that opportunities for play will be influenced by children's gender and socioeconomic status and provide resources and encouragement when necessary.

- Allow children to change the rules of a game in mid-play, as long as the other players agree with the new terms.

- Encourage children to develop hobbies or become involved in sports during their leisure time.

- Help children to play cooperatively with others by coaching a sport or after-school activity, such as the computer club.

---

community as well as create *avatars,* or actors with their own faces and identities, to interact with heroes and villains using a "values dictionary" that is meant to promote caring, connection, and other prosocial behaviors (Bers, 2006). Similarly, in Project Inter-Action, parents and elementary-age children can create virtual robots together and discuss the family and cultural values that they have ascribed to them (Bers, 2006).

STOP What were your favorite games, sports, or hobbies in middle childhood?

Social Skills

Social skills are socially acceptable learned behaviors, such as sharing, helping, initiating conversations, and giving compliments, that enable children to interact with others in ways that elicit positive responses and avoid negative ones (Elliott, Malecki, & Demaray, 2001). "What all such efforts share is an assumption that children who have peer-relationship difficulties lack the necessary skills to initiate and maintain relationships" (Asher et al., 1996, p. 370). In studying the development of social skills, most middle childhood researchers have focused on two opposing types of social interactions, *prosocial* (e.g., helping, protecting) and *antisocial* (e.g., fighting, bullying), both described in the previous chapter. Social skills that are prosocial generally strengthen or enhance interpersonal relationships (Elliott et al., 2001). For example, children who are similar in levels of prosocial and antisocial behavior are more likely to become friends than those who are not (Haselager, Hartup, van Lieshout, & Rilke-Walraven, 1998). In addition, having prosocial friends may serve as a protective factor against antisocial behavior (see Berndt, 2002, for a review).

Social skills discriminate between children who get along with their peers versus those who do not. Many researchers, for example, have found that socially skilled children are more often nominated by their peers as popular (Chan et al., 2000). In addition, a high-quality friendship is typically characterized by high levels of positive behavior and low levels of conflict (Berndt, 2002). Thus, the study of social skills in middle childhood often involves identifying how children who differ in skill level respond when they encounter conflict (Cillessen & Bellmore, 2002).

In a study of 9- to 12-year-olds, for example, level of peer acceptance was related to the ability of children to resolve interpersonal conflicts with peers. Interestingly, acceptance was also related to the causal attributions they made about disagreements between friends (Joshi & Ferris, 2002). School-age children ascribed conflicts between friends to one of four causes:

1. *Relationship characteristics.* Conflict is attributable to an inevitable characteristic of the relationship or to human nature in general (e.g., *"Friends have a lot in common but not everything"* or *"Because people are different"*).

2. *Interactional condition.* Conflict is the result of a specific situation, such as conflicting goals (e.g., *"One person wants something the other has"*).

3. *Person characteristics.* Conflict is caused by the characteristics, attributes or actions of a specific person, either self or other (e.g., *"Because someone is in a bad mood"*).

4. *Extraneous characteristics.* Conflict is the result of factors unrelated to the friendship (e.g., *"God thinks you need to fight in your life"*). (adapted from Joshi & Ferris, 2002, pp. 68–69)

Most children attribute the cause of conflicts with friends to specific features of the interaction rather than to individual personality characteristics of themselves and their friends (Joshi & Ferris, 2002).

> *If José were to argue with his friends, for example, he would likely attribute the cause of their disagreement to conflicting goals in a specific situation, such as letting Emilio join in a game.*

Social Skills Assessment. Because the ability to resolve conflicts is important to maintaining peer relations and friendships in middle childhood, varied techniques have been developed to assess and remediate school-age children's social skills. Because most children think that conflicts are situational, these methods typically assess children's social skills in context. A contextual approach to social skills assessment has multiple goals (adapted from Sheridan, Hungelmann, & Maughan, 1999):

- Identifying behaviors and skills that are important in a particular social context (e.g., home or school)
- Determining the norms and expectations for those skills in that environment
- Analyzing the conditions that support or discourage social skills
- Identifying individual children's social skills in a specific situation
- Designing interventions to improve children's social skills in that setting
- Measuring outcomes in the relevant social context

Social skills are usually assessed using parent or teacher rating scales, supplemented by structured observation of children's classroom behavior or attainment of social goals, such as successfully initiating conversation with peers (Elliott et al., 2001; see Demaray, Ruffalo, Carlson, & Busse, 1995, for a review of measures). A widely used measure, the *Social Skills Rating System* (SSRS) (Gresham & Elliott, 1990), includes items on the teacher's version such as:

- Makes friends easily
- Cooperates with peers without prompting
- Gets along with people who are different

The SSRS also allows school-age children to rate their own social skills on a scale of 0 to 3 (0 = Never, 1 = Sometimes, 3 = Always). The SSRS instrument can raise elementary-school children's awareness of social behaviors that are valued by their peers, such as asking their classmates to join an activity or game.

Social Skills Training. **Coaching** is a method of social skills training in which an adult models and explains skills, allows the child to practice them, and provides feedback to improve the child's performance (Shaffer, 2005). For example, a successful intervention program with third and fourth graders taught children cooperation skills (e.g., taking turns, sharing materials), participation skills (e.g., getting started paying attention), communication skills (e.g., talking with the other person, listening), and validation skills (e.g., smiling, offering encouragement). The children improved in social skills and gained status in their peer group (see Oden & Asher, 1977). Other social skills training programs have delivered intervention through such varied techniques as live or video-taped models, play sessions with peers, social role-playing, and problem-solving tasks (for reviews, see Asher et al., 1996; Elliott et al., 2001). An example of a training program in social problem-solving was provided in chapter 9 (refer to Box 9.1).

Children are usually selected for social skills training on the basis of poor social skills and low sociometric status. In most cases, although children's overall peer acceptance is improved by social skills training, the frequency of friendship nominations is not as likely to improve. As a result, scholars have suggested that lasting friendships may require a different set of social skills from more incidental peer interactions. To maintain friendships, children must (adapted from Asher et al., 1996):

- Conceive of friendship as a relationship that demands contact outside the context where children normally interact (e.g., school), and possess skills for initiating contact with friends in that setting (e.g., home or neighborhood).
- Possess the dispositions to be perceived as fun, resourceful, and enjoyable companions.
- Recognize and respect that friendship requires a spirit of equality.
- Have the ability to self-disclose if they are to share intimacies with friends.
- Be able to express caring, concern, admiration, and affection in acceptable ways.
- Be willing to help when their friends are in need and be a reliable partner.
- Manage disagreements, resolve conflicts, and be able to forgive.
- Recognize that friendship exists within a broader social context, including cliques and crowds.

Considerable evidence exists for considering friendships important contexts for developing social skills (Berndt, 2002; Ladd & Kochenderfer, 1996; Hartup, 1996). For example, the quality of children's friendships may influence social skill acquisition because friends

- Communicate with each other more effectively than nonfriends.
- Provide more support and assistance than nonfriends.
- Problem-solve together in a "climate of agreement" compared to nonfriends.
- Seek ways of resolving disagreements that support continued interaction. (adapted from Hartup, 1996)

In our case example, Emilio's attempt at a friendship with José may help him to practice social skills with a supportive peer, and thus lessen Emilio's rejection by the other boys in their neighborhood.

Newer approaches to social skills training involve interventions in the context of children's naturalistic environments, such as the classroom (Elliott et al., 2001) or school (Kilian, Fish, & Maniago, 2007). For example, an approach termed the Responsive Classroom integrates teaching social skills as part of everyday classroom

Guideposts for Working with School-Age Children

- Carefully monitor children's participation in Internet friendships by helping them to develop their profiles for sites such as myspace.com.
- Assist children to recognize social skills through youth literature that describes common situations faced by school-agers.
- Help children to problem-solve when facing challenging social situations rather than assume

a disagreement is due to differences in personalities.
- Teach school-agers conflict negotiation skills by modeling, coaching, or role-playing solutions to common everyday disagreements they have recently experienced.

STOP How did you resolve conflicts with your friends during middle childhood?

life. In this model, which stresses group activities and teamwork, students exhibited more social skills, greater gains in both social and academic areas, and fewer problem behaviors than students in more traditional classrooms (Elliott et al., 2001).

FRIENDS AND PEER RELATIONS IN CONTEXT

Families, school, and neighborhoods are important contexts for peer interaction and the development of children's friendships. For example, the quality of parents' friendships has been associated with the quality of children's friendships (Simpkins & Parke, 2001). Positive school climates also promote positive peer relations and friendships. And, finally, neighborhood factors—especially the presence of community-based activities for school-age children—support middle childhood peer interaction. In addition, it is important to recognize that the meanings and desirability of social behaviors, such as cooperation versus competition, may vary from context to context (Rubin et al., 2005).

Family Contexts

A great deal of debate has centered around the relative impact of parents and peers in middle childhood, but despite the claims of socialization theorists that emphasize the importance of peers over parents (see Harris, 1998), most scholars maintain that parents have an important influence on middle childhood (and adolescent) values, attitudes, and behaviors. For example, when fifth- to ninth-grade students reported to whom they talked over the course of a week, time spent talking to friends increased dramatically with age, as expected, but *did not* replace talk with family members (Raffaelli & Duckett, 1989). In addition, when children trust parents not to overreact or ridicule their behaviors, future positive communication is promoted (Kerr et al., 2003).

Parents' supportive behavior during middle childhood promotes adolescents' positive behavior toward friends, whereas parents' hostile behavior predicts adolescents' negative behavior toward friends (Cui, Conger, Bryant, & Elder, 2002). Fifth graders who perceived greater support from their parents, for example, had higher friendship quality and greater psychological adjustment. Support from fathers, in particular, also predicted lower peer rejection and victimization (Rubin et al., 2004). Similarly, parents' supportive behaviors promoted their seventh graders' positive behaviors toward their

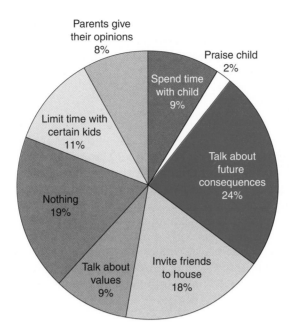

FIGURE 10.3
Parental Influences on Choosing Friends

Parents use a variety of strategies to influence their children's choices of friends.

Source: From "Parental Management of Adolescent Peer Relationships" by N. S. Mounts in K. A. Kerns, J. M. Contreras, & A. M. Neal-Barnett (Eds.), *Family and peers: Linking two social worlds* (p. 174), 2000, Westport, CT: Praeger. Copyright © 2000 by Katherine A. Kerns, Josefina M. Contreras, & Angela M. Neal-Barnett. Reprinted by permission of Greenwood Publishing Group, Inc., Westport, CT.

siblings and friends, in turn, predicted the quality of teenagers' friendships four years later. Even after controlling for the effects of contextual factors (e.g., gender, income, education) family interaction processes still predicted peer interaction and friendship quality (Cui et al., 2002).

Parents not only influence their children through direct interaction but also function as managers of their children's lives (Parke & Buriel, 1998). For example, see Figure 10.3 for ways parents can influence children's choice of friends. Family theorists have recently proposed models that integrate parent and peer contexts through the mechanisms of children's disclosure of their daily activities to parents (e.g., Kerr et al., 2003) or parental monitoring of their children's activities and whereabouts (e.g., Dishion & McMahon, 1998).

By supporting their children's extracurricular activities, parents can structure and influence children's friendships.

Adamsmith/Getty Images, Inc. — Taxi

For example, since José's parents work until 5 P.M., he goes straight to his new friend's house after school so that Emilio's mother can keep an eye on them. She also does not allow the boys to stray off the block.

School Contexts

The context that is most frequently cited in studies of peer interaction in middle childhood is schools. Past research has shown that characteristics of schools (e.g., structure, composition, and emotional climate) predict friendships and peer inter-action. For example, curriculum tracking and availability of extracurricular activities are key organizers of friendships by determining the available peers for such relationships to develop (Crosnoe, 2000).

As we saw in chapter 7, students report higher social and affective competence in schools that present them with appropriate challenges, that help them to see value in participation, and where they feel safe and cared for by others (Roesner, Eccles, & Sameroff, 2000). In a study of fifth- and sixth-grade girls, students kept week-long diaries of important peer activities and liked and disliked peer behaviors in those activities (Zarbatany et al., 1990). Students preferred school activities that provided:

- A context for sociability
- Concern for achievements
- Integrity of the self
- Opportunities for instruction and learning

A growing body of literature describes the importance of "place" for children's development. A sense of **place** affords children a feeling of belonging. When over 300 school-age children from 100 Italian elementary and middle schools were given the opportunity to tell community developers what they wanted in their schools and communities, they composed a "Children's Manifesto" that focused on their social needs, such as "Gathering places where we can meet friends." With respect to schools, they included "To use courtyards to play in and meet our friends" (Francis & Lorenzo, 2006). Social places, such as school lunch or recess areas, provide opportunities for children to develop a sense of responsibility to and respect for others (Derr, 2006; see also Thorne, 2005).

In an observational study of how middle-school students spent their time during recess over the entire school year, social interaction was more prevalent than the physical play commonly seen during recess in elementary school (see Jarrett & Duckett-Hedgebeth, 2003). Most students went outside during recess, although some chose to play computer or board games indoors. Overall, the middle school provided very little play equipment (e.g., 2 jump ropes and a few balls of various kinds). Across grades 5 to 8, hanging out and talking or playing football were the most observed activities. Although boys dominated the play area with football, as expected, about one-third of the time, 2 to 3 girls were involved in football games as active players. Very few fights were observed, but teasing was frequent, with most cross-sex teasing initiated by girls toward boys and most same-sex teasing by boys toward other boys. Boys, however, engaged in most of the chasing (of girls) and roughhousing. In addition, about 60% of the solitary behavior was among boys, compared to about 40% among girls. When the students were surveyed regarding their suggestions for improving recess, most ideas centered on providing more equipment and places for both indoor and outdoor play (Jarrett & Duckett-Hedgebeth, 2003).

Taken together, these findings suggest that school contexts provide valuable opportunities for peer interaction and play.

Recall our case study one more time. Once school begins, the "neighborhood boys," including José and Emilio, will eat lunch as quickly as they can so they will have time to go outside and play.

Community Contexts

An ecological perspective (refer to chapter 1) considers peer relations in the context of the larger cultural community in which they are embedded (e.g., McHale et al., 2003). For example, school-age children tend to draw their friends from their communities (Crosnoe, 2000). Efforts to capture variation in children's life circumstances have often relied on global indexes, such as social class or ethnic background, called **social address** variables. However, cultural anthropologists have described children's social ecologies, called **niches** (McHale et al., 2003; see also Weisner, 2001). Ecological niches have direct implications for social development in middle childhood. Examples of niches include how and where school-age children spend their time, their companions in everyday activities, and accompanying cultural scripts (McHale et al., 2003), such as *"be nice to your friends."*

Despite developmental psychologists' use of ecological theory, however, they often focus on individual child outcomes rather than the paths that children must travel during development (Crosnoe, 2000). Sociologists and social psychologists, on the other hand, have utilized life-course theory (described in detail in chapter 12). A life-course perspective operates on the premise that social behavior depends on carefully analyzing the potential role of community-level agents of socialization, including friends, social clubs, youth organizations, religious groups, informal peer associations, and even gangs (Mussen & Eisenberg, 2001). For example, changes in growth, technology, schooling, family patterns, community organization, and the rights and responsibilities of youth could affect their orientation to friends, the influences exerted by friends, and the control of friendship by adults (Crosnoe, 2000).

Recently, a global United Nations (UNESCO) project was implemented to engage children in evaluating their own communities, determining their priorities for change, and helping to implement local improvements. The Growing Up in Cities project initiates ongoing processes for community improvement in which school-age children participate. Methods to understand how a community functions for its children, what the existing resources for children, youth, and families are, and the areas that need improvement include (adapted from Chawla, 2002):

- Drawings, maps, models, and photographs to document local environmental conditions and desired changes (see Figure 10.4 for an example)
- Interviews with community residents, parents, and community officials
- Child-led tours of neighborhoods
- Focus group discussions and role-playing
- Visioning and ranking exercises
- Observations of public places and other spaces that children use

To encourage inclusive community development, the project may be school-based or community-based, depending on the resources available (Chawla, 2002).

 In what family activities, school groups or community organizations did you participate during middle childhood?

FIGURE 10.4
Child's Drawing of
Special Places

This fifth-grade pro-
posal gives promi-
nence to a pea patch
surrounded by special
places and tree-lined
pathways.

Source: From "Young Peo-
ple's Participation in Con-
structing a Socially Just
Public Sphere" by Sharon
Egretta Sutton and Susan
P. Kent, in C. Spencer &
M. Blades (Eds.), *Children
and Their Environments:
Learning, Using and De-
signing Spaces* (p. 263),
2006, New York: Cam-
bridge University Press.
Copyright © 2006 by
Cambridge University
Press. Reprinted with the
permission of Cambridge
University Press.

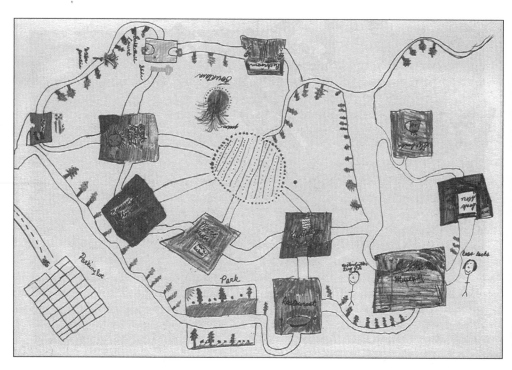

CHAPTER REVIEW

Peer Relations

- Relationships with peers and friends are important contexts in middle childhood.

- Peer relations may fulfill communal, survival, or agentic needs, also called social provisions.

Theoretical Viewpoints

- Friendships during middle childhood change from occasional interactions into enduring reciprocal relationships involving trust and mutual support.

- Popularity, or social status, becomes a central concern in middle childhood and predicts school-agers' social skills and school adjustment.

Peer Interaction

- Peer acceptance fulfills school-agers' communal needs for support and companionship with others.
- Friendship networks in middle childhood are usually composed of same-sex, same-age peers.

- Cliques are small friendship groups, whereas crowds are larger peers networks.
- Middle childhood same-sex peer relations are commonly augmented by cross-sex interactions and group dating in early adolescence.

Play and Social Skills

- Social competence is defined as the ability to interact effectively with others.
- Typical play in middle childhood is a cooperative game with rules.

- Social skills differentiate children who get along with their peers versus those who do not.
- Social skills training is an effective way of increasing peer acceptance of socially unskilled children.

Friends and Peers in Context

- Peer relations supplement, but do not replace, family relations and the importance of parenting during middle childhood.

- Schools with a positive social climate among students, staff, and teachers encourage positive peer relations.

- Neighborhoods with high levels of social integration (frequent contact among adults and children) and places to play support peer interaction.

TABLE 10.4   Summary of Developmental Theories

Chapter	Theory	Focus
10: Friends, Play, and Peer Relations	Friendship Understanding	Developmental sequence of understanding the meaning and function of friendship
	Ethology	Social behavior and social status in peer relations and peer networks

---

KEY TERMS

Agentic needs
Associative play
Chums
Cliques
Close friendships
Coaching
Communal needs
Constructive play
Controversial

Cooperative play
Crowds
Ethological theory
Extensive networks
Functional play
Friends
Friendship stages
Games with rules
Intensive networks

Neglected
Niches
Parallel play
Peers
Peer acceptance
Place
Popular
Popularity
Rejected

Social address
Social competence
Social provisions
Social skills
Sociogram
Sociometric
Solitary play
Symbolic play
Survival needs

SUGGESTED ACTIVITIES

1. Select a novel for young readers from the youth literature section of a library or bookstore. Describe the nature of the peer interactions and friendships portrayed in the story.

2. Interview a school-age child about his or her friendships. Ask about the child's best friend, peer network (clique), and social group (crowd).

3. Read a school-ager's online diary (Web log, or "blog") at http://clubpenguin.com. Analyze the site's content

and related peer commentary for evidence of peer support or friendship.

4. Play a card game, board game, or video game with a school-age child. Does the child follow or change the rules of play? How does the child react if you break or attempt to revise the rules?

5. Attend a sports meet or competition that involves school-age children. How do the children interact with each other? Do you see evidence of social skill development? What social skills do they need to learn?

RECOMMENDED RESOURCES

Suggested Readings

Blume, L. B., & Isbey, J. A. (2002). Youth fiction: Using chapter books and novels for young readers to teach about middle childhood. *Journal of Teaching in Marriage and Family: Innovations in Family Science Education, 2*(4), 454–474.

Piaget, J. (1962). *Play, dreams, and imitation in childhood* (C. Gattegno & F. M. Hodgson, Trans.). New York: W. W. Norton.

Seiter, E. (2004). The Internet playground. In J. Goldstein, D. Buckingham & G. Brougere (Eds.), *Toys, games, and media* (pp. 93–108). Mahwah, NJ: Erlbaum.

Simmons, R. (2004). *Odd girl speaks out: Girls write about bullies, cliques, popularity, and jealousy.* New York: Harvest.

Strasburger, V. C., & Wilson, B. J. (2002). *Youth and media: Opportunities for development or lurking dangers? Children, adolescents, and the media.* Thousand Oaks, CA: Sage.

Suggested Online Resources

Children's Technology Review. http://www.childrenssoftware.com/

Computer and Internet Use by Students in 2003. http://nces.ed.gov/pubs2006/2006065.pdf

Overlap Between Peer Networks and Friends and Its Implications. http://www.sonet.pdx.edu/PeerNetworks/GroupID/Overlap-Net&Frnds.htm

Wired Kids, Inc. http://wiredsafety.org/

Young people in Canada: Their health and well-being. Chapter 4: The peer group. http://www.phac-aspc.gc.ca/dca-dea/publications/hbsc-2004/chapter_4_e.html

Suggested Web Sites

Club Penguin. http://www.clubpenguin.com/

International Play Association. http://www.ipaworld.org/home.html

Parent's Guide to Internet Safety. http://www.fbi.gov/publications/pguide/pguidee.htm

Social Networks Research Group: Peer Networks. http://www.sonet.pdx.edu/PeerNetworks/index.htm

Sociometry in the Classroom: How to Do It. http://www.users.muohio.edu/shermalw/sociometryfiles/socio_introduction.htmlx

Suggested Films and Videos

Child's play: Growing up in America (1999). Films for the Humanities and Sciences (30 minutes)

Friendship . . . Put it to the test (2000). Films for the Humanities and Sciences (13 minutes)

Growing up in video world: Media and the developing child (2007). Learning Seed (24 minutes)

Peer pressure: Why are all my friends staring at me? (1991). Insight Media (15 minutes)

The wonder years, Episode #29: "Odd man out" (1989). New World Entertainment (25 minutes)

CHAPTER 11

Social Identity and Gender Development in Middle Childhood

Cindy Charles/PhotoEdit Inc.

Chapter Objectives

After reading this chapter, students will be able to:

▶ Define social identities, personal fables, and imaginary audiences in middle childhood.

▶ Summarize social identity and gender schema theories.

▶ Describe gender development in middle childhood.

▶ Discuss current research on racial/ethnic identities of school-age children.

▶ Explain the contributions of family, school, and community contexts to social identity development in middle childhood.

Mina is a 12-year-old with a burning desire to try out for the local soccer team. Mina's parents, however, disapprove of her passion for sports and think that she should come right home after school to do her homework and then help her mother cook dinner for the family, not to go to soccer practice. But they allow her older brother Ramaswami, who is applying to the university next year, to attend the computer science club after school every single day! Mina just wants to play soccer. She carries her soccer ball everywhere, hoping that eventually she can change her parents' minds. She can be a good Hindu daughter and a soccer player, too. Can't she?

SOCIAL IDENTITIES IN MIDDLE CHILDHOOD

During middle childhood, school-agers are just beginning to develop a sense of who they are and what they can do well, as we discussed in chapter 7. This feeling of competence—resulting from what Erikson (1968) referred to as a "sense of industry"—will eventually lead school-age children to explore a "sense of identity" in adolescence (discussed in chapter 12). Even before then, however, school-age children form social identities based on their membership in social groupings, such as same-sex groups (i.e., boys or girls) or racial/ethnic groups (e.g., African American or Latino). The development of *social* identity in middle childhood has been primarily studied by social psychologists and family sociologists. Identity theorists ask questions derived from the ideas of Mead and Cooley regarding the "I" and the "Me," such as:

- What is the relationship between the self as "knower" and the self as "known"?
- Is there such a thing as a "unified" self or is it more appropriate to think of multiple selves, depending on the situation? (Côté & Levine, 2002)

A developmental model of self-understanding is illustrated in Figure 11.1. In middle childhood, according to this model, the development of identity involves defining yourself according to your abilities (the "I") and responding to the approval or disapproval of others (the "Me") (Damon & Hart, 1988). Recall from chapter 7 that

FIGURE 11.1
Developmental Model of Self-Understanding

In this 3-dimensional model, the "I" is represented by the definitional self (front), and the "Me" is the subjective self (side).

Source: From "A Developmental Model of Self-Understanding" (p. 56) by W. Damon and D. Hart in *Self-Understanding in Childhood and Adolescence,* 1988, New York: Cambridge University Press. Copyright © 1988 by Cambridge University Press. Reprinted with the permission of Cambridge University Press.

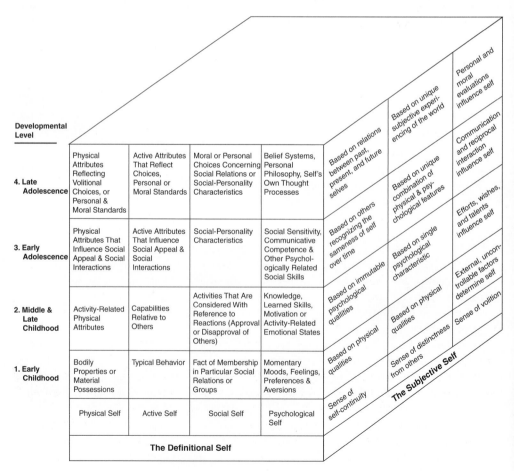

school-agers are able to consider their own values and present a "false self" to others (Harter, 1998). Such a charade implies that they must also have a sense of their "true self." But who is that person? Is it who you are (your actual self) or who you wish to become (your ideal self)? Beginning in middle childhood, preteens construct multiple selves in different contexts, causing internal conflicts between opposing roles. These contradictions probably begin in late middle childhood because cognitive development allows school-age children to detect—but not resolve—conflicting selves (Harter, Bresnick, Bouchey, & Whitesell, 1997; Harter, Waters, & Whitesell, 1998).

> *Let's think about Mina. Is her true self a dutiful daughter or the soccer player she dreams of becoming? Does it matter how her family perceives her?*

In middle childhood and early adolescence, as school-age children are sorting out "who they are" while at the same time imagining "who they want to become," they often construct *personal fables* and *imaginary audiences* (Elkind, 1967, 1985; see also Alberts, Elkind, & Ginsberg, 2007). Developmental psychologists generally support the idea that during middle childhood and early adolescence, school-age children may use this type of thinking to try on new social and gender roles.

An **imaginary audience** represents children's presumption that everyone is looking at and judging them, when in fact they are not. This construct may help explain the extreme self-consciousness that many early adolescents experience regarding their appearance, behavior, personality characteristics, and abilities (Muuss, 1982). It may also explain the embarrassment that they experience when something trivial happens to them in public (e.g., tripping over the curb).

> *Mina, for example, is fearful that everyone she meets can tell that she is wearing her soccer uniform underneath her sari!*

Personal fables are created when individuals become preoccupied with their own thoughts, view their thoughts and themselves as unique, and therefore see themselves as invulnerable to that which happens to others. It is an intriguing explanation for why school-age children engage in high-risk behaviors, such as drinking or smoking. Although familiar with the risks, they underestimate the risks *to themselves* or deny the possibility that anything will happen *to them* (Gardner & Herman, 1990; Halpern-Felsher et al., 2001; Moore & Rosenthal, 1991). For example, a recent study examined the perception of invulnerability in fifth, seventh, and ninth graders and its relationship to their alcohol and tobacco use. The results showed that, indeed, all students underestimated the risks of alcohol and tobacco use, supporting the notion of a personal fable (Goldberg, Halpern-Felsher, & Millstein, 2002). Although imaginary audience and personal fable hold an intuitive explanatory appeal, they are not well supported by research (for a review, see Vartanian & Powlishta, 1996). The constructs are difficult to measure and are not consistently related to high-risk behavior (Frankenberger, 2004; Jacobs Quadrel, Fischhoff, & Davis, 1993).

Some critics also have proposed that these constructs are better reflected by developmental changes in children's social perspective-taking skills and interpersonal understanding as outlined by Selman (1980) and presented in chapter 9 (Jahnke & Blanchard-Fields, 1993; Lapsley & Rice, 1988). However, despite an increasing ability to take multiple perspectives, school-age children tend to be preoccupied with their own points of view. This egocentrism has been described as a failure to differentiate between the cognitive concerns of others and those of the self (Elkind, 1967, 1978). Researchers have also suggested that personal fables may play an important role in becoming a separate person, for example, in believing that you are unique within a social group (Goossens, Beyers, Emmen, & van Aken, 2002).

As part of a normative developmental process, personal fables may also protect individuals from undue anxiety about separation and may impart a sense of mastery, coping, and self-worth (Aalsma & Lapsley, 1999; Lapsley, Flannery, Gottschalk, & Raney, 1996). However, scholars also acknowledge that feeling that you are unique (i.e., a personal fable) may be more characteristic of Western cultures, which emphasize individualism, than non-Western cultures, which are more communal (Vartanian, 2000).

> *Mina's personal fable is that no one else is going through what she is experiencing as an aspiring, but misunderstood, soccer player.*

THEORETICAL VIEWPOINTS

Two primary theoretical perspectives inform the study of middle childhood group identities: social identity and gender schema theories. Both of these approaches help to explain how school-age children construct their identities as social group members. According to social identity perspectives, the social context is of primary importance for developing a sense of self that integrates multiple, intersecting identities, such as your gender and ethnicity. Group identities, therefore, are the result of social interactions in various contexts, such as the family or peer group.

From this perspective, individuals construct meanings through interaction with others, called **symbolic interactions.** Symbolic interaction places the origin of identity in a person's enactment of social roles, which always takes place in a social context. Although some symbolic interaction theorists focus more on constructing an identity through social interaction while others focus more on the roles available in society (Côté & Levine, 2002), what all symbolic interactionists share is an emphasis on the importance of the social context in figuring out "who you are."

> *Mina, for example, is trying to figure out who she is in terms of how her family views her, referred to in chapter 7 as her "looking-glass self."*

In this chapter, we have adopted a contextual perspective to examine socially constructed differences in school-age children's social identities, such as gender and race/ethnicity. For example, middle childhood gender exploration might involve experimenting with makeup, dress, or hairstyles, reflecting changing images in popular culture (Blume & Blume, 2003). In this contextual approach to gender, school-age children are thinking, feeling social agents who reflect on the prevailing cultural discourse and on the options available to them (DeReus, Few, & Blume, 2005; see also Ochs, 1993).

> *Mina alters her identity by wearing her soccer shorts and jersey under her sari, which she removes as soon as she is out of her mother's sight.*

Social Identity Theory

Group identities that are collectively based, such as ethnicity, race, class, gender, or sexual orientation, are called **social identities** (e.g., Tajfel, 1981; Turner, 1987). Social-identity theory states that identity develops not only from an individual's sense of belonging to a particular group but also from an affective component in which one's self-esteem is based on positive feelings about one's group (Umaña-Taylor, Yazedjian, & Bámaca-Gomez, 2004). For example, school-age children often derive a sense of belonging and connection from their family identity (e.g., Fuligni et al., 2005). However, if society does not value the group to which one belongs (e.g., ethnic group), the individual will likely experience prejudice or discrimination and may exhibit lowered self-esteem (Phinney, Cantu, & Kurtz, 1997).

Social identity theory (SIT) explains children's intragroup and intergroup attitudes and beliefs, but it is not a developmental theory. Like its predecessor—social learning theory (discussed in chapter 9)—social identity theory describes how group attitudes are formed, regardless of age. "According to SIT, individuals' perceptions of, and attitudes toward, in-group and out-group members ultimately derive from their desire to identify with and belong to groups that are comparatively superior, as a means of enhancing their own self-esteem" (Nesdale & Flesser, 2001, p. 506). An **in-group** is a social group whose members are similar to oneself; **out-group** members, on the other hand, are perceived to be different from oneself. In addition, in-groups are seen as possessing more favorable qualities than out-groups.

Across middle childhood, in addition to understanding group membership, children also become more aware of what is normative and deviant about their in-groups. For example, English children between ages 6 and 11 were asked to imagine English football (soccer) fans talking about the England team playing against Germany for the World Cup. Normative statements were positive remarks about the home team, such as "I think England is the best team" and "Even if we lost the game to Germany, I'd still say that England are the better team." Deviant statements were positive comments about Germany, such as "When Germany plays well, I always stand up and cheer" (Abrams et al., 2003, p. 1844). As expected, children of all ages expressed intergroup bias, preferring England. However, their differential evaluation against in-group deviants (England liking Germany) and in favor of out-group deviants (Germany liking England) strengthened with age. These results suggest that social identity first involves intergroup biases and later, intragroup biases (Abrams et al., 2003).

Stereotyping. Both in-groups and out-groups can be stereotyped. A **stereotype** is a set of beliefs about a person based on the person's group membership rather than personal characteristics (see Jahoda, 2001). For example, a gender stereotype is the belief that all boys are strong and that all girls are weak. Developmental researchers have successfully used social identity theory to describe children's knowledge of others and acquisition of group stereotypes in children as young as 5 years (see Nesdale & Flesser, 2001). In cross-cultural research in 25 countries, the percentage of stereotyped responses related to gender, for example, accelerated during middle childhood from 60% at age 5 to around 70% by age 11 (Best, 2004).

Like research with adults on stereotyping and prejudice, most of these studies utilize experimental methods (for a description of experiments, refer to the Appendix). For example, in a study of children between ages 7 and 11, children in a summer program were randomly assigned to either "red" or "green" groups. Consistent with the theory, both groups showed in-group favoritism after 4 weeks, regardless of age or gender (Bigler, 1995; see also Bigler, Jones, & Lobliner, 1997). In a similar study, 7- and 11-year-old children who had been randomly assigned to groups allocated rewards to their own group more than to the other group (Vaughan, Tajfel, & Williams, 1981).

Awareness of others' endorsement of stereotypes is called **stereotype consciousness.** For example, children as young as 6 years who observed an interracial exchange in which a White person exhibits prejudice toward a Black person could infer the White individual's stereotype of African Americans. The related term **prejudice** refers to negative behaviors enacted toward members of a stereotyped group. Developmental research has revealed that between ages 6 and 10, school-age children's stereotype consciousness increases dramatically, as does their awareness of stereotypes that are widely held in society—especially if they are members of stereotyped groups themselves, such as ethnic minorities (McKown & Weinstein, 2003).

Multiple Identities. A contextual view of identity contrasts with Erikson's emphasis on the continuity of identity over time, even under varying conditions (Côté & Levine, 2002). Contextual researchers are more interested in how people configure an integrated identity when presented with potentially conflicting identifications, such as their gender identity and their cultural values (Schachter, 2004). For example, given the prevalence of gender-linked racial stereotypes, African Americans must understand not just what it means to be Black, but what it means to be an African American male or female (Swanson, Spencer, Dell'Angelo, Harpalani, & Spencer, 2002).

> *Mina, too, is struggling with what it means to be an American girl from a Hindu family who immigrated to the United States from India.*

Feminist theorists have described such situations as the *intersection* of multiple identities (Collins, 1991). **Intersectionality** refers to the ways that social identities (e.g., race, ethnicity, class, gender, sexuality, nationality, ability, and religion) mutually construct one another. The concept of intersectionality requires us to examine how social institutions, patterns of social interactions, and other social practices may influence the choices, opportunities, and identities that individuals and groups make and claim as their own (De Reus, Few, & Blume, 2005). In fact, contemporary scholars often view identity as a series of autobiographical stories that are actively constructed during social interaction (e.g., Gergen, 1991; Ochs, 1993; Thorne, 2004).

Gender Schema Theory

Gender schemas are concepts and beliefs about gender that children actively construct from their interactions with others in the social context—whether family, school, or community. In this sense, a cognitive-constructivist approach to gender is consistent with both feminism and symbolic interactionism, as discussed earlier. According to gender schema theory, once a child has constructed gender cognitions, these beliefs are expected to influence gender understandings of self and others (Liben & Bigler, 2002).

In early childhood, for example, children are able to use gender-related information to infer what toys a child might like; however, they base their predictions solely on the target child's sex. By contrast, in middle childhood, children use information on the target child's *interests* to predict their toy preferences (Martin, 1989). However, when preschool-age and school-age children are asked to predict the likelihood of a target child with a feminine or masculine characteristic having *other* feminine or masculine characteristics, school-agers' stereotyping is *greater* than that of younger children (Martin, Wood, & Little, 1990). In addition, when school-age children hold egalitarian attitudes about gender, they are more likely to perceive gender discrimination (Brown & Bigler, 2004). Taken together, these findings suggest that by middle childhood, gender schemas strongly influence children's understanding of gender.

For example, Mina likes to play soccer and thinks that her mother's disapproval of female sports involvement is old-fashioned.

Although some scholars have hypothesized that gender schemas influence children's own behaviors *first*, from which they derive attitudes about others' gendered behaviors, most researchers have found that gender schemas about *others*—such as parents, siblings, teachers, or peers—strongly influence children's *own* behaviors (Powlishta, 2002; Ruble & Martin, 2002). For instance, parents' gendered perceptions of their children's abilities predict children's confidence and interest in certain activities, such as science, math, music, or sports (Eccles et al., 1993; Eccles, Frome, Yoon, Freedman-Doan, & Jacobs, 2000). For an example of parents' socialization of school-age children's sports participation, see Box 11.1.

 BOX 11.1 Roadmap to Understanding Theory and Research
Gender, Families, and Sports in Middle Childhood

Researcher Jacquelynne Eccles has proposed that parents influence school-age children's athletic competence and beliefs about the value of sports activities (Fredricks et al., 2005). Parents not only serve as managers of children's daily activities but also as interpreters of their children's experiences, for example, by stressing mastery over skills, such as passing a ball, rather than performance goals, such as winning. Parents can:

- Be a role model either as a coach or by participating in sports themselves.
- Interpret their children's experiences and give children supportive messages about their athletic abilities.
- Provide emotional support for children's involvement in sports.
- Provide positive experiences during athletic activities.
- Do sports with their children.
- Provide needed equipment and clothing.
- Arrange for children's participation in sports activities.

Parents' beliefs about their children's abilities also play an important role in determining children's own rating of their athletic abilities. For example, parents' rating of elementary-age children's sports ability helped to explain children's belief in their athletic competence through the 12th grade, regardless of their actual ability (Fredricks & Eccles, 2002).

In both middle childhood and adolescence, however, parents think that their sons have more athletic ability than their daughters. They also believe that sports are more important for girls than boys. These results illustrate the importance of parents' gender-stereotypic beliefs in children's sports participation.

As part of the *Childhood and Beyond Study*, Eccles and her colleagues analyzed data from middle-class children in grades 2 through 6. Mothers and fathers separately reported on their own attitudes and involvement in sports activities and on their beliefs and behaviors related to their children's sports involvement. Children responded to a questionnaire about their time involvement in competitive sports and their self-perceived competence. To control for differences in children's actual athletic ability, children were also administered a motor skills test. The researchers then examined each family's pattern of responses to the socialization items in terms of their promotion of children's sports involvement.

Results indicated that parents of boys were more likely to create contexts that supported their child's athletic motivation and participation than parents of girls. Few parents of girls provided

(continued)

BOX 11.1   Roadmap to Understanding Theory and Research *(Continued)*
Gender, Families, and Sports in Middle Childhood

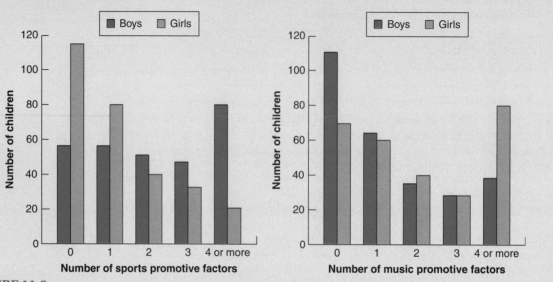

FIGURE 11.2
Parental Socialization of Sports and Music by Child Gender

Parents promote sports with boys more than with girls and music with girls more than with boys.

Source: From "Family Socialization, Gender, and Participation in Sports and Instrumental Music" by Jennifer A. Fredericks, Sandra Simpkins, and Jacquelynne S. Eccles, in C. R. Cooper, C. T. García Coll, W. T. Bartko, H. Davis, & C. Chatman (Eds.), *Developmental Pathways Through Middle Childhood: Rethinking Context and Diversity as Resources* (p. 53), 2005, Mahwah, NJ: Erlbaum. Copyright 2005 by Lawrence Erlbaum Associates, Inc. Reprinted by permission.

support for athletic activities at home. In contrast, parents of boys provided more encouragement, time, and athletic opportunities than parents of girls. Overall, parents thought that boys were better at sports and that sports were more important for boys than girls.

Although the focus of this brief summary is sports, it is interesting to note that Eccles and her colleagues also examined data from these same parents on the promotion of music activities. Just the opposite results were obtained! See Figure 11.2 for a gender comparison of the number of factors promoting sports or music with sons and daughters.

In addition, each of the parenting beliefs and practices—along with the child's gender, age, and aptitude—was examined as predictors of children's self-competence beliefs and participation rates in both sports and instrumental music. The parents' beliefs about their children's abilities and about the value of participating were the strongest predictors

of children's involvement in either sports or music; parents' actual behaviors (encouragement, participation with children, enrolling their child in an activity) were much less important. When the cumulative effect of *both* parental beliefs and behaviors was examined, however, parental socialization had a significant effect on children's beliefs about their competence and their actual involvement in sports or music. These results suggest that a climate of family support is important to children's interests and participation in skill-based activities in middle childhood.

Source: Based on "Family Socialization, Gender, and Participation in Sports and Instrumental Music," by J. A. Fredricks, S. Simpkins, and J. S. Eccles, in C. R. Cooper, C. T. García Coll, W. T. Bartko, H. Davis, & C. Chatman (Eds.), *Developmental Pathways Through Middle Childhood: Rethinking Context and Diversity as Resources* (pp. 41–62), 2005, Mahwah, NJ: Erlbaum. Copyright 2005 by Lawrence Erlbaum Associates, Inc.

GENDER DEVELOPMENT IN MIDDLE CHILDHOOD

Socialization theories of gender development hypothesize that others—including parents and peers—regulate social interactions by endorsing rules for gender-appropriate activities, including the separateness of boys' and girls' play activities during the school years. From a developmental-contextual perspective, however, children actively participate in constructing their own gendered identities (Cahill, 1986; for a review, see Coltrane, 1997).

Developmental researchers have documented the growth of gender schemas, gender-role attitudes, and gendered behaviors during the early and middle childhood periods. For example, research on gender development has documented that, by early childhood, children are able to enact behaviors that conform to their gender. By school age, most children show a range of behaviors from stereotypically male to stereotypically female (see Tolman, Spencer, Rosen-Reynoso, & Porche, 2003). Gender differences can be observed in virtually all cultures, although marked variation exists with respect to how much and how often they are evident (Liben & Bigler, 2002).

Gender Differentiation

Research on **gender differentiation,** or how children develop an understanding of gender differences, examines the emergence of attitudes (e.g., what people should be like) and behaviors (e.g., what people should do) (for a review, see Liben & Bigler, 2002). In general, middle childhood gender differentiation is seen as the degree to which school-age children follow their cultures' prescriptions for gender-stereotyped attitudes and behaviors, including identifying with their own sex. **Gender identity** refers to one's biological sex as well as to one's identification with **gender roles,** a set of attitudes and behaviors associated with the cultural conventions of being male or female (Bailey, 1996; Green, 1985; O'Brien, 1992). Gender identity is composed of five major components (Egan & Perry, 2001):

1. *Membership knowledge.* Knowledge of membership in a gender category (e.g., "I am a girl")
2. *Gender typicality.* The degree to which one feels like a typical member of a gender category (e.g., "I'm just like the other girls")
3. *Gender contentedness.* How happy one is with one's gender assignment (e.g., "I like being a girl")
4. *Pressure for gender conformity.* The degree to which one feels pressure from parents, peers, and oneself for conformity to gender stereotypes (e.g., "I ought to act like a girl")
5. *Intergroup bias.* The extent to which one believes one's sex is superior to the other (e.g., "Girls are better than boys") (adapted from Carver, Yunger, & Perry, 2003)

In middle childhood, most children recognize that social expectations for the activities of boys and girls are stereotyped by sex (e.g., boys are football players, girls are cheerleaders). In addition, most school-age children conform to gender rules for self-presentation (e.g., dress, hairstyle) that are strictly enforced by peer culture (Martin, Ruble, & Szkrybalo, 2002; Thorne, 1993). By adolescence, however, most children will recognize that gender-role stereotypes are social conventions. Nevertheless, most school-agers still choose the "safe" alternative of behaving in

---

TABLE 11.1   Gender-Role Acquisition

The understanding of gender roles is a gradual process that continues through adolescence.

Age Period	Gender-Role Acquisition process
0–3 years	Acquisition of culturally defined gender categories
3–7 years	Stereotyped attitudes about gender, encompassing activities, clothing, social roles, personal attributes; male and female seen as opposites
7–12 years	Flexibility of gender concepts arising from separation of external characteristics and core identity
12–15 years	Reemergence of gender-role salience, especially in cross-sex relationships
15–18 years	Establishment of sexual preference; selection of adult social roles, initial career choices; for some, emergence of individual identity incorporating masculine and feminine characteristics

Source: From "Gender Identity and Sex Roles" by M. O'Brien, in V. Van Hasselt & M. Hersen (Eds.), *Handbook of Social Development: A Lifespan Perspective* (p. 332), 1992, New York: Plenum. Copyright © 1992 by Plenum Press. Reprinted by permission. With kind permission from Springer Science and Business Media.

---

sex-stereotypic ways (O'Brien, 1992). Table 11.1 provides examples of the typical developmental sequence of gender-role acquisition.

Gender-Role Orientation. Gender-role behaviors that are more or less stereotypic are called **sex-typed** (e.g., *masculine, feminine*) or **nonsex-typed** (e.g., *androgynous, undifferentiated*) (Bem, 1974, 1981; see also Spence & Helmreich, 1980):

- ***Masculine.*** Behaviors that are male-stereotypic (e.g., competitive, aggressive; interested in instrumental, or goal-oriented, activities)
- ***Feminine.*** Behaviors that are female-stereotypic (e.g., nurturing, expressive, interested in relationships)
- ***Androgynous.*** Behaviors that combine male and female characteristics (e.g., instrumental *and* expressive)
- ***Undifferentiated.*** Behaviors that are not typical of either sex-role stereotype (e.g., acts differently in varying contexts)

Let's reflect again on the case study. Exploring her desire to play soccer, Mina must consider her abiding interest in sports in interaction with her gender and ethnic identities. She is pretty sure that she knows what is coming: Her mother will say that girls shouldn't act like boys and that she should behave like a good Hindu daughter!

But how accurate are stereotypes about sex differences between males and females? Some developmental theorists have argued that gendered behaviors will intensify in late middle childhood as a result of the onset of puberty, called the **gender intensification hypothesis** (Hill & Lynch, 1983). As early adolescents begin to adopt male or female roles in anticipation of dating and other adult behaviors, they seem to act in more sex-stereotyped ways. For example, if they associate with older teens during adolescence, early maturing adolescents are more likely to become wives and mothers than attend college (Stattin & Magnusson, 1990).

Research in support of gender intensification is mixed. One study found that sex differences in masculinity, but not femininity, increased from ages 11 to 13 years (Galambos, Almeida, & Petersen, 1990). **Masculinity ideology** is the belief that men and boys ought to adhere to culturally defined standards for male behavior. The girls may not have shown as dramatic a rise in femininity as boys did in masculinity because masculinity is more highly valued in American society. The form of masculinity that is culturally dominant in a given setting is called **hegemonic masculinity.** Furthermore, hegemonic masculinity can be highly visible in school-age peer groups, where a small number of highly influential boys are admired by many others (Connell, 1996; Renold, 2007). Box 11.2 provides a compelling case for rethinking cultural expectations for boys' masculinity.

Recently, scholars have criticized gender-role orientations as outdated because they are based on dichotomous sex categories (i.e., male is the opposite of female) that no longer reflect 21st-century constructions of gender as fluid and context dependent (Bailey, 1996; Bem, 1993; Hegarty, 2002). Because of their cognitive constructions of gender (i.e., gender schemas), children may either act in sex-typed ways or may transcend stereotypic gender roles (Eccles, 1987).

According to gender-schema theory, gender-role transcendence involves reducing dependence on gender-based stereotypes as a basis for determining one's own actions and beliefs and for judging the behavior of others (O'Brien, 1992). For example, gender development researchers have studied the relationship between school-age children's attitudes about others and their self-characterizations in middle childhood. They found that girls who held fewer stereotypes of masculine activities for others showed greater acceptance of masculine attitudes in themselves. Boys, on the other hand, who endorsed more feminine traits in themselves in grade 6 held increasingly egalitarian gender attitudes by grade 7 (Liben & Bigler, 2002). From this perspective, an individual's ability to move past traditional concepts of male and female represents a processing of gender schemas that incorporates aspects of both masculine and feminine into an integrated identity (O'Brien, 1992).

Let's examine Mina's social construction of gender in the chapter case. She sees her conservative Indian family's gender traditionality as coming up against contemporary American norms of gender egalitarianism.

Stages of Gender Development. Based on gender-schema theory, developmental psychologists proposed a sequence of gender-role stages from undifferentiated gender identity in infancy to the transcending of gender roles in adolescence, as shown in Table 11.2 (Eccles & Bryan, 1994; Rebecca, Hefner, & Oleshansky, 1976). In this developmental sequence, early childhood understandings of gender are both descriptive (i.e., "she's a girl") and prescriptive (i.e., "only girls play with dolls"). By school age, children are cognitively able to separate external manifestations (e.g., appearance) from internal stable constructs like gender identity (e.g., boys can do many things girls do without altering their sex) (Eccles & Bryan, 1994).

In late middle childhood and early adolescence (roughly ages 10 to 15), however, because of the appearance of the secondary sex characteristics associated with puberty and the increasing social pressure to conform to traditional gender-role expectations, such as dating, many teens may "regress" to gender-role stereotypes (Eccles & Bryan, 1994). This process is consistent with the gender intensification hypothesis described earlier. In seventh grade, for example, physically mature boys spent more

BOX 11.2   Roadmap to Successful Practice
Hearing and Healing the Pain of "Real Boys"

Clinical psychologist William Pollack (2006) describes the current socialization and treatment of boys in American society as the "boy code." Through warnings like "Stand on your own two feet," "Don't be a wimp," and "Be a man," boys are subject to what Pollack calls **gender straightjacketing,** or overly rigid gender guidelines. In this instance of masculinity ideology, boys have been cut off from emotionality and attachment to others.

In his clinical practice at the Centers for Men and Young Men, Pollack has found that socialization for masculinity has led to increased school failure, depression and suicide, isolation, and violence. In addition, the suffering of boys is often difficult to detect because of the pressure that society places on boys to "tough it out" and hide their emotions at all costs—especially by middle childhood. Both parents and clinicians, according to Pollack, are often fooled by boys' external demeanor of rambunctiousness when they are really doing poorly at school, failing at friendships, or feeling depressed.

In the Listening to Boys' Voices project, an empirical study at the Harvard Medical School, and his clinical practice, Pollack and his colleagues recorded the sentiments of healthy middle-class adolescent boys "in their own voices." They hypothesized that boys would reveal unconscious feelings of loneliness and separation, high outward self-esteem but inner insecurity, ambivalence about "becoming a man," and resistance to society's rules about male behavior and masculinity. By interviewing adolescent boys individually rather than in groups to reduce peer pressure, the researchers asked about

- Their emotional connections to their families
- How expressing their emotions affects their relationships
- Advice they would give to younger boys about their identities
- Handling feelings such as anger, sadness, and vulnerability
- The role of sports, mentors, and heroes in their lives

Overall, the study hypotheses were supported. The findings revealed that, "underneath the mask of masculinity—underneath the bragging, braggadocio, shame hardening, and puffed-up self-confidence—were *relational* boys, boys who worried a lot about the quality of their relationships with friends and families and who were eminently sensitive to the emotional needs of others" (Pollack, 2006, p. 194).

Although these interviews were conducted with adolescents, Pollack's study holds several important implications for parents and practitioners raising and working with school-age children:

1. As boys get older, they increasingly feel the pressure to be perceived as strong, confident, and masculine. Parents and practitioners need to give boys safe spaces to talk privately about their worries and fears. Let boys know that no feelings are forbidden to them.

2. Boys often harden themselves against the expression of feelings, hiding their emotions from others. Be empathic with boys who are "afraid of being afraid" and remain calm and supportive even when boys attempt to push you away.

3. Because boys may have a limited or stereotyped view of masculinity, create a broader sense of what it means to become a man or, for that matter, become a person. Treat them with the care and affection you would have them show to others.

Using a hegemonic metaphor, Pollack—ironically—calls for a "war" *for* boys, concluding that that contemporary society needs to engage in a rethinking of boyhood in the midst of changing attitudes about masculinity.

Source: Based on "The 'War' *For* Boys: Hearing 'Real Boys" Voices, Hearing Their Pain," by W. S. Pollack, 2006, in *Professional Psychology: Research and Practice, 37*(2), 190–195. Copyright © 2006 by the American Psychological Association.

TABLE 11.2 Stages of Gender-Role Identity

Adolescent gender roles are usually intensely stereotypical, but this rigidity often declines with identity formation during middle adolescence.

Stage	Age Period	Description
Stage I	0–2 years	UNDIFFERENTIATED GENDER ROLES
		The child is unaware of gender as a social category and has not yet learned gender-role stereotypic beliefs.
Stage II	2–7 years	HYPER-GENDER-ROLE DIFFERENTIATION
		Gender becomes a very important and salient social category. Children actively seek to learn their culture's gender-role system, and, in so doing, generate their own gender-role stereotypes that are consistent with the commonly held stereotypes in their culture.
Stage III	7–11 years	GENDER-ROLE DIFFERENTIATION
		Cognitively, the emergence of conventional moral thought and a growing awareness of social roles may lead the child to maintain a belief in the prescriptive nature of stereotypes, particularly if this view is reinforced by the social actors in a child's life.
Stage IV	12–16 years	TRANSITION PHASE 1
		Despite the cognitive capacity to transcend the prescriptive function of stereotypes, sociocultural forces may produce a rigidification of gender-role schema and a reemergence of confusion between gender identity and gender-role identity.
		TRANSITION PHASE 2
		If the sociocultural milieu provides the necessary stimuli and adolescents have not committed to traditional gender roles, they may transcend the gender role identity as one element of the resolution of their identity crisis.
Stage V	16–22 years	IDENTITY AND GENDER-ROLE TRANSCENDENCE
		The ambivalent crises of Stage IV have been resolved into an integration of masculinity and femininity that transcends gender roles.

Source: Based on "Adolescence: Critical Crossroad in the Path of Gender-Role Development" by J. Eccles & J. Bryan, in M. R. Stevenson (Ed.), *Gender Roles Through the Lifespan: A Multidisciplinary Perspective* (pp. 132–134), 1994, Muncie, IN: Ball State University Press, 1994. Copyright 1994 by Ball State University Press.

time playing sports, whereas physically mature girls spent less time on sports. More mature seventh graders of both sexes, however, spent more time socializing with the opposite sex than did their less mature peers (Eccles & Bryan, 1994).

In a more recent study, sixth graders were asked to keep monthly after-school activity diaries during their first two years of middle school. When the diary entries were later coded for gender stereotypicality, researchers found that although both boys and girls increased in the flexibility of their gender-role attitudes from sixth to seventh grade, their self-perceptions and behavior did not change significantly (Bartini, 2006). The legacy of same-sex peer groups in middle childhood, when boys and girls acquire different experiences, may foster potential conflicts for heterosexual dating relationships later in adolescence (Leaper, 1994; Leaper & Anderson, 1997).

Growth toward gender-role transcendence means reducing the salience of biological sex as a defining property of one's identity (Eccles & Bryan, 1994). For example, school-age children exposed to an egalitarian child-rearing environment in which men and women, and boys and girls, are treated equally are more likely to transcend traditional gender roles (Risman, 1998; Risman & Johnson-Sumerford, 1998; Risman & Myers, 1997; see also Weisner & Wilson-Mitchell, 1990).

Gender Nonconformity. When individuals transgress gender categories, they are referred to as **gender nonconforming.** Generally, cross-gender behavior receives greater disapproval when done by boys than girls (Ruble & Martin, 1998). Girls are not often considered masculine if they play competitive sports, but boys may be seen as effeminate if they pursue creative arts or literature (Owens, 1998; Savin-Williams, 1996). For example, recalling his childhood, a 19-year-old gay youth stated that, as far back as he could remember, he was always teased about not being very masculine and was called a "sissy" and a "fairy" (Savin-Williams, 1996). According to social-identity theory, males are the high-status group. Therefore, boys tend to emphasize sex-stereotypic behaviors more than girls in order to maintain their social advantage. In middle childhood, feeling like a "typical" boy or girl is also positively related to self-esteem, whereas pressure to conform to gender stereotypes is negatively related (Carver et al., 2003; Egan & Perry, 2001).

When one's gender identity differs from one's biological or genetic sex, the descriptive term is **transgender** (i.e., feeling, looking, or acting like the other sex). Although many school-agers try to "fit in" by wearing gender-neutral or gender-typical clothing, some adolescents may start high school as clearly transgendered, and their families may have made an arrangement with the school for them to be registered in the "new" sex and adopt an opposite-sex name (Cohen-Kettenis & Pflafflin, 2003). Some may eventually fall in love and have relationships with same-sex peers. However, *transgender* refers only to gender identity, not to sexuality. **Sexual identity** is "an organized set of self-perceptions and attached feelings that an individual holds about self with regard to some social category [such as gay or straight]" (Cass, 1984, p. 110).

> *Gender nonconformity could be used to describe Mina's early development. As a child, she avoided playing inside with the other girls in the neighborhood. Her mother always tried to get Mina interested in sewing or cooking, but she—not her brother Ram—was always the athlete in the family.*

Sexual orientation, on the other hand, is defined as "a consistent pattern of sexual arousal toward persons of the same gender encompassing fantasy, conscious attractions, emotional and romantic feelings, and sexual behaviors" (Remafedi, 1987, p. 331). Can we predict the sexual orientation of children with atypical *gender* identities? Studies of very feminine boys suggest that most will become gay or bisexual. Studies of masculine girls suggest that they have a higher-than-average chance of becoming lesbians, although most will be heterosexual (Bailey, 1996). For example, fourth- to eighth-grade boys and girls who viewed themselves as gender nonconforming also questioned their heterosexuality (Carver et al., 2003; Carver et al., 2004; Egan & Perry, 2001). In addition, an extensive review of studies of gender-atypical play in childhood revealed that, as adults, both homosexual men and women recall substantially more cross-sex-typed play in childhood than do heterosexuals, although effects were strongest for gay men (Bailey & Zucker, 1995).

STOP What were your favorite activities in childhood and adolescence? Were they gendered?

Gender Segregation

Gender researchers frequently study the degree of *physical* separation between boys and girls in middle childhood, called **gender segregation** (Leaper, 1994). Recall from chapter 10 that in middle childhood children's social interaction is usually characterized by activities with same-sex, same-age peers. For example, the play of boys is usually organized into larger, more hierarchical groups while girls' play is usually more intimate and egalitarian. As discussed in chapter 3, boys also engage in more rough-and-tumble play than girls (Pellegrini & Smith, 1998). As a result, most social groups on school playgrounds—as well as in classroom work groups selected by children—are typically segregated by gender, with about 80% same-sex and only about 20% mixed-sex. In addition, one "token" girl accounted for the gender integration in over half of the mixed-sex groupings (for a review, see Thorne, 1993).

Borderwork. Occasionally, school-age children join mixed-sex, cross-age, or socially integrated play groups, effectively crossing boundaries or "borders," referred to as **borderwork** by ethnographers and anthropologists (Barth, 1993; Thorne, 1993, 2005). In border-crossing situations, gender is no longer viewed as the salient category, and boys and girls interact together on an equal basis. Borderwork usually involves play, as in organized games pitting the girls versus the boys or spontaneous

Children usually form same-sex play groups during middle childhood.

Elizabeth Crews/Elizabeth Crews Photography

episodes of boys chasing girls. Moving from same-sex to cross-sex play, however, sometimes *activates* gender boundaries by making them more visible. For example, gender borders—when evoked—may result in play characterized by more intense emotions, a stylized sense of performance, a mixture of play and aggression, and increasingly sexual overtones, as seen in the example in Box 11.3. In addition, as early adolescents begin to be perceived by their peers as potential dating partners, they may be subject to increased heterosexual teasing, which also pushes the sexes further apart (Thorne, 1993).

> *Usually, Mina is the only South Asian girl on the soccer field. She gets plenty of teasing, too, from her Indian friends!*

Nevertheless, when school-age children successfully cross into groups and activities of the "other" sex they challenge the dichotomous structure of male/female gender relations, often referred to as the **gender binary.** If a child were accepted on the majority's terms, such as a girl playing with the boys "as if one of them"—or vice

---

BOX 11.3   Roadmap to Understanding Theory and Research
Borderwork in Middle Childhood Play

On a paved area of the Oceanside playground a game of team handball took shape. . . . Kevin arrived with the ball, and, seeing potential action, Tony walked over with interest on his face. Rita and Neera already stood on the other side of the yellow painted line that designated the center of a playing court. Neera called out, "Okay, me and Rita against you two," as Kevin and Tony moved into position. The game began in earnest with serves and returns punctuated by game-related talk—challenges between the opposing teams ("You're out!" "No, exactly on the line") and supportive comments between team members ("Sorry, Kevin," Tony said, when he missed a shot; "That's okay," Kevin replied). The game proceeded for about five minutes, and then the ball went out of bounds. Neera ran after it, and Tony ran after her, as if to begin a chase. As he ran, Rita shouted with annoyance, "C'mon, let's play." Tony and Neera returned to their positions, and the game continued.

Then Tony slammed the ball, hard, at Rita's feet. She became angry at the shift from the ongoing, more cooperative mode of play . . . calling Sheila to join their side. The game continued in a serious vein until John ran over and joined Kevin and Tony, who cheered; then Bill arrived, and there was more cheering. Kevin called out, "C'mon, Ben," to draw

in another passing boy; then Kevin added the numbers up on each side, looked across the yellow line, and triumphantly announced, "We got five and you got three." The game continued, more noisy than before, with the boys yelling "wee, haw" each time they made a shot. The girls—and that's how they now seemed, since the sides were increasingly defined in terms of gender—called out "Bratty boys! Sissy boys!" When the ball flew out of bounds, the game dissolved, as Tony and Kevin began to chase after Sheila. Annoyed by all these changes, Rita had already stomped off.

In this sequence, an earnest game with no commentary on the fact that boys and girls happened to be on different sides gradually transformed into a charged sense of girls-against-the-boys/boys-against-the-girls. . . . The frame of a team handball game was altered and eventually overwhelmed when the kids began to evoke gender boundaries.

Source: From "Creating a Sense of Opposite Sides," by B. Thorne, in *Gender Play: Girls and Boys in School* (pp. 65–66), 1994, New Brunswick, NJ: Rutgers University Press. Copyright © 1994 by Barrie Thorne. Reprinted by permission of the author.

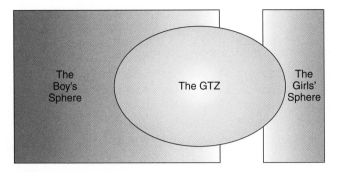

FIGURE 11.3

Gender Boundaries in Middle Childhood

The gender transgression zone and its boundaries.

Source: From "Playing in the Gender Transgression Zone: Race, Class, and Hegemonic Masculinity in Middle Childhood" (p. 617) by C. Shawn McGuffey and B. Lindsay Rich, 1999, *Gender & Society, 19,* 608–627. Copyright © 1999 by Sociologists for Women in Society. Reprinted by permission.

versa—gender binaries would be weakened. By fourth grade, however, most sports are seen as masculine, and many artistic activities are seen as feminine, for example. Furthermore, school-age children's beliefs about masculinity and femininity effectively "police" gender transgressions (McGuffey & Rich, 1999; Thorne, 1993).

School-age children's transgressions of gender boundaries were the subject of a participant observation at a summer camp for children between 5 and 12 years of age. Researchers found that high-status boys (older, athletic, leaders)—irrespective of race or class—were the enforcers of gender boundaries by deciding what behaviors were accepted and valued, reflecting hegemonic masculinity (described earlier). In addition, boys discouraged playing in what the researchers referred to as the "gender transgression zone" (GTZ) more often than girls, suggesting that boys' enforcement of the GTZ maintained their preferred status in the gender hierarchy (McGuffey & Rich, 1999). Refer to Figure 11.3 for a diagram of the gender transgression zone. Notice also that the boys' territory is larger than the girls' territory, as is typical of spatial differences in middle childhood play.

Play and Gender.   In an extensive ethnography of children's play on elementary-school playgrounds, age interacted with gender in interesting ways (see Thorne, 1993, 1997b). In middle childhood, when gender segregation peaks, boys and girls were likely to also self-segregate into same-age than into mixed-age groups. These findings suggest that when same-sex children are roughly the same age, they may be more likely to share interests and skills, and therefore search out each others' similarities (Thorne, 1993).

In addition to age, other contextual factors also influence the gender-segregated play of school-age children. Gender segregation is more likely to occur (adapted from Thorne, 1993):

- *In crowded settings* (e.g., school playgrounds or lunchrooms)
- *During publicly witnessed situations* (e.g., choosing teams or classroom work groups)
- *When few or no adults are present* (e.g., riding the school bus or walking home)

Guideposts for Working with School-Age Children

- Promote cooperative play between boys and girls using criteria other than gender.
- Affirm and reinforce the values of all children, regardless of social categories, by using groupings such as "our class" or "our family."
- Whenever possible, organize children into small, heterogeneous work groups and encourage cross-sex activities.

- Facilitate school-age children's access to all activities, for example, arts activities for boys, sports activities for girls.
- Actively challenge stereotyping and social exclusion on the basis of age, gender, racial/ethnic group, or social class. (adapted from Thorne, 1993)

However, gender is not the only social identity category to separate school-age children. Other social identity categories are also used by children to separate themselves into social groupings by similarity, such as grade level, language spoken, racial/ethnic group, and social class (Thorne, 1993).

Gender Appearance

In determining the sex of each person we encounter and in presenting ourselves to others, we rely extensively on displays of gender (Lucal, 1999). A **gender display** refers to our physical enactment of gender—including our bodies, hairstyles, clothing, jewelry, and cosmetics—as well as our repeated performances of gender in social interaction with others (Goffman, 1979). Gender displays are also enacted in visual media, such as video and film, and in print media, such as books and magazines. Gender images pervade the media and popular culture, especially in advertising campaigns for preteen fashion, music, and movies in which the pubescent body is sexualized (Durham, 1998).

In middle childhood, children who are heavy viewers of television (25 hours or more per week) score higher on measures of sex-stereotyping than lighter viewers (10 hours or less per week). In addition, a meta-analysis of television viewing concluded that watching sex-stereotyped TV programs is related to greater acceptance of gender stereotypes and sex-stereotyping of household chores. On the other hand, counter-stereotypical programming can undermine sex-typing. For example, school-age children who were exposed to the nonsexist program *Freestyle* in grades 4 to 6 were more accepting of diverse gender roles (for a review, see Huesmann & Taylor, 2006).

By adolescence, media exposure has been estimated at 40 to 45 hours per week (compared to about 35 to 50 hours of school and 55 to 75 hours of sleep) (Turner, 2003). Through magazines, television, movies, the Internet, and music, girls—in particular—in most industrialized countries are encouraged to see themselves as sexualized (Durham, 1998; Jones, Vigfusdottir, & Lee, 2004; L'Engle, Brown, & Kenneavey, 2006; Strouse, Goodwin, & Roscoe, 1994; Ward, 2003). For example, in a content analysis of popular teen magazines read by many late-elementary and middle-school students, several areas of cultural influence were apparent (Durham, 2003):

- *Bodies and appearance.* Cosmetics and grooming, diet and weight, clothing and fashion
- *Gendered sexuality.* Feminine ideal of beauty, looking "sexy" and attractive to boys

- *Love and romance.* Dating and boyfriends, family and relationship advice, and weddings

Such content raises concern about girls' social constructions of their sexuality through media images (Chapin, 2000; Durham, 2003; Fingerson, 1999; Huesmann & Taylor, 2006; Hyde & Jaffee, 2000; Ward, 2003; Ward, Hansbrough, & Walker, 2005).

Gendered Bodies. The ways in which cultural images are incorporated into our body image is called **embodiment.** Recall from chapter 3 that girls are more likely to think that they are overweight even when they are average or underweight. On the other hand, boys are as likely to think they are underweight as overweight. Most girls want to be thinner, while most boys want to be more muscular, taller, and heavier. In addition, for third- and sixth-grade girls, body satisfaction is related to positive self-concept. Criticism by their peers, however, has been associated with negative attitudes about their bodies in sixth-grade girls and boys (Guiney & Furlong, 2000). Taken together, these findings demonstrate that the cultural construction of bodies may be problematic for *both* girls and boys as they approach puberty.

Developmental scholars have recently examined three types of influences as risk or protective factors of body image in adolescence (Barker & Galambos, 2003):

- *Physical factors.* Pubertal status, body weight, and weight management behaviors (e.g., dieting and exercise)
- *Contextual factors.* Teasing about one's appearance by family or peers, and being involved in popular culture (e.g., TV, music, movies, magazines)
- *Resource factors.* Protections from body dissatisfaction (e.g., parental acceptance, sports involvement)

The risk factors of weighing more, dieting more, and being teased predicted girls' dissatisfaction with their bodies compared to boys', for whom the only significant risk factor was teasing. Of the protective factors, parental acceptance was a significant predictor of body satisfaction for girls but not for boys. However, none of the protective resource factors moderated the effects of significant risk factors for either sex, such as teasing or media influences (Barker & Galambos, 2003).

Gendered Sexuality. In middle childhood, early-maturing girls in the United States report more interest than late-maturing girls in sexual content in movies, television, magazines, and music, regardless of age or race. They are also more likely to listen to music, see R-rated movies, and read magazines with sexual content. Children in late middle childhood also interpret the messages they see in the media as approving of teens having sexual intercourse. As a result of these findings, researchers have suggested that the mass media may be serving as a kind of sexual "super peer" that provides girls with sexual content and information (Brown, Halpern & L'Engle, 2005). During a five-year period, for instance, more than 1,300 middle childhood girls between the ages of 8 and 13 reported having sexual conversations in chat rooms throughout the day. In addition, they reported that their parents were unaware of their sexual chatting (Atwood, 2006).

Gendered Romance. In a study exploring school-age children's social discourse, British children responded to the sexualized behaviors they encountered when watching television programs, such as soap operas and dating game shows. Although the younger group (6- to 7-year-olds) were less likely to watch either soaps or

Guideposts for Working with School-Age Children

- Be a model for nonsexist language and teach nonsexist usage in the school curriculum.

- Discourage comments based on physical appearance, such as "She's sexy!" or "He's gorgeous!"

- Help both boys and girls recognize male privilege in school and society by analyzing

institutions in which hegemonic masculinity is common, such as gendered media.

- Ask school-agers to find examples of sexist attitudes in magazines and media as a way to reflect on the origin of such beliefs.

STOP How did magazines, television, books, movies or the Internet influence your response to gender norms in middle childhood?

dating games as preferred viewing, boys also decried any *hint* of romance, such as the relationship between Superman and Lois Lane! On the other hand, program choices of the older group (10- to 11-year-olds) were frequently shows that explored sexual attraction. In addition, the 10- to 11-year-old girls often talked about watching soaps with older sisters or mothers (Kelley, Buckingham, & Davies, 1999).

The social pressure to conform to normative gender roles and to identify with heterosexuality is referred to by sociologists as **heteronormativity** (Oswald, Blume, & Marks, 2005). In fact, feminist theorists usually refer to this compelling cultural force as "compulsory heterosexuality" (e.g., Rich, 1980). From this perspective, the social discourse surrounding sexuality may compel school-age children to enact traditional gender roles (Raymond, 1994).

RACIAL/ETHNIC IDENTITIES IN MIDDLE CHILDHOOD

For most children, race/ethnicity—like gender—is a highly salient feature of their identity. In the 21st century, however, it is becoming increasingly difficult to define what we mean by race or ethnicity. Like other social identities, race/ethnicity defines one's sense of belonging to a *social* group. Today's scientists widely acknowledge that race is not a *biological* category, because across the world's populations there is only a small amount of total human genetic variation (Blume & De Reus, 2007; Cooper, García Coll, Thorne, et al., 2005). Instead, current scholars prefer to identify members of racial/ethnic groups that are defined by a shared culture or national heritage, such African Americans or Polish Americans. In addition, some children are often referred to as **biracial** or **biethnic** because their parents have two differing racial/ethnic backgrounds.

The more inclusive term **multiethnic** represents children whose identity includes two or more of the current U.S. Census Bureau (2000) categories:

- White (non-Latino)
- Latino/Spanish/Hispanic
- Black (not Hispanic or Latino)
- American Indian or Alaska Native
- Asian

For example, respondents to the U.S. Census can now check more than one category, write in their own self-descriptions, and answer an additional question about national origin, allowing people to further identify their cultural heritage (Cooper,

Dominguez, & Rosas, 2005; see also Anderson & Fienberg, 2000 for a history of the Census). Recently, the United States also began allowing immigrants to retain their former citizenship, resulting in many children from transnational families to hold dual citizenship. Many developmental scholars now refer to children with two or more racial/ethnic backgrounds and two or more national citizenships as **third-culture** children (Wardle & Cruz-Janzen, 2004).

STOP If you were responding to the U.S. Census, how would you self-identify?

Deconstructing demographic categories, such as race/ethnicity, has special significance for immigrant or transnational children and families (defined in chapter 8). Developmental scholars studying middle childhood have recently outlined several reasons why racial/ethnic categorization is problematic (adapted from Cooper et al., 2005):

1. Mutually exclusive demographic categories neglect children and families who describe themselves with more than one national, ethnic, or racial identity label.

2. Race/ethnicity is not a fixed and stable characteristic but rather conveys a variety of possible meanings in different settings and at different times, for example, in their home country versus their adopted country.

3. Research that treats demographic categories as causal factors in children's development (i.e., independent variables) omits consideration of contextual influences, such as community economic resources or disparities in school funding.

Using social-identity theory as a framework, scholars studying immigrant school-age children have suggested that developmental researchers and practitioners pay close attention to the processes children use to construct their identities in varied settings, such as schools. For example, educational practices—from teaching English as a second language (ESL) to grouping all English-speaking children together regardless of racial/ethnic backgrounds—have implications for children's self-constructions of their social identities. From this perspective, a concern of researchers is to understand how children "bridge" multiple environments—without fostering stereotypes based on race, ethnicity, gender, social class, and country of origin (see Cooper, 1999; Cooper, Garcia Coll, Bartko et al., 2005). Called the **multiple worlds model,** it describes how students must navigate through many—sometimes diverse—cultural contexts, such as home, school, or neighborhood (Phelan, Davidson, & Yu, 1998). In everyday interactions with family and friends, for instance, children actively construct their racial/ethnic identities (Cooper, Garcia Coll, Thorne et al., 2005).

Racial Identity

Racial identity refers to one's sense of self compared to other perceived racial groups (for a recent review, see Helms, 2003). This definition is based on the assumption that racial categories are socially constructed. For example, people are usually treated as if they belong to only one racial group (e.g., White or Black) even though such racial groupings have no biological basis. Racial categories are often based solely on physical appearance (i.e., skin color) (Helms, 2003). Consistent with social-identity theory, most studies of racial identity describe stages of identification: from low racial or ethnic awareness, often with a preference for the majority culture, to an appreciation and acceptance of one's own racial/ethnic group (Phinney & Rosenthal, 1992; see also Vandiver, Cross, & Worrell, 2002; Wardle & Cruz-Jantzen, 2004).

STOP How did your middle childhood experiences create a sense of racial belonging and ethnic pride?

TABLE 11.3   Stages of Racial Identity

Positive racial identity develops gradually, from little or no identification with your racial-ethnic group to the eventual integration of your culture with your personal identity.

Stage	Description	Example
1. Pre-encounter	Preferring the dominant culture's values to your own culture	Perceiving your physical features as unattractive
2. Encounter	Wanting to identify with your racial-minority group, but not knowing how	Realizing you will never belong to the majority culture
3. Immersion/Emersion	Immersing yourself in your minority culture and rejecting the dominant society	Participating in cultural explorations and discussions of racial issues
4. Internalization/Commitment	Experiencing a sense of fulfillment by integrating your personal and racial identities	Becoming socially active by fighting racial discrimination

Source: Based on "Racial Identity and Racial Socialization as Aspects of Adolescents' Identity Development," by J. E. Helms, in R. M. Lerner, F. Jacobs & D. Wertleib (Eds.), 2003, *Handbook of Applied Developmental Science: Promoting Positive Child, Adolescent, and Family Development Through Research, Policies, and Programs, Vol. 1* (pp. 143–163). Thousand Oaks, CA: Sage.

Four stages in the development of racial identity have been described, as shown in Table 11.3. From the social-identity perspective, racial identity is influenced by direct interactions (e.g., parents, teachers) and indirect influences (e.g., media, peers) in the sociocultural environment, often called *racial socialization*. **Racial/ ethnic socialization** refers to the laws, customs, or traditions that teach individuals to value (or disparage) their own racial/ethnic groups or themselves as group members (Helms, 2003). In a study of African American parents, positive socialization messages were less frequent than were messages promoting mistrust or preparing their 9- to 14-year-olds for bias (Hughes & Chen, 1997). Compared to their peers, African American school-age children have more differentiated ideas about racism and negative evaluations of their own group. However, by age 10, 80% of African American and Latino children and 63% of White and Asian American children are aware of racism (McKown, 2004).

In middle childhood, parents, teachers, and other practitioners increasingly help children cope with racism and discrimination (see Pfeifer, Brown, & Juvonen, 2007, for a recent review). Parental racial socialization, for example, includes messages that communicate to children how they are to perceive and respond to discrimination and prejudice based on race (Johnson, 2005). In a contextual approach to understanding children's racial coping, family factors—such as parental socialization— are as seen as proximal influences, whereas societal factors—such as discrimination— are viewed as distal influences. Furthermore, a contextual model suggests that gender, race/ethnicity, and social class—and the segregation or discrimination that may result from racism or prejudice—influence children's developmental opportunities in either supportive or unsupportive environments, such as schools and neighborhoods (García Coll et al., 1996). Figure 11.4 illustrates how these contexts directly and indirectly influence the creation of adaptive cultures (described in chapter 1) and developmental competencies in children of color.

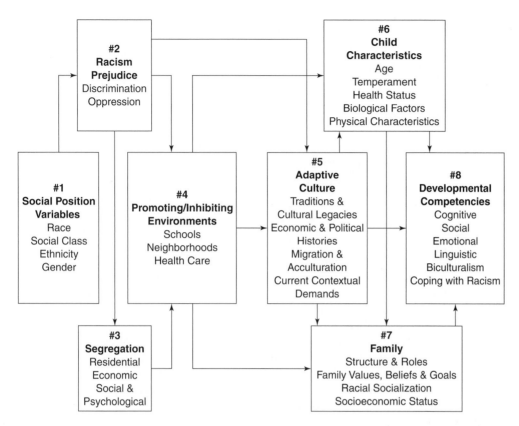

FIGURE 11.4
An Integrative
Model of
Development in
Minority Children

Integrative model for
the study of develop-
ment competencies
in minority children.

Source: From "An Inte-
grative Model for the
Study of Developmental
Competencies in Minor-
ity Children," by C. Gar-
cía Coll et al., 1996, *Child
Development, 67,* 1996.
Copyright © 1996 by the
Society for Research in
Child Development.
Reprinted by permission
of the society.

Using this contextual model to study school-age children's strategies for coping with racial discrimination, researchers created hypothetical conflict stories
based on social identity theory. One story, for example, was about between-group
competition:

> Jacob (Janice) is about your age. (S)he is very smart and his/her classmates really like
> him/her. Jacob (Janice) is the only Black person in his/her classroom; all of the other
> children and the teacher are White. Sometimes Jacob (Janice) raises his/her hand to
> answer the questions the teacher asks. Almost all the time the teacher chooses some-
> one else to answer the question. Jacob (Janice) feels this is unfair because (s)he al-
> most always knows the answer. What should Jacob (Janice) do about this problem?
> (Johnson, 2005, p. 103)

Researchers then classified children's racial-coping strategies in three school settings: a predominantly (75% or more) African American school, a mixed-race school,
and a racially homogeneous school where Black students were a minority (less than
25%). In the mostly African American school, children did not anticipate discrimination (e.g., raising your hand will result in the teacher calling on you). In the mixed-
race school, children used moral reasoning strategies (e.g., asserting your right to fair
treatment). In the racial-minority school, children more often sought support from
adults in authority (e.g., asking parents, other teachers, or principals for help). These
findings suggest that the school context significantly influences how school-age children cope with racism.

Ethnic Identity

A closely related construct, **ethnic identity,** refers to a sense of belonging to an ethnic group, such as Latinos (Phinney & Rosenthal, 1992; Rotheram & Phinney, 1987). Most, but not all, ethnic-identity research has been conducted with members of racial/ethnic minorities. Individuals who belong to racial/ethnic minorities may differ with respect to their

- Self-identification as a group member
- Feelings of commitment to the group
- Positive or negative attitudes toward the group
- Sense of shared values, traditions, and customs (Phinney & Rosenthal, 1992)

During early childhood, children become aware of individual differences in physical appearance, such as skin color, or of linguistic differences, such as speaking a different language. At this age, young children may also seem to stereotype others, partly because they may still need a single label to describe others. In the early years, preoperational thinkers (refer to chapter 5) are unable to engage in class inclusion, for example, to understand what it means to be Black and at the same time African American or Afro-Caribbean in ethnicity (Wardle & Cruz-Jantzen, 2004).

By the beginning of middle childhood (about age 8), school-age children can recognize peers from other racial/ethnic groups based on group membership, not just appearance or behavior. Because school-age children are concrete thinkers, they are now also increasingly able to conserve racial/ethnic categories and other social identities, such as gender. For example, they may describe peers as "White girls" or "Japanese boys." By around the end of middle childhood (about age 12) most children have achieved a sense belonging to their own ethnic group (Wardle & Cruz-Janzen, 2004).

In early adolescence, children begin a developmental sequence of ethnic-identity formation that may last into adulthood in which they may explore their ethnic heritage and resolve what their ethnic identity means to them (Phinney, 1989). Not surprisingly, higher levels of family racial/ethnic socialization have been associated with greater exploration and resolution of teenagers' ethnic identity (Umaña-Taylor, Yazedjian, & Bámaca-Gomez, 2004). A sense of ethnic identity and the ability to be **bicultural** (i.e., navigate between one's ethnic-minority culture and the majority culture) have also been found to be protective factors against such problem behaviors as youth violence, whereas **acculturation,** or assimilating into the majority culture, is a potential risk factor (Soriano, Rivera, Williams, Daley, & Reznik, 2004).

> *What does her Indian heritage mean to Mina? Ethnic socialization is evidenced by her parents' expectations of academic achievement and gender appropriateness. However, at her school or in the wider community context, it appears that Mina does not feel very Hindi.*

In recent investigation of first- and fourth-grade children of Dominican, Portuguese, and Cambodian immigrants, researchers asked children "Are you _____?" in response to a list that included labels for:

- *Gender*
- *Role* (e.g., student)
- *Race* (e.g., Black)

A sense of ethnic identity involves developing a sense of belonging through the sharing of values, traditions, and customs.

David Young-Wolff/PhotoEdit Inc.

- *Nationality* (e.g., Cambodian)
- *Pan-ethnic group* (e.g., Asian)

The most salient label was the one that children mentioned first. The meanings of their identities were then assessed by asking, "Why do you think you are _____ ?" for each label they chose (Cooper et al., 2005; see also García Coll et al., 2005).

On average, children chose seven labels, with even the first-graders choosing one ethnic label and a gender label. The fourth-graders, however, chose more labels than younger children. In addition to gender and ethnicity, 77% of the entire sample chose a label for their family role, 36% chose a racial label, and 26% chose a religious label, leading researchers to conclude that gender, ethnicity, and family were the labels that are most important to school-agers. Across the ethnic groups in the study, most children chose nationality, followed by culture and language labels (e.g., Khmer or Spanish), hyphenated labels (e.g., Portuguese-American), and finally pan-ethnic labels (e.g., Asian or Latino) (Cooper et al., 2005). In addition, fourth-grade children were able to explain the meaning of their identities in complex terms:

> For example, after Carlos, a fourth-grade Dominican boy chose "Boy," "Dominican," "Dominican-American," "Latino," and "White," he explained as follows: "I am a boy, because God made me one; I am Dominican because my parents were born in Dominican Republic [holds dual citizenship]; I am Dominican-American because I was born here; I am Latino because that's what they call people here who speak Spanish, and I am White because my skin is light." (Cooper et al., 2005, p. 192)

Processes children use to construct their identities in varied social contexts, such as with their peers, were evident in the comments of a fifth-grade girl in the same study, whose primary identity label was her religion:

> I am happy to be Muslim. It is a good religion for me. We [her family] pray and we give money to the poor . . . I like that this religion is unique because a lot of people practice it and other people know who you are because only Muslims wear this headpiece . . . When I was in kindergarten, they [other children] tried to tease me and pull my headpiece off. It made me feel very angry and sad because they treated me bad because I am different. I do not think they should try to be so mean because they are different. You should try to be friends . . . to learn about the difference. (Cooper et al., 2005, p. 192)

Racial/Ethnic Stereotyping

Racial/ethnic identities are frequent sources of categorizing, stereotyping, and exclusion on the basis of group membership. Developmental research illustrates why it is important to pay attention to social identities in middle childhood. Researchers have found that when exclusion occurs on the basis of group membership, children are at risk for negative self-esteem, lower academic achievement, and increased bullying, as described in chapter 9.

Furthermore, recent findings also suggest that stereotyping and prejudice is seen as wrong or unfair by a majority of school-age children. In a study combining moral (i.e., fairness) and social-identity (i.e., stereotyping) theories of development, researchers investigated how school-age children evaluate both gender and racial/ethnic exclusion. Children in grades 4, 7, and 10 were asked to evaluate the appropriateness of excluding target children who differed by gender and race/ethnicity from each of three contexts: schools, peer groups, and friendships. The researchers were interested in whether children would use moral reasoning (e.g., "Everyone should be treated the same") or social-identity reasoning (e.g., "Black kids like different music than White kids") to justify exclusions (Killen, Lee-Kim, McGlothlin, & Stangor, 2002).

Overall, exclusion based on gender or race/ethnicity was viewed as wrong by almost 80% of participants. Not surprisingly, older children were more likely to use fairness as a justification than younger children (refer to chapter 9 for a discussion of fairness reasoning). The majority of children also made clear distinctions between contexts. Friendship was often viewed as a personal decision in which it is acceptable to use gender or race as a basis for exclusion, whereas children's reasoning about excluding someone from a peer group (e.g., music club) was more often on the basis of social identity and promoting successful group functioning. In the school context, however, gender and racial/ethnic exclusion was overwhelmingly rejected as wrong by 98% of children! For example, a fourth-grade girl said,

> "It's not okay (for Jerry not to be friends with Damon because he's Black)." *Why not?*
> "That makes me think of history." *Why?*
> "Because in Martin Luther King times, Blacks would have to drink at the Black water fountain and Whites would have to drink at the White water fountain. They go to different schools everyplace. It was unfair. And now that the world has changed, Blacks and Whites can play together. If they become friends they will learn to live with each other." (Killen et al., 2002, p. 89)

Stereotypes about race/ethnicity, nevertheless, still affect children's intergroup relations, as seen in the ethnographic study of children's lunchroom behavior described earlier (Thorne, 2005). Speaking a language other than English set children apart, often marking them as immigrants, despite the fact that in an elementary school lunch group of Chinese girls, four out of five were U.S.-born and bilingual. When asked why they speak Cantonese, one girl replied, "We speak Cantonese when we want to talk about someone, and when it's more personal, and when we don't know some words in English" (p. 194). Interestingly, the group broke up when they entered a middle school known for racial divisions among Blacks, Asians, and Mexicans. All but one girl started affiliating with several Vietnamese girls, stopped speaking Cantonese at school, and started referring to themselves as Asian as well as Chinese. Findings such as these suggest that ethnic labels can be redefined and that school-age children may use multiple identities to avoid fights or intergroup rivalry, resulting in renegotiated identities in school contexts (Cooper et al., 2005; see also Dillon, 2006).

STOP In elementary or middle school, did you work, play, eat, or sit with other children of the same race/ethnicity as you?

Guideposts for Working with School-Age Children

- Ask school-agers to name their racial/ethnic identities, avoiding racial categorizations based on appearance.
- Encourage school-age children to explore their ethnicity through discussions of films, literature, music, poetry, and cultural celebrations.
- Recognize that children's ethnic or racial identities may "feel" stronger or weaker depending on the context (e.g., home or school) and with whom they are interacting (e.g., parents or peers).
- Create a positive school climate for all ethnic-minority groups by avoiding comparisons to the majority culture.
- Because White students also belong to ethnic groups, help them explore their family histories of immigration.

SOCIAL IDENTITIES IN CONTEXT

The term *context* has been used in two ways by identity researchers: "that which surrounds" and "that which weaves together" (Goossens & Phinney, 1996). School-age children are surrounded by others who—like them—belong to social identity groups, such as parents, siblings, teachers, and peers. Furthermore, each person's identity (as mother or father, son or daughter, brother or sister, student or friend) intersects with gender and race/ethnicity, weaving a complex fabric of interconnected identities in the multiple contexts of family, school, and community (see also Shweder et al., 2006).

Family Contexts

As discussed in this chapter, gender theorists have suggested that children in late middle childhood and early adolescence become increasingly stereotypical in their sex-role behavior, called gender intensification. The influence of families on gender intensification in middle childhood was the focus of a longitudinal study of children who were between 9 and 11 years of age initially and then followed for one year (Crouter, Manke, & McHale, 1995). Researchers examined three aspects of children's socialization:

- Participation in "masculine" or "feminine" chores
- Involvement in activities with mothers or fathers
- Monitoring by parents of children's activities, companions, and whereabouts

In addition, the researchers asked whether these influences might have different effects depending, in part, on differing family contexts. Specifically, they examined two characteristics of the family environment:

1. Whether families engaged in a sex-stereotypic division of housework
2. Presence of a younger sibling of the opposite sex from the target child

If gender intensification were present, girls would engage in more traditionally feminine tasks, do more activities with their mothers than their fathers, and receive more parental monitoring than boys. Boys would, of course, demonstrate the opposite pattern, engaging in more traditionally masculine tasks, doing more activities with their fathers than their mothers, and receiving less parental monitoring than girls.

Support for the hypotheses was mixed. There was no difference in the parents' monitoring of either boys or girls. The traditionality of parents' division of household labor, however, was related to increasingly sex-typed behaviors on the part of children, but not to involvement with a same-sex parent. In addition, gender intensification was most pronounced for girls with younger brothers, suggesting that sex-role traditional parents may assign their older daughters more feminine tasks when the family is composed of both boys and girls. Taken together, these findings confirm that the family context is a significant influence on gender attitudes and behavior.

School Contexts

As we discussed in chapter 10, school climate (i.e., the quality of interactions between adults and students in a school community) is a powerful influence on middle childhood (and adolescent) attitudes and behaviors (Crosnoe et al., 2004). For example, middle-school students' perceptions of school climate predicted their self-esteem (e.g., Hoge, Smit, & Hanson, 1990). Perceptions of school climate also explained African American and White early adolescents' psychological adjustment after controlling for their perceptions of family and peers (Eccles et al., 1997). Similarly, support from the school staff contributed to a decrease in African American and White early adolescents' psychological distress, over and above the support of family and friends (DuBois, Feiner, Brand, Adin, & Evans, 1992).

One of the challenges many teachers face in creating a positive classroom climate is that ethnicity often serves as a euphemism for race (Hollins, 1999; Root, 1999). In 2006, American schools are expected to be the most ethnically diverse since waves of European immigrants arrived in the United States in the early 20th century. If trends continue, ethnic-minority students appear likely to outnumber White students within a decade, as they do already in six states: California, Hawaii, Louisiana, Mississippi, New Mexico, and Texas (Dillon, 2006).

Racial/ethnic diversity—while viewed as positive by most school districts—can result in stereotyping and have a negative impact on school climate if

- Schools code racial/ethnic groups in their records.
- Ethnic groups are perceived as homogeneous.
- Appearance, language, dress, food, family lineage, or birthplace are highly visible.
- Teachers use racial/ethnic labels in discussing intergroup conflicts. (Cooper et al., 2005)

Parents, practitioners, and educators, therefore, must continuously engage in a critical self-examination to increase their individual awareness and sensitivity to the experience of others (Blume & De Reus, 2007). Reflecting on one's *own* racism and position of relative privilege is a central component of **reflective practice.** Furthermore, educators recommend that practitioners focus on self-understanding from four different perspectives:

- Examine the meaning of your own childhood, recalling and documenting as many school experiences as possible in relation to your own parenting or teaching philosophy and practice.
- Examine how images of yourself as a parent or teacher are influenced by past experiences and prevailing cultural ideologies.

- Examine how your own racial/ethnic identity and attitudes about others reflect your personal feelings and perceptions.
- Examine how your own background and definition of culture shapes your thoughts and responses to other people, events, and situations. (adapted from Hollins, 1999)

Parents, teachers, and other practitioners who work with school-age children need to evaluate not only their own racial/ethnic biases but also bias in the curriculum (Root, 1999). For example, Box 11.4 describes questions to ask when evaluating gender and racial/ethnic stereotyping in literature for middle childhood.

Community Contexts

An issue that has been largely unexamined in middle childhood research is the effect of being an undocumented immigrant (Cooper, Dominguez, & Rosas, 2005). Millions of undocumented children are currently in the United States (U.S. Immigration and Naturalization Service, 2000). **Undocumented immigrants** have either entered the United States illegally or hold expired temporary visas (also called "green cards"). A recent longitudinal study of undocumented children who eventually obtained a green card found that the process of becoming documented usually takes between 8 and 10 years. If the children of undocumented immigrants were born in the United States, however, those children are U.S. citizens (see Cooper & Villagomez, 2003; Green, 2003).

The institutional responses and opportunity structures available within communities shape the resources available to immigrant children and their families. For example, three types of governmental responses in the receiving country have been identified:

- Legal definitions of who can become a citizen
- Public discourse about immigration
- Migrant-worker public policy initiatives (Landolt & Da, 2005)

Recall also (from chapter 8) that many migrant families maintain enduring ties to their homelands even as they are incorporated into the community in their countries of resettlement. For example, transnational families typically keep in touch and give care over long distances, send children to learn English abroad or back to their home countries to be educated by grandparents, manage multiple residences, and send or receive money between their homeplaces.

Differences in community participation often depend on the contexts of departure and arrival of different immigrant groups. For example, immigrants and refugees coming from rural areas tend to form nonpolitical hometown civic committees in support of the localities left behind. Immigrants from more urban areas more often become involved in the politics and the cultural life of their countries as a whole, especially if political parties, churches, and cultural institutions there seek to maintain an active presence in their communities (Portes, Escobar, & Radford, 2005).

Some scholars assert that the identities of immigrants and children can be conceptualized as social positions that develop from their goal-directed use of community resources. For example, undocumented Mexican immigrants involved with a community organization were found to change from an "illegal" to an "undocumented" identity that functioned to make their presence visible, claim their rights,

BOX 11.4 Roadmap to Successful Practice
Evaluating Children's Books for Stereotypes

To critique the gender or racial/ethnic content in children's books, teachers, parents, or other practitioners can conduct content evaluations of a book's story, language, and pictures:

Story Critique

- Note the race/ethnicity of characters that receive the most focus throughout the book.
- List the major problems and tasks overcome in the book and the gender/race/ethnicity of characters involved.
- To what extent are females or racial/ethnic minorities portrayed as causing problems? Resolving problems?
- What other people appear in the book, how much attention do they receive, and what do they accomplish?
- Which characters generate sympathy/respect?
- Which characters does the reader learn more about?
- Note any gender/racial/ethnic stereotypes.
- Does the story relate to one group or to a multicultural experience? If it relates to one group, does the book imply that it is better/more successful?
- Does the story communicate a need for belonging/loyalty/solidarity?
- As far as you can tell, is the author the same gender or race/ethnicity of the characters in the book? Do you think the author is qualified to write a book from that particular perspective?

Language Critique

- Does the book use nonsexist language to refer to both genders?
- List any stereotypical words used and the gender and race/ethnicities of the characters to whom they are linked.
- What adjectives are used to describe White and non-White racial/ethnic people? Are those words positive or negative?

- Look carefully for words like *progress, successful, civilized* and the gender and race/ethnicity of the people they describe. Are they more often White males?
- Look carefully for words like *ashamed, marginalized, coping* and the gender and race/ethnicity of the people they describe. Are they more often females or racial/ethnic minorities?
- What image is portrayed by the use of dialects, accents, non-English phrases, etc.?

Picture Critique

- Note any racial or ethnic stereotypes.
- Note any multiethnic/multicultural stereotypes.
- Note any gender-role stereotypes.

Analysis of the Critiques

Consider people with differing backgrounds in analyzing the results of this critique, but remember categories can intersect.

1. Determine how much space and attention—both text and pictures—is devoted to each group.
2. Does the book provide roles and characters with whom students can identify and who give the impression that students can aspire to reach their goals?
3. Does the book provide an opportunity for a student who identifies with the characters to have positive and empowering impressions?
4. Does the book provide complex characters who give richness to gender or racial/ethnic diversity?
5. To what extent does the book portray people of different backgrounds experiencing life and solving problems together?

Source: Based on "How to Evaluate a Textbook/Reading Book for P–12 Programs," by F. Wardle and M. I. Cruz-Janzen, in *Meeting the Needs of Multiethnic and Multiracial Children in Schools* (pp. 156–160), 2004, Boston: Allyn and Bacon. Copyright 2004 by Pearson Education, Inc.

and counter societal claims about their legitimacy and citizenship entitlement. In fact, children living in immigrant families have described their experiences of illegality as a form of community violence (Solis, 2002). Clearly, a contextual approach that examines how immigration assistance to children is enacted by adults in schools, community organizations, and government agencies can inform our understanding of **multicultural** societies and the meanings of racial/ethnic identities (Cooper et al., 2005).

STOP Who were the most recent immigrants in the community where you lived as a school-ager?

CHAPTER REVIEW

Social Identity

- School-age children integrate their self-understandings and others' perceptions into a sense of self.
- Social identities are based on one's membership in social groups, such as gender or racial/ethnic groups.
- Early adolescents may construct personal fables to imagine how they want to be seen and imaginary audiences to imagine how others see them.

Theoretical Viewpoints

- According to social identity theory, children's group identities are based on their positive or negative feelings about their group membership(s).
- According to symbolic interactionists, children construct personal meaning and identity through their interactions with others.
- According to gender schema theory, children's gender beliefs are reflected in the understandings of self and others and influence children's behavior.

Gender Development

- Gender identity refers to your biological sex as well as to your identification with gender roles.
- Gender roles are a set of attitudes and behaviors associated with the cultural conventions of being male or female. Gender-role orientation can be feminine, masculine, androgynous, or undifferentiated.
- Developmental psychologists have proposed a sequence of gender-role stages moving from undiffer-
- entiated gender identity in infancy to gender identity that transcends gender roles in adolescence.
- Media images influence how school-age children see themselves, especially in the areas of gender and sexuality.
- Embodiment refers to the ways in which cultural images are incorporated into body image, or how individuals think or feel about their bodies.

Racial/Ethnic Identities

- Ethnic-minority adolescents typically navigate diverse cultures, such as family, peer, and school contexts, called "multiple worlds."
- Racial identity refers to one's sense of self compared to other perceived racial groups.
- Ethnic identity refers to a sense of belonging to your ethnic group.
- School-age children may engage in stereotyping by gender, race/ethnicity, and group membership.
- Practitioners need to examine their own gender and racial/ethnic stereotypes and bias.

Social Identities in Context

- The family context influences gender intensification in early adolescence, especially in sex-role traditional families.

- A positive school climate and positive gender and racial/ethnic attitudes of teachers reduce school-age children's psychological distress.

- Community attitudes and government policies affect immigrant children's well-being, especially if they live in transnational families.

TABLE 11.4 Summary of Developmental Theories

Chapter	Theories	Focus
11. Social Identities and Gender Development in Middle Childhood	Social Identity	Identification and belonging to social groups, such as gender and race/ethnicity, as well as explaining in-group and out-group attitudes
	Gender Schema	Gender beliefs reflected in the understanding of self and others and influencing children's behavior

---

KEY TERMS

Acculturation
Androgynous
Biethnic
Biracial
Bicultural
Borderwork
Embodiment
Ethnic identity
Feminine
Gender binary
Gender differentiation
Gender display
Gender identity

Gender intensification hypothesis
Gender nonconforming
Gender roles
Gender schemas
Gender segregation
Gender straightjacketing
Hegemonic masculinity
Heteronormativity
Imaginary audience
In-group
Intersectionality
Masculine

Masculinity ideology
Multicultural
Multiethnic
Multiple worlds model
Nonsex-typed
Out-group
Personal fables
Prejudice
Racial identity
Racial/ethnic socialization
Reflective practice
Sex-typed
Sexual identity

Sexual orientation
Social identity theory
Stereotype
Stereotype consciousness
Symbolic interactions
Third-culture
Transgender
Undocumented immigrants
Undifferentiated

SUGGESTED ACTIVITIES

1. Select a popular magazine with an ethnic-minority target audience, such as *blackgirl*. Read the letters to the editor. What identity issues do you find to be salient in readers' responses?

2. Look through a magazine for girls, such as *YM* or *Seventeen*, or go to their Web sites. Count the number of sexist or sexual images and topics. Overall, what influence do you think this media source has on teens—both boys and girls?

3. Interview the parents of a multiethnic or multiracial child. How are they raising their children? What aspects of their culture or national heritage are important to them? Which are difficult to maintain and why?

4. Use the instrument described in Box 11.4 to evaluate a children's book or textbook used with school-age children. How well does it represent gender, cultural, racial-ethnic diversity?

5. Walk through a public building, such as a school or community center, and observe how information is presented. Are the signs, art, or other visible symbols biased or unbiased with respect to gender, race-ethnicity, sexual orientation, or language? What messages do they convey to school-age children? How could they be changed to be more representative of diversity?

RECOMMENDED RESOURCES

Suggested Readings

Edut, O. (1998). *Adios, Barbie: Young women write about body image and identity.* Emeryville, CA: Seal Press.

McAdoo, H. P. (Ed.)(1999). *Family ethnicity: Strength in diversity.* Thousand Oaks, CA: Sage.

O'Reilly, P., Penn, E. M., & deMarrais, K. (Eds.) (2001). *Educating young adolescent girls.* Mahwah, NJ: Erlbaum.

Pollack, W. S. (1998). *Real boys: Rescuing our sons from the myth of boyhood.* New York: Random House.

Wardle, F., & Cruz-Janzen, M. (2004). *Meeting the needs of multiethnic and multiracial children in schools.* Boston: Allyn & Bacon.

Suggested Online Resources

Child Trends: Racial and Ethnic Composition of the Child Population. http://www.childtrendsdatabank.org/indicators/60RaceandEthnicComposition.cfm

The Girls' Report http://www.ncrw.org/research/girlsrpt.htm *Shortchanging Girls, Shortchanging America.* http://www.aauw.org/research/sasa.cfm

Suggested Web Sites

Center for Migration and Development.
    http://cmd.princeton.edu

National Institute on Media and the Family.
    http://www.mediafamily.org/

National Organization for Multiethnic and Multiracial Students.
    http://www.mavin.net

The New Americans.
    http://www.pbs.org/independent-lens/newamericans/

Suggested Films and Videos

Boys will be men (2001). Insight Media (57 minutes)

Everybody's ethnic: Your invisible culture. (2007). Learning Seed (21 minutes)

Identity crisis (2005). Films for the Humanities & Sciences (60 minutes)

Self, identity & sex role development (1993). Magna Systems (29 minutes)

Talking gender (1999). Insight Media (23 minutes)

What a girl wants (2003). Media Education Foundation (33 minutes)

CHAPTER 12

Beyond Middle Childhood: Adolescence

Photolibrary.com

Chapter Objectives

After reading this chapter, students will be able to:

▶ Define adolescence and the timing of adolescent transitions.

▶ Discuss historical and contemporary portrayals of adolescence as a distinct period of development.

▶ Name the developmental achievements of adolescence.

▶ Describe the diverse ecological contexts of adolescence.

▶ Compare research perspectives on risk and opportunity in the teen years.

▶ Explain the goals of an applied focus that translates practice into policy.

Leticia is worried. She's 15, and she hasn't yet been on a real date. She frequently goes to movies or parties on the weekends, but always in a group. Leticia looks grown up. She is tall for her age, has a great figure, and wears the latest styles. Fitting in and having lots of friends is becoming more important to Leticia than getting good grades. But her mother insists that Leticia pick up her younger brother Raúl from elementary school and come right home, so she can't hang out like the other kids. She fixes Raúl a snack, does her homework, and then calls her girlfriend Marina on the phone. Leticia complains, "Now if I can just convince my mother to let me go to the mall on school nights! After all, I'm almost 16!"

DEFINING ADOLESCENCE

Adolescence is the developmental period between puberty and young adulthood, roughly ages 13 to 18. The problems faced by Leticia are part of a normative dilemma experienced by many adolescents. Caught between childhood and adulthood, their struggle is to find a place in family, school, society, and peer cultures consistent with the ways in which adolescence is defined in each of these developmental contexts. Problems arise, however, because—as with middle childhood—our society defines adolescence differently depending on your perspective as a parent, teacher, program provider, employer, or policy maker. Teens themselves—whether just 13 or almost 18—may think that their lives are "on hold," as illustrated in Figure 12.1. In addition, teen self–help books, such as *What Teens Need to Succeed: Proven, Practical Ways to Shape Your Own Future* (Benson, Espeland, & Galbraith, 1998) often characterize teens as future adults.

🛑 What self-help books or teen magazines did you read as an adolescent? How did they portray adolescents?

A recurring question frequently asked by adolescents is *"Am I old enough now [to drive, to work, to date . . .]?"* A corresponding question asked by many parents and teachers is *"How do I know when adolescence begins, and when it ends?"* Still a third question often asked by community leaders is *"How will adolescents fit into the adult world?"* These three questions correspond to three underlying assumptions that will guide our study of middle adolescent development in this chapter:

- The primary developmental achievement of adolescents is maturing into adults—whether in the physical, cognitive, affective, or social domains of development.

- Adolescence is a cultural construction that may be differently defined across cultures, ethnic groups, or nationalities, or perhaps not exist at all in some societies.

- A society's ultimate goal for adolescents is to prepare for adulthood by minimizing possible risks and maximizing potential opportunities for youth development.

Therefore, we view adolescence as *both* a stage of development and as a developmental transition, echoing the approach to middle childhood used in this textbook. For example, when we examine whether the socially constructed meanings of "being adolescent" have changed historically or are essentially unchanged from G. Stanley Hall's (1904) turn-of-the-20th-century description, we find that current developmental researchers often conceptualize adolescence as affording either opportunities or risks to teens in transition. For example, a book called *Youth Crisis: Growing Up in a High Risk Society* (Davis, 1999) portrays the social

FIGURE 12.1
Teenagers

Teenagers are often impatient when it comes to acquiring the privileges that accompany increasing maturity.

Source: From G. Evans, "Luann," February 20, 1994. LUANN: © GEC Inc./Dist. by United Feature Syndicate, Inc.

conditions of adolescence at the end of the 20th century as affording many *risks*, such as homelessness, addiction, and violence, but little *protection* by society.

The contemporary perspective (i.e., that youth-in-crisis occurs in the context of a high-risk environment), contrasts with Hall's earlier idea that a crisis in adolescence is developmental (i.e., that all adolescents experience a normative crisis). Hall's hypothesis was that adolescence is a normative period of ***"sturm und drang"*** ("storm and stress") that must be endured on the pathway to adulthood. This viewpoint has affected not only today's popular notion of the teen years as troubled but also the scientific study of adolescents in crisis in such fields as psychology, psychiatry, education, criminal justice, sociology, and social work.

HISTORICAL CONTEXT OF ADOLESCENCE

The English word *adolescent* is derived from a Latin root meaning "to nourish or to grow." Western societies saw adolescence as a time for education, training in practical arts, or apprenticeship. This formative view of adolescence persisted in Europe throughout the Middle Ages and the Enlightenment and was subsequently brought to the United States by the early colonists. Apprenticeship, however, was seen as more important than formal schooling for most adolescents in colonial America, as we discussed in chapter 1.

Most children did not stay in school beyond the primary grades, except for wealthy boys (and a few privileged girls) who attended private academies intended to prepare them for elite colleges. Most adolescents worked on farms, in mines, or in factories as soon as they could legally leave school (i.e., at age 16, or at age 14 if their labor was needed to support their families). Native American and African American children often could not attend school at all (Hine, 1999).

Modern Contributions to the Construction of Adolescence

The first public high school, in Boston, opened in 1821, partly as a result of a national committee called the Committee on Secondary School Studies (Hine, 1999). Also known as the "Committee of Ten," this group directed the work of 90 subcommittee

Modern high schools are an important context for adolescent development.

Anthony Magnacca/Merrill

members from all parts of the United States (National Education Association, 1969). They identified three major problems with secondary education:

- Wide divergence in courses of study
- Uncertain standards of admission
- Minimal requirements for graduation

In their final report to the U.S. Bureau of Education in 1893, the committee concluded that secondary schools were the most "defective" part of education in the United States.

Ten years later, in 1913, the National Education Association appointed a commission to reorganize secondary education. Their report, called *The Cardinal Principles of Secondary Education*, stated broad social goals for schools and for society, such as education for living in a democracy and preparation for the workplace (Boyer, 1983). But despite the best efforts of educators, secondary schools were not prevalent in all U.S. communities until the 1930s. Even then, high schools served only 47% of the adolescent age group, with separate schools for Black students (Hine, 1999).

By the 1950s, a majority of White American teenagers completed high school. Box 12.1 highlights a now-classic study that describes the segregated education of adolescents in Elmtown, a prototypical Midwestern town (Hollingshead, 1949). However, in 1954, the U.S. Supreme Court mandated equal access to education for racial minorities with the *Brown vs. Board of Education* decision (Boyer, 1983). America struggled to improve secondary education—not only as a response to the civil rights movement but also to satisfy a popular desire for scientific superiority during the cold war of the 1950s and 1960s. For example, a Carnegie-funded study of American high schools urging a more comprehensive academic curriculum called *The American High School Today* became a bestseller (Conant, 1959/1967).

 BOX 12.1   Roadmap to Understanding Theory and Research
Elmtown's Youth

August B. Hollingshead's ethnographic research in the 1940s was one of the first studies to highlight the impact of social class on youth development. A professor at Yale University, he studied a typical midwestern U.S. town he called Elmtown (pop. 6,200). According to Hollingshead, Elmtown teenagers knew more about the family, the school, the church, the grocery, and the butcher than they did about the county government or banking institutions, as would be expected. Nevertheless, although there were not *supposed* to be class differences in America, most high-schoolers knew that their families' economic status would subtly affect them as they faced the transition from child to adult.

Hollingshead also found that adolescents, no matter what their class position, who could not obtain money from their families to participate in their peer group's activities faced the dilemma of entering the workforce or staying in school. "If he takes the school road, he will move into an entirely different social world from the one he will traverse if he takes the work road. A middle road between the two is traveled by those who combine school with part-time work out of school hours" (p. 148). Hollingshead concluded that sometime between ages 14 and 18, Elmtown's teens made this choice, a decision that affected their social relations with practically every institution in the community throughout the adolescent years and into adult life.

Source: Based on "The Adolescent in the Community" by A. E. Hollingshead, 1949, in *Elmtown Youth* (pp. 148–159), New York: Wiley. Copyright © 1949 by John Wiley & Sons, Inc.

During the 1960s and 1970s, concerns about the academic preparedness of adolescents were replaced by an even more democratic concern. An emphasis on community service and youth leadership arose from a focus on disadvantaged students during the federal "War on Poverty" (Boyer, 1983; Tucker, 1999). By the early 1980s, the Carnegie Foundation for the Advancement of Teaching issued a comprehensive report on secondary education in the United States, affirming two goals for improving public education:

- To recognize that all students must be prepared for a lifetime of both work and further education
- To give students more opportunities for service in anticipation of their growing civic and social responsibilities as they become adults (Boyer, 1983)

Box 12.2 outlines five items from the agenda developed by the Carnegie Commission. These recommendations are significant because they focused the nation's attention on the importance of educational opportunity for all adolescents.

 BOX 12.2   Roadmap to Successful Practice
High School: Five Items from "An Agenda for Action"

1. ***Clarifying Goals.*** A high school, to be effective, must have a clear and vital mission. Educators must have a shared vision of what, together, they are trying to accomplish. That vision should go beyond keeping students in school and out of trouble, and be more significant than adding up the Carnegie course units the student has completed.

2. ***The Centrality of Language.*** The next priority is language. Formal schooling has a special obligation to help all students become skilled in the written and oral use of English. Those who do not become proficient in the primary language of the culture are enormously disadvantaged in school and out of school as well.

3. ***The Curriculum Has a Core.*** A core of common learning is essential. The basic curriculum should be a study of those consequential ideas, experiences, and traditions common to all of us by virtue of our membership in the human family at a particular moment in history. The content of the core curriculum must extend beyond the specialties, and focus on more transcendent issues, moving from courses to coherence.

4. ***Transition to Work and Learning.*** The high school should help all students move with confidence from school to work and further education. Today, we track students into programs for those who "think" and those who "work," when, in fact, life for all of us is a blend of both. Looking to the future, we conclude that, for most students, twelve years of schooling will be insufficient. Today's graduates will change jobs several times. New skills will be required, new citizenship obligations will be confronted. Of necessity, education will be lifelong.

5. ***Service: The New Carnegie Unit.*** Beyond the formal academic program the high school should help all students meet their social and civic obligations. During high school young people should be given opportunities to reach beyond themselves and feel more responsibly engaged. They should be encouraged to participate in the communities of which they are a part.

Source: From "High School: An Agenda for Action" by E. L. Boyer, 1983, in *High School: A Report on Secondary Education in America* (pp. 301–319), New York: Harper & Row. Copyright © 2007 by the Carnegie Foundation for the Advancement of Teaching. Reprinted with permission.

At about the same time, the Commission on Work, Family, and Citizenship was formed by the William T. Grant Foundation to study the economic conditions affecting adolescents in the United States who did *not* attend college after completing high school (Youth and America's Future, 1988). In their report, called *The Forgotten Half,* they cited factors that inordinately affected teenagers from working-class families:

- High unemployment
- A 27% decrease in the median income levels of American families
- Greater numbers of single-parent households

STOP Did you feel prepared for college or a job when you left high school?

As the 1990s began, high school students felt an unrelenting pressure, not for real academic accomplishment, but "to get their tickets punched so that they could get to the next stage in an increasingly competitive economy" (Tucker, 1999, p. 21).

Adolescence as a Transition. The dominant view of adolescence during the 20th century was that the teenage years constituted *a developmental transition* between childhood and adulthood. (This view is similar to the assertion of current researchers discussed in chapter 1 that middle childhood falls in between early childhood and adolescence.) For example, during the social upheaval of the 1960s, many sociologists considered adolescents to be "characterized by the confusion and uncertainty of not knowing exactly what [their] role expectations are during the period of transition from childhood to adulthood. It is this vague no man's land that is defined as *adolescence"* (Sebold, 1968, p. vii). Many developmental scholars who described adolescence as a transition did not focus on the developmental achievements of this age group (i.e., from 13 to 18), but rather emphasized their progress toward becoming adults (Offer, Ostrow, & Howard, 1981). Adulthood scholars have recently used the term **adultification** to refer to an acceleration of adult responsibilities in childhood, particularly among high-risk teens (Burton, 2002). However, as with both middle childhood and adolescence, the study of adults has also been stymied by a lack of clear definitions (Côté, 2000b). *When does adolescence end and adulthood begin?*

Some developmental researchers have suggested that the term *adultoid* be used to describe adolescents who have assumed adult behaviors, such as working, but do not have the psychological maturity of adults (Greenberger & Steinberg, 1986). In a person-centered study of adolescents from ages 10 to 18 who were classified as either immature, adultoid, or mature on the basis of personal profiles, researchers found that "adultoid" adolescents had more advanced physical maturity, earlier expectations for attaining privileges, and higher social involvement than adolescents who were either more or less mature (Galambos & Tilton-Weaver, 2000). (For an explanation of person-centered research, refer to chapter 2.) These results suggest that a successful adolescent transition to adulthood may vary from person to person depending on the fit between an individual's maturity level and the demands of the environment.

In late modern societies, the average transition to "adulthood" has became more prolonged and difficult, partly because of economic factors, such as unemployment trends, or because of social trends, such as delaying marriage or parenthood. Popular books, such as *Grownups: A Generation in Search of Adulthood* (Merser, 1987), underscore the social construction of both adolescence and adulthood and emphasize our society's cultural idealization of "youth" in both age groups.

Today, many developmental psychologists see the functional significance of adolescence (i.e., as a transition to adulthood) as equal in significance to the formal maturational changes that occur in adolescents' reproductive status or appearance brought about by puberty. For example, by the 1990s, three simultaneous and equally significant research efforts were documented in the adolescent literature:

- *At the Threshold* (Feldman & Elliott, 1990), supported by the Carnegie Council on Adolescent Development, published by a collaborative group of researchers
- *Pathways through Adolescence* (Crockett & Crouter, 1995), supported in part by the Reproductive Transition Group of the MacArthur Foundation
- *Transition through Adolescence* (Graber et al., 1996), the report of a conference held by the Policy, Research, and Intervention for Development in Early Adolescence (PRIDE) project and supported by the Carnegie Corporation

Most research on adolescence as a transitional period has focused on the educational pathways available to teenagers as they journey from middle childhood to adolescence, such as the transition from middle to high school (e.g., Barber & Olsen, 2004).

Leticia has just started high school. As a ninth grader, she has expectations that her life should change somehow! She wants to start dating and to be given new privileges in recognition of this important transition.

To clarify the *developmental* transitions of adolescents for their families, and often for the wider community, many U.S. ethnic or religious subcultures mark entrance into "maturity" by observing formal **rites of passage**, or ritual ceremonies marking a person's movement from one stage to another (Delaney, 1995; Markstrom & Iborra, 2003). For example, rites of passage may be used to facilitate family members' understanding of the *transitional* function of adolescence:

- African American boys may participate in a church- or school-based program modeled after African rites-of-passage traditions.
- American Indian boys may fast and stay in a "sweat lodge" to be purified by heat and prayer. Girls may participate in a formal ritual celebrating their first menstrual cycles.
- Jewish boys and girls may celebrate their *Bar* or *Bat Mitzvah* at age 13 by reading aloud a portion of the Old Testament in the synagogue or temple.
- Latina girls may celebrate their 15th birthday, or *quinceañera*, with a religious mass and family party.

In contemporary U.S. society, however, many adolescent rites of passage are often informal, such as getting keys to the family car on your 16th birthday. Family therapists have recommended instead that more formalized rituals, such as graduation parties or changes in living arrangements (e.g., moving from a room shared with younger siblings to a private bedroom), be used to identify *structural* changes in an adolescent's developmental status (Quinn, Newfield, & Protinsky, 1985).

Adolescence as a Stage. An alternative to the view of adolescence as a *transition* is that the teen years constitute a *distinct* developmental *stage*, characterized by unique developmental achievements and stresses. More importantly, stage approaches theorize adolescence as a **structural period** that begins with a biological event (i.e., puberty) and typically ends with a sociological event (i.e., graduating from high school or college, marrying, or joining the workforce). If these structural markers occur out of the normative order, such as bearing a child before graduating from high school, then the onset or termination of adolescence may seem ambiguous.

Biological or behavioral changes associated with puberty, in combination with structural conditions (e.g., compulsory secondary schooling, laws prohibiting child labor, a juvenile justice system that operates on the basis of age), may also lead to increasing stress in the relationship between the adolescent and others (Quinn et al., 1985). For example, in a classic portrait of an adolescent, Rousseau (1762/1970) described the interaction with his student Emile as suddenly troubling at the age of puberty, "He no longer listens to his schoolmaster's voice. He is a lion in a fever. He mistrusts his teacher and is averse to control" (p. 96).

Reflecting Rousseau's 18th-century case study description of Emile as a youth overcome by adolescent drives, G. Stanley Hall (1904) theorized that adolescence was a maturational period in individual human growth and development, or **ontogeny**, echoing the evolution of the entire human species, or **phylogeny**. Hall proposed this process, known as **recapitulation theory**, to account for adolescents' immaturity compared to "fully evolved" adults! Hall saw adolescents as primitives, prone to disruptive emotions and impulsive behaviors, who would eventually—like the species as a whole—grow out of their savagery. As humorously written by the author of a popular book called *The Rise and Fall of the American Teenager,* "If your teenager is a Neanderthal, you can take heart. It's only a phase he's going through" (Hine, 1999, p. 36).

Recall also the influential work of Arnold Gesell (discussed in chapter 1) who carefully documented the normative stages of child and adolescent development in the early 20th century. Gesell, Ilg, and Ames (1956) wrote the following description of an "average" adolescent: "He glimpsed the future and what he wanted to become . . . but all too often he became discouraged, lost his incentive, and expressed himself more in rebellion than in cooperation" (p. 262).

Leticia thinks, "Maybe I should stop studying so hard. Then I'd have more time to spend with my friends, and the boys wouldn't think I'm so smart."

Even as late as the 1980s, David Elkind, a well-known child development expert, described children who are physically mature but have no "place" in society (Elkind, 1984). He claimed that adolescents have lost adults' support for their struggle to achieve a sense of personal identity. According to psychologists, the popular phrase *identity crisis* that is so commonly associated with teenagers is a normal experience. Normative adolescence involves a **moratorium**, or delay, in making commitments during the years between childhood and adulthood; instead, it is a time for testing and discovery (Erikson, 1968).

Leticia's older brother Lorenzo, a junior, just wants to have fun in high school. These are the best years of their life, right? Why waste them on studying, anyway. "Pretty soon," he plans, "I'll turn 18, graduate, and get a full-time job."

In advanced industrial societies like the United States, formally structured institutional settings, such as schools, often provide adolescents with a time-out before taking on adult responsibilities (Côté & Allahar, 1996). In theory, these adolescent contexts (e.g., high schools; youth programs; music, arts, or sports subcultures) can provide teenagers with opportunities to experiment with roles, ideas, beliefs, and lifestyles that they might follow in later life (Côté & Allahar, 1996).

To the present day, social discourse on the storm and stress of adolescence has endured despite the fact that there is little, if any, scientific evidence to support the culturally constructed myth of rebellion. Empirical research on adolescence from

---

Guideposts for Working with School-Age Children

- Because teens may not know exactly what role expectations will accompany the transition to adulthood, be specific in articulating your expectations for their behavior.

- Avoid stereotyping all teens as rebellious, especially when they are exploring new or controversial ideas.

- Mark teens' normative rites of passage, such as getting a driver's license, finding a first job, or taking the SAT exam, as a special occasion.

- Talk with adolescents about their future options, whether furthering their education, entering the military, or getting a job.

---

the 1950s to 1990s has indicated that most teens share their parents' values and attitudes and progress through early, middle, and late adolescence with few serious problems (Barnes & Olsen, 1985; Laursen, Coy, & Collins, 1998; Lerner & Knapp, 1975; Offer, 1969). For example, researchers studying American adolescents' responses to national events from 1966 (in early 10th grade) to 1970 (one year after high school graduation) reported that adolescent boys' dissent over military involvement in Vietnam increased, along with that of many adults who also became increasingly frustrated with the war (Bachman & Van Duinen, 1971), as is true with respect to the war in Iraq. Even in the turbulent 1970s, a large cross-cultural study of adolescent self-image revealed that American teenagers—like teens from Israel, Ireland, and Australia—held very positive feelings toward their families and tended to be only slightly more rebellious than adolescents from other cultures (Offer et al., 1981). Then, as today, in the great majority of families, parents and adolescents actually hold similar attitudes about sexuality, drug use, war and peace, and human rights (Lerner, 2002a).

MEANINGS OF ADOLESCENCE IN POSTMODERN SOCIETIES

In 2002, the Society for Research on Adolescence issued a groundbreaking report by the Study Group on Adolescence in the 21st Century that examined how the demands of the new millennium are reshaping adolescents' experiences and their preparation for adulthood (Larson, Brown, & Mortimer, 2002a). Because global communication, increased emigration, and a shared geopolitical climate have made an international perspective on adolescence seem necessary, the study group went beyond a strictly Western conception of adolescence. "What is emerging across the world are postmodern assemblages of local and global elements combined in different and challenging ways. It is important to ask whether the assemblages shape pathways that are secure or precarious" (Larson et al., 2002b, p. 2).

As we discussed in chapter 1 with respect to middle childhood, postmodern scholars often emphasize diversity in the study of adolescence. At the turn of the 21st century, adolescent researchers have increasingly emphasized the importance of differences in context on developmental processes (Silbereisen & Todt, 1994). For example, the meaning of being an adolescent in a working-class, single-mother family where a teenager is expected to assume responsibilities for household chores or for the child care of younger siblings may be quite different from its meaning in an upper-income, two-parent family where the primary household and child care chores are the responsibilities of either a stay-at-home parent or a paid household employee.

After school, Leticia has to watch Raúl until their mother gets off work. Sometimes, when her mother is going to be late, she even cooks dinner for the whole family.

Diverse Ecological Contexts

In varied cultural, social, or economic contexts, divergent pathways, or what scholars have termed the "new adolescences," result from factors such as increased education, delayed employment, and later marriage and parenthood (Larson, 2002). In most industrialized cultures, adolescence as a transitional period has been lengthened over the past half century. For example, the average age of marriage has changed from 12 to 16 in rural India and from 22 to 26 in Europe (Larson et al., 2002b). According to sociologists, adolescence is longer in societies with greater technological complexity, with urban adolescents requiring a longer time to reach adulthood than adolescents from rural communities or agrarian societies (Chatterjee et al., 2001).

In developing countries, high birthrates also mean that the numbers of adolescents will grow over the next several decades, straining employment and educational resources and possibly limiting adolescents' opportunities and transition into adult roles (Larson, 2002). For example, 56% of Saudis are under age 20 (Saudi Arabia Information Resource, 2005). Similarly, the United States also has both high immigration rates and an expected 18% increase in the numbers of 15- to 25-year-olds by 2010 (U.S. Census Bureau, 2001).

But there are also many differences in adolescent experiences across nations (Larson, 2002). Trends in Japan, Europe, and the former Soviet states are just the opposite! In Japan, for instance, many 21st-century youth are postponing or forgoing marriage in favor of a prolonged and self-focused single life—they are referred to by Japanese adults as "single parasites." Psychologists studying later adolescence have termed this period of the life span *emerging adulthood* (Arnett, 2002). Thus, the length of adolescence may be very different throughout the world, depending on diverse cultural responses to increased socioeconomic opportunities caused by globalization.

Effects of Globalization

Globalization refers to increases in communication, shared economic influences, and political alliances among the nations of the world. Globalization has existed for many centuries as cultures became more alike through trade, immigration, and the exchange of ideas; however, recent advances in telecommunications and increases in financial interdependence have accelerated globalization in the 21st century (Arnett, 2002). For example, current trends in **economic globalization** have increased the stratification between rich and poor, in which adolescents in successful global markets see improved educational and job opportunities while adolescents in poorer countries may see fewer.

Economic globalization also has disrupted **social reproduction**, or the ways that adolescents receive the knowledge and skills necessary for the world in which they will come of age as workers. In Third World countries like Sudan, for example, agricultural development has displaced rural populations to its cities, resulting in "street children" in the towns of Sudan as an unwanted outcome of economic globalization. Similarly, in the so-called First World cities of the United States, disinvestments in manufacturing have dimmed the prospects for well-paying, stable, and meaningful jobs for many working-class adolescents while deteriorating school budgets have diminished their access to quality education (Katz, 1998).

At the same time, adolescents living in global economies may experience **cultural globalization**, or the effects of material culture on societies, such as the spread of brand-named products or music and film icons, thus increasing their commonalities (Larson, 2002). Although fundamental differences in cultural values are likely to persist, adolescents in the future may know more about each other than in past centuries because of satellite communication, cable news networks, and the Internet (see Lim & Renshaw, 2001). A simultaneous trend toward economic and cultural globalization may mean that differences in adolescence could be minimized across cultures, as seen in Box 12.3. In fact, a 1998 United Nations report identified a market for brand-name music, videos, T-shirts, and soft drinks among "global teens" (Arnett, 2002).

BOX 12.3   Roadmap to Understanding Theory and Research
The Construction of Youth Cultures

While filming in Mexico, Doreen Massey interviewed a group of women in their Yucatán homes. With light from an open fire, they sat on stones on the earth floor in an adobe house with a thatched roof. While they talked, the women were making tortillas "by hand, as it had always been done" and talking about their lives. Massey recorded what she called a truly indigenous culture intent on preserving its customs, clothing, food, and beliefs.

When the interview was over, the filmmakers walked back to their jeep. As they approached the road, they heard electronic sounds, American slang, and Western music. From another building—this one wired for electricity—a dozen or so youth were playing computer games. Machines were lined up around the walls of the shack, and every one was surrounded by players. Of course, they filmed the adolescents, too.

The filmmakers later suggested that the youth culture of the Yucatán countryside may serve as an entry point for external influences into, and maybe the eventual breakup of, inherited Mayan culture. Because the cultures of the young seemed more internationalized than those of older generations, Massey asked, "Was this a local culture, or were these youngsters part of the emerging global culture of youth?"

The answer depended on how she conceptualized culture: Was it *global* in the full sense that

everyone, everywhere, has access to it? Massey saw the roomful of computer games as a link between this small cluster of houses in eastern Mexico and something that might be characterized as global (or American) culture—for example, the T-shirts with slogans in English, the baseball caps, the athletic shoes, the litter of cola cans. Nevertheless, the filmmakers suggested that the youth culture here was quite different from that of San Francisco, or a small American town, or England, or Tokyo, for example.

In each place, T-shirts and computer games are mixed in with locally distinct cultures that have their own histories. For example, the meaning of what is and what is not a status symbol, or of how particular slogans or music are interpreted, changes. In Mexico, global elements were embedded in Mayan family relations, in the culture's unique understanding of ancient cosmology, or in Mexico's particular Latin American consciousness. Massey concluded that local variations in youth cultures can be constantly reinvented even while international influences are accepted and incorporated.

Source: Based on "The Spatial Construction of Youth Cultures," by Doreen Massey, in T. Skelton and G. Valentine (Eds.), *Cool Places: Geographies of Youth Cultures* (pp. 121–129), 1998, London: Routledge. Copyright 1998 by Tracey Skelton and Gill Valentine.

But despite the trends toward globalization, many world cultures resist its influence. Orthodox Islam, for example, has organized opposition to globalization in the Middle East among its youth by promoting traditional religious values (Larson, 2002). In Samoa, postmodern adolescents have revived an ancient rite-of-passage custom of tattooing as an overt sign of maintaining their indigenous culture in the face of increasing globalization (Arnett, 2002). If adolescents are in the forefront of these religious and political movements, what is the current cultural construction of adolescence in these nations?

Poststructural Ideas

Most scholars in the 20th century subscribed to the structural view of adolescence as a distinct stage of development, bounded by puberty on one side and by adulthood on the other. *Structuralism* implies that adolescence is a defined stage. On the other hand, **poststructuralism** rejects physical metaphors (i.e., that adolescence has distinct age boundaries).

Cross-cultural research supports a *poststructural* view of adolescence, which has increasingly influenced developmental scholars in the 21st century (see Maira & Soep, 2004). Sociologists and anthropologists, in particular, have explained that the cultural construction of adolescence—like that of middle childhood—does not exist in some cultures. For example, Islamic youth are generally regarded as interchangeable with adults. Also recall (from chapter 1) that Mead (1928) described a smooth transition to adulthood for Samoan adolescents because their culture did not structure adolescence as a separate stage. Mead's hypothesis was that the "storm and stress" of adolescence—postulated by Hall (1904) as biologically universal—is, in fact, not universal at all.

Such conclusions regarding the cultural diversity of adolescence have been carefully examined and are supported by a majority of contemporary scholars (Côté, 2000b). For example, in India most adolescents and young adults—even though they often participate in a global high-tech culture—prefer to have an arranged marriage in accordance with Indian tradition (Arnett, 2002). Variations in the social construction of adolescence suggest that the meanings of adolescence are not universal in either their structure (e.g., timing or duration) or in their function (e.g., preparation for adulthood).

STOP Was your adolescence "stormy" or "stressful" and, if so, how?

Guideposts for Working with Adolescents

- Remember that adolescence has different meanings in diverse cultures.

- Ask teens to keep a log of comments they hear in the media or in the community about teenagers. Talk with teens about the social construction of adolescence in contemporary culture.

- Help teenagers understand parental, educational, and societal expectations for adolescents by reading and discussing youth fiction from around the world.

- Encourage today's global teens to learn about their similarities to adolescents from other countries by using e-mail, Internet chat rooms, or Web logs (blogs).

DEVELOPMENTAL MILESTONES IN ADOLESCENCE

In adolescence, as in middle childhood and in all other periods of the life span, biological maturation (e.g., physiological or genetic factors) and environmental influences (e.g., social or cultural influences) interact to produce change over time, or *development*. Recall from chapter 1 that a developmental interaction is a dynamic exchange of reciprocal influences between maturation and experience. For example, a given 13- or 14-year-old might not have developed the abstract reasoning ability to engage in moral reasoning about ethical dilemmas sometimes facing adolescents (e.g., abortion vs. adoption decisions by pregnant teens), whereas at age 16 or 17 the same adolescent may be able to think hypothetically about possible alternatives. Developmental educators refer to this phenomenon as **readiness**.

Developmental theories are useful because they concentrate our attention on "time-dependent *phenomena of becoming* or emergence of a new structural order of the phenomena from their previous state" (Valsiner, 1997, p. 3). The developmental milestones along the road to maturity can be summarized using normative expectations for adolescent development in the same four domains we discussed in chapter 1 of the text, as depicted in Figure 12.2:

1. *Physical development.* As in middle childhood, this domain includes biological and physiological development. In adolescence, children experience changes associated with puberty. Onset of puberty occurs at varied ages, with 11 years the average age for girls and 13 years for boys, marked by hormonal and reproductive changes (i.e., primary sexual characteristics) and by observable changes in physical appearance (i.e., secondary sexual characteristics).

2. *Cognitive development.* As in younger children, this domain includes intellectual and language skills, reasoning abilities, and memory capacities. Adolescence is characterized by a qualitative change in logical understanding involving hypothetical reasoning, probabilistic thinking, and complex information processing, such as higher problem solving in science or math.

3. *Affective development.* As seen previously, this developmental domain includes personality, emotional development, motivation, and self-esteem. During the adolescent years, teens are developing a sense of personal identity; are beginning to experience more intimacy in romantic relationships; and are feeling emotions and moods with a deepening intensity.

4. *Social Development.* As in middle childhood, this domain includes social skills and interpersonal understanding, moral and ethical development, and maintaining close relationships. Adolescents develop intimate, mutual relations with others by increasing interactions beyond their families, by deepening friendships, and by seeking emergent roles in the adult community.

Let's think about Leticia. Her physical appearance (i.e., tall, with enlarged breasts and hips) indicates that she has probably undergone menarche and is now reproductively mature. Cognitively, Leticia demonstrates the hypothetical thinking about her future that typically distinguishes adolescents from school-age children (e.g., she anticipates the challenges of adolescence). Emotionally, Leticia appears quite mature. She keeps up a B average and is active in her church. Socially, however, Leticia could be considered preoccupied with "silly" concerns that—from an adult's perspective—are just "growing pains," such as making friends or getting a date. But Leticia's experience is typical of most adolescents who ask impatiently, "If not now, when?"

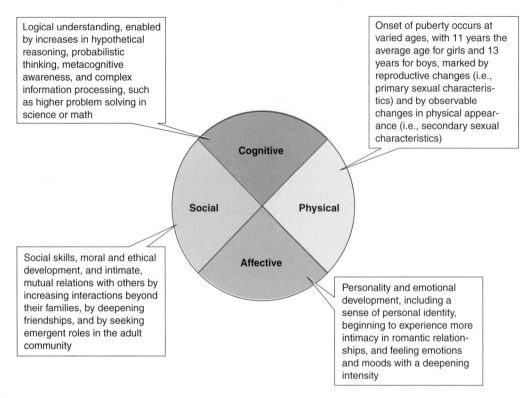

Logical understanding, enabled by increases in hypothetical reasoning, probabilistic thinking, metacognitive awareness, and complex information processing, such as higher problem solving in science or math

Onset of puberty occurs at varied ages, with 11 years the average age for girls and 13 years for boys, marked by reproductive changes (i.e., primary sexual characteristics) and by observable changes in physical appearance (i.e., secondary sexual characteristics)

Cognitive

Social

Physical

Affective

Social skills, moral and ethical development, and intimate, mutual relations with others by increasing interactions beyond their families, by deepening friendships, and by seeking emergent roles in the adult community

Personality and emotional development, including a sense of personal identity, beginning to experience more intimacy in romantic relationships, and feeling emotions and moods with a deepening intensity

FIGURE 12.2

Developmental Domains of Adolescence

The development milestones of adolescence correspond to the domains of middle childhood development.

Anticipation of major life transitions, such as graduating, getting a job, or leaving home, is called **life-course development**. Social historians have successfully employed this concept to analyze changing patterns in individual development across a generation, a culture, or a particular historical context (Mintz, 1993). Since the 20th century, life-course decisions have increasingly reflected individualized choices or social norms (Mintz, 1993). (Recall that a developmental norm is the average age at which a particular behavior typically occurs in the adolescent population.) In the case of legally sanctioned activities, however, such as getting a driver's license or a work permit, age norms have been institutionalized by society. Other social norms may be particular to families or communities, such as the age at which a teenager is allowed to date.

Marina just started going out with a boy from church named James. Leticia certainly doesn't want to feel like a "third wheel." More to the point, how will she ever meet someone?

THEORETICAL VIEWPOINTS

Two complementary theoretical perspectives provide a developmental framework for the study of middle adolescence: (1) life-span theory, and (2) life-course theory. Life-span approaches examine adolescence in relation to other developmental *stages* in the life span. On the other hand, life-course approaches examine major life *transitions* over a lifetime. These complementary approaches allow us to see how adolescence is *at once* a developmental stage and a transition to adulthood.

Life-Span Theory

Life-span psychology is the study of development from conception to death. Life-span theorists and researchers expect each period in the life span (e.g., infancy, childhood, adolescence, adulthood, old age) to have its own developmental agenda and to contribute to continuity and change across the life course (Baltes, Reese, & Lipsett, 1980; Baltes, Lindenberger, & Staudinger, 2006). The three major goals of life-span theorizing (Baltes, 1987) are to obtain knowledge about:

1. General principles of development across the life course, called **ontogenesis**
2. Differences *between* people, called **interindividual differences**
3. Changes *within* a person, called **intraindividual change**

Although adulthood and aging have been the primary interest of many life-span researchers, they have contributed several important theoretical propositions to a general view of development that will assist us in examining adolescence as a stage in the life span:

- *Development is **multidirectional**, or comprised of the capacity both for gains and for losses.* For example, in adolescence, as teenagers move toward new levels of abstract logical reasoning and probabilistic thinking, their peer conformity may decline, and they may start to think for themselves.

- *Development can vary substantially with history, called **historical embeddedness**.* How age-related development proceeds is markedly influenced by sociocultural conditions in a given historical period. For example, adolescents born after 1980 may be much more likely than previous generations to practice "safe sex" because of the threat of HIV/AIDS.

- *Any particular individual's development can be understood as the outcome of developmental influences that are **age-graded** (e.g., the onset of puberty); **history-graded** (e.g., beginning middle school); and **nonnormative** (e.g., moving to a new community).* Much like developmental-contextual and bioecological theories (described in chapter 1), life-span psychology uses **contextualism** as its **metatheoretical paradigm**, or worldview, and thus considers development to be highly dependent on life experiences in a specific time and place.

- *Life-span theory is **multidisciplinary**.* Life-span researchers often employ many diverse disciplinary perspectives on adolescence (e.g., social history, sociology, or anthropology).

Figure 12.3 illustrates the interplay of age-graded, history-graded, and nonnormative influences as taking place throughout our lives. The life span also unfolds in *ontogenetic time,* during which the forces of biology and the environment continuously interact.

Recently, life-span theory has been discussed in terms of evolutionary psychology, discussed in chapter 4 (Baltes, 1997). A long developmental period, such as human childhood and adolescence, is thus seen as allowing enough time to

FIGURE 12.3
Theoretical Model of Life-Span Development

Source: From "Life-Span Theory in Developmental Psychology" by P. B. Baltes, U. Lindenberger, U. M., & Staudinger, 1998, in W. Damon (Series Ed.) & R. M. Lerner (Vol. Ed.), *Handbook of child psychology, Vol. 1: Theoretical models of human development* (5th ed., pp. 1049), 1998, New York: Wiley. Copyright © 1998 by John Wiley & Sons, Inc. Reprinted by permission of the publisher.

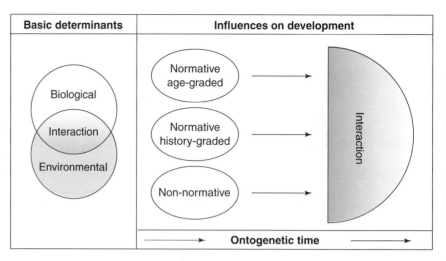

refine the physical, social, and cognitive competencies that support survival and reproduction of the species. Seen from this perspective, life-span theory asserts that adolescence provides **selective optimization**, or movement toward increased efficiency and higher levels of functioning, such as increasing autonomy in adolescence; and **compensation**, or making up for a level of functioning no longer present, such as spending more time with friends than family (Baltes, 1997).

Life-Course Theory

Like life-span theory, **life-course theory** also focuses on systematic changes experienced by individuals as they move through their lives. But instead of focusing on developmental changes as does life-span theory, life-course theory focuses on life *events,* such as starting school, graduating, entering the workforce, getting married, or having children. According to its major proponent, Glen Elder (1998), the life-course perspective includes four central principles:

1. The life-course of individuals is embedded in and shaped by the historical times and places they experience over their lifetime.

2. The developmental impact of a life transition or event is contingent on when it occurs in a person's life.

3. Lives are lived interdependently, and social and historical influences are expressed through a network of shared relationships.

4. Individuals construct their own life course through the choices and actions they take within the constraints and opportunities of history and social circumstances. (Elder, 1998, p. 961)

The significance of life-course theory for studying adolescence is its ability to weave the development of *individuals* into the social fabric of developmental *contexts,* that is, to explain how lives are socially organized. Life-course theorists view the ontogeny of individuals and the development of history as one system (Lerner, 2002b). This emphasis on the simultaneous contributions of individual and historical development leads life-course researchers to use the following methods:

- Analysis of **life histories**, or the examination of the transitions between major life events
- Investigation of the timing and sequencing of **life events**, or major milestones within any individual's life history
- Emphasis on accepted variations in individuals' life histories as a way to investigate the strength of norms in any given cohort or historical period

According to life-course methodology, your birth year is your point of entry into the social system, and your life course is constructed by your location along three temporal dimensions, including:

- **Developmental time** (i.e., birth to death)
- **Family time** (i.e., your location relative to preceding or successive generations)
- **Historical time** (i.e., the social and cultural system that exists during your lifetime)

Refer to Figure 12.4 for an illustration of developmental, family, and historical time portraying our lives as existing in a three-dimensional space created by successive

STOP What life events signaled to you that you were becoming an adolescent?

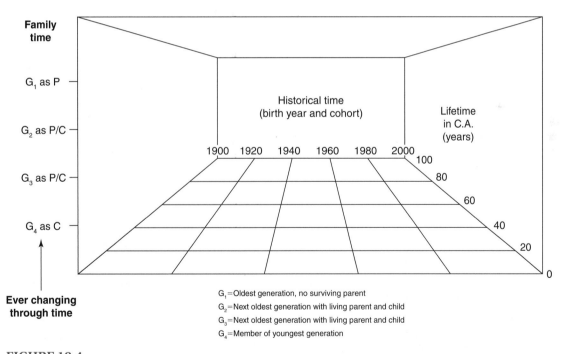

FIGURE 12.4

Theoretical Model of Life-Course Development

Source: From "The Life Course and Human Development" by G. E. Elder, G. H., Jr., in W. Damon (Series Ed.) & R. M. Lerner (Vol. Ed.), *Handbook of Child Psychology, Vol. 1: Theoretical Models of Human Development* (5th ed., pp. 1998), New York: Wiley. Copyright © 1998 by John Wiley & Sons, Inc. Reprinted by permission of the publisher.

generations born at different points in history. According to life-course theory, changing environments, social relationships, and historical influences have developmental implications for individuals, who are active participants in shaping the course of their lives (Elder & Shanahan, 2006).

Recently, family theorists have proposed a variation of life-course theory called **family development theory** (White, 1991; White & Klein, 2002). The emphasis in family development theory is on the concept of transitions through what was traditionally called the **family life cycle**, depicted in Figure 12.5 (Duvall, 1957; White, 1991). For example, like biological organisms, families may go through developmental stages: formation, growth, maintenance, shrinkage, and dissolution (White & Klein, 2002). Family members may also be seen as progressing through **family careers** (Aldous, 1996), such as the sibling career in childhood and adolescence (assuming you have brothers and/or sisters); the marital career (if you are married); and the parental career (provided you have children).

For most developmentalists, the newer concept of the family life course has replaced the earlier concept of the family life cycle because it better reflects variations in norms across cultures and societies (White & Klein, 2002). For example,

FIGURE 12.5
Traditional Model of Family Development

In the 1950s, family scholars diagrammed an idealized family life cycle.

Source: From "The Family Life Cycle" by E. M. Duvall, in *Marriage and Family Development* (5th ed.). Published by Allyn and Bacon, Boston, MA. Copyright © 1977 by Pearson Education, Inc. Reprinted by permission of the publisher.

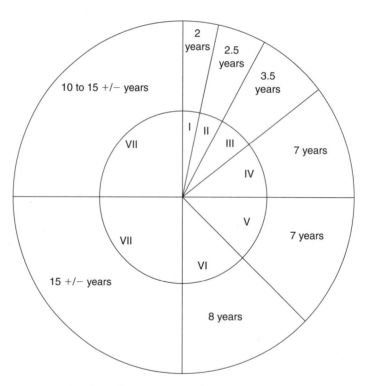

I. Married couples (without children).

II. Childbearing families (oldest child, birth–30 months).

III. Families with preschool children (oldest child 30 months–6 years).

IV. Families with school children (oldest child 6–13 years).

V. Families with teenagers (oldest child 13–20 years).

VI. Families with launching centers (first child gone to last leaving home).

VII. Middle-aged parents (empty nest to retirement).

VIII. Aging family members (retirement to death of both spouses).

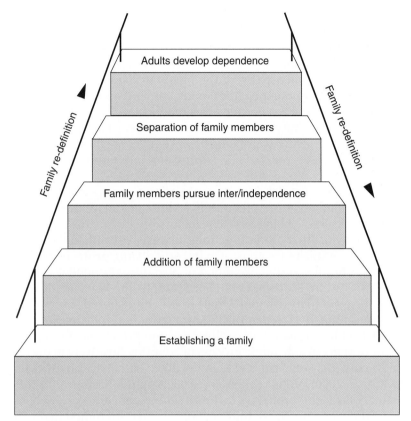

FIGURE 12.6
A New Family Development Framework
Today, family scholars recognize that diverse families vary in the ways they are established, develop, and change.

Source: From "A Framework for Teaching Family Development for the Changing Family" by Jack M. Richman & Patricia G. Cook, 2004, *Journal of Teaching in Social Work, 24*(1/2), 1–18. Copyright © 2004 by The Haworth Press. Reprinted by permission.

not all families progress through similar stages at the same rate (e.g., adolescents whose youngest sibling is born after they leave home) or sequence (e.g., a teenage mother who becomes a parent before marrying). In this view, the deviation of a large number of individuals or families from a normative path would be seen as an indication of social change (White & Klein, 2002). A recent revision of the family developmental model, illustrated in Figure 12.6, accommodates the variations in timing and structure common to diverse families in contemporary society, such as single parents, gay or lesbian families, or intergenerational households (Richman & Cook, 2004).

Guideposts for Working with Adolescents

- Remember that there is *often wide variation in the norms* for individual development across domains, and expect adolescents to be more mature in some areas than others.

- When considering teens' readiness for new experiences, discuss their fears and expectations as well as their individual development.

- Have teens diagram their family life course, creating a family tree or a historical timeline across the generations.

- Engage teens in group discussions with other adults and adolescents to help them see how their lives may be socially organized by family, school, or community norms.

RESEARCH ON RISK AND OPPORTUNITY IN ADOLESCENCE

During adolescence, teens may be learning to deal with their own and others' potentially risky behaviors (e.g., abusing substances like tobacco, alcohol, and other drugs; engaging in sexual activity; dropping out of school) as well as potentially risky environments (e.g., poor neighborhoods, violent schools, stressful families) (Furstenberg, 2001). In the last decade, researchers have focused on the relative influences of risk and opportunity in adolescence (see Boyer, 2006, for a review). This abiding concern for adolescents' well-being has also reflected the debate (discussed earlier) over whether the teen years are (a) stormy and inherently stressful or (b) relatively calm and normal.

Conceptually, **risk factors** are conditions or variables associated with a higher likelihood of negative outcomes in a variety of areas, from health and well-being to socially desirable behaviors. Risk factors operate by instigating or supporting problem behaviors that promote actions inconsistent with, for example, staying in school or avoiding substance abuse. On the other hand, **protective factors** have the reverse effect—they lessen the likelihood of negative consequences from exposure to risks (Jessor, Turbin, & Costa, 1998). For example, the Kauai study described in chapter 2 conceived of high-risk individuals who demonstrated successful outcomes in adulthood as *resilient* (Werner, 1993). Although some child development researchers have criticized the construct of resilience as too broad, most scholars agree that it commonly refers to a dynamic process of adapting positively in the context of significant adversity (Benson, Scales, & Mannes, 2003; Luthar, Cicchetti, & Becker, 2000; Masten & Curtis, 2000; Perkins & Borden, 2003; Wright & Masten, 2006). Box 12.4 describes a study of risk and protective factors in adolescence.

Many psychologists and sociologists have attempted to predict adolescents' risk behaviors. Yet there is a second, increasingly strong view, grounded in developmental theory, that is closer to "risk-taking as opportunity." In this view, adolescent problem behaviors are seen as normative, involving typical teenage experimentation, autonomy, and identity development (Lightfoot, 1997). Whether you are a high school teacher, social service provider, youth program specialist, or child development student, it is important to review the research on adolescent behavior from each of these two perspectives: risks and opportunities.

Teens living in high-risk environments can be protected from negative outcomes by a sense of competence, family support, and involvement in constructive activities.

Ken Karp/PH College

BOX 12.4   Roadmap to Understanding Theory and Research
Risk and Protection in Successful Outcomes Among Disadvantaged Adolescents

In a study of 1,638 socioeconomically disadvantaged middle school and high school students (40% Hispanic, 37% White, and 23% Black) from a large suburban school district, Richard Jessor and his colleagues Mark Turbin and Frances Costa assessed the role of risk and protective factors in promoting successful adolescent development. Despite adverse circumstances—such as poverty, dilapidated neighborhoods, inadequate resources, and exposure to dangers—many, if not most, teenagers "make it."

Conceptually, risk factors were defined as conditions associated with a lower likelihood of positive outcomes; protective factors were defined as the opposite; that is, as lessening the likelihood of negative consequences from exposure to risk. This study used the theoretical perspective of life-course development, in which successful outcomes are defined by the developmental stage of the person's life course—in this case, adolescence. Success was measured by two important tasks of adolescence: engaging in school and avoiding problem behavior.

Five risk factors and seven protective factors were examined in this study, as follows:

Risk Factors

- Low expectations for success
- Low self-esteem
- Sense of hopelessness
- Greater orientation to friends than parents
- Friends as models for problem behavior

Protective Factors

- Intolerance of deviance
- Positive orientation to health

- Religiosity
- Positive relations with adults
- Perception of social controls
- Friends as models for conventional behavior
- Involvement in prosocial activities

Socioeconomic disadvantage and risk factors were found to have significant negative effects on success, whereas protective factors had significant positive effects. In addition, protection moderated the effects of risk, especially for more disadvantaged youth. Key risk factors were low expectation for success, low self-esteem, hopelessness, and having friends as models for problem behavior. Key protective factors were intolerance of deviance, positive orientation to health, and having friends as models for conventional behavior.

The authors concluded that strengthening protective factors, as well as reducing risks, may enhance successful development:

> Overall the findings from this study begin to tell a story about how adolescents manage to make it despite the risk, the adversity, and the disadvantage that may have characterized their lives. A large part of that story, a part that is emerging more insistently in recent years, has to do with protection. The direct and the moderator effects of protection would seem to warrant further attention from researchers and interventionists alike. (p. 207)

Source: Based on "Risk and Protection in Successful Outcomes among Disadvantaged Adolescents" by R. Jessor, M. S. Turbin, & F. M. Costa, 1998. *Applied Developmental Science, 2,* pp. 194–208. Copyright © 1998 by Lawrence Ertbaum Associates, Inc.

Perspectives on Teen Risks

Researchers examining teen risks have attempted to identify overlapping problem behaviors (e.g., delinquency, substance use, teenage pregnancy, and school failure). Six common characteristics have predicted high-risk involvement (Dryfoos, 1990):

1. *Age.* Early initiation or occurrence of any problem behavior predicts heavy involvement and more negative consequences.

2. *Expectations for education and school grades.* Doing poorly in school, and expecting to do poorly, are associated with more problem behaviors, such as delinquency.

3. *General behavior.* Acting out, truancy, antisocial behavior, and other conduct disorders are related to high-risk behaviors, like substance abuse.

4. *Peer influence.* Having low resistance to peer pressure and having friends who participate in the same behaviors are common to high-risk adolescents.

5. *Parental role.* Having parents who do not monitor, supervise, offer guidance, or communicate with their children, or who are too authoritarian or too permissive, is related to being at high risk for problem behaviors.

6. *Neighborhood quality.* Living in a poverty area or in an urban, high-density community predicts high-risk behavior in adolescents.

Researchers have estimated that as many as one in four adolescents between ages 10 and 17 are in need of assistance because they are at high risk of engaging in multiple problem behaviors. Although ethnic-minority youth seem to have higher prevalence rates (i.e., because they may more often live in poorer, urban environments), the majority of multiproblem youth are White and male (Dryfoos, 1997). Researchers have compared inner-city youth to suburban adolescents and found that both groups experienced emotional distress and substance abuse, with higher levels among the more affluent teens (Luthar & Latendresse, 2002). In addition, so-called "normative risks," such as depression, may have different outcomes for sexual-minority youth who simultaneously experience peer harassment and discrimination (Russell, 2005). Unique risk factors for sexual minority adolescents include (adapted from Russell, 2005)

- *Coming out at a young age* (e.g., associated with increased suicide)
- *Coming out at school* (e.g., related to peer harassment)
- *Conflict with parents over coming out* (e.g., linked to running away)

In defining who is *at risk*, adolescents needing prevention services should include not only those teenagers who may not yet have initiated a problem behavior (e.g., smoking or drinking) that can have negative outcomes (i.e., lung cancer or drunk driving) but also those whose demographic, social, or personal characteristics predict that they are vulnerable (Dryfoos, 1997). Recent research on adolescents' judgments of "what is risky" has found that teenagers were likely to perceive themselves as vulnerable to personal risks, such as getting drunk, injured, or pregnant—even when controlling for experience and age differences (Millstein & Halpern-Felsher, 2002).

Perspectives on Teen Opportunities

Psychologists have suggested that an important developmental capacity of adolescence is **initiative**, or the motivation and ability to direct attention and effort toward a challenging goal (Larson, 2000). Much of the research on the normal developmental tasks of adolescence minimizes problem behaviors and instead considers adolescent risk-taking as a potential growth experience, associated with feelings of maturity and independence (Lightfoot, 1997; see also Jessor et al., 1998). Although some teen behaviors may be seen by parents as rebellious (e.g., spiking your hair or dressing "goth"), in fact they may be no more risky than many acceptable expressions of adolescent autonomy, such as learning to drive or beginning to date.

Research on teen opportunities emphasizes positive youth development despite the presence of risks in the environment. This area of study is known as **developmental strengths**, an approach to conducting adolescent research and preventive interventions with teens that focuses on three major elements (Benson et al., 2003):

1. *Competence.* **Competence** refers to successfully completing the developmental tasks expected at a given age in a particular cultural and historical and context (Masten & Curtis, 2000). Research with adolescents has found that areas of competence may include academic, social, athletic, romantic, and job competencies.

2. *Protective factors.* **Protective factors** refer to factors that play a role in protecting adolescents from risk, including intelligence, parenting, high commitment to school, positive orientation to health, having friends as models for conventional behavior, high self-efficacy, and a support system that encourages coping and positive values.

3. *Connectedness.* **Connectedness** refers to the quality and stability of the emotional bonds of support and caring that exist between teens and families, peers, and other adults. The National Longitudinal Study of Adolescent Health (Resnick et al., 1997) found that young people who experienced closer connections to their families and schools were less likely than other adolescents to engage in a variety of risk-taking behaviors, such as violence and substance abuse.

Some researchers referred to "the five C's of positive youth development: *Competence, Confidence, Character, Connection, and Caring*" (Lerner, Brentano et al., 2002, p. 23; see also Lerner, Almerigi, Theokas, & Lerner, 2005). When youth possess these Five Cs, a "Sixth C," *Contribution*, may emerge that enables them to transcend themselves and support their communities (Balsano, 2005; Lerner, Dowling, & Anderson, 2003).

Researchers studying developmental strengths have also identified sets of **developmental assets**, or strengths that serve a protective function in adolescence, similar to those listed in chapter 1 for middle childhood (see Table 1.4). The average number of assets decreases from 23 in sixth grade to 18 in twelfth grade, with boys averaging fewer assets than girls overall despite variations across communities (Benson, 2002). However, as assets rise in number, risk behavior patterns are reduced: alcohol, tobacco, and illicit drug use; antisocial behavior; violence; school failure; sexual activity; attempted suicide; and gambling. The cumulative effect is equally predictive of increases in positive behaviors: academic achievement; school grades; leadership; prosocial behavior; delay of gratification; and affirmation of diversity (Benson, 2002).

Leticia and her youth group at church are highly motivated to raise money for a good cause. They will work hard, hoping to raise $1,000 to buy new shoes for the children at the homeless shelter.

Built into the developmental asset model are external, **ecological assets**: support, empowerment, boundaries and expectations, and structured time use (Benson, 2002; Mancini & Huebner, 2004). Of course, what is protective may not be the same across differing contexts or cultures (Benson et al., 2003). For example, African American or Latino adolescents living in urban and/or high-risk environments may benefit from stricter parenting than teens whose parents think their neighborhoods are high in quality and safety (see reviews in Furstenberg, 2001; and O'Neil et al., 2001).

Developmental scholars, in particular, have reexamined risk and resilience concepts as they apply to adolescence and have incorporated culture and diversity (Arrington & Wilson, 2000). For example, in revising risk and opportunity models for studying ethnic-minority youth, who comprise one in three American adolescents (U.S. Bureau of the Census, 2000), researchers have asserted that several major factors affect the development of youth of color (García Coll et al., 1996):

- *Social position* (e.g., social class, gender, or race)
- *Racism and discrimination* (e.g., residential and psychological segregation)
- *Promoting/inhibiting environments* (e.g., schools and health care)
- *Adaptive culture* (e.g., traditions and legacies)
- *Children's characteristics and developmental competencies* (e.g., age or temperament)
- *Family values and beliefs* (e.g., ethics and religion)

The display of developmental competence despite possible adversity constitutes **resilience,** or successful adaptation (refer again to Figure 11.4). For example, new immigrants who settle in the downtown areas of large U.S. cities often achieve success despite being surrounded by poverty (Arrington & Wilson, 2000; Coatsworth, Pantin, & Szapocznik, 2002).

STOP What risks and what opportunities did you face as a teenager?

Sometimes, families may need supportive community programs to help them reduce the risks to adolescents that are too often associated with poor, urban environments. For example, Box 12.5 describes Familias Unidas, a community program designed to help Hispanic families build a strong parent support network and strengthen their culturally relevant parenting strategies (Coatsworth et al., 2002).

BOX 12.5   Roadmap to Successful Practice
Familias Unidas

Familias Unidas is a family-centered, multilevel prevention program designed to link together groups of recently immigrated Hispanic parents and to empower them to take leadership in structuring their adolescents' social ecology. The intervention aims to accomplish this goal by enhancing parents' knowledge about adolescent development in a multicultural urban environment and by assisting parents in developing the kinds of skills that will help them reduce risks and enhance protection in important developmental domains.

The program's philosophy is a blend of cognitive change strategies, behavioral skills training, and empowerment. The goal is the creation of a social ecology that is rich with positive, supportive interconnections, including a parenting network.

The intervention goals and activities are pictured in Figure 12.7.

In Familias Unidas, all intervention activities are organized around strengthening the family and placing it in charge of enhancing protective processes and decreasing risk within and across social systems. There are four phases: engagement, skill-building, restructuring, and evaluation.

Results from analysis of the effectiveness of Familias Unidas showed more improvement in parental investment and more consistent declines in behavior problems of adolescents than in control groups. In addition, families who participated in more intervention sessions showed significantly greater investment by parents, especially for higher socioeconomic and more acculturated families.

(continued)

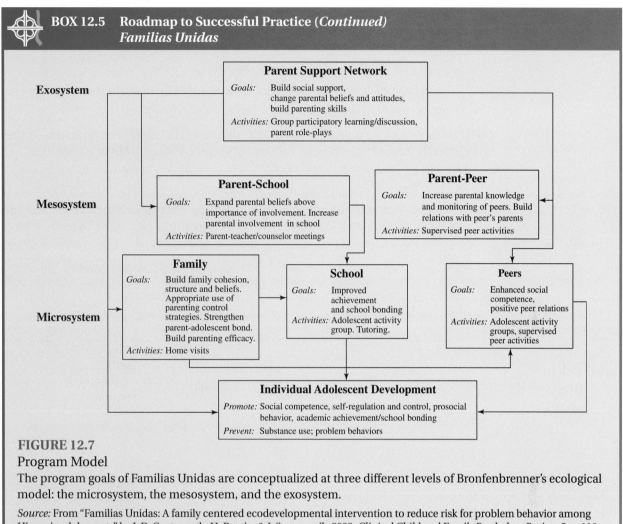

BOX 12.5   Roadmap to Successful Practice (*Continued*)
Familias Unidas

FIGURE 12.7

Program Model

The program goals of Familias Unidas are conceptualized at three different levels of Bronfenbrenner's ecological model: the microsystem, the mesosystem, and the exosystem.

Source: From "Familias Unidas: A family centered ecodevelopmental intervention to reduce risk for problem behavior among Hispanic adolescents" by J. D. Coatsworth, H. Pantin, & J. Szapocznik, 2002, *Clinical Child and Family Psychology Review*, 5, p. 116. Copyright © 2002 by Plenum Publishing Corporation. Reprinted with kind permission from Springer Science and Business Media.

Developmental scholars have found that "youth development programs seek to enhance not only adolescents' skills but also their confidence in themselves and their futures, their character, and their connections to other people and institutions by creating environments, both at and away from the programs, where youth can feel supported and empowered" (Roth & Brooks-Gunn, 2003, p. 219). In studies of sixth to twelfth graders in more than 200 U.S. communities, asset-building strategies that went beyond "village rhetoric" (i.e., it takes a village to raise a child) created healthy communities through economic development, neighborhood revitalization, and civic engagement (Scales, Benson, Leffert, & Blyth, 2000; Lerner, Taylor, & von Eye, 2002). Developmental assets, such as school success, leadership, valuing diversity, physical health, helping others, delaying gratification, and overcoming adversity have predicted thriving among adolescents across six ethnic groups. Furthermore, these developmental assets contribute significantly to positive adolescent outcomes over and above the influence of demographic variables, such as social class and geography (Scales et al., 2000; see also Theokas et al., 2005; Wright & Masten, 2006).

To support and foster positive youth development, we need to examine the key features of youth programs in schools, in communities, and in youth organizations (Oden, 1995):

- To learn how and why programs are effective
- To expand knowledge of outcomes for the youth who participate
- To guide policy or program replications from place to place

Refer to Table 12.1 for a description of effective youth development programs as they are currently being implemented in both community-based and school settings.

Social Policy Implications

As we have seen, the social construction of adolescence has changed from the earlier notion of a *problem* stage to the current conceptualization of the teen years as

---

TABLE 12.1   Characteristics of Youth Development Programs

Effective programs for youth development involve improving adolescent outcomes, creating a positive atmosphere, and offering activities to teens.

Outcomes	Definition
Competence	Interpersonal skills, cognitive abilities, school performance, work habits, and career choice
Confidence	Self-esteem, self-concept, self-efficacy, identity, and belief in the future
Connections	Building and strengthening relationship with other people and institutions, such as school
Character	Increased self-control, decreasing problem behaviors, respect for culture and society, morality, and spirituality
Caring	Improved empathy, compassion, and identification with others
Atmosphere	
Supportive	Encourage supportive relationships with adults and/or peer mentors
Empowering	Encourage useful roles, self-determination, and develop or clarify goals for the future
Expecting	Communicate expectations for positive behavior, clear rules, consequences; foster prosocial norms and healthy behaviors
Rewarding	Reward positive behaviors or structure opportunities for public recognition of skills
Lasting	Offer enduring support and opportunities for meaningful relationships that are ongoing
Activities	
Build skills	Engage in real and challenging activities, such as life skills training, or academic instruction
Authentic activities	Employment, leadership opportunities, such as peer mentoring or tutoring, and community service
Broaden horizons	Field trips, cultural activities, exposure to new people, places, or opportunities
Other contexts	Improve at least one other context: family, school, or community, e.g., parent activities, or teacher training

Source: Based on "What Is a Youth Development Program? Identification of Defining Principles" by J. L. Roth & J. Brooks-Gunn, in R. M. Lerner, F. Jacobs, & D. Wertleib (Eds.), *Handbook of Applied Developmental Science, Vol. 2: Enhancing the Life Chances of Youth and Families: Contributions of Programs, Policies, and Service Systems* (p. 218), 2003, Thousand Oaks, CA: Sage. Copyright 2003 by Sage Publications, Inc.

a *positive* developmental transition toward adulthood. Researchers have found that even if youths were vulnerable (i.e., had fewer developmental strengths or lived in less developmentally attentive communities), the percentage of vulnerable adolescents who successfully avoided problem behavior was higher in healthy communities (19% vs. 35%) (Blyth & Leffert, 1995). This finding means that vulnerable youth with fewer personal assets, in particular, may benefit from living in healthier communities. The policy implication is to improve neighborhood quality and community environment rather than to focus exclusively on adolescent problem behaviors.

Today, applied developmental researchers are attempting to reframe adolescence to policy makers. Public opinion of adolescents is too often framed by negative media reports. For example, public opinion polls have shown that 71% of Americans (and 74% of parents) believe that teenagers are disrespectful, irresponsible, and wild and that only 15% (and 12% of parents) think teens are smart, curious, or helpful (Public Agenda, cited in Roth & Brooks-Gunn, 2000). To counter these perceptions, youth policy advocates suggest four remedies (Roth & Brooks-Gunn, 2000):

1. Conduct positive media campaigns, legislative briefings, and liaisons with journalists and politicians.

2. Publish research reports that focus on the positive, not just on preventing problems, such as the percentage of youth who are engaged in volunteer activities, after-school programs, and school clubs.

3. Stress the intersections among the different settings influencing adolescents, such as schools, families, and peer groups.

4. Initiate community mobilization efforts, such as the Search Institute's *Healthy Communities–Healthy Youth Initiative* or the Social Development Research Group's *Communities That Care*.

A common framework emphasizing positive youth development has been developed to guide worldwide social policy makers using a broad set of principles applicable to wide-ranging contexts. Social policies should (adapted from Pittman, Diversi, & Ferber, 2002):

- Aim not only at preventing youth problems but also at promoting youth development and youth engagement in their communities.

- Be written in a way that presents clear pathways and trajectories of support from birth through adulthood.

- Reach across a range of settings, providing a full range of services, supports, and opportunities.

- Feature the voices and actions of young people themselves as agents of positive change.

Developing social policy for adolescents in the 21st century has become more challenging as societies become increasingly diverse, global, and postmodern. The changing view of adolescence has influenced youth policies in most American communities. Instead of the earlier focus on reducing problem behaviors, most policy makers now emphasize creating healthy communities as contexts for positive youth development (see Benson, Scales, Sesma, & Hamilton, 2006).

STOP If you were a policy maker or legislator, what youth policies or laws would you work to change?

Guideposts for Working with Adolescents

- Acknowledge adolescents' positive development in multiple contexts—home, school, and neighborhood—by attending local sporting events or extracurricular activities.

- Visit the communities in which teens live, work, and play and meet their families and friends.

- Remember that even if teens face numerous risk factors, such as poverty, they may be resilient due to protective factors in their environment, such as parental support.

- Make a list with teenagers of their "developmental assets" and design activities or create opportunities that build on their strengths.

Contexts of Middle Adolescence

From the perspective of positive youth development, adolescents' social contexts are central to understanding dynamic developmental change (see Lerner, Almerigi, Theokas, & Lerner, 2005). In a fascinating experiment, low-income youth who moved from economically and racially segregated neighborhoods to middle-class, primarily White neighborhoods responded to surveys two years after relocating. Compared to demographically similar youth who did not relocate, 8- to 9-year-olds experienced less victimization, fewer family and peer problems, and lower delinquency. However, 16- to 18-year-olds who moved to a "low-risk" neighborhood experienced *more* problems than youth who stayed in "high-risk" communities! Few effects were found for 10- to 15-year-olds (Fauth, Leventhal, & Brooks-Gunn, 2005). These results suggest that residential moves can have complex implications for developmental outcomes, especially in adolescence.

In adolescence, as in middle childhood, three contexts are salient: family, school, and community. Although developmental contexts are often viewed as separate environments, they are, in fact, overlapping. From a life-course perspective, studying context-context interactions also presents a changing picture over time, as adolescents move through normative developmental transitions, like getting a job or beginning to date. Most studies of the impact of context on adolescent behaviors have shown that the effects of families, schools, and neighborhoods are independent but, when added together, may exert a powerful influence on adolescent development (Furstenberg, 2001; see also Silbereisen, 2003).

Family Contexts

Researchers studying the interplay of family, schools, peers, and work in adolescence have found that the parent-adolescent relationship seems to be a major mediating link between experiences in various contexts outside the family and adolescents' psychosocial development (Silbereisen & Todt, 1994; see also Sheridan, Eagle, & Dowd, 2006). Recent surveys also indicate that many Americans believe that most parents provide too little supervision of their teenagers (Furstenberg, 2001). Several recent studies of family relations during adolescence have demonstrated that parenting influences many areas of adolescent development, such as temperament, autonomy, school achievement, and problem behavior (Borkowski, Ramey, & Bristol-Power, 2002). For example, in a recent study, parents' prior stereotypes about adolescence and their specific beliefs about their own children were related to their teens' social behaviors and relationships with deviant peers three years later (Jacobs, Chhin, & Shaver, 2005).

Michelle D. Bridwell/PhotoEdit Inc.

A supportive and involved family life is a developmental asset for adolescents.

In addition, interrelationships between the family context and other environments change as a function of adolescent development. Parents, for example, typically relax their rules for older adolescents. Adolescence is a time of major developmental transitions and of significant realignments in family relations as parenting demands change (Small & Eastman, 1995). Contextual sources of support for parenting, such as informal support networks through the child's school, need to change as adolescents develop relationships in the wider community. Leticia illustrates a central issue in understanding the importance of context in the study of adolescence:

> *Leticia is still worried. Her parents and older brother Lorenzo still see her as a child and won't accept the fact that she is responsible. "Why won't they let me grow up?" she asks Marina in frustration. At school, no one questions her judgment. Even her youth minister thinks that she is a good leader. If only her family could see her at school or volunteering at the homeless shelter! Leticia's involvement in youth ministry increases the likelihood that her mother will see her as able to make more of her own decisions in the near future.*

Children become more active in the selection of contexts when they reach adolescence. Time spent outside the home in adolescence generally increases at the expense of family time, although parents may choose neighborhoods, schools, churches, and other voluntary organizations in order to situate their adolescents in communities that are consistent with their own values (Furstenberg, 2001).

Studies of adolescent work have consistently demonstrated important linkages between contexts (Mortimer & Finch, 1996). For example, farming traditions in rural communities contribute to higher levels of prosocial behaviors, such as helping the family, among rural youth than among adolescents who leave the farm (Elder & Conger, 2000). In addition, researchers studying the relationships between work and family contexts have suggested that, due to gender-specific role expectations, females see home and work as conflictual, whereas male adolescents see these two contexts as compatible (Bowlby, Evans, & Mohammad, 1998; Camarena, Stemmler, & Petersen, 1994).

Some researchers have also pointed out harmful effects for both sexes of working during adolescence on school performance and educational commitment, such as getting good grades and staying in school (Greenberger & Steinberg, 1986). Other researchers have pointed out potential benefits of employment for gaining skills, psychological maturity, and social contacts (Mortimer & Finch, 1996). Most researchers studying adolescents with jobs agree that the consequences of working depend on the quality and safety of the context in which it occurs, the amount of adult supervision provided, and the limiting of long hours (Furstenberg, 2001).

> *Lorenzo works at the public library after school and on weekends. He wanted to work at an all-night diner, but his mother said no, emphatically. The library is well supervised, safe, and educational.*

School Contexts

Recently, community schools have emerged as a framework within which schools and many different community agencies, or partners, can come together to improve learning and development while strengthening families and communities (Blank, Shah, Johnson, Blackwell, & Ganley, 2003). In a summary report called *Learning Together*, the Institute for Educational Leadership described four major strategies of community schools: (a) service reform, (b) youth development, (c) community development, and (d) education reform (Melaville, 1998), as summarized in Table 12.2.

A significant shift in thinking about what adolescents need to become successful adults has been behind these recent efforts of the federal government to fund community-based schools, called *21st Century Learning Centers* (Roth & Brooks-Gunn,

---

TABLE 12.2   Strategies of Community Schools

Strategy	Goal	Objectives
Service Reform	Remove the nonacademic barriers to school performance by providing access to improved health and human services to young people and families	Create family support centers, health clinics, mental health services, crisis intervention programs, and other supports for students and their families, and sometimes residents, in the school
Youth Development	Help students develop their talents and abilities to participate fully in adolescence and adult life by increasing young people's opportunities to be involved in learning, decision making, service, and supportive relationships with others	Provide after-school mentoring, community service, service learning, recreation, leadership development, and career development programs
Community Development	Enhance the social, economic, and physical capital of the community by focusing on economic development	Create jobs, engage in community organizing, advocacy, and leadership development among community members, students, and parents
Education Reform	Improve educational quality and academic performance by improving the management, curriculum, instruction, and general culture within schools and classrooms	Engage parents, families, and teachers in school-based decision making, engage the private sector in a range of activities described in the previous objectives

Source: From *Learning Together: The Developing Field of School-Community Initiatives* by A. I. Melaville, 1998, pp. 14–15, Washington, DC: Mott Foundation. Available from http://www.mott.org/publications/pdf/SPECIALlearningtogether.pdf. Copyright © 1998 by the Charles Stewart Mott Foundation. Adapted by permission.

2003). Twenty-first-century schools were originally a response to a 1983 report of the National Commission on Excellence in Education, called *A Nation at Risk*. Complex studies of peer groups, especially in classroom and school contexts, have demonstrated how factors such as learning communities have shaped the course of adolescents' social and academic development (Furstenberg, 2001; Wigfield, Eccles, & Rodriguez, 1998). Researchers studying community schools have found significant improvements in the following areas (Dryfoos, 2000):

- *Achievement.* Academic gains in the areas of math and reading over a two- or three-year period
- *Attendance.* Lower drop-out rates, including the rate for pregnant teens
- *Suspensions.* Reductions in suspensions, suggesting improved school climate
- *High-risk behaviors.* Lower rates of substance abuse, teen pregnancy, and disruptive behavior
- *Parent involvement.* Heightened sense of adult support and parent involvement
- *Neighborhood.* Less violence and safer streets in their communities

A 21st-century school would provide Leticia's younger brother Raúl with an after-school program while she participates in a school youth group. It could even provide career counseling and job placement for their older brother Lorenzo.

Community Contexts

Youth development programs focus on communities to build the developmental strengths of adolescents and to promote their health and well-being (Benson et al., 2003). A **developmentally attentive community** is an environment that encourages the strength-building capacity of both youth and adults (as in Familias Unidas). In order to sustain a developmentally attentive community, adult engagement with adolescents is encouraged through the application of financial resources, social norms, and policies. Five types of community capacity have been described by researchers (Benson et al., 2003):

1. *Adult engagement.* Community adults build sustained, strength-building relationships with youth, both within and beyond family.
2. *Child, and especially youth, engagement.* Adolescents use their asset-building capacities with peers and younger children and in activities that enhance the quality of their communities.
3. *Community engagement.* Families, neighborhoods, schools, congregations, and youth organizations activate strength-building potentials.
4. *Programs.* A community infrastructure of quality after-school, weekend, and summer programs is available and used by children and youth.
5. *Community supports.* Financial, leadership, media, and policy resources are mobilized to sustain youth development.

The intersection of adolescent and community development has recently been termed **community-based human development** (Benson et al., 2003). This approach involves the social construction of adolescence as a *positive* period in human development and stresses the interplay of action and reflection, or *praxis*, in which teens and adults together engage in contemplating their own experiences as change agents in their communities. In this view, youth civic engagement is a component of social capital because the more civic engagement a society can secure across its citizens, the more social capital the society will have at its disposal (Balsano, 2005).

Participation in community service activities provides a context for youth civic participation (Youniss et al., 2002). More importantly, these experiences may provide adolescents with reflective opportunities at a critical juncture in the development of their adult identity (Larson, 2000). Ideally, a community-based human development approach would allow youth to become adults who contribute to their own self-development *and* to their communities in a way that advances social justice and a civil society (Lerner et al., 2002).

> *Leticia is able to reflect on the needs of homeless children and on how to raise money for the local shelter. As a result, Leticia not only sees herself as a change agent but also has enhanced her future identity as a socially responsible citizen.*

Studies have consistently demonstrated the influences of the community context on individual outcomes and positive adolescent development, but not on risky individual behaviors (Gilliam & Bales, 2001; Pittman et al., 2002). For example, "overcoming the odds" against positive development, African American male adolescents in urban gangs demonstrate developmental assets remarkably similar to those of youth living in the same communities but belonging to community-based organizations instead of gangs (Taylor et al., 2002a, 2002b; Taylor et al., 2005). Acknowledging the resilience of ethnic minority adolescents, applied developmental researchers have recognized the multiple contexts of school, family, neighborhoods, and religious institutions as a framework for the positive development of African American youth (Swanson et al., 2002). Thus, community-based researchers have integrated developmental scholarship with the promotion of positive youth development (Lerner, Fisher, & Weinberg, 2000; Lerner, Taylor et al., 2002; Roth & Brooks-Gunn, 2003; Whitlock & Hamilton, 2003).

CHAPTER REVIEW

History of Adolescence

- Adolescence is defined as the developmental period between puberty and young adulthood, roughly ages 13 to 18, although some researchers divide adolescence into early (10 to 14), middle (15 to 18), and late (18 to 24) adolescence.

- Adolescence has historically been viewed as a period of storm and stress, although current empirical research does not support this negative view. Recently, adolescence is more often viewed as a positive transition to adulthood.

- Rapid globalization has influenced adolescents across diverse societies, but due to variations in the social construction of adolescence, the meanings of adolescence are not universal in either their structure (e.g., timing or duration) or in their function (e.g., preparation for adulthood).

Developmental Perspectives

- Adolescent research is commonly divided into physical, cognitive, affective, and social domains of development.

- Life-span theory suggests that adolescence is a stage in the life span characterized by intraindividual change, interindividual differences, and historical embeddedness.

- Life-course theory suggests that adolescence can be studied by examining the timing, sequencing, and transitions between major life events in any given cohort or historical period.

Risk and Opportunity

- Researchers examining teen risks have attempted to identify overlapping problem behaviors that predict vulnerability during adolescence.

- Researchers examining teen opportunities have attempted to identify developmental assets or strengths that predict resilience to adversity during adolescence.

- Youth policies reflect a changing focus from preventing problem behaviors to enhancing developmental and ecological assets and positive youth development.

Contexts of Adolescence

- The interrelated contexts of positive development in adolescence include families, schools, and communities.

- Policy makers are increasingly involving community members and adolescents themselves in formulating youth policies.

TABLE 12.3   Summary of Developmental Theories

Chapter	Theory	Focus
12: Beyond Middle Childhood: Adolescence	Life Span	Development in relation to preceding and subsequent stages with a focus on both individual differences and developmental changes over time
	Life Course	Normative and nonnormative life events that are shaped by both historical events and adolescents' personal life histories

---

KEY TERMS

Adolescence
Adultification
Age-graded
Community-based human development
Compensation
Competence
Connectedness
Contextualism
Cultural globalization
Developmental assets
Developmental strengths
Developmental time

Developmentally attentive communities
Ecological assets
Economic globalization
Family careers
Family development theory
Family life cycle
Family time
Globalization
Historical embeddedness
Historical time
History-graded
Initiative

Interindividual differences
Intraindividual change
Life events
Life histories
Life-course development
Life-course theory
Life-span psychology
Metatheoretical paradigm
Moratorium
Multidirectional
Multidisciplinary
Nonnormative
Ontogenesis

Ontogeny
Phylogeny
Poststructuralism
Protective factors
Readiness
Recapitulation theory
Resilience
Risk factors
Rites of passage
Selective optimization
Social reproduction
Structural period
Sturm und drang

SUGGESTED ACTIVITIES

1. Talk with adolescents about the daily ups and downs in their lives. How supportive do they think their parents, siblings, and peers are of their concerns? Do you think these are typical concerns of most adolescents? Do they face any unusual stress? Do they show any unusual strengths?

2. Interview the parent(s) of a teenager. How has being the parent of an adolescent differed from what they expected? How do other people react when told the age of their teenager? Is their adolescent typical of teenagers today? How?

3. Look through a teen magazine of your choice. What is the magazine's general attitude about adolescence? Are the articles, advertisements, and photographs consistent with a positive image of adolescence, or do they reinforce negative stereotypes and problem behaviors?

4. Modify the traditional family development cycle pictured in Figure 12.5 so that it accurately represents your family of origin by enlarging or decreasing time spent in each stage, or changing the order of life-course events. Note how your family differs from Duvall's (1957) model family!

5. Ask an adolescent and/or a young adult to examine the list of personal risks and protective factors provided in Box 12.4. Ask them to imagine the various situations described and to make risk judgments for themselves in similar situations. Which risks were judged more likely to occur? How protected do they seem overall? How might personal experience and context have influenced their ratings?

6. Analyze an existing policy for youth in your state or local area. Who were the framers of the policy? Were youth involved in the establishment of the policy? Does the policy conform to the framework described in this chapter emphasizing positive youth development? If not, how could it be modified?

RECOMMENDED RESOURCES

Suggested Readings

Brown, B. B., Larson, R. W., & Saraswathi, T. S. (2002). *The world's youth: Adolescence in eight regions of the globe.* Cambridge, UK: Cambridge University Press.

Elkind, D. (1997). *All grown up and no place to go: Teenagers in crisis* (rev. ed.). New York: Perseus.

Gesell, A., Ilg, F. L., & Ames, L. B. (1956). *Youth: The years from ten to sixteen.* New York: Harper & Row.

Hersch, P. (1998). *A tribe apart: A journey into the heart of American adolescence.* New York: Ballantine.

Nichols, S. L., & Good, T. L. (2004). *America's teenagers— myths and realities: Media images, schooling, and the social costs of indifference.* Mahwah, NJ: Erlbaum.

Turning points: Preparing American youth for the 21st century. (1989). Available from the Carnegie Council on Adolescent Development, P.O. Box 753, Waldorf, MD 20604.

Villarruel, F. A., et al. (2003). *Community youth development: Programs, policies, and practices.* Thousand Oaks, CA: Sage.

Suggested Online Resources

Adolescents' Preparation for the Future: Perils and Promise (2002). http://www.s-r-a.org/studygroup.html

Building a Better Teenager: A Summary of "What Works" in Adolescent Development (2002). http://www.childtrends.org/files/k7Brief.pdf

Community Programs to Promote Youth Development (2002). Available online from the National Academies Press: http://books.nap.edu/books/0309072751/html/index.html

Forum for Youth Investment: Youth Development Resources. http://forumforyouthinvestment.org/_portalcat.cfm?LID=D662C83D-BEEE-4E8E-A926F89515009A78

Great Transitions: Preparing Adolescents for a New Century (1995). http://www.carnegie.org/sub/pubs/reports/great_transitions/gr_intro.html

Suggested Web Sites

Advocates for Youth.
    http://www.advocatesforyouth.org/
Carnegie Council on Adolescent Development.
    http://www.carnegie.org/sub/research/#adol
Center for Youth Development and Policy Research.
    http://www.aed.org/Youth/

Communication with Your Adolescent.
    http://www.aap.org/pubed/ZZZGP4ZUR7C.htm?&sub_cat=106
Society for Research on Adolescence.
    http://www.s-r-a.org/about.html

Suggested Films and Videos

American adolescence (1999). Films for the Humanities & Sciences (30 minutes)

Coming of age: Ethnographic profiles from a global perspective (2005). Films for the Humanities & Sciences (60 minutes)

A kind of childhood (2003). Direct Cinema. (52 minutes)

My so-called life (2002). Ventura Distribution. (60 minutes)

Sixteen candles (2003). Universal Studios. (93 minutes)

The teen years (*Ages 13 to 18*). (2000). Films for the Humanities & Sciences. (41 minutes)

Thirteen (2003). Fox Searchlight. (100 minutes)

Tough times, resilient kids: The documentary. (2002). Insight Media. (58 minutes)

APPENDIX

A Primer in Research Design

After you have asked a research question and formed a hypothesis, your next step is to develop the research design, or overall plan for your study. Research designs differ in the number of persons studied, the length of time needed for completion, and the applicability of their conclusions. The best research design will be determined by what you want to know. In this primer, we will describe some of the most common research designs used in developmental research, the types of questions each design best answers, and the strengths and limitations of each.

EXPERIMENTAL DESIGNS

If your research question were "to what extent does watching violence on television *cause* children to behave more aggressively," you might answer this question empirically using an experimental research design. Experimental designs are used to examine cause-and-effect relationships. Experimental studies typically include more than one group (e.g., an experimental and a control group) in which a variable is manipulated (i.e., the independent variable) and the effects of that manipulation are measured (i.e., the dependent variable). The specific components and procedural issues of designing an experiment are presented in Figure A.1.

An experimental design allows inferences about causation to be made because of the strict control it exercises over other variables that could influence the results. If an experiment is well designed and executed, much can be learned about causal influences on human development. However, results from a single experiment rarely define developmental phenomena. Rather, they initiate a systematic study of the phenomena over many trials, manipulating many different variables, under many different settings until we begin to have some understanding of, for example, how violence on television influences *some* children under certain circumstances.

Not all developmental phenomena can be manipulated in an experimental setting. This is a limitation of the experimental design. In fact, some researchers think that when children are studied in a laboratory setting rather than their homes, classrooms, or neighborhoods, the ecological validity, or authenticity of the setting, has been threatened (Bronfenbrenner, 1979; Bronfenbrenner & Morris, 2006). The importance of studying the developmental dynamics of a child within multiple contexts

FIGURE A.1

Sample Experimental Design

This figure shows how two groups of participants are exposed to the independent variable and how the outcome of the manipulation is measured in the dependent variable.

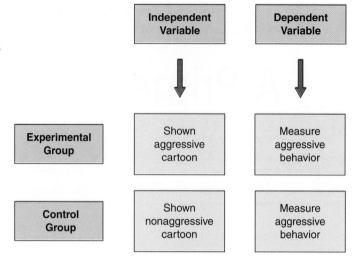

is emphasized in chapter 1 and is not translated easily into a laboratory experiment. In addition, there are interesting and important research questions which practically, or ethically, cannot be fit into an experimental design. Many psychologists, educators, and practitioners who read this textbook may not find the use of an experimental design feasible in their current or future work environment, but there are several alternative designs that are much more likely to be seen in a classroom, day care center, or after-school program.

ALTERNATIVE EXPERIMENTAL DESIGNS

In some circumstances not all of the control features in an experiment are possible to institute, most notably the random assignment of participants. For example, a teacher may be interested in trying a new pedagogical technique for teaching science to a fourth-grade class and would like to know if the students learn more using the new teaching technique. According to the procedural rules of a laboratory experiment, students should be randomly assigned to either the experimental or control group. But due to logistical constraints, such as time and space, the teacher cannot feasibly separate the class for the purposes of the experiment. To answer this research question, a pretest-posttest design could be used instead, where the researcher would test the participants *before* and *after* the manipulation or treatment. In this example, the teacher could establish a baseline measure of science knowledge by administering a pretest, introduce the new pedagogy, and then retest the students. The difference in performance between the pre- and posttest scores would be an indication of the success or failure of the new teaching technique.

A time-series design allows the researcher to administer two or more treatments or manipulations to the same participants at different times and then measure their behavior after each treatment or manipulation. Using the same class of science students, the teacher could present a lesson on the planet Neptune using a pedagogical technique that involves small group projects, and assess the learning after that session. This assessment would then be followed by the presentation of material on the planet Uranus, using a pedagogical technique that involves more experiential learning, such as creating a planet out of material that mimics the composition, weight, and density of the planet. This learning would be assessed and the overall amount of learning could be compared between the two pedagogical techniques.

Both the pretest-posttest and time-series designs allow for the use of a single group of research participants, thereby keeping intellectual, personality, and behavioral characteristics constant throughout the study and providing us with information about children's behaviors in their natural settings. These designs, however, do not rule out all factors that may be causing the change in students' science performance, such as motivation or illness, or a difference in the level of enthusiasm or competency the teacher offered when teaching similar material in two different ways. Also, they do not allow for a comparison to a similar group of students who have not been exposed to the new pedagogical techniques.

In natural experiments, researchers take advantage of different treatments or manipulations that already exist, such as different parenting styles, neighborhood resources, or after-school programs, and compare them. Bush and Simmons (1987) in a classic study of pubertal timing and school transitions, compared similar groups of girls who were either early, on-time, or later maturers, and then compared the self-esteem of those who transitioned to a new school in sixth or seventh grade. They found that those girls who matured early and made a school transition *simultaneously* (sixth grade) exhibited the lowest self-esteem scores compared to those who transitioned later (seventh grade) and began their pubertal change at the same time, or later than the other girls. This study illustrates how a natural experiment does not *assign* participants to a group, but rather capitalizes on conditions that exist in the societal structure. They include only groups of participants who are very similar in characteristics that could potentially influence the results. If differences were found between groups, then we could conclude that the differences were more likely the result of the program or, in this case, the interaction of puberty and transition, rather than differences among the participants.

Field experiments allow the researchers to manipulate an independent variable within the child's natural environment. These alternative designs have the advantage of working with participants in their natural environments, but the disadvantage of not allowing the elimination of other explanations for the differences between groups or changes in behavior.

CORRELATIONAL DESIGNS

A correlational study examines the relationship between two variables. If your research question were to ask the extent to which peer rejection and aggression are related, a correlational research design would be the appropriate organizational scheme. It would allow you to take two pieces of information and assess the strength of their relationship. For example, you could assess peer acceptance or rejection by asking a group of boys to list three boys whom they like most and least, and then correlate these peer nominations with your observational data of aggressive play behavior on the playground. If there were a relationship between peer rejection and aggression, then a statistical technique called a correlational analysis would yield a significant correlation coefficient, which is a numerical value between $+1.0$ and -1.0, indicating a relationship between the two variables. More

FIGURE A.2
Scatterplots of Positive and Negative Correlations

The top panel shows how an increase in aggressive behaviors is related to an increase in peer rejection. The bottom panel illustrates how an increase in peer rejection is related to a decrease in aggressive behvior.

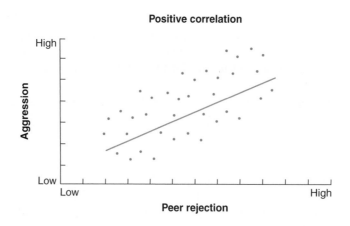

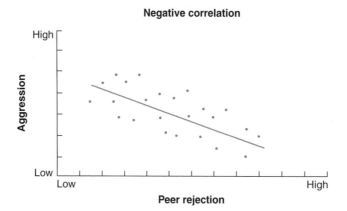

information about coefficient values and the meaning of correlational findings are presented in Figure A.2.

Correlational designs should be used when you are trying to establish a relationship between two or more phenomena and you have a large group of research participants. It is also a useful design to employ when conducting an experiment would be unethical. For example, a researcher interested in studying the relationship between glue sniffing and later cognitive deficits cannot force a group of middle-schoolers to sniff inhalants in order to compare them to children who were *not* exposed to inhalants. Many interesting research questions exist that cannot be experimentally manipulated, and therefore we must rely on correlational analyses to measure the possible connections between related variables. The major disadvantage associated with using a correlational design is that you *cannot imply causation*. For example, if you found that peer rejection and aggressive behavior were strongly correlated, you could not conclude that aggressive behavior *causes* peer rejection; it may be that peer rejection causes a child to respond more aggressively toward those by whom he is rejected. It is impossible to establish the direction of causality using a correlational design. It also may be that a third variable, such as a developmental disability, is having a causal effect on both peer rejection and aggression. Therefore, you cannot conclude that aggression causes peer rejection, acknowledging that the variables may or may not be significantly related to one another.

TABLE A.1   A Summary of Select Research Designs with Their Strengths and Limitations

Different types of research designs provide the researcher with different tools by which to answer a question about development.

Design	Strengths	Limitations
Experimental designs	• Causal relationships can be inferred	• Not all phenomena can be treated within this strictly controlled design
Alternative designs		
• Pretest/posttest	• One sample • Compares behavior before and after intervention	• Less control of variables that may influence results
• Time series	• One sample • Administration of two or more interventions to the same participants • Observe behavior after each intervention	• Less control of variables that may influence results
• Natural experiments	• Studying participants in their natural conditions	• Unable to match participants in groups on critical variables
• Field experiments	• Studying participants in their natural environment, but the researcher manipulates the independent variable	• Cannot control for other variables that may influence results
Correlational designs	• Can be used with large participant groups to understand the relationship between two variables	• Cannot infer cause and effect • Cannot determine the causal direction between two variables

---

Table A.1 is a summary of possible research designs and their accompanying strengths and limitations.

References

Aalsma, M. C., & Lapsley, D. K. (1999). Religiosity and adolescent narcissism: Implications for values counseling. *Counseling & Values, 44*(1), 17–30.

Aarnio, M., Winter, T., Kujala, U. M., & Kaprio, J. (1997). Familial aggregation of leisure-time physical activity—a three generation study. *International Journal of Sports Medicine, 18*, 549–556.

Abe, J. A., & Izard, C. E. (1999). Compliance, noncompliance strategies, and the correlates of compliance in 5-year-old Japanese and American children. *Social Development, 8*, 1–20.

Aber, J. L., Brown, J. L., & Jones, S. M. (2003). Developmental trajectories toward violence in middle childhood: Course, demographic differences, and response to school-based intervention. *Developmental Psychology, 39*(2), 324–348.

Abma, J., Driscoll, A., & Moore, K. (1998). Young women's degree of control over first intercourse: An exploratory analysis. *Family Planning Perspectives, 30*, 12–18.

Abrams, D., Rutland, A., & Cameron, L. (2003). The development of subjective group dynamics: Children's judgments of normative and deviant in-group and out-group individuals. *Child Development, 74*, 1840–1856.

Abroms, L., Simons-Morton, B., Haynie, D. L., & Chen, R. (2005). Psychosocial predictors of smoking trajectories during middle and high school. *Addiction, 100*, 852–861.

Adair, L. S., & Gordon-Larsen, P. (2001). Maturational timing and overweight prevalence in U.S. adolescent girls. *American Journal of Public Health, 91*, 642–644.

Adler, P. A., & Adler, P. (1998). *Peer power: Preadolescent culture and identity.* Brunswick, NJ: Rutgers University Press.

Administration for Children and Families. (2006). Healthy Marriage Initiative. Retrieved July 27, 2006, from http://www.acf.hhs.gov/healthymarriage/index.html.

Aftab, P. (2000). *The parent's guide to protecting your children in cyberspace.* New York: McGraw-Hill.

Agnew, R. (1991). The interactive effects of peer variables on delinquency. *Criminology, 29*, 47–72.

Ahrons, C. (1994). *The good divorce: Keeping your family together when your marriage comes apart.* New York: HarperCollins.

Ainsworth, M. D. S., & Bell, S. M. (1970). Attachment, exploration, and separation: Illustrated by the behavior of one-year-olds in a strange situation. *Child Development, 41*(1), 49–67.

Ainsworth, M. D. S., Bell, S., & Stayton, D. J. (1971). Individual differences in the development of some attachment behaviors. *Merrill-Palmer Quarterly, 18*, 123–143.

Ainsworth, M. D. S., Blehar, M. C., Waters, E., & Wall, S. (1978). *Patterns of attachment: A psychological study of the strange situation.* Hillsdale, NJ: Erlbaum.

Alan Guttmacher Institute. (1998). *Sex and America's teenagers.* New York: Author.

Alberts, A., Elkind, D., & Ginsberg, S. (2007). The personal fable and risk-taking during early adolescence. *Journal of Youth and Adolescence, 36*, 71–76.

Albrecht, S., Semrau, K., Kasonde, P., Sinkala, M., Kankasa, C., Vwalika, C. et al. (2006). Predictors of nonadherence to single-dose nevirapine therapy for the prevention of mother-to child HIV transmission. *JAIDS Journal of Acquired Immune Deficiency Syndromes, 41*, 114–118.

Aldous, J. (1996). *Family careers: Rethinking the developmental perspective.* Thousand Oaks, CA: Sage.

Aljughaiman, A., Mowrer-Reynolds, E. (2005). Teachers' conceptions of creativity and creative students. *Journal of Creative Behavior, 39*, 17–34.

Allington, R. L., & Johnston, P. H. (Eds.). (2002). *Reading to learn: Lessons from exemplary fourth-grade classrooms.* New York: Guilford Press.

Alsaker, F. D. (1992). Pubertal timing, overweight, and psychological adjustment. *Journal of Early Adolescence, 12*(4), 396–419.

Alvarez, J. M., Ruble, D. N., & Bolger, N. (2001). Trait understanding or evaluative reasoning? An analysis of children's behavioral predispositions. *Child Development, 72*, 1409–1425.

Amabile, T. M. (1982). Social psychology of creativity: A consensual assessment technique. *Journal of Personality and Social Psychology, 43*, 997–1013.

Amabile, T. M. (1983). *The social psychology of creativity.* New York: Springer-Verlag.

Amabile, T. M. (1996). *Creativity in context: Update to The Social Psychology of Creativity.* Boulder, CO: Westview Press.

Amato, P. R. (2000). The consequences of divorce for adults and children. *Journal of Marriage and Family, 62*(4), 1269–1287.

Amato, P. R., & Booth, A. (1996). A prospective study of divorce and parent-child relationships. *Journal of Marriage and Family, 58*, 356–365.

Amato, P. R., & Booth, A. (2001). The legacy of parents' marital discord: Consequences for children's marital quality. *Journal of Personality & Social Psychology, 81*(4), 627–638.

Amato, P. R., & Fowler, F. (2002). Parenting practices, child adjustment, and family diversity. *Journal of Marriage and Family, 64*, 703–716.

Amato, P. R., & Gilbreth, J. (1999). Nonresident fathers and children's well-being: A meta-analysis. *Journal of Marriage and Family, 61*, 557–573.

Amato, P. R., & Keith, B. (1991). Parental divorce and the well-being of children: A meta-analysis. *Psychological Bulletin, 110*, 26–46.

American Association of University Women. (1992). *The AAUW report: How schools shortchange girls.* Washington, DC: The AAUW Educational Foundation and National Education Association.

American Psychiatric Association. (2000). *Diagnostic and statistical manual of mental disorders: DSM-IV-TR* (4th ed.). Washington, DC: Author.

Ammaniti, M., Speranza, A. M., & Fedle, S. (2005). Attachment in infancy and in early and late childhood. In K. A. Kerns & R. A. Richardson (Eds.), *Attachment in middle childhood* (pp. 115–136). New York: Guilford Press.

Andersen, S. L. (2003). Trajectories of brain development: Point of vulnerability or window of opportunity? *Neuroscience and Biobehavioral Reviews, 27*, 3–18.

Anderson, C. A., Funk, J. B., & Griffiths, M. D. (2004). Editorial: Contemporary issues in adolescent video game playing: Brief overview and introduction to the special issue. *Journal of Adolescence, 27*, 1–3.

Anderson, D. R., Huston, A. C., Schmitt, K., Linebarger, D., & Wright, J. C. (2001). Adolescent outcomes associated with early childhood television viewing: The Recontact Study. *Monographs of the Society for Research in Child Development, 66*, vii–147.

Anderson, K. M. (1992). Self-complexity and self-esteem in middle childhood. In R. P. Lipka & T. M. Brinthaupt (Eds.), *Self-perspectives across the life span* (pp. 11–51). Albany: State University of New York.

Anderson, M., & Fienberg, S. E. (2000). Race and ethnicity and the controversy over the U.S. Census. *Current Sociology, 48*(3), 87–110.

Anderson-Butcher, D., Newsome, W. S., & Ferrari, T. M. (2003). Participation in boys and girls clubs and relationships to youth outcomes. *Journal of Community Psychology, 31*, 39–55.

Andersson, T., & Magnusson, D. (1990). Biological maturation in adolescence and the development of drinking habits and alcohol abuse among young males: A prospective longitudinal study. *Journal of Youth and Adolescence, 19*, 33–41.

Andersson-Ellstrom, A., Forssman, L., & Milsom, I. (1996). Age of sexual debut related to life-style and reproductive health factors in a group of Swedish teenage girls. *Acta Obstetricia et Gynecologica Scandinavica, 75*(5), 484–489.

Andre, T., Whigham, M., Hendrickson, A., & Chambers, S. (1999). Competency beliefs, positive affect, and gender stereotypes of elementary students and their parents about science versus other school subjects. *Journal of Research in Science Teaching, 36*, 719–747.

Andrews, G., Skinner, D., & Zuma, K. (2006). Epidemiology of health and vulnerability among children orphaned and made vulnerable by HIV/AIDS in sub-Saharan Africa. *AIDS Care, 18*, 269–276.

Anfara, V. A., Jr. (2001). *Handbook of research in middle level education*. Greenwich, CT: Information Age Publishing.

Annett, M. (1999). Left-handedness as a function of sex, maternal versus paternal inheritance, and report bias. *Behavior Genetics, 29*, 103–114.

Anthias, F. (2002). Where do I belong? Narrative collective identity and translocational positionality. *Ethnicities, 2*(4), 491–514.

Aries, P. (1962). *Centuries of childhood: A social history of family life*. (R. Baldick, Trans.). New York: Random House. (Original work published 1960).

Arnett, J. J. (2002). The psychology of globalization. *American Psychologist, 57*, 774–783.

Arrington, E. G., & Wilson, M. N. (2000). A reexamination of risk and resilience during adolescence: Incorporating culture and

diversity. *Journal of Child and Family Studies, 9*, 221–230.

Arsenio, W. F., & Lemerise, E. A. (2001). Varieties of childhood bullying: Values, emotion processes, and social competence. *Social Development, 10*(1), 59–73.

Asher, S. R., Parker, J. G., & Walker, D. L. (1996). Distinguishing friendship from acceptance: Implications for intervention and assessment. In W. M. Bukowski & A. F. Newcomb (Eds.), *The company they keep: Friendship in childhood and adolescence* (pp. 366–405). New York: Cambridge University Press.

Aten, M. J., Siegel, D. M., Enaharo, M., & Auinger, P. (2002). Keeping middle school students abstinent: Outcomes of a primary prevention intervention. *Journal of Adolescent Health, 31*, 70–78.

Atwood, J. D. (2006). Mommy's little angel, daddy's little girl: Do you know what your preteens are doing? *American Journal of Family Therapy, 34*, 447–467.

Averett, S. L., Rees, D. I., & Argys, L. M. (2002). The impact of government policies and neighborhood characteristics on teenage sexual activity and contraceptive use. *American Journal of Public Health, 92*, 1773–1778.

Azmitia, M., Kamprath, N. A., & Linnet, J. (1998). Intimacy and conflict: The dynamics of boys' and girls' friendships during middle childhood and early adolescence. In L. H. Meyer & H. Park (Eds.), *Making friends: The influences of culture and development: Vol. 3. Children, youth, and change: Sociocultural perspectives* (pp. 171–187). Baltimore, MD: Paul H. Brooks.

Bachman, J. G., & Van Duinen, E. (1971). *Youth look at national problems: A special report from the youth in transition project*. Ann Arbor, MI: Institute for Social Research.

Baenen, J. (2002). *Exploring the 'cusp culture' helps adolescents navigate the way to adulthood*. Retrieved July 7, 2002, from http://www.nmsa.org.

Bailey, J. M. (1996). Gender identity. In R. C. Savin-Williams & K. M. Cohen (Eds.), *The lives of lesbians, gays, and bisexuals: Children to adults* (pp. 71–93). Belmont, CA: Thomson.

Bailey, J. M., & Zucker, K. L. (1995). Childhood sex-typed behavior and sexual orientation: A conceptual analysis and quantitative review. *Developmental Psychology, 31*, 43–55.

Baillie, L., Lovato, C. Y., Johnson, J. L., & Kalaw, C. (2005). Smoking decisions from a teen perspective: A narrative study. *Journal of Health Behavior, 29*, 99–106.

Baker, D., & Leary, R. (1995). Letting girls speak out about science. *Journal of Research in Science Teaching, 32*, 3–27.

Balsano, A. B. (2005). Youth civic engagement in the United States: Understanding and addressing the impact of social impediments on positive youth and commu-

nity development. *Applied Developmental Science, 9*, 188–201.

Baltes, P. B. (1987). Theoretical propositions of life-span developmental psychology: On the dynamics between growth and decline. *Developmental Psychology, 23*, 611–626.

Baltes, P. B. (1997). On the incomplete architecture of human ontogeny: Selection, optimization, and compensation as foundation of developmental theory. *American Psychologist, 57*, 366–380.

Baltes, P. B., Lindenberger, U., & Staudinger, U. M. (2006). Life-span theory in developmental psychology. In W. Damon & R. M. Lerner (Series Ed.) & R. M. Lerner (Vol. Ed.), *Handbook of child psychology: Vol. 1. Theoretical models of human development* (6th ed., pp. 569–664). New York: Wiley.

Baltes, P. B., Reese, H. W., & Lipsett, L. P. (1980). Life-span developmental psychology. *Annual Review of Psychology, 31*, 65–110.

Bancroft, J., Herbenick, D. L., & Reynolds, M. A. (2003). Masturbation as a marker of sexual development: Two studies 50 years apart. In J. Bancroft (Ed.), *Sexual development in childhood* (pp. 156–185). Bloomington, IN: Indiana University Press.

Bandura, A. (1971). *Social learning theory*. Englewood Cliffs, NJ: Prentice Hall.

Bandura, A. (1981). Self-referent thought: A developmental analysis of self-efficacy. In J. H. Flavell & L. Ross (Eds.), *Social cognitive development: Frontiers and possible futures* (pp. 200–239). Cambridge, UK: Cambridge University Press.

Bandura, A. (1987). *Social foundations of thought and action: A social cognitive theory*. Englewood Cliffs, NJ: Prentice Hall.

Bandura, A. (1990). Conclusion: Reflections on nonability determinants of competence. In R. J. Sternberg & J. Kolligian (Eds.), *Competence considered* (pp. 315–362). New Haven, CT: Yale University Press.

Bandura, A. (1994). *Self-efficacy: The exercise of control*. New York: Freeman.

Bandura, A. (2001). Social cognitive theory: An agentic perspective. *Annual Review of Psychology, 52*, 1–26.

Bank, L., Burraston, B., & Snyder, J. (2004). Sibling conflict and ineffective parenting as predictors of adolescent boys' antisocial behavior and peer difficulties: Additive and interactive effects. *Journal of Research on Adolescence, 14*, 99–125.

Barber, B. K., & Olsen, J. A. (2004). Assessing the transitions to middle and high school. *Journal of Adolescent Research, 9*, 3–30.

Barbour, A. C. (1999). The impact of playground design on the play behaviors of children with differing levels of physical competence. *Early Childhood Research Quarterly, 14*, 75–98.

Barker, E. T., & Galambos, N. L. (2003). Body dissatisfaction of adolescent girls and boys: Risk and resource factors. *Journal of Early Adolescence, 23*, 141–165.

Barkley, R. A. (1998). *Attention-deficit/hyperactivity disorder: A handbook for diagnosis and treatment* (2nd ed.). New York: Guilford Press.

Barkley, R. A. (2000). *Taking charge of ADHD: The complete, authoritative guide for parents.* New York: Guilford Press.

Barnes, H. L., & Olsen, D. H. (1985). Parent-adolescent communication and the Circumplex model. *Child Development, 56,* 438–447.

Barnes, H. V. (1975). Physical growth and development during puberty. *Medical Clinics of North America, 59,* 1305–1317.

Barnett, W. S., & Camilli, G. (2002). Compensatory preschool education, cognitive development, and "race." In J. M. Fish (Ed.), *Race and intelligence: Separating science from myth* (pp. 369–406). Mahwah, NJ: Lawrence Erlbaum.

Barth, F. (Ed.) (1993). *Ethnic groups and boundaries.* Boston: Little, Brown.

Bartholomew, K., & Horowitz, L. M. (1991). Attachment styles among young adults: Test of a four-category model. *Journal of Personality and Social Psychology, 61,* 226–244.

Bartini, M. (2006). Gender role flexibility in early adolescence: Developmental change in attitudes, self-perceptions, and behaviors. *Sex Roles, 55,* 233–245.

Bates, J. E. (2000). Temperament as an emotion construct: Theoretical and practical issues. In M. Lewis & J. M. Haviland-Jones (Eds.), *Handbook of emotions* (2nd ed., pp. 382–396). New York: Guilford Press.

Baumann, J. F., Font, G., Edwards, E. C., & Boland, E. (2005). Strategies for teaching middle-grade students to use word-part and context clues to expand reading vocabulary. In E. H. Hiebert & M. L. Kamil (Eds.), *Teaching and learning vocabulary: Bringing research to practice* (pp. 179–205). Mahwah, NJ: Erlbaum.

Baumrind, D. (1971). Current patterns of parental authority. *Developmental Psychology Monographs, 4*(1, Pt. 2).

Baumrind, D. (1978). Parental disciplinary patterns and social competence in children. *Youth and Society, 9,* 239–276.

Baumrind, D. (1991). Effective parenting during the early adolescent transition. In P. A. Cowan & M. Hetherington (Eds.), *Family transitions.* Hillsdale, NJ: Erlbaum.

Bauer, N. S., Lozano, P., & Rivara, F. P. (2007). The effectiveness of the Olweus prevention program in public middle schools: A controlled trial. *Journal of Adolescent Health, 40,* 266–274.

Bauserman, R. (2002). Child adjustment in joint-custody versus sole-custody arrangements: A meta-analytic review. *Journal of Family Psychology, 16,* 91–102.

Bauserman, R., & Davis, C. (1996). Perceptions of early sexual experiences and adult sexual adjustment. *Journal of Psychology and Human Sexuality, 8,* 37–59.

Beaumont, S. (2000). Conversational styles of mothers and their preadolescent and middle adolescent daughters. *Merrill-Palmer Quarterly, 46,* 119–139.

Beers, K. (2003). *When kids can't read: What teachers can do: A guide for teachers 6–12.* Portsmouth, NH: Heinemann.

Beighle, A., & Pangrazi, R. P. (2006). Measuring children's activity levels: The association between step-counts and activity time. *Journals of Physical Activity and Health, 3*(2), 221–229.

Belsky, J., Steinberg, L., & Draper, P. (1991). Childhood experience, interpersonal development, and reproductive strategy: An evolutionary theory of socialization. *Child Development, 62,* 647–670.

Bem, S. L. (1974). The measurement of psychological androgyny. *Journal of Consulting and Clinical Psychology, 42,* 155–162.

Bem, S. L. (1981). Gender schema theory: A cognitive account of sex typing. *Psychological Review, 88*(4), 354–364.

Bem, S. L. (1993). *The lenses of gender: Transforming the debate on sexual inequality.* New Haven, CT: Yale University Press.

Benjet, C., & Hernandez-Guzman, L. (2002). A short-term longitudinal study of pubertal change, gender, and psychological well-being of Mexican early adolescents. *Journal of Youth and Adolescence, 31*(6), 429–442.

Benson, P. L. (2002). Adolescent development in social and community context: A program of research. *New Directions for Youth Development, 95,* 123–147.

Benson, P. L. (2004). Emerging themes in research on adolescent spiritual and religious development. *Applied Developmental Science, 8*(1), 47–50.

Benson, P. L., Espeland, P., & Galbraith, J. (1998). *What teens need to succeed: Proven, practical ways to shape your own future.* Minneapolis: Free Spirit.

Benson, P. L., Scales, P. C., & Mannes, M. (2003). Developmental strengths and their sources: Implications for the study and practice of community building. In R. M. Lerner, F. Jacobs & D. Wertleib (Eds.), *Handbook of applied developmental science: Vol. 1. Applying developmental science for youth and families: Historical and theoretical foundations* (pp. 369–406). Thousand Oaks, CA: Sage.

Benson, P. L., Scales, P. C., Sesma, A. Jr., & Hamilton, S. F. (2006). Positive youth development: Theory, research, and applications. In W. Damon & R. M. Lerner (Series Eds.) & R. M. Lerner (Vol. Ed.), *Handbook of child psychology: Vol. 1. Theoretical models of human development* (6th ed., pp. 894–941). New York: Wiley.

Berenbaum, S. A., Korman, K., & Leveroni, C. (1995). Early hormones and sex differences in cognitive abilities. *Learning and Individual Differences, 7,* 303–321.

Bergen, D., & Mauer, D. (2000). Symbolic play, phonological awareness, and literacy skills at three age levels. In K. A. Roskos & J. F. Christie (Eds.), *Play and literacy in early childhood: Research from multiple perspectives* (pp. 45–62). Mahwah, NJ: Erlbaum.

Berger, K. S. (2007). Update on bullying at school: Science forgotten? *Developmental Review, 27,* 90–126.

Berger, R. (2001). Gay stepfamilies: A triple-stigmatized group. In J. M. Lehmann (Ed.), *The gay and lesbian marriage & family reader: Analyses of problems and prospects for the 21st century* (pp. 171–194). New York: Gordian Knot/Altschuler.

Bergman, L. R., Magnusson, D., & El-Khouri, B. M. (2003). *Studying individual development in an interindividual context: A person-oriented approach.* Mahwah, NJ: Lawrence Erlbaum Associates.

Berk, L. (2003). *Child development* (6th ed.). New York: Pearson Education.

Berkey, C. S., Gardner, J. D., Frazier, A. L., & Colditz, G. A. (2000). Relation of childhood diet and body size to menarche and adolescent growth in girls. *American Journal of Epidemiology, 152,* 446–452.

Berndt, T. J. (1989). Obtaining support from friends during childhood and adolescence. In D. Belle (Ed.), *Children's social networks and social supports* (pp. 173–188). New York: Wiley.

Berndt, T. J. (2002). Friendship quality and social development. *Current Directions in Psychological Science, 11*(1), 7–10.

Bers, M. U. (2006). The role of new technologies to foster positive youth development. *Applied Developmental Science, 10,* 200–219.

Berscheid, E., Snyder, M., & Omoto, A. M. (1989). The Relationship Closeness Inventory: Assessing the closeness of personal relationships. *Journal of Personality and Social Psychology, 57,* 792–807.

Best, D. L. (2004). Gender roles in childhood and adolescence. In U. P. Gielen & J. Roopnarine (Eds.), *Childhood and adolescence: Cross-cultural perspectives and applications* (pp. 199–228). Westport, CT: Praeger.

Betancur, C., Leboyer, M., & Gillberg, C. (2002). Increased rate of twins among affected sibling pairs with autism. *American Journal of Human Genetics, 70,* 1381–1383.

Bigelow, B. J. (1977). Children's friendship expectations: A cognitive-developmental study. *Child Development, 48,* 246–253.

Bigelow, B. J., & LaGaipa, J. J. (1995). The development of friendship values and choice. In H. C. Foot, A. L. Chapman & J. R. Smith (Eds.), *Friendship and social relations in children* (pp. 15–44). New Brunswick, NJ: Transaction.

Bigler, R. S. (1995). The role of classification skill in moderating environmental influences on children's gender stereotyping: A study of the functional use of gender in the classroom. *Child Development, 66,* 1072–1087.

Bigler, R. S., Jones, L.C., & Lobliner, D. B. (1997). Social categorization and the formation of intergroup attitudes in children. *Child Development, 68,* 530–543.

Biro, F. M., McMahon, R. P., Striegel-Moore, R., Crawford, P. B., Obarzanek, E., & Morrison, J. A. (2001). Impact of timing of pubertal maturation on growth in black and white female adolescents: The National Heart, Lung, and Blood Institute Growth and Health Study. *Journal of Pediatrics, 138,* 636–643.

Bjorklund, D. A., & Schneider, W. (1996). The interaction of knowledge, aptitudes, and strategies in children's memory performance. In H. W. Reese (Ed.), *Advances in child development and behavior* (Vol. 26, pp. 59–89). San Diego, CA: Academic Press.

Bjorklund, D. F. (1997). The role of immaturity in human development. *Psychological Bulletin, 122,* 153–169.

Bjorklund, D. F. (2000). *Children's thinking: Developmental function and individual differences* (3rd ed.). Belmont, CA: Wadsworth.

Bjorklund, D. F., & de Marchena, M. R. (1984). Developmental shifts in the basis of organization in memory: The role of associative versus categorical relatedness in children's free-recall. *Child Development, 55,* 952–962.

Blanck, G. (1992). Vygotsky: The man and his cause. In L. C. Moll (Ed.), *Vygotsky and education: Instructional implications and applications of sociohistorical psychology* (pp. 31–58). New York: Cambridge University Press.

Blank, M., Melaville, T., & Shah, B. (2003). *Making the difference: Research and practice in community schools.* Washington, DC: Coalition of Community Schools.

Blank, M. J., Shah, B., Johnson, S., Blackwell, W., & Ganley, M. (2003). Reforming education: Developing twenty-first century community schools. In R. M. Lerner, F. Jacobs, & D. Wertleib (Eds.), *Handbook of applied developmental science: Vol. 2. Enhancing the life chances of youth and families: Contributions of programs, policies, and service systems* (pp. 291–310). Thousand Oaks, CA: Sage.

Bloom, B. (Ed.). (1985). *Developing talent in young people.* New York: Ballentine.

Bloom, L. (1998). Language acquisition in its developmental context. In W. Damon (Series Ed.) & D. Kuhn & R. S. Siegler (Vol. Eds.), *Handbook of child psychology: Vol. 2. Cognition, perception, and language* (5th ed., pp. 309–370). New York: Wiley.

Blume, L. B. (2001, August). *Body, self, creativity, and identity in adolescent female dancers.* Paper presented at the annual meetings of the American Psychological Association, San Francisco, CA.

Blume, L. B., & Blume, T. W. (1997). Negotiating identity in parent-adolescent relationships. *Theory Construction and Research Methodology, Vol. 27.* Available from the National Council on Family Relations, 5989 Central Avenue, NE, Suite 550, Minneapolis, MN, 55421.

Blume, L. B., & Blume, T. W. (2003). Toward a dialectical model of family gender discourse: Body, identity, and sexuality. *Journal of Marriage and Family, 65*(4), 785–794.

Blume, T. W. (2006). *Becoming a family counselor: A bridge to family therapy, theory, and practice.* New York: Wiley.

Blume, L. B., & DeReus, L. A. (2007). Transnational families and the social construction of identity: Whiteness matters. In R. L. Dalla, J. DeFrain, J. Johnson, & D. Abbott (Eds.), *Strengths and challenges of new immigrant families: Implications for research, policy, education, and service.* New York: Lexington Press.

Blumenfeld, P., Modell, J. Bartko, W. T., Secada, W. G., Fredricks, J. A., Friedel, J., et al., (2005). School engagement of inner-city students during middle childhood. In C. R. Cooper, C. T. Garcia Coll, W. T. Bartko, H. Davis, & C. Chatman (Eds.), *Developmental pathways through middle childhood: Rethinking contexts and diversity as resources* (pp. 145–170). Mahwah, NJ: Erlbaum.

Blyth, D. A., & Leffert, N. (1995). Communities as contexts for adolescent development: An empirical analysis. *Journal of Adolescent Research, 10,* 64–87.

Blythe, J., & Rosenthal, S. L. (2000). Female adolescent sexuality: Promoting healthy sexual development. *Obstetrics and Gynecology in Clinics of North America, 27,* 125–141.

Bock, R. D. (2004). Multiple prepubertal growth spurts in children of the Fels Longitudinal Study: Comparison with results from the Edinburgh Growth Study. *Annals of Human Biology, 31,* 59–74.

Bohlin, G., Hagekull, B., & Rydell, A. (2000). Attachment and social functioning: A longitudinal study from infancy to middle childhood. *Social Development, 9,* 24–39.

Bolger, K. E., & Patterson, C. (2001). Developmental pathways from child maltreatment to peer rejection. *Child Development, 72,* 549–568.

Bonino, S., & Cattelino, E. (1999). The relationship between cognitive abilities and social abilities in childhood: A research on flexibility in thinking and co-operation with peers. *International Journal of Behavioral Development, 23*(1), 19–36.

Boocock, S. S., & Scott, K. A. (2005). *Kids in context: The sociological study of children and childhoods.* Lanham, MD: Rowman & Littlefield.

Boomer, L. (Executive Producer). (2000). *Malcolm in the middle* [Television series]. Beverly Hills, CA: Fox Broadcasting.

Booth-LaForce, C., Rubin, K. H., Rose-Krasnor, L., & Burgess, K. (2005). Attachment and friendship predictors of psychosocial functioning in middle childhood and the mediating roles of social support and self-worth. In K. A. Kerns & R. A. Richardson (Eds.), *Attachment in middle childhood* (pp. 161–188). New York: Guilford Press.

Borkowski, J. G., Ramey, S. L., & Bristol-Power, M. (2002). *Parenting and the child's world: Influences on academic, intellectual, and social-emotional development.* Mahwah, NJ: Erlbaum.

Bourdieu, P. (1977). *Outline of a theory of practice.* New York: Cambridge University Press.

Bowen, M. (1978). *Family therapy in clinical practice.* New York: Aronson.

Bowen, N. K., Bowen, G. L., & Cook, W. B. (2000). Neighborhood characteristics and supportive parenting among single mothers. In G. L. Fox & M. L. Benson (Eds.), *Contemporary perspectives in family research. Vol 2. Families, crime, and criminal justice* (pp. 183–206). New York: Elsevier.

Bowlby, J. (1969). *Attachment and loss, Vol. 1.* New York: Basic.

Bowlby, J. (1973). *Attachment and loss, Vol. 2.* New York: Basic.

Bowlby, J. (1988). *A secure base: Parent-child attachment and healthy human development.* New York: Basic.

Bowlby, S., Evans, S. L., & Mohammad, R. (1998). In T. Skelton & G. Valentine (Eds.), *Cool places: Geographies of youth cultures* (pp. 229–248). London: Routledge.

Boyatzis, C., Dollahite, D., & Marks, L. (2005). The family context of children's spiritual and religious development. In P. E. King & E. C. Roehlkepartain (Eds.), *Handbook of spiritual development in childhood and adolescence* (pp. 297–309). Thousand Oaks, CA: Sage.

Boyce, W., Doherty, M., Fortin, C., & MacKinnon, D. (2003). *Canadian youth, sexual health and HIV/AIDS study: Factors influencing knowledge, attitudes and behaviours.* Toronto, ON: Council of Ministers of Education.

Boyce, W. T., & Ellis, B. J. (2005). Biological sensitivity to context: I. An evolutionary developmental theory of the origins and functions of stress reactivity. *Development and Psychopathology, 17,* 271–310.

Boyer, E. L. (1983). *High school: A report on secondary education in America of the Carnegie Foundation for the Advancement of Teaching.* New York: Harper & Row.

Boyer, T. W. (2006). The development of risk-taking: A multi-perspective review. *Developmental Review, 26,* 291–345.

Bradley, R. H., & Corwyn, R. F., (2002). Socioeconomic status and child development, *Annual Review of Psychology, 53,* 371–399.

Brendgen, M., Vitaro, F., & Doyle, A. (2002). Same-sex peer relations and romantic relationships during early adolescence: Interactive links to emotional, behavioral, and academic adjustment. *Merrill-Palmer Quarterly, 48,* 77–103.

Bretherton, I., & Munholland, K. A. (1999). Internal working models in attachment relationship: A construct revisited. In J. Cassidy & P. R. Shaver (Eds.), *Handbook of attachment: Theory, research, and clinical applications* (pp. 89–111). New York: Guilford Press.

Brody, G., Stoneman, Z., & McCoy, J. (1994). Contributions of family relationships and child temperaments to longitudinal variations in sibling relationship quality and sibling relationship styles. *Journal of Family Psychology, 8,* 274–286.

Bronfenbrenner, U. (1979). *The ecology of human development: Experiments by nature and design.* Cambridge, MA: Harvard University Press.

Bronfenbrenner, U., & Ceci, S. J. (1994). Nature-nurture reconceptualized in developmental perspective: A bioecological model. *Psychology Review, 101,* 568–586.

Bronfenbrenner, U., & Crouter, A. C. (1983). The evolution of environmental models in developmental research. In W. Kessen (Series Ed.) & P. H. Mussen (Vol. Ed.), *Handbook of child psychology: Vol. 1. History, theory, and methods* (4th ed., pp. 357–414). New York: Wiley.

Bronfenbrenner, U., & Morris, P. A. (2006). The ecology of developmental processes. In W. Damon & R. M. Lerner (Series Eds.) & R. M. Lerner (Vol. Ed.), *Handbook of child psychology: Vol. 1. Theoretical models of human development* (6th ed., pp. 793–828). New York: Wiley.

Brooks-Gunn, J., Petersen, A. C., & Eichorn, D. (1985). The study of maturational timing effects in adolescence. *Journal of Youth and Adolescence, 14*(3), 149–161.

Brooks-Gunn, J., & Reiter, E. O. (1990). The role of pubertal processes. In S. S. Feldman & G. R. Elliot (Eds.), *At the threshold: The developing adolescent* (pp. 16–53). Cambridge, MA: Harvard University Press.

Brooks-Gunn, J., & Warren, M. P. (1989). Biological and social contributions to negative affect in young adolescent girls. *Child Development, 60,* 40–55.

Broude, G. J. (1994). *Marriage, family, and relationships: A cross-cultural encyclopedia.* Santa Barbara, CA: ABC-CLIO.

Broude, G. J. (1995). *Growing up: A cross-cultural encyclopedia.* Santa Barbara, CA: ABC-CLIO.

Brown, B. B., Eicher, S. A., & Petrie, S. (1986). The importance of peer group ("crowd") affiliation in adolescence. *Journal of Adolescence, 9,* 73–96.

Brown, B. B., Feiring, C., & Furman, W. (1999). Missing the love boat: Why researchers have shied away from adolescent romance. In W. Furman, B. B. Brown, & C. Feiring (Eds.), *The development of romantic relationships in adolescence* (pp. 1–16). Cambridge, UK: Cambridge University Press.

Brown, B. B., Mory, M. S., & Kinney, D. (1994). Casting adolescent crowds in a relational perspective: Caricature, channel, and context. In R. Montemayor, G. R. Adams, & T. P. Gulotta (Eds.), *Personal relationships during adolescence: Advances in adolescent development* (Vol. 3, pp. 125–167). Thousand Oaks, CA: Sage.

Brown, C. S., & Bigler, R. S. (2004). Children's perception of gender discrimination. *Developmental Psychology, 40,* 714–726.

Brown, E. C., Catalano, R. F., Fleming, C. B., Haggerty, K. P., & Abbott, R. D. (2005). Adolescent substance use outcomes in the Raising Healthy Children Project: A two-part latent growth curve analysis. *Journal of Consulting and Clinical Psychology, 73,* 699–710.

Brown, J. D., Halpern, C. T., & L'Engle, K. L. (2005). Mass media as a sexual super peer for early maturing girls. *Journal of Adolescent Health, 36*(5), 420–427.

Brown, J. L., & Pollitt, E. (1996, November). Malnutrition, poverty and intellectual development. *Scientific American, 274,* 38–43.

Brown, L. M., & Gilligan, C. (1992). *Meeting at the crossroads.* New York: Ballantine.

Brownell, M. D., & Yogendran, M. S. (2001). Attention-deficit hyperactivity disorder in Manitoba children: Medical diagnosis and psychostimulant treatment rates. *Canadian Journal of Psychiatry, 46,* 264–272.

Bryant, A. L., Schulenberg, J. E., Bachman, J. G., O'Malley, P. M., & Johnston, L. D. (2000). Understanding the links among school misbehavior, academic achievement and cigarette use during adolescence: A national panel study of adolescents. *Prevention Science, 1,* 71–87.

Bryant, A. L., Schulenberg, J. E., O'Malley, P. M., Bachman, J. G., & Johnston, L. D. (2003). How academic achievement, attitudes, and behaviors relate to the course of substance use during adolescence: A 6-year, multiwave national longitudinal study. *Journal of Research on Adolescence, 13,* 361–397.

Brydon-Miller, M. (1997). Participatory action research: Psychology and social change. *Journal of Social Issues, 53,* 657–666.

Brydon-Miller, M. (2001). Education, research, and action: Theory and methods of participatory action research. In D. L. Tolman & M. Brydon-Miller (Eds.), *From subjects to subjectivities: A handbook of interpretive and participatory methods* (pp. 76–94). New York: New York University Press.

Buehler, C., & Gerard, J. (2002). Marital conflict, ineffective parenting, and children's and adolescents' maladjustment. *Journal of Marriage and Family, 64,* 78–92.

Buhrmester, D. (1990). Intimacy of friendship, interpersonal competence, and adjustment during preadolescence and adolescence. *Child Development, 61,* 1101–1111.

Buhrmester, D. (1996). Need fulfillment, interpersonal competence, and the developmental contexts of early adolescent friendship. In W. M. Bukowski & A. F. Newcomb (Eds.), *The company they keep: Friendship in childhood and adolescence* (pp. 158–185). New York: Cambridge University Press.

Bukowski, W. M., Sippola, L. K., & Newcomb, A. F. (2000). Variations in patterns of attraction to same- and other-sex peers during early adolescence. *Developmental Psychology, 36*(2), 147–154.

Bulik, C. M. (2002). Eating disorders in adolescents and young adults. *Child and Adolescent Psychiatric Clinics of North America, 11,* 201–218.

Burns, M. S., Griffin, P., & Snow, C. E. (Eds.). (1999). *Starting out right: A guide to promoting children's reading success.* Washington, DC: National Academy Press.

Burt, C. W., & Fingerhut, L. A. (1998). Injury visits to hospital emergency departments: United States, 1992–1995. *Vital Health Statistics, 13,* 1–76.

Burton, L. (2002, May). *Adultification in childhood and adolescence: A matter of risk and resilience.* Paper presented at the Center for the Development of Peace and Well-Being, University of California. Berkeley, CA.

Bush, D., & Simmons, R. (1987). Gender and coping with the entry into early adolescence. In R. Barnett, L. Biener, & G. Baruch (Eds.), *Gender and stress* (pp. 185–217). New York: Free Press.

Byers, J. A. (1998). The biology of human play. *Child Development, 69,* 599–600.

Cahill, S. E. (1986). Childhood socialization as a recruitment process: Some lessons from the study of gender development. *Sociological Studies of Child Development, 1,* 163–186.

Cain, K., Oakhill, J. V., & Elbro, C. (2003). The ability to learn new word meanings from context by school-age children with and without language comprehension difficulties. *Journal of Child Language, 30,* 681–694.

Caird, J. K., & Hancock, P. A. (1994). The perception of arrival time for different oncoming vehicles at an intersection. *Ecological Psychology, 6,* 83–109.

Cairns, R. B. (2000). Developmental science: Three audacious implications. In L. R. Bergman, R. B. Cairns, L. Nilsson, & L. Nystedt (Eds.), *Developmental science and the holistic approach* (pp. 49–62). Mahwah, NJ: Erlbaum.

Call, K. T., & Mortimer, J. T. (2001). *Arenas of comfort in adolescence: A study of adjustment in context.* Mahwah, NJ: Erlbaum.

Calvert, S. L., & Kotler, J. A. (2003). Lessons from children's television: The impact of the Children's Television Act on children's learning. *Applied Developmental Psychology, 24,* 275–335.

Camarena, P. M., Stemmler, M., & Petersen, A. C. (1994). The gender-differential significance of work and family: An exploration of adolescent experience and expectation. In. R. K. Silbereisen & E. Todt (Eds.), *Adolescence in context: The interplay of family, school, peers, and work in adjustment* (pp. 201–221). New York: Springer-Verlag.

Camic, P. M., Rhodes, J. E., & Yardley, L. (2003). Naming the stars: Integrating qualitative methods into psychological research. *Qualitative research in psychology: Expanding perspectives in methodology and design* (pp. 3–15). Washington, DC: American Psychological Association.

Campbell, J. R., Hombo, C. M., & Mazzeo, J. (2000). *NAEP 1999: Trends in academic progress.* Washington, DC: Department of Education.

Campos, J. J., Mumme, D. L., Kermoian, R., & Campos, R. G. (1994). A functionalist perspective on the nature of emotion. In N. A. Fox (Ed.), *Monographs of the Society for Research in Child Development, 59*(2–3, Serial No. 240), 284–303.

Capaldi, D. M., & Rothbart, M. K. (1992). Development and validation of an early adolescent temperament measure. *Journal of Early Adolescence, 12,* 153–173.

Caprara, G. V., Barbaranelli, C., Pastorelli, C., Bandura, A., & Zimbardo, P. G. (2000). Prosocial foundations of children's academic achievement. *Psychological Science, 11,* 302–306.

Caputo, R. K. (2001). Grandparents and coresident grandchildren in a youth cohort. *Journal of Family Issues, 22*(5), 541–546.

Carlo, G., Hausmann, A., Christiansen, S., & Randall, B. A. (2003). Sociocognitive and behavioral correlates of a measure of prosocial tendencies for adolescents. *Journal of Early Adolescence, 23*(1), 107–134.

Carnegie Council on Adolescent Development. (1989). *Turning points: Preparing American youth for the 21st century.* New York: Carnegie Corporation of New York.

Carnegie Council on Adolescent Development. (1995). *Great transitions: Preparing adolescents for a new century.* New York: Carnegie Corporation of New York.

Caron, A. H., & Caronia, L. (2001). Active users and active objects: The mutual construction of families and communication technologies. *Convergence, 7*(3), 38–61.

Carpendale, J. I. M. (2000). Kohlberg and Piaget on stages and moral reasoning. *Developmental Review, 20,* 181–205.

Carr, M., & Schneider, W. (1991). Long-term maintenance of organizational strategies in kindergarten children. *Contemporary Educational Psychology, 16,* 61–72.

Carver, P. R., Egan, S. K., & Perry, D. G. (2004). Children who question their heterosexuality. *Developmental Psychology, 40,* 43–53.

Carver, P. R., Yunger, J. L., & Perry, D. G. (2003). Gender identity and adjustment in middle childhood. *Sex Roles, 49*(3/4), 95–109.

Case, R. (1991). Stages in the development of the young child's first sense of self. *Developmental Review, 11,* 210–230.

Case, R. (1992). *The mind's staircase: Exploring the conceptual underpinnings of children's thought and knowledge.* Hillsdale, NJ: Erlbaum.

Case, R., Kurland, M., & Goldberg, J. (1982). Operational efficiency and the growth of short-term memory span. *Journal of Experimental Child Psychology, 33,* 386–404.

Casella, R., & Burstyn, J. (2002). Linking academics and social learning: Perceptions of school staff to a violence prevention program at an alternative school. *Journal of School Violence, 1*(1), 83–102.

Casey, B. J., Giedd, J. N., & Thomas, K. M. (2000). Structural and functional brain development and its relation to cognitive development. *Biological Psychiatry, 54,* 241–257.

Casey, B. M., Nuttall, R. L., & Pezaris, E. (2001). Spatial-mechanical reasoning skills versus mathematical self-confidence as mediators of gender differences on mathematics subtests using cross-national gender-based items. *Journal for Research in Mathematics Education, 32,* 28–57.

Caspi, A., & Moffitt, T. E. (1991). Individual differences are accentuated during periods of social change: The sample case of girls at puberty. *Journal of Personality and Social Psychology, 61,* 157–168.

Cass, V. (1984). Homosexual identity: A concept in need of a definition. *Journal of Homosexuality, 4,* 105–126.

Ceballo, R., McLoyd, V. C., & Toyokawa, T. (2004). The influence of neighborhood quality on adolescents' educational values and school effort. *Journal of Adolescent Research, 19,* 716–739.

Ceci, S. J., & Roazzi, A. (1994). The effects of context on cognition: Postcards from Brazil. In R. Sternberg & R. K. Wagner (Eds.), *Mind in context: Interactionist perspectives on human intelligence* (pp. 74–101). New York: Cambridge University Press.

Ceci, S. J., Rosenblum, T. B., & Kumpf, M. (1998). The shrinking gap between high- and low-scoring groups: Current trends and possible causes. In U. Neisser (Ed.), *The rising curve* (pp. 287–302). Washington, DC: American Psychological Association.

Center for Mental Health in Schools at UCLA. (1999, October). *Expanding educational reform to address barriers to learning: Restructuring student support services and enhancing school-community partnerships.* Los Angeles, CA: Author.

Centers for Disease Control and Prevention. (1997). Guidelines for school and community programs to promote lifelong physical activity among young people. *Morbidity and Mortality Weekly Reports, 46,* 1–36.

Centers for Disease Control and Prevention. (1999). *Youth Risk Behavior Survey* [Online]. Retrieved April 22, 2003, from http://www.cdc.gov/epo/mmwr/preview/mmwr.html/ss4905a.htm.

Centers for Disease Control and Prevention. (2003). *Press release archive: More American children and teens are overweight.* Retrieved April 22, 2003, from http://www.cdc.gov/nccdphp/dnpa/press/archive/overweight.htm.

Centers for Disease Control and Prevention. (2004). *Web-based injury statistics query and reporting system (WISQARS).* National Center for Injury Prevention and Control. Retrieved April 22, 2003, from http://www.cdc.gov/ncipc/wisqars.

Centers for Disease Control and Prevention. (2005). *Results from the Youth Risk Behavior Survey on sexual activity.* Retrieved August 31, 2006, from http://apps.nccd.cdc.gov/yrbss/QuestYearTable.asp

Chall, J. S. (1983). *Stages of reading development.* New York: McGraw-Hill.

Chambers, M. L., Hewitt, J. K., Schmitz, S., Corley, R. P., & Fulker, D. W. (2001). Height, weight, and body mass index. In R. N. Emde & J. K. Hewitt (Eds.), *Infancy to early childhood: Genetic and environmental influences on developmental change* (pp. 292–306). New York: Oxford University Press.

Champion, K., Vernberg, E., & Shipman, K. (2003). Nonbullying victims of bullies: Aggression, social skills, and friendship characteristics. *Journal of Applied Developmental Psychology, 24,* 535–551.

Chan, D., Ramey, S., Ramey, C., & Schmitt, N. (2000). Modeling intraindividual change in children's social skills at home and at school: A multivariate latent growth approach to understanding between-settings differences in children's social skill development. *Multivariate Behavioral Research, 35,* 365–396.

Changeux, J-P., & Dehaene, S. (1989). Neuronal models of cognitive functions. *Cognition, 33,* 63–109.

Chao, R. K. (2001). Extending research on the consequences of parenting style for Chinese Americans and European Americans. *Child Development, 72,* 1832–1843.

Chapin, J. R. (2000). Adolescent sex and mass media: A developmental approach. *Adolescence, 35,* 799–811.

Chassin, L., Presson, C. C., Pitts, S. C., & Sherman, S. J. (2000). The natural history of cigarette smoking from adolescence to adulthood in a midwestern community sample: Multiple trajectories and their psychosocial correlates. *Health Psychology, 19,* 223–231.

Chatterjee, P., Bailey, D., & Aronoff, N. (2001). Adolescence and old age in twelve communities. *Journal of Sociology and Social Welfare, 28*(4), 121–159.

Chawla, L. (2002). "Insight, creativity and thoughts on the environment": Integrating children and youth into human settlement development. *Environment & Urbanization, 14*(2), 11–22.

Cheek, D. B., Grumbach, M. M., Grave, G. D., et al. (1974). *Control of onset of puberty.* New York: Wiley.

Chen, C., Lee, S. Y., & Stevenson, H. W. (1996). Long-term prediction of academic achievement of American, Chinese, and Japanese adolescents. *Journal of Educational Psychology, 18,* 750–759.

Chen, C., & Stevenson, H. W. (1988). Cross-linguistic differences in digit span of preschool children. *Journal of Experimental Child Psychology, 46,* 150–158.

Chen, C., & Tonegawa, S. (1997). Molecular genetic analysis of synaptic plasticity, activity-dependent neural development, learning, and memory in the mammalian brain. *Annual Review of Neuroscience, 20,* 157–184.

Chen, H. (2005). *Practical program evaluation: Assessing and improving planning, implementation, and effectiveness.* Thousand Oaks, CA: Sage.

Cherlin, A. J., & Furstenberg Jr., F. F. (1992). *The new American grandparent: A place in the family, a life apart.* New York: Basic.

Cherlin, A. J., Furstenberg Jr., F. F., Chase-Lansdale, P. L., Kiernan, K., Robins, P. K., Morrison, D. R., et al. (1991). Longitudinal studies of effects of divorce on children in Great Britain and the United States. *Science, 252,* 1386–1389.

Chi, M. T. H. (1978). Knowledge structure and memory development. In R. Siegler (Ed.), *Children's thinking: What develops?* (pp. 73–96). Hillsdale, NJ: Erlbaum.

Chicago Department of Transportation (1999). *The walking school bus training manual.* Chicago: Department of Transportation.

Child Trends. (2005). Racial and ethnic composition of the child population. Retrieved July 16, 2005, from http://www.childtrendsdatabank.org/figures/60-Figure-2.gif.

Child Trends. (2006). *What does marriage mean for children? A brief review of the research.* Retrieved July 30, 2006, from http://www.healthymarriageinfo.org/research/?d={5AB600D8-C23A-49FD-9DD5CE88A935DC4E}.

Children's Bureau, Administration of Children and Families, U.S. Department of Health and Human Services (2005). *Child*

maltreatment 2003. Washington, DC: U.S. Government Printing Office.

Chodorow, N. J. (1999). *The reproduction of mothering: Psychoanalysis and the sociology of gender.* Berkeley, CA: University of California Press.

Christenson, S. L., & Sheridan, S. M. (2001). *Schools and families: Creating essential connections for learning.* New York: Guilford Press.

Chugani, H. T. (1994). Development of regional brain glucose metabolism in relation to behavior and plasticity. In G. Dawson & K. Fischer (Eds.), *Human behavior and the developing brain* (pp. 153–175). New York: Guilford Press.

Cicchetti, D., & Toth, S. L. (1998). The development of depression in children and adolescents. *American Psychologist, 53,* 221–241.

Cillessen, A. H. N., & Bellmore, A. B. (2002). Social skills and interpersonal perception in early and middle childhood. In P. K. Smith & C. H. Hart (Eds.), *Handbook of childhood social development* (pp. 356–374). Malden, MA: Blackwell.

Civil Rights Project and the Southern Poverty Law Center. (2002). Positive interracial outcomes in the classroom. Retrieved July 11, 2005, from http://www.civilrightsproject.harvard.edu/convenings/splc/synopsis.php.

Clarke-Stewart, A., & Brentano, C. (2006). *Divorce: Causes and consequences.* New Haven, CT: Yale University Press.

Claxton, A. F., Pannells, T. C., & Rhoads, P. A. (2005). Developmental trends in the creativity of school-age children. *Creativity Research Journal, 17,* 327–335.

Clayton, P. E., & Trueman, J. A. (2000). Leptin and puberty. *Archives of Disease in Childhood, 83,* 1–4.

Clifford, B. R., Gunter, B., & McAleer, J. (1995). *Television and children: Program evaluation, comprehension, and impact.* Hillsdale, NJ: Erlbaum.

Coatsworth, J. D., Pantin, H., & Szapocznik, J. (2002). Familias Unidas: A family-centered ecodevelopmental intervention to reduce risk for problem behavior among Hispanic adolescents. *Clinical Child and Family Psychology Review, 5*(2), 113–132.

Cohane, G. H., & Pope, H. G., Jr. (2001). Body image in boys: A review of the literature. *International Journal of Eating Disorders, 29,* 373–379.

Cohen-Kettenis, P. T., & Pfafflin, F. (2003). *Transgenderism and intersexuality in childhood and adolescence.* Thousand Oaks, CA: Sage.

Coie, J. D., & Dodge, K. A. (1998). Aggression and antisocial behavior. In W. Damon (Series Ed.) & N. Eisenberg (Vol. Ed.), *Handbook of child psychology: Vol. 3. Social, emotional, and personality development* (5th ed., pp. 779–862). New York: Wiley.

Colby, A., & Kohlberg, L. (1987a). *The measurement of moral judgment: Vol. 1. Theoretical foundations and research validation.* New York: Cambridge University Press.

Colby, A., & Kohlberg, L. (1987b). *The measurement of moral judgment: Vol. 2. Standard issue scoring manual.* New York: Cambridge University Press.

Colby, A., Kohlberg, L., & Gibbs, J. (1983). A longitudinal study of moral judgment. *Monographs of the Society for Research in Child Development, 48* (Serial No. 1–2).

Colby, S. M., Tiffany, S. T., Shiffman, S., & Niaura, R. S. (2000). Are adolescent smokers dependent on nicotine? A review of the evidence. *Drug & Alcohol Dependence, 59,* S83–S95.

Cole, A., & Kerns, K. (2001). Perceptions of sibling qualities and activities of early adolescents. *Journal of Early Adolescence, 21,* 204–226.

Cole, D. A., Maxwell, S. E., Martin, J. M., Peeke, L. G., Tram, J. M., Hoffman, K. B., et al., (2001). The development of multiple domains of child and adolescent self-concept: A cohort sequential longitudinal design. *Child Development, 72,* 1723–1746.

Cole, M. (1990). Cognitive development and formal schooling: The evidence from cross-cultural research. In L. C. Moll (Ed.), *Vygotsky and education.* Cambridge, UK: Cambridge University Press.

Cole, M. (1996). *Cultural psychology: A once and future discipline.* Cambridge, MA: Harvard University Press.

Coleman, M., Ganong, L., & Fine, M. (2000). Reinvestigating remarriage: Another decade of progress. *Journal of Marriage and the Family, 62*(4), 1288–1307.

Coleman, P. K. (2003). Perceptions of parent-child attachment, social self-efficacy, and peer relationships in middle childhood. *Infant & Child Development, 12,* 351–368.

Coleman, P. K., & Karraker, K. H. (2000). Parenting self-efficacy among mothers of school-age children: Conceptualization, measurement, and correlates. *Family Relations, 49,* 13–24.

Coles, R. L. (2002). Black single fathers: Choosing to parent full-time. *Journal of Contemporary Ethnography, 31,* 411–439.

Collins, M. A., & Amabile, T. M. (1999). Motivation and creativity. In R. J. Sternberg (Ed.), *Handbook of creativity* (pp. 297–312). Cambridge, UK: Cambridge University Press.

Collins, P. H. (1991). *Black feminist thought: Knowledge, consciousness, and the politics of empowerment.* London: Routledge.

Collins, W. A. (1984). *Development during middle childhood: The years from six to twelve.* Washington, DC: National Academy Press.

Collins, W. A. (1990). Parent-child relationships in the transition to adolescence:

Continuity and change in interaction, affect, and cognition. In R. Montemayor, G. R. Adams, & T. P. Gullotta (Eds.), *From childhood to adolescence: A transitional period?* Newbury Park, CA: Sage.

Collins, W. A. (2005). Foreword. In C. R. Cooper, C. T. García Coll, W. T. Bartko, H. Davis, & C. Chatman (Eds.), *Developmental pathways through middle childhood: Rethinking context and diversity as resources* (pp. ix–xi). Mahwah, NJ: Erlbaum.

Collins, W. A., Maccoby, E. E., Steinberg, L., Hetherington, E. M., & Bornstein, M. H. (2000). Contemporary research on parenting: The case for nature and nurture. *American Psychologist, 55,* 218–232.

Collins, W. A., & Repinski, D. J. (1994). Relationships during adolescence: Continuity and change in developmental perspective. In R. Montemayor, G. R. Adams, & T. P. Gulotta (Eds.), *Personal relationships during adolescence: Advances in adolescent development* (Vol. 3, pp. 7–36). Thousand Oaks, CA: Sage.

Collins, W. A., & van Dulman, M. (2006). The significance of middle childhood peer competence for work and relationships in early adulthood. In A. C. Huston & M. N. Ripke (Eds.), *Developmental contexts in middle childhood: Bridges to adolescence and adulthood* (pp. 23–40). Cambridge, UK: Cambridge University Press.

Coltrane, S. (1997). Children and gender. In T. Arendell (Ed.), *Contemporary parenting: Challenges and issues* (pp. 219–253). Thousand Oaks, CA: Sage.

Combrinck-Graham, L. (1985). A developmental model for family systems. *Family Process, 24,* 139–150.

Comings, D. E., Muhleman, D., Johnson, J. P., & MacMurray, J. P. (2002). Parent-daughter transmission of the androgen receptor gene as an explanation of the effect of father absence on age of menarche. *Child Development, 73,* 1046–1051.

Committee on the Prevention of Reading Difficulties in Young Children. (1998). *Preventing reading difficulties in young children.* Washington, DC: National Academy Press.

Conant, J. B. (1959/1967). *The American high school today: A first report to interested citizens.* New York: McGraw-Hill.

Conger, K. J., & Conger, R. D. (1994). Differential parenting and change in sibling differences in delinquency. *Journal of Family Psychology, 8*(3), 287–302.

Connell, R. (1996). Teaching the boys: New research on masculinity and gender strategies for schools. *Teachers College Record, 98,* 206–235.

Connelly, M. L., Conaglen, H. M., Parsonson, B. S., & Isler, R. B. (1998). Child pedestrian's crossing gap thresholds. *Accident Analysis and Prevention, 30,* 443–453.

Connolly, J., Craig, W., Golberg, A., & Pepler, D. (2004). Mixed-gender groups, dating, and romantic relationships in early adolescence. *Journal of Research on Adolescence, 14*(2), 185–207.

Cooley, C. H. (1902). *Human nature and the social order.* New York: Charles Scribner and Sons.

Coontz, S. (2003). The American family today is not worse off than in the past. In M. Coleman & L. Ganong (Eds.), *Points & counterpoint: Controversial relationship and family issues in the 21st century* (pp. 222–225). Los Angeles, CA: Roxbury.

Cooper, C. R. (1999). Multiple selves, multiple worlds: Cultural perspectives on individuality and connectedness in adolescent development. In A. S. Masten (Ed.), *Cultural processes in child development* (pp. 25–57). Mahwah, NJ: Erlbaum.

Cooper, C. R., Dominguez, E., & Rosas, S. (2005). Soledad's dream: How immigrant children bridge their multiple worlds and build pathways to college. In C. R. Cooper, C. T. García Coll, W. T. Bartko, H. Davis, & C. Chatman (Eds.), *Developmental pathways through middle childhood: Rethinking context and diversity as resources* (pp. 235–260). Mahwah, NJ: Erlbaum.

Cooper, C. R., García Coll, C. T., Bartko, W. T., Davis, H., & Chatman, C. (Eds.) (2005). Editor's introduction. In C. R. Cooper, C. T. García Coll, W. T. Bartko, H. Davis, & C. Chatman (Eds.), *Developmental pathways through middle childhood: Rethinking context and diversity as resources* (pp. 1–13). Mahwah, NJ: Erlbaum.

Cooper, C. R., García Coll, C. T., Thorne, B., & Orellana, M. F. (2005). Beyond demographic categories: How immigration, ethnicity, and "race" matter for children's identities and pathways through school. In C. R. Cooper, C. T. García Coll, W. T. Bartko, H. Davis, & C. Chatman (Eds.), *Developmental pathways through middle childhood: Rethinking context and diversity as resources* (pp. 1–13). Mahwah, NJ: Erlbaum.

Cooper, D. C., & Villagomez, S. (2003). *Pathways to the green card.* Santa Cruz, CA: University of California Press.

Cooper, H., Nye, B., Charlton, K., & Lindsay, J. (1996). The effects of summer vacation on achievement test scores: A narrative and meta-analytic review. *Review of Educational Research, 66,* 227–268.

Cooper, H. M., Jackson, K., & Nye, B. A. (2001). A model of homework's influence on the performance evaluations of elementary school students. *Journal of Experimental Education, 69,* 181–199.

Cooper, H. M., Lindsay, J. J., & Nye, B. (2000). Homework in the home: How student, family, and parenting-style differences relate to the homework process. *Contemporary Educational Psychology, 25,* 464–487.

Coopersmith, S. (1967). *The antecedents of self-esteem.* San Francisco: Freeman.

Corbin, C. B., & Pangrazi, R. (2000). *Physical activity for children: A statement of guidelines* (pp. 1–21). Reston, VA: Council for Physical Education for Children (COPEC) of the National Association for Sport and Physical Education (NASPE).

Cota-Robles, S., Neiss, M., & Rowe, D. C. (2002). The role of puberty in violent and nonviolent delinquency among Anglo American, Mexican American, and African American boys. *Journal of Adolescent Research, 17,* 364–376.

Côté, J. E. (2000a). The Mead-Freeman controversy in review. *Journal of Youth and Adolescence, 29,* 525–538.

Côté, J. E. (2000b). *Arrested development: The changing nature of maturity and identity.* New York: New York University Press.

Côté, J. E., & Allahar, A. L. (1996). *Generation on hold: Coming of age in the late twentieth century.* New York: New York University Press.

Côté, J. E., & Levine, C. G. (2002). *Identity formation, agency, and culture: A social psychological synthesis.* Mahwah, NJ: Erlbaum.

Cowan, P. A., Powell, D., & Cowan, C. P. (1998). Parenting interventions: A family systems perspective. In W. Damon (Series Ed.) & N. Eisenberg (Vol. Ed.), *Handbook of child psychology: Vol. 3. Social, emotional, and personality development* (5th ed., pp. 3–72). New York: Wiley.

Cox, B., Ornstein, P. A., Naus, M. J., Maxfield, D., & Zimler, J. (1989). Children's concurrent use of rehearsal and organizational strategies. *Developmental Psychology, 25*(4), 619–627.

Craig, H. K. & Washington, J. A. (2004). Grade-related changes in the production of African American English. *Journal of Speech, Language, and Hearing Research, 47,* 450–463.

Crain, W. (2000). *Theories of development: Concepts and applications* (4th ed.) Upper Saddle River, NJ: Prentice Hall.

Cratty, B. J. (1986). *Perceptual and motor development in infants and children* (3rd ed.). Englewood Cliffs, NJ: Prentice Hall.

Creswell, J. W., & Maietta, R. C. (2002). Qualitative research. In D. C. Miller & N. J. Salkind (Eds.), *Handbook of research design and social measurement* (6th ed., pp. 145–194). Thousand Oaks, CA: Sage.

Creusere, M. A. (2000). A developmental test of theoretical perspectives on the understanding of verbal irony: Children's recognition of allusion and pragmatic insincerity. *Metaphor & Symbol, 15,* 29–45.

Crick, N. R. (1996). The role of overt aggression, relational aggression, and prosocial behavior in the prediction of children's future social adjustment. *Child Development, 67,* 2317–2327.

Crick, N. R. (2007). *What does relational aggression look like at different ages?* Paper presented at the Second Annual Teaching Institute at the Biennial Meeting of the Society for Research on Child Development, Boston, MA, March 29.

Crick, N. R., Bigbee, M. A., & Howes, C. (1996). Gender differences in children's normative beliefs about aggression: How do I hurt thee? Let me count the ways. *Child Development, 67,* 1003–1014.

Crick, N. R., & Dodge, K. A. (1994). A review and reformulation of social information-processing mechanisms in children's social adjustment. *Psychological Bulletin, 115*(1), 74–101.

Crick, N. R., & Dodge, K. A. (1999). "Superiority" is in the eye of the beholder: A comment on Sutton, Smith and Swettenham. *Social Development, 8,* 128–131.

Crick, N. R., & Grotpeter, J. K. (1995). Relational aggression, gender, and social-psychological adjustment. *Child Development, 66,* 710–722.

Criss, M. M., Shaw, D. S., & Ingoldsby, E. M. (2003). Mother-son positive synchrony in middle childhood: Relation to antisocial behavior. *Social Development, 12,* 379–400.

Crockett, L. J., & Crouter, A. C. (1995). *Pathways through adolescence: Individual development in relation to social contexts.* Mahwah, NJ: Erlbaum.

Crockett, L. J., Raffaelli, M., & Moilanen, K. L. (2003). Adolescent sexuality: Behavior and meaning. In G. R. Adams & M. D. Berzonsky (Eds.), *Blackwell Handbook of Adolescence* (pp. 371–392). Malden, MA: Blackwell Publishing.

Croll, J., Neumark-Sztainer, D., Story, M., & Ireland, M. (2002). Prevalence and risk and protective factors related to disordered eating behaviors among adolescents: Relationship to gender and ethnicity. *Journal of Adolescent Health, 31,* 166–175.

Crosby, R. A., & Miller, K. S. (2002). Family influences on adolescent females' sexual health. *Handbook of women's sexual and reproductive health* (pp. 113–127). New York: Kluwer Academic/Plenum.

Crosnoe, R. (2000). Friendships in childhood and adolescence: The life course and new directions. *Social Psychology Quarterly, 63,* 377–391.

Crosnoe, R., Johnson, M. K., & Elder, G. H. Jr. (2004). Intergenerational bonding in school: The behavioral and contextual correlates of student-teacher relationships. *Sociology of Education, 77,* 60–81.

Crosnoe, R., & Muller, C. (2004). Body mass index, academic achievement, and school context: Examining the educational experiences of adolescents at risk of obesity. *Journal of Health and Social Behavior, 45,* 393–407.

Crouter, A. C., Helms-Erikson, H., Updegraff, K., & McHale, S. M. (1999). Conditions underlying parents' knowledge about children's daily lives in middle childhood: Between- and within-family comparisons. *Child Development, 70,* 246–259.

Crouter, A. C., Manke, B. A., & McHale, S. M. (1995). The family context of gender intensification in early adolescence. *Child development, 66,* 317–329.

Csikszentmihalyi, M. (1990). *Flow: The psychology of optimal experience.* New York: Harper & Row.

Csikszentmihalyi, M. (1990). The domain of creativity. In M. A. Runco & R. S. Albert (Eds.), *Theories of creativity* (pp. 190–212). Newbury Park, CA: Sage.

Csikszentmihalyi, M., & Rathunde, K. (1992). The measurement of flow in everyday life: Toward a theory of emergent motivation. In S. Harter, J. S. Eccles, & L. L. Carstensen (Eds.), *Developmental perspectives on motivation* (pp. 57–97). Lincoln, NB: University of Nebraska Press.

Cui, M., Conger, R., Bryant, C. M., & Elder, G. H. (2002). Parental behavior and the quality of adolescent friendships: A social-contextual perspective. *Journal of Marriage and Family, 64,* 676–689.

Cunningham, M., & Spencer, M. B. (2000). Conceptual and methodological issues in studying minority adolescents. In R. Montemayor, G. R. Adams, & T. R. Gulotta (Eds.), *Adolescent diversity in ethnic, economic, and cultural contexts* (pp. 235–257). Thousand Oaks, CA: Sage.

Czerwinski, S. A., Lee, M., Choh, A. C., Wurzbacher, K., Demerth, E. W., Towene, B., & Siervogel, R. M. (2007). Genetic factors in physical growth and development and their relationship to subsequent health outcomes. *American Journal of Human Biology: The Official journal of the Human Biology Council, 19*(5), 684–691.

Dadisman, K., Vandell, D. L., & Pierce, K. (2002). *Experience sampling provides a window into after-school program experiences.* Paper presented at the Biennial Meeting of the Society for Research on Adolescence, New Orleans, April 14, 2002.

Dahl, R. E., & Lewin, D. S. (2002). Pathways to adolescent health, sleep regulation, and behavior. *Journal of Adolescent Health, 31,* 175–184.

Dahlberg, L. L., & Potter, L. B. (2001). Youth violence: Developmental pathways and prevention challenges. *American Journal of Preventative Medicine, 20,* 3–14.

Damon, W. (1975). Early conceptions of positive justice as related to the development of logical operations. *Child Development, 46,* 301–312.

Damon, W. (1983). *Social and personality development.* New York: Norton.

Damon, W., & Hart, D. (1988). *Self-understanding in childhood and adolescence.* New York: Cambridge University Press.

Danesco, E. R., Miller, T. R., & Spicer, R. S. (2000). Incidence and costs of 1987–1994 childhood injuries: Demographic breakdowns. *Pediatrics, 105* [Online]. Retrieved April 22, 2003, from www.pediatrics.org/cgi/content/full/105/2/e27.

Darling, N., & Steinberg, L. (1993). Parenting style as context: An integrative model. *Psychological Bulletin, 113,* 487–496.

Darwin, C. (1859). *On the origin of species by means of natural selection.* London: John Murray.

Davidson, J. E., & Sternberg, R. J. (1984). The role of insight in intellectual giftedness. *Gifted Child Quarterly, 28,* 58–64.

Davies, D. (2004). *Child development: A practitioner's guide.* New York: Guilford Press.

Davis, G. A. (2001). Point to point: Turning points to Turning Points 2000. In V. A. Anfara (Ed.), *The handbook of research in middle level education* (pp. 215–239). Greenwich, CT: IAP.

Davis, N. J. (1999). *Youth crisis: Growing up in the high-risk society.* Westport, CT: Praeger.

Davis-Kean, P. E., & Sandler, H. M. (2001). A meta-analysis of measures of self-esteem for young children: A framework for future measures. *Child Development, 72*(3), 887–906.

Dawkins, M. P. (1997). Drug use and violent crime among adolescents. *Adolescence, 32,* 396–405.

Deater-Deckard, K., Dunn, J., & Lussier, G. (2002). Sibling relationships and social-emotional adjustment in different family contexts. *Social Development, 11,* 571–590.

De Bellis, M. D. (2005). The psychobiology of neglect, *Child Maltreatment, 10,* 150–172.

De Bellis, M. D., & Keshavan, M. S. (2003). Sex differences in brain maturation in maltreatment-related pediatric posttraumatic stress disorder. *Neuroscience and Biobehavioral Reviews, 27,* 103–117.

De Bellis, M. D., Keshavan, M. S., Clark, D. B., Casey, B. J., Giedd, J. N., Boring, A. M., et al., (1999). Developmental traumatology part II: Brain development. *Biological Psychiatry, 45,* 1271–1284.

De Bellis, M. D., Keshavan, M. S., & Harenski, K. A. (2001). Anterior cingulated *N*-acetylaspartate/creatine ratios during clonidine treatment in a maltreated child with post-traumatic stress disorder. *Journal of Child and Adolescent Psychopharmacology, 11,* 311–316.

Deci, E. L., & Ryan, R. M. (1985). *Intrinsic motivation and self-determination in human behavior.* New York: Plenum.

Delaney, C. H. (1995). Rites of passage in adolescence. *Adolescence, 30,* 891–897.

De Lisi, R., & Wolford, J. L. (2002). Improving children's mental rotation accuracy with computer game playing. *Journal of Genetic Psychology, 163,* 272–282.

Demaray, M. K., Ruffalo, S. L., Carlson, J., & Busse, R. T. (1995). Social skills assessment: A comparative evaluation of six published rating scales. *School Psychology Review, 24,* 648–671.

deMause, L. (1995). *The history of childhood.* Northville, NJ: Jason Aronson.

Dempster, F. N. (1981). Memory span: Sources of individual and developmental differences. *Psychological Bulletin, 89,* 63–100.

Dempster, F. N. (1995). Interference and inhibition in cognition: An historical perspective. In F. N. Dempster & C. J. Brainerd (Eds.), *Interference and inhibition in cognition* (pp. 3–26). San Diego, CA: Academic Press.

Denzin, N. K., & Lincoln, Y. S. (Eds.). (2000). *Handbook of qualitative research* (2nd ed.). Thousand Oaks, CA: Sage.

DeReus, L. A., & Blume, L. B. (2008). Special issue of *Family Relations, 57*(4).

DeReus, L. A., Few, A. M., & Blume, L. B. (2005). Multicultural and critical race feminisms: Theorizing families in the third wave. In A. Acock, K. Allen, V. Bengtson, D. Klein, & P. Dilworth-Anderson (Eds.), *Sourcebook of family theory and research* (pp. 447–468). Thousand Oaks, CA: Sage.

Derr, T. (2006). "Sometimes birds sound like fish": Perspectives on children's place experiences. In C. Spencer & M. Blades (Eds.), *Children and their environments: Learning, using and designing spaces* (pp. 108–123). New York: Cambridge University Press.

Dick, D. M. Rose, R. J., Pulkkinen, L., & Kaprio, J. (2001). Measuring puberty and understanding its impact: A longitudinal study of adolescent twins. *Journal of Youth and Adolescence, 30*(4), 385–400.

Dillon, S. (2006, August 27). In schools across the U.S., the melting pot overflows. *The New York Times,* pp. A1, A16.

Dinkmeyer, D., & McKay, G. (1989). *The parents' handbook.* Circle Pines, MN: American Guidance Service.

Dishion, T. J., Andrews, D. W., & Crosby, L. (1995). Antisocial boys and their friends in early adolescence: Relationship characteristics, quality, and friendship processes. *Child Development, 66,* 139–151.

Dishion, T. J., McCord, J., & Poulin, F. (1999). When interventions harm: Peer groups and problem behavior. *American Psychologist, 54,* 755–764.

Dishion, T. J., & McMahon, R. J. (1998). Parental monitoring and the prevention of child and adolescent problem behavior: A conceptual and empirical foundation. *Clinical Child and Family Psychology Review, 1,* 61–75.

Donovan, J. E. (2004). Adolescent alcohol initiation: A review of psychosocial risk factors. *Journal of Adolescent Health, 35,* 529.e7–529.e18.

Dowdney, L., Skuse, D., Morris, K., & Pickles, A. (1998). Short normal children and environmental disadvantage: A longitudinal study of growth and cognitive development from 4 to 11 years. *Journal of Child Psychology & Psychiatry, 39,* 1017–1029.

Downs, T. (1999). Children's and parents' discourses about computers in the home and school. *Convergence, 5,* 4, 104–111.

Dreher, J., & Grafman, J. (2003). Dissociating the roles of the rostral anterior cingulate and the lateral prefrontal cortices in performing two tasks simultaneously or successively. *Cerebral Cortex, 13,* 329–339.

Drewnowski, A. (2004). Obesity and the food environment: Dietary energy density and diet costs. *American Journal of Preventive Medicine, 27,* 154–162.

Dryfoos, J. D. (1990). *Adolescents at risk: Prevalence and prevention.* New York: Oxford University Press.

Dryfoos, J. D. (1997). The prevalence of problem behaviors: Implications for programs. In R. P. Weissberg & T. P. Gulotta (Eds.), *Healthy children 2010: Enhancing children's wellness.* Thousand Oaks, CA: Sage.

Dryfoos, J. D. (2000). *Evaluation of community schools: Findings to date.* Washington, DC: Coalition for Community Schools. Retrieved December 19, 2002, from http://www.communityschools.org.

Dryfoos, J. G. (2005). The effects of health and social welfare factors on literacy development in urban schools. In J. Flood & P. L. Anders (Eds.), *Literacy development of students in urban schools* (pp. 35–57).

DuBois, D. L., Feiner, R. D., Brand, S., Adin, A. M., & Evans, E. G. (1992). A prospective study of life stress, social support, and adaptation in early adolescence. *Child Development, 63,* 542–57.

DuBois, D. L., Lockerd, E. M., Reach, K., & Parra, G. R. (2003). Effective strategies for esteem-enhancement: What do young adolescents have to say? *Journal of Early Adolescence, 23,* 405–434.

Duncan, G. J., & Brooks-Gunn, J. (2000). Family poverty, welfare reform, and child development. *Child Development, 71,* 188–196.

Dunlop, S. A., Archer, M. A., Quinlivan, J. A., Beazley, L. D., & Newnham, J. P. (1997). Repeated prenatal corticosteroids delay myelination in the ovine contral nervous system. *Journal of Maternal-Fetal Medicine, 6,* 309–313.

Dunn, M. S., Eddy, J. M., Wang, M. Q., Nagy, S., Perko, M. A., & Bartee, R. T. (2001). The influence of significant others on attitudes, subjective norms and intentions regarding dietary supplement use among adolescent athletes. *Adolescence, 36,* 583–591.

Durham, M. G. (1998). Dilemmas of desire: Representations of adolescent sexuality in two teen magazines. *Youth and Society, 29,* 369–389.

Durham, M. G. (2003). Girls, media, and the negotiation of sexuality: A study of race, class, and gender in adolescent peer groups. In J. M. Henslin (Ed.), *Down to earth sociology: Introductory readings* (pp. 332–348). New York: Free Press.

Durkin, K. (1995). *Developmental social psychology: From infancy to old age.* London: Blackwell.

Duvall, E. (1957). *Family development.* Philadelphia: Lippincott.

Eaton, W. O., McKeen, N. A., & Campbell, D. W. (2001). The waxing and waning of movement: Implications for psychological development. *Developmental Review, 21,* 205–223.

Eccles, J. S. (1987). Adolescence: Gateway to gender-role transcendence. In D. B. Carter (Ed.), *Current conceptions of sex roles and sex typing: Theory and research* (pp. 225–241). New York: Praeger.

Eccles, J. S. (1992). School and family effects on the ontogeny of children's interests, self-perceptions, and activity choices. In S. Harter, J. S. Eccles, & L. L. Carstensen (Eds.), *Developmental perspectives on motivation* (pp. 145–208). Lincoln, NE: University of Nebraska Press.

Eccles, J., Barber, B., Jozefowicz, D., Malenchuk, O., & Vida, M. (1999). Self-evaluations of competence, task values, and self-esteem. In N. G. Johnson, M. C. Roberts, & J. Worell (Eds.), *Beyond appearance: A new look at adolescent girls* (pp. 53–83). Washington, DC: American Psychological Association.

Eccles, J., & Bryan, J. (1994). Adolescence: Critical crossroad in the path of gender-role development. In M. R. Stevenson (Ed.), *Gender roles through the lifespan: A multidisciplinary perspective* (pp. 11–147). Muncie, IN: Ball State University Press.

Eccles, J. S., & Buchanan, C. M. (1996). School transitions in early adolescence: What are we doing to our young people? In J. Graber, J. Brooks-Gunn, & A. Petersen (Eds.), *Transitions through adolescence: Interpersonal domains and context* (pp. 251–284). Mahwah, NJ: Erlbaum.

Eccles, J. S., Frome, P., Yoon, K. S., Freedman-Doan, C., & Jacobs, J. (2000). Gender-role socialization in the family: A longitudinal approach. In T. Eckes & H, M. Trautner (Eds.), *The developmental social psychology of gender* (pp. 333–360). Mahwah, NJ: Erlbaum.

Eccles, J. S., & Harold, R. D. (1993). Parent-school involvement during the early adolescent years. *Teachers College Record, 94,* 560–587.

Eccles, J. S., Jacobs, J. E., Harold, R. D., Yoon, K. S., Arbreton, A., & Freedman-Doan, C. (1993). Parents and gender-role socialization during the middle childhood and adolescent years. In S. Oskamp & M. Costanzo (Eds.), *Gender issues in contemporary society* (pp. 59–83). Thousand Oaks, CA: Sage.

Eccles, J. S., Midgley, C., Wigfield, A., Miller Buchanan, C., Rueman, D., Flanagan, C., et al. (1997). Development during adolescence: The impact of stage-environment fit on young adolescents' experiences in schools and in families. *American Psychologist, 48,* 90–101.

Eccles, J. S., & Wigfield, A. (2002). Motivational beliefs, values, and goals. *Annual Review of Psychology, 53,* 109–132.

Eccles, J. S., Wigfield, A., & Schiefele, U. (1998). Motivation to succeed. In N. Eisenberg (Ed.), *Handbook of child psychology: Vol. 3. Social, emotional, and personality development* (5th ed., pp. 1017–1095). New York: Wiley.

Eccles-Parsons, J., Adler, T. F., Futterman, R., Goff, S. B., Kaczala, C. M., Meece, J. L., et al. (1983). Expectancies, values, and academic behaviors. In J. T. Spence (Ed.), *Achievement and achievement motivation* (pp. 75–146). San Francisco: Freeman.

Economos, C. D. (2001). Less exercise now, more disease later? The critical role of childhood exercise interventions in reducing chronic disease burden. *Nutrition in Clinical Care, 4,* 306–313.

Edwards, C. P. (2000). Children's play in cross-cultural perspective: A new look at the Six Cultures study. *Cross-Cultural Research, 34,* 318–338.

Egan, S. K., & Perry, D. G. (2001). Gender identity: A multidimensional analysis with implications for psychosocial adjustment. *Developmental Psychology, 37,* 451–463.

Eichhorn, D. H. (1966). *The middle school.* New York: Center for Applied Research in Education.

Eichhorn, D. H. (1980). The school. In M. Johnson (Ed.), *Toward adolescence: The middle school years, 79th yearbook of the National Society for the Study of Education.* Chicago: National Society for the Study of Education.

Eisenberg, N., & Fabes, R. A. (1998). Prosocial development. In W. Damon & N. Eisenberg (Eds.), *Handbook of child psychology: Vol. 3. Social emotional and personality development* (5th ed., pp. 701–778). New York: Wiley.

Eisenberg, N., Fabes, R. A., & Spinrad, T. L. (2006). Prosocial development. In W. Damon & R. M. Lerner (Series Eds.) & R. M. Lerner (Vol. Ed.), *Handbook of child psychology: Vol. 1. Theoretical models of human development* (6th ed., pp. 646–718). New York: Wiley.

Eisenberg, N., Guthrie, I. K., Murphy, B. C., Shepard, S. A., Cumberland, A., & Carlo, G. (1999). Consistency and development of prosocial dispositions: A longitudinal study. *Child Development, 70,* 1360–1372.

Elder, G. H., Jr. (1998). The life course and human development. In W. Damon (Series Ed.) & R. M. Lerner (Vol. Ed.), *Handbook of child psychology: Vol. 1. Theoretical models of human development* (5th ed., pp. 939–991). New York: Wiley.

Elder, G. H., Jr., & Conger, R. D. (2000). *Children of the land: Adversity and success in rural America.* Chicago: University of Chicago Press.

Elder, G. H., & Shanahan, M. J. (2006). The life course and human development. In W. Damon & R. M. Lerner (Series Eds.) & R. M. Lerner (Vol. Ed.), *Handbook of child psychology: Vol. 1. Theoretical models of human development* (6th ed., pp. 716–792). New York: Wiley.

Elicker, J., Englund, M., & Sroufe, A. L. (1992). Predicting peer competence and peer relationships in childhood from early parent-child relationships. In R. D. Parke & G. W. Ladd (Eds.), *Family-peer relationships: Models of linkage* (pp. 71–106). Hillsdale, NJ: Erlbaum.

Elkind, D. (1967). Egocentrism in adolescence. *Child Development, 38,* 1025–1034.

Elkind, D. (1978). *The child's reality: Three developmental themes.* Hillsdale, NJ: Erlbaum.

Elkind, D. (1984). *All grown up and no place to go: Teenagers in crisis.* Reading, MA: Addison-Wesley.

Elkind, D. (1985). Egocentrism, redux. *Developmental Review, 5,* 218–226.

Ellickson, P. L., D'Amico, E. J., Collins, R. L., & Klein, D. J. (2005). Marijuana use and later problems: When frequency of recent use explains age of initiation effects (and when it does not). *Substance Use and Misuse, 40,* 343–359.

Elliott, S. N., Malecki, C. K., & Demaray, M. K. (2001). New directions in social skills assessment and intervention for elementary and middle school students. *Exceptionality, 9* (1 & 2), 19–32.

Ellis, B. J. (2005). Determinants of pubertal timing: An evolutionary developmental approach. In *Origins of the social mind: Evolutionary psychology and child development* (pp. 164–188). New York: Guilford Press.

Ellis, B. J., Bates, J. E., Dodge, K. A., Fergusson, D. M., Horwood, J. L., et al. (2003). Does father absence place daughters at special risk for early sexual activity and teenage pregnancy? *Child Development, 74,* 801–821.

Ellis, B. J., & Garber, J. (2000). Psychosocial antecedents of variation in girls' pubertal timing: Maternal depression, stepfather presence, and marital and family stress. *Child Development, 71,* 485–501.

Ellis, B. J., McFayden-Ketchum, S., Dodge, K. A., Pettit, G. S., & Bates, J. E. (1999). Quality of early family relationships and individual differences in the timing of pubertal maturation in girls: A longitudinal test of an evolutionary model. *Journal of Personality and Social Psychology, 77,* 387–401.

Ellis, S., Klahr, D., & Siegler, R. S. (1993, March). *Effects of feedback and collaboration on changes in children's use of mathematical rules.* Paper presented at the meeting of the Society for Research in Child Development, New Orleans.

El-Sheikh, M., Buckhalt, J. A., Mize, J., & Acebo, C. (2006). Marital conflict and disruption of children's sleep. *Child Development, 77,* 31–43.

El-Sheikh, M., Harger, J., & Whitson S. M. (2001). Exposure to interparental conflict and children's adjustment and physical health: The moderating role of vagal tone. *Child Development, 72,* 1617–1636.

Ely, R. (1997). Everything including talk and why you hafta listen. *Journal of Narrative & Life History, 7*(1–4), 351–357.

Emery, R. E. (1994). *Renegotiating family relationships: Divorce, child custody, and mediation.* New York: Guilford Press.

Emery, S., Wakefield, M. A., Terry-McElrath, Y., Saffer, H., Szczypka, G., O'Malley, P. M., et al. (2005). Televised state-sponsored antitobacco advertising and youth smoking beliefs and behavior in the United States, 1999–2000. *Archives of Pediatrics & Adolescent Medicine, 159,* 639–645.

Entwisle, D. R., Alexander, K. L., & Olson, L. S. (2001). Keep the faucet flowing: Summer learning and home environment. *American Educator, 25,* 10–15.

Entwisle, D. R., Alexander, K. L., & Olson, L. S. (2006). Educational tracing within and between schools: From first grade through middle school and beyond. In A. C. Huston & M. N. Ripke (Eds.), *Developmental contexts in middle childhood: Bridges to adolescence and adulthood* (pp. 173–197). Cambridge, UK: Cambridge University Press.

Erikson, E. H. (1950). *Childhood and society.* New York: W. W. Norton.

Erikson, E. H. (1968). *Identity, youth, and crisis.* New York: W. W. Norton.

Erkut, S., Marx, F., Fields, J. P., & Sing, R. (1999). Raising confident and competent girls: One size does not fit all. In L. A. Peplau, S. C. DeBro, R. C. Veniegas, & P. L. Taylor (Eds.), *Gender, culture, and ethnicity: Current research about women and men* (pp. 83–101). Mountain View, CA: Mayfield.

Ernest, P. (2000). Teaching and learning mathematics. In V. Koshy, P. Ernest, & R. Casey (Eds.), *Mathematics for primary teachers.* New York: Routledge.

Espelage, D. L., & Asidao, C. S. (2002). Conversations with middle school students about bullying and victimization: Should we be concerned? In R. A. Geffner, M. Loring, & C. Young (Eds.), *Bullying behavior: Current issues, research, and interventions* (pp. 49–62). New York: Haworth.

Evans, M. A., Whigham, M., & Wang, M. C. (1995). The effect of a role model project upon the attitudes of ninth-grade science students. *Journal of Research in Science Teaching, 32*, 195–204.

Ewing, M. E., Gano-Overway, L. A., Branta, C. F., & Seefeldt, V. D. (2002). The role of sports in youth development. In M. Gatz & M. A. Messner (Eds.), *Paradoxes of youth and sport* (pp. 31–47). Albany, NY: State University of New York Press.

Ewing, M. E., & Seefeldt, V. D. (1989). *Participation and attrition patterns in American agency sponsored and interscholastic sports: An executive summary.* Final report to the Athletic Footwear Council of the Sporting Goods Manufacturers Association.

Fahrmeier, E. D. (1978). The development of concrete operations among the Hausa. *Journal of Cross-Cultural Psychology, 9*, 23–44.

Falicov, C. J. (2005). Emotional transnationalism and family identities. *Family Process, 44*, 399–406.

Falk, B., & Eliakim, A. (2003). Resistance training, skeletal muscle, and growth. *Pediatric Endocrinology Reviews: PER, 1*(2), 102–127.

Farkas, G., & Beron, K. (2004). The detailed age trajectory of oral vocabulary knowledge: Differences by class and race. *Social Science Research, 33*, 464–497.

Fashola, O. S. (1998). *Review of extended-day and after-school programs and their effectiveness.* Report No. 24, Center for Research on the Education of Students Placed At-Risk, Johns Hopkins University.

Faulkner, D. L., Farrelly, M. C., & Hersey, J. C. (2000). Race, grade level, and cigarette smoking: The 1999 National Youth Tobacco Survey. *Journal of the National Cancer Institute, 92*, 1360.

Fauth, R. C., Leventhal, T., & Brooks-Gunn, J. (2005). Early impacts of moving from poor to middle-class neighborhoods on low-income youth. *Journal of Applied Developmental Psychology, 26*, 415–439.

Federal Interagency Forum on Child and Family Statistics (2003). *America's children: Key national indicators on wellbeing, 2003.* Federal Interagency Forum on Child and Family Statistics, Washington, DC: U.S. Government Printing Office.

Feinstein, L., & Bynner, J. (2004). The importance of cognitive development in middle childhood for adult socioeconomic status, mental health, and problem behavior. *Child Development, 75*, 1329–1339.

Feiring, C. (1993, March). Developing concepts of romance from 13 to 18 years. In W. Furman (Chair), *Adolescent romantic relationships: A new look.* Symposium conducted at the biennial meetings of the Society for Research in Child Development, New Orleans, LA.

Feist, G. J. (1999). The influence of personality on artistic and scientific creativity. In R. J. Sternberg (Ed.), *Handbook of creativity* (pp. 273–296). New York: Cambridge University Press.

Feldman, D. H. (1999). The development of creativity. In R. J. Sternberg (Ed.), *Handbook of creativity* (pp. 169–186). New York: Cambridge University Press.

Feldman, D. H. (2003). Cognitive development in childhood. In R. M. Lerner, M. A. Easterbooks, & J. Mistry (Eds.), *Handbook of psychology*: Vol. 6. *Developmental psychology* (pp. 195–210). New York: Wiley.

Feldman, S. S., & Elliott, G. R. (1990). *At the threshold: The developing adolescent.* Cambridge, MA: Harvard University Press.

Fennema, E., Sowder, J., & Carpenter, T. P. (1999). Creating classrooms that promote understanding. In E. Fennema & T. A. Romberg (Eds.), *Mathematics classrooms that promote understanding* (pp. 185–199). Mahwah, NJ: Erlbaum.

Fenzel, L. M. (2000). Prospective study of changes in global self-worth and strain during the transition to middle school. *Journal of Early Adolescence, 20*, 93–116.

Feshbach, N. D., & Feshbach, S. (1982). Empathy training and the regulation of aggression: Potentialities and limitations. *Academic Psychology Bulletin, 4*, 399–413.

Feshbach, N. D., & Feshbach, S. (1983). *Learning to care: Classroom activities for social and affective development.* Glenview, IL: Scott, Foresman.

Field, A., Camargo, C., Taylor, C. B., Berkey, C., Frazier, L., Gillman, M., et al. (1999). Overweight, weight concerns, and bulimic behaviors among girls and boys. *Journal of the American Academy of Adolescent Psychiatry, 38*, 754–760.

Fingerson, L. (1999). Active viewing: Girls' interpretations of family television programs. *Journal of Contemporary Ethnography, 28*(4), 389–418.

Finkelstein, J. S., Neer, R. M., Biller, B. M., Crawford, J. D., Klibanski, A., et al. (1992). Osteopenia in men with a history of delayed puberty. *The New England Journal of Medicine, 326*, 600–604.

Finnegan, R. A., Hodges, E. V. E., & Perry, D. C. (1996). Preoccupied and avoidant coping during middle childhood. *Child Development, 67*, 1318–1328.

Fisch, S. (1998). The children's television workshop: The experiment continues. In R. G. Noll & M. E. Price (Eds.), *A communications cornucopia: The Markle Foundation essays of information policy.* Washington, DC: Brookings Institute Press.

Fischer, K. W., Shaver, P., & Carnochan, P. (1990). How emotions develop and how they organize development. *Cognition and Emotion, 4*, 81–127.

Fisher, C. B., & Lerner, R. L. (1994). Foundations of applied developmental psychology. In C. B. Fisher & R. M. Lerner (Eds.), *Applied developmental psychology* (pp. 3–20). New York: McGraw-Hill.

Flanagan, C., & Van Horn, B. (2003). Youth civic development: Next step in community youth development. In F. A. Villarruel, D. F. Perkins, L. M. Borden, L. M. & J. G. Keith (Eds.), *Community youth development: Programs, policies, and practices* (pp. 273–296). Thousand Oaks, CA: Sage.

Flavell, J. H. (2000). Development of children's knowledge about the mental world. *International Journal of Behavioral Development, 24*, 15–23.

Flavell, J. H., & Miller, P. H. (1998). Social cognition. In W. Damon (Series Ed.) & D. Kuhn & R. S. Siegler (Vol. Eds.), *Handbook of child psychology, Vol. 2. Cognition, perception, and language* (5th ed., pp. 851–898). New York: Wiley.

Flavell, J. H., Miller, P. H., & Miller, S. A. (2002). *Cognitive development* (4th ed.). Upper Saddle River, NJ: Prentice Hall.

Fletcher, A. C., Darling, N. E., Steinberg, L., & Dornbusch, S. L. (1995). The company they keep: Relation of adolescents' adjustment and behavior to their friends' perceptions of authoritative parenting in the social network. *Developmental Psychology, 31*, 300–310.

Flick, U. (2002). *An introduction to qualitative research* (2nd ed.). Thousand Oaks, CA: Sage.

Fonagy, P. (1999). Psychoanalytic theory from the viewpoint of attachment theory and research. In J. Cassidy & P. R. Shaver (Eds.), *Handbook of attachment: Theory, research, and clinical applications* (pp. 595–624). New York: Guilford Press.

Ford, D. H., & Lerner, R. M. (1992). *Developmental systems theory: An integrative approach.* Newbury Park, CA: Sage.

Foucault, M. (1978). *The history of sexuality: An introduction: Vol. 1.* (R. Hurley, Trans.). New York: Vintage. (Original work published 1976).

Fowler, J. W. (1981). *Stages of faith: The psychology of human development and the quest for meaning.* San Francisco: Harper & Row.

Fowler, J. W. (1991). Stages in faith consciousness. In F. K. Oser & W. G. Scarlett (Eds.), *Religious development in childhood and adolescence* (pp. 27–45). *New Directions for Child Development*, No. 52. San Francisco: Jossey-Bass.

Fowler, J. W. (2005). Stages of faith from infancy through adolescence: Reflections on three decades of faith development theory. In P. E. King & E. C. Roehlkepartain (Eds.), *Handbook of spiritual development in childhood and adolescence* (pp. 34–45). Thousand Oaks, CA: Sage.

Fox, C., Porter, R., & Wokler, R. (Eds.) (1995). *Inventing human science.* Berkeley, CA: University of California Press.

Fox, N. A. (Ed.) (1994). The development of emotion regulation: Biological and behavioral considerations. *Monographs of the Society for Research in Child Development, 59* (2–3, Serial No. 240).

Francis, M., & Lorenzo, R. (2006). Children and city design: Proactive process and the 'renewal' of childhood. In C. Spencer & M. Blades (Eds.), *Children and their environments: Learning, using and designing spaces* (pp. 217–237). New York: Cambridge University Press.

Franke, M. L. (2003). Fostering young children's mathematical understanding. In C. Howes (Ed.), *Teaching 4- to 8-year-olds: Literacy, math, multiculturalism, and classroom community* (pp. 93–112). Baltimore, MD: Paul H. Brooks.

Frankenberger, K. D. (2004). Adolescent egocentrism, risk perceptions, and sensation seeking among smoking and nonsmoking youth. *Journal of Adolescent Research, 19,* 576–590.

Fredricks, J. A., & Eccles, J. S. (2002). Children's competence and value beliefs from childhood through adolescence: Growth trajectories in two male sex-typed domains. *Developmental Psychology, 38,* 519–533.

Fredricks, J. A., Simpkins, S., & Eccles, J. S. (2005). Family socialization, gender, and participation in sports and instrumental music. In C. R. Cooper, C. T. García Coll, W. T. Bartko, H. Davis, & C. Chatman (Eds.), *Developmental pathways through middle childhood: Rethinking context and diversity as resources* (pp. 41–62). Mahwah, NJ: Erlbaum.

Fredriks, A. M., Van Buuren, S., Burgmeijer, R. J. F., Muelmeester, J. F., Roelien, J., Brugman, E. et al. (2000). Continuing positive secular growth change in the Netherlands 1955–1997. *Pediatric Research, 47,* 316–323.

Freedman, D. S., Kettel Khan, L., Serdula, M. K., Srinivasan, S. R., & Berenson, G. S. (2000). Secular trends in height among children during 2 decades. *Archives of Pediatrics and Adolescent Medicine, 154,* 155–161.

Freeman, C. E. Trends in educational equity of girls & women: 2004. *Education Statistics Quarterly, 6.* Retrieved April 22, 2003, from http://nces.ed.gov/programs/quarterly/vol_6/6_4/8_1.asp.

Freitag, M. K., Belsky, J., Grossmann, K., Grossmann, K. E., & Scheuerer-Englisch, H. (1996). Continuity in parent-child relationships from infancy to middle childhood and relations with friendship competence. *Child Development, 67,* 1437–1454.

French, S. A., Fulkerson, J. A., & Story, M. (2000). Increasing weight-bearing physical activity and calcium intake for bone mass growth in children and adolescents: A review of intervention trials. *Preventative Medicine, 31,* 722–731.

Frenn, M., & Malin, S. (2003). Diet and exercise in low-income culturally diverse middle school students. *Public Health Nursing, 20,* 361–368.

Freud, S. (1959). *The collected works of Sigmund Freud.* London: Hogarth Press and the Institute of Psycho-Analysis.

Frey, K. S., & Ruble, D. N. (1990). Strategies for comparative evaluation: Maintaining a sense of competence across the life span. In R. J. Sternberg & J. Kolligian (Eds.), *Competence considered* (pp. 167–189). New Haven, CT: Yale University Press.

Fuligni, A. J., Alvarez, J., Bachman, M., & Ruble, D. N. (2005). Family obligation and the academic motivation of young children from immigrant families. In C. R. Cooper, C. T. García Coll, W. T. Bartko, H. Davis, & C. Chatman (Eds.), *Developmental pathways through middle childhood: Rethinking context and diversity as resources* (pp. 261–282). Mahwah, NJ: Erlbaum.

Fuligni, A. J., Eccles, J. S., Barber, B. L., & Clements, P. (2001). Early adolescent peer orientation and adjustment during high school. *Developmental Psychology, 37*(1), 28–36.

Furman, W., & Shaffer, L. (2003). The role of romantic relationships in adolescent development. In P. Florsheim (Ed.), *Adolescent romantic relations and sexual behavior: Theory, research, and practical implications* (pp. 3–22). Mahwah, NJ: Erlbaum.

Furman, W., & Wehner, E. A. (1994). Romantic views: Toward a theory of adolescent romantic relationships. In R. Montemayor, G. R. Adams, & T. P. Gulotta (Eds.), *Personal relationships during adolescence: Advances in adolescent development* (Vol. 3, pp. 168–195). Thousand Oaks, CA: Sage.

Furstenberg, F. F., Jr. (1988). Child care after divorce and remarriage. In E. M. Hetherington & J. Arasteh (Eds.), *Impact of divorce, single-parenting, and stepparenting on children* (pp. 245–261). Hillsdale, NJ: Erlbaum.

Furstenberg, F. F., Jr. (2001). The sociology of adolescence and youth in the 1990s: A critical commentary. In R. M. Milardo (Ed.), *Understanding families into the new millennium: A decade in review.* Minneapolis, MN: National Council on Family Relations.

Furstenberg, F. F., Cook, T. D., Eccles, J. S., Elder, G. H., & Sameroff, A. (1999). *Managing to make it: Urban families and adolescent success.* Chicago: University of Chicago Press.

Fury, G., Carlson. E. A., & Sroufe, L. A. (1997). Children's representations of attachment relationships in family drawings. *Child Development, 68,* 1154–1164.

Gable, S., & Lutz, S. (2000). Household, parent, and child contributions to childhood obesity. *Family Relations, 49,* 293–300.

Galambos, N. L., Almeida, D. M., & Petersen, A. C. (1990). Masculinity, femininity, and sex role attitudes in early adolescence: Exploring gender identification. *Child Development, 61,* 1905–1914.

Galambos, N. L., & Leadbeater, B. J. (2000). Trends in adolescent research for the new millennium. *International Journal of Behavioral Development, 24,* 289–294.

Galambos, N. L., & Tilton-Weaver, L. C. (2000). Adolescents' psychosocial maturity, problem behavior, and subjective age: In search of the adultoid. *Applied Developmental Science, 4,* 178–192.

Galvin, K. (2005). Diversity's legacy: The rise of discourse-dependent families. *NCFR Report, 50*(2), F4–F5.

Garbarino, J., Hammond, W. R., Mercy, J., & Yung, B. R. (2004). Community violence and children: Preventing exposure and reducing harm. In K. I. Maton & C. J. Schellenbach (Eds.), *Investing in children, youth, families, and communities: Strengths-based research and policy* (pp. 303–320). Washington, DC: American Psychological Association.

García Coll, C., Lamberty, G., Jenkins, R., McAdoo, H. P., Crnic, K., Wasik, B. H., et al. (1996). An integrative model for the study of developmental competencies in minority children. *Child Development, 67,* 1891–1914.

García Coll, C., & Szalacha, L. A. (2004). The multiple contexts of middle childhood. *Future of Children, 14*(2), 81–97.

García Coll, C., Szalacha, L. A., & Palacios, N. (2005). Children of Dominican, Portuguese, and Cambodian immigrant families: Academic attitudes and pathways during middle childhood. In C. R. Cooper, C. T. García Coll, W. T. Bartko, H. Davis, & C. Chatman (Eds.), *Developmental pathways through middle childhood: Rethinking context and diversity as resources* (pp. 207–234). Mahwah, NJ: Erlbaum.

Gardner, H. (1982). Giftedness: Speculations from a biological perspective. *New Directions for Child Development* (No. 171982) (pp. 47–60). San Francisco: Jossey-Bass.

Gardner, H. (1983). *Frames of mind: The theory of multiple intelligences.* New York: Basic Books.

Gardner, H. (1993). *Creating minds: An anatomy of creativity seen through lives of Freud Einstein, Picasso, Stravinsky, Eliot, Graham, and Gandhi.* New York: Basic.

Gardner, H. (1999). *Intelligence reframed.* New York: Basic Books.

Gardner, H. (2004). *Frames of mind: The theory of multiple intelligences.* New York: Basic Books.

Gardner, H., Kornhaber, M., & Wake, W. (1996). *Intelligence: Multiple perspectives.* Fort Worth, TX: Harcourt Brace.

Gardner, R. M., Stark, K., Friedman, B. N., & Jackson, N. A. (2000). Predictors of eating disorder scores in children ages 6 through 14: A longitudinal study. *Journal of Psychosomatic Research, 49,* 199–205.

Gardner, W., & Herman, J. (1990). Adolescents' AIDS risk taking: A rational choice perspective. In W. Gardner, S. Millstein, & B. Wilcox (Eds.), *Adolescents in the AIDS epidemic* (pp. 17–34). San Francisco: Jossey-Bass.

Garlick, D. (2002). Understanding the nature of the general factor of intelligence: The role of individual differences in neural plasticity as an explanatory mechanism. *Psychological Review, 109,* 116–136.

Garrity, C., Jens, K., Porter, W., Sager, N., & Short-Camilli, C. (1995). *Bully-proofing your school: A comprehensive approach for elementary schools.* Longmount, CO: Sopris West.

Garry, J. P., Morrissey, S. L., & Whetstone, L. M. (2003). Substance use and weight loss tactics among middle school youth. *International Journal of Eating Disorders, 33,* 55–63.

Gaskins, S. (1999). Children's daily lives in a Mayan village: A case study of culturally constructed roles and activities. In A. Goncu (Ed.), *Children's engagement in the world: Sociocultural perspectives* (pp. 25–60). New York: Cambridge University Press.

Gauvain, M. (1999). Everday opportunites for the development of planning skills: Sociocultural and family influences. In A. Goncu (Ed.), *Children's engagement in the world: Sociocultural perspectives* (pp. 173–201). UK: Cambridge University Press.

Gauvain, M. (2001). *The social context of cognitive development.* New York: Guilford Press.

Gauvain, M. & Huard, R. D. (1999). Family interaction, parenting style, and the development of planning: A longitudinal analysis using archival data. *Journal of Family Psychology, 13,* 1–18.

Gauvain, M. & Savage, S. (1995, August). *Everyday opportunities for the development of planning skills.* Paper presented at the meeting of the American Psychological Association, New York.

Gauvain, M., Savage, S., & McCollum, D. (2000). Reading at home and at school in the primary grades: Cultural and social influences. *Early Education and Development, 11,* 447–463.

Ge, X., Conger, R. D., & Elder, G. H., Jr. (1996). Coming of age too early: Pubertal influences on girls' vulnerability to psychological distress. *Child Development, 67,* 3386–3400.

Ge, X., Conger, R. D., & Elder, G. H., Jr. (2001). The relation between puberty and psychological distress in adolescent boys. *Journal of Research on Adolescence, 11,* 49–70.

Ge, X., Kim, I. J., Brody, G. H , Conger, R. D., Simons, R. L., Gibbons, F. X., et al. (2003). It's about timing and change: Pubertal transition effects of symptoms of major depression among African American youths. *Developmental Psychology, 39*(3), 430–439.

Geary, D. C. (1998). *Male, female: The evolution of human sex differences.* Washington, DC: American Psychological Association.

Geary, D. C. (2000). Attachment, caregiving, and parental investment. *Psychological Inquiry, 11*(2), 84–86.

Geary, D. C., & Bjorkland, D. F. (2000). Evolutionary developmental psychology. *Child Development, 71*(1), 57–65.

Gentile, D. A., & Walsh, D. A. (2002). A normative study of family media habits. *Applied Developmental Psychology, 23,* 157–178.

Gergen, K. J. (1991). *The saturated self: Dilemmas of identity in contemporary life.* New York: Basic Books.

Gershoff, E. T., & Aber, J. L. (Eds.) (2004a.). Special issue: Part 1: Assessing the impact of September 11th, 2001 on children, youth, and parents in the United States: Lessons from applied developmental science. *Applied Developmental Science, 8,* 106–169.

Gershoff, E. T., & Aber, J. L. (Eds.) (2004b.). Special issue: Part 2: Assessing the impact of September 11th, 2001 on children, youth, and parents in the United States: Lessons from applied developmental science. *Applied Developmental Science, 8,* 172–225.

Gesell, A., & Ilg, F. L. (1943). *Infant and child in the culture of today.* New York: Harper & Row.

Gesell, A., & Ilg, F. L. (1946). *The child from five to ten.* New York: Harper & Row.

Gesell, A., Ilg, F. L., & Ames, L. B. (1956). *Youth: The years from ten to sixteen.* New York: Harper & Row.

Giedd, J. N., Blumenthal, J., Jeffries, N. D., Castellanos, F. X., Lui, H., Zijdenbos, A., et al. (1999). Brain development during childhood and adolescence: A longitudinal MRI study. *Nature Neuroscience, 2,* 861–863.

Gilbert, M. C. (1996). Attributional patterns and perceptions of math and science among fifth-grade through seventh-grade girls and boys. *Sex Roles, 35,* 489–506.

Giles, H. C. (2005). Three narratives of parent-educator relationships: Toward counselor repertoires for bridging the urban parent-school divide. *Professional School Counseling, 8,* 228–235.

Gilliam, F. D., Jr., & Bales, S. N. (2001). Strategic frame analysis: Reframing America's youth. *Social Policy Report, Vol. 15, No. 3.* Retrieved March 21, 2005, from http://www.srcd.org/spr.html.

Gilligan, C. (1977). In a different voice: Women's conceptions of the self and of morality. *Harvard Educational Review, 47,* 481–517.

Gilligan, C. (1982). *In a different voice: Psychological theory and women's development.* Cambridge, MA: Harvard University Press.

Gilligan, C., & Brown, L. M. (1992). *Meeting at the crossroads: Women's psychology and girls' development.* Cambridge, MA: Harvard University Press.

Gilligan, C., Lyons, N. P., & Hanmer, T. J. (1990). *Making connections: The relational worlds of adolescent girls at Emma Willard School.* Cambridge, MA: Harvard University Press.

Gilpin, E. A., Choi, W. S., Berry, C., & Pierce, J. P. (1999). How many adolescents start smoking each day in the United States? *Journal of Adolescent Health, 25,* 248–255.

Gjerde, P. F., & Onishi, M. (2000). In search of theory: The study of "ethnic groups" in developmental psychology. *Journal of Research on Adolescence, 10,* 289–298.

Glaser, D. (2000). Child abuse and neglect and the brain: A review. *Journal of Child Psychology and Psychiatry, 41,* 97–116.

Goffman, E. (1979). *Gender advertisements.* Cambridge, MA: Harvard University Press.

Gogate, N., Giedd, J., Janson, K., & Rapoport, J. L. (2001). Brain imaging in normal and abnormal brain development: New perspectives for child psychiatry. *Clinical Neuroscience Research, 1,* 283–290.

Goldberg, J. H., Halpern-Felsher, B. L., & Millstein, S. G. (2002). Beyond invulnerability: The importance of benefits in adolescents' decision to drink alcohol. *Health Psychology, 21,* 477–484.

Goldsmith, H. H. (1993). Temperament: Variability in developing emotion systems. In M. Lewis & J. M. Haviland (Eds.), *Handbook of emotions* (pp. 353–364). New York: Guilford Press.

Goldsmith, H. H., & Gottesman, I. I. (1996). In M. F. Lenzenweger & J. J. Haugaard (Eds.), *Frontiers of developmental psychopathology* (pp. 5–43). New York: Oxford University Press.

Goldsmith, L. T. (1990). The timing of talent: The facilitation of early prodigious achievement. In M. J. A. Howe (Ed.), *Encouraging the development of exceptional skills and talents* (pp. 17–31). Oxford, UK: British Psychological Society.

Golombok, S. (2006). New family forms. In A. Clarke-Stewart & J. Dunn (Eds.), *Families count: Effects on child and adolescent development* (pp. 273–298). New York: Cambridge University Press.

Golombok, S., & MacCallum, F. (2003). Practitioner review: Outcomes for parents and children following non-traditional conception: What do clinicians need to know? *Journal of Child Psychology and Psychiatry, 44*(3), 303–315.

Golombok, S., MacCallum, F., Goodman, E., & Rutter, M. (2002). Families with children conceived by donor insemination: Follow-up at age twelve. *Child Development, 73,* 952–968.

Golombok, S., & Tasker, F. (1996). Do parents influence the sexual orientation of their children? Findings from a longitudinal study of lesbian families. *Developmental Psychology, 32,* 3–11.

Gonzalez, V. (2005). Cultural, linguistic, and socioeconomic factors influencing monolingual and bilingual children's cognitive development. In V. Gonzalez and J. Tinajero (Eds.), *Review of research and practice* (Vol. 3, pp. 67–104). Mahwah, NJ: Erlbaum.

Goossens, L., Beyers, W., Emmen, M., & van Aken, M. A. G. (2002). The imaginary audience and personal fable: Factor analyses and concurrent validity of the "new look" measures. *Journal of Research on Adolescence, 12,* 193–215.

Goossens, L., & Phinney, J. S. (1996). Commentary: Identity, context, and development. *Journal of Adolescence, 19,* 491–496.

Gootman, J. A. (Ed.). (2000). *After-school programs that promote child and adolescent development: Summary of a workshop.* Washington, DC: National Academy Press. Retrieved March 21, 2005, from http://books.nap.edu/books/0309071798/html/index.html.

Gottesman, I. I., & Hanson, D. R. (2005). Human development: Biological and genetic processes. *Annual Review of Psychology, 56,* 263–286.

Gottfredson, L. S. (1997). Why *g* matters: The complexity of everyday life. *Intelligence, 24,* 79–132.

Gottfried, A. E., Fleming, J. S., & Gottfried, A. W. (2001). Continuity of academic intrinsic motivation from childhood through late adolescence: A longitudinal study. *Journal of Educational Psychology, 93,* 3–13.

Graber, J., Brooks-Gunn, J., & Petersen, A. (1996). Adolescent transitions in context. *Transitions through adolescence: Interpersonal domains and context* (pp. 369–383). Mahwah, NJ: Erlbaum.

Graber, J. A., Lewisohn, P. M., Seeley, J. R., & Brooks-Gunn, J. (1997). Is psychopathology associated with the timing of pubertal development? *Journal of the American Academy of Child and Adolescent Psychiatry, 36,* 1768–1776.

Graham, S., & Taylor, A. Z. (2002). Ethnicity, gender, and the development of achievement values. In A. Wigfield & J. S. Eccles (Eds.), *The development of achievement motivation* (pp. 121–146). San Diego, CA: Academic.

Granic, I., Dishion, T. J., & Hollenstein, T. (2003). The family ecology of adolescence: A dynamic systems perspective on normative development. In G. R. Adams & M. D. Berzonsky (Eds.), *Blackwell handbook of adolescence* (pp. 60–91). Malden, MA: Blackwell.

Granot, D., & Mayseless, O. (2001). Attachment security and adjustment to school in middle childhood. *International Journal of Behavioral Development, 25*(6), 530–541.

Grant, B. F. (1997). Prevalence and correlates of alcohol use and DSM-IV alcohol dependence in the United States: Results of the national longitudinal alcohol epidemiologic survey. *Journal of Studies on Alcohol,* 464–473.

Grant, C. A., & Gomez, M. L. (2001). *Campus and classroom: Making schooling multicultural* (2nd ed.). Upper Saddle River, NJ: Merrill/Prentice Hall.

Grantham-McGregor, S., Ani, C., & Fernald, L. (2001). The role of nutrition in intellectual development. In R. J. Sternberg & E. L. Grigorenko (Eds.), *Environmental effects on cognitive abilities* (pp. 119–155). Mahwah, NJ: Erlbaum.

Graue, M. E., & Walsh, D. J. (1998). *Studying children in context.* Thousand Oaks, CA: Sage.

Gray, M. R., & Steinberg, L. (1999). Unpacking authoritative parenting: Reassessing a multidimensional construct. *Journal of Marriage and the Family, 61,* 574–587.

Green, P. E. (2003). The undocumented: Educating the children of migrant workers in America. *Bilingual Research Journal, 27,* 51–71.

Green, R. C. (1985). Potholes on the research road to sexual identity development. *Journal of Sex Research, 21,* 96–101.

Greenberger, E., & Steinberg, L. (1986). *When teenagers work: The psychological and social costs of adolescent employment.* New York: Basic Books.

Greener, S., & Crick, N. R. (1999). Normative beliefs about prosocial behavior in middle childhood: What does it mean to be nice? *Social Development, 8*(3), 349–363.

Greenough, W., & Black, J. (1992). Induction of brain structure by experience: Substrate for cognitive development. In M. R. Gummar & C. A. Nelson (Eds.), *Minnesota symposia on child psychology: Vol. 24. Developmental behavioral neuroscience* (pp. 155–200). Hillsdale, NJ: Erlbaum.

Greer, B., & Mulhern, G. (2002). *Making sense of data and statistics in psychology.* New York: Palgrave.

Gresham, F. M., & Elliott, S. N. (1990). *Social Skills Rating System manual.* Circle Pines, MN: American Guidance Service.

Grigorenko, E. L., Meier, E., Lipka, J., Mohatt, G., Yanez, E., & Sternberg, R. J. (2004). Academic and practical intelligence: A case study of the Yup'ik in Alaska. *Learning and Individual Differences, 14,* 183–207.

Grinwis, B., Smith, A. B., & Dannison, L. L. (2004). Custodial grandparent families: Steps for developing responsive health care systems. *Michigan Family Review, 9*(1), 37–44.

Grissmer, D. W., Williamson, S., Kirby, S. N., & Berends, M. (1998). Exploring the rapid rise in black achievement scores in the United States (1970–1990). In U. Neisser (Ed.), *The rising curve: Long-term gains in IQ and related measures* (pp. 251–285). Washington, DC: American Psychological Association.

Grolnick, W. S. (2003). *The psychology of parental control: How well-meant parenting backfires.* Mahwah, NJ: Erlbaum.

Grolnick, W. S., Gurland, S. T., Jacob, K. F., & Decourcey, W. (2002). The development of self-determination in middle childhood and adolescence. In A. Wigfield & J. S. Eccles (Eds.), *The development of achievement motivation* (pp. 147–171). San Diego, CA: Academic Press.

Gross, E. F., Juvonen, J., & Gable, S. L. (2002). Internet use and well-being in adolescence. *Journal of Social Issues, 58,* 75–90.

Growing up: W. K. Kellogg Foundation 2001 annual report. Retrieved August 1, 2002, from http://www.wkkf.org/pubs/Pub3363.pdf.

Gruber, H., & Davis, S. (1988). Inching our way up Mount Olympus: The evoking systems approach to creative thinking. In R. Sternberg (Ed.), *The nature of creativity* (pp. 243–270). UK: Cambridge University Press.

Grueneich, R. (1982). The development of children's integration rules for making moral judgments. *Child Development, 53,* 887–894.

Grumbach, M. M., & Styne, D. M. (1998). Puberty: Ontogeny, neuroendocrinology, physiology, and disorders. In J. D. Wilson, D. W. Foster, & H. M. Kronenberg (Eds.), *Williams textbook of endocrinology* (pp. 1509–1625). Philadelphia: W. B. Saunders.

Grusec, J., Goodnow, J. J., & Kuczynski, L. (2000). New directions in analyses of parenting contributions to children's acquisition of values. *Child Development, 71,* 205–211.

Grusec, J. E., & Mammone, N. (1995). Features and sources of parents' attributions about themselves and their children. In N. Eisenberg (Ed.), *Social development* (pp. 49–73). Thousand Oaks, CA: Sage.

Guba, E. G., & Lincoln, Y. S. (2005). Paradigmatic controversies, contradictions, and emerging confluences. In N. K. Denzin and Y. S. Lincoln (Eds.), *The Sage handbook of qualitative research* (pp. 191–215). Thousand Oaks, CA: Sage.

Guberman, S. R. (1999). Supportive environments for cognitive development: Illustrations from children's mathematical activities outside of school. In A. Goncu (Ed.), *Children's engagement in the world: Sociocultural perspectives* (pp. 202–227). Cambridge, UK: Cambridge University Press.

Guddemi, M., Jambor, T., & Moore, R. (1998). Advocacy for the child's right to play. In D. P.

Fromberg & D. Bergen (Eds.), *Play from birth to twelve and beyond* (pp. 519–529). New York: Garland.

Guillaume, M., Lapidus, L., Bjorntorp, P., & Lambert, A. (1997). Physical activity, obesity, and cardiovascular risk factors in children: The Belgian-Luxembourg child study II. *Obesity Research, 5*, 549–556.

Guiney, K. M., & Furlong, N. E. (2000). Correlates of body satisfaction and self-concept in third- and sixth-graders. *Current Psychology, 18*, 353–367.

Guttentag, R. E. (1995). Children's associative learning: Automatic and deliberate encoding of meaningful associations. *American Journal of Psychology, 108*, 99–114.

Guttentag, R. E., Ornstein, P. A., & Siemens, L. (1987). Children's spontaneous rehearsal: Transitions in strategy acquisition. *Cognitive Development, 2*, 307–326.

Guy, J. A., & Michell, L. J. (2001). Strength training for children and adolescents. *Journal of the American Academy of Orthopaedic Surgeons, 9*(1), 29–36.

Haddow, J. L. (2006). Residual effects of repeated bullying victimization before the age of 12 on adolescent functioning. *Journal of School Violence, 5*(2), 37–52.

Hager-Ross, C., & Rosblad, B. (2002). Norms for grip strength in children aged 4–16 years. *Acta Paediatrica, 91*, 617–625.

Halberstadt, A. G., Dunsmore, J. C., Denham, S. A. (2001). Spinning the pinwheel, together: More thoughts on affective social competence. *Social Development, 10*, 130–136.

Hall, E. R., Esty, E. T., & Fisch, S. M. (1990). Television and children's problem-solving behavior: A synopsis of an evaluation of the effects of Square One TV. *Journal of Mathemtatical Behavior, 9*, 161–174.

Hall, G. S. (1904). *Adolescence: Psychology and its relation to physiology, anthropology, sociology, sex, crime, and education.* New York: Appleton.

Halpern, C. T., Udry, J. R., Campbell, B., & Suchindran, C. (1993). Testosterone and pubertal development as predictors of sexual activity: A panel analysis of adolescent males. *Psychosomatic Medicine, 55*, 436–447.

Halpern, C. T., Udry, J. R., & Suchindran, C. (1997). Testosterone predicts initiation of coitus in adolescent females. *Psychosomatic Medicine, 59*, 161–171.

Halpern, C. T., Udry, J. R., Suchindran, C., & Campbell, B. (2000). Adolescent males' willingness to report masturbation. *The Journal of Sex Research, 37*, 327–332.

Halpern, D. (2004). A cognitive-process taxonomy for sex differences in cognitive abilities. *Current Directions in Psychological Science, 13*, 135–139.

Halpern-Felsher, B., Millstein, S., Ellen, J., Adler, N., Tschann, J., & Biehl, M. (2001). The role of behavioral experience in

judging risks. *Health Psychology, 20*, 120–126.

Hammersley, M. (1992). *What's wrong with ethnography?* New York: Routledge.

Hancox, R. J., Milne, B. J., & Poulton, R. (2004). Association between child and adolescent television viewing and adult health: A longitudinal birth cohort study. *Lancet, 364*, 257–262.

Hardy, C. L., Bukowski, W. M., & Sippola, L. K. (2002). Stability and change in peer relationships during the transition to middle-level school. *Journal of Early Adolescence, 22*(2), 117–142.

Hare, J., & Richards, L. (1993). Children raised by lesbian couples: Does context of birth affect father and partner involvement? *Family Relations, 42*, 249.

Harlow, H. F., & Harlow, M. K. (1962). Social deprivation in monkeys. *Scientific American, 207*(5), 136.

Harris, J. R. (1998). *The nurture assumption: Why children turn out the way they do.* New York: Touchstone.

Harter, S. (1982). The Perceived Competence Scale for Children. *Child Development, 53*, 87–97.

Harter, S. (1985). *The Self-Perception Profile for Children.* Unpublished manual. Denver, CO: University of Denver.

Harter, S. (1987). The determinants and mediational role of global self-worth in children. In N. Eisenberg (Ed.), *Contemporary topics in developmental psychology* (pp. 219–242). New York: Wiley.

Harter, S. (1992). Visions of self: Beyond the me in the mirror. In S. Harter, J. S. Eccles, & L. L. Carstensen (Eds.), *Developmental perspectives on motivation* (pp. 99–144). Lincoln, NB: University of Nebraska Press.

Harter, S. (1996a). Developmental changes in self-understanding across the 5 to 7 shift. In A. J. Sameroff & M. M. Haith (Eds.), *The five to seven year shift* (pp. 207–236). Chicago: University of Chicago Press.

Harter, S. (1996b). Historical roots of contemporary issues involving self-concept. In B. A. Bracken (Ed.), *Handbook of self-concept: Developmental, social, and clinical considerations* (pp. 1–37). New York: Wiley.

Harter, S. (1998). The development of self-representations. In W. Damon (Series Ed.) & N. Eisenberg (Vol. Ed.), *Handbook of child psychology: Vol. 3. Social, emotional, and personality development* (5th ed., pp. 553–617). New York: Wiley.

Harter, S. (1999). Symbolic interactionism revisited: Potential liabilities for the self constructed in the crucible of interpersonal relationships. *Merrill-Palmer Quarterly, 45*, 677–701.

Harter, S. (2006). The self. In W. Damon & R. M. Lerner (Series Eds.) & R. M. Lerner (Vol. Ed.), *Handbook of child psychology: Vol. 1. Theoretical models of human development* (6th ed., pp. 505–570). New York: Wiley.

Harter, S., Bresnick, S., Bouchey, H. A., & Whitesell, N. R. (1997). The development of multiple role-related selves during adolescence. *Development and Psychopathology, 9*, 835–853.

Harter, S., & Pike, R. (1984). The pictorial scale of perceived competence and social acceptance for young children. *Child Development, 55*, 1969–1982.

Harter, S., Stocker, C., & Robinson, N. S. (1996). The perceived directionality of the link between approval and self-worth: The liabilities of a looking glass self-orientation among young adolescents. *Journal of Research on Adolescence, 6*, 285–308.

Harter, S., Waters, P., & Whitesell, N. R. (1998). Relational self-worth: Differences in perceived worth as a person across interpersonal contexts among adolescents. *Child Development, 69*, 756–766.

Harter, S., & Whitesell, N. R. (1989). Developmental changes in children's understanding of single, multiple, and blended emotion concepts. In C. Saarni & P. Harris (Eds.), *Children's understanding of emotion* (pp. 81–116). Cambridge, UK: Cambridge University Press.

Harter, S., Whitesell, N. R., & Kowalski, P. (1992). Individual differences in the effects of educational transitions on young adolescents' perceptions of competence and motivational orientation. *American Educational Research Journal, 29*, 777–807.

Hartup, W. W. (1996). The company they keep: Friendships and their developmental significance. *Child Development, 67*, 1–13.

Haselager, G. J. T., Hartup, W. W., & van Lieshout, C. F. M. (1998). Similarities between friends and nonfriends in middle childhood. *Child Development, 69*(4), 1198–1208.

Hashey, J. M., & Connors, D. J. (2003). Learn from our journey: Reciprocal teaching action research. *The Reading Teacher, 57*, 224–232.

Haste, H., & Torney-Purta, J. (Eds.) (1992). *The development of political understanding: A new perspective. New Directions for Child Development*, No. 56. San Francisco: Jossey-Bass.

Hatchett, S. J., & Jackson, J. S. (1993). African American extended kin systems: An assessment. In H. P. McAdoo (Ed.), *Family ethnicity: Strength in diversity* (pp. 90–107). Newbury Park, CA: Sage.

Hauser-Cram, P., Erickson Warfield, E., Stadler, J., & Sirin, S. R. (2006). School environments and the diverging pathways of students living in poverty. In A. C. Huston & M. N. Ripke (Eds.), *Developmental contexts in middle childhood: Bridges to adolescence and adulthood* (pp. 198–216). New York: Cambridge University Press.

Hauspie, R. C., Bergman, P., Bielicki, T., & Susanne, C. (1994). Genetic variance in the pattern of the growth curve for height: A longitudinal analysis of male twins. *Annals of Human Biology, 21,* 347–362.

Hawkins, D. L., Pepler, D. J., & Craig, W. M. (2001). Naturalistic observations of peer interventions in bullying. *Social Development, 10*(4), 512–527.

Hayes, N. (2000). *Doing psychological research: Gathering and analyzing data.* Buckingham, UK: Open University Press.

Haynes, N. M., Emmons, C. L., & Woodruff, D. W. (1998). School development program effects: Linking implementation to outcomes. *Journal of Education for Students Placed at Risk, 3,* 71–85.

Hayslip, B., Jr., & Kaminski, P. L.(2005). Grandparents raising their grandchildren: A review of the literature and suggestions for practice. *The Gerontologist, 45*(2), 262–269.

Haywood, K. M., & Getchell, N. (2001). *Life span motor development* (3rd ed.). Champaign, IL: Human Kinetics.

Hazan, C., & Shaver, P. R. (1987). Romantic love conceptualized as an attachment process. *Journal of Personality and Social Psychology, 52,* 511–524.

Heary, C. M., & Hennessy, E. (2002). The use of focus group interviews in pediatric health care research. *Journal of Pediatric Psychology, 27,* 47–57.

Hedges, L. V., & Nowell, A. (1995). Sex differences I mental test scores: Variability and numbers of high-scoring individuals. *Science, 269,* 41–45.

Heelan, K. A., Donnelly, J. E., Jacobsen, D. J., Mayo, M. S., Washburn, R., & Greene, L. (2005). Active commuting to and from school and BMI in elementary school children—Preliminary data. *Child: Care, Health & Development, 31,* 341–349.

Hegarty, P. (2002). "More feminine than 999 men out of 1000": Measuring sex roles and gender nonconformity in psychology. In T. Lester (Ed.), *Gender nonconformity, race, and sexuality: Charting the connections* (pp. 62–83). Madison, WI: University of Wisconsin Press.

Heinberg, L. J. (1996). Theories of body image disturbance: Perceptual, developmental and sociocultural factors. In J. K. Thompson (Ed.), *Body image, eating disorders, and obesity: An integrative guide for assessment and treatment* (pp. 27–47). Washington, DC: American Psychological Association.

Heinberg, L. J., Thompson, J. K., & Matson, J. L. (2001). Body image dissatisfaction as a motivator for healthy lifestyle change: Is some distress beneficial? In R. Striegel-Moore & L. Smolak (Eds.), *Eating disorders: Innovative directions for research and practice* (pp. 215–232). Washington, DC: American Psychological Association.

Helms, J. E. (2003). Racial identity and racial socialization as aspects of adolescents'

identity development. In R. M. Lerner, F. Jacobs, & D. Wertleib (Eds.), *Handbook of applied developmental science: Promoting positive child, adolescent, and family development through research, policies, and programs: Vol. 1. Applying developmental science for youth and families: Historical and theoretical foundations* (pp. 143–163). Thousand Oaks, CA: Sage.

Henderson, T. L. (2005). Grandparent visitation rights: Justices' interpretation of the best interests of the child standard. *Journal of Family Issues, 26,* 638–664.

Henderson, V. L., & Dweck, C. S. (1990). Motivation and achievement. In S. Feldman & G. R. Elliott (Eds.), *At the threshold: The developing adolescent* (pp. 308–329). Cambridge, MA: Harvard University Press.

Herdt, G., & Boxer, A. (1993). *Children of horizons.* New York: McGraw-Hill.

Herdt, G., & McClintock, M. (2000). The magical age of 10. *Archives of Sexual Behavior, 29,* 587–606.

Herman-Giddens, M. E., Slora, E. J., Wasserman, R. C., Bourdony, C. J., Bhapkar, M. V., Koch, G. G., et al. (1997). Secondary sexual characteristics and menses in young girls seen in office practice: A study from the Pediatric Research in Office Settings Network. *Pediatrics, 99,* 505–512.

Herman-Giddens, M. E., Wang, L., & Koch, G. (2001). Secondary sexual characteristics and menses in boys: Estimates from the National Health and Nutrition Examination Survey III, 1988–1994. *Archives of Pediatrics and Adolescent Medicine, 155,* 1022–1028.

Hetherington, E. M. (1994). Siblings, family relationships, and child development. *Journal of Family Psychology, 8,* 251–253.

Hetherington, E. M., Stanley-Hagan, M., & Anderson, E. R. (1989). Marital transition: A child's perspective. Special issue: Children and their development: Knowledge base, research agenda, and social policy application. *American Psychologist, 44*(2), 303–312.

Hewitt, J. P. (1998). *The myth of self-esteem: Finding happiness and solving problems in America.* New York: St. Martin's Press.

Higgins, E. T. (1991). Development of self-regulatory and self-evaluative processes: Costs, benefits, and trade-offs. In M. R. Gunnar & L. A. Sroufe (Eds.), *Self processes in development. Twenty-third Minnesota Symposium on Child Psychology.* Hillsdale, NJ: Erlbaum.

Hildebrand, D. K., & Ledbetter, M. F. (2001). Assessing children's intelligence and memory: The Wechsler Intelligence Scale for Children—Third Edition and and the Children's Memory Scale. In J. J. C. Andrews, D. H. Saklofske, & H. L. Janzen (Eds.), *Handbook of psychoeducational assessment* (pp. 13–32). San Diego, CA: Academic Press.

Hill, J. P., & Lynch, M. E. (1983). The intensification of gender-related role expectations during early adolescence. In J. Brooks-Gunn & A. C. Petersen (Eds.), *Girls at puberty: Biological and psychological perspectives* (pp. 201–228). New York: Plenum.

Hill, K., & Pomeroy, C. (2001). Assessment of physical status of children and adolescents with eating disorders and obesity. In J. K. Thompson & L. Smolak (Eds.), *Body image, eating disorders, and obesity in youth: Assessment, prevention, and treatment* (pp. 171–191). Washington, DC: American Psychological Association.

Hill, K. G., Hawkins, J. D., Catalano, R. F., Abbott, R. D., & Guo, J. (2005). Family influences on the risk of daily smoking initiation. *Journal of Adolescent Health, 37,* 202–210.

Hine, T. (1999). *Rise and fall of the American teenager.* New York: Avon.

Hines, A. N. (1997). Divorce-related transitions, adolescent development, and the role of the parent-child relationship: A review of the literature. *Journal of Marriage and the Family, 59,* 375–388.

Hinson, J., DiStefano, C., & Daniel, C. (2004). The Internet Self-Perception Scale: Measuring elementary students' levels of self-efficacy regarding Internet use. *Journal of Educational Computing Research, 29,* 209–228.

Ho, E., & Willms, J. D. (1996). Effects of parental involvement on eighth-grade achievement. *Sociological Quarterly, 69,* 126–141.

Hoff, E. V. (2005). Imaginary companions, creativity, and self-image in middle childhood. *Creativity Research Journal, 17,* 167–180.

Hoff, E., & Tian, C. (2005). Socioeconomic status and cultural influences on language. *Journal of Communication Disorders, 38,* 271–278.

Hofferth, S. L. (2003). Race/ethnic differences in father involvement in two-parent families: Culture, context, or economy? *Journal of Family Issues, 24,* 185–216.

Hofferth, S. L., & Sandberg, J. F. (2001). How American children spend their time. *Journal of Marriage and Family, 63,* 295–308.

Hoge, D. R., Smit, E. K., & Hanson, S. K. (1990). School experiences predicted changes in self-esteem of sixth- and seventh-grade students. *Journal of Educational Psychology, 82,* 117–127.

Hollingshead, A. B. (1949). *Elmtown's youth: The impact of social classes on adolescents.* New York: Wiley.

Hollins, E. R. (1999). Relating ethnic and racial identity to teaching. In R. H. Sheets & E. R. Hollins (Eds.), *Racial and ethnic identity in school practices: Aspects of human development* (pp. 183–193). Mahwah, NJ: Erlbaum.

Holtzman, M. (2005). The family definitions continuum. *NCFR Report, 50*(2), F1–F3.

Hoover, H. D., Dunbar, S. B., & Frisbie, D. A. (2001). *Iowa Tests of Basic Skills.* Boston: Riverside.

Hoover-Dempsey, K. V., Walker, J. M. T., Jones, P., & Reed, R. P. (2002). Teachers Involving Parents (TIP): Results from an in-service teacher education program for enhancing parental involvement. *Teaching & Teacher Education, 18*, 843–867.

Horn, M. (1993). Childhood and children. In M. K. Cayton, E. J. Gorn, & P. W. Williams (Eds.), *Encyclopedia of American social history* (Vol. 3, pp. 2023–2036). New York: Scribner.

Horner, S. D. (2000). Using focus group methods with middle school children. *Research in Nursing & Health, 23*, 510–517.

Howe, N., & Strauss, W. (2000). *Millennials rising: The next great generation.* New York: Vintage.

Howes, C. (Ed.). (2003). *Teaching 4- to 8-year olds: Literacy, math, multiculturalism, and classroom community.* Baltimore, MD: Paul H. Brooks.

Huddleston, J., & Ge, X. (2003). Boys at puberty: Psychosocial implications. In C. Hayward (Ed.), *Gender differences at puberty* (pp. 113–134). New York: Cambridge University Press.

Hudson, J., & Fivush, R. (1991). Planning in the preschool years: The emergence of plans from general event knowledge. *Cognitive Development, 6*, 393–415.

Huebner, A. J., & Mancini, J. A. (2003). Shaping structured out-of-school time use among youth: The effects of self, family, and friend systems. *Journal of Youth and Adolescence, 32*(6), 453–463.

Huesmann, L. R., Dubow, E. F., Eron, L. D., & Boxer, P. (2006). Middle childhood family contextual and personal factos as predictors of adult outcomes. In A. C. Huston & M. N. Ripke (Eds.), *Developmental contexts in middle childhood: Bridges to adolescence and adulthood* (pp. 62–85). Cambridge, UK: Cambridge University Press.

Huesmann, L. R., & Taylor, L. D. (2006). Media effects in middle childhood. In A. C. Huston & M. N. Ripke (Eds.), *Developmental contexts in middle childhood: Bridges to adolescence and adulthood* (pp. 303–326). Cambridge, UK: Cambridge University Press.

Huffman, H. A. (1994). *A character education program: One school district's experience.* Alexandria, VA: Association for Supervision and Curriculum Development.

Hughes, D., & Chen, L. (1997). When and what parents tell children about race: An examiniation of race-related socialization among African American families. *Applied Developmental Science, 1*(4), 200–214.

Humphreys, L. G., & Davey, T. C. (1988). Continuity in intellectual growth from 12 months to 9 years. *Intelligence, 12*, 183–197.

Hunter, A. G. (1997). Counting on grandmothers: Black mothers' and fathers' reliance on grandmothers for parenting support. *Journal of Family Issues, 18*, 251–269.

Hurks, P. P. M., Hendriksen, J. G. M., Vles, J. S. H., Kalff, A. C., Feron, F. J. M., Kroes, M., et al. (2004). Verbal fluency over time as a measure of automatic and controlled processing in children with ADHD. *Brain and Cognition, 55*, 535–544.

Huston, A. C. (2005). Connecting the science of child development to public policy. *SRCD Social Policy Report, 19*(4), 3–18.

Huston, A. C., & Ripke, M. N. (2006a). Middle childhood: Contexts of development. In A. C. Huston & M. N. Ripke (Eds.), *Developmental contexts in middle childhood: Bridges to adolescence and adulthood* (pp. 1–22). Cambridge, UK: Cambridge University Press.

Huston, A. C., & Ripke, M. N. (2006b). Experiences in middle childhood and children's development: A summary and integration of research. In A. C. Huston & M. N. Ripke (Eds.), *Developmental contexts in middle childhood: Bridges to adolescence and adulthood* (pp. 409–434). Cambridge, UK: Cambridge University Press.

Huston, A. C., & Wright, J. C. (1997). Mass media and children's development. In W. Damon (Series Ed.), I. Sigel & A. Renniger (Vol. Eds.), *Handbook of child psychology: Vol. 4. Child psychology in practice* (5th ed., pp. 999–1058). New York: Wiley.

Huttenlocher, P. R., & Dabholkar, A. S. (1997). Regional differences in synaptogenesis in human cerebral cortex. *Journal of Comparative Neurology, 387*, 167–178.

Hyde, J. S., & Jaffee, S. R. (2000). Becoming a heterosexual adult: The experiences of young women. *Journal of Social Issues, 56*, 283–296.

Iglowstein, I., Jenni, O. G., Molinari, L., & Largo, R. H. (2003). Sleep duration from infancy to adolescence: Reference values and generational trends. *Pediatrics, 111*, 302–307.

Ihinger-Tallman, M., & Cooney, T. M. (2005). *Families in context: An introduction.* Los Angeles, CA: Roxbury.

Illick, J. E. (2002). *American childhoods.* Philadelphia, PA: University of Pennsylvania Press.

International Association for the Evaluation of Education Achievement. (n.d.). PIRLS 2001 report. Retrieved from http://www.iea.nl/Home/Studies/PIRLS2001/pirls2001.html.

International Play Association. (1990). *Declaration of the child's right to play.* Retrieved August 20, 2006, from http://www.ipaworld.org/ipa_declaration.html.

Isaacs, D. (2001). *Character building: A guide for parents and teachers.* Dublin, Ireland: Four Courts Press.

Isen, A. M. (2000). Positive affect and decision making. In M. Lewis & J. M. Haviland-Jones (Eds.), *Handbook of emotions* (2nd ed., pp. 417–435). New York: Guilford Press.

Izard, M. K. (1990). Social influences on the reproductive success and reproductive endocrinology of prosimian primates. In T. E. Ziegler & F. B. Bercovitch (Eds.), *Socioendocrinology of primate reproduction* (pp. 159–186). New York: Wiley-Liss.

Jackson, A. W., & Davis, G. A. (2000). *Turning points 2000: Educating adolescents in the 21st century.* New York: Teachers College Press.

Jackson, L. A., von Eye, A., Biocca, F. A., Barbatsis, G., Zhao, Y, & Fitzgerald, H. E. (2006). Does home Internet use influence the academic performance of low-income children? *Developmental Psychology, 42*, 429–435.

Jacobs, B. A. (2002). Where the boys aren't: Non-cognitive skills, returns to school and the gender gap in higher education. *Economics of Education Review, 21*, 589–598.

Jacobs, J. E., Chhin, C. S., & Shaver, K. (2005). Longitudinal links between perceptions of adolescence and the social beliefs of adolescents: Are parents' stereotypes related to beliefs held about and by their children? *Journal of Youth and Adolescence, 34*, 61–72.

Jacobs, J. E., Bleeker, M. M., & Constantino, M. J. (2003). The self-system during childhood and adolescence: Development, influences, and implications. *Journal of Psychotherapy Integration, 13*, 33–65.

Jacobs Quadrel, M., Fischoff, B., & Davis, W. (1993). Adolescent (in)vulnerability. *American Psychologist, 48*, 102–116.

Jacobsen, T., & Hofmann, V. (1997). Children's attachment representations: Longitudinal relations to school behavior and academic competency in middle childhood and adolescence. *Developmental Psychology, 33*(4), 703–710.

Jahnke, H. C., & Blanchard-Fields, F. (1993). Two models of adolescent egocentrism. *Journal of Youth and Adolescence, 22*, 313–326.

Jahoda, G. (2001). Beyond stereotypes. *Culture and Psychology, 7*(2), 181–197.

James, W. (1890). *Principles of psychology.* New York: Henry Holt.

Jankowski, S. M. (1992). Ethnic identity and political consciousness in different social orders. In H. Haste & J. Torney-Purta (Eds.), *The development of political understanding: A new perspective* (pp. 79–93). *New Directions for Child Development,* No. 56. San Francisco: Jossey-Bass.

Janz, K. (2002). Physical activity and bone development during childhood and adolescence: Implications for the prevention of osteoporosis. *Minerva Pediatrics, 54,* 93–104.

Jarrett, O. S., & Duckett-Hedgebeth, M. (2003). Recess in a middle school: What do the students do? In J. L. Roopnarine (Series Ed.) & D. E. Lytle (Vol. Ed.), *Play and culture series: Vol. 5. Play and educational theory and practice* (pp. 227–241). Westport, CT: Praeger.

Jarrett, R. L. (1995). Growing up poor: The family experiences of socially mobile youth in low income African-American neighborhoods. *Journal of Adolescent Research, 10,* 111–135.

Jarrett, R. L. (1997). African American family and parenting strategies in impoverished neighborhoods. *Qualitiative Sociology, 20,* 275–288.

Jenkins, D., & Reaburn, P. (2000). *Guiding the young athlete: All you need to know.* St Leonards, NSW: Allen & Unwin.

Jenkins, J. M., Dunn, J., O'Connor, T. G., Rasbash, J., & Behnke, P. (2005). Change in maternal perception of negativity: Within- and between-family influences. *Journal of Family Psychology, 19*(4), 533–541.

Jenkins, J. M., Rasbash, J., & O'Connor, T. G. (2003). The role of the shared family context in differential parenting. *Developmental Psychology, 39*(1), 99–113.

Jenkins, J. M., Simpson, A., Dunn, J., Rasbash, J., & O'Connor, T. G. (2005). Mutual influence of marital conflict and children's behavior problems: Shared and nonshared family risks. *Child Development, 76,* 24–39.

Jennings, N., & Wartella, E. (2004). Technology and the family. In A. Vangelisti (Ed.), *Handbook of family communication* (pp. 593–608). Mahwah, NJ: Erlbaum.

Jensen, A. R. (1998). *The g factor: The science of mental ability.* Westport, CT: Praeger.

Jensen, A. R. (2001). Spearman's hypothesis. In J. M. Collis & S. Messick (Eds.), *Intelligence and personality: Bridging the gap in theory and measurement* (pp. 3–24). Mahwah, NJ: Erlbaum.

Jensen, A. R., & Reynolds, C. R. (1982). Race, social class and ability patterns on the WISC-R. *Personality and Individual Differences, 3,* 423–438.

Jessor, R., Turbin, M. S., & Costa, F. M. (1998). Risk and protection in successful outcomes among disadvantaged adolescents. *Applied Developmental Science, 2*(4), 194–208.

Johnson, C. M., & Johnson, S. (2002). Construct stability of the Cognitive Abilities Scale—Second Edition for infants and toddlers. *Journal of Psychoeducational Assessment, 20,* 144–151.

Johnson, D. J. (2005). The ecology of children's racial coping: Family, school, and community influences. In T. S. Weisner (Ed.), *Discovering successful pathways in children's development: Mixed methods in the study of childhood and family life* (pp. 87–109). Chicago: University of Chicago Press.

Johnson, M. (1980). *Toward adolescence: The middle school years, 79th yearbook of the National Society for the Study of Education.* Chicago: National Society for the Study of Education.

Johnson, M. H. (2005). Sensitive periods in functional brain development: Problems and prospects. *Developmental Psychology, 46,* 287–292.

Johnson, R. (2002). Pathways to adolescent health: Early intervention. *Journal of Adolescent Health, 31,* 240–250.

Johnston, L. D., O'Malley, P. M., & Bachman, J. G., & Schulenberg, J. E. (2006). *Monitoring the Future national results on adolescent drug use: Overview of the key findings, 2005.* (NIH Publication No. 06–5882). Bethesda, MD: National Institute on Drug Abuse.

Jones, D. C., Vigfusdottir, F. H., & Lee, Y. (2004). Body image and the appearance culture among adolescent girls and boys: An examination of friend conversations, peer criticism, appearance magazine, and the internalization of appearance ideals. *Journal of Adolescent Research, 19*(3), 323–339.

Jones, M. C., & Bayley, N. (1950). Physical maturing among boys as related to behavior. *Journal of Educational Psychology, 41,* 129–148.

Joshi, A., & Ferris, J. C. (2002). Causal attributions regarding conflicts between friends in middle childhood. *Social Behavior and Personality, 30,* 65–74.

Kafai, Y. B. (1998). Play and technology: Revised realities and potential perspectives. In D. P. Fromberg & D. Bergen (Eds.), *Play from birth to twelve and beyond* (pp. 93–99). New York: Garland.

Kafai, Y. B., Fishman, B. J., Bruckman, A. S., & Rockman, S. (2002). Models of educational computing @ home: New frontiers for research on technology in learning. *Educational Technology Review* [Online serial], *10*(2), 52–68.

Kafai, Y. B., & Sutton, S. (1999). Elementary school students' computer and Internet use at home: Current trends and issues. *Journal of Educational Computing, 21,* 345–362.

Kagan, J. (2003). Biology, context, and developmental inquiry. *Annual Review of Psychology, 54,* 1–23.

Kagan, J., & Saudino, K. (2001). Behavioral inhibition and related temperaments. In R. M. Emde & J. K. Hewitt (Eds.), *Infancy to early childhood: Genetic and environmental influences on developmental change* (pp. 111–119). London: Oxford University Press.

Kagan, J., Snidman, N., Kahn, V., & Towsley, S. (2007). The preservation of two infant temperaments into adolescence. In W. A. Collins (Ed.), *Monographs of the Society for Research in Child Development, 72*(2, Serial No. 287), 1–75.

Kahle, J. B., & Lakes, M. K. (2003). The myth of equality in science classrooms. *Journal of Research in Science Teaching, 40,* S58–S67.

Kail, R. (1995). Processing speed, memory, and cognition. In F. E. Weinert, & W. Schneider (Eds.), *Memory performance and competencies: Issues in growth and development* (pp. 71–88). Hillsdale, NJ: Lawrence Erlbaum Associates.

Kandel, D. B., & Chen, K. (2000). Types of marijuana user by longitudinal course. *Journal of Studies on Alcohol, 61,* 367–378.

Kaplan, S. J., Pelcovitz, D., & Labruna, V. (1999). Child and adolescent abuse and neglect research: A review of the past 10 years. Part I: Physical and emotional abuse and neglect. *Journal of the American Academy of Child & Adolescent Psychiatry, 38,* 1214–1222.

Karavasilis, L., Doyle, A., & Markiewicz, D. (2003). Associations between parenting style and attachment to mother in middle childhood and adolescence. *International Journal of Behavioral Development, 27*(2), 153–164.

Karcher, M. J. (2002). The cycle of violence and disconnection among middle school students: Teacher disconnection as a consequence of violence. *Journal of School Violence, 1*(1), 35–51.

Karofsky, P. S., Zeng, L., & Kosorock, M. R. (2001). Relationship between adolescent-parental communication and initiation of first intercourse by adolescents. *Journal of Adolescent Health, 28,* 41–45.

Katz, C. (1998). Disintegrating developments: Global economic restructuring and the eroding ecologies of youth. In T. Skelton & G. Valentine (Eds.), *Cool places: Geographies of youth cultures.* London: Routledge.

Keeney, B. P., & Ross, J. M. (1985). *Mind in therapy.* New York: Basic.

Keller, M., & Edelstein, W. (1991). The development of socio-moral meaning-making: Domains, categories, and perspective-taking. In W. M. Kurtines & J. L. Gewirtz (Eds.), *Handbook of moral behavior and development: Vol. 1. Theory* (pp. 89–114). Hillsdale, NJ: Erlbaum.

Kelley, H. H., Berscheid, E., Christiensen, A., Harvey, J. H., Huston, T. L., Levinger, G., et al. (1983). *Close relationships.* New York: Freeman.

Kelley, P., Buckingham, D., & Davies, H. (1999). Talking dirty: Children, sexual knowledge, and television. *Childhood, 6,* 221–242.

Kelly, J. B. (2003). Changing perspectives on children's adjustment following divorce: A view from the United States. *Childhood, 10,* 237–254.

Kelly, J. B., & Emery, R. E. (2003). Children's adjustment following divorce: Risk and resilience perspectives. *Family Relations, 52,* 352–362.

Kennedy, C., Kools, S., & Krueger, R. (2001). Methodological considerations in children's focus groups. *Nursing Research, 50,* 184–187.

Kennedy, S. G., Washburn, G., & Martinez, M. (1998, January 13). Volunteer shield stands up for Taylor Homes' children. *Chicago Tribune,* 1.

Kerns, K. A., Klepac, L., & Cole, A. K. (1996). Peer relationships and preadolescents' perceptions of security in the mother-child relationship. *Developmental Psychology, 32,* 457–466.

Kerns, K. A., & Richardson, R. A. (Eds.) (2005). *Attachment in middle childhood.* New York: Guilford Press.

Kerns, K. A., Schlegelmilch, A., Morgan, T. A., & and M. M. Abraham, M. M. (2005). Assessing attachment in middle childhood. In K. A. Kerns & R. A. Richardson (Eds.), *Attachment in middle childhood* (pp. 46–70). New York: Guilford Press.

Kerns, K. A., Tomich, P. L., Aspelmeier, J. E., & Contreras, J. M. (2000). Attachment-based assessment of parent-child relationships in middle childhood. *Developmental Psychology, 36,* 614–626.

Kerns, S. E. U., & Prinz, R. J. (2002). Critical issues in the prevention of violence-related behavior in youth. *Clinical Child and Family Psychology Review, 5*(2), 133–160.

Kerr, M., Stattin, H., Biesecker, G., & Ferrer-Wreder, L. (2003). Relationships with parents and peers in adolescence. Emotion and personality development in childhood. In R. M. Lerner & M. A. Easterbrook (Eds.), *Handbook of psychology: Vol. 6. Developmental psychology* (pp. 395–419). New York: Wiley.

Kilian, J. M., Fish, M. C., & Maniago, E. B. (2007). Making schools safe: A system-wide school intervention to increase student prosocial behaviors and enhance school climate. *Journal of Applied School Psychology, 23,* 1–30.

Killen, J., Taylor, C., Hayward, C., Haydel, K., Wilson, D., Hammer, L., et al. (1996). Weight concerns influence the development of eating disorders: A four year prospective study. *Journal of Consulting and Clinical Psychology, 64,* 936–940.

Killen, M., Lee-Kim, J., McGlothlin, & Stangor, C. (2002). How children and adolescents evaluate racial and gender exclusion. *Monographs of the Society for Research in Child Development, 67* (4, Serial No. 271).

Kim, S., Brody, G. H., & Murry, V. M. (2003). Factor structure of the Early Adolescent Temperament Questionnaire and measurement invariance across gender. *Journal of Early Adolescence, 23,* 268–294.

King, P. E., & Boyatzis, C. J. (2004). Exploring adolescent spiritual and religious development: Current and future theoretical and empirical perspectives. *Applied Developmental Science, 8,* 2–6.

King, P. E., Dowling, E. M., Mueller, R. A., White, K., Schultz, W., Obsborn, et al. (2005). *Journal of Early Adolescence, 23,* 94–112.

Kinsman, S. B., Romer, D., Furstenberg, F. F., & Schwartz, D. F. (1998). Early sexual initiation: The role of peer norms. *Pediatrics, 102,* 1185–1192.

Kirby, D. (2001). *Emerging answers: Research findings on programs to reduce teen pregnancy.* Washington, DC: National Campaign to Prevent Teen Pregnancy.

Kirby, D. (2002a). Antecedents of adolescent initiation of sex, contraceptive use, and pregnancy. *American Journal of Health Behavior, 26,* 473–485.

Kirby, D. (2002b). Effective approaches to reducing adolescent unprotected sex, pregnancy, and childbearing. *The Journal of Sex Research, 39,* 51–57.

Klintsova, A. Y., & Greenough, W. T. (1999). Synaptic plasticity in cortical systems. *Current Opinion in Neurobiology, 9,* 203–208.

Knoth, R., Boyd, K., & Singer, B. (1988). Empirical tests of sexual selection theory: Predictions of sex differences in onset, intensity, and time course of sexual arousal. *Journal of Sex Research, 24,* 73–89.

Kolb, B. (1989). Brain development, plasticity, and behavior. *American Psychologist, 44,* 1203–1212.

Kolb, B., Gibb, R, & Robinson, T. E. (2003). Brain plasticity and behavior. *Current Directions in Psychological Science, 12,* 1–5.

Kolb, B., & Wishaw, I. Q. (1998). Brain plasticity and behavior. *Annual Review of Psychology, 49,* 43–64.

Kolecki, P, & Shih, R. (2004). Inhalant abuse. In J. Brick (Ed.), *Handbook of the medical consequences of alcohol and drug abuse* (pp. 303–318). New York: Haworth Press.

Kontula, O., & Haavio-Mannila, E. (2002). Masturbation in a generational perspective. *Journal of Psychology and Human Sexuality, 14,* 49–83.

Kowal, A., Kramer, L., Krill, J. L., & Crick, N. R. (2002). Children's perceptions of the fairness of parental preferential treatment and their socioemotional well-being. *Journal of Family Psychology, 16,* 297–306.

Kreutzer, M. A., Leonard, C., & Flavell, J. H. (1975). An interview study of children's knowledge about memory. *Monographs of the Society for Research in Child Development, 40*(1, Serial No. 159).

Krogman, W. M. (1972). *Child growth.* Ann Arbor, MI: The University of Michigan Press.

Krotz, F. (2001). Who are the new media users? In S. Livingstone (Ed.), *Children and their changing media environment: A European comparative study* (pp. 245–262). Mahwah, NJ: Erlbaum.

Krueger, R. A., & Casey, M. A. (2000). *Focus groups: A practical guide for applied research* (3rd ed.). Thousand Oaks, CA: Sage.

Kuo, Y-Y. (1996). Taoistic psychology of creativity. *Journal of Creative Behavior, 30,* 197–212.

Kupek, E. (2001). Sexual attitudes and number of partners in young British men. *Archives of Sexual Behavior, 30,* 13–27.

Kurdek, L. A. (1994). Family transitions: Divorce and remarriage. In S. Price (Series Ed.) & P. C. McHenry & S. M. Gravazzi (Issue Eds.), *Vision 2010: Families and adolescents.* Minneapolis, MN: National Coumcil on Family Relations.

Kuttler, A. F., Parker, J. G., & La Greca, A. M. (2002). Developmental and gender differences in preadolescents' judgments of the veracity of gossip. *Merrill-Palmer Quarterly, 48,* 105–132.

Ladd, G. W. (1999). Peer relationships and social competence during early and middle childhood. *Annual Review of Psychology, 50,* 333–359.

Ladd, G. W., & Kochenderfer, B. J. (1996). Linkages between friendship and adjustment during early school transitions. In W. M. Bukowski & A. F. Newcomb (Eds.), *The company they keep: Friendship in childhood and adolescence* (pp. 322–345). New York: Cambridge University Press.

Lagana, L. (1999). Psychosocial correlates of contraceptive practices during late adolescence. *Adolescence, 34,* 463–482.

Laitinen-Krispijn, S., Van der Ende, J., Hazebroek-Kampschreur, A. A. J. M., & Verhulst, F. C. (1999). Pubertal maturation and the development of behavioural and emotional problems in early adolescence. *Acta Psychiatrica Scandinavica, 99*(1), 16–25.

Lam, T. H., Shi, H. J., Ho, L. M., Stewart, S. M., & Fan, S. (2002). Timing of pubertal maturation and heterosexual behavior among Hong Kong Chinese adolescents. *Archives of Sexual Behavior, 31*(4), 359–366.

Lam, T. H., Stewart, S. M., Leung, G., Ho, S. Y., Fan, A. H., & Ma, A. L. T. (2002). Sex differences in body satisfaction, feeling fat and pressure to diet among Chinese adolescents in Hong Kong. *European Eating Disorders Review, 10,* 347–358.

Lamanna, M. A., & Riedmann, A. (2006). *Marriages and families: Making choices in a diverse society* (9th ed.). Belmont, CA: Thomson Wadsworth.

Landers-Potts, M., & Grant, L. (1999). Competetitive climates, athletic skill, and children's status in after-school recreational sports programs. *Social Psychology of Education, 2,* 297–313.

Landolt, P., & Da, W. W. (2005). Spatially ruptured practices of migrant families: A comparison of immigrants from El Salvador and People's Republic of China. *Current Sociology, 53,* 625–653.

Landrine, H. (1995). *Bringing cultural diversity to feminist psychology: Theory, research, and practice.* Washington, DC: American Psychological Association.

Langille, D. B., & Curtis, L. (2002). Factors associated with sexual intercourse before age 15 among female adolescents in Nova Scotia. *The Canadian Journal of Human Sexuality, 11,* 91–99.

Lapsley, D. K. (1996). *Moral psychology.* Boulder, CO: Westview.

Lapsley, D. K., Flannery, D. J., Gottschalk, H., & Raney, M. (1996, March). *Sources of risk and resilience in adolescent mental health.* Poster at the Sixth Biennial Meetings of the Society for Research on Adolescence, Boston, MA.

Lapsley, D. K., & Narvaez, D. (2006). Character education. In W. Damon & R. M. Lerner (Series Eds.) & R. M. Lerner (Vol. Ed.), *Handbook of child psychology: Vol. 1. Theoretical models of human development* (6th ed., pp. 248–296). New York: Wiley.

Lapsley, D. K., & Rice, K. (1988). The "new look" at the imaginary audience and the personal fable: Toward a general model of adolescent ego development. In D. K. Lapsley & F. C. Power (Eds.), *Self, ego, identity: Integrative approaches* (pp. 109–129). New York: Springer.

Lareau, A. (2000). Social class and the daily lives of children: A study from the United States. *Childhood: A Global Journal of Child Research, 7*(2), 155–171.

Larson, R. W. (1994). Youth organizations, hobbies, and sports as developmental contexts. In R. K. Silbereisen & E. Todt (Eds.), *Adolescence in context: The interplay of family, school, peers, and work in adjustment* (pp. 46–65). New York: Springer-Verlag.

Larson, R. W. (2000). Toward a psychology of positive youth development. *American Psychologist, 55,* 170–183.

Larson, R. W. (2001). How U.S. children and adolescents spend time: What it does (and doesn't) tell us about their development. *Current Directions in Psychological Science, 10,* 160–164.

Larson, R. W. (2002). Globalization, societal change, and new technologies. What they mean for the future of adolescence. *Journal of Research on Adolescence, 12,* 1–30.

Larson, R. W., Brown, B. B., & Mortimer, J. T. (2002a). *Adolescents' preparation for the future: Perils and promise.* Preface to the report of the Study Group on Adolescence in the Twenty-first Century. *Journal of Research on Adolescence, 12,* iii–v.

Larson, R. W., Brown, B. B., & Mortimer, J. T. (2002b). *Adolescents' preparation for the future: Perils and promise.* Malden, MA: Blackwell.

Larson, R. W., & Richards, M. H. (1989). The changing life space of early adolescence [Special issue]. *Journal of Youth and Adolescence, 18,* 501–509.

Larson, R. W., & Richards, M. H. (1991). Daily companionship in late childhood and early adolescence: Changing developmental contexts. *Child Development, 62,* 284–300.

Larson, R. W., Richards, M. H., Sims, B. & Dworkin, J. (2001). How urban African American young adolescents spend their time: Time budgets for locations, activities, and companionship. *American Journal of Community Psychology, 29,* 565–597.

Larsson, I., & Svedin, C. (2002). Sexual experiences in childhood: Young adults' recollections. *Archives of Sexual Behavior, 31,* 263–272.

Latendresse, C. (2004). Literature circles: Meeting reading standards, making personal connections, and appreciating other interpretations. *Middle School Journal, 35,* 13–20.

Laursen, B., Coy, K. C., & Collins, W. A. (1998). Reconsidering changes in parent-adolescent conflict across adolescence: A meta-analysis. *Child Development, 69,* 817–832.

Leaper, C. (1994). Exploring the consequences of gender segregation on social relationships. In C. Leaper (Ed.), *Childhood gender segregation: Causes and consequences* (pp. 67–86). *New Directions for Child Development,* No. 65. San Francisco: Jossey-Bass.

Leaper, C., & Anderson, K. J. (1997). Gender development and heterosexual romantic relationships during adolescence. In S. Shulman & W. A. Collins (Eds.), *Romantic relationships in adolescence: Developmental perspectives* (pp. 85–103). San Francisco: Jossey-Bass.

Lease, A. M., & Axelrod, J. J. (2001). Position in the peer group's perceived organizational structure: Relation to social status and friendship. *Journal of Early Adolescence, 21,* 377–404.

Lease, A. M., McFall, R. M., & Viken, R. J. (2003). Distance from peers in the group's perceived organizational structure: Relation to individual characteristics. *Journal of Early Adolescence, 23*(2), 194–217.

Lederer, J. M. (2000). Reciprocal teaching of social studies in inclusive elementary classrooms. *Journal of Learning Disabilities, 33,* 91–106.

Lee, R. E., & Cubbin, C. (2002). Neighborhood context and youth cardiovascular health behaviors. *American Journal of Public Health, 92,* 428–436.

Lee, V. E. & Burkam, D. T. (2002). *Inequality at the starting gate: Social background differences in achievement as children begin school.* Washington, DC: Economic Policy Institute.

Lefebvre, C., & Reid, G. (1998). Prediction in ball catching by children with and without

a developmental coordination disorder. *Adapted Physical Activity Quarterly, 15,* 299–315.

Leitenberg, H., & Saltzman, H. (2000). A state-wide survey of age at first intercourse for adolescent females and age of their male partners: Relation to other risk behaviors and statutory rape implications. *Archives of Sexual Behavior, 29,* 203–215.

L'Engle, K. L., Brown, J. D., & Kenneavy, K. (2006). The mass media are important context for adolescents' sexual behavior. *Journal of Adolescent Health, 38,* 186–192.

Lengua, L. J. (2003). Associations among emotionality, self-regulation, adjustment problems, and positive adjustment in middle childhood. *Journal of Applied Developmental Psychology, 24,* 595–618.

Lengua, L. J., & Long, A. C. (2002). The role of emotionality and self-regulation in the appraisal-coping process: Tests of direct and moderating effects. *Journal of Applied Developmental Psychology, 23,* 471–493.

Lenhart, A., Rainie, L., & Lewis, O. (2001). Teenage life online: The rise of the instant-message generation and the Internet's impact on friendships and family relationships. Washington, DC: Pew Internet and American Life Project. Retrieved August 23, 2006, from http://www.pewinternet.org/pdfs/PIP_Teens_Report.pdf.

Lennard, S. H. C., & Lennard, H. (1977). Architecture: Effect of territory, boundary, and orientation on family functioning. *Family Process, 16,* 49–66.

Lenroot, R. K., & Giedd, J. N. (2006). Brain development in children and adolescents: Insights from anatomical magnetic resonance imaging. *Neuroscience and Biobehavioral Reviews, 30*(6), 718–729.

Lerner, R. M. (1996). Relative plasticity, integration, temporality, and diversity in human development: A developmental contextual perspective about theory, process, and method. *Developmental Psychology, 32,* 781–786.

Lerner, R. M. (2002a). *Adolescence: Development, diversity, context, and application.* Upper Saddle River, NJ: Prentice Hall.

Lerner, R. M. (2002b). *Concepts and theories of human development* (3rd ed.). Mahwah, NJ: Erlbaum.

Lerner, R. M., Alberts, A. E., Anderson, P. M., & Dowling, E. M. (2005). On making humans human: Spirituality and the promotion of positive youth development. In P. E. King & E. C. Roehlkepartain (Eds.), *Handbook of spiritual development in childhood and adolescence* (pp. 60–72). Thousand Oaks, CA: Sage.

Lerner, R. M., Almerigi, J. B., Theokas, C., & Lerner, J. V. (2005). Positive youth development: A view of the issues. *Journal of Early Adolescence, 25,* 10–16.

Lerner, R. M., Brentano, C., Dowling, E. M., & Anderson, P. M. (2002). Positive youth development: Thriving as the basis of personhood and civil society. *New Directions for Youth Development, 95*, 11–33.

Lerner, R. M., Dowling, E. M., & Anderson, P. M. (2003). Positive youth development: Thriving as the basis of personhood and civil society. *Applied Developmental Science, 7*, 172–180.

Lerner, R. M., Fisher, C. B., & Weinberg, R. A. (2000). Toward a science for and of the people: Promoting civil society through the application of developmental science. *Child Development, 71*, 11–20.

Lerner, R. M., & Knapp, J. R. (1975). Actual and perceived intrafamilial attitudes of late adolescents and their parents. *Journal of Youth and Adolescence, 4*, 17–36.

Lerner, R. M., Lerner, J. V., Almerigi, J. B., Theokas, C., Phelps, et al. (2005). Positive youth development, participation in community youth development programs, and community contributions of fifth-grade adolescents: Findings from the first wave of the 4-H Study of Positive Youth Development. *Journal of Early Adolescence, 25*, 17–71.

Lerner, R. M., Taylor, C. S., & von Eye, A. (Eds.). (2002). *Pathways to positive development among diverse youth. New Directions for Youth Development*, No. 95. New York: Jossey-Bass.

Leventhal, T., & Brooks-Gunn, J. (2003a). Children and youth in neighborhood contexts. *Current Directions in Psychological Science, 12*, 27–31.

Leventhal, T. & Brooks-Gunn, J. (2003b). Moving on up: Neighborhood effects on children and families. In M. H. Bornstein & R. H. Bradley (Eds.), *Socioeconomic status, parenting, and child development* (pp. 209–230). Mahwah, NJ: Erlbaum.

Levine, M., Smolak, L., Moodey, A., Shuman, M., & Hessen, L. (1994). Normative developmental challenges and dieting and eating disturbances in middle school girls. *International Journal of Eating Disorders, 15*, 11–20.

Levinson, S. C. (1997). Language and cognition: The cognitive consequences of spatial description in Guugu Yimithirr. *Journal of Linguistic Anthropology, 7*, 98–131.

Lewis, C. C. (1995). *Educating hearts and minds: Reflections on Japanese preschool and elementary education*. Cambridge, UK: Cambridge University Press.

Lewis, M., Feiring, C., & Rosenthal, S. (2000). Attachment over time. *Child Development, 71*, 707–720.

Lewis, M. D. (2000). The promise of dynamic systems approaches for an integrated account of human development. *Child Development, 71*(1), 36–43.

Lewis, T. L. & Maurer, D. (2005). Multiple sensitive periods in human visual development: Evidence from visually deprived

children. *Developmental Psychobiology, 46*, 163–183.

Li, S., Chen, W., Srinivasan, S. R., Bond, M. G., Tang, R., Urbina, E. M., et al. (2003). Childhood cardiovascular risk factors and carotid vascular changes in adulthood: The Bogalusa heart study. *JAMA: Journal of the American Medical Association, 290*, 2271–2275.

Li, T., & Noseworthy, M. D. (2002). Mapping the development of white matter tracts with diffusion tensor imaging. *Developmental Science, 5*, 293–300.

Liben, L. S., & Bigler, R. S. (2002). The developmental course of gender differentiation. *Monographs of the Society for Research in Child Development, 67*(2, Serial No. 269).

Liberman, I. Y. (1973). Segmentation of the spoken word and reading acquisition. *Bulletin of the Orton Society, 23*, 65–77.

Lickona, T. (1991). *Educating for character: How our schools can teach respect and responsibility*. New York: Bantam.

Liddell, C. (2002). Emic perspectives on risk in African childhood. *Developmental Review, 22*, 97–116.

Lightfoot, C. (1997). *The culture of adolescent risk-taking*. New York: Guilford Press.

Lightfoot, C. (2001). Breathing lessons: Self as genre and aesthetic. In T. Brown & L. Smith (Eds.), *Reductionism and the development of knowledge* (pp. 177–198). Mahwah, NJ: Erlbaum.

Lightfoot, C., & Bullock, M. (1990). Interpreting contradictory communications: Age and context effects. *Developmental Psychology, 26*, 830–836.

Lim, L., & Renshaw, P. (2001). The relevance of sociocultural theory to culturally diverse partnerships and communities. *Journal of Child and Family Studies, 10*, 9–21.

Lin, C. H., Hsiao, C. K., & Chen, W. J. (1999). Development of sustained attention assessed using the Continuous Performance Test among children 6–15 years of age. *Journal of Abnormal Child Psychology, 27*, 403–412.

Lincoln, Y. S., & Cannella, G. S. (2004). Dangerous discourses: Methodological conservatism and governmental regimes of truth. *Qualitative Inquiry, 10*, 5–14.

Lincoln, Y. S., & Guba, E. G. (2000). Paradigmatic controversies, contradictions, and emerging confluences. In N. K. Densin & Y. S. Lincoln (Eds.), *The handbook of qualitative research* (2nd ed., pp. 163–188). Beverly Hills, CA: Sage.

Lipsitz, J. S. (1980). In M. Johnson (Ed.), *Toward adolescence: The middle school years, 79th yearbook of the National Society for the Study of Education* (pp. 7–31). Chicago: National Society for the Study of Education.

Lively, W. L., & Bromley, D. B. (1973). *Person perception in childhood and adolescence*. Chichester, UK: Wiley.

Livingstone, M. B. E., Robson, P. J., Wallace, J. M. W., & McKinley, M. C. (2003). How active are we? Levels of routine physical activity in children and adults. *Proceedings of the Nutrition Society, 62*, 681–701.

Livingstone, S. (2003). Children's use of the Internet: Reflections on the emerging research agenda. *New Media & Society, 5*, 147–166.

Lochman, J. E. & Wells, K. C. (2004). The Coping Power Program for preadolescent aggressive boys and their parents: Outcome effects at the 1-year follow-up. *Journal of Consulting and Clinical Psychology, 72*, 571–578.

Lochman, J. E., Wells, K. C., & Murray, M. (2007). The Coping Power Program: Preventative intervention at the middle school transition. In P. Tolan, J. Szapocznik, & S. Sambrano (Eds.), *Preventing youth substance abuse: Science-based programs for children and adolescents* (pp. 185–210). Washington, DC: American Psychological Association.

Loovis, E. M., & Butterfield, S. A. (2000). Influence of age, sex and balance on mature skipping by children in grades K–8. *Perceptual & Motor Skills, 90*, 974–978.

Lorch, E. P., Diener, M. B., Sanchez, R. P., Milich, R., Welsh, R., & van den Broek, P. (1999). The effects of story structure on the recall of stories in children with attention deficit hyperactivity disorder. *Journal of Educational Psychology, 92*, 273–283.

Lorch, E. P., Eastman, D., Milich, R., & Lemberger, C. C. (2004). Difficulties in comprehending causal relations among children with ADHD: The role of cognitive engagement. *Journal of Abnormal Psychology, 113*, 1–8.

Lorch, E. P., Milich, R., & Sanchez, R. P. (1998). Story comprehension in children with ADHD. *Clinical Child and Family Psychology Review, 1*, 163–178.

Lorch, E. P., O'Neil, K., Berthiaume, K. S., Milich, R., Eastham, D., & Brooks, T. (2004). Story comprehension and the impact of studying on recall in children with attention deficit hyperactivity disorder. *Journal of Clinical Child and Adolescent Psychology, 33*, 506–515.

Lorenz, K. (1970). *Studies in animal and human behaviour: Vol. 1* (R. Martin, Trans.). Oxford, UK: Harvard University Press.

Lozoff, B., Jimenez, E., Hagen, J., Mollen, E., & Wolf, A. W. (2000). Poorer behavioral and developmental outcome more than 10 years after treatment for iron deficiency in infancy. *Pediatrics, 105*, E51.

Lubart, T. I. (1999). Creativity across cultures. In R. J. Sternberg (Ed.), *Handbook of creativity* (pp. 339–350). Cambridge, UK: Cambridge University Press.

Lucal, B. (1999). What it means to be gendered me: Life on the boundaries of a dichotomous gender system. *Gender & Society, 13,* 781–797.

Luke, C. (1999). Cyborg pedagogy in cyborg culture. *Teaching Education, 10,* 69–72.

Luna, B., Garver, K. E., Urban, T. A., Lazar, N. A., & Sweeney, J. A. (2004). Maturation of cognitive processes from late childhood to adulthood. *Child Development, 75,* 1357–1372.

Lunner, K., Werthem, E. H., Thompson, J. K., Paxton, S. J., McDonald, F., & Halverson, K. S. (2000). A cross-cultural examination of weight-related teasing, body image, and eating disturbance in Swedish and Australian samples. *International Journal of Eating Disorders, 28,* 430–435.

Lussier, G., Deater-Deckard, K, Dunn, J., & Davies, L. (2002). Support across two generations: Children's closeness to grandparents following parental divorce and remarriage. *Journal of Family Psychology, 16*(3), 363–376.

Luthar, S. S., Cicchetti, D., & Becker, B. (2000). Research on resilience: Response to commentaries. *Child Development, 71,* 573–575.

Luthar, S. S., & Latendresse, S. J. (2002). Adolescent risk: The costs of affluence. *New Directions for Youth Development, 95,* 101–121.

Lyon, R. (1999). *Testimony to the Committee on Education and the Workforce, U.S. House of Representatives: Hearing on Title I of the Elementary and Secondary Education Act.* Retrieved from http://156.40.88.3/about/crmc/cdb.

Lypaczewski, G., Lappe, J., & Stubby, J. (2002). "Mom & me" and healthy bones: An innovative approach to teaching bone health. *Orthopedic Nursing, 21,* 35–42.

Ma, X., Stewin, L. L., & Mah, D. L. (2001). Bullying in school: Nature, effects, and remedies. *Research Papers in Education, 16*(3), 247–270.

Mabbott, D. J., & Bisanz, J. (2003). Developmental change and individual differences in children's multiplication. *Child Development, 74,* 1091–1107.

MacArthur Network on Successful Pathways Through Middle Childhood research initiatives. (1997). Retrieved October 21, 2002, from http://midchild.soe.umich.edu/research/.

MacArthur Network on Successful Pathways Through Middle Childhood. (2002). Retrieved October 22, 2002, from http://www.macfound.org/research/hcd/hcd_15.htm.

Maccoby, E. E. (1990). Gender and relationships: A developmental account. *American Psychologist, 45,* 513–520.

Maccoby, E. E. (1998). *The two sexes: Growing up apart, coming together.* Cambridge, MA: Harvard University Press.

Maccoby, E. E. (2000). Parenting and its effects on children: On reading and mis-

reading behavior genetics. *Annual Review of Psychology, 51,* 1–27.

Macdonald, D., Ziviani, J., & Abbott, R. (2006). Children's participation in physical activity at school. In S. Rodger & J. Ziviani (Eds.), *Occupational therapy with children: Understanding children's occupations and enabling participation* (pp. 261–279). Malden, MA: Blackwell Publishing.

MacKinnon, C., Volling, B. L., & Lamb, M. (1994). A cross-contextual analysis of boys' social competence: From family to school. *Developmental Psychology, 30,* 325–333.

Madanes, C. (1981). *Strategic family therapy.* San Francisco: Jossey-Bass.

Madden-Derdich, D. A., & Leonred, S. A. (2000). Parental role identity and fathers' involvement in coparental interaction after divorce: Fathers' perspectives. *Family Relations, 49,* 311–318.

Maffulli, N., Baxter-Jones, A. D. G., & Grieve, A. (2005). Long term sport involvement and sport injury rate in elite young athletes. *Archives of Disease in Childhood, 90,* 525–527.

Magee, V. (2002, January). Perspective and balance: Considering qualitative research methods in psychology. Review essay: M. Kopala & L. A. Suzuki (Eds.) (1999). Using qualitative methods in psychology [40 paragraphs]. *Forum Qualitative Sozialforschung/Forum: Qualitative Social Research* [Online Journal], *3*(1). Retrieved March 21, 2005, from http://www.qualitative-research.net/fqs-eng.htm.

Magnuson, K., Duncan, G. J., & Kalil, A. (2006). The contribution of middle childhood contexts to adolescent achievement. In A. C. Huston & M. N. Ripke (Eds.), *Developmental contexts in middle childhood: Bridges to adolescence and adulthood* (pp. 150–172). Cambridge, UK: Cambridge University Press.

Magnusson, D. (1995). Individual development: A holistic, integrated model. In P. Moen, G. H. Elder, & K. Lusher (Eds.), *Examining lives in context: Perspectives on the ecology of human development* (pp. 19–60). Washington, DC: American Psychological Association.

Magnusson, D. (2000). The individual as the organizing principle in psychological inquiry: A holistic approach. In L. R. Bergman, R. B. Cairns, L. Nilsson, & L. Nystedt (Eds.), *Developmental science and the holistic approach* (pp. 33–48). Mahwah, NJ: Erlbaum.

Magnusson, D., & Stattin, H. (2006). The person in the environment: Toward a general model for scientific inquiry. In W. Damon & R. M. Lerner (Series Eds.) & R. M. Lerner (Vol. Ed.), *Handbook of child psychology: Vol. 1. Theoretical models of human development* (6th ed., pp. 400–464). New York: Wiley.

Magnusson, D., Stattin, H., & Allen, V. (1985). Biological maturation and social development: A longitudinal study of some adjustment processes from mid-adolescence to adulthood. *Journal of Youth and Adolescence, 14,* 267–283.

Mahler, M. S., Pine, F., & Bergman, A. (1975). *The psychological birth of the human infant: Symbiosis and individuation.* New York: Basic Books.

Mahoney, J. L. (2000). School extracurricular activity participation as a moderator in the development of antisocial patterns. *Child Development, 71,* 502–516.

Mahoney, J. L., Harris, A. L., & Eccles, J. S. (2006). Organized activity participation, positive youth development, and the overscheduling hypothesis. *Social Policy Report, 20*(4), 3–30.

Main, M., Kaplan, K., & Cassidy, J. (1985). Security in infancy, childhood and adulthood: A move to the level of representation. In I. Bretherton & E. Waters (Eds.), *Growing points in attachment theory and research* (pp. 66–104). *Monographs of the Society for Research in Child Development, 50* (1–2, Serial No. 209).

Main, M., & Solomon, J. (1990). Procedures for identifying infants as disorganized/disoriented during the Ainsworth strange situation. In M. T. Greenberg, D. Cicchetti, & E. M. Cummings (Eds.), *Attachment in the preschool years* (pp. 121–160). Chicago: University of Chicago Press.

Mainess, K. J., Champion, T. B., & McCabe, A. (2002). Telling the unknown story: Complex and explicit narration by African American preadolescents—preliminary examination of gender and socioeconomic issues. *Linguistics and Education, 13,* 151–173.

Maira, S., & Soep, E. (2004). United States of adolescence? Reconsidering U.S. youth culture studies. *Youth: Nordic Journal of Youth Studies, 12,* 245–269.

Mancini, J. A., & Huebner, A. J. (2004). Adolescent risk behavior patterns: Effects of structured time-use, interpersonal connections, self-system characteristics, and socio-demographic influences. *Child and Adolescent Social Work Journal, 21,* 647–668.

Manning, M. L. (1998). Play development from ages eight to twelve. In D. P. Fromberg & D. Bergen (Eds.), *Play from birth to twelve and beyond* (pp. 154–161). New York: Garland.

Manning, M. L., & Bucher, K. T. (2000). Middle schools should be both learner-centered and subject-centered. *Childhood Education, 77,* 41–42.

Manning, W. D. (2002). The implications of cohabitation for children's well-being. In A. Booth & A. C. Crouter (Eds.), *Just living together: Implications of cohabitation* on families, children, and social policy (pp. 121–152). Mahwah, NJ: Erlbaum.

Marcus, B. H., Forsyth, L. H., Stone, E. J., Dubbert, P. M., McKenzie, T. L., Dunn, A. L., et al. (200). Physical activity behavior change: Issues in adoption and maintenance, *Health Psychology, 19*(1S), 32–41.

Margolin, G., & Gordis, E. B. (2000). The effects of family and community violence on children. *Annual Review of Psychology, 51*, 445–479.

Marion, M. (1999). *Guidance of young children*. Columbus, OH: Merrill.

Markstrom, C. A., & Iborra, A. (2003). Adolescent identity formation and rites of passage: The Navaho Kinaaldá ceremony for girls. *Journal of Research on Adolescence, 13*, 399–425.

Marsh, H. W., & Hattie, J. (1996). Theoretical perspectives on the structure of self-concept. In B. A. Bracken (Ed.), *Handbook of self-concept: Developmental, social, and clinical considerations* (pp. 38–90). New York: Wiley.

Marshall, W. A., & Tanner, J. M. (1969). Variations in patterns of pubertal change in girls. *Archives of Disease in Childhood, 44*, 291–303.

Martin, C. L. (1989). Children's use of gender-related information in making social judgments. *Developmental Psychology, 25*, 80–88.

Martin, C. L., Ruble, D. N., & Szkrybalo, J. (2002). Cognitive theories of early gender development. *Psychological Bulletin, 128*(6), 903–933.

Martin, C. L., Wood, C. H., & Little, J. K. (1990). The development of gender stereotype components. *Child Development, 61*, 1891–1904.

Martindale, C. (1999). Biological bases of creativity. In R. J. Sternberg (Ed.), *Handbook of creativity* (pp. 137–152). New York: Cambridge University Press.

Maslow, A. H. (1962). *Toward a psychology of being*. New York: Van Nostrand.

Maslow, A. H. (1962). Some basic propositions of a growth and self-actualizing psychology. In *Perceiving, behaving, becoming: A new focus for education*. Washington, DC: Association for Supervision and Curriculum Development.

Maslow, A. H. (1971). *The farther reaches of human nature*. New York: Viking.

Maslow, A. H. (1987). *Motivation and personality* (3rd ed.). New York: Harper & Row.

Masten, A. S., & Curtis, W. J. (2000). Integrating competence and psychopathology: Pathways toward a comprehensive science of adaptation in development. *Development and Psychopathology, 12*, 529–550.

Mathematics Achievement. (1996). *Mathematics achievement in the middle school years: IEA's third international mathematics and science report*. Chestnut Hill, MA: Boston College, Center for the Study of Testing, Evaluation, and Educational Policy.

Mattanah, J. F., Pratt, M. W., Cowan, P. A., & Cowan, C. P. (2005). Authoritative parenting, parental scaffolding of long-division mathematics, and children's academic competence in fourth grade. *Applied Developmental Psychology, 26*, 85–106.

Maurer, D. (2005). Introduction to the special issue on critical periods reexamined: Evidence from human sensory development. *Developmental Psychobiology, 46*, [np].

Maynard, A. E. (2004). Sibling interactions. In U. P. Gielen & J. Roopnarine (Eds.), *Childhood and adolescence: Cross-cultural perspectives and applications* (pp. 229–252). Westport, CT: Praeger.

Maynard, A. E., & Greenfield, P. M. (2003). Implicit cognitive development in cultural tools and children: Lessons from Maya Mexico. *Cognitive Development, 18*, 489–510.

Mayseless, O. (2005). Ontogeny of attachment in middle childhood: Conceptualization of normative changes. In K. A. Kerns & R. A. Richardson (Eds.), *Attachment in middle childhood* (pp. 1–23). New York: Guilford Press.

Mazur, L. J., Yetman, R. J., & Risser, W. L. (1993). Weight-training injuries: Common injuries and preventative methods. *Sports Medicine, 16*(1), 57–63.

McAdoo, H. P. (1999). *Family ethnicity: Strength in diversity* (2nd ed.). Thousand Oaks, CA: Sage.

McBride, C. K., Paikoff, R. L., & Holmbeck, G. N. (2003). Individual and familial influences on the onset of sexual intercourse among urban African American adolescents. *Journal of Consulting & Clinical Psychology, 71*, 159–167.

McCabe, M. P., & Ricciardelli, L. A. (2003). A longitudinal study of body change strategies among adolescent males. *Journal of Youth and Adolescence, 32*, 105–113.

McCall, R. B., Evahn, C., & Kratzer, L. (1992). *High school underachievers: What do they achieve as adults?* Newbury Park, CA: Sage.

McCall, R. B., & Groark, C. J. (2000). The future of applied child development research and public policy. *Child Development, 71*, 197–204.

McCarthy, R. J. (1972). *The ungraded middle school*. West Nyack, NJ: Parker.

McClintock, M .K., & Herdt, G. (1996). Rethinking puberty: The development of sexual attraction. *Current Directions in Psychological Science, 5*, 178–183.

McCurdy, D. W., Spradley, J. P., & Shandy, D. J. (2005). *The cultural experience: Ethnography in complex society* (2nd ed.). Long Grove, IL: Waveland Press.

McGhee, P. E. (1976). Children's appreciation of humor: A test of the cognitive congruency principle. *Child Development, 47*, 420–426.

McGill, H. C., & McMahan, C. A. (2003). Starting earlier to prevent heart disease. *JAMA: Journal of the American Medical Association, 290*, 2320–2322.

McGoldrick, M., & Carter, B. (2003). The family life cycle. In F. Walsh (Ed.), *Normal family process: Growing diversity and complexity* (3rd. ed., pp. 375–398). New York: Guilford Press.

McGoldrick, M., & Carter, B. (2005). Self in context: The individual life cycle in systemic perspective. In B. Carter & M. McGoldrick (Eds.), *The expanded family life cycle: Individual, family, and social perspectives* (3rd ed., pp. 27–46). New York: Allyn & Bacon.

McGuffey, C. S., & Rich, B. L. (1999). Playing in the gender transgression zone: Race, class, and hegemonic masculinity in middle childhood. *Gender & Society, 19*, 608–627.

McGuire, S., Manke, B., Eftekhari, A., & Dunn, J. (2000). Children's perceptions of sibling conflict during middle childhood: Issues and sibling (dis)similarity. *Social Development, 9*(2), 173–190.

McGuire, S., Manke, B., Saudino, K. J., Reiss, D., Hetherington, E. M., & Plomin, R. (1999). Perceived competence and self-worth during adolescence: A longitudinal behavioral genetic study. *Child Development, 70*, 1283–1296.

McHale, S. M., Crouter, A. C., & Tucker, C. J. (1999). Family context and gender role socialization in middle childhood: Comparing girls to boys and sisters to brothers. *Child Development, 70*, 990–1004.

McHale, S. M., Crouter, A. C., & Tucker, C. J. (2001). Freetime activities in middle childhood: Links with adjustment in early adolescence. *Child Development, 72*(6), 1764–1778.

McHale, S. M., Dariotis, J. K., & Kauh, T. J. (2003). Social development and social relationships in middle childhood. In R. M. Lerner & M. A. Easterbrook (Eds.), *Handbook of psychology:* Vol. 6. *Developmental psychology* (pp. 241–265). New York: Wiley.

McHale, S. M., Updegraff, K. A., Helms-Erikson, H., & Crouter, A. C. (2001). Sibling influences on gender development in middle childhood and early adolescence: A longitudinal study. *Developmental Psychology, 37*, 115–125.

McHale, S. M., Updegraff, K. A., Tucker, C. J., & Crouter, A. C. (2000). Step in or stay out? Parents' roles in adolescent siblings' relationships. *Journal of Marriage and Family, 62*, 746–760.

McKay, A. (2004). Oral sex among teenagers: Research, discourse, and education. *The Canadian Journal of Human Sexuality, 13*, 3–4.

McKay, H. A., Bailey, D. A., Mirwald, R. L., Davison, K. S., & Faulkner, R. A. (1998). Peak bone mineral accrual and age at menarche in adolescent girls: A 6-year longitudinal study. *The Journal of Pediatrics, 133,* 682–687.

McKechnie, J., & Hobbs, S. (1999). Child labour: A global phenomenon? *Child Abuse Review, 8,* 87–90.

McKechnie, J., & Hobbs, S. (2002). Work by the young: The economic activity of school-aged children. In M. Tienda & W. J. Wilson (Eds.), *Youth in cities: A cross-national perspective* (pp. 217–245). Cambridge, UK: Cambridge University Press.

McKown, C. (2004). Age and ethnic variation in children's thinking about the nature of racism. *Applied Developmental Psychology, 25,* 597–617.

McKown, C., & Weinstein, R. S. (2003). The development and consequences of stereotype consciousness in middle childhood. *Child Development, 74,* 498–515.

McLoyd, V. C. (1998). Socioeconomic disadvantage and child development. *American Psychologist, 53,* 185–204.

McNamara, C. A. (1998). *Basic guide to program evaluation.* Retrieved July 16, 2005, from http://www.mapnp.org/library/evaluatn/fnl_eval.htm.

McNeely, C., Shew, M. L., Beuhring, T., Sieving, R., Miller, B. C., & Blum, R. W. (2002). Mothers' influence on the timing of first sex among 14- and 15-year-olds. *Journal of Adolescent Health, 31,* 256–265.

McNeill, K. L., Lizotte, D. J., Krajcik, J., & Marx, R. W. (2006). Supporting students' construction of scientific explanations by fading scaffolds in instructional materials. *The Journal of the Learning Sciences, 15,* 153–191.

McWhirter, J. J., McWhirter, B. T., McWhirter, E. H., & McWhirter, R. J. (2007). *At-risk youth: A comprehensive response for counselors, teachers, psychologists, and human services professionals,* 4th ed. Belmont, CA: Thomson Brooks/Cole.

Mead, G. H. (1934). *Mind, self, and society from the standpoint of a social behaviorist.* Chicago: University of Chicago Press.

Mead, M. (1973/1928). *Coming of age in Samoa: A psychological study of primitive youth for Western civilization.* New York: Morrow.

Meerum Terwogt, M., & Olthof, T. (1992). Awareness and self-regulation of emotion in young children. In C. Saarni & P. Harris (Eds.), *Children's understanding of emotion* (pp. 209–237). Cambridge, UK: Cambridge University Press.

Melaville, A. (1998). *Learning together: The developing field of community-school initiatives.* Washington, DC: Charles Stewart Mott Foundation.

Menzulis, A. H., Hyde, J. S., & Abramson, L. Y. (2003, June). *Can temperament provide protection against risk for depression? Relationships between temperament and cognitive style in middle childhood.* Poster presented at the MacArthur Conference on Successful Pathways through Adolescence, Washington, DC.

Merriam-Webster's collegiate dictionary (10th ed.) (2002). Springfield, MA: Merriam-Webster.

Merrick, E. (1999). An exploration of quality in qualitative research: Are "reliability" and "validity" relevant? In M. Kopala & L. Suzuki (Eds.), *Using qualitative methods in psychology* (pp. 25–36). Thousand Oaks, CA: Sage.

Merser, C. (1987). *Grownups: A generation in search of adulthood.* New York: Putnam.

Middle Start Initiative. (2002). *Starting again in the middle.* Available from the Michigan League for Human Services, 300 N. Washington Square, Suite 401, Lansing, MI, 48933.

Mikulincer, M., & Selinger, M. (2001). The interplay between attachment and affiliation systems in adolescents' same-sex friendships: The role of attachment style. *Journal of Social and Personal Relationships, 18,* 81–106.

Miles, M. B., & Huberman, A. M. (1994). *Qualitative data analysis.* Thousand Oaks, CA: Sage.

Milgram, R. M., & Hong, E. (1999). Creative out-of-school activities in intellectually gifted adolescents as predictors of their life accomplishment in young adults: A longitudinal study. *Creativity Research Journal, 12,* 77–87.

Millard, E. (2006). Up for debate: As blogs and social networking sites grow even more popular, is it up to schools to set the brakes? *District Administration, 42*(9), 60–62.

Miller, B. C., Benson, B., & Galbraith, K. A. (2001). Family relationships and adolescent pregnancy risk: A research synthesis. *Developmental Review, 21,* 1–38.

Miller, P. H. (2002). *Theories of developmental psychology* (4th ed.). New York: Worth.

Millstein, S. G., & Halpern-Felsher, B. L. (2002). Judgments about risk and perceived invulnerability in adolescents and young adults. *Journal of Research on Adolescence, 12*(4), 399–422.

Mintz, S. (1993). Life stages. In M. K. Cayton, E. J. Gorn, & P. W. Williams (Eds.), *Encyclopedia of American social history* (Vol. 3, pp. 2011–2022). New York: Scribner.

Minuchin, S. (1974). *Families and family therapy.* Cambridge, MA: Harvard University Press.

Mistry, J., & Saraswathi, T. S. (2003). The cultural context of child development. In R. M. Lerner, M. A. Easterbrooks, & J. Mistry (Vol. Eds.), *Handbook of psychology: Vol. 6. Developmental psychology* (pp. 267–291). New York: Wiley.

Modell, J., & Elder, G. H. (2002). Children develop in history: So what's new? In W. W. Hartup & R. A. Weinberg (Eds.), *Child psychology in retrospect and prospect: Vol. 32. The Minnesota symposia on child psychology.* Mahwah, NJ: Erlbaum.

Modey, B. E., Heart, S. S., Leal, L., Santulli, K. A., Rao, N., & Johnson, T., et al., (1992). The teacher's role in facilitating memory and study strategy development in the elementary school classroom. *Child Development, 63,* 653–672.

Moely, B. E., Santulli, K. A., & Obach, M. S. (1995). Strategy instruction, metacognition, and motivation in the elementary school classroom. In F. E. Weinert, & W. Schneider (Eds.), *Memory performance and competencies: Issues in growth and development* (pp. 301–321). Hillsdale, NJ: Lawrence Erlbaum Associates.

Moinian, F. (2006). The construction of identity on the Internet: Oops! I've left my diary open to the whole world! *Childhood, 13,* 49–68.

Montemayor, R. (2000). The variety of adolescent experiences. In R. Montemayor, G. R. Adams, & T. P. Gullotta (Eds.), *Adolescent diversity in ethnic, economic, and cultural contexts* (pp. 256–271). Thousand Oaks, CA: Sage.

Montemayor, R., Adams, G. R., & Gullotta, T. P. (1990). *From childhood to adolescence: A transitional period?* Newbury Park, CA: Sage.

Montemayor, R., & Flannery, D. J. (1990). Making the transition from childhood to early adolescence. In R. Montemayor, G. R. Adams, & T. P. Gullotta. *From childhood to adolescence: A transitional period?* (pp. 291–301). Newbury Park, CA: Sage.

Moore, S., & Rosenthal, D. (1991). Adolescent invulnerability and perceptions of AIDS risk. *Journal of Adolescent Research, 6,* 164–180.

Morgan, D. L. (1996). Focus groups. *Annual Review of Sociology, 22,* 129–153.

Morgan, D. L. (1997). *Focus groups as qualitative research* (2nd ed.). Thousand Oaks, CA: Sage.

Morgan, M., Gibbs, S., Maxwell, K., & Britten, N. (2002). Methodological issues in conducting focus groups with children ages 7–11 years. *Qualitative Research, 2,* 5–20.

Morris, P., & Kalil, A. (2006). Out-of-school time use during middle childhood in a low-income sample. In A. C. Huston & M. N. Ripke (Eds.), *Developmental contexts in middle childhood: Bridges to adolescence and adulthood* (pp. 237–259). Cambridge, UK: Cambridge University Press.

Morrison, F. J., McMahon Griffith, E., & Frazier, J. A. (1996). Schooling and the 5 to 7 shift: A natural experiment. In A. J. Sameroff & M. M. Haith (Eds.), *The five to seven year shift: The age of reason and responsibility.* Chicago: The University of Chicago Press.

Morrow, S. L. (2005). Quality and trustworthiness in qualitative research in counseling psychology. *Journal of Counseling Psychology, 52*, 250–260.

Mortimer, J. T., & Finch, M. D. (1996). Work, family, and adolescent development. In J. T. Mortimer & M. D. Finch (Eds.), *Adolescents, work and family: An intergenerational developmental analysis* (pp. 1–24). Thousand Oaks, CA: Sage.

Mosher, C., Rotolo, T., Phillips, D., Krupski, A., & Stark, K. D. (2004). Minority adolescents and substance use risk/protective factors: A focus on inhalant use. *Adolescence, 39*, 399–502.

Moving an out-of-school agenda: Lessons and challenges across cities (Executive summary). Retrieved September 8, 2002, from http://www.forumforyouthinvestment.org/grasp/execsumm.htm.

Mruk, C. (1995). *Self-esteem: Research, theory, practice*. New York: Springer.

Muir, S. L., Wertheim, E. H., & Paxton, S. J. (1999). Adolescent girls' first diets: Triggers and the role of multiple dimensions of self-concept. *Eating Disorders: The Journal of Treatment and Prevention, 7*, 259–270.

Muller, C., & Kerbow, D. (1993). Parent involvement in the home, school, and community. In B. Schneider & J. S. Coleman (Eds.), *Parents, their children, and schools* (pp. 13–42). Boulder, CO: Westview.

Murphy, K. R., & Davidshofer, C. O. (2001). *Psychological testing: Principles and applications*. Upper Saddle River, NJ: Prentice Hall.

Murphy, M. M. (2002). *Character education in America's blue ribbon schools: Best practices for meeting the challenge* (2nd ed.). Lanham, MD: Scarecrow Press.

Murray-Close, D., Ostrov, J. M., & Crick, N. R. (2007). A short-term longitudinal study of growth of relational aggression during middle childhood: Associations with gender, friendship intimacy, and internalizing problems. *Development and Psychopathology, 19*, 187–203.

Mussen, P., & Eisenberg, N. (2001). Prosocial development in context. In A. C. Bohart & D. J. Stipek (Eds.), *Constructive & destructive behavior: Implications for family, school, & society* (pp. 103–126). Washington, DC: American Psychological Association.

Mussen, P. H., & Jones, M. C. (1957). Self-conceptions, motivations, and interpersonal attitudes of late- and early-maturing boys. *Child Development, 28*, 243–256.

Must, A., & Tybor, D. J. (2005). Physical activity and sedentary behavior: A review of longitudinal studies of weight and adiposity in youth. *International Journal of Obesity, 29*, S84–S96.

Muuss, R. E. (1982). Social cognition: David Elkind's theory of adolescent egocentrism. *Adolescence, 17*, 249–265.

Muuss, R. E. (1996). *Theories of adolescence* (6th ed.). New York: McGraw-Hill.

Myers, M. G., & MacPherson, L. (2004). Smoking cessation efforts among substance abusing adolescents. *Drug & Alcohol Dependence, 73*, 209–213.

Nagin, D., & Tremblay, R. E. (1999). Trajectories of boys' physical aggression, opposition, and hyperactivity on the path to physically violent and nonviolent juvenile delinquency. *Child Development, 70*, 1181–1196.

Naimi, T. S., Brewer, R. D., Mokdad, A., Denny, C., Serdula, M. K., & Marks, J. S. (2003). Binge drinking among U.S. adults. *Journal of the American Medical Association, 289*, 70–75.

Nakkula, M. J., & Nikitopoulos, C. E. (2001). Negotiation training and interpersonal development: An exploratory study of early adolescents in Argentina. *Adolescence, 36*, 1–20.

Närvänen, A., & Näsman, E. (2004). Childhood as generation or life phase? *Young: Nordic Journal of Youth Research, 12*(1), 71–91.

National Association for Sport and Physical Education (NASPE) (1998). *Physical activity for children: A statement of guidelines*. Reston, VA: NASPE Publications.

National Center for Education Statistics. (2003). *International comparisons in fourth-grade reading literacy: Findings from the progress in international reading literacy study (PIRLS) of 2001*. (NCES 2003–073). Washington, DC: U.S. Government Printing Office.

National Center for Education Statistics. (2006). Computer and Internet use by children and adolescents in 2003: Statistical analysis report. Washington, DC: U.S. Department of Education.

National Center for Health Statistics. (2001). *Prevalence of overweight among children and adolescents: United States, 1999*. Centers for Disease Control and Prevention, Health E-Stats.

National Center for Health Statistics. (2004). *Trends in Childhood Overweight*. Centers for Disease Control and Prevention, Health E-stats.

National Education Association (1969). *Report of the Committee on Secondary School Studies*. New York: Arno/New York Times.

National Research Council and Institute of Medicine. (2003). *Engaging schools: Fostering high school students' motivation to learn*. Washington, DC: National Academy Press.

National Science Board (1998). Science and engineering indicators—1998. (NSB 98–1). Arlington, VA: National Science Foundation.

Neary, L. (2007, January 19). Club Penguin beckons to preteen surfers. *All Things Considered*. National Public Radio broadcast. Retrieved March 8, 2007, from http://www.npr.org/templates/story/story.php?storyId=6923823.

Neisser, U., Boodoo, G., Bouchard, T. J., Jr., Boykin, A. W., Brody, N., Ceci, S. J., et al. (1996). Intelligence: Knowns and unknowns. *American Psychologist, 51*, 77–101.

Nesdale, D., & Flesser, D. (2001). Social identity and the development of children's group attitudes. *Child Development, 72*, 506–517.

Nesselroade, J. R., & Baltes, P. B. (1974). Adolescent personality development and historical changes: 1970–1972. *Monographs of the Society for Research in Child Development, 39*(1, Serial No. 154).

Neumark-Sztainer, D., Story, M., Falkner, N. H., Beuhring, T., & Resnick, M. D. (1999). Sociodemographic and personal characteristics of adolescents engaged in weight loss and weight/muscle gain behaviors: Who is doing what? *Preventive Medicine, 28*, 40–50.

Newcomb, A. E., Bukowski, W., & Pattee, L. (1993). Children's peer relations: A meta-analytic review of popular, rejected, neglected, controversial, and average sociometric status. *Psychological Bulletin, 113*, 99–128.

Newman, R. S. (2002). What do I need to do to succeed … when I don't understand what I'm doing!?: Developmental influences on students' adaptive help-seeking. In A. Wigfield & J. S. Eccles (Eds.), *The development of achievement motivation* (pp. 285–305). San Diego, CA: Academic Press.

Nickerson, A. B., & Nagle, R. J. (2005). Parent and peer attachment in late childhood and early adolescence. *Journal of Early Adolescence, 25*(2), 225–249.

Nickerson, R. S. (1999). Enhancing creativity. In R. J. Sternberg (Ed.), *Handbook of creativity* (pp. 392–430). New York: Cambridge University Press.

Ninio, A., & Snow, C. E. (1996). *Pragmatic development*. Boulder, CO: Westview Press.

Nippold, M. A., Taylor, C. L., & Baker, J. M. (1996). Idiom understanding in Australian youth: A cross-cultural comparison. *Journal of Speech and Hearing Research, 39*, 442–447.

Niu, W., & Sternberg, R. J. (2003). Societal and school influences on student creativity: The case of China. *Psychology in the Schools, 40*, 103–114.

Novick, N., Cauce, A. M., & Grove, K. (1998). Competence self-concept. In B. A. Bracken (Ed.), *Handbook of self-concept: Developmental, social, and clinical considerations* (pp. 210–258). New York: Wiley.

Nowson, C. (2006). Reaching peak bone mass. *Nutridate, 17*(1), 1–4.

Nucci, L. P. (2001). *Education in the moral domain*. New York: Cambridge University Press.

Nussbaum, M. C. (2000). Emotions and social norms. In L. P. Nucci, G. B. Saxe, & E. Turiel (Eds.), *Culture, thought, and development* (pp. 41–63). Mahwah, NJ: Erlbaum.

Nyborg, H., & Jensen, A. R., (2001). Occupation and income related to psychometric g. *Intelligence, 29*, 45–56.

Obradović, J., van Dulmen, M. H. M., Yates, T. M., Carlson, E. A., & Egeland, B. (2006). Developmental assessment of competence from early childhood to middle adolescence. *Journal of Adolescence, 29*, 857–889.

O'Brien, M. (1992). Gender identity and sex roles. In V. B. Van Hasselt & M. Hersen (Eds.), *Handbook of social development: A lifespan perspective* (pp. 325–345). New York: Plenum.

Ochs, E. (1993). Constructing social identity: A language socialization perspective. *Research on Language and Social Interaction, 26*(3), 287–306.

O'Connell, E. J., & Logan, G. B. (1974). Parental smoking in childhood asthma. *Annals of Allergy, 32*, 142–145.

Oden, S. (1995). Studying youth programs to assess influences on youth development: New roles for researchers. *Journal of Adolescent Research, 10*(1), 174–186.

Oden, S., & Asher, S. R. (1997). Coaching children in social skills for friendship making. *Child Development, 48*, 495–506.

Offer, D. (1969). *The psychological world of the teenager*. New York: Basic Books.

Offer, D., Ostrow, E., & Howard, K. I. (1981). *The adolescent: A psychological self-portrait*. New York: Basic Books.

Ogden, C. L., Carroll, M. D., Curtin, L. R., McDowell, M. A., Tabak, C. J., & Flegal, K. M. (2006). Prevalence of overweight and obesity in the United States, 1999–2004. *Journal of the American Medical Association, 295*, 1549–1555.

O'Grady, W. (1997). *Syntactic development*. Chicago: University of Chicago Press.

Ohayan, M. M., Carskadon, M. A., Guilleminault, C., & Vitiello, M. V. (2004). Meta-analysis of quantitative sleep parameters from childhood to old age in healthy individuals: Developing normative sleep values across the human lifespan. *Sleep: Journal of Sleep and Sleep Disorders Research, 27*, 1255–1273.

Okin, S. M. (1989). *Justice, gender, and the family*. New York: Basic Books.

Olweus, D., Mattsson, A., Schalling, D., & Low, H. (1988). Circulating testosterone levels and aggression in adolescent males: A causal analysis. *Psychosomatic Medicine, 3*, 261–272.

O'Moore, M., & Kirkham, C. (2001). Self-esteem and its relationship to bullying behaviour. *Aggressive Behavior, 27*, 269–283.

O'Neil, M. L. (2002). Youth curfews in the United States: The creation of public spheres for some young people. *Journal of Youth Studies, 5*, 49–67.

O'Neil, R., Parke, R. D., & McDowell, D. J. (2001). Objective and subjective features of children's neighborhoods: Relations to parental regulatory strategies and children's social competence. *Journal of Applied Developmental Psychology, 22*, 135–155.

Oppenheim, D., & Waters, H. S. (1995). Narrative processes and attachment representations: Issues of development and assessment. In E. Waters, B. E. Vaughn, G. Posada, & K. Kondo-Ikemura (Eds.), *Caregiving, cultural, and cognitive perspectives on secure-base behavior and working models: New growing points of attachment theory and research* (pp. 197–214). *Monographs of the Society for Research in Child Development, 60*(2–3, Serial No. 244).

Orenstein, P. (1994). *Young women, self-esteem, and the confidence gap*. New York: Anchor.

Ornstein, P. A., Naus, M. J., & Liberty, C. (1975). Rehearsal and organizational processes in children's memory. *Child Development, 46*, 818–830.

Oser, F. K. (1991). The development of religious judgement. *New Directions for Child Development, 52*, 5–25.

Oser, F. K., & Gmünder, P. (1991). *Religious judgement: A developmental perspective*. Birmingham, AL: Religious Education Press.

Oser, F. K., Scarlett, W. G, & Bucher, A. (2006). Religious and spiritual development throughout the lifespan. In W. Damon (Series Ed.) & R. M. Lerner (Vol. Ed.), *Handbook of child psychology, Vol. 1: Theoretical models of human development* (6th ed., pp. 942–998). New York: Wiley.

O'Sullivan, J. T. (1996). Children's metamemory about the influence of conceptual relations on recall. *Journal of Experimental Child Psychology, 62*, 1–29.

Oswald, R. F., Blume, L. B., & Marks, S. (2005). Decentering heteronormativity: A model for family studies. In A. Acock, K. Allen, V. Bengtson, D. Klein, & P. Dilworth-Anderson (Eds.), *Sourcebook of family theory and research* (pp. 447–468). Thousand Oaks, CA: Sage.

Owens, J. A., Stahl, J., Patton, A., Reddy, U., & Crouch, M. (2006). Sleep practices, attitudes, and beliefs in inner city middle school children: A mixed-methods study. *Behavioral Sleep Medicine, 4*, 114–134.

Owens, R. E. (1996). *Language development: An introduction* (4th ed.). Boston: Allyn & Bacon.

Owens, R. E., Jr. (1998). *Queer kids: The challenges and promises for lesbian, gay, and bisexual youth*. Binghamton, NY: Haworth.

Ozturk, C., Durmazlar, N., Ural, B., Karaagaoglu, E., Yalaz, K., & Anlar, B. (1999). Hand and eye preference in normal preschool children. *Clinical Pediatrics, 38*, 677–680.

Pace, K. L. (2003). The character of moral communities: A community youth development approach to enhancing character development. In F. A. Villarruel, D. F. Perkins, L. M. Borden, L. M. & J. G. Keith (Eds.), *Community youth development: Programs, policies, and practices* (pp. 248–272). Thousand Oaks, CA: Sage.

Palinscar, A. S., & Brown, A. L. (1984). Reciprocal teaching of comprehension-fostering and comprehension monitoring activities. *Cognition and Instruction, 1*, 117–175.

Parke, R. D., & Buriel, R. (1998). Socialization in the family: Ethnic and ecological perspectives. In W. Damon (Series Ed.) & N. Eisenberg (Vol. Ed.), *Handbook of child psychology: Vol. 3. Social, emotional, and personality development* (5th ed., pp. 463–552). New York: Wiley.

Parker, J. G., & Asher, S. R. (1993). Friendship and friendship quality in middle childhood: Links with peer group acceptance and feelings of loneliness and social dissatisfaction. *Developmental Psychology, 29*, 611–621.

Parker, J. G., & Seal, J. (1996). Forming, losing, renewing, and replacing friendships: Applying temporal parameters to the assessment of children's friendship experiences. *Child Development, 67*, 2248–2268.

Parrish, M. (2004). Urban poverty and homelessness as hidden demographic variables relevant to academic achievement. In D. Boothe and J. C. Stanley (Eds.), *In the eyes of the beholder: Critical issues for diversity in gifted education* (pp. 203–211). Waco, TX: Prufrock Press.

Parten, M. B. (1933). Social play among preschool children. *Journal of Abnormal & Social Psychology, 28*, 136–147.

Pasley, K., Dollahite, D. C., & Ihinger-Tallman, M. (1993). Bridging the gap: Clinical applications of research findings on the spouse and stepparent roles in remarriage. *Family Relations, 42*, 315–322.

Patterson, G. R., & Fisher, P. A. (2002). Recent developments in our understanding of parenting: Bidirectional effects, causal models, and the search for parsimony. In M. Bornstein (Ed.), *Handbook of parenting. Vol. 5: Practical and applied parenting* (2nd ed., pp. 59–88). Mahwah, NJ: Erlbaum.

Patton, M. Q. (2002). *Qualitative evaluation and research methods* (3rd ed.). Thousand Oaks, CA: Sage.

Paus, T., Zijdenbos, A., Worsley, K., Collins, D. L., Blumenthal, J., Giedd, J. N., et al. (1999). Structural maturation of neural pathways in children and adolescents: In vitro study. *Science, 283*, 1908–1911.

Pechman, C. (1997). Does anti-smoking advertising combat underage smoking? A review of past practices and research. In M. E. Goldberg, M. Fishbein, & S. E. Middlestadt (Eds.), *Social marketing: Theoretical and practical perspectives* (pp. 189–216). Mahwah, NJ: Erlbaum.

Pedersen, S. (2005). Urban adolescents' out-of-school activity profiles: Associations with youth, family, and school transition characteristics. *Applied Developmental Science, 9,* 107–124.

Peevers, B. H., & Secord, P. F. (1973). Developmental changes in attribution of descriptive concepts to persons. *Journal of Personality and Social Psychology, 27,* 120–128.

Pellegrini, A. D. (2001). A longitudinal study of heterosexual relationships, aggression, and sexual harassment during the transition from primary school through middle school. *Journal of Applied Developmental Psychology, 22*(2), 119–133.

Pellegrini, A. D., & Bjorklund, D. F. (1997). The role of recess in children's cognitive performance. *Educational Psychologist, 32,* 35–40.

Pellegrini, A. D., & Bohn, C. M. (2005). The role of recess in children's cognitive performance and school adjustment. *Educational Researcher, 34,* 13–19.

Pellegrini, A. D., & Smith, P. K. (1998). Physical activity play: The nature and function of a neglected aspect of play. *Child Development, 69,* 577–598.

Pellegrini, A. D., & Smith, P. K. (2003). Development of play. In J. Valsiner & K. Connolly (Eds.), *Handbook of Developmental Psychology* (pp. 276–291). London: Sage.

Penza-Clyve, S. M., Mansell, C., & McQuaid, E. L. (2004). Why don't children take their asthma medications? A qualitative analysis of children's perspectives of adherence. *Journal of Asthma, 41,* 189–197.

Perkins, D. F., & Borden, L. M. (2003). Positive behaviors, problem behaviors, and resiliency in adolescence. In I. B. Weiner (Series Ed.) & R. M. Lerner, M. A. Easterbrooks, & J. Mistry (Vol. Eds.), *Handbook of psychology: Vol. 6. Developmental psychology* (pp. 373–394). New York: Wiley.

Perkins, D. F., Jacobs, J. E., Barber, B. L., & Eccles, J. S. (2004). Childhood and adolescent sports participation as predictors of participation in sports and physical fitness activities during young adulthood. *Youth & Society, 35,* 495–520.

Perleth, C., & Heller, K. A. (1994). The Munich longitudinal study of giftedness. In R. F. Subotnik & K. D. Arnold (Eds.), *Beyond Terman: Contemporary longitudinal studies of giftedness and talent* (pp. 77–114). Westport, CT: Ablex Publishing.

Perugini, E. M., Harvey, E. A., Lovejoy, D. W., Sandstrom, K., & Webb, A. H. (2000). The predictive power of combined neuropsychological measures for attention-deficit/hyperactivity disorder in children. *Child Neuropsychology, 6,* 101–114.

Petersen, A. C., & Taylor, B. (1980). The biological approach to adolescence: Biological change and psychological adaptation. In J. Adelson (Ed.), *Handbook of adolescent psychology* (pp. 117–155). New York: Wiley.

Peterson, G. W., Madden-Derdich, D., & Leonard, S. A. (2000). Parent-child relations across the life course: Autonomy within the context of connectedness. In S. J. Price, P. C. McHenry, & M. J. Murphy (Eds.), *Families across time: A life course perspective* (pp. 187–203). Los Angeles, CA: Roxbury.

Pexman, P. M., Glenwright, M., Krol, A., & James, T. (2005). An acquired taste: Children's perceptions of humor and teasing in verbal irony. *Discourse Processes, 40,* 259–288.

Pfeifer, J. H., Brown, C. S., & Juvonen, J. (2007). Teaching tolerance in schools: Lessons learned since *Brown v. Board of Education* about the development and reduction of children's prejudice. *Social Policy Report, 21*(2), 3–15.

Phelan, P., Davidson, A. L., & Yu, H. C. (1998). Students' multiple worlds: Navigating the borders of family, peer, and school cultures. In P. Phelan & A. L. Davidson (Eds.), *Adolescents' worlds: Negotiating family, peers, and school* (pp. 52–88). New York: Teachers College Press.

Phillips, D. A., & Zimmerman, M. D. (1990). The developmental course of perceived competence and incompetence among competent children. In R. J. Sternberg & J. Kolligian (Eds.), *Competence considered* (pp. 41–66). New Haven, CT: Yale University Press.

Phinney, J. S. (1989). Stages of ethnic identity development in minority group adolescents. *Journal of Early Adolescence, 9,* 34–49.

Phinney, J. S., Cantu, C. L., & Kurtz, D. A. (1997). Ethnic and American identity as predictors of self-esteem among African American, Latino, and White adolescents. *Journal of Youth and Adolescence, 26,* 165–185.

Phinney, J. S., & Rosenthal, D. A. (1992). Ethnic identity in adolescence: Process, context, and outcome. In G. R. Adams, T. P. Gullotta, & R. Montemayor (Eds.), *Adolescent identity formation* (pp. 145–172). Newbury Park, CA: Sage.

Piaget, J. (1962). *Play, dreams, and imitation in childhood* (C. Gattegno & F. M. Hodgson, Trans.). New York: W. W. Norton. (Original work published 1952.)

Piaget, J. (1963). *The origins of intelligence in children* (M. Cook, Trans.). New York: W. W. Norton. (Original work published 1953.)

Piaget, J. (1965). *The moral judgment of the child* (M. Gabain, Trans.). New York: W. W. Norton. (Original work published 1932.)

Piaget, J. (1977). *Piaget on Piaget* [Motion Picture]. New Haven, CT: Yale University Press. (Distributed by Yale University Media Design Studio, New Haven, CT, 06520.)

Piaget, J., & Inhelder, B. (1969). *The psychology of the child* (H. Weaver, Trans.). New York: Basic Books.

Pianta, R. C., Stuhlman, M. W., & Hamre, B. K. (2002). How schools can do better: Fostering stronger connections between teachers and students. In J. E. Rhodes (Ed.), *A critical view of youth mentoring* (pp. 91–107). San Francisco: Jossey-Bass.

Pike, A. (2002). Behavioral genetics, shared and nonshared environment. In P. K. Smith & C. H. Hart (Eds.), *Blackwell handbook of childhood social development* (pp. 27–43). Malden, MA: Blackwell.

Pipher, M. B. (1994). *Reviving Ophelia: Saving the selves of adolescent girls.* New York: Putnam.

Pitcairn, T. K., & Edlmann, T. (2000). Individual differences in road crossing ability in young children and adults. *British Journal of Psychology, 91,* 391–410.

Pittman, K., Diversi, M., & Ferber, T. (2002). Social policy supports for adolescence in the twenty-first century: Framing questions. *Journal of Research on Adolescence, 12,* 149–158.

Plomin, R. (2004). Genetics and developmental psychology. *Merrill-Palmer Quarterly, 50*(3), 341–352.

Plomin, R., & Asbury, K. (2005). Nature and nurture: Genetic and environmental influences on behavior. *Annals of the American Academy of Political and Social Science, 600,* 86–98.

Plomin, R., & Petrill, S. A. (1997). Genetics and intelligence: What's new? *Intelligence, 24,* 53–77.

Plumert, J. M., Kearney, J. K., & Cremer, J. F. (2004). Children's perception of gap affordances: Bicycling across traffic-filled intersections in an immersive virtual environment. *Child Development, 75,* 1243–1253.

Polakow Suransky, V. (1982). *The erosion of childhood.* Chicago: University of Chicago Press.

Pollack, W. S. (2006). The 'war' *for* boys: Hearing 'real boys' voices, hearing their pain. *Professional Psychology: Research and Practice, 37*(2), 190–195.

Pomerantz, E. M., & Ruble, D. N. (1997). Distinguishing multiple dimensions of conceptions of ability: Implication for self-evaluation. *Child Development, 68,* 1165–1180.

Pomerantz, E. M., Ruble, D. N., Frey, K. S., & Greulich, F. (1995). Meeting goals and confronting conflict: Children's changing perceptions of social comparison. *Child Development, 66,* 723–738.

Pomerantz, E. M., & Saxon, J. L. (2001). Conceptions of ability as stable and self-evaluative processes: A longitudinal evaluation. *Child Development, 72,* 152–173.

Ponterotto, J. G. (2005). Qualitative research in counseling psychology: A primer on research paradigms and philosophy of science. *Journal of Counseling Psychology, 52,* 126–136.

Portes, A., Escobar , C., & Radfird, A. W. (2005). *Immigrant transnational organizations and development: A comparative study: Working Paper #05–07.* Princeton, NJ: Princeton University Center for Migration and Development. Retrieved August 13, 2006, from http://cmd.princeton.edu/papers/wp0507.pdf.

Posner, J. K., & Vandell, D. L. (1999). After-school activities and the development of low-income urban children: A longitudinal study. *Developmental Psychology, 35,* 868–879.

Poteat, P. V., & Espelage, D. L. (2007). Predicting psychosocial consequences of homophobic victimization in middle school students. *The Journal of Early Adolescence, 27,* 175–191.

Powlishta, K. K. (2002). Commentary: Measures and models of gender differentiation. In W. F. Overton (Ed.), *Developmental course of gender differentiation* (pp. 167–178). *Monographs of the Society for Research in Child Development, 67*(2, Serial No. 269).

Pratt, S., & George, R. (2005). Transferring friendship: Girls' and boys' friendships in the transition from primary to secondary school. *Children & Society, 19,* 16–26.

Pressley, M., Gaskins, I. W., Solic, K., & Collins, S. (2006). A portrait of Benchmark School: How a school produces high achievement in students who previously failed. *Journal of Educational Psychology, 98,* 282–306.

Price-Williams, D. R., Gordon, W., & Ramirez, M., III. (1969). Skill and conservation: A study of pottery-making children. *Developmental Psychology, 1,* 769.

Prinstein, M. J., & La Greca, A. M. (2002). Peer crowd affiliation and internalizing distress in childhood and adolescence: A follow-back study. *Journal of Research on Adolescence, 12,* 325–351.

Prochaska, J. O., & Norcross, J. C. (2002). *Systems of psychotherapy: A transtheoretical analysis* (5th ed.). Pacific Grove, CA: Wadsworth.

Prout, A. (2005). Reflections on childhood, diversity, pathways, and context. In C. R. Cooper, C. T. García Coll, W. T. Bartko, H. Davis, & C. Chatman (Eds.), *Developmental pathways through middle childhood: Rethinking context and diversity as resources* (pp. 313–328). Mahwah, NJ: Erlbaum.

Provins, K. A. (1997). The specificity of motor skill and manual asymmetry: A review of the evidence and its implications. *Journal of Motor Behavior, 29,* 183–192.

Puckett, M. B., & Black, J. K. (2001). *The young child: Development from prebirth through age eight* (3rd ed.). Upper Saddle River, NJ: Merrill/Prentice Hall.

Pugh, S., Wolff, R., DeFrancesco, C., Gilley, W., & Heitman, R. (2000). A case study of elite male youth baseball athletes' perception of the youth sports experience. *Education, 120,* 773–781.

Quinn, W., Newfield, N. A., & Protinsky, H. O. (1985). Rites of passage in families with adolescents. *Family Process, 24,* 101–111.

Raffaelli, M., & Duckett, E. (1989). "We were just talking . . .": Conversations in early adolescence. *Journal of Youth and Adolescence, 18,* 567–581.

Raikes, H. A., & Thompson, R. A. (2005). Relationships past, present, and future: Reflection on attachment in middle childhood. In K. A. Kerns & R. A. Richardson (Eds.), *Attachment in middle childhood* (pp. 255–282). New York: Guilford Press.

Rathunde, K., & Csikszentmihalyi, M. (2006). The developing person: An experiential perspective. In W. Damon & R. M. Lerner (Series Eds.) & N. Eisenberg (Vol. Ed.), *Handbook of child psychology, Vol. 3: Social, emotional and personality development* (6th ed., pp. 465–515). New York: Wiley.

Raymond, D. (1994). Homophobia, identity, and the meaning of desire: Reflections on the cultural construction of gay and lesbian adolescent sexuality. In J. M. Irvine (Ed.), *Sexual cultures and the construction of adolescent identities* (pp. 115–150). Philadelphia, PA: Temple University Press.

Rebecca, M., Hefner, R., & Oleshansky, B. (1976). A model of sex-role transcendence. *Journal of Social Issues, 32*(3), 197–207.

Ree, M. J., & Earles, J. A. (1992). Intelligence is the best predictor of job performance. *Current Directions in Psychological Science, 1,* 86–89.

Reiss, D., Neiderhiser, J. M., Hetherington, E. M., & Plomin, R. (2000). *The relationship code: Deciphering genetic and social influences on adolescent development.* Cambridge, MA: Harvard University Press.

Remafedi, G. (1987). Adolescent homosexuality: Psychosocial and medical implications. *Pediatrics, 79,* 331–337.

Renold, E. (2007). Primary school "studs": (De)constructing young boys' heterosexual masculinities. *Men and Masculinities, 9,* 275–297.

Resnick, M. D., et al. (1997). Protecting adolescents from harm: Findings from the National Longitudinal Study on Adolescent Health. *Journal of the American Medical Association, 278,* 823–832.

Rest, J., Narvaez, D., Bebeau, M. J., & Thoma, S. J. (1999). *Postconventional moral thinking: A neo-Kohlbergian approach.* Mahwah, NJ: Erlbaum.

Reynolds, M. A., Herbenick, D. L., & Bancroft, J. (2003). The nature of childhood sexual experience: Two studies 50 years apart. In J. Bancroft (Ed.), *Sexual development in childhood* (pp. 134–155). Bloomington, IN: Indiana University Press.

Rhodes, G. M. (2005, June). *Estimated HIV prevalence in the United States at the end of 2003.* Paper presented at the National HIV Prevention Conference, Atlanta, GA.

Rich, A. (1980). Compulsory heterosexuality and lesbian existence. *Signs, 5,* 198–210.

Richman, J. M., & Cook, P. G. (2004). A framework for teaching family development for the changing family. *Journal of Teaching in Social Work, 24,* 1–18.

Ridenour, T. A., Greenberg, M. T., & Cook, E. T. (2006). Structure and validity of people in my life: A self-report measure of attachment in late childhood. *Journal of Youth and Adolescence, 35,* 1037–1053.

Ridley, M. (2003). *Nature via nurture.* New York: HarperCollins.

Riegel, K. F. (1976). The dialectics of human development. *American Psychologist, 31,* 689–700.

Ringel, B. A., & Springer, C. J. (1980). On knowing how well one is remembering: The persistence of strategy use during transfer. *Journal of Experimental Child Psychology, 29,* 322–333.

Ripke, M. N., Huston, A. C., & Casey, D. M. (2006). Low-income children's activity participation as a predictor of psychosocial and academic outcomes in middle childhood and adolescence. In A. C. Huston & M. N. Ripke (Eds.), *Developmental contexts in middle childhood: Bridges to adolescence and adulthood* (pp. 260–282). Cambridge, UK: Cambridge University Press.

Risman, B. J. (1998). *Gender vertigo: American families in transition.* New Haven, CT: Yale University Press.

Risman, B. J., & Johnson-Sumerford, D. (1998). Doing it fairly: A study of postgender marriages. *Journal of Marriage and the Family, 60,* 23–40.

Risman, B. J., & Myers, K. (1997). As the twig is bent: Children reared in feminist households. *Qualitative Sociology, 20,* 229–252.

Roberton, M. A., & Konczak, J. (2001). Predicting children's overarm throw ball velocities from their developmental levels in throwing. *Research Quarterly for Exercise & Sport, 72,* 91–103.

Roberts, D. F., Foehr, U. G., & Rideout, V. (2005). *Generation M: Media in the lives of 8–18 year olds.* Menlo Park, CA: Kaiser Family Foundation.

Roberts, L., White, G., & Yeomans, P. (2004). Theory development and evaluation of Project WIN: A violence reduction program for early adolescents. *Journal of Early Adolescence, 24,* 460–483.

Robinson, N. M., & Noble, K. D. (1991). Socio-emotional development and adjustment of gifted children. In M. C. Wang, M. C. Reynolds & Walberg, H. J. (Eds.), *Handbook of special education: Vol. 4. Research and practice* (pp. 57–76). Elmsford, NY: Pergamon Press.

Robinson, T. L. (1999). The intersections of dominant discourses across race, gender, and other identities. *Journal of Counseling and Development, 77,* 73–79.

Rodkin, P. C., Farmer, T. W., Pearl, R., & Van Acker, R. (2000). Heterogeneity of popular boys: Antisocial and prosocial configurations. *Developmental Psychology, 36*(1), 14–24.

Roehlkepartain, E. C., Benson, P. L., King, P. E., & Wagener, L. M. (2005). Spiritual development in childhood and adolescence: Moving to the scientific mainstream. In P. E. King & E. C. Roehlkepartain (Eds.), *Handbook of spiritual development in childhood and adolescence* (pp. 1–15). Thousand Oaks, CA: Sage.

Roesner, R. W., Eccles, J. S., & Sameroff, A. J. (2000). School as a context of early adolescents' academic and social-emotional development: A summary of research findings. *The Elementary School Journal, 100,* 443.

Roffman, J. G., Pagano, M. E., & Hirsch, B. J. (2001). Youth functioning and experiences in inner-city after-school programs among age, gender, and race groups. *Journal of Child and Family Studies, 10,* 85–100.

Rogers, C. R. (1961). *On becoming a person.* Boston: Houghton Mifflin.

Rogers, C. R. (1969). *Freedom to learn.* Columbus, OH: Merrill.

Rogers, C. R. (1980). *A way of being.* Boston: Houghton Mifflin.

Rogoff, B. (1990). *Apprenticeship in thinking: Cognitive development in social context.* New York: Oxford University Press.

Rogoff, B. (1996). Developmental transitions in children's participation in sociocultural activities. In A. J. Sameroff & M. M. Haith (Eds.), *The five to seven year shift: The age of reason and responsibility.* Chicago: University of Chicago Press.

Rogoff, B. (1998). Cognition as a collaborative process. In W. Damon (Series Ed.), & D. Kuhn & R. S. Siegler (Vol. Eds.), *Handbook of child psychology: Cognition, perception, and language* (pp. 679–744). New York: Wiley.

Rogoff, B. (2003). *The cultural nature of human development.* New York: Oxford University Press.

Rogoff, B., Paradise, R., Mejia Arauz, R., Correa-Chavez, M., & Angelillo, C. (2003). Firsthand learning through intent participation. *Annual Review of Psychology, 54,* 175–203.

Rogoff, B., & Waddell, K. J. (1982). Memory for information organized in a scene by children from two cultures. *Child Development, 53,* 1224–1228.

Rogol, A. D., Roemmich, J. N., & Clark, P. A. (2002). Growth at puberty. *Journal of Adolescent Health, 31,* 192–200.

Roid, G. H. (2003). *Stanford-Binet Intelligence Scales* (5th ed.). Itasca, IL: Riverside.

Root, M. P. P. (1999). The biracial baby boom: Understanding the ecological constructions of racial identity in the 21st century. In R. H. Sheets & E. R. Hollins (Eds.), *Racial and ethnic identity in school practices: Aspects of human development* (pp. 67–89). Mahwah, NJ: Erlbaum.

Rose, B., Larkin, D., & Berger, B. G. (1997). Coordination and gender influences on the perceived competence of children. *Adapted Physical Activity Quarterly, 14,* 210–221.

Roth, J., & Brooks-Gunn, J. (2000). What do adolescents need for healthy development? Implications for youth policy. *Social Policy Report,* Vol. 14, No. 1. Retrieved March 21, 2005, from http://www.srcd.org/spr.html.

Roth, J., & Brooks-Gunn, J. (2003). What is a youth development program? Identification of defining principles. In R. M. Lerner, F. Jacobs, & D. Wertlieb (Eds.), *Handbook of applied developmental science: Vol. 2. Enhancing the life chances of youth and families: Contributions of programs, policies, and service systems* (pp. 197–223). Thousand Oaks, CA: Sage.

Roth, J., Brooks-Gunn, J., Murray, L., & Foster, W. (1998). Promoting healthy adolescence: Synthesis of youth development program evaluations. *Journal of Research on Adolescence, 8,* 432–459.

Rothbart, M. K., & Bates, J. E. (1998). Temperament. In W. Damon (Series Ed.) & N. Eisenberg (Vol. Ed.), *Handbook of child psychology: Vol. 3. Social, emotional, and personality development* (5th ed., pp. 105–176). New York: Wiley.

Rothbaum, F., & Trommsdorff, G. (2007). Do roots and wings complement or oppose one another?: The socialization of relatedness and autonomy in cultural context. In J. E. Grusec & P. Hastings (Eds.), *Handbook of socialization: Theory and research* (pp. 461–489). New York: Guilford Press.

Rotheram, M. J., & Phinney, J. S. (1987). Definitions and perspectives in the study of children's ethnic socialization. In. J. S. Phinney & M. J. Rotheram (Eds.), *Children's ethnic socialization: Pluralism and development* (pp. 10–31). Newbury Park, CA: Sage.

Rousseau, J. J. (1970). *The Emile* (W. Boyd, Trans.). New York: Teacher's College Press. (Original work published 1762.)

Roy, R., Benenson, J. F., & Lilly, F. (2000). Beyond intimacy: Conceptualizing differences in same-sex friendships. *The Journal of Psychology, 134,* 93–101.

Royse, D., Thyer, B. A., Padgett, D. K., & Logan, T. K. (2006). *Program evaluation:*

An introduction. Belmont, CA: Thomson Brooks/Cole.

Rubin, K. H. (1998). Social and emotional development from a cultural perspective. *Developmental Psychology, 34,* 611–615.

Rubin, K. H., Bukowski, W., & Parker, J. G. (1998). Peer interactions, relationships, and groups. In W. Damon (Series Ed.) & N. Eisenberg (Vol Ed.), *Handbook of child psychology: Vol. 3. Social, emotional, and personality development* (5th ed., pp. 619–695). New York: Wiley.

Rubin, K. H., Bukowski, W., & Parker, J. G. (2006). Peer interactions, relationships, and groups. In W. Damon & R. M. Lerner (Series Eds.) & N. Eisenberg (Vol. Ed.), *Handbook of child psychology, Vol. 3: Social, emotional and personality development* (6th ed., pp. 571–645). New York: Wiley.

Rubin, K. H., Coplan, R., Chen, X., Buskirk, A. A., & Wojslawlowski, J. C. (2005). Peer relationships in childhood. In M. H. Bornstein & M. E. Lamb (Eds.), *Developmental science: An advanced textbook* (5th ed., pp. 469–512). Mahwah, NJ: Erlbaum.

Rubin, K. H., Dwyer, K. M., Booth-LaForce, C., Kim, A. H., Burgess, K. B., & Rose-Krasnor, L. (2004). Attachment, friendship, and psychosocial functioning in early adolescence. *Journal of Early Adolescence, 24,* 326–356.

Rubinstein, J. S., Meyer, D. E., & Evans, J. E. (2001). Executive control of cognitive processes in task switching. *Journal of Experimental Psychology: Human Perception and Performance, 27,* 763–797.

Ruble, D. N. (1987). The acquisition of self-knowledge: A self-socialization perspective. In N. Eisenberg (Ed.), *Contemporary topics in developmental psychology* (pp. 243–270). New York: Wiley.

Ruble, D. N. & Dweck, C. S. (1995). Self-conceptions, person conceptions, and their development. In N. Eisenberg (Ed.), *Social development* (pp. 109–139). Thousand Oaks, CA: Sage.

Ruble, D. N., Eisenberg, R., & Higgins, E. T. (1994). Developmental changes in achievement motivation: Motivational implications of self-other differences. *Child Development, 65,* 1095–1110.

Ruble, D. N., & Martin, C. L. (1998). Gender development. In W. Damon (Series Ed.) & N. Eisenberg (Vol. Ed.), *Handbook of child psychology: Vol. 3. Social, emotional, and personality development* (5th ed., pp. 993–1016). New York: Wiley.

Ruble, D. N., & Martin, C. L. (2002). Conceptualizing, measuring, and evaluating the developmental course of gender differentiation: Compliments, queries, and quandaries: Commentary. In W. F. Overton (Ed.), *Developmental course of gender differentiation* (pp. 148–166). *Monographs of* the Society for Research in Child Development, 67(2, Serial No. 269).

Ruiselova, Z. (1998). Relationships with parents and teachers in connection with pubertal maturation timing in girls. *Studia Psychologica, 40*(4), 277–281.

Ruiz-de-Velasco, J., Fix, M., & Clewell, B. C. (2000). *Overlooked and underserved: Immigrant status in U.S. secondary schools.* Washington, DC: The Urban Institute.

Rumbaut, R. G. (2005). Sites of belonging: Acculturation, discrimination, and ethnic identity among children of immigrants. In T. S. Weisner (Ed.), *Discovering successful pathways in children's development: Mixed methods in the study of childhood and family life* (pp. 111–163). Chicago: University of Chicago Press.

Runion, B. P., Langendorfer, S. J., & Roberton, M. A. (2003). Forceful overarm throwing: A comparison of two cohorts measured 20 years apart. *Research Quarterly for Exercise & Sport, 74*, 324–330.

Russ, S. W. (2003). Play and creativity: Developmental issues. *Scandinavian Journal of Educational Research, 47*, 291–303.

Russell, S. T. (2005). Beyond risk: Resilience in the lives of sexual-minority youth. *Journal of GLBT Issues in Education, 2*(3), 5–18.

Saarni, C. (1990). Emotional competence: How emotions and relationships become integrated. In R. A. Thompson (Ed.), *Nebraska symposium on motivation: Vol. 36. Socioemotional development* (pp. 115–182). Lincoln, NB: University of Nebraska Press.

Saarni, C. (1998). Issues of cultural meaningfulness in emotional development. *Developmental Psychology, 34*, 647–652.

Saarni, C. (2000). The social context of emotional development. In M. Lewis & J. M. Haviland-Jones (Eds.), *Handbook of emotions* (2nd ed., pp. 306–322). New York: Guilford Press.

Saarni, C. (2001a). Epilogue: Emotion communication and relationship context. *International Journal of Behavioral Development, 25*, 354–356.

Saarni, C. (2001b). Cognition, context, and goals: Significant components in social-emotional effectiveness. *Social Development, 10*, 125–129.

Saarni, C., Campos, J., Camras, L. A., & Witherington, D. (2006). Emotional development: Action, communication and understanding. In W. Damon & R. M. Lerner (Series Eds.) & R. M. Lerner (Vol. Ed.), *Handbook of child psychology: Vol. 1. Theoretical models of human development* (6th ed., pp. 226–299). New York: Wiley.

Saarni, C., Mumme, D. L., & Campos, J. L. (1998). Emotional development: Action, communication, and understanding. In W. Damon (Series Ed.) & N. Eisenberg (Vol. Ed.), *Handbook of child psychology: Vol. 3.*

Social, emotional, and personality development (5th ed., pp. 237–309). New York: Wiley.

Sadeh, A., Raviv, A., & Gruber, R. (2000). Sleep patterns and sleep disruptions in school-age children. *Developmental Psychology, 36*, 291–301.

Sadker, M., & Sadker, D. (1994). *Failing at fairness: How America's schools cheat girls.* New York: Charles Scribner's Sons.

Sallis, J. F., Woodruff, S. I., Vargas, R., Deosaransingh, K., Laniado-Laborin, R., Moreno, C., et al., (1997). Reliability and validity of a cigarette refusal skills test for Latino youth. *American Journal of Health Behavior, 21*, 345–355.

Salovey, P., Bedell, B. T., Detweiler, J. B., & Mayer, J. D. (2000). Current directions in emotional intelligence research. In M. Lewis & J. M. Haviland-Jones (Eds.), *Handbook of emotions* (2nd ed., pp. 504–520). New York: Guilford Press.

Sameroff, A. J., & Haith, M. M. (1996). *The five to seven year shift: The age of reason and responsibility.* Chicago: University of Chicago Press.

Sampson, R. J., & Morenoff, J. (1997). Ecological perspectives on the neighborhood context of urban poverty: Past and present. In J. Brooks-Gunn, G. J. Duncan, & J. L. Aber (Eds.), *Neighborhood poverty: Vol. 2. Policy implications in studying neighborhoods* (pp. 1–22). New York: Russell Sage Foundation.

Sandberg, D. E., Bukowski, W. M., Fung, C. M., & Noll, R. B. (2004). Height and social adjustment: Are extremes a cause for concern and action? *Pediatrics, 114*, 744–750.

Sandberg, D. E., Kranzler, J., Bukowski, W. M., & Rosenbloom, A. L. (1999). Psychosocial aspects of short stature and growth hormone therapy. *The Journal of Pediatrics, 135*, 133–134.

Sandberg, D. E., Ognibene, T. C., Brook, A. E., Barrick, C., Shine, B., & Grundner, W. (1998). Academic outcomes among children and adolescents receiving growth hormone therapy. *Children's Health Care, 27*, 265–282.

Sarampote, N. C., Bassett, H. H., & Winsler, A. (2004). After-school care: Child outcomes and recommendations for research and policy. *Child and Youth Care Forum, 33*, 329–348.

Saudi Arabia Information Resource. (2005). Riyadh population by age groups. Retrieved June 26, 2005, from http://www.saudinf.com/main/y7938.htm.

Savelsbergh, G. J. P., & van der Kamp, J. (2000). Information in learning to coordinate and control movements: Is there a need for specificity of practice. *International Journal of Sport Psychology, 31*, 467–484.

Savin-Williams, R. C. (1994a). Dating those you can't love and loving those you can't

date. In R. Montemayor, G. R. Adams, & T. P. Gullotta (Eds.), *Advances in adolescent development: Vol. 3. Personal relationships during adolescence* (pp. 196–215). Thousand Oaks, CA: Sage.

Savin-Williams, R. C. (1994b). Verbal and physical abuse as stressors in the lives of lesbian, gay male and bisexual youths: Associations with school problems, running away, substance abuse, prostitution, and suicide. *Journal of Consulting and Clinical Psychology, 62*, 261–269.

Savin-Williams, R. C. (1996). Memories of childhood and early adolescent sexual feelings among gay and bisexual boys: A narrative approach. In R. C. Savin-Williams & K. M. Cohen (Eds.), *The lives of lesbians, gays, and bisexuals: Children to adults* (pp. 94–109). Belmont, CA: Thomson.

Savin-Williams, R. C., & Diamond, L. M. (2000). Sexual-identity trajectories among sexual-minority youth: Gender comparisons. *Archives of Sexual Behavior, 29*, 607–627.

Savin-Williams, R. C. & Diamond, L. M. (2004). Sex. In R. M. Lerner & L Steinberg (Eds.), *Handbook of adolescent psychology* (2nd ed., pp. 189–231). New York: Wiley.

Saxe, G. B. (1988). The mathematics of street vendors. *Child Development, 59*, 1415–1425.

Scaglione, J., & Scaglione, A. M. (2006). *Bully-proofing children: A practical hands-on guide to stop bullying.* Lanham, MD: Rowman & Littlefield.

Scales, P. C., Benson, P. L., Leffert, N., & Blyth, D. A. (2000). Contribution of developmental assets to the prediction of thriving among adolescents. *Applied Developmental Science, 4*, 27–46.

Scanlan, T. K., Babkes, M. L., & Scanlan, L. A. (2005). Participation in sport: A developmental glimpse at emotion. In J. L. Mahoney, R. W. Larson, & J. S. Eccles (Eds.), *Organized activities as contexts of development: Extracurricular activities, after-school and community programs* (pp. 275–309). Mahwah, NJ: Erlbaum.

Scarborough, H. S. (1998). Early identification of children at risk for reading disabilities: Phonological awareness and some other promising predictors. In B. K. Shapiro, P. J. Accardo, & A. J. Capute (Eds.), *Specific reading disability: A view of the spectrum* (pp. 75–119). Timonium, MD: York Press.

Scarr, S. (1997). Behavior-genetic and socialization theories of intelligence: Truce and reconciliation. In R. J. Sternberg & E. L. Grigorenko (Eds.), *Intelligence, heredity, and environment* (pp. 3–41). New York: Cambridge University Press.

Scarr, S., & McCartney, K. (1983). How people make their own environments: A theory of genotype-environment effects. *Child Development, 54*, 424–435.

Schachter, E. P. (2004). Identity configurations: A new perspective on identity formation in contemporary society. *Journal of Personality, 72*, 167–199.

Schneider, W. (1986). The role of conceptual knowledge and metamemory in the development of organizational processes in memory. *Journal of Experimental Child Psychology, 42*, 218–236.

Schneider, W. (1998). Performance prediction in young children: Effects of skill, metacognition, and wishful thinking. *Developmental Science, 1*, 291–297.

Schneider, W., & Bjorklund, D. (2003). Memory and knowledge development. In J. Valsiner & K. J. Connolly (Eds.), *Handbook of developmental psychology* (pp. 370–403). Thousand Oaks, CA: Sage.

Schneider, W., Bjorklund, D. A., & Maier-Bruckner, W. (1996). The effects of expertise and IQ on children's memory: When knowledge is, and when it is not enough. *International Journal of Behavioral Development, 19*, 773–796.

Schneider, W., & Lockl, K. (2002). The development of metacognitive knowledge in children and adolescents. In T. J. Perfect & B. L. Schwartz (Eds.), *Applied metacognition* (pp. 224–257). New York: Cambridge University Press.

Schneider, W., & Pressley, M. (1997). *Memory development between 2 and 20* (2nd ed.). Mahwah, NJ: Erlbaum.

Schunk, D. H., & Pajares, F. (2002). The development of academic self-efficacy. In A. Wigfield & J. S. Eccles (Eds.), *The development of achievement motivation* (pp. 15–31). San Diego, CA: Academic Press.

Schuster, M. A., Bell, R. M., Berry, S. H., & Kanouse, D. E. (1998). Impact of a high school condom availability program on sexual attitudes and behaviors. *Family Planning Perspectives, 30*, 67–72.

Schwebel, D. C., & Plumert, J. M. (1999). Longitudinal and concurrent relations between temperament, ability estimation, and injury proneness. *Child Development, 70*, 700–712.

Schwebel, D. C., Plumert, J. M., & Pick, H. L. (2000). Integrating basic and applied research: A new model for the twenty-first century. *Child Development, 71*(1), 220–230.

Sebold, H. (1968). *Adolescence: A sociological analysis*. Englewood Cliffs, NJ: Prentice Hall.

Seccombe, K., & Warner, R. L. (2004). *Marriages and families: Relationships in social context.* Belmont, CA: Wadsworth.

Sefton-Green, J., & Buckingham, D. (1996). Digital visions: Children's "creative" uses of multimedia technologies. *Convergence, 2*(2), 47–79.

Seiter, E. (2004). The Internet playground. In J. Goldstein, D. Buckingham & G. Brougere

(Eds.), *Toys, games, and media* (pp. 93–108). Mahwah, NJ: Erlbaum.

Sellers, D. E., McGraw, S. A., & McKinlay, J. B. (1994). Does the promotion and distribution of condoms increase teen sexual activity? Evidence from an HIV prevention program for Latino youth. *American Journal of Public Health, 84*, 1952–1959.

Selman, R. L. (1980). Four domains, five stages: A summary portrait of interpersonal understanding. In *The growth of interpersonal understanding: Developmental and clinical implications* (pp. 131–155). New York: Academic Press.

Selman, R. L. (2003). *The promotion of social awareness*. New York: Russell Sage Foundation.

Serbin, L. A., Marchessault, K., McAffer, V., Peters, P., & Schwartzman, A. E. (1993). Patterns of social behavior on the playground in 9- to 11-year-olds girls and boys: Relation to teacher perceptions and to peer ratings of aggression, withdrawal, and likeability. In C. H. Hart (Ed.), *Children on playgrounds: Research perspectives and applications* (pp. 162–183). Albany, NY: State University of New York Press.

Shaffer, D. R. (2005). *Social and personality development* (5th ed.). Belmont, CA: Wadsworth.

Shantz, C. U. (1983). Social cognition. In P. H. Mussen (Series Ed.) & J. H. Flavell & E. M. Markman (Vol. Eds.), *Handbook of child psychology: Vol. 3. Cognitive development* (4th ed., pp. 495–555). New York: Wiley.

Shapiro, L. J., & Azuma, H. (2004). Intellectual, attitudinal, and interpersonal aspects of competence in the United States and Japan. In R. J. Sternberg & E. L. Grigorenko (Eds.), *Culture and competence: Contexts of life success* (pp. 187–205). Washington, DC: American Psychological Association.

Sharp, S., & Smith, P. K. (1994). *Tackling bullying in your school: A practical handbook for teachers*. London: Routledge.

Sheldon, S. B. (2002). Parents' social networks and beliefs as predictors of parent involvement. *Elementary School Journal, 102*, 301–316.

Sheldon, S. B. (2003). Linking school-family-community partnerships in urban elementary schools to student achievement on state tests. *The Urban Review, 35*, 149–165.

Shemilt, I., Harvey, I., Shepstone, L., Swift, L., Reading, R., Mugford, M., et al. (2004). A national evaluation of school breakfast clubs: Evidence from a cluster randomized controlled trial and an observational analysis. *Child: Care, Health and Development, 30*, 413–427.

Sher, L. (2006). Functional magnetic resonance imaging in studies of neurocognitive effects of alcohol use on adolescents and young adults. *International Journal of Adolescent Medicine and Health, 18*, 3–7.

Sheridan, S. M., Eagle, J. W., & Dowdf, S. E. (2006). Families as contexts for children's adaptation. In S. Goldstein, & R. B. Brooks (Eds.), *Handbook of resilience in children* (pp. 165–179). New York: Springer.

Sheridan, S. M., Hungelmann, A., & Maughan, D. P. (1999). A contextualized framework for social skills assessment, intervention, and generalization. *School Psychology Review, 28*, 84–103.

Sherr, J. (1982). The universal structures and dynamics of creativity: Maharishi, Plato, Jung, and various creative geniuses on the creative process. *Journal of Creative Behavior, 16*, 155–175.

Shiffrin, R. M., & Atkinson, R. C. (1969). Storage and retrieval processes in long-term memory. *Psychological Review, 76*, 179–193.

Shirk, S. R., & Renouf, A. G. (1992). The tasks of self-development in middle childhood and early adolescence. In R. P. Lipka, & T. M. Brinthaupt (Eds.), *Self-perspectives across the life span* (pp. 53–90). Albany, NY: State University of New York.

Shisslack, C. M., & Crago, M. (2001). Risk and protective factors in the development of eating disorders. In J. K. Thompson & L. Smolak (Eds.), *Body image, eating disorders, and obesity in youth: Assessment, prevention, and treatment* (pp. 103–125). Washington, DC: American Psychological Association.

Shisslack, C. M., Crago, M., & Estes, L. S. (1995). The spectrum of eating disturbances. *International Journal of Eating Disorders, 18*, 209–219.

Shisslack, C. M., Crago, M., McKnight, K., Estes, L., Gray, N., & Parnaby, O. (1998). Potential risk factors associated with weight control behaviors in elementary and middle school girls. *Journal of Psychosomatic Research, 44*, 301–314.

Shweder, R. A. (1991). *Thinking through cultures*. Cambridge, MA: Harvard University Press.

Shweder, R. A., Goodnow, J., Hatano, G., LeVine, R. A., Markus, H., & Miller, P. (2006). The cultural psychology of development: One mind, many mentalities. In W. Damon & R. M. Lerner (Series Eds.) & R. M. Lerner (Vol. Ed.), *Handbook of child psychology: Vol. 1. Theoretical models of human development* (6th ed., pp. 716–792). New York: Wiley.

Siegel, J. M., Yancey, A. K., Aneshensel, C. S., & Schuler, R. (1999). Body image, perceived pubertal timing, and adolescent mental health. *Journal of Adolescent Health, 25*, 155–165.

Siegler, R. S. (1996). *Emerging minds: The process of change in children's thinking*. New York: Oxford University Press.

Silbereisen, R. K. (2003). Contextual constraints on adolescents' leisure. In S. Verma & R. Larson (Eds.), *Examining adolescent leisure time across cultures: Developmental opportunities and risks* (pp. 95–101). *New Directions for Child and Adolescent Development*, No. 99. San Francisco: Jossey-Bass.

Silbereisen, R. K., & Todt, E. (1994). *Adolescence in context: The interplay of family, school, peers, and work in adjustment.* New York: Springer-Verlag.

Simmons, R. (2003, October 2). Cyberbullying stalks students. *The Detroit News*, 13A, 17A.

Simmons, R. G., & Blyth, D. A. (1987). *Moving into adolescence: The impact of pubertal change and school context.* New York: Aldine de Gruyter.

Simons-Morton, B. G. (2004). Prospective association of peer influence, school engagement, drinking expectancies, and parent expectations with drinking initiation among sixth graders. *Addictive Behaviors, 29,* 299–309.

Simons-Morton, B. G., Haynie, D. L., Crump, A. D., Saylor, K. E., Eitel, P., & Yu, K. (1999). Expectancies and other psychosocial factors associated with alcohol use among early adolescent boys and girls. *Addictive Behaviors, 24,* 229–238.

Simons-Morton, B. G., Haynie, D. L., Saylor, K. E., Crump, A. D., & Chen, R. (2005). The effects of the Going Places Program on early adolescent substance use and antisocial behavior. *Prevention Science, 6,* 187–197.

Simpkins, S. D., Fredricks, J. A., Davis-Kean, P. E., & Eccles, J. S. (2006). Healthy minds, healthy habits: The influence of activity involvement in middle childhood. In A. C. Huston & M. N. Ripke (Eds.), *Developmental contexts in middle childhood: Bridges to adolescence and adulthood* (pp. 283–302). Cambridge, UK: Cambridge University Press.

Simpkins, S. D., & Parke, R. D. (2001). The relations between parental friendships and children's friendships: Self-report and observational analysis. *Child Development, 72,* 569–582.

Singer, J. L., & Brink, N. (2003). The genius of play. *Imagination, Cognition and Personality, 22,* 95–96.

Skuse, D., Gilmour, J., Tian, C. S., & Hindmarsh, P. (1994). Psychosocial assessment of children with short stature: A preliminary report. *Acta Paediatrica* (Suppl. 406), 11–16.

Slattery, P. (1999). The excluded middle: Postmodern conceptions of the middle school. In C. W. Walley & W. G. Gerrick (Eds.), *Affirming middle grades education* (pp. 26–37). Boston: Allyn & Bacon.

Sleet, D. A., & Mercy, J. A. (2003). Promotion of safety, security, and well-being. In M. H. Bornstein, L. Davidson, C. L. M. Keyes, K. A. Moore, & The Center for Child Well-Being (Eds.), *Well-being: Positive develop-*

ment across the life course (pp. 81–97). Mahwah, NJ: Erlbaum.

Small, S. A., & Eastman, G. (1995). Rearing adolescents in contemporary society: A conceptual framework for understanding the responsibilities and needs of parents. In D. H. Demo & A. Ambert (Eds.), *Parents and adolescents in changing families* (pp. 50–61). Minneapolis: National Council on Family Relations.

Smilansky, S. (1968). *The effects of sociodramatic play on disadvantaged preschool children.* Oxford, UK: Wiley.

Smith, A., & Dannison, L. (2002). Educating educators: Programming to support grandparent headed families. *Contemporary Education, 72,* 47–51.

Smith, A., Dannison, L. & Vacha-Haase, T. (1998). When "Grandma" is "Mom": What today's teachers need to know. *Childhood Education, 75*(1), 12–16.

Smith, D. A., Sprengelmeyer, P. G., & Moore, K. J. (2004). Parenting and antisocial behavior. In M. Hoghughi & N. Lond (Eds.), *Handbook of parenting: Theory and research for practice* (pp. 237–255). London: Sage.

Smith, G. J., & Carlsson, I. M. (1990). *The creative process: A functional model based on empirical studies from early childhood to middle age.* Madison, CT: International Universities Press.

Smock, P. J. (2006). *Promises and perils of proposals to promote marriage: Experts list from council on contemporary families.* Council on Contemporary Families. Retrieved July 27, 2006, from http://www.contemporaryfamilies.org/subtemplate.php?t=briefingPapers&ext=ppp.

Smolak, L., Levine, M., & Thompson, J. K. (2001). Body image in adolescent boys and girls as assessed with the Sociocultural Attitudes Towards Appearance Scale. *International Journal of Eating Disorders, 29,* 216–223.

Snow, C. E., Burns, M. S., & Griffin, P. (1998). *Preventing reading difficulties in young children.* Washington, DC: National Academy Press.

Solis, J. (2002). The (trans)formation of illegality as an identity: A study of the organization of undocumented Mexican immigrants and their children in New York City. *Dissertation Abstracts International: Section B: The Sciences and Engineering, 63*(3-B).

Solomon, J., & George, C. (1999). The measurement of attachment security in infancy and childhood. In J. Cassidy & P. R. Shaver (Eds.), *Handbook of attachment: Theory, research, and clinical applications* (pp. 287–316). New York: Guilford Press.

Soriano, F. I., Rivera, L. M., Williams, K. J., Daley, S. P., & Reznik, V. M. (2004). Navigating between cultures: The role of culture

in youth violence. *Journal of Adolescent Health, 34*(3), 169–176.

Spence, J. T., & Helmreich, R. L. (1980). Masculine instrumentality and feminine expressiveness: Their relationships with sex-role attitudes and behaviors. *Psychology of Women Quarterly, 5,* 147–163.

Stacey, J., & Bilbarz, T. (2001). (How) does the sexual orientation of parents matter? *American Sociological Review, 66,* 159–183.

Stacey, J., & Davenport, E. (2002). Queer families quack back. In D. Richardson & S. Seidman (Eds.), *Handbook of gay and lesbian studies* (pp. 355–374). London: Sage.

Stack, C. (1990). Different voices, different visions: Race, gender, and moral reasoning. In R. Ginsberg & A. Tsing (Eds.), *The negotiation of gender in American society* (pp. 19–27). Boston: Beacon Press.

Stafford, L. (2004). Communication competencies and sociocultural priorities of middle childhood. In A. Vangelisti (Ed.), *Handbook of family communication* (pp. 311–332). Mahwah, NJ: Erlbaum.

Stanger, J. D., & Gridina, N. (1999). *Media in the home 1999: The fourth annual survey of parents and children (Survey Series No. 5).* Norwood, NJ, & Philadelphia: Annenberg Public Policy Center of the University of Pennsylvania.

Stattin, H., & Magnusson, D. (1990). *Pubertal maturation in female development.* Hillsdale, NJ: Erlbaum.

Steele, H., & Steele, M. (2005). The construct of coherence as an indicator of attachment security in middle childhood: The friends and family interview. In K. A. Kerns & R. A. Richardson (Eds.), *Attachment in middle childhood* (pp. 137–160). New York: Guilford Press.

Steinberg, L. (1986). Latchkey children and susceptibility to peer pressure: An ecological analysis. *Developmental Psychology, 22,* 433–439.

Steinberg, L. (1995). Commentary: On developmental pathways and social contexts in adolescence. In L. J. Crockett & A. C. Crouter (Eds.), *Pathways through adolescence: Individual development in relation to social contexts* (pp. 245–253). Mahwah, NJ: Erlbaum.

Steinberg, L. (1996). *Beyond the classroom: Why school reform has failed and what parents need to do.* New York: Touchstone.

Steinberg, L. (2001). We know some things: Parent-adolescent relationships in retrospect and prospect. *Journal of Research on Adolescence, 11,* 1–19.

Steinberg, L., & Cauffman, E. (2001). Adolescents as adults in court: A developmental perspective on the transfer of juveniles to criminal court. *Social Policy Report,* Vol. 15, No. 4. Retrieved March 21, 2005, from http://www.srcd.org/spr.html.

Steinberg, L., Dornbusch, S. M., & Brown, B. B. (1992). Ethnic differences in adolescent achievement: An ecological perspective. *American Psychologist, 47,* 723–729.

Sternberg, R. J. (1985). *Beyond IQ: A triarchic theory of human intelligence.* New York: Cambridge University Press.

Sternberg, R. J. (1999). *Handbook of creativity.* New York: Cambridge University Press.

Sternberg, R. J. (2000). Creativity is a decision. In A. L. Costa (Ed.), *Teaching for intelligence II* (pp. 85–106). Arlington Heights, IL: Skylight Training and Publishing.

Sternberg, R. J. (2003a). Our research program validating the triarchic theory of successful intelligence: Reply to Gottfredson. *Intelligence, 31,* 399–413.

Sternberg, R. J. (2003b). Creative thinking in the classroom. *Scandinavian Journal of Educational Research, 47,* 325–338.

Sternberg, R. J., Forsythe, G. B., Hedlund, J., Horvath, J., Snook, S., Williams, W. M., et al. (2000). *Practical intelligence in everyday life.* New York: Cambridge University Press.

Sternberg, R. J., Grigorenko, E. L., Ferrai, M., & Clinkenbeard, P. (1999). A triarchic analysis of an aptitude-treatment interaction. *European Journal of Psychological Assessment, 15,* 1–11.

Sternberg, R. J., & Lubart, T. I. (1995). *Defying the crowd: Cultivating creativity in a culture of conformity.* New York: Free Press.

Sternberg, R. J., & Lubart, T. I. (1996). Investing in creativity. *American Psychologist, 51,* 677–688.

Sternberg, R. J., & Lubart, T. I. (1999). The concept of creativity: Prospects and paradigms. In R. J. Sternberg (Ed.), *Handbook of creativity* (pp. 3–15). New York: Cambridge University Press.

Sternberg, R. J., Nokes, K., Geissler, P. W., Okatcha, F., Bundy, D. A., et al. (2001). The relationship between academic and practical intelligence: A case study in Kenya. *Intelligence, 29,* 401–418.

Sternberg, R. J., & O'Hara, L. A. (1999). Creativity and intelligence. In R. J. Sternberg (Ed.), *Handbook of creativity* (pp. 251–272). New York: Cambridge University Press.

Sternberg, R. J., & Williams, W. M. (1996). *How to develop student creativity.* Alexandria, VA: Association for Supervision and Curriculum Development.

Stetsenko, A., Little, T. D., Gordeeva, T., Grasshof, M., & Oettingen, G. (2000). Gender effects in children's beliefs about school performance: A cross-cultural study. *Child Development, 71,* 517–527.

Stevenson, H. W. (1998). Cultural interpretations of giftedness: The case of East Asia. In R. C. Friedman & K. B. Rogers (Eds.), *Talent in context: Historical and social perspectives on giftedness* (pp. 61–77). Washington, DC: American Psychological Association.

Stevenson, H. W., & Lee, S. Y. (1990). *Contexts of achievement: A study of American,*

Chinese, and Japanese children. Chicago: University of Chicago Press.

Stevenson, H. W., Lee, S. Y., & Stigler, J. W. (1986). Mathematics achievement of Chinese, Japanese, and American children. *Science, 231,* 693–699.

Stewart, S. D. (2003). Nonresident parenting and adolescent adjustment: The quality of nonresident father-child interactions. *Journal of Family Issues, 24,* 217–244.

Stice, E., & Martinez, E. E. (2005). Cigarette smoking prospectively predicts retarded physical growth among female adolescents. *Journal of Adolescent Health, 37,* 363–370.

Stice, E., Presnell, K., & Bearman, S. K. (2001). Relation of early menarche to depression, eating disorders, substance abuse, and comorbid psychopathology among adolescent girls. *Developmental Psychology, 37,* 608–619.

Stipek, D. (2005). Children as unwitting agents in their developmental pathways. In C. R. Cooper, C. T. García Coll, W. T. Bartko, H. Davis, & C. Chatman (Eds.), *Developmental pathways through middle childhood: Rethinking context and diversity as resources* (pp. 99–120). Mahwah, NJ: Erlbaum.

Stocker, C. M., Burwell, R. A., & Briggs, M. L. (2002). Sibling conflict in middle childhood predicts children's adjustment in early adolescence. *Journal of Family Psychology, 16,* 50–57.

Stone, E., Gomez, E., Hotzoglou, D., & Lipnitsky, D. Y. (2005). Transnationalism as a motif in family stories. *Family Process, 44,* 381–398.

Stone, E. J., McKenzie, T. L., Welk, G. J., & Booth, M. L. (1998). Effects of physical activity interventions in youth. Review and synthesis. *American Journal of Prevention Medicine, 15,* 298–315.

Stoneman, Z., & Brody, G. H. (1993). Sibling temperaments, conflict, warmth, and role asymmetry. *Child Development, 64,* 1786–1800.

Story, M., & Alton, I. (1996). Adolescent nutrition: Current trends and critical issues. *Topics in Clinical Nutrition, 11,* 56–69.

Strasberger, V. C., & Wilson, B. J. (2002). *Children, adolescents, and the media.* Thousand Oaks, CA: Sage.

Stratton, P. (2003). Contemporary families as contexts for development. In J. Valsiner & K. Connolly (Eds.), *Handbook of Developmental Psychology* (pp. 333–357). London: Sage.

Striegel-Moore, R., Schreiber, G. B., Lo, A., Crawford, P., Obarzanek, E., & Rodin, J. (2000). Eating disorder symptoms in a cohort of 11- to 16-year-old Black and White girls: The NHLBI Growth and Health Study. *International Journal of Eating Disorders, 27,* 49–66.

Strouse, J. S., Goodwin, M., & Roscoe, B. (1994). Correlates among attitudes toward

sexual harassment among early adolescents. *Sex Roles, 31,* 559–578.

Suarez-Orozco, C., & Suarez-Orozco, M. (2001). *Children of immigration.* Cambridge, MA: Harvard University Press.

Subrahmanyam, K., Greenfield, P., Kraut, R., & Gross, E. (2001). The impact of computer use on children's and adolescents' development. *Applied Developmental Psychology, 22,* 7–30.

Subrahmanyam, K., Kraut, R. E., Greenfield, P. M., & Gross, E. F. (2000). The impact of computer use on children's activities and development. *The Future of Children, 10,* 123–144.

Sullivan, H. S. (1953/1981). *The interpersonal theory of psychiatry.* New York: Norton.

Sun, Y., & Li, Y. (2002). Children's well-being during parents' marital disruption process: A pooled time-series analysis. *Journal of Marriage and Family, 64,* 472–488.

Sussman, S., Lichtman, K., Ritt, A., & Pallonen, U. (1999). Effects of thirty-four adolescent tobacco use cessation and prevention trials on regular users of tobacco products. *Substance Use and Misuse, 34,* 1469–1505.

Sutton, J., Smith, P. K., & Swettenham, J. (1999a). Bullying and "theory of mind": A critique of the "social skills deficit" view of anti-social behaviour. *Social Development, 8,* 117–127.

Sutton, J., Smith, P. K., & Swettenham, J. (1999b). Socially undesirable need not be incompetent: A response to Crick and Dodge. *Social Development, 8,* 132–134.

Swanson, D. P., Spencer, M. B., Dell'Angelo, T., Harpalani, V., & Spencer, T. R. (2002). Identity processes and the positive development of African Americans: An explanatory framework. *New Directions for Youth Development, 95,* 73–99.

Swearer, S. M., & Doll, B. (2002). Bullying in schools: An ecological framework. In R. A. Geffner, M. Loring, & C. Young (Eds.), *Bullying behavior: Current issues, research, and interventions* (pp. 7–23). New York: Haworth.

Tajfel, H. (1981). *Human groups and social categories: Studies in social psychology.* Cambridge, UK: Cambridge University Press.

Tanapat, P., Hastings, N. B., & Gould, E. (2001). Adult neurogenesis in the hippocampal formation. In C. A. Nelson & M. Luciana (Eds.), *Handbook of developmental cognitive neuroscience.* Cambridge, MA: MIT Press.

Tanner, J. M. (1978). *Education and physical growth* (2nd ed.). New York: International Universities Press.

Tanner, J. M. (1986). Normal growth and techniques of growth assessment. *Clinics in Endocrinology and Metabolism, 15,* 411–451.

Tanner, J. M. (1990). *Fetus into man: Physical growth from conception to maturity* (2nd ed.). Cambridge, MA: Harvard University Press.

Tasker, F. L., & Golombok, S. (1997). *Growing up in a lesbian family: Effects on child development.* New York: Guilford Press.

Taylor, C. S., Lerner, R. M., von Eye, A., Balsano, A. B., Dowling, E. M., Anderson, P. M., et al. (2002a). Individual and ecological assets and positive developmental trajectories among African American male youth involved in gangs and in community-based organizations serving youth. *New Directions for Youth Development, 95,* 57–72.

Taylor, C. S., Lerner, R. M., von Eye, A., Balsano, A. B., Dowling, E. M., Anderson, P. M., et al. (2002b). Stability of attributes of positive functioning and of developmental assets among African American male gang and community-based organization members. *New Directions for Youth Development, 95,* 35–55.

Taylor, C. S., Smith, P. R., Taylor, V. A., von Eye, A., Lerner, R. M., Balsano, A. B., et al. (2005). Individual and ecological assets and thriving among African American adolescent male gang and community-based organization members. *Journal of Early Adolescence, 23,* 72–93.

Taylor, M. (1996). A theory of mind perspective on social cognitive development. In R. Gelman & T. Kit-Fong (Eds.), *Perceptual and cognitive development* (pp. 283–329). San Diego, CA: Academic Press.

Taylor, R. D. (2000). An examination of the association of African American mothers' perceptions of their neighborhoods with their parenting and adolescent adjustment. *Journal of Black Psychology, 26*(3), 267–287.

Teachman, J. D. (2002). Childhood living arrangements and the intergenerational transmission of divorce. *Journal of Marriage and Family, 64,* 719–729.

Teasley, S. D. (1995). The role of talk in children's peer collaboration. *Developmental Psychology, 31,* 207–220.

Teicher, M. H., Andersen, S. L., Polcari, A., Anderson, C. M., Navalta, C. P., & Kim, D. M. (2003). The neurobiological consequences of early stress and childhood maltreatment. *Neuroscience & Biobehavioral Reviews, 27,* 33–44.

Teitelman, A. M. (2004). Adolescent girls' perspectives of family interactions related to menarche and sexual health. *Qualitative Health Research, 14,* 1292–1308.

Theokas, C., Almerigi, J. B., Lerner, R. M., Dowling, E. M, Benson, P. L., Scales, P. C., et al. (2005). Conceptualizing and modeling individual and ecological asset components of thriving in early adolescence. *Journal of Early Adolescence, 25,* 113–143.

Theokas, C., Lerner, J. V, Phelps, E., & Lerner, R. M. (2006). Cacophony and change in youth after school activities: Findings from the 4-H Study of Positive Youth Development. *Journal of Youth Development: Bridging Research into Practice, 1,* 1–8.

Thomas, S. (2006). Pervasive learning games: Explorations of hybrid educational gamescapes. *Simulation and Gaming, 37,* 41–55.

Thomas, S. P., & Smith, H. (2004). School connectedness, anger behaviors, and relationships of violent and nonviolent American youth. *Perspectives on Psychiatric Care, 40,* 4, 135–148.

Thompson, A. M., Baxter-Jones, A. D. G., & Mirwald, R. L. (2003). Comparison of physical activity in male and female children: Does maturation matter? *Medicine and Science in Sports and Exercise, 35,* 1684–1690.

Thompson, A. M., Humbert, L. M., & Mirwald, R. L. (2003). A longitudinal study of the impact of childhood and adolescent physical activity experiences on adult physical activity perceptions and behaviors. *Qualitative Health Research, 13,* 358–377.

Thompson, D., Arora, T., & Sharp, S. (2002). *Bullying: Effective strategies for long-term improvement.* London: Routledge Falmer.

Thompson, J. K., & Smolak, L. (2001). Body image, eating disorders, and obesity in youth—the future is now. In J. K. Thompson and L. Smolak (Eds.), *Body image, eating disorders, and obesity in youth: Assessment, prevention, and treatment* (pp. 1–18). Washington, DC: American Psychological Association.

Thompson, R. A. (1990). Emotion and self-regulation. In R. A. Thompson (Ed.), *Nebraska symposium on motivation: Vol. 36. Socioemotional development* (pp. 367–467). Lincoln, NE: University of Nebraska Press.

Thompson, R. A. (1998). Early sociopersonality development. In W. Damon (Series Ed.) & N. Eisenberg (Vol. Ed.), *Handbook of child psychology: Vol. 3. Social, emotional, and personality development* (5th ed., pp. 25–104). New York: Wiley.

Thompson, R. A. (1999). Early attachment and later development. In J. Cassidy & P. R. Shaver (Eds.), *Handbook of attachment: Theory, research, and clinical applications* (pp. 265–286). New York: Guilford Press.

Thompson, R. A., & Nelson, C. A. (2001). Developmental science and the media: Early brain development. *American Psychologist, 56,* 5–15.

Thompson, S. H., Rafiroiu, A. C., & Sargent, R. G. (2003). Examining gender, racial, and age differences in weight concern among third, eighth, and eleventh graders. *Eating Behaviors, 3,* 307–323.

Thorndike, R. M. (2005). *Measurement and evaluation in psychology and education* (7th ed.). Upper Saddle River, NJ: Pearson Education.

Thorne, A. (1993). On contextualizing Loevinger's stages of ego development. *Psychological Inquiry, 4*(1), 53–55.

Thorne, A. (2004). Putting the person into social identity. *Human Development, 47,* 361–365.

Thorne, B. (1993). *Gender play: Girls and boys in school.* New Brunswick, NJ: Rutgers University Press.

Thorne, B. (1997a). Children and gender: Constructions of difference. In M. M. Gergen & S. N. Davis (Eds.), *Toward a psychology of gender: A reader* (pp. 185–202). New York: Routledge.

Thorne, B. (1997b). Girls and boys together, but mostly apart: Gender arrangements in elementary schools. In W. W. Hartup & Z. Rubin (Eds.), *Relationships and development.* Hillsdale, NJ: Erlbaum.

Thorne, B. (2005). Unpacking school lunchtime: Structure, practice, and the negotiation of differences. In C. R. Cooper, C. T. García Coll, W. T. Bartko, H. Davis, & C. Chatman (Eds.), *Developmental pathways through middle childhood: Rethinking context and diversity as resources* (pp. 63–87). Mahwah, NJ: Erlbaum.

Thurstone, L. L. (1938). Primary mental abilities. *Psychometric Monographs,* No. 1.

Tobler, N. S., Roona, M. R., Ochshorn, P., Marshall, D. G., Streke, A. V., & Stackpole, K. M. (2000). School-based adolescent drug prevention programs: 1998 meta-analysis. *Journal of Primary Prevention, 20,* 275–336.

Toblin, R. L., Schwartz, D., Gorman, A. H., & Aboudezzeddine, T. (2005). Social-cognitive and behavioral attributes of aggressive victims of bullying. *Journal of Applied Developmental Psychology, 26,* 329–346.

Todd, R. D. (1992). Neural development is regulated by classical neuro-transmitters: Dopamine D receptor stimulation enhances neurite outgrowth. *Biological Psychiatry, 31,* 794–807.

Tolman, D. L., Spencer, R., Rosen-Reynoso, M., & Porche, M. V. (2003). Sowing the seeds of violence in heterosexual relationships: Early adolescents narrate compulsory heterosexuality. *Journal of Social Issues, 59,* 159–178.

Tolman, J., Pittman, K., Yohalem, N., Thomases, J., & Trammel, M. (2002). *Moving an out-of-school agenda: Lessons and challenges across cities.* Takoma Park, MD: The Forum for Youth Investment.

Torrance, E. P. (1967). *Understanding the fourth grade slump in creative thinking* (Report No, BR-5–0508; CRP-994). Washington, DC: U.S. Office of Education. (ERIC No. ED018273)

Torrance, E. P. (1974). *The Torrance Tests of Creative Thinking.* Lexington, MA: Personnel Press.

Trawick-Smith, J. (2006). *Early childhood development: A multicultural perspective.*

Upper Saddle River, NJ: Merrill-Prentice Hall.

Tremblay, R. E. (2000). The development of aggressive behaviour during childhood: What have we learned in the past century? *International Journal of Behavioral Development, 24,* 129–141.

Tschann, J. M., Adler, N. E., Irwin, C. E., Millstein, S. G., Turner, R. A., & Kegeles, S. M. (1994). Initiation of substance use in early adolescence: The roles of pubertal timing and emotional distress. *Health Psychology, 13*(4), 326–333.

Tucker, M. S. (1999). How did we get here and where should we be going? In D. D. Marsh & J. B. Codding (Eds.), *The new American high school.* Thousand Oaks, CA: Corwin/Sage.

Turiel, E. (1998). The development of morality. In W. Damon (Series Ed.) & N. Eisenberg (Vol. Ed.), *Handbook of child psychology: Vol. 3. Social, emotional, and personality development* (5th ed., pp. 863–932). New York: Wiley.

Turiel, E. (2006). The development of morality. In W. Damon & R. M. Lerner (Series Eds.) & R. M. Lerner (Vol. Ed.), *Handbook of child psychology: Vol. 1. Theoretical models of human development* (6th ed., pp. 789–857). New York: Wiley.

Turkheimer, E. (2000). Three laws of behavior genetics and what they mean. *Current Directions in Psychological Science, 9,* 160–166.

Turkheimer, E., Haley, A., Waldron, M., D'Onofrio, B., & Gottesman, I. (2003). Socioeconomic status modifies heritability of IQ in young children. *Psychological Science, 14,* 623–628.

Turner, J., & Simmons, A. (2006). Transnational resilience and resistance: Key concepts for working with refugees. *Immigrant families and immigration: Therapeutic work. American Family Therapy Academy Monograph Series, Vol. 2*(1), 6–22.

Turner, J. C. (1987). *Rediscovering the social group: A self-categorization theory.* Oxford, UK: Basil Blackwell.

Turner, J. S. (2003). *Dating and sexuality in America: A reference handbook.* Santa Barbara, CA: ABC-CLIO.

Twenge, J. M., & Baumeister, R. F. (2002). Self-control: A limited yet renewable resource. In Y. Kashima, M. Foddy, & M. Platow (Eds.), *Self and identity: Personal, social, and symbolic* (pp. 57–70). Mahwah, NJ: Erlbaum.

Udry, J. R. (1988). Biological predispositions and social control in adolescent sexual behavior. *American Sociological Review, 53,* 709–722.

Udry, J. R., & Campbell, B. C. (1994). Getting started on sexual behavior. In A. S. Rossi (Ed.), *Sexuality across the life course. The John D. and Catherine T. MacArthur Foundation series on mental health and devel-*

opment: Studies on successful midlife development (pp. 187–207). Chicago: University of Chicago Press.

Udry, J. R., Talbert, L., & Morris, N. M. (1986). Biosocial foundations of adolescent female sexuality. *Demography, 23,* 217–230.

Umaña-Taylor, A., Yazedjian, A., & Bámaca-Gomez, M. (2004). Developing the ethnic identity scale using Eriksonian and social identity perspectives. *Identity: An International Journal of Theory and Research, 4,* 9–38.

UNAIDS/UNICEF, & USAID (2004). *Children on the brink 2004: Joint report of new orphan estimates and a framework for action.* New York: UNICEF.

UNAIDS/WHO (2006). *Report on the global AIDS epidemic.* Retrieved August 31, 2006, from http//www.unaids.org/en/HIV_data/2006GlobalReport/default.asp.

Underwood, M. K. (2003). *Social aggression among girls.* New York: Guilford Press.

Underwood, M. K., Galen, B. R., & Paquette, J. A. (2001). Top ten challenges for understanding gender and aggression in children: Why can't we all just get along? *Social Development, 10*(2), 248–266.

Underwood, M. K., & Hurley, J. C. (1999). Emotion regulation in peer relationships in middle childhood. In L. Balter & C. S. Tamis-LeMonda (Eds.), *Child psychology: A handbook of contemporary issues* (pp. 237–258). Philadelphia, PA: Psychology Press.

Ungar, M. (2001). Constructing narratives of resilience with high-risk youth. *Journal of Systemic Therapies, 20,* 58–73.

Ungar, M. (2004). A constructionist discourse on resilience: Multiple contexts, multiple realities among at-risk children and youth. *Youth & Society, 35,* 341–365.

Ungar, M. & Teram, E. (2005). Qualitative resilience research: Contributions and risks. In M. Ungar (Ed.), *Handbook for working with children and youth: Pathways to resilience across cultures and contexts* (pp. 149–163). Thousand Oaks, CA: Sage.

UNICEF (2005). *The state of the world's children: Childhood under threat.* New York: UNICEF.

United Nations. (1986). *The situation of youth in the 1980s and prospects and challenges for the year 2000.* New York: Author.

U.S. Bureau of the Census. (2000, August 28). *Census bureau facts for features.* Retrieved July 18, 2002, from http://www.census.gov/Press-Release/www/2000/cb00ff09.html.

U.S. Bureau of the Census. (2001a). *School enrollment in the United States: Social and economic characteristics of students.* (U.S. Bureau of the Census Publication No. P20–533). Washington, DC: Government Printing Office.

U.S. Bureau of the Census. (2001b). *Age: 2000.* (U.S. Bureau of the Census Publica-

tion No. C2KBR/01–12). Washington, DC: Government Printing Office.

U.S. Bureau of the Census. (2001c). *Home computers and Internet use in the United States: August 2000.* (U.S. Bureau of the Census Publication No. P23–207). Washington, DC: Government Printing Office.

U.S. Commission on Online Child Protection (COPA) (2000). *Report to Congress, October 21, 2001.* Washington, DC: COPA.

U.S. Department of Education and U.S. Department of Justice. (2000). *Working for children and families: Safe and smart after-school programs.* Retrieved July 31, 2002, from http://www.ed.gov/pubs/parents/SafeSmart.

U.S. Department of Health and Human Services (1986). *The health consequences of involuntary exposure to tobacco smoke: A report of the surgeon general: executive summary.* Rockville, MD: U.S. Department of Health and Human Services, Public Health Service, Centers for Disease Control, Center for Health Promotion and Education, Office on Smoking and Health.

U.S. Department of Health and Human Services. (1994). *Preventing tobacco use among young people: A report of the Surgeon General.* Atlanta, GA: U.S. Department of Health and Human Services, Public Health Service, Centers for Disease Control and Prevention, National Center for Chronic Disease Prevention and Health Promotion, Office on Smoking and Health.

U.S. Department of Health and Human Services. (2006). *The health consequences of involuntary exposure to tobacco smoke: A report of the surgeon general—executive summary.* Rockville, MD: U.S. Department of Health and Human Services, Public Health Service, Centers for Disease Control, Center for Health Promotion and Education, Office on Smoking and Health.

U.S. Immigration and Naturalization Service. (2000). *2000 statistical yearbook of the Immigration and Naturalization Service.* Washington, DC: U.S. Department of Justice.

Updegraff, K. A., Madden-Derdich, D. A., Estrada, A. U., Sales, L. J., & Leonard, S. A. (2002). Young adolescents' experiences with parents and friends: Exploring the connections. *Family Relations, 51,* 72–80.

Updegraff, K. A., McHale, S. M., & Crouter, A. (2000). Adolescents' sex-typed friendship experiences: Does having a sister versus a brother matter? *Child Development, 71,* 1597–1610.

Useem, E. L. (1992). Middle schools and math groups: Parents' involvement in children's placement. *Sociology of Education, 65,* 263–279.

Valkenburg, P. M., Peter, J., & Schouten, A. P. (2006). Friend networking sites and their relation to adolescents' well-being and social self-esteem. *CyberPsychology and Behavior, 9,* 584–590.

Valsiner, J. (1997). *Culture and the development of children's action* (2nd ed.). New York: Wiley.

van Baal, G. C. M., Boomsma, D. I., & de Geus, E. J. C. (2001). Longitudinal genetic analysis of EEG coherence in young twins. *Behavior Genetics, 31,* 637–651.

Van Voorhis, F. L. (2000). *The effects of interactive (TIPS) homework on family involvement and science achievement of middle grade students.* Unpublished doctoral dissertation, University of Florida, Gainesville.

Vander Wal, J. S., & Thelen, M. H. (2001). Predictors of body image dissatisfaction in elementary-age school girls. *Eating Behaviors, 1,* 1–18.

Vandiver, B. J., Cross, W. E., Jr., & Worrell, F. C. (2002). Validating the Cross Racial Identity Scale. *Journal of Counseling Psychology, 49,* 71–85.

Vartanian, L. R. (2000). Revisiting the imaginary audience and personal fable constructs of adolescent egocentrism: A conceptual review. *Adolescence, 35,* 639–661.

Vartanian, L. R., & Powlishta, K. K. (1996). A longitudinal examination of the social-cognitive foundations of adolescent egocentrism. *Journal of Early Adolescence, 16,* 157–178.

Vaughan, G., Tajfel, H., & Williams, J. A. (1981). Bias in reward allocation in an intergroup and an interpersonal context. *Social Psychology Quarterly, 44,* 37–42.

Vergnaud, G. (1996). Education, the best portion of Piaget's heritage. *Swiss Journal of Psychology, 55,* 112–118.

Verhaagen, D. (2005). *Parenting the millennial generation: Guiding our children born between 1982 and 2000.* Westport, CT: Praeger.

Verma, S., & Sharma, D. (2006). Cultural dynamics of family relations among Indian adolescents in varied contexts. In K. H. Rubin & O. B. Chung (Eds.), *Parenting beliefs, behaviors, and parent-child relations: A cross-cultural perspective.* New York: Psychology Press.

Videon, T. M. (2002). The effects of parent-adolescent relationships and parental separation on adolescent well-being. *Journal of Marriage and Family, 64*(2), 489–503.

Vion, M., & Colas, A. (2004). On the use of the connective 'and' in oral narration: A study of French-speaking elementary school children. *Journal of Child Language, 31,* 399–419.

von Bertalanffy, L. (1975). *Perspectives on general system theory: Scientific-philosophical studies.* New York: George Braziller.

von Busschbach, J. J., Hinten, M., Rikken, B., Grobbee, D. E., De Charro, F. T., et al.

(1999). Some patients with an idiopathic short stature see their short stature as a problem, but others do not: Why this difference? In U. Eiholzer, F. Haverkamp, & L. Voss (Eds.), *Growth, stature, and psychosocial well-being* (pp. 27–35). Ashland, OH: Hogrefe and Huber.

Voss, L. D. (2001). Short normal stature and psychosocial disadvantage: A critical review of the evidence. *Journal of Pediatric Endocrinology Metabolism, 14,* 701–711.

Voyer, D., Voyer, S., & Bryden, M. P. (1995). Magnitude of sex differences in spatial abilities: A meta-analysis and consideration of critical variables. *Psychological Bulletin, 117,* 250–270.

Vygotsky, L. S. (1988). On inner speech. In M. B. Franklin & S. S. Barten (Eds.), *Child language: A reader* (pp. 181–187). New York: Oxford University Press.

Wadsworth, B. J. (1996). *Piaget's theory of cognitive and affective development: Foundations of constructivism* (5th ed.). White Plains, NY: Longman.

Walcott, D. D., Pratt, H. D., & Patel, D. R. (2003). Adolescents and eating disorders: Gender, racial, ethnic, sociocultural, and socioeconomic issues. *Journal of Adolescent Research, 18,* 223–243.

Walker, A. J., Manoogian-O'Dell, M., McGraw, L. A., & White, D. L. (2001). *Families in later life: Connections and transitions.* Thousand Oaks, CA: Sage.

Walker, L. J., de Vries, B., & Trevethan, S. D. (1987). Moral stages and moral orientations in real life and hypothetical dilemmas. *Child Development, 58,* 842–858.

Wallis, C. (2006). The multitasking generation. *Time, 167*(13), 48–55.

Walsh, F. (1998). *Strengthening family resilience.* New York: Guilford Press.

Wang, R., Bianchi, S. M., & Raley, S. B. (2005). Teenagers' Internet use and family rules: A research note. *Journal of Marriage and Family, 67,* 1249–1258.

Wang, Y. (2002). Is obesity associated with early sexual maturation? A comparison of the association in American boys versus girls. *Pediatrics, 10,* 903–910.

Ward, L. M. (2003). Understanding the role of entertainment media in the sexual socialization of American youth: A review of empirical research. *Developmental Review, 23,* 347–388.

Ward, L. M., Hansbrough, E., & Walker, E. (2005). Contributions of music video exposure to Black adolescents' gender and sexual schemas. *Journal of Adolescent Research, 20,* 143–166.

Ward, T. B., Smith, S. M., & Finke, R. A. (1999). Creative cognition. In R. J. Sternberg (Ed.), *Handbook of creativity* (pp. 189–212). New York: Cambridge University Press.

Wardle, F., & Cruz-Janzen, M. I. (2004). *Meeting the needs of multiethnic and mul-*

tiracial children in schools (pp. 156–160). Boston: Allyn and Bacon.

Warren, M. P. (1983). Physical and biological aspects of puberty. In J. Brooks-Gunn & A. C. Petersen (Eds.), *Girls at puberty: Biological and psychosocial perspectives* (pp. 3–28). New York: Plenum.

Wartella, E., Caplovitz, A. G. & Lee, J. H. (2004). From Baby Einstein to Leapfrog, from Doom to the Sims, from instant messaging to Internet chat rooms: Public interest in the role of interactive media in children's lives. *Social Policy Report,* Vol. 18, No. 4. Retrieved March 21, 2005, from http://www.srcd.org/spr.html.

Waters, E., & Cummings, E. M. (2000). A secure base from which to explore close relationships. *Child Development, 71,* 164–172.

Watson, M. W., & Fischer, K. W. (1980). Development of social roles in elicited and spontaneous behavior during the preschool years. *Developmental Psychology, 16,* 483–494.

Wattigney, W. A., Srinivasan, S. R., Chen, W., Greenlund, K. J., & Berenson, G. S. (1999). Secular trend of earlier onset of menarche with increasing obesity in black and white girls: The Bogalusa Heart Study. *Ethnicity and Disease, 9,* 181–189.

Watts, R., Liston, C., Niogi, S., & Ulug, A. M. (2003). Fiber tracking using magnetic resonance diffusion tensor imaging and its applications to human brain development. *Mental Retardation and Developmental Disabilities Research Reviews, 9,* 168–177.

Wechsler, D. (1939). *The measurement of adult intelligence.* Baltimore, MD: Williams and Wilkins.

Wechsler, D. (1997). *Wechsler Adult Intelligence Scale* (3rd ed.). San Antonio, TX: Psychological Corporation.

Wechsler, D. (2002). *WPPSI—III manual.* San Antonio, TX: Psychological Corporation.

Wechsler, D. (2003). *Wechsler Intelligence Scale for Children* (4th ed.). San Antonio, TX: Psychological Corporation.

Weichold, K., Silbereisen, R. K., & Schmitt-Rodermund, E. (2003). Short-term and long-term consequences of early versus late physical maturation in adolescents. In C. Hayward (Ed.), *Gender differences at puberty* (pp. 241–276). New York: Cambridge University Press.

Weigel, D. J., Martin, S. S., & Bennett, K. K. (2005). Ecological influences of the home and the child-care center on preschool-age children's literacy development. *Reading Research Quarterly, 40,* 204–233.

Weinfeld, N. S., Sroufe, L. A., & Egeland, B. (2000). Attachment from infancy to adulthood in a high-risk sample: Continuity, discontinuity, and their correlates. *Child Development, 71,* 695–702.

Weisner, M., & Ittel, A. (2002). Relations of pubertal timing and depressive symptoms to substance use in early adolescence. *Journal of Early Adolescence, 22*(1), 5–23.

Weisner, T. S. (1996). The 5 to 7 transition as an ecocultural project. In A. J. Sameroff & M. M. Haith (Eds.), *The five to seven year shift: The age of reason and responsibility* (pp. 295–396). Chicago: University of Chicago Press.

Weisner, T. S. (1998). Human development, child well-being, and the cultural project of development. In D. Sharma & K. Fischer (Eds.), *Socio-emotional development across cultures* (pp. 69–85). *New Directions in Child Development*, No. 81. San Francisco: Jossey-Bass.

Weisner, T. S. (2001). Childhood: Anthropological aspects. In D. L. Sills (Ed.), *The international encyclopedia of the social sciences* (pp. 1697–1701). New York: Macmillan.

Weisner, T. S. (2005). Introduction. In T. S. Weisner (Ed.), *Discovering successful pathways in children's development: Mixed methods in the study of childhood and family life* (pp. 1–18). Chicago: University of Chicago Press.

Weisner, T. S., & Wilson-Mitchell, J. E. (1990). Nonconventional family lifestyles and sex-typing in six-year-olds. *Child Development, 61*, 1915–1933.

Weiss, H. B., Dearing, E., Mayer, E., Kreider, H., & McCartney, K. (2005). Family educational involvement: Who can afford it and what does it afford? In C. R. Cooper, C. T. Garcia, W. T. Barko, H. Davis, & C. Chatman (Eds.), *Developmental pathways through middle childhood: Rethinking contexts and diversity as resources* (pp. 17–39). Mahwah, NJ: Erlbaum.

Welch, J. M., & Weaver, C. M. (2005). Calcium and exercise affect the growing skelton, *Nutrition Reviews, 63*(11), 361–373.

Wentzel, K. R. (2003). Sociometric status and adjustment in middle school: A longitudinal study. *Journal of Early Adolescence, 23*(1), 5–28.

Werner, E. E. (1989). Children of the garden island. *Scientific American, 260*(4), 106–111.

Werner, E. E. (1993). Risk, resilience, and recovery: Perspectives from the Kauai longitudinal study. *Development and Psychopathology, 5*, 503–515.

Werner, E. E., & Smith, R. S. (2001). *Journeys from childhood to midlife: Risk, resilience, and recovery*. Ithaca, NY: Cornell University Press.

Wheeler, M. D. (1991). Physical changes of puberty. *Endocrinology and Metabolism Clinics of North America, 20*, 1–14.

White, J. M. (1991). *Dynamics of family development: The theory of family development*. New York: Guilford Press.

White, J. M., & Klein, D. M. (2002). *Family theories* (2nd ed.). Thousand Oaks, CA: Sage.

White, R. W. (1959). Motivation reconsidered: The concept of competence. *Psychological Review, 66*, 233–297.

White, S. H. (1996). The child's entry into the "age of reason." In A. J. Sameroff & M. M. Haith (Eds.), *The five to seven year shift: The age of reason and responsibility* (pp. 17–30). Chicago: University of Chicago Press.

Whitesell, N. R., & Harter, S. (1989). Children's reports of conflict between simultaneous opposite-valence emotions. *Child Development, 60*, 673–682.

Whiting, B. B. (Ed.). (1963). *Six cultures: Studies of child rearing*. New York: Wiley.

Whiting, B. B., & Edwards, C. P. (1973). A cross-cultural analysis of sex differences in the behavior of children aged 3–11. *Journal of Social Psychology, 91*, 171–188.

Whiting, B. B., & Edwards, C. P. (1988/1992). *Children of different worlds: The formation of social behavior*. Cambridge, MA: Harvard University Press.

Whiting, B. B., & Edwards, C. P. (1992). *Children of different worlds*. Cambridge, MA: Harvard University Press.

Whiting, B. B., & Whiting, J. W. M. (1975). *Children of six cultures: A psycho-cultural analysis*. Cambridge, MA: Harvard University Press.

Whitlock, J. L., & Hamilton, S. F. (2003). The role of youth surveys in community youth development initiatives. *Applied Developmental Science, 7*, 39–51.

Wigfield, A., Battle, A., Keller, L. B., & Eccles, J. S. (2002). Sex differences in motivation, self-concept, career aspiration, and career choice: Implications for cognitive development. In A. McGillicuddy-De Lisi & R. De Lisi (Eds.), *Biology, society, and behavior: The development of sex differences in cognition* (pp. 93–124). Westport, CT: Ablex Publishing.

Wigfield, A., & Eccles, J. S. (2002). The development of competence beliefs, expectancies for success, and achievement values from childhood to adolescence. In A. Wigfield & J. S. Eccles (Eds.), *The development of achievement motivation* (pp. 91–121). San Diego, CA: Academic Press.

Wigfield, A., Eccles, J. S., & Rodriguez, D. (1998). The development of children's motivation in school contexts. *Review of Research in Education, 23*, 73–118.

Wiles, J., & Bondi, J. (2001). *The new American middle school: Educating preadolescents in an era of change* (3rd ed.). Upper Saddle River, NJ: Merrill/Prentice Hall.

Williams, J. M., & Currie, C. (2000). Self-esteem and physical development in early adolescence: Pubertal timing and body image. *Journal of Early Adolescence, 20*(2), 129–149.

Wilson, B. J. (2004). The mass media and family communication. In A. Vangelisti (Ed.), *Handbook of family communication* (pp. 563–591). Mahwah, NJ: Erlbaum.

Wilson, D. M., Killen, J. D., Hayward, C., Robinson, T. N., Hammer, L. D., Kraemer, H. C., et al. (1994). Timing and rate of sexual maturation and the onset of cigarette and alcohol use among teenage girls. *Archives of Pediatrics and Adolescent Medicine, 148*, 789–795.

Wilson, J. F. (2003). *Biological foundations of human behavior*. Belmont, CA: Wadsworth/Thomson Learning.

Wilson, N., Syme, S. L., Boyce, W. T., Battistich, V. A., & Selvin, S. (2005). Adolescent alcohol, tobacco, and marijuana use: The influence of neighborhood disorder and hope. *American Journal of Health Promotion, 20*, 11–19.

Windle, M. (1992). Revised Dimensions of Temperament Survey (DOTS-R): Simultaneous group confirmatory factor analysis for adolescent gender groups. *Psychological Assessment, 4*, 1–21.

Windle, M., Hooker, K., Lenerz, K., East, P. L., Lerner, J. V., & Lerner, R. M. (1986). Temperament, perceived competence, and depression in early and late adolescents. *Developmental Psychology, 22*, 384–392.

Witzke, K. A., & Snow, C. M. (2000). Effects of plyometric jump training on bone mass in adolescent girls. *Medicine and Science in Sports and Exercise, 32*, 1051–1057.

Wolfson, A. R., Tzischinsky, O., Brown, C., Darley, C., Acebo, C., & Carskadon, M. (1995). Sleep, behavior, and stress at the transition to senior high school. *Sleep Research, 24*, 115.

Wong, M. M., Nigg, J. T., Zucker, R. A., Puttler, L. I., Fitzgerald, H. E., Jester, J. M., et al. (2006). Behavioral control and resiliency in the onset of alcohol and illicit drug use: A prospective study from preschool to adolescence. *Child Development, 77*, 1016–1033.

Wood, K. C., Becker, J. A., & Thompson, J. K. (1996). Body image dissatisfaction in preadolescent children. *Journal of Applied Developmental Psychology, 17*, 85–100.

Woodard, E. H., & Gridina, N. (2000). *Media in the home 2000: Survey series no. 7*. Washington, DC: Annenberg Public Policy Center.

Woodson, S. E. (1999). Mapping the cultural geography of childhood or, performing monstrous children. *Journal of American Culture, 22*(4), 31–43.

Woodward, L., Fergusson, D. M., & Belsky, J. (2000). Timing of parental separation and attachment to parents in adolescence: Results of a prospective study from birth to age 16. *Journal of Marriage and the Family, 62*(1), 162–174.

Wormeli, R. (2001). *Meet me in the middle: Becoming an accomplished middle-level teacher*. Portland, ME: Stenhouse Publishers.

Wright, J. C., Huston, A. C., Vandewater, E. A., Bickham, D. S., Scantlin, R. M., Kotler, J. A.

et al. (2001). American children's use of electronic media in 1997: A national survey. *Applied Developmental Psychology, 22,* 31–47.

Wright, M. O., & Masten, A. M. (2006). Resilience processes in development: Fostering positive adaptation in the context of adversity. In S. Goldstein & R. B. Brooks (Eds.), *Handbook of resilience in children* (pp. 17–37). New York: Springer.

Wu, L. T., Pilowsky, D. J., & Schlenger, W. E. (2004). Inhalant abuse and dependence among adolescents in the United States. *Journal of the American Academy of Child & Adolescent Psychiatry, 43,* 1206–1214.

Wu, L. T., Schlenger, W. E., & Ringwalt, C. L. (2005). Use of nitrite inhalants ("poppers") among American youth. *Journal of Adolescent Health, 37,* 52–60.

Wyatt, G., Durvasula, R. S., Guthrie, D., LeFranc, E., & Forge, N. (1999). Correlates of first intercourse among women in Jamaica. *Archives of Sexual Behavior, 28,* 139–157.

Wyn, J., & White, R. (1997). *Rethinking youth.* London: Sage.

Xue, Y, Leventhal, T., Brooks-Gunn, J., & Earls, F. (2005). Neighborhood residence and mental health problems of 5- to 11-year-olds. *Archives of General Psychiatry, 62,* 554–563.

Yan, J. H., & Jevas, S. (2004). Young girls' developmental skills in underarm throwing. *Perceptual & Motor Skills, 99,* 39–47.

Yan, Z. (2005). Age differences in children's understanding of the complexity of the Internet. *Journal of Applied Developmental Psychology, 26,* 385–396.

Yates, M., & Youniss, J. (1998). Community service and political identity. *Journal of Social Issues, 54,* 495–512.

Youniss, J. (1980). *Parents and peers in social development: A Sullivan-Piaget perspective.* Chicago: University of Chicago Press.

Youniss, J., Bales, S., Christmas-Best, V., Diversi, M., McLaughlin, M., & Silbereisen, R. (2002). Youth civic engagement in the twenty-first century. *Journal of Research on Adolescence, 12,* 121–148.

Youth and America's Future. (1988). *The forgotten half: Pathways to success for America's youth and young families.* Washington, DC: William T. Grant Foundation Commission on Work, Family and Citizenship.

Zametkin, A. J., Zoon, C. K., Klein, H. W., & Munson, S. (2004). Psychiatric aspects of child and adolescent obesity: A review of the past 10 years. *Journal of the American Academy of Child & Adolescent Psychiatry, 43,* 134–150.

Zarbatany, L., Hartmann, D. P., & Rankin, D. B. (1990). The psychological functions of preadolescent peer activities. *Child Development, 61,* 1067–1080.

Zauszniewki, J. A., Chung, C., Chang, C., & Krafcik, K. (2002). Predictors of resourcefulness in school-aged children. *Journal of Mental Health Nursing, 23,* 385–401.

Zeller, M., Vanatta, K., Schaffer, J., & Noll, R. B. (2003). Behavioral reputation: A cross-age perspective. *Developmental Psychology, 39,* 129–139.

Zimet, G. D., Cutler, M., Litvene, M., Dahms, W., et al. (1995). Psychological adjustment of children evaluated for short stature: A preliminary report. *Journal of Developmental & Behavioral Pediatrics, 16,* 264–270.

Zimmer-Gembeck, M. J., Geiger, T. C., & Crick, N. R. (2005). Relational and physical aggression, prosocial behavior, and peer relations: Gender moderation and bidirectional associations. *Journal of Early Adolescence, 25,* 421–452.

Zinnbauer, B. J., Pargament, K. I., & Cole, B. (1997). Spirituality and religion: Unfuzzying the fuzzy. *Journal for the Scientific Study of Religion, 36,* 549–564.

Zionts, L. (2005). Examining relationships between students and teachers: A potential extension of attachment theory? In K. A. Kerns & R. A. Richardson (Eds.), *Attachment in middle childhood* (pp. 231–254). New York: Guilford Press.

Name Index

Subject Index